THE LEE ROSE STORY

A Horseshoe-Pitching Chronicle

1920–1960

The Lee Rose Story

A Horseshoe-Pitching Chronicle
1920–1960

- - - - - - - - - - - - -

As Recorded in the Journals
of Lee Rose and Compiled by
Bob Dunn, NHPA Historian

BEAVER'S POND
PRESS

ISBN: 978-1-59298-926-3
Library of Congress Control Number: 2014915251

Printed in the United States of America
Designed by Mayfly Design and Typeset in the Whitman and Myriad Pro typefaces
First Printing: 2014

18 17 16 15 14   5 4 3 2 1

Beaver's Pond Press, Inc.
7108 Ohms Lane
Edina, MN 55439
(952) 829-8818
www.BeaversPondPress.com

To order, visit www.BeaversPondBooks.com
or call (800) 901-3480. Reseller discounts available.

CONTENTS

FOREWORD

- - - - - - - - - - - - - - - - -

One of the most interesting chapters in the long history of horseshoe pitching is the story of Lee Rose. Much of Lee's story can be written in his own words thanks to the five handwritten journals he created between 1933 and 1950. We're fortunate that these journals still exist and are available. Steve Summerlin, a long-time member of the Michigan Horseshoe Pitchers Association and its regional director for more than 20 years, acquired the journals from Lee's family shortly after Lee's death in 1998.

Lee Rose, born February 24, 1906, was a champion-class horseshoe pitcher at a very young age. He started pitching when he was 14 and just seven years later, he qualified for the men's Championship Class, placing 22nd at the 1927 World Tournament. He also appeared in the 1928 World Tournament, where he placed 25th. He went on to win three Michigan state championships (1934, 1944, and 1955) and was runner-up in 1928, 1930, and 1932.

Rose was also was a prominent promoter of the sport. His most significant effort was publishing *The Horseshoe Compendium* in 1940. He was elected as secretary-treasurer of the National Horseshoe Pitchers Association (NHPA) in 1939, and the compendium was his first project in that role—and what a major project it was.

The Horseshoe Compendium is a substantial contribution to the recording of NHPA's history, as the association has produced just three books: *Horseshoe Pitching: How to Play the Game*, by D. D. Cottrell in 1927, Lee's book in 1940, and then Gary T. Kline's *Official N.H.P.A. History of the World Tournament 1909 to 1980*, which was published in 1980.

The Horseshoe Compendium provides a tremendous look at the history of the sport up to 1940 and its content is included in this book in its entirety. Rose's respect for history and the value of recording it, as demonstrated by the compendium, must have also been the energy behind his decades-long efforts to record his own involvement in the sport.

Rose's involvement in the sport even included owning a shoe manufacturing business. He purchased the Lattore Horseshoe Company in 1946, and maintained their production right up to his death on July 23, 1998, at age 92.

In honor of his lifetime dedication to the sport of horseshoe pitching, Lee Rose was inducted into the NHPA Hall of Fame in 1984.

Some of his journal entries record specific games and the results of various tournaments he participated in. Some of this may seem like less than exciting reading, but the information was important enough for Lee to record and is therefore reprinted in its entirety. The details offer a singular perspective of our sport 60 to 70 years ago, and some of it is very interesting.

As our story begins, take note that we are about to find out that Rose was not his real name. He was actually Lee Jacobs, and as a young teenager he took an assumed name to use for horseshoe pitching—as a way to avoid a confrontation with his father, who forbid Lee to play the game!

Our story begins with a 1935 newspaper clipping enclosed in one of the early Rose journals. This is a delightful article that gives us the story behind his assumed name.

- - - - - - -

Champion Had to Overcome Father's Horseshoe Phobia

False Modesty and a Stage Name Taken by Rose

You won't believe it, but Lee Rose, champion horseshoe pitcher of Michigan, had to run away when he was a little boy and even assume a stage name to keep his father from knowing that he was learning to pitch horseshoe.

And so it develops that the champion horseshoe pitcher of Michigan isn't Lee Rose at all, but Lee Jacobs.

Before Lee's story is told however, it should be explained that he and his father, Julius Jacobs, prominent Detroit horse dealer and auctioneer are not mad at each other and actually lived as neighbors on Shaw Avenue.

Lee on Monday morning will begin his training for the world's championship in Moline, Illinois.

His struggle to reach the peak of the ancient sport in his home state is loaded with much incident.

Papa Loved Horses, But...

The whole trouble started because Papa Jacobs loved horses and hated horseshoe pitchers, while Lee hated horses and admired horseshoe pitchers.

"Yep, my Dad wanted me to become a great horseman and be a great rider like the polo players," said Champion Jacobs in relating his rise to fame. "But I was 13 years old and if ever there was anything I didn't like it was horses. I just liked horseshoes and the people that threw 'em on the stakes."

"That's right," interrupted Bob Omans, widely known sports enthusiast, who devotes most of his spare time to telling the Free Press about chess and checker champions and what a swell horseshoe pitcher is Lee. "Yes sir, do you know that when we were kids all of us used to cry for nickels to go see cowboy pictures and we couldn't get Lee to go—just because he hated horses so."

Had To Dodge Cameras

Champion Jacobs continued, "Well. I loved horseshoes, so I would run away to tournaments. I knew my Dad would be mad if he caught me, so I told the people at the tournaments that my name was Lee Rose, and boy was I glad I did, for I won the first tournament I ran away to and because I was only 13 the papers wanted pictures of me. I ran back home before they could get any pictures but the papers the next day told what a great feat a thirteen-year-old boy has accomplished against a lot of guys old enough to be his grandfather. But they used the name of Lee Rose and nobody at home knew I was that little guy. You know it's funny, because I never wanted my picture taken, everybody thought I was modest and I'm not at all. I wanted my picture taken all the time."

Just then Booster Oman interrupted again with: "Tell him about your boy, go wan, tell 'em."

"He means how funny it is about my boy and my father," Champion Jacobs explained. "You see I hated horses and my father loved them. And my boy, Lee Jr., (he's 5 years old) has made my Dad happy by being crazy about horses. He won the juvenile riding contest last week at the Northville Fair."

Lee then revealed that horseshoe pitching is getting too rough and unruly and that the national organization intends to do something about it. It seems that a lot of new boys are breaking into the game [who] don't know the ethics. You are not supposed to yell and scream at your opponent or walk in front of him.

"You can throw a horseshoe pitcher off his stride easier than you can a golfer," Jacobs explained. "Horseshoe pitchers are a very temperamental lot, most of them. I'm talking professionals, of course, I guess maybe all the publicity they get goes to their heads."

30 Ringers in a Row

"On Champion Jacob's good days, using the regulation forty-ounce shoe, he can throw 30 consecutive ringers and on his off days around 14." Boswell Omans interjected with pride.

The horseshoe pitcher was more astounded, however, at the information that city boys are better than country boys at horseshoe. Champion Jacobs was unable to explain.

Before Omans took his horseshoe champion away, he wanted his chess and checker public to understand he has not deserted his favorite pastime. "Tell 'em that the reason I want to see Champion Jacobs get along with the papers is because he and I used to be kids together and I like to beat him at checkers and he likes to show me up at horseshoes."

- - - - - - -

His journals suggest that Lee may not have been the most modest person. However, he did a fascinating job of recording his career performances, and in the process, shares a most unique and wonderful view of the past. When he was handwriting his journals, it is doubtful he had any idea what a time capsule he was creating.

He played against each and every star of the beginning era of horseshoe pitching as an organized sport. And he won many of the encounters. Most importantly for us, he took the time to record those games and his recollections. His record helps us capture an insider's view of the sport in those early days. Some entries may have only meant something to Lee, but the rest of us get a fascinating glimpse of just how serious Lee was about horseshoe pitching and what the sport meant to him.

Lee's journals also contain a few great photographs and some newspaper photos. They are also included in this book along with an image of the 1948 World Tournament finals report mailed out to all the participants. This is an unusual tournament finals report because it was printed on linen paper that feels almost like cloth—and because it records Guy Zimmerman's perfect game, the only Men's Division World Tournament perfect game in the first five decades of World Tournament play.

It All Began at Age 14

As we open the first of the five journals, three photos are revealed. On the left are two snapshots of Lee in his youth—one of him taking a practice toss in his backyard, and the other a pose of him with one of his latest trophies with his shoes set out before him.

Notice that the shoes are hookless, so we know the photo was taken prior to 1932, when all tournament players had the availability of hooked horseshoes. One is of Lee Rose in his youth, on this page and one is on the cover with Lee Rose posing with one of his lastest trophies and his pitching shoes set out in front of him. In those days, these would have been the picnic variety of pitching shoes and would have been the least expensive to purchase, which is probably the reason a young teenager would be using them. The shoes were hammered out of a single blade of steel with the heel calks simply bent around to form the calk. The toe calk on these early shoes was formed quite differently as contemporary shoes—by scooping some metal out of the blade and hammering it down to create the toe calk.

Lee Rose at age 14 in 1920

This is the only photo I've seen that indicates a tournament player had chosen the Leader shoe.

The third image (page 4) was almost certainly clipped out of a *Horseshoe World* magazine, but is a great shot of a very young Ted Allen and Caroline Schultz (middle), the 1933 World champions. The lady on the left presenting the championship trophies is Mrs. James Miller, part of the World's Fair host committee. The 1933 World Horseshoe Tournament took place at the 1933 World's Fair in Chicago.

On the next page is another photo clipped from the August 1933 edition of *Horseshoe World*. It shows the 1933 World Tournament participants and dignitaries. Few photos are more historic than this shot. Lee has penciled in some player identification, which is quite helpful in deciphering the image. There are at least 12 hall of fame members in this photo, and a few more who are significant in various ways to our sport's history.

The hall of fame members pictured include: Frank Jackson; Charles Clyde Davis; Bert Duryee; Jimmy Risk; Jack Claves, who coined the term "Four Dead" and was elected NHPA president in 1940; John A. Gordon, owner of the Gordon Horseshoe Company; Ted Allen; L. E. Tanner, elected NHPA president in 1935; Blair Nunamaker; Fernando Isais; R. B. Howard, publisher of *Horseshoe World* and NHPA secretary-treasurer; and Ben Leighton, NHPA's first president.

Other players of note in the photo are Lyle Brown, the 1938 Iowa state champion; Alex Cumming, a long-time NHPA vice president who was elected NHPA president in 1933; Glover Hawley, five-time Ohio state champion (1941, 1943, 1944, 1945, and 1949) and designer of the Hawley bronze pitching shoe in 1939; Milton Tate, who qualified for the men's World Tournament Championship Class eight times and was a four-time Illinois state champion and Utah state champion in 1961; James Lecky, who was the Arizona state champion 22 times; Ed Walls, a five-time Michigan state champion; and Leo G. Lattore, who along with Edward Levagood was the founder of the Lattore Horseshoe Company in 1933—the company that was later purchased by Lee Jacobs.

The 1933 World Tournament was historic because it was Ted Allen's first, and the first of his ten World Championships. He won that year in a three-game playoff against C. C. Davis, who was probably the best horseshoe pitcher up to that time. No less than five hall of fame pitchers were on hand, and there were another five or six who should have received that honor.

The 1933 World Tournament men's final standings were clipped out of *Horseshoe World* and pasted into Lee's journal.

Page Two   THE HORSESHOE WORLD   August, 1933

OFFICIAL TOURNAMENT PICTURE

Pictured here are the 24 finalists, a number of those who did not qualify, and horseshoe enthusiasts who watched the tournament. Officials of the tournament are also in the picture. In the front row, starting with the man second from left is William Blair, John Hogan and L. E. Tanner, members of the tournament committee. Next to Tanner is Alex. Cumming, president of the National Association. Next in line are R. B. Howard, editor of The Horseshoe World and newly-elected secretary-treasurer of the National Association; B. G. Leighton, chairman of the Interim Committee; V. W. Kimball, member of the Tournament Committee; Jack Claves, of St. Louis; Rev. P. V. Harris, second vice-president of the National Association; John A. Gordon, equipment manufacturer, and F. M. Kohler, one of the scorekeepers.

1933 World Tournament Men's Championship Class

Carolyn Schultz (middle) and Ted Allen (right) receiving their 1933 World Championship awards.

The Lee Rose Story

The 1933 Men's Championship Finals

Name and Address	W	L	R	SP	Pct.
Ted Allen, California	23	3	1127	1532	73.5
C. C. Davis, Missouri	20	3	1119	1382	71.9
Blair Nunamaker, Ohio	18	5	1034	1504	68.9
Fernando Isais, California	18	5	1087	1502	72.0
Jimmy Risk, Indiana	18	5	1016	1580	70.9
James Lecky, Arizona	16	7	1004	1516	65.4
Russell Signer, Illinois	16	7	947	1488	67.5
Bert Duryee, Kansas	15	8	1003	1538	64.4
G. C. Hawley, Ohio	14	9	932	1472	63.9
Ed Walls, Michigan	13	10	933	1574	62.1
Harold Scheets, Wisconsin	12	11	946	1492	64.1
Howard Collier, Illinois	12	11	869	1414	48.8
Hanford Jackson, Kansas	10	13	781	1410	60.0
Lloyd Woodard, Kansas	10	13	823	1388	58.5
John Colao, Illinois	10	13	805	1384	52.7
Verne Licht, Wisconsin	8	15	990	1654	56.1
Vyrl Jackson, Iowa	9	14	852	1456	48.8
Lefty Steinmann, St. Louis	9	14	808	1426	53.9
Carroll Jackson, Illinois	9	14	786	1280	52.5
Orville Harris, Indiana	6	17	813	1466	49.9
Clarence Pfeiffer, Iowa	5	18	928	1540	51.1
Alton Wood, Illinois	4	19	738	1378	46.8
Jack Hoecksema, Michigan	2	21	504	942	53.8
Milton Tate, Illinois	0	23	446	850	48.1

The journal also contains four short, undated newspapers clippings. Context suggests that they are from 1933 as well.

The first article asserts that 1933 was Michigan's first state championship. It was actually something like the ninth, but it was Rose's first title and that's likely how the reporter got mixed up.

The next clipping is about a California league contest and must have appeared in a Detroit newspaper. It's interesting to speculate about why this particular piece would be considered news so far away, but clearly Rose found compelling at the time. Alhambra, California, was the hometown of the great Ted Allen.

- - - - - - -

Horseshoe Title Is Won by Rose

Lee Rose outclassed a field of 14 entries to capture the first horseshoe championship of the State of Michigan at the Paradise courts.

Al Field defeated Harold Arold in a playoff for the runner-up position. Others to place, finishing in the order named, were Dick Prediger, Jim Burt, Tom Cleary and Tom Tipton.

Lots of Ringers

To defeat the Alhambra, California horseshoe team, the Culver City varsity was forced to set a new mark of ringers per man per stake, averaging 66.1 ringers per team member.

Boy Wonder Wins

On the evening of August 16, at the Dearborn horseshoe courts, Bobby Hitt, sensational 11-year-old horseshoe star, who pitches from 37 feet, defeated both Lee Rose and Leo Lattore two games each. A large crowd cheered loudly for the tiny player who stands less than four feet and weight only 50 pounds.

Summary of the games follows:

	P	R	DR	SP	Pct.
Hitt	50	63	20	92	.684
Rose	43	60	20	92	.657
Hitt	50	47	18	66	.712
Rose	37	41	13	66	.621
Hitt	50	40	13	56	.714
Lattore	23	32	11	56	.571
Hitt	50	78	27	106	.736
Lattore	49	78	28	106	.736

Hitt pitched 228 ringers of 320 shoes for 71.25%.

The last game certainly drew applause as Bobbie held Lattore on 49 for the last eight innings and came from behind to go out. All three players pitch on the Dearborn team of the International League.

Lee Rose Is Winner in Horseshoe Tournament

Lee Rose of Dearborn won the open horseshoe pitching tournament, having 11 victories and two defeats. Field defeated Arold in the playoff for second place. Each had won nine matches and lost four. Bobby Hitt, 11-year-old star, will meet all comers in an exhibition Saturday at the Paradise Club Courts, Harper and Canton Avenues at 2:30 p.m.

- - - - - - -

Next is an incredible example of record keeping that demonstrates just how interested Lee was in keeping detailed records of his involvement in the sport. He meticulously recorded the results of his first nine state tournaments and his performance against each opponent.

- - - - - - -

Won/Loss Record in 11 State Tournaments

1925-26-27-28-29-30-31-32-33

W	Player	L	W	Player	L	W	Player	L
4	H. Ellerby	0	1	J. DeLeeuw	0	2	J. Latzko	1
2	J. Hoekjema	0	1	S. DeLeeuw	0	7	J. Skinner	4
2	D. Stephens	0	1	G. G. Smith	0	3	J. Burt	4
2	A. Zeiter	0	1	Wilson	0	3	R. Prediger	2
2	G. Middling	0	1	E, Stewart	0	2	L. Lattore	2
2	H. Hoeksema	0	1	G. Stewart	0	2	B. Emerson	2
2	F. O'Melay	0	1	George	0	2	L. Harrison	2
2	R. Wrobbel	0	1	Case	0	1	Cadwalladar	1
1	A Field	0	1	Oatzes	0	1	J. McDonald	1
1	H. Arold	0	1	DePottey	0	1	W. Wrobbel	1
1	T. Tipton	0	1	Marsch	0	1	James	1
1	Remus	0	1	G. Portt	0	1	D. Latzko	1
1	S. Esper	0	1	Sheppardson	0	1	A. Bush	1
1	L. Wilkes	0	1	W. Davidson	0	2	Ed Walls	3

(Continued on next page)

W	Player	L	W	Player	L	W	Player	L
1	H. Stanlake	0	1	Babcock	0	1	Ed Combs	2
1	A. Seals	0	1	T. Cleary	0	0	F. Seals	1
1	P. Harper	0	1	Taylor	0	0	Yarnell	1
1	C. Sebo	0	1	Kozlowski	0	0	J. Forten	1
1	Rial	0	6	R. H. Rizor	1	0	K. Crouse	1
1	Maurer	0	4	R. Armstrong	1	0	W. Emerson	1
1	Faurot	0	3	R. Gorsline	1	0	Ira Knight	1
1	H. J. Oates	0	3	W. Wulf	1	0	M. B. Getz	1
1	C. Emerson	0	3	A. Koppitsch	1	0	H. Askey	1
1	J. Kossen	0	3	R. Middleton	1	0		
1	O. Kossen	0	4	R. D. Baxter	2	0	H. Askey	1

In eleven tournaments, I won first place in 1933, took second in 1928, 1930, 1932. My overall record was 109 games won, 44 games lost and I have played in more tournaments and won more games than any other player in Michigan.

- - - - - - -

In the middle of Lee's list the name "G. Portt" appears. That is none other than Glen Portt, past NHPA president, Senior Men's World Champion in 1980 and 1984, and member of the NHPA Hall of Fame. Portt was born in Michigan in 1914, and as a youth toured with Jimmy Risk and participated in Risk's pitching exhibitions. Portt was 18 when he pitched against Lee Rose in 1932. No one could have foreseen what a productive and distinguished career he would have as an NHPA member.

Rose also set up some other grids that are just amazing. He took record keeping beyond imagination. He recorded win/loss records by year from 1920 through 1933. This is some fascinating reading, especially the years that include his attendance at World Tournaments, because he faced so many of the key stars from the early days of our sport. Sure, most of the names mean little to us now, but it is extraordinary to see the record keeping Lee maintained, and keep in mind the years that he recorded at least in part because his records are evidence that official horseshoe-pitching contests were being held. In his words:

Following is a list or recapitulation of all the horseshoe games I ever engaged in that I have any record of. This list includes only games played in state, world, county, city, special, sectional or any kind of tournament, also games played in team matches or special match games. An 'x' is by each player that I met for the first that year.

1920

Wins		Lose	Win		Lose
6	Boye **x**	0	1	Joe LaBurt	0
5	Belford Rose	0	1	Lewis **x**	0
2	Richard Pawlitz	0	1	Scott Jr. **x**	0
2	Victor Trousseau	0	4	Dean **x**	1
2	Brown **x**	0	4	Ben Mersdorf **x**	1
1	Leslie Evans x	0	3	Scott Sr. **x**	2
1	Herbert Smitling	0	5	William Peschke	4
1	Burnette	0	2	Alfred Reid	3

Won 41   Lost 11

1921

Wins		Lose	Win		Lose
10	Fred Kruger **x**	0	5	Albert Salinger **x**	0
10	Homer **x**	0	5	Clarence Salinger **x**	0
5	Fred Beter **x**	0	5	Burdette House	0
5	Russell Rymus x	0	5	Williams **x**	0
5	Richard Pawlitz	0	5	Harry Underhill **x**	0
5	Blaire Dwelle x	0	5	Gustave Kinsky **x**	0
5	Burnette	0	5	Floyd Brennan **x**	0
5	Victor Trousseau	0	5	Raymond Faes **x**	0
5	Belford Rose	0	5	Arthur Scott **x**	0
5	Herbert Smitling	0	5	Dominic Bernardi	1
5	Jack Fiske **x**	0	5	William Peschke	2
5	Joe LaBurt	0	5	Alfred Reid	3
5	Charles Johnson **x**	0			

Won 135   Lost 6

1922

Wins		Lose	Win		Lose
5	Belford Rose	0	4	Dominic Bernardi	0
4	Burdette House	0	3	Robert Metzger x	0
4	Kenneth Perry x	0	5	William Peschke	1

Won 25   Lost 1

1923

Wins		Lose	Win		Lose
5	Alfred Reid	0	5	William Peschke	1
1	Ned Martin x	0	0	C. W. Huntington x	1

Won 11   Lost 2

1924

Wins		Lose	Win		Lose
1	Taylor (Dearborn) x	0	1	Robert Omans x	0
1	Freddie Theisen x	0	1	Foster Kockenderfer x	0
1	Panko x	0	2	Elmer Yungs x	1
1	Karalash x	0	0	'Doc' Taylor x	2
1	Manneback x	0			

Won 9   Lost 3

1925

Wins		Lose	Win		Lose
1	E. Stewart x	0	0	Yarnell	1
1	Faurot	0	0	Eddie Combs	1
1	H. J. Oates	0	0	Joe Forten	1
1	Allie Seals x	0	0	Frank Seals x	1
1	Wilson	0			

Won 5   Lost 4

The Lee Rose Story

1926

Wins		Lose	Win		Lose
1	Lew Wilkes x	0	1	Faurdt	0
1	John Rossen x	0	1	Forten	0
1	High Stanlake x	0	1	Moersch x	0
1	G. G. Smith x	0	9	Smith (Clark Park) x	1
1	J. DeLeeuw x	0	2	Albert ___ x	1
1	Claude Emerson x	0	1	Ed. Combs	1
1	S. DeLeeuw x	0	1	McKonkey	1
1	Orra Koosen x	0	1	Vanderpool x	2
5	Harley Rizor x	0	0	Varnell	1
1	H. J. Oates	0	0	Ira Knight x	1
1	Guthrie x	0	0	Kenneth Crouse x	1
1	Wilson x	0	0	Wayne Emerson x	1
1	Cunningham x	0			

Won 34   Lost 10

- - - - - - -

His statistics from 1927 include his visit to the 1927 World Tournament (summer) held in Duluth, Minnesota. After the qualifying rounds, the top 35 players formed the men's Championship Class. Rose qualified and played in the semifinals. His record was 12–21 and he placed 22nd, short of the cutoff for the 12-man finals. Most of his games in 1927 were from the World Tournament, suggesting that the only pitching he did in 1927 was at that event and, most likely, the Michigan state tournament.

- - - - - - -

1927

Wins		Lose	Wins		Lose	Wins		Lose
1	Putt Mossman x	0	1	Al Zeiter	0	0	Harvey Elmerson	1
1	William Yocum x	0	1	Solomon Beaver	0	0	Vyrl Jackson	1
1	Wesley Gibson x	0	1	Graumlich x	1	0	Verne Licht x	1
1	Hopkins x	0	0	Carroll Jackson	1	0	Elmer Lewis x	1
1	Sidney Plott x	0	0	C. C. Davis	1	0	Johns Anderson x	1
1	Roy Slater x	0	0	Seymour Johnson	1	0	Emmett Mossman	1
1	R. Rasmussen x	0	0	John Dahl x	1	0	R. D. Baxter	1
1	R. Shewsbury x	0	0	Collier x	1	0	Louis Harrison	2
1	Fred Qualley x	0	0	Harvey Reese x	1	0	R. Cadwalladar	1
1	Perkins x	0	0	R. Ransdell x	1	0	James Skinner	1
1	Ira Vail x	0	0	James Risk	1	0	McKonkey	1

(Continued on next page)

(Continued from previous page)

Wins		Lose	Wins		Lose	Wins		Lose
1	Frederickson **x**	0	0	Art Cumming **x**	1	0	Raybourne	1
1	Kenneth Hart **x**	0	0	Hans. Jackson	1	0	Ed Walls	1
1	Frank Stinson **x**	0	0	George Hilst **x**	1	0	Joe Latzko	1
1	Ray Gorsline	0	0	Milton Tate **x**	1	0	Dan Latzko	1
1	George Middling	0	0	Cecil Freel **x**	1	0	R. H. Rizor	1
1	Fred O'Melay	0	0	Frank Jackson	1	0	Ed Combs	1
1	Mauer **x**	0	0	Bert Duryee	1			

Won 23   Lost 34

- - - - - - -

Lee's record of games played in 1928 includes his visit to the 1928 World Tournament, held in St. Petersburg, Florida, from February 20 to March 1. The winter event was the only men's World Tournament held in 1928. (Although there was a summer event for the women in Rochester, New York.) Similarly, in 1929 the winter event was the last World Tournament held until 1933.

Note that Lee records three games against Mrs. Mildred Brouillette. Brouillette was a two-time World Champion and the defending women's World Champion when she arrived at the tournament in Florida. This suggest that there must have been an exhibition held between the two players. Note also that Lee picked up first-time matches against some well-known players, such as hall-of-famers Harold Falor and Blair Nunamaker.

- - - - - - -

1928

Wins		Lose	Wins		Lose	Wins		Lose
2	Warren Wulf	0	1	Tony Bush	0	0 0	Jim Hough **x**	1
2	Dan Latzko	0	1	Heinie Freidman **x**	0	0 0	Vyrl Jackson	1
2	Jack Walsh	0	1	Claude Gebhardt **x**	0	0	Jimmy Risk	1
2	Ed Miller	0	1	Van Huizen	0	0	Putnam **x**	1
1	Harry Robinson **x**	0	1	Perry Harper **x**	0	0	Herbert Jackson **x**	1
1	Emmett Mossman	0	1	Ray Gorsline	0	0	Fred Brundige **x**	1
1	Les Evans **x**	0	1	Harry Ellerby	0	0	Hansford Jackson	1
1	Abner Whipple **x**	0	4	R. H. Rizor	1	0	Les Robison **x**	1
1	Lyemance **x**	0	1	Joe Latzko	1	0	Harvey Elmerson	1
1	Charles Brundice **x**	0	1	Jim Skinner	1	0	C. R. Thompson **x**	1
1	Parker Moore **x**	0	1	Ben Emerson	2	0	Carol Jackson	1
1	Lloyd Eaton **x**	0	1	Ed Combs	2	0	John Estep **x**	1
1	Cliff Moylan	0	1	M. Brouillette **x**	2	0	Putt Mossman	1

(Continued on next page)

(Continued from previous page)

Wins		Lose	Wins		Lose	Wins		Lose
1	Winters x	0	1	Ed Walls	3	0	Blair Nunamaker x	1
1	Art Scovel	0	0	Harold Falor x	1	0	D. T. Leonard x	1
1	Brewster x	0	0	Bert Duryee	1	0	R. Caldwallader	1
1	Joe Galesky x	0	0	Glenn Porter x	1	0	C. C. Davis	1
1	Perino Allagreen x	0	0	Frank Jackson	1			

Won 39   Lost 34

- - - - - - -

Rose didn't attend the 1929 World Tournament and, for the most part, his opponents were just one or two games during the year. There are a few exceptions, and certainly the eight matches with Leo G. Lattore stand out. As mentioned previously, Leo Lattore, with a partner named Edward Levagood, started the Lattore Horseshoe Company. They filed for a patent on December 21, 1932, and after what seems like a long delay, their patent was granted on August 20, 1935. Lee purchased their company sometime in the 1940s and maintained management of it into the 1980s.

Also note the game with Ed Besancon. Ed never qualified for a men's final at the World Tournaments, but his wife did three times—1924, 1925, and 1926. She had two third-place finishes and one fourth-place finish.

- - - - - - -

1929

Wins	Lose		Wins		Lose	Wins		Lose
3	R. Cadwalladar	0	1	Ridge x	0	1	Case x	0
3	John Collins x	0	1	Cooper x	0	1	Oates x	0
2	'No. 12' Ontario x	0	1	Johnson	0	1	Depotty x	0
2	Don Walls	0	1	Guy Williams	0	1	Marsh x	0
2	George Roberts	0	1	Huggard x	0	1	Jim Burt	0
2	Wm. Bierwirth x	0	1	Walsh (Essex)x	0	1	Hector Rivers	0
2	Ed Besancon x	0	1	G. Lickman	0	1	Sam LaJoie x	0
2	Albert Zeiter	0	1	Art Scovel	0	1	Holden	0
2	Harry Ellerby	0	1	Van Huizen	0	4	Dale Huntington	1
2	Fred O'Melay	0	1	Bartlett x	0	4	Ed Combs	1
2	Ralph D. Baxter	0	1	Dan Latzko	0	3	Ben Emerson	1
2	Oostdyke	0	1	Jack Hoeksema	0	3	R. H. Rizor	1
2	Hicks	0	1	Cliff Moylan	0	5	Leo Lattore	3
2	Warren Wulf	0	1	Mays x	0	1	Wm Struthers x	1
2	Lou Harrison	0	1	Jack Walsh	0	1	Richard Prediger	2

(Continued on next page)

(Continued from previous page)

Wins	Lose	Wins	Lose	Wins	Lose
2 Ed Walls	0	1 Harold Davis	0	0 A. Bush	1
1 Struthers x	0	1 Ray Wrobbel	0	0 Bruckman	1
1 Buchingham x	0	1 R. Middleton	0	0 Jim Skinner	2
1 Petrie	0	George x	0	0 Joe Latzko	2

Won 86   Lost 16

1930

Wins	Lose	Wins	Lose	Wins	Lose
5 D. Huntington	0	1 George Levagood	0	1 Leo Lattore	0
4 Ricard Prediger	0	1 Ed Curran x	0	1 Harry Ellerby	0
3 'Cannon Ball'		1 McDonald Sr. x	0	1 Roy Middleton	0
Tierney x	0	1 Art Scovel	0	1 Ray Gorsline	0
2 Parisot x	0	1 George Pillman	0	1 Joe Latzko	1
2 Blakely x	0	1 Stevens x	0	1 George Stewart	0
2 Krock x	0	1 Rittenger x	0	3 R. H. Rizor	*1
2 'Red' Hanning x	0	1 Jim Burt	0	2 Jim Skinner	1
2 Ed Miller	0	1 Ed Combs	0	1 Dan Kasko	1
2 Jack Walsh	0	1 Seyforth x	0	1 R.D. Cadwalladar	1
2 Harold Davis	0	1 Stanley Burt x	0	1 C. James x	1
2 W. MacDonald	0	1 'Slim' (Monroe) x	0	1 James Risk	6
2 Rhineheart x	0	1 'Glasses'(Monroe) x	0	0 Randall x	1
2 'Doc' Meyer x	0	1 Pekkola x	0	0 O. A. Zimmerman x	1
2 Neddo x	0	1 'Heavey' (Monroe) x	0	0 Cliff Maylan	1
2 Riekartz x	0	1 Pearl Fisher	0	0 Bruckman x	1
1 Smith (Ft Wayne) x	0	1 Sprague x	0	0 Lemke x	1
1 J. C. Hahn x	0	1 Elmer Fought x	0	0 Ed Walls	1
1 Hartman x	0	1 Lew Harrison	0	0 Guy Binkley x	2
1 Funderburg x	0	1 Clarence Peck x	0		
1 Jimmy Lee x	0	1 Sellers x	0		

Won 81   Lost 20

Wins	Lose	Wins	Lose
1 Overholtzer Sr x	0	1 Jack Hoeksema x	0
1 Overholtzer Jr x	0	1 Scheets x	0

- - - - - - -

Rose had another successful year in 1930, when he boasted an 81 and 20 record. Most of the records are from single games, except for seven matches against Jimmy Risk, who is a hall of fame member known for his traveling exhibitions of horseshoe pitching. It appears that Rose participated in one or two of Risk's shows.

Rose played considerably more games (and more opponents) in 1931, but without the kind of league setup we know today. Most of the games are just one or two matches, but the majority of the year's games were team challenges with neighboring towns. Lee included some newspaper clippings that illustrate those challenges.

There is one new name on the 1931 list that should capture our attention. After spending many years collecting pitching shoes, I became very familiar with many of the toy shoes also. Occasionally a set of old toy rubber shoes under the brand name Si Perkins comes up for sale on eBay. I always thought that was a made-up name for marketing purposes, but it turns out that in 1931 Lee Rose played two games with a Si Perkins. It must be the same Si Perkins who inspired or made the toy rubber shoes.

- - - - - - -

1931

Wins		Lose	Wins		Lose	Wins		Lose
4	Melvin Best x	0	1	German x	0	1	Tom Wolf x	0
4	Wm. Kettler x	0	1	George Perkins	0	1	Oostdyke	0
3	Bristol x	0	1	McConkey	0	1	Bock x	0
3	Currin x	0	1	Baker x	0	1	Julius Walker x	0
3	Jack Polanskix	0	1	Kear x	0	1	Reynolds x	0
3	Albert Hallup	0	1	Collins x	0	1	Mrs. Lee Rose x	0
3	A. R. Turbett	0	1	Tess x	0	1	Provo x	0
3	John Walls	0	1	Webster x	0	1	Hayes	0
3	Leo Lattore	0	1	Strayer x	0	1	Steska x	0
2	Archie Gray x	0	1	Ehrat x	0	1	Blake x	0
2	McCrumb x	0	1	Price x	0	1	Harold Arold	0
2	Johnston x	0	1	Rosecrans x	0	1	McLain x	0
2	Si Perkins x	0	1	Allen x	0	1	J. Moylan x	0
2	Jack Walsh	0	1	Art Scovel	0	1	Harry Ellerby	0
2	Tom Tipton	0	1	Art Theisen x	0	4	Frank Koppitsch	1
2	G. Levagood	0	1	Trudall x	0	9	R. Harley Rizor	3
2	Asseumacker x	0	1	Bernard Korte x	0	1	K.E. Armstrong	2
2	Bob Bixman	0	1	Lute x	0	2	Myers x	1
2	Shears x	0	1	Kleinknan x	0	2	Warren Wrobbel	1
2	Petrie	0	1	Mullaney	0	2	M. B. Getz	1
2	Johnson(Romulus)	0	1	Sweeney x	0	3	Ed Walls	3
2	W. MacDonald	0	1	Vincent Kolb x	0	2	Tony Bush	2
2	Ray Wrobbel	0	1	Johnson (Detroit)x	0	4	Jim Burt	6
2	Stanley Daid x	0	1	Ed Combs	0	0	Pearl Fisher	1
2	Roy Hayden x	0	1	Cameron x	0	0	Jones x	1

(Continued on next page)

(Continued from previous page)

Wins		Lose	Wins		Lose	Wins		Lose
2	Harold Davis x	0	1	Aude x	0	0	Art Moser	1
2	Paul Fitch	0	1	Don Stephens	0	0	Stanley Esper	1
2	Holden	0	1	Chas. Roulier	0	0	Jim Skinner	1
2	Hicks	0	1	Ray Craig x	0	3	Cliff Moylan	0
2	Lickman	0	1	Gardener x	0			
2	Belford Rose	0	1	Foster	0			

Won 153   Lost 25

1932

Wins		Lose	Wins		Lose	Wins		Lose
4	Rouhier	0	1	Clark x	0	1	'No. 3' x	0
5	Rizor	0	1	Sovullkin x	0	1	'No. 4' x	0
4	Harrington x	0	1	Bixman	0	1	Pierce	0
4	J. Campeau	0	1	Austin x	0	1	Lou Harrison	0
4	Stephens	0	1	Wilcot x	0	1	H. Holksema	0
4	Skinner	0	1	Williams x	0	1	J. Holksema	0
3	McCann	0	1	Tony x	0	1	Wright x	0
3	Stockwell x	0	1	Harris x	0	1	Heaton x	0
2	Lanoue	0	1	'No. 1' x	0	1	T. Haley x	0
2	Davis	0	1	Turbett	0	5	H. Rivers	1
2	Jewett	0	1	Marsh x	0	11	Jim Burt	3
2	Kruger x	0	1	Kramer x	0	2	Martin x	1
2	R. Wrobbel	0	1	Stradley	0	2	S. Esper	1
2	W. Wrobbel	0	1	T. Buck	0	2	Al Field	1
2	Mullaney	0	1	Miller x	0	2	A. Bush	1
2	Ingman x	0	1	De Merchant x	0	4	H. Rose x	3
2	Forster	0	1	Drouillard	0	1	Baltzer x	1
2	Hayes	0	1	Mann x	0	1	Bohley x	1
2	Gravenkemper x	0	1	Hess x	0	1	Hallup	1
2	O'Dell x	0	1	Connor x	0	1	Ray Brown x	1
2	Wolfe	0	1	Kitilla x	0	1	Middleton	1
2	Getz	0	1	Arold	0	1	W. Wulf	1
2	King x	0	1	Cleary	0	4	Belair x	5
2	Baxter	0	1	Pichotte x	0	5	Prediger	9
2	Freeman x	0	1	Fitch	0	1	Labodie x	2
1	G. Dillman x	0	1	McArthur x	0	0	Gorsline	1
1	Ruhl x	0	1	Portt x	0	0	Lattore	1
1	Kelly x	0	1	Koppitsch	0	0	Les Allen x	2
1	Ivan Bader x	0	1	G. Perkins	0	0	R. Haley x	2
1	Winder x	0	1	Moser	0	0	J. McDonald	4
1	Shires x	0	1	C. Moylan	0	0	Ed Walls	9
1	Philps x	0	1	F. Levagood x	0	2	Armstrong	1
1	Johnson x	0	1	'No 2' x	0			

Won 162   Lost 53

The Lee Rose Story

- - - - - - -

There was not much of significance in the 1932 listing, other than it was the largest list of games played so far. You might notice a 0–9 record against Ed Walls. Walls clearly had the upper hand against Rose. He should, after all, Walls was a five-time Michigan state champion (1927, 1928, 1930, 1931, and 1932). I noticed seven games against H. Rose and wondered if that might have been a relative, but then I recalled that Lee's real surname wasn't Rose, it was Jacobs.

Lee's diary of games played continued with the 1933 list. There were a number of new opponents—and a win against Casey Jones. Jones was just entering the national scene in 1933 and he became one of the greatest players of all time. He is arguably the greatest player never to have won a World Championship. It's also worthy of remark that 11-year-old Bobbie Hitt held a 7–2 edge over 27-year-old Lee Rose.

- - - - - - -

1933

Wins		Lose	Wins		Lose	Wins		Lose
6	Prediger	0	1	L. Stage x	0	1	J. McDonald	0
3	Al Field	0	1	Hewer x	0	1	Davidson x	0
3	Don Walls	0	1	Godby x	0	1	Demus x	0
3	Arold	0	1	Tony Bush	0	1	H. Hoeksema	0
2	F. Campeau x	0	1	Mullaney	0	1	Tipton	0
2	McCann	0	1	Stradley	0	1	Sipple x	0
2	Howard x	0	1	Johnson x	0	1	Beck x	0
2	J. Hart x	0	1	Drouillard	0	1	'Toledo 1' x	0
2	Lovas x	0	1	York x	0	2	H. Rivers	1
2	Lamet x	0	1	Getz	0	2	Lou Harrison	1
2	C. Westerly x	0	1	Fitch	0	2	Stephens	1
2	Ward	0	1	Olin x	0	2	R.D. Baxter	1
2	J. Walls	0	1	M. Westerby x	0	1	S. Esper	1
2	R. Wrobbel	0	1	Bates x	0	1	Wolfe	1
2	Russeau x	0	1	Valleau x	0	1	H. Askey x	1
2	Pierce	0	1	Mangan x	0	9	Jim Burt	5
2	T. Buck	0	1	Rayma x	0	4	Ed Walls	6
2	Lanoue	0	1	McArthur (RO) x	0	2	Bobbie Hitt x	7
2	J. Campeau x	0	1	Yarnell	0	0	Joe Bennett x	1
2	Sheppardson x	0	1	Haines x	0	0	Lattore	1
2	C. Buck x	0	1	Harris x	0		Leo Ingram x	1
2	Taylor x	0	1	Denio x	0	0	Antill x	1

(Continued on next page)

(Continued from previous page)

Wins		Lose	Wins		Lose	Wins		Lose
2	Kozlowski **x**	0	1	Casey Jones **x**	0	0	'Toledo 2' **x**	1
2	Babcock **x**	0	1	Armstrong	0	0	Birchard **x**	1
2	Rizor	0	1	Jewett	0	0	Emerson	2
2	Ed Combs	0	1	Koppitsch	0	0	Skinner	2
1	Rouhier	0	1	Davis	0	2	W. Wrobbel	0
1	Boos	0	1	J. Hoeksema	0			

Won 137   Lost 35

A careful study of the foregoing records will show that during 14 years of horseshoe pitching, I have met in match games a total of 413 different players. The players who have an 'x' after their name are new opponents whom I met in that year. In the last 3 years, I have met 141 new men and women, with 48 in 1931, 50 in 1932 and 43 in 1933. My most ancient rival is Eddie Combs, whom I met for the first time in 1925, but I have played him only 16 times, winning 10. I also met Yarnell in 1925 and again in 1926. I did not play him again until 1933. My most durable rival however is R. Harley Rizor, whom I met first in 1926. I have played him every year and have now met him 38 times. I have been victorious 31 times over him. My worst hoodoo is Ed Walls. In 33 games over a span of 7 years, he has defeated me 23 times. My most prolific rival is Jim Burt. In a span of 5 years, I have played him 40 games, winning 26 and losing 14.

In 1925, the leading pitchers in Michigan were Eddie Combs, Ben Emerson, Warren Wulf, Frank Seals, Allie Seals, Perry Baxter, Harley Rizor and possible a few others. Of these men, Combs, the Seals boys, Harper, Wilkes, Ellerby and Caldwalladar have dropped out of the first rank, or else given up the game entirely. Emerson dropped out after 1929, but made a comeback in 1933. Wulf has pitched steadily through the years, but did not attend any tournaments from 1929 until 1932. Again in 1933, Wulf did not appear. Baxter was out of the state in 1930 & 1931, but has never quit pitching. Rizor has never been a threat, but is always a tough customer. In 1926, Joe and Dan Latzko established themselves, as did Hugh Stanlake, Ira Knight, Kenneth Crouse, Jim Skinner, Ray Gorsline, Lou Harrison and others. Of these, only Skinner, Gorsline and Harrison are still going and only Skinner has been active in every year.

I would have eventually conquered my own state, had not an interloper appeared in 1927—Ed Walls! Walls had been several times state champion in Nebraska and was already to step right in and take over the state of Michigan. He swept through two years without losing a game until I finally downed him in the state tournament in 1928. In 1929, I played him only twice, once in a team match and then in the state tournament. I won both games! I played him only one game in 1930, which he won and in 1931, in 6 games, I earned an even break. In 1932, he won nine straight games off me and he also won every game in 1933 until that last glorious meeting when I defeated him 4 to 3 in a 7 game duel. Perhaps this may be the turning point in my 7-year quest to down Walls.

While the Walls–Rose feud was raging, other shoe luminaries flashed from over the horizon and many have flashed back again. Prediger moved in from Ohio in 1929, dropped out of horseshoe in 1931, came back strong in 1932, but took some heavy wallops in the latter part of 1933. Jim Burt broke in, in 1928, and has been going strong ever since. But there are none to dispute my claim to being the "oldest inhabitant" in horseshoes in Michigan, being always right near the top for nine years, more than any other player. My really greatest year just passed and I intend to make 1934 a year [that] will see Lee Rose reach newer and greater heights than ever before. Over the next page is my standing against my leading opponents, rated by the number of years I have met each one.

- - - - - - -

In his summary, Rose writes that Ed Walls won some state championships in Nebraska. Well, actually, it was Missouri. Walls won state titles there in 1925 and 1926.

This seems like a good time to recall that Lee Rose did not have the advantage of a computer program Microsoft Excel to do his recording and organizing of these extensive reports. His work was all done in longhand on regular old ledger paper. As we glance over these lists, even though the reports may mean little to us and may seem rather monotonous, it surely is a testimony to Lee's dedication to the sport and his own participation in it. Here is his all-inclusive report of his games played over eight years.

- - - - - - -

Years	Won	Player	Lost	Years	Won	Player	Lost	Years	Won	Player	Lost
8	31	R.H. Rizor	7	3	4	Ben Emerson	5	2	4	Hicks	0
8	10	Ed Combs	6	3	6	Warren Wrobbel	1	2	3	Lickman	0
7	10	Ed Walls	23	3	5	Warren Wulf	1	2	2	Geo Perkins	0
5	8	C. H. Davis	0	3	3	Ray Middleton	1	2	3	Forester	0
5	6	Cliff Moylan	1	3	2	McConkey	2	2	3	Oostdyke	0
7	7	Jim Skinner	8	3	1	Jimmy Risk	8	2	3	Hayes	0
5	6	Tony Bush	4	3	12	Al Reid	6	2	9	Dale Huntington	1
5	6	Lou Harrison	3	2	5	Al Field	1	2	4	Ed Miller	0
5	26	Jim Burt	14	2	5	Don Walls	0	2	3	Albert Zeiter	0
5	9	Leo Lattore	5	2	5	McCann	0	2	3	Fred O'Melay	0
4	16	Dick Prediger	11	2	5	John Walls	0	2	3	Johnson	0
4	7	Ray Wrobbel	0	2	3	Tom Buck	0	2	2	Van Huizen	0
4	4	Jack Hoeksema	0	2	4	Lanoue	0	2	2	George Middling	0
4	6	Ralph Baxter	2	2	6	Joel Campeau	0	2	1	Emmett Mossman	1
4	3	Ray Gorsline	1	2	2	J.R. Stradley	0	2	0	Bert Duryee	2
4	7	Jack Walsh	0	2	2	Drouillard	0	2	0	Frank Jackson	2
4	17	Belford Rose	0	2	1	Pearl Fisher	1	2	0	Vyrl Jackson	2
4	4	Art Scovel	0	2	3	Jewett	0	2	0	Hans. Jackson	2
4	5	Harry Ellerby	0	2	1	J, McDonald	4	2	0	Harvey Elmerson	2
4	2	Joe Latzko	5	2	2	H. Hoeksema	0	2	0	Carroll Jackson	2
4	4	Dan Latzko	5	2	3	Tom Tipton	0	2	1	Putt Mossman	1
4	4	R. Cadwalladar	3	2	2	Tom Cleary	0	2	0	C.C. Davis	3
4	20	Wm. Peschke	8	2	3	Joe Wolfe	1	2	2	H.J. Oastes	0
3	5	Harold Arold	0	2	0	Bruckman	2	2	2	Wilson	0
3	7	Char. Rouhier	0	2	3	Pierce	0	2	2	Faurot	0
3	4	Dick Mullaney	0	2	3	Bob Bixman	0	2	1	Joe Forten	1
3	5	M.B. Getz	1	2	4	A.R. Turbett	0	2	9	Burdette House	0
3	4	Paul Fitch	0	2	1	Art Mosher	1	2	9	Dominic Bernardi	1
3	1	Yarnell	2	2	4	Albert Hallup	1	2	7	Richard Pawlitz	0
3	7	K.E. Armstrong	3	2	2	George Dillman	0	2	6	Burnett	0
3	6	Frank Koppitsch	1	2	3	Geo. Levagood	0	2	7	Vic Trousseau	0
3	8	Hector Rivers	2	2	4	Wm. McDonald	0	2	5	Herb Smitling	0
3	7	Don Stephens	1	2	3	Petrie	0	2	6	Joe LaBurt	0
3	3	Stanley Esper	3	2	3	Holden	0				

Won 433   Lost 171

- - - - - - -

Lee's work and attention to detail for the International Horseshoe Pitchers Association, as then self-appointed secretary-treasurer, was impeccable; it could almost be called amazing. At the end of the 1933 season, Rose wrote out the following league records, another impressive display of record keeping.

- - - - - - -

Association Records

Team Records –

Highest Pct. in One Match	Dearborn
Highest Pct. for Season	Dearborn
Most Points Scored for Season	Dearborn
Most Ringers in One Match	Dearborn
Most Ringers for Season	Dearborn
Most Doubles in One Match	Dearborn
Most Double for Season	Dearborn
Most Shoes in One Match	Birmingham/East Dearborn
Most Shoes for Season	John R.
Least Shoes in One Match	Dearborn/Birmingham
Most Games Won	Dearborn

Individual Records –

Highest Pct. in One Game	Lattore	.893
Highest Pct. in Five-Game Match	Ed Walls	.760
Highest Pct. for Season	Ed Walls	.679
Most Points Scored for season	Rose	3,664
Most Ringers in One Game	Hitt	78
Most Ringers in One Match	Ed Walls	262
Most Ringers for Season	Rose	2,406
Most Double in One Game	Hitt	28
Most Doubles in One Match	Ed Walls	90
Most Doubles for Season	Rose	737
Most Shoes in One Game	Ed Walls vs. Hitt	
Most Shoes in One Match	Smith	404
Most Shoes for Season	Rose	3,954
Most Games Pitched	Rose	75
Most Games Won	Rose	69
Highest Winning Average	Ed Walls	.937
Least Shoes in One Game	Several tie	24
Least Shoes in Five-Game Match	Armstrong	152

- - - - - - -

Present-day league reports contain many more categories than he recorded in 1933. Of course, the Rose method of reporting makes more sense when we recall that they were playing 50-point games. Surprisingly, there were no "4-On" categories, at least up to this point in time. That is a neat term, since "Four-Dead" had not yet been coined.

His First State Championship

The 1934 journal pages began with a couple of short newspaper clippings about setting up the year's league play; in fact, this chapter is almost completely dedicated to league play and his record over the years. Rose did not expound on the method of play, but it is safe to assume that this league played 50-point games with no handicap. Here's Lee's account, as recorded in his own hand.

- - - - - - -

To Organize Horseshoe Team Sunday

The first meeting of Dearborn's championship horseshoe team will be held at two o'clock on Sunday, April 22 at their courts located at Park and Monroe Boulevard.

The meeting will be held for the purpose of lining up the team members for the coming season. Manager Lee Rose expects to see the following players at the courts: Leo Lattore, Kenneth Armstrong, Frank Koppitsch, George Levagood, John Harris, Harold Davis, A. R. Tubett, Albert Hallup, Charles Bohley, Leonard Lademann, John Forster, Alve Hayes, William Bertrand and Leonard Marsh. Any other player interested in trying out for the team is cordially invited to attend. If enough players can be found, there will be two teams formed this year.

In three years of league play, Dearborn has won the championship each year, compiling a record unequaled anywhere in the country, winning 46 and losing only four matches.

Twenty-six different players have helped the team hang up this record, but only six of them have played all three seasons. Their won and lost record is as follows:

	W	L
Lee Rose	201	26
Kenneth Armstrong	155	57
Frank Koppitsch	144	68
Leo Lattore	93	9
George Levagood	65	43
A. R. Turbett	2	7

Horseshoe Pitching Association To Meet

The International Horse Shoe Pitching Association will meet in the Dearborn City Hall next Wednesday evening at 8 o'clock. This league comprises some of the best teams and individuals in Michigan and Ontario.

Plans will be made for activities of the present season and a schedule of games drawn. Officers of the league are as follows: Henry D. Schubert, president; Walter Plumb of Pleasant Ridge, vice president and Lee Rose of Dearborn, secretary.

It was a very difficult task to get the horseshoe league together and going. After much dickering and running around, six teams were finally lined up: 1. Dearborn, 2. Northwestern, 3. Lincoln Park, 4. Detroit H.S.C., 5. Detroit Reserves, 6. Plymouth Motor Co.

Dearborn's first game was to have been with Detroit, but it was postponed. Members of the 2 Dearborn teams:

Dearborn	Dearborn Reserves
1. Rose	1. Lademann
2. Lattore	2. Bertrand
3. Koppitsch	3. Herbert
4. Davis	4. J. Field
5. Armstrong	5. O. Field
6. A. Field	6. Bohley
7. W. Field	7. Ropp
8. Mrs. Rose	8. Forster
9. Mrs. Davis	9. Hallup
10. Cleveland	
11. Valleau	

Champions Whip Reserves 19–6

The Dearborn Champions spanked their Reserves to open the International season. The game was played at Dearborn on the evening of May 24th.

It was a savage encounter with scrubs showing surprising strength and fight. Frank Koppitsch led the assault for the champs by hammering out the best night's work he has ever produced when he shot .675%. Rose followed right on his heels with .658%.

Without Lattore or Davis and with Al Field laid up with a bad foot, the Champs faced a confident Reserve Team which had a chance to win. But the paralyzing stream of ringers poured on the stakes by Koppitsch and Rose inspired the balance of the team and they trampled the fighting scrubs underfoot.

League standings on May 24, 1934

	W	L	Rose's scores	
1. Northwestern	2	0	50 Ropp	7
2. Dearborn	1	0	50 Bertrand	18
3. Dearborn Reserves	0	1	50 Herbert	9
4. Detroit	0	1	50 Lademann	43
5. Lincoln Park	0	1	50 J. Field	28
6. Plymouth Motor	0	0		

Scores

Northwestern	21	vs.	Lincoln Park	4
Northwestern	19	vs.	Detroit	6
Dearborn	19	vs.	Dearborn Reserves	6

Lincoln Park is Easy Victim

Dearborn easily won its second start on May 29, when they entertained the Lincoln Park team. Dearborn won, 21–4. Koppitsch again showed the way by pounding out .576.

Charlie Davis was right behind with .563. Al Field, with his foot still a little sore, crashed out .548 and Manager Rose made .540. These four players each won 5 straight. Bill Cleveland lost his first two and Bill Field replaced him and won 1 out of 3.

The next game for Dearborn is against Northwestern, there. Northwestern is the John R. team transplanted to Northwestern Field and includes: Ed Walls, Burt, Prediger, Arold, Tripton, Ron Wells and others.

Standing of Dearborn Players

Player	W	L	Pts	OP	R	OR	SP	Pct
Koppitsch	10	0	500	158	283	86	458	.618
Rose	10	0	500	189	267	74	450	.593
Davis	5	0	250	73	124	36	220	.563
Armstrong	4	0	200	88	116	33	206	.563
Al Fiend	5	1	296	150	159	42	304	.523
W. Field	4	4	333	245	170	28	488	.348
Cleveland	2	5	248	316	135	21	408	.331

League Standings	W	L
1. Northwestern	3	0
2. Dearborn	2	0
3. Detroit	1	1
4. Dearborn Reserves	0	2
5. Lincoln Park	0	2
6. Plymouth	0	1

Dearborn Crushes Northwestern Team
Champions Assume League Lead as They Trample Rivals
Koppitsch Leads Team Again

Flashing too much power for their old enemies to cope with, the Dearborn Champions squelched Northwestern at Northwestern Field, 16–9, and became the only undefeated team in the league. Both teams were minus a star, Ed Walls being absent from NW and Lattore from Dearborn. Manager Rose dropped a 50–48 game to Getz in the 1st round and Northwest led 3-2 and it seemed that Dearborn was to be in for a nip and tuck struggle. But from there on, the Dearborn superiority was well defined.

Koppitsch stamped himself as the league's leading player by blasting out 5 more victories with a .579 average. After his poor start, Rose wheeled around and crashed down his other four opponents with a .553 average. Al Field waded through 4 out of 5 games with a .509 mark.

Detroit Swamps Reserves

Detroit came out to Dearborn on May 31 and walloped the Reserves 21–4.

Ladermann battled hard for the Reserves and hung up a .436 average, better than anyone on either team. Herppich and Anderson led the way for Detroit with 5 wins apiece, while the Askey brothers, Roy and Harry, took 4 out of 5.

[On] June 6 at Lincoln Park, the reserves took it on the chin again, 16–9. J. Field won all 5 for the Reserves team.

Dearborn Massacres Monroe

Another massacre took place on the banks of the River Raisin on the evening of June 11, when Dearborn moved in to play the Monroe team a 6-man team match. Lattore, Al Field, Armstrong, Davis and Rose started the game and promptly began to slaughter and scalp the hapless home team. The final score was 35–1, the one Monroe victory being scored by J. Field, who was loaned to Monroe to help them fill out a team. Jimmy defeated Armstrong and was a source of annoyance to all the other Dearborn players, who had to go good to best him. Koppitsch pounced on Jimmy in the last round with 38 ringers in 42 shoes for a .904 game. Rose ran up an .882 game with 30 out of 34, while all the other players crowded 70% consistently. No records were kept of the match, but the team average was close 60% and for 6-men teams, this would constitute a world record.

Northwestern Beats Reserves

Northwestern won from the Dearborn Reserves on June 13 at the N.W. Field, 17–8. The scrubs put up a stubborn battle and Northwestern was forced to hurl their best game of the season to come out on top. The Reserves [had] their best game of the season also and fought their stronger rivals tooth and nail. Jimmy Field, who promised to become a star player, even though a southpaw, won 3 games and Lademann, won 2. For N.W., Burt won 5 and Tipton won 4.

June 17 – At Northwestern Field
Rose vs. Burt, 6 out of 11 games

Game	Player	Pts	R	DR	SP	Pct.
1	Rose	35	39	9	76	.513
	Burt	50	43	11	76	.566
2	Rose	49	45	14	78	.577
	Burt	50	41	12	78	.525
3	Rose	50	35	12	66	.530
	Burt	47	33	6	66	.533
4	Rose	25	20	5	54	.370
	Burt	50	27	10	54	.500
5	Rose	50	43	13	70	.603
	Burt	46	41	13	70	.586
6	Rose	50	28	10	44	.636
	Burt	8	14	4	44	.318
7	Rose	50	38	10	80	.475
	Burt	47	37	9	80	.462
8	Rose	50	31	10	42	.738
	Burt	9	17	2	42	.404
9	Rose	44	30	7	58	.517
	Burt	50	32	9	58	.552
10	Rose	28	37	12	70	.528
	Burt	50	43	15	70	.614
11	Rose	50	25	8	42	.595
	Burt	19	13	3	42	.309
Totals	**Rose**	**781**	**371**	**110**	**680**	**.546**
	Burt	**726**	**341**	**94**	**680**	**.501**

This match lasted nearly 4 hours and was played in a glaring sun and before a very small crowd. In justice to Rose, it must be said that he had been to a wedding anniversary celebration the night before and didn't feel so good. Rose was challenged by Prediger for a match on July 1st and it will be played if Dearborn doesn't have a team match out-state that day.

Detroit Falls Before Champions

Detroit came out to Dearborn on June 20 and took a 17–8 licking from the champs. Bohley and Valleau played in the Dearborn line-up just for the experience. Davis hung up the best % hurling .571, but dropped a game to Taylor, while Rose and Field won all their games. Rose hurled a .581 and Field .529. Valleau, in his first start, won 3 games, while Bohley dropped all five.

Dearborn invades Lansing on July 1st and will make a stride toward a state title should they defeat the Lansing team. It will be a 5-man match.

June 24 – At Northwestern Field
Rose vs. Arold, 6 out of 11 games

Game	Player	Pts	R	DR	SP	Pct
1	Rose	50	24	6	54	.444
	Arold	26	18	2	54	.333
2	Rose	50	31	7	60	.516
	Arold	25	23	4	60	.383
3	Rose	50	31	10	76	.407
	Arold	42	28	3	76	.368
4	Rose	50	35	7	72	.485
	Arold	37	34	11	72	.472
5	Rose	50	35	6	70	.500
	Arold	39	31	6	70	.442
6	Rose	50	33	7	66	.500
	Arold	36	28	4	66	.424
	Totals	**300**	**189**	**43**	**398**	**.475**
		205	**162**	**30**	**398**	**.407**

Ringers Deluge Dearborn Reserves

Dearborn again spanked the reserves on June 27, this time by a score of 21–4. Lee Rose led the way with the record percentage of the year for the league with 164 ringers in 232 shoes for .707. He also turned in the high game of the year when he landed on W. Field with 34 ringers in 40 shoes for .850.

Davis blasted out .638, the best he has ever turned in, while Armstrong looked like the man he used to be in turning back 5 opponents with .555. Ray Wrobbel, recently manager of Plymouth, having dropped out with his team, joined the Reserves and won 2 of their 4 victories. Mrs. Lee Rose started for the Champs, but was removed after losing the first game, [then] entered the fray again in the last round to pitch a game for the Reserves. Dearborn set the record for he year so far when they hung up .563 for the team %.

Won and Lost for Dearborn Players

Champions	W	L	Reserves	W	L
1. Koppitsch	17	0	1. Lademann	10	9
2. Rose	24	1	2. J. Field	15	15
3. Davis	17	3	3. R. Wrobbel	6	9
4. A. Field	16	3	4. Herbert	4	11
5. Armstrong	9	5	5. W. Field	6	20
6. Valleau	4	9	6. Cleveland	2	10
7. Bohley	2	7	7. Bertrand	1	9
8. Mrs. Rose	0	2	8. O. Field	1	10
9. Ropp	0	8			

~~ Bulletin ~~

Dearborn will also meet Battle Creek at Lansing on July 1, in the second game of a double-header. The first game is with Lansing.

Dearborn Captures Important Double-Header
Roses' Men Approach State Title
as They Win From Lansing And Battle Creek

Dearborn grabbed a stranglehold on the Michigan team title on July 1st when they won both ends of a double-header from Lansing and Battle Creek, played at Potter Park in Lansing.

```
Dearborn...4 2 3 33 – 15
Lansing.... 1 3 2 22 – 10
```

Dearborn	W	L	Pts	OP	R	DR	SP	Pct
Lattore	5	0	250	109	169	47	278	.608
Rose	4	1	246	136	156	49	278	.561
Davis	3	2	216	191	141	31	304	.463
Armstrong	2	3	157	235	121	23	304	.394
Koppitsch	1	4	155	249	122	17	312	.391
	15	10	1024	920	709	167	1476	.482

Lansing	W	L	Pts	OP	R	DR	SP	Pct
Fisher	3	2	226	171	155	42	294	.534
Graham	3	2	211	168	157	31	308	.509
Allen	2	2	182	179	134	30	292	.458
Fought	1	4	144	210	104	18	266	.399
Strayer	1	4	138	246	97	17	260	.373
Moore	0	1	19	50	21	3	56	.375
	10	15	920	1024	668	141	1476	.453

The big first round practically clinched the game with Lansing, but the game with Battle Creek was a much tougher affair.

Dearborn Ekes Narrow Win
From Battle Creek

This game was a rip-roaring affair that was anybody's until the last shoe was thrown. It was a savage clash as horseshoe games go and his most ancient and hated rivals, Emerson, Harrison and Skinner. After battling even for half a game with Emerson, Rose slammed on seven consecutive doubles and ran right out, much to Ben's chagrin. Harrison hung on like a leech and the last part of the game was a nightmare of ringers, but Rose kept a small lead intact by smashing on ringer for ringer and finally came out on top. Skinner proved to be easy and Babcock easier. Then, in the last round, Rose met the new sensation, Brown and this game was probably the greatest game ever pitched in Potter Park. After an even start, Rose put on a spurt and ran up a lead of 27–11. Here, Brown threw off his hat and smacked on 12 straight doubles to go ahead 32–27. But once again Rose began to creep ahead and was leading 48–36 when Brown slammed on another string of ringers to go out and win. Each man tossed on 61 ringers in 92 shoes.

Lattore easily won all his games and Davis came through with 3 victories after dropping his first and third games. Koppitsch blew up badly all day, losing 9 straight games after winning his first 50–49.

Dearborn	W	L	Pts	R	DR	SP	Pct
Lattore	5	0	250	189	56	302	.626
Rose	4	1	248	200	57	336	.595
Davis	3	2	201	147	36	302	.487
Armstrong	1	4	183	127	27	316	.402
Koppitsch	0	5	200	146	29	318	.459
Totals	13	12	1084	809	205	1574	.514

Battle Creek	W	L	Pts	R	DR	SP	Pct
Brown	4	1	232	186	55	308	.604
Skinner	3	2	219	166	37	332	.500
Dryer	2	2	150	98	18	228	.430
Harrison	1	2	206	164	39	354	.463
Emerson	2	3	112	69	18	156	.442
Babcock	0	3	115	84	14	196	.429
Totals	12	13	1034	767	181	1034	.487

There is now only one other team in Michigan [that] could give Dearborn a good game. This team is Grand Rapids, which recently beat Battle Creek 15–10. It is planned to have Dearborn meet Grand Rapids in Battle Creek for a state title game.

A big double-header is being arranged for sometime soon at Springfield, Ohio, where Dearborn will meet Willis Ave. and the Ohio Horseshoe Co. team of Columbus.

It is planned to sign Ed Walls for these out-of-state games.

Lincoln Park is Walloped Again

Dearborn made a visit to Lincoln Park on July 3 and smothered the Parkers 22–3. Rose attempted to insert Mrs. Rose and Mrs. Davis into the Dearborn line-up, but the Lincoln Park players refused to pitch against them. The result was that an angry Dearborn five took to the courts and roundly trounced their hosts.

Rose led the way, winning five with an average of .583. Al Field and Orv Valleau also won five. Davies dropped one to the surprising Vaughan and Koppitsch, still in a slump, fell from the league lead when he dropped games to Lovas and Osteen.

Rose Walks Away with Tournament

On July 10, a tournament was held at the old John R. Courts and Lee Rose shocked the John R. crowd when he easily took first money, seven dollars. He won 8 consecutive victories, but it was the first game that decided the whole thing. It was the game between Rose and Ed Walls.

Walls got the pitch and started right out by scoring 6 in the first inning. After hurling 6 out of eight, Walls was leading 10–0 and the John R. crowd was grinning and nodding when Rose launched a terrific offensive that sewed the game up within a few throws. Rose slammed on 18 ringers in his next 20 shoes and was leading the white-faced, perspiring Walls 20–10. The rest of the game was fairly even, Rose out-playing Walls 30–21 from then on to win 50–31.

	Pts	R	DR	SP	Pct	4 On
Rose	50	62	20	88	.704	9
Walls	31	54	14	88	.613	9

Ringers per 10 shoes

Rose	5	9	8	8	7	5	8	6	6
Walls	7	8	5	5	7	3	8	6	5

From then on, it was a walk for Rose and here are his other scores:

50	Rizor	14	50	Freeman	27
50	Arold	15	50	Burt	34
50	Langlands	26	50	Singer	1
50	McIntyre	16			

A rainstorm halted the tournament with one round unfinished, but first place was conceded to Rose, Walls took second and Burt got 3rd.

Dearborn Comes From Behind to Win
Fighting Spirit Proves Better Than Northwestern's
Rose Loses to Walls

Northwestern came out to Dearborn on July 11 all primed to defeat the home team as Ed Walls was with them, while Lattore was absent from Dearborn. None of the Dearborn rooters could see anything but a defeat for the Champions. The Northwestern cohorts were jubilent, believing they had certain win.

Getz was off to a fast start and ran up a lead of 23–1 on Valleau. Orville got over his stage fright then and outplayed Getz the rest of the game, but Getz had too long a lead and won 50–33.

Al Field insisting on throwing a 1 1/4 turn (a turn he cannot do good with) fell an easy victim of Burt 50–36. Davis didn't have much trouble in stowing away Prediger 50–24. Koppitsch nosed a win out over the slow-pitching McIntyre 50–45.

Walls and Rose clashed in the big game of the evening. Rose pumped on 15 out of 18 to take the lead on Walls 10–3, but Walls was out for revenge and was pitching as though his life hung on every shoes and he came up to lead Rose 15–10. Nine ringers in his next 10 shoes enabled Rose to bring it to 19–17. Walls made it 22–17 and then Rose spurted and ran ahead of Walls 25–22. Walls rallied again and took the lead 29–25. Rose made it 29–28 and Ed made it 33–28. Rose shot ahead 34–33. Walls again forged ahead 39–34. Rose brought it up to 39–37 and then Walls pushed ahead to make it 45–37. Rose rallied again to make it 45–41, Walls picked up a point and then Rose with a last desperate rush, took the lead on Walls 48–46. Two final doubles put Walls out 50–48.

	Pts	R	DR	SP	Pct	4On
Walls	50	63	21	90	.700	11
Rose	48	60	21	90	.667	11

Northwestern was leading 3–2 and things looked black for Dearborn.

Second Round

Rose pounced on Burt and wound the game up in a few minutes, 50–12, planking on 22 out of 32. Prediger led Valleau several times but Valleau hung on and rallied to finally win out 50–40. Field took a lead of 26–7 on McIntyre, but could not hold his lead and was downed 50–41. Walls tossed on 25 ringers out of his first 34 shoes to lead Davis 28–10, but fell off and Davis rushed up to go ahead 36–29. Walls got it going again to lead 48–36 and although Davies battled hard, Walls finally won 50–43. Getz rallied in mid-game to smear Koppitsch 50–35. Northwestern was then leading 6–4 and things looked even bleaker than ever for Dearborn.

The Lee Rose Story

Third Round

Koppitsch and Prediger battled evenly until it stood 36–36 and then Koppitsch went out with 3 doubles as Prediger missed. Rose easily defeated McIntyre 50–20. Valleau, in need of a rest, was removed for the round and Mrs. Davis took his place. She lost to Walls 50–2, Walls throwing 25 ringers in 32 shoes.

Getz walloped Field 50–40. Burt ran up a lead of 40–23 on Davis, but Davis rallied very nicely to come up and win out 50–41. The score was now 8–7 in favor of Northwestern and the Northwestern players got into knots discussing things while the Dearborn men ran up and down encouraging one another.

Fourth Round

McIntyre and Davis put on a terrific fight. Davis led 6–0 and then McIntyre ran up a lead of 17–6. Davis brought it up to 17–16, but Mac ran ahead again 30–16. Davis rallied here and made it 30–29. McIntyre kept going and was leading Davis 43–37, but Charley ploughed on 12 out of his last 14 to win 50–43. Walls slapped Koppitsch down 50–25. Rose gave Getz his first defeat of the evening 50–15. Valleau ripped on 13 out of 18 to lead Burt 27–0 and took it easy from then on to whip Burt 50–17. Field came to life and walked all over Prediger 50–7. Dearborn was pitching like a team possessed and had now taken the lead 11–9.

Fifth Round

Walls slaughtered Field 50–14, throwing 35 out of 46. Davis led Getz throughout to win 50–39. Koppitsch beat Burt 50–29. Rose romped over Prediger 50–15. Valleau easily turned back McIntyre 50–34 and Dearborn had won 15–10.

This victory not only clinched the first half title, but also stamped Dearborn as one of the most powerful teams in the country. Valleau is now a real regular, having thrown .531 in this match.

On July 24th, another tournament was held at John R., and this time Rose ran second to Walls. After beating down Ray Wrobbel, Arold and Getz, Rose lost a ringerful battle to Walls 50–47, after leading 47–38. Rose nosed Davis out 50–48 to take second, four dollars.

And Now !!!
We Come to the End

This is where the powerful Dearborn Team disintegrates and the league falls apart.

It seems that the faction led by Lattore finally became too obnoxious for Rose to put up with any longer and the old pals who had stuck together for years finally fell out and became enemies.

Simultaneously, Northwestern and Detroit lost interest in league games and there was no more league. Horseshoe practically vanished as a sport in Detroit.

August 1 – Lincoln Park (Evening)

Al Field defeated Lee Rose 6–5 in an eleven game match after Rose had led 5–2.

Rose had one 80% game, 57 ringers in 72 shoes. Field averaged 59% and Rose shot 58%.

City Tournament

Held at Northwestern Field on Saturday & Sunday, Aug. 25 and 26. The tournament was supposed to be a Detroit championship affair but was opened to almost anyone who came along. Rose, Lattore, Field, Davis and the defending title-holder, Burt, were pre-tourney favorites.

On both days, a terrific wind blew across the courts, swirling around and blowing sand in whirlpools. I had switched to Gordon shoes for this tournament and was handicapped very much by the wind.

August 26th

I was called upon to meet McIntyre in my first game and "Mac" was not much opposition. I rolled up 10 before he scored and led later by scores of 27–3, 42–11 and finally, 50–19. Score:

	Pts	R	DR	SP	Pct.
Rose	50	29	9	54	.537
McIntyre	19	18	2	54	.333

Burt had beaten Field in their game, while Rizor had upset Davis. I met Field next.

He started weakly and I ran up a lead of 19–1. I built my lead to 23–5 and here Field began to throw plenty of ringers and began to overhaul me. I led 29–13 and later 30–22. He threw a double and it looked like the end of "Tiger" Rose. But I managed to top his double and then to the discomfiture of Field and the crowd, I flung 3 more doubles on the stake and Field failed to even stop one of them and I shot out to win the game 50–46. Score:

	Pts	R	DR	SP	Pct
Rose	50	36	11	66	.545
Field	46	34	8	66	.515

Burt and Lattore also won again. I met Freeman next. Freeman played hard, but I was too strong for him and gradually forged ahead all the way through. Score:

	Pts	R	DR	SP	Pct
Rose	50	35	11	62	.564
Freeman	33	30	5	62	.484

Arold sprang a surprise in this round by Beating Lattore. Burt won his game and Rose and Burt, ancient enemies in city tournaments, were not in front once more. In my next game, I eked out a victory over Millar 50–38. The game was not as close as the score would indicate. The wind was blowing harder than ever. Score:

	Pts	R	DR	SP	Pct
Rose	50	26	7	60	.433
Millar	38	23	5	60	.383

Burt was defeated by Lattore in this round. I was now alone at the top and thus became a shining mark for the other players to shoot at and for most of my "public" life to boo at.

I met Davies next. I flung 7 out of 10 to take the lead on him 11–3. He then ploughed on 9 out of 10 to run ahead of me 22–11. I painfully rallied to make it 22–19. Here I missed both shoes and he smacked on a double to lead 28–19. Again I dug in and crawled up to 31–27. Again Davis shot ahead 37–27 and it seemed that I could never quite catch up. All the other games had ended and most of the players were gathered around our game.

I picked up a point and then shot on 3 doubles in a row. Davis could only get a single on each time and I had at last tied the score, 37–37. Davis got another point and then I went ahead 46–38. Here, Charley laid on 3 doubles in a row and once more shot ahead 47–46. He missed one shoe and I popped on a double to go ahead 49–47. I came back with another double and Davis after putting his first shoe on, at last missed and I had won out. Score:

	Pts	R	DR	SP	Pct
Rose	50	39	10	70	.557
Davis	47	39	11	70	.557

In the last round of the day, I met Leo Lattore. After my terrific fight with Davis, I hadn't much left to battle Lattore.

At the end of 3 innings Lattore was ahead 7–0. I then made a terrific attempt to swing the game my way. Throwing everything I had into every pitch, I smashed on 19 ringers in the next 22 shoes and rolled ahead of Lattore 21–12. After this burst, I missed both shoes 3 straight times and Lattore went ahead 25–21. I rallied again to go ahead 28–25 but Lattore kept piling 'em on and took the lead again 38–28. He missed both shoes and taking a minute for each shoe, I put on a double to come up to 38–34. Another point for me made it 38–35, then I fell off again and Lattore went ahead 45–35. In a last rally I made it 45–39 and then Lattore went out to win. Score:

	Pts	R	DR	SP	Pct
Rose	39	40	12	68	.588
Lattore	50	43	14	68	.632

This left the leaders standing thus:

	W	L
Rose	5	1
Lattore	5	1
Burt	5	1
Field	4	2
Arold	4	2

August 26th

I met Valleau first and took it easy to win going away. Score:

	Pts	R	DR	SP	Pct
Rose	50	29	5	68	.412
Valleau	26	25	5	68	.368

Lattore and Burt also won in this round. Arold was my next opponent and I led nearly all the way in a cat-and-dog fight to emerge a winner 50–40. Score:

	Pts	R	DR	SP	Pct
Rose	50	35	10	64	.547
Arold	40	34	8	64	.531

Valleau had toppled Burt and this left the leaders thus:

	W	L
Rose	7	1
Lattore	7	1
Burt	6	2
Field	5	3
Arold	5	3

The wind was blowing a regular gale as I engaged Koppitsch. The wind favored Hank very much as his low driving shoe was not affected much, while my high dropping shoe was whisked hither and thither by the wind. He leaped ahead 6–0. I brought it up to 6–4 and I took the lead 7–6. This was the only time in the game I ever got up to Koppitsch. He pitched an inspired game, fighting every inch of the way, while I wobbled at times, saddened that a player I once was so good to and whom I looked upon as a true friend and pal should be so bitterly against me. He shot ahead 15–7. I made it 15–13. He made it 21–12; I

21–16; he 27–16. I brought it up to 27–20 and he made it 30–20. Here I topped a double and came back with a double which got away to make it 30–26. But I missed here and he bent far over to plough on a double to lead 36–26. I made it 36–30 and he made it 39–30. I rallied here to bring it up to 39–37, but missed here and Frank leaned over again and laid on a double to make it 45–37. In a last, desperate push, I made it 45–43 but could not get any further and missed twice, while Koppitsch went out on 2 singles. This practically clinched the tournament for Lattore, as he had only 2 weak players to meet. Score:

	Pts	R	DR	SP	Pct
Rose	43	35	11	68	.515
Koppitsch	50	38	11	68	.559

I beat Rizor as follows:

	Pts	R	DR	SP	Pct
Rose	50	22	4	50	.440
Rizor	24	18	4	50	.360

I met Burt in a frame of mind that didn't care whether I won or lost. Burt rolled up to 13–3 before he fell off a bit and I came to the front 16–13. I the fell off some and he began to plank on doubles and took a lead of 23–16. I got 3 and Burt rang up 12 more to lead 35–19. Burt continued to lead and soon was ahead 48–29. I made a last rally and came rushing up on Burt. I kept going on — on — on until I tied the score at 49 all! Here I missed one shoe and Burt put on his first double I 8 frames to win out. Score:

	Pts	R	DR	SP	Pct
Rose	49	46	12	80	.575
Burt	50	46	14	80	.575

Final standing of the first four:

	W	L
Lattore	10	1
Burt	9	2
Rose	8	3
Field	8	3

So much for the city Tournament!

Complete Four-Year Record for Dearborn under the Rose Regime

League Game – 1931

Date	W	Opponent	L
July 9	17	Scovels	8
July 16	16	John R.	9
July 23	15	Detroit	10
July 30	18	Rizors	7
Aug 6	19	Pleasant Ridge	6
Aug 13	17	Scovels	8
Aug 20	11	John R.	14
Aug 27	17	Detroit	8
Sept 3	15	East Dearborn	10
Sept 10	25	Fords	0
Sept 11	20	Pleasant Ridge	5
Sept 17	13	Rizors	12
Sept 24	14	John R.	11
Oct 1	16	East Dearborn	9
Oct 2	19	Fords	6
Oct 8	15	Rizors	10
1931 Won 15			**Lost 1**

League Games – 1932

Date	W	Opponent	L
May 24	19	Pontiac	6
May 31	18	East Dearborn	7
June 7	22	Wrobbels	3
July 5	22	Challengers	3
July 12	23	Royal Oak	2
July 19	19	Ferndale	6
July 31	16	East Windsor	9
Aug 2	10	Wrobbels	15
Aug 9	14	Pleasant Ridge	11
Aug 16	16	Pontiac	9
Aug 23	13	John R.	12
Aug 25	14	East Dearborn	11
Aug 30	24	Challengers	1
Sept 7	18	Royal Oak	7
Sept 16	14	Pontiac	11
Sept 20	11	John R.	14
Oct 2	16	East Windsor	9
Oct 5	13	Pleasant Ridge	3
1932 Won 16			**Lost 2**

League Game – 1933

Date	W	Opponent	L
May 23	21	East Windsor	4
May 24	21	Lincoln Park	4
May 31	25	Birmingham	0
June 7	12	John R.	13
June 16	20	East Dearborn	5
June 26	16	Royal Oak	9
June 29	21	Pleasant Ridge	4
July 2	16	East Windsor	9
July 12	25	Lincoln Park	0
July 17	25	Birmingham	0
July 26	19	John R.	6
Aug 2	20	East Dearborn	5
Aug 9	23	Royal Oak	2
Aug 16	25	Pleasant Ridge	0
Aug 22	15	John R.	10
Aug 29	18	John R.	7
Won	**13**	**Lost**	**1**

League Games – 1934

Date	W	Opponent	L
May 24	19	Dearborn Res.	6
May 29	21	Lincoln Park	4
June 6	16	Northwestern	9
June 13	25	Plymouth Mtr. Co	0
June 20	17	Detroit	8
June 27	21	Dearborn Res.	4
July 3	22	Lincoln Park	3
July 11	15	Northwestern	10
Won	**8**	**Lost**	**0**

Dearborn's Four-Year Record – Non-League Games

1931

May 10	20	Franklin	16
May 21	28	Franklin	8
May 24	18	Northwestern	18
May 26	19	Lincoln Park	6
June 19	19	East Dearborn	6
June 23	14	Romulus	11
July 1	20	Romulus	4
Oct 4	17	Franklin	8

Won 7   Lost 0   Tied 1

1932

Mar 13	18	East Windsor	14
Apr 3	17	East Windsor	15
May 1	12	East Windsor	13
May 7	13	Cass City	3
May 8	16	Bad Axe	0
May 15	15	East Windsor	10
May 17	16	Northwestern	9
May 29	10	East Windsor	15
June 5	17	Woodward Temple	8
June 12	10	Eloise	2
June 20	19	Lincoln Park	6
June 25	20	Lincoln Park	5
July 10	20	Willis Ave (Ohio)	16
July 13	8	Eloise	4
Aug 4	13	Northwestern	23
Sept 11	15	Willis Ave	21

Won 12   Lost 4

1933

July 11	5	Battle Creek	4
Aug 26	14	Paradise	2
Aug 27	12	Jackson	2
Aug	27	15 Battle Creek	10
Oct 8	14	Toledo, Ohio	12

Won 5   Lost 0

1934

June 11	35	Monroe	1
July 1	15	Lansing	10
July 1	13	Battle Creek	12

Recapitulation (4-Year total)

League Games	Won 54	Lost 4	
Non-League	W–27	L–4	T–1
Over-all	W–81	L–8	T–1

- - - - - - -

The incredible statistics recording continues as Rose lists every player to pitch a game for the Dearborn team between 1931 and 1934. Here is his chart:

Four-Year Individual Records

Players	W	L	Pct.	Players	W	L	Pct.
Lee Rose	347	50	.875	E. Lucas	4	9	.308
K.E. Armstrong	246	94	.724	W. Cleveland	2	5	.286
F. Koppitsch	256	126	.670	L. Lademann	2	6	.250
Leo Lattore	149	12	.925	W. Kettler	2	8	.200
Geo. Levagood	120	76	.612	J. Field	1	3	.250
C.H. Davis	85	39	.685	C. Smith	1	9	.100
Bobbie Hitt	55	5	.916	W. Gibson	0	10	.000
J.W. Harris	51	47	.520	B. Rose	0	1	.000
R.H. Rizor	40	17	.702	R. Omans	0	1	.000
Al Field	33	8	.805	P. Petrie	0	2	.000
A. Hallup	21	34	.382	McLean	0	2	.000
A.R. Turbett	16	28	.364	F. Levagood	0	4	.000
V. Kolb	15	2	.872	Hunsicker	0	2	.000
O. Valleau	11	3	.786	O. Field	0	2	.000
John McKay	11	17	.393	McGarvey	0	3	.000
W. Bertstrand	10	5	.667	Ed. Levagood	0	5	.000
Tom Tipton	9	8	.529	Mrs. L. Rose	0	3	.000
Charles Bohley	4	19	.173	Mrs. Davis	0	3	.000
W. Field	4	4	.500				

As Rose's account of 1934 comes to a close, another name pops up that invites a story. Leo Lattore has been mentioned previously as the co-founder and co-owner of the Lattore Horseshoe Company. Lattore was a rather accomplished horseshoe pitcher and was heavily involved in the game. His partner Edward Levagood, on the other hand, had a one-time appearance over a four-year period. If he wasn't an avid player of the game, perhaps he brought something else to the partnership, such as business expertise or money. Both Lattore and Levagood signed the shoe-design patent application filed on December 21, 1932. The shoe went on the market in 1933, though the patent wasn't approved until August 20, 1935. The first two players to endorse the Lattore shoe—in an advertisement that appeared in NHPA's publication *Horseshoe World*—were Ed Walls and our own Lee Rose.

Here's my 1934 record complete:

Rose	Name	Opp	Rose	Name	Opp
9	Harold Arold	0	1	Leo Ingraham	0
4	Jimmy Field	0	1	Omar Herppich	0
4	McIntyre	0	1	Sam Godfrey	0
2	Herman Reinas	0	1	William Field	0
2	Lawrence Vaughan	0	1	Orville Field	0
2	Richard Prediger	0	1	Pearl Fisher	0
2	Ray Wrobbel	0	1	Allen	0
2	Orville Valleau	0	1	Elmer Fought	0
2	C. H. Davis	0	1	Strayer	0
2	R. H. Rizor	0	1	Jim Skinner	0
2	Freeman	0	1	Lou Harrison	0
1	William Bertrand	0	1	Ben Emerson	0
1	William Herbert	0	1	Babcock	0
1	Leonard Ladermann	0	1	Osteen	0
1	William Howard	0	1	Lovas	0
1	John Hart	0	1	William Langland	0
1	Ballish	0	1	Singer	0
1	Tom Tipton	0	2	M. B. Getz	1
1	Sahrer	0	9	Jim Burt	6
1	'Monroe 1'	0	6	Al Field	6
1	'Monroe 2'	0	1	Ed Walls	2
1	'Monroe 3'	0	0	Brown	1
1	'Monroe 4'	0	0	Graham	1
1	Al Taylor	0	0	Koppitsch	1
1	Zugga	0	0	Lattore	1
			Wins 84		**Lost 19**

- - - - - - -

Lee Rose was the Michigan state champion in 1934, but for some strange reason he declined to write about the event. He included only a small newspaper clipping that records his achievement. It's curious that Rose's accounts elsewhere suggest that he was not the most modest person, yet when he finally claimed the big prize in the state of Michigan (in a period when that was about as glorious a triumph a young player could gain) he didn't even mention it.

A Tremendous Career Is On Its Way

A s we review this next chapter, notice the shift in the subject matter recorded by Rose. Rose moves away from recording the escapades of his summer league to a higher level of the sport's activity. The league he describes in previous years no longer existed and Rose's interests or focus seemed to have changed also.

It may be helpful to point out that the national association was in struggling during a difficult period of national economic recovery. Much of that struggle trickled down to the state or charter levels. There had been a four-year period of no World Tournaments and when the annual event was held again in 1933 and 1934, Rose didn't enter, even though the 1933 event was held in nearby Chicago. There was a World Tournament again in Illinois in 1935. We will hear all about that event from Lee, since both Mr. and Mrs. Rose traveled to Moline, Illinois, and entered the tournament. Then there was another five-year gap in which no summertime World Championships were held. In fact, there were only two national men's events over the next 11 years and there wasn't another women's national event until 1947, a 12-year lag.

This chapter has some good reading.

- - - - - - -

December 28. 1934, I wrote to R. B. Howard, secretary of the National Association, asking him if the Battle Creek bunch had renewed their state charter for 1935 and if not, could a group from Detroit obtain it. January 3, 1935, received a reply; here it is:

45

Replying to your letter of December 28, the records show that the charter held by the Michigan Association was not renewed when it ran out this fall. You ask if it would be possible for another group to secure this charter. The National Horseshoe Pitchers Association is not particularly interested in what group holds the charter so long as it can be satisfactorily shown that the group to which the charter is issued represents the best interest of horseshoe in the state and that this organization will satisfactory promote the game throughout the year.

My personal belief is that your factionalism in Michigan will ruin the game, no matter whether your group or the Battle Creek group operates the state association. The mere fact that you have two groups in positive proof to me that there is need for some "missionary" work in Michigan. Undoubtedly, you feel that your group is the most fair and the best able to handle the state organization. You may be correct in this assumption. Undoubtedly, the other group feels the same way. As a matter of fact, in order to accomplish anything, you fellows should all bury the hatchet and get under one tent. Could that be accomplished?

I am open for suggestions and I am personally willing to work with you so long as I feel that the best interest of horseshoe pitching is being served.

R. B. Howard

I immediately got in touch with Rizor and Davis to see if we three could raise the $25.00 necessary to obtain a state charter, but neither of them could see their way to expend the sum at the time. Had to let things ride.

January 12 – It was fairly nice weather, so I got out the shoes and gloves and went out on my court to throw a few. After warming up a while, I threw 51 ringers in 200 shoes.

January 22 – Much colder, but the first day I could do any more pitching. I threw 71 ringers in 200 shoes.

January 26 – I threw 56 ringers in 200 shoes.

January 27 – I threw 58 ringers in 200 shoes.

January 28 – I went to see Leo Lattore and told him of our chance to get the state charter and he agreed to help.

January 29 – Threw 46 ringers in 150 shoes.

January 30 – Threw 38 ringers in 100 shoes.

January 31 – Threw 43 ringers in 100 shoes. Had a meeting at my home, of Lattore, Rizor, Davis and me. We talked over plans for the year and discussed a state constitution I had written. I also sent a letter to Marion, Ohio, asking for a team match for February 9, on which day we had expected to go to London for the charter. However, I had received a reply from Marion saying that they no longer had indoor courts, but recommended [that I write] to Galvin, Ohio. At our meeting, we set the date of February 16 to go London for the charter, believing we could have the money by then.

February 1 – A little warmer today and I got almost into summer form by tossing 112 ringers in 200 shoes.

I also wrote two letters, one to R. B. Howard saying we would be in London on February 16 to get the charter and one to Galion, Ohio, asking for a team match on February 16.

February 3 – A very heavy snowfall stopped all horseshoe practice.

February 7 – Here is the reply I received today from Galion, Ohio:

Mr. Lee Rose
5228 Shaw Ave.
Detroit, Mich.

Dear Mr. Rose,
In regards to the team match on the Galion courts, Feb. 16, this will be O.K. We are having a game the following week with the greater

Cleveland team of which the results will be broadcast by Tom Manning over the National Broadcasting Station W.T.A.M. on Monday 25th at 6:35 p.m. We can do likewise with this game.

We have six courts on which to play the contest. There will be no delay in pitching it off.

Yours for more ringers,
G. D. Roop
Pres. N.C.O.L.
656 W. Church Street
Galion, Ohio

On February 9, Rizor came out and we pitched on my court, which had been shoveled free of snow and filled with sawdust. We played 4 games and Rizor won them all. The scores were 50–18, 50–42, 50–37 and 50–49. I was leading 16–9 in the next game when Rizor ripped the skin off his finger and we quit pitching.

February 10 – I pitched quite a lot and got my swing going pretty well.

Here is R. B. Howard's reply, which I received on February 7:

Dear Lee,

So far as I know I will be able to be in my office on February 16. I certainly will work toward that program and in case I am not able to be here, I will get in touch with you. If you still want to come. As for the Charter, I will have it ready for you, assuming, of course, that that is the thing, which we should do. I very much prefer seeing your proposed constitution and knowing something of your plans for 1935. I have not entirely got it out of my head that two factions of Horseshoe Pitchers in Michigan should be represented in any set-up, which is made in Michigan. As bad as the Horseshoe Association needs the $25.00 fee for a charter, I would much prefer to do without it than issue a charter that does not fully cover all of the Horseshoe interests in the state.

I imagine that you feel that I am very obstinate in this matter and perhaps looking at it as you do from your viewpoint, you undoubtedly have a difficult time to see it my way. At any rate, we are all friends and all interested in the general welfare of the sport and I am sure that we can iron the matter out satisfactorily to all concerned."

Sincerely yours,
R. B. Howard

On February 10, I visited Al Field and Ed Walls and they both said they would go to Galion if they did not have to work. The six men I have in mind for a team are: Rose, Lattore, Rizor, Koppitsch, Walls and Field. These men would make a very powerful team in the summer, but now out of practice as they are, it is a big question.

February 11 – Warmed up about an hour – Not so good!

February 15 – Lattore, Koppitsch and Ed Levagood to go in Lattore's car and Rose, Rizor, Walls, A. Field and W, Field to go in my car, is the arrangement for tomorrow.

February 16 – I arose at 4:30 a.m., dressed and went after the Field boys, Walls and Rizor. Got under way at 6:15 a.m. and rolled off the 185 miles to London, Ohio, by 10:15 a.m. We met R. B. Howard and were discussing things when Lattore, Levagood and Koppitsch came in at 10:45. It was not long after that we had been issued a charter for the Wolverine State Horseshoe Pitchers' Association. Rizor and Lattore each loaned the association ten dollars, while Ed Levagood loaned five. Lattore was appointed president, while I was made secretary. Taking leave of London and Mr. Howard, we set out for Galion. We ate at Marion and not long afterwards we were in Galion and found the courts.

They had six nice courts in what used to be an old theatre or auditorium and the balcony was still there for spectators. We all warmed up for a while and then the match began. For the first four rounds it was nip and tuck, but in the last 2 rounds our men tired rapidly and we were beaten 22–14. Score by rounds:

North Central Ohio All-Stars

3 2 4 3 5 5 = 22

Detroit Stars

3 4 2 3 1 1 = 14

A quart and pint of gin warmed our ride home in a snowstorm.

- - - - - - -

The results of the match and the individual performances were recorded in a typed letter mailed to Lee by G. D. Roop. That letter is tacked into the journal.

- - - - - - -

Lee Rose
5228 Shaw Ave.
Detroit, Michigan

Dear Mr. Rose:

We want to congratulate your men on your excellent horseshoe pitching on the Galion courts last Saturday afternoon.

The results of this contest were flashed over the wires to Columbus and from there to all the big newspapers of the country.

Here are the totals of the game:

Detroit	W	L	Pts	R	DR	SP	Pct
Lattore	5	1	278	233	71	376	62
Walls	4	2	279	229	73	380	60
Rose	3	3	247	179	37	410	44
Koppitsch	1	5	202	217	56	408	53
Field	1	5	232	213	57	416	51
Rizor	0	6	195	160	33	366	44
	14	22	1442	1231	328	2356	52

NCO Stars	W	L	Pts	R	DR	SP	Pct
Listensidner	6	0	300	221	57	386	57
Biller	5	1	299	227	72	372	61
E. Pry	4	2	284	265	78	440	60
J. Campbell	3	3	224	193	47	372	52
Shoup	2	4	240	202	50	404	50
Meyers	2	4	208	173	36	382	45
	22	14	1555	1281	340	2356	55

Yours Truly,

G. D. Roop

Pres. N.C.O. League

On March 16 – Rizor, Omans and I went to Flint, We met Lattore there and we all talked to Ed Jones regarding the formation of an Eastern Michigan Association. Nothing definite was done.

On March 30 – At N.W. Field I played Lattore 3 practice games. I won all three 50–43, 50–21, 50–9, hurling 65, 75 and 90 percent.

- - - - - - -

Then comes a letter from R. B. Howard.

- - - - - - -

Dear Lee,

I have just received a letter from Lee McGinley, Care of Lawrence Scudder & Co., First National Bank Bldg., Marquette, Michigan, who state they are organizing a horseshoe association at Marquette. I believe your state association should contact them.

Sincerely Yours,

R. B. Howard

Publisher

The Horseshoe World

I wrote a letter to Marquette and I soon got an answer. Then I called a big meeting and practice tournament for Dearborn on April 14:

April 8, 1935

Dear Mr. Rose,
Thank you for your letter of the 6th.

We have just about completed organization of the Marquette Horseshoe Club, consisting of four squads, each squad comprising four two-man teams. Will send you copies of our constitution, by-laws, playing rules, score sheets, etc. as soon as they are available.

We would like to have further information regarding the state association. I have mentioned it to some of the boys and the idea appeals to them. For example, there is a club at the Soo who could probably be enrolled and by the looks of it there will be another club here shortly as we received many more than 52 applications, our present limit. Also, Ironwood, Escanaba, Iron Mountain and other towns in the U.P. should be interested.

Sincerely,
Mc/DJ
Lee McGinley

P.S. The writer travels considerably around the U.P. and gets down to Detroit every couple of months. Perhaps we could get together at Detroit some time shortly.

- - - - - - -

A newspaper clipping is pasted in next, followed by another journal entry with a letter Rose received.

- - - - - - -

Michigan Champion Wins Tournament

On April 14, at the Dearborn courts, Lee Rose, Michigan State Champion, scuttled six opponents with ease to win the invitation tournament. He walloped Getz, Lattore, W. Field, A. Field, Rizor and Valleau in order and none of them threatened at any time to upset the champ who streamed doubles on the stake steadily to run each of his opponents into the ground. How they finished:

1. Rose	6–0	5. Rizor	3–3
2. A. Field	4–2	6. Valleau	1–5
3. Getz	4–2	7. W. Field	0–6
4. Lattore	3–3		

I wrote letters and challenges to Galion, Ohio, and Battle Creek. Here's the reply from Galion:

Dear Mr. Rose,

We have just organized our summer league, six clubs have entered, namely, Marion, Bucyrus, Galion, Sulfur Springs, Shelby and Willard.

If you can come Saturday, May 18th, it would be more suitable for us, we will have this game well advertised and should have a big crowd. If this date is O.K. with you please drop me a card at once so we can get things started, state the time you want to begin the game.

We have some work to do at our club and would like to have it done before you come, the 18th will give us the necessary time.

Yours Truly,
G. D. Roop
Pres. N.C.O. League

I answered, saying we'd be there at about noon of May 18.

In some practice games on April 28, at Northwestern Field, I played Ed Walls 11 games. I threw 417 ringers for an average of .601. He threw 439 ringers for an average of .632. I had the high game with 41 out of 54 for .759. I experimented with Gordons and new and old Lattores and finally came to the conclusion that the 1935 model Lattore shoes are the best, as I averaged .619 with them as against .585 with the others.

April 29 – Threw 87 ringers in 120 shoes (72.5%) with 1935 Lattores.

Notice Lee's comments about the Lattore shoes; he has more to say later in an article that discusses his purchase of the Lattore Horseshoe Company. But let's consider the Gordons shoes, which were probably manufactured longer than most present-day players realize, even those who pitched Gordon shoes before production was discontinued in 2004. The first Gordon horseshoes were on the market by 1931, as proven by a 1931 advertisement in the *Horseshoe World* magazine. The shoes were named after their inventor and designer, company owner John Gordon. They were initially manufactured in Los Angeles, California. Gordon applied for a patent May 26, 1931, and received approval on November 7, 1933. The first Gordons did not have full-size hooks—that feature didn't come along until 1934. From that year until the last year of production, there was little change to the shoe. By 1934, all production had been transferred to Queen City forge in Cincinnati, Ohio. The Gordon shoe is a popular shoe for horseshoe collectors because shoes manufactured from about 1939 through 1965 were dated.

Ted Allen was a primary endorser of the shoe and now we see that Lee Rose gave the shoe a try, which might be construed as an unsolicited endorsement. Rose stuck with the Lattore shoe, but records show that Gordons were a much larger seller than Lattore and probably were exceeded in sales only by Allens and Ohio shoes. John Gordon was known for his generosity to the game and his efforts in promotion. He was inducted to the NHPA Hall of Fame in 1971.

The following newspaper article was inserted in the journal, probably clipped from a Galion newspaper.

---- ----

Horseshoe Pitching Season To Open Here For Summer Season

League All-Stars to Compete Against Detroit Team May 18

The strong Wolverine horseshoe team from Detroit, Michigan, will be here on Saturday afternoon, May 18, to play the All-Stars of the north Central Ohio League in a contest on the Galion City Hall Courts. The contest will start promptly at 1:30 o'clock. The Wolverines comprise the strongest horseshoe team in Michigan. They have such players on their team as Lee Rose, the present Michigan state champion, Ed Walls, six times Michigan champion, Leo Lattore, president of the Michigan State Horseshoe Pitchers Association and manufacturer of the famous Lattore horseshoes, R. H. Rizor, Frank Koppitsch, Mr. Fields and others. These men are highly skilled in the art of horseshoe pitching.

The N.C.O. Stars are the strongest team in the state of Ohio. They played six contests last winter with no defeats, playing such teams as the Akron City team, which previously had been considered the strongest in Ohio.

The All-Stars of the Greater Cleveland league, the All-Stars of the Central Ohio League and the team from Detroit were also victims of the N.C.O. All-Stars.

The N.C.O. League will start playing their regular scheduled games within the next two weeks. Six teams have entered to date, namely: Marion, Bucyrus, Sulfur Springs, Galion, Shelby and Willard.

No change was made in the election of league officers. G. D. Roop of Galion was re-elected president. Roop was also elected manager of the All-Star team. James Campbell, Bucyrus, was re-elected vice president and F. Van Wagner, Shelby, secretary-treasurer.

The line-up for the N.C.O. stars will include Myron Forbit and Ace Titus, Marion, (Forbit tied for second place in the state tournament at Springfield last fall); E. Pry, F. Ulmer, G. Weiner and G. D. Roop, Galion, (E. Pry finished in third place in the Open State Tournament at Lakeside last August); Wayne and James Campbell, Bucyrus; John Meyers and John Listensidner, Mansfield; Howard Biller and Shoup, Shelby. These men are all horseshoe artists and very hard to defeat. Horseshoe fanes from all over the North Central Ohio district will be here May 18 to see the big game with the Wolverine team.

---- ----

After reading the newspaper announcement and public invitation of the big upcoming match, and knowing that the Detroit team in the winter match, it was hard telling how successful Rose and the boys would be. Rose's account of the match is even more interesting than the newspaper article.

- - - - - - -

On May 18, 1935, two cars set out from Detroit for Galion and in them were Rose, Lattore, Valleau, Koppitsch, Rizor, Ed Walls, Mrs. Walls, Armstrong and Mrs. Rose. Arrived there all o.k., except Rose who lost his gloves en route and was forced to hurl in match without them. Lattore had lumbago, Field and Rizor had hand cuts and Koppitsch was out of practice. Rizor and Valleau started against the powerful N.C.O. All-Stars. Walls, Rose, Valleau and Field won their games in the first round and the Wolverines led 4–2.

The second round was even with Walls, Rose and Valleau winning and the score stood 7–5. In the third round, Walls, Valleau, Field and Koppitsch cracked out wins and Detroit led 11–7, at half time.

In the fourth round, Walls, Rose and Field cracked out victories to make the score 15–10. In the fifth round, Lattore replaced Rizor and he, Walls, Rose and Koppitsch smashed out wins to put Detroit ahead 18–12. In the last round, the boisterous visitors pounded out 5 more victories, Valleau only losing and sent the powerful All-Stars down to a 23–13 defeat.

Had lotsa fun coming home! Ask Koppitsch and Rizor about the Dago Red!

June 2 – at Northwestern Field

Rose vs. Field – 4 out of 7 games

Game	Player	Pts	R	DR	SP	Pct	4 On
1	Rose	50	44	14	62	.709	4
	Walls	26	37	10	62	.596	
2	Rose	50	48	18	66	.727	4
	Walls	27	40	9	66	.606	
3	Rose	50	47	17	74	.635	3
	Walls	39	42	12	74	.567	
4	Rose	26	24	8	50	.480	4
	Walls	50	34	14	50	.680	
5	Rose	36	32	8	68	.471	3
	Walls	50	37	12	68	.544	
6	Rose	50	37	10	66	.561	2
	Walls	32	32	8	66	.484	
Totals	Rose	262	232	75	386	.601	20
	Walls	224	222	65	386	.575	

Rose vs. Burt – 4 out of 7 games

Game	Player	Pts	R	DR	SP	Pct	4 On
1	Rose	50	31	10	46	.673	1
	Burt	14	17	3	46	.369	
2	Rose	50	37	15	52	.711	5
	Burt	21	26	8	52	.500	
3	Rose	50	34	9	60	.566	3
	Burt	34	29	9	60	.483	
4	Rose	50	37	14	68	.544	4
	Burt	37	31	5	68	.455	
Totals	Rose	200	139	48	226	.615	13
	Burt	106	103	25	226	.456	

Wolverines Smash Battle Creek

Rose Leads Way For Detroit Team As Visitors Pile Up Huge Lead Over Western Michigan Rivals

On July 7, at the Postum Courts in Battle Creek, the powerful Wolverines administered the most crushing and overwhelming defeat to a Western Michigan team ever doled out. Lee Rose, Wolverine manager, showed his men the proper way to play against out-state boys by slamming down seven consecutive opponents for a perfect day. C. Davis, Rizor and Koppitsch yapped closely on their leader's heels as they smacked down six foemen while dropping only one each. Jim Burt, arriving a bit late, took five out of six, while Lattore, after winning three out four, dropped out. Hicks, Langlands, L. Davis and Valleau played the other games. In one of Rose's games, he and Skinner were slated to put on a great battle, but Rose stepped on the gas and roared over Skinner 50–4, while the audience looked aghast. Score:

Wolverines	4 5 5 4 5 5 6 – 34
Battle Creek	3 2 2 3 2 2 1 – 15

Wolverines	W	L	Battle Creek	W	L
Rose	7	0	Cadwalladar	2	0
C. Davis	6	1	Brown	3	4
Koppitsch	6	1	Skinner	3	4
Rizor	6	1	Jones	3	4
Burt	5	1	Zeedyke	2	5
Lattore	3	1	Kraft	1	6
Valleau	1	5	Harrison	1	6
Hicks	0	1	Gorsline	0	5
L. Davis	0	1			
Langlands	0	3			

Rose Qualifies in Detroit

District Tournament

On July 9, Lee Rose pitched his five 50-shoe qualifying games in the preliminaries of the Detroit District Tournament, at N.W. Field. R. Harley Rizor opposed him, but Rizor did not count his scores. Rose won all five games, with .720 ringer average for the match and a high game of .800. Score summary:

	Pts	R	DR	SP	Pct.
Rose	227	180	67	250	.720
Rizor	113	144	42	250	.576

On Saturday evening, August 3, World Champion Ted Allen gave an exhibition at the Dearborn courts, I played him two games. In the first game I gave him a real fight.

	Pts	R	SP	Pct.
Rose	33	65	90	72
Allen	50	73	90	82

In the second game he only threw 72%, but I fell down badly to 50% and was beaten 50–22.

Rose Defeats World Champion

August 7 – Center Line Courts

Lee Rose overcame Ted Allen, 50–47, coming up from behind in a magnificent uphill fight after trailing 35–16 at one time. Scoring by inning – (Beg pardon, my wife threw the score sheet away.) #!!*##*

	Pts	R	SP	Pct.
Rose	50	53		
Allen	47	54		

The game was played on poor stakes, under poor lights, in a slight drizzle of rain and before a very, very vociferous audience.

Lee Rose Wins Central Michigan Tourney at Ionia Free Fair
Crushes Eleven Consecutive Opponents to Earth
as He Marches to Overwhelming Victory

On August 14, at the Ionia Free Fair, Lee Rose of Detroit captured the Central Michigan Championship at the tournament held on the sand courts there. After qualifying only 6th high with 61% and 211 points in 100 shoes, Rose ran 11 foemen into the ground to easily capture the first prize of $25.00.

Game 1 — Rose 50, Davis 38 – After rolling up a lead of 40–18 on his friend, Rose coasted out.

Game 2 – Rose 50, Remus 38 – Remus gave Rose a hard fight, playing even for a while and then going ahead 34–29.

Here, Rose rallied and slammed on a bunch of ringers to score 21 while holding his Grand Rapids opponent to 4.

Game 3 – Rose 50, Harrison 21 – This game was just a lunch for Rose, who toyed with his old rival for a while and then clouded up and rained all over him.

Game 4 – Rose 50, Hoeksema 23 – Hoeksema started in as though to "clean Roses' clock," in a hurry and rolled up a lead of 20–4. Then, just as things looked bad for him, Rose turned calmly to work, threw 4 doubles, a single, six doubles, a single and two doubles and the game was all over, leaving a stunned Hoeksema wondering what had struck him.

Dinner was in order at the time and Rose & Brown had each won 4 games.

Game 5 – Rose 50, Fisher 10 – Pearl Fisher of Lansing was just so much cannon fodder to Rose's big guns. After missing in the first two innings while Fisher picked up 6 points, Rose smashed in 33 out of 42 and ran out in a hurry.

Game 6 – Rose 50, Craft 36 – Rose easily defeated his Kalamazoo foe, rolling up a lead of 48–21 and then easing out in spite of a storm of last minute ringers by Craft.

Game 7 – Rose 50, Skinner 16 – Rose committed pure and unadulterated assault and battery on "Old Man" Skinner when he pounced on him with 38 ringers in 50 shoes to pitch his best game of the day. Skinner never had a chance, although he put up a spirited fight in the early stages. But as Rose's ringers kept pouring on, Jim weakened badly.

Game 8 – Rose 50, Parker 6 – Marking time for his next game with Brown, Rose polished off Parker with 28 out of 40. By this time, hundreds were gathered around court 5 to see Rose play Brown. Neither man had lost a game, and a "lulu" of a battle was expected.

Game 9 – Rose 50, Brown 27 – Brown started out bravely enough, taking a 5–0 lead with 3 out of 6 while Rose was getting only 2 out of 6. Brown then threw his first double, but Rose promptly topped it. Rose then laid on an unholy string of ringers and in a few minutes had run up an almost insurmountable lead of 34–5. Brown rallied gamely to make it 34–23, but Rose smeared him,

16–4 from then on to take undisputed possession of 1st place. Rose threw 38 out of 54 in this game.

Game 10 – Rose 50, Rizor 39 – Rizor rolled up an early lead and held it for quite a while before Rose's late rallies finally pulled him down.

Game 11 – Rose 50, Cadwallader 44 – Rose rolled up an early lead and easily held it until the score stood 48–23. "Cad" then instituted his usual late rally and got all the way to 44 before Rose topped Ross's double and came back with one of his own to go out.

Final Standings

Place	Player	Won	Lost
1.	Lee Rose	11	0
2.	C. Brown	9	2
3.	Jim Skinner	8	3
4.	Jack Hoeksema	7	4
5.	R. Cadwallader	7	4
6.	R. H. Rizor	5	6
7.	Remus	5	6
8	C. H. Davis	4	7
9.	Pearl Fisher	4	7
10.	Craft	4	7
11.	Parker	1	10
12.	Harrison	1	10

August 17 – John R. Ferris Courts, Rose played a 2 out of 3 exhibition match against Davis and won as follows:

		Pts	R	DR	SP	Pct
Game 1	Rose	50	32	12	46	.695
	Davis	21	23	5	46	.500
Game 2	Rose	50	44	16	60	.734
	Davis	29	35	9	60	.584

- - - - - - -

A newspaper clipping announcing a big event is included in between Lee's handwritten description.

- - - - - - -

Horseshoe Tournament
Starts Next Saturday

Greater Detroit's annual singles horseshoe pitching tournament will be held August 24 and 25 at Northwestern Field. The meet will be run in two classes, A and B. Class A shall be for the pitchers of proven ability, while B will be for beginners. All players wishing to compete are requested to be on hand at Northwestern Field by 9 o'clock next Saturday.

- - - - - - -

The sport was not without controversy, even back in the times of Rose, as we see in this next newspaper article. Lattore's refusal to qualify was the correct call on his part, unless there were specific guidelines to cover the matter previously established by the event coordinators. This issue become prevalent at the World Tournaments starting in 1948. During the 1950s, the defending World Champion did not have to qualify but was just seeded as the number-one player in the Championship Class finals. That practice continued right up to the 1980s when qualifying was eliminated.

- - - - - - -

Horseshoe Meet
To Close Today

With more than a score of pitchers qualified by Saturday's play, finals of the Greater Detroit Horseshoe Pitching Tournament open today at Northwestern Field. Trials Saturday were marked by the refusal of Leo Lattore, defending champion, to seek to qualify.

He held he should be qualified for the final match by virtue of his championship. He said he did not care to risk the chance of wearing himself out just before going to Moline, Ill., to participate in the world tournament there. A decision based on a vote of those entered was to be reached today.

The feature of the trials was the score of 241 recorded by Edward Walls, former Michigan champion. He made 11 consecutive double ringers and amassed during the course of his qualifying trial, a total of 75 out of 100 shoes. His score was the highest ever made in tournament competition here.

Those who qualified and their scores include: Edward Walls, 241; Ray Wrobbel, 222; Lee Rose, 218; Al Field, 216; Harold Arold, 203; Charles Lundgren, 201; James Burt, 200; C. H. Davis, 200; Orville Valleau, 196; R. H. Rizor, 195; Charles Kish, 183; John Hart, 177; John Elmer, 171; Lawrence Vaughan, 168; Edward Nieman, 150; Thomas Cameron, 144; Frank Koppitsch, 140; Dan Wininger, 139; Mark Goodell, 115.

I defeated John Hart two straight games in the first round of play, 50–11, 50–7, averaging .611 and .666 for a 2-game average of .643.

In the second round I met the new Detroit sensation, Charles Lundgren. I won the first game, 50–25, hurling 45 out of 60 for .750.

In the second game, I led 27–13, only to finally lose a long, hard-fought game, 50–48. Lundgren had 61 ringers to my 58, out of 90 shoes. He made .668 and I made .644.

He took an early lead in the last game and I could never catch up. He won 50–40, throwing .666 and I threw .616. For the three games I had .662 and he had .658.

Ed Walls won the tournament, winning 10 straight games.

And now, ON TO MOLINE!!

- - - - - - -

And so on to Moline, Illinois, we shall go along with Mr. Rose and Mrs. Rose and visit the 1935 World Horseshoe Pitching Tournament. This was an noteworthy World Tournament that was well covered by the media and Rose did a thorough job of tacking clippings into his journal.

The 1935 event defined and confirmed Ted Allen as the top player in the sport. The reigning women's champion, Carolyn Schultz from Illinois, the greatest women pitcher in the first 50 years of the sport, was there to defend her title. In fact, all who attended the event were probably ready to just hand her the first-place trophy. There was a Class B event, the first of its kind, but under a different label. The event was the final championship challenge for a number of all-time great players.

My Fourth World Tournament

Held at Moline, Illinois, August 29, 30, 31 and September 1, 2. Bertie, Rizor and I drove to Moline on Tuesday, August 27.

WORLD'S CHAMPIONSHIP HORSE SHOE TOURNAMENT
RIVERSIDE PARK COURTS.   MOLINE, ILLINOIS
AUG. 29 TO SEPT. 2, 1935.

Davis Leads in National
Shoe Meet with 266

Seventy-five Pitchers Enter Moline Tourney;
High Scores in Qualifying.
Jimmy Risk of Indiana Also Ahead of Ted Allen in Morning Play

C. C. Davis of Kansas City, L. F. Gray of Long Beach, Cal., and Jimmy Risk of Montpelier, Ind., fired a broadside at Ted Allen of Alhambra this morning as they dominated the qualifying for the national horseshoe pitching tournament at Riverside Park.

Davis, the Missouri veteran who formerly held the title now held by owned by Allen, set the pace with a stupendous 266, one point better than Gray compiled and two more than Risk's total. All three marks were exceptionally high.

The champion qualified easily with 255, but he has been given fair warning that he is in for a merry battle when the boys start clashing in match games tomorrow afternoon.

Seventy-four men and five women had filed entries at the riverside courts at noon today and several others were expected this afternoon. Nearly fifty of the men completed their 200 shoe qualifying this morning while the rest were busy this afternoon fighting for places in the tourney finals.

Risk Leads in Ringers

Risk had the highest average for the morning rounds. Davis had 84 percent ringers, Gray 83 and Allen 80. A dozen or more other stars were in the high 70s.

The early scoring spree indicated that a count of 240 would qualify among the first twenty-four, but it was doubtful if much under that total would put a pitcher into the title quest. The second twenty-four qualifiers, of course, will be eligible for the Dispatch Tournament, which will be run at night.

Frank Jackson of Blue Mound, Kansas, the veteran "Champion of Champions," pitched his way into the finals with a great 256, hitting 79 percent ringers. The genial traveler appears to be on his game and undoubtedly will give a great battle for the big money.

Casey Jones, 16-year-old Waukesha lad who is Wisconsin state champion, qualified with 252.

Gray is Real Threat

One of the new title threats appears to be Gray of Long Beach, who is assured of a high place in the standing because of his 263 score. He had not been mentioned in the pre-tournament dope and while his record was known among horseshoe men, his success in qualifying was a surprise to some of the experts.

Two of the eastern contingent apparently landed in the money unless there is an outbreak of scoring miracles this afternoon. They are Roy Addington of Dunkirk, N.Y., the Erie representative who got 247, and James O'Shea of Brockton, Mass., who qualified with 249.

Tournament Program

Here is a program of events for the next four days and nights of the big meet:

Banquet and dance at 7 tonight in LeClaire Hotel.

National convention tomorrow morning.

Match play, championship flight (six games) at 1 tomorrow afternoon.

Match play, Dispatch Tourney (six games) at 7:30 tomorrow night.

That program will continue through Saturday and Sunday with the women qualifying Saturday morning and afternoon and starting their match play Sunday afternoon.

Match games in both men's and women's championships will be played Monday morning and afternoon, while the final games in the Dispatch Tourney will be played Monday night.

Two Canadian Indians Enter Shoe Tourney
Towering Roy Addington from Erie, Pa.,
Wins Trip to National Event
Allen Remains Favorite
Courts Filled with Pitchers Warming Up for
Qualifying Tests Today

Two Canadian Indians from London, Ontario, both former champions of the dominion, were among those warming up for the national horseshoe tournament yesterday afternoon.

They are John Riley and John Simons, title-holders in 1929 and 1933, respectively, and they traveled more than 500 miles in a small truck to take part in the battle for the world championship now held by Ted Allen of Alhambra, California, who is defending his crown today on the elaborate Moline courts.

With Riley and Simons is Fred Harbourn of Stratford, Ontario, the 1934 Canadian king of the horseshoe courts, who gave the onlookers and many of the contestants a treat with a display of ringers tossing during the afternoon.

Wanted – White Trousers

Not only were the Canadians faced with problem of pitching ringers against the greatest field of horseshoe men ever assembled on one layout, but also they were confronted with another handicap which threatened to keep them from participating in the classic event.

Rules of the national association require all contestants to be garbed in white trousers. The visitors from the dominion have none. Neither are they blessed with an abundance of money with which to purchase said outfits.

They agreed to buy the trousers if they qualify in either the national or the dispatch tourney and asked the meet officials for permission to pitch in the clothes they brought with them on the long trip. Said officials were puzzled for a time, but they assured the Canadians that some arrangement could be made to solve their problem to get into action today.

New Yorker Wins Trip

One of the outstanding entries in the tournament is a 6-fooot, 7-inch youth from Dunkirk, N.Y., who won his way into the national by capturing a district championship in Erie, Pa., a few weeks ago. He is Roy Addington, 20-year-old ringer tosser, who proved yesterday that he is capable of locating the peg with enough consistency to give him a great chance today of landing in the Dispatch Tournament.

Addington had to beat the best pitchers in sections of three eastern states to win his trip to Moline. He triumphed over champions of Erie, Pa., Ashtabula, Ohio, and Meadville, Pa., in the finals of the meet, which attracted eighty pitchers.

The tournament was conducted by an Erie newspaper and a large manufacturing concern in that city and is to be an annual event.

Casey, Mahoney Arrive

The two youngsters who are expected to give the veterans a run for the money were among the arrivals yesterday. Charles "Casey" Jones of Waukesha, the Wisconsin champion, and Larry Mahoney of New Jersey, the eastern open title-holder, were the center of attention as they gave the courts a fling.

Jones is regarded as a real threat in spite of the fact that he is only 16 years old and has been pitching in big time meets only two years. He is small and may not be able to stand up under the grind of the long tournament, but he throws a great shoe and seems to have the temperament of an old-time campaigner.

Mahoney is unbeaten in eastern play this year and must be figured in the running, but experts point to a low ringer average and express a doubt that he will be able to stand up with the veterans in the heat of the title battle.

Fans and experts alike are speculating on the chances of Ted Allen keeping his world championship and the consensus seems to be that the title-holder should repeat unless the breaks of the game all go against him.

Allen came through the Midwest championship in Des Moines earlier this week with the loss of only two games in the finals. That triumph leads observers to believe that Ted is on his game after a full year of campaigning on all sorts of courts throughout the United States and that he should be rated No. 1 again on the Moline courts.

However, there are dozens of good pitchers in Moline ready to take advantage of any lapse in the champion's game and it is not altogether out of the question for a new king of the courts to rise from the ranks Monday afternoon.

All sixteen courts at Riverside were in use almost constantly yesterday afternoon and evening as the pitchers practiced for the long grind which opened this morning.

Davis Becomes Contender for Allen's Crown

Twenty-four horseshoe pitchers extraordinary and twenty-four others, just a step behind, were ready today and tonight to start off the campaigns for title honors in the national championship and Dispatch Invitation Tournament on the elegant Riverside Courts.

Those forty-eight stars of the ringer-making game earned the right to complete in the money classes the rest of this week and next Monday by qualifying yesterday in one of the greatest bursts of scoring ever recorded in the archives of the association which governs the sport.

The troupe was paced by the veteran campaigner, C. C. Davis of Kansas City, whom many believe is on the way to regaining the world title he once held but which since has been the property of younger stars of the first magnitude. Charley put together eighty-four ringers and fourteen other points yesterday morning to set a new qualifying record of 266 in the national tournament. He had one less ringer than Jimmy Risk of Montpelier, who was third, but managed extra points on his missed attempts.

First Night Play

Fans will get their first opportunity to see real competition under lights at 7:30 this evening when the matches in the Dispatch tourney will be started off. Pitching in the national, of course, was to have started at 1:30 this afternoon with each of the twenty-four contenders testing his ability under fire in six games.

There will be six games each for the nighthawks in this evenings show, also.

The championship and distribution of prize money in each tournament is determined on a games won and lost basis. Each pitcher must play every other performer in his division between now and Monday night, twenty-three games in all. The one with the highest percentage of victories will be crowned champion and walk off with the largest slice of the money.

Fans will be admitted to each session for 25 cents apiece, or they may secure season tickets for the daytime pitching for 50 cents and likewise 50-cent season ducats for the nocturnal meetings.

Banquet is Success

The visitors and home guard went social in a pleasant way last night in the roof garden of the LeClaire Hotel. An excellent banquet was consumed by approximately seventy-five persons. There was a brief program of speaking and dancing followed until a late hour.

Delegates to the national convention gathered in the city hall to discuss business affairs of the association and to plan for expansion in the future. They were to resume the convention this morning.

With the conclusion of the dancing last night, the tournament and convention settled down to the serious business of finding a new world champion or to that of seeing the present title-holder, Ted Allen of Alhambra, recrowned for another year.

While many were picking Davis to dethrone the wandering king of the game, the fact remained that Allen is a great campaigner and apparently in form to withstand the threats of the Missouri champ and all his helpers who are gunning to upset the present leader.

Gray Is Dark Horse

A dark horse competitor loomed today as a result of yesterday's performance in the person of L. F. Gray of Long Beach, Cal. The coast sensation gave the folks something to talk about by finishing one point back of Davis and setting up a ringer average of 83% percent. What he will do in hand to hand encounters with the other favorites remains to be seen in the next few days, but he undoubtedly will make it uncomfortable for any and all of the performers.

Dopesters aren't forgetting Frank Jackson, the old-timer, either when figuring out the possibilities for the coming matches. Frank, who failed to qualify in Chicago two years ago and who has been out of the title picture for a number of years, seems to be in full stride again. He has a cunning smile on his face when anyone talks about titles with him, giving a hint of a probable comeback, which would make horseshoe history, if it did come to pass.

Moline Is Praised

The program which followed the banquet last night provided an opportunity for words of praise for the Moline Horseshoe Club and its handling of the big tournament.

"We need more Andy Petersons and Dave Swansons and more Moline Horseshoe Clubs," declared Jack Claves of St. Louis, who gave one of the talks at the hotel.

"If the game of horseshoe pitching is to go ahead, we have got to stick together and promote the sport through the national association."

Claves, who is leader of the Missouri Association and assistant manager of the Moline tournament, likened the game to bowling, but stated that the indoor sport had made strides far beyond the outdoor pastime.

Judge N. A. Larson of circuit court was toastmaster. Mayor A. Henry Arp, Harry A. Sward of the Dispatch, C. C. Lydick of the Chamber of Commerce, and R. B. Howard, secretary of the national association from London, Ohio, gave talks. The Rev. E. V. Stevens of Marlboro, Mass., delivered the invocation. Chris Oberlander entertained at the close of the meeting.

Praise for Courts

Almost everyone had words of praise for the courts, which the city of Moline, through its park department, provided in Riverside Park for the tournament. The fact that the greatest scoring rampage in tournament history was staged yesterday indicates that the layout must be to the liking of the pitchers.

Yesterday's rain held off until the last qualifier was winding up his second 100 shoes. It was cool and cloudy all morning and then threatening in the afternoon, but no rain came until about 5 in the evening.

Half a dozen of the women pitchers took advantage of an opportunity to get in some practice during the slack moments of the men's qualifying. The feminine stars will qualify tomorrow and at least a dozen are expected to seek the eight places in the championship flight. The title will be defended by Miss Caroline Schultz of Harvey, Illinois.

Casey Jones Leads Youthful Qualifiers
Mahoney is in Dispatch Event

Moline will be represented in the championship flight of the national horseshoe tournament by only one player, Joe Bennett, the 1932 Illinois champion from Congerville who has adopted the Plow City as his new home. Joe tied for seventeenth place with two other pitchers, Guy Zimmerman of Sac City, Iowa, and Leo Rollick of Chicago. They each scored 246 points.

Little Larry Mahoney of Red Bank, N.J., the youngest player in the tournament, will have to be satisfied with a shot at the money in the Dispatch night meet. The highly rated eastern champion ran into a series of tough breaks and into the greatest field of stars he ever has seen and finished out the title running with a 232 qualifying score.

The youngsters are well represented, however, in the championship class, being led by Casey Jones of Waukesha, Wis., who landed eighth in the standing with a 252 total. Casey's fellow townsman, Harold Scheets, was one notch behind with 251.

Addington, O'Shea Score

Two other young pitchers, who have become popular with the fans that have been crowding the rails since the arrival of the stars at Riverside. They are Addington, the angular Dunkirk, N.Y., lad from the Erie, Pa., district and James O'Shea, the young Massachusetts title-holder from Brockton.

O'Shea pitched 249 to assure himself a place in the finals, while Addington, participating for the first time in major competition turned in a 247 which placed him fourteenth in the standing.

It will be a profitable trip for Addington regardless of how he comes out in the match games. He won an all-expenses trip to Moline by taking first in a district tourney at Erie, Pa., and now is assured of a share in the $1,400 which will be divided among the twenty-four finalists in proportion to their positions in the final standing next Monday afternoon.

Bad Luck and Good

What was bad luck for one proved to be good luck for another yesterday in the qualifying round. Carl Hoff of Lewisburg, Ohio, tossed a 247 to land among the survivors in the national, only to be ruled out because it was discovered that his shoes were not regulation. He was required to pitch his 200 shoes over and his score fell off 10 points and eliminated him from the title flight.

The ill wind that was Hoff's "blew some good" for Gaylord Peterson of Varna, the 1934 Illinois champ who is a member of the Moline Club. Gaylord had 242 for his qualifying score and had been relegated to first rank in the Dispatch tourney, but Hoff's drop to the second division automatically moved Gaylord into the championship flight.

The Hoff incident was practically the only cause for official action yesterday. Everything seemed to be run off smoothly with a minimum of complaint from any and all quarters.

One Indian Survives

One of the Canadian Indians came through with enough points to land in the Dispatch tourney. John Simon of London, Ontario, piled up 229 marks to get safely into the second flight along with his fellow countryman, Fred Harburn of Cromarty, Ontario, who had a 231. John Riley, veteran of the horseshoe wars and Canadian champion in 1929, failed to reach 200 and dropped out of the competition. He accepted defeat stoically in typical Indian fashion.

Illinois pitchers led in gaining qualifying places in the championship flight with eight. Wisconsin was next with four entries. Missouri, California and Kansas each placed two in the finals. States with one representative remaining are Indiana, Ohio, Michigan, Massachusetts, New York and Iowa.

The low qualifying mark of 242 is by far the largest last place score ever noted in national horseshoe history. Likewise, C. C. Davis' 266 is the largest top score. The 222 minimum in the second twenty-four is one point more than the last qualifying score in the recent Illinois state meet.

Carey Davis in Running

Moline has one representative in the Dispatch tournament, Carey Davis, the city and county champion, who scored 227 points. Dave Swanson took part in the qualifying in spite of the handicap of a shoulder and back ailment, which developed overnight, and fell down to 215, failing to get over the line.

Blair Nunamaker of Cleveland, Ohio, the 1929 world champion who was expected to be one of Ted Allen's leading contenders for the title, decided to pass up the national at the last minute and defend his Ohio crown at the state fair in Columbus this week.

The list of players in the Dispatch tourney is dotted with big names in the horseshoe world. Among those is that of Johnny Caleo, the handsome young Chicagoan who is popular in Moline and the Midwest. Johnny produced a 229 yesterday to get into the second division.

- - - - - - -

By the way, the shoes that Hoff was using when his qualifying score was disqualified (because they didn't meet the official dimensions) were Isaacs AIR-FLO. They were relatively new, having just being patented on May 25, 1935. The shoe had a novel streamlined shape, triple-notch ringer breaker, and rounded aerodynamic heel calks. Hoff was from Ohio, as was the shoe's designer, W. L. Isaacs of Hamilton, Ohio. Not many Isaacs AIR-FLO shoes were sold and they are a mighty rare to find today. In 2005, a set of four Isaacs AIR-FLO shoes sold on eBay for $184.75. Now back to newspaper accounts of the competition.

Casey to Meet Shoe Champion in Sunday Game
Youthful Jones and Ted Allen Only Undefeated Pitchers
Moline Star Ties C.C. Davis, One Game out of First;
Zimmerman Shines

Climax of the national horseshoe tournament which reached the half way point late this afternoon at Riverside Park, is expected to come tomorrow as the twenty-four pitchers enter the third round of six games in their fight to determine the championship of the world.

The fortunate twenty-four tossed off six games yesterday in rapid fashion and were battling in six more today. With the competition of the third set Sunday afternoon the title quest should be narrowed down to a handful of men with the fate of any one of them hanging on the antics of every shoe pitched.

Already the faithful who have crowded the rails at the Moline courts are on edge awaiting the classic struggle of the meet, the clash between Champion Ted Allen and the 16-year-old Wisconsin titleholder, Charles "Casey" Jones. Yesterday Ted and Casey set the pace with a perfect afternoon of shooting six wins and no losses. Tomorrow they come together in the final match of the afternoon, the eighteenth game of the tournament for each.

Crucial Struggle

It is scarcely probably that either will go into that game undefeated. Allen had to turn back the threat of C. C. Davis this afternoon and many were picking the former champion to be the first to upset the titleholder. However, most of the fans believe [the match] between Casey and Ted will go far toward picking the ultimate winner.

After tomorrow's shooting, five games will remain for each pitcher. Three of those will be played Labor Day morning and two in the afternoon. The rest of the day will be devoted to playing off ties for various positions in the standing and their respective cash award.

Tomorrow also will bring the first match in the woman's title tournament in which Caroline Schultz, of Harvey, Illinois will defend her title. The feminine tossers staged their qualifying rounds today and eight survivors were lined up against each other in the match games Sunday.

Brilliant pitching was continued on every hand yesterday afternoon. Allen swept through his six games with little or no trouble, piling up ringer averages of better than 71 percent in every game.

Casey Jones fell below the 70 mark in one game, but won that with a margin of 42 points, his easiest triumph of the day. He hit 80.9 recent ringers in one battle.

Guy Is Ringer Champ

Guy Zimmerman, who tied with four others for fifth place in the early standings, collected a 6-game ringer average of 78.4 percent, scoring the highest single-game average of the day with 85.7 percent ringers.

Charlie Davis and Joe Bennett tied for third place behind Allen and Jones with five victories and one loss apiece. Davis handed Bennett his lone setback 50 to 43, while Jimmy Risk tripped Davis in the final game of the afternoon.

Risk is one of the boys who tied for fifth place with Zimmerman at four wins and two losses. The others in that group were Frank Jackson, the oldest pitcher in the tournament and the many times holder of the world title, Harold Scheets and Harvey Elmerson.

Zimmerman's two defeats were registered by Allen and Jones, leaving Guy a much easier path to the finals than most of the other contenders. He upset Risk in the first match of the afternoon and disposed of Elmerson in a later match, leaving only Davis, Bennett and Scheets of the first nine in the present standing to play in the remaining games of the tournament.

The Sac City star, who claims the trick shot championship of the world, staged the most thrilling comeback of the opening day's play when he downed Risk in the first game. The Indiana title-holder held a 42 to 25 lead over Zimmerman at one time, but a succession of doubles and very timely point getting lifted Guy to the top with a final score of 52 to 43.

Risk Sets Record

Risk set a tournament record in the match, throwing twelve consecutive doubles. It was that string which gave him such a commanding lead in the early part of the match, a margin which crumbled under the relentless firing of the Iowan.

Not a pitcher extended the national champion, although Allen had to come from behind early in his opening game with W. O. Maxwell of Hicksville, Ohio. Ted finally won out 50–27. His greatest margin was over Glenn Rust, who failed to win a game yesterday, 50–16.

Jones had to rally in the closing innings to win his opening match from Ellis Griggs of Plainsville, the Illinois state champion. Ellis had Casey 49 to 43 at one stage, but the careful little Badger poured on the doubles to triumph by one point.

Casey followed that with an easy win over Frank Jackson, 50 to 29, and continued with a minimum of difficulty until he met Zimmerman in the sixth game. With almost the entire gallery of about 200 persons crowded about his section of the court, Jones appeared to be cracking and Zimmerman quickly collected a lead. Guy got a dose of his own medicine, however, as the battle wore along. Casey tied it up at the halfway mark and taking advantage of the Iowan's every lapse, finally forged into the lead to win, 50 to 38.

Gray Starts Slowly

One of the disappointments of the opening rounds was the showing of L. F. Gray of Long Beach, Cal., who had qualified second to Charley Davis. Gray dropped three straight games before he found himself and finally broke even for the afternoon's work.

Roy Addington, the 6–foot, 7-inch lad from Dunkirk, N.Y., who gratified his backers from Erie, Pa., by his qualifying in the national, could not get going in the match games, dropping five out of the six.

James O'Shea of Brockton, Mass., state champion for the last three years, broke even in the six games and remained within striking distance of the top, although he is not expected to get much higher in the standing as the going gets rougher.

- - - - - - -

Then the women finally got their opportunity to qualify and there seemed to be lots of excitement brewing.

Michigan Woman Sets Record in Horseshoe Meet

Mrs. Esther James at Hastings this morning in the qualifying round of the national women's horseshoe tournament at Riverside Park when she qualified with a total of 266 points. She led a field of eight contestants into the match play tomorrow and Monday.

Mrs. James' total equaled that of C. C. Davis of Kansas, City, the leading qualifier in the men's tournament Thursday. She bested the men's ringer record by throwing 86 percent in her 100 qualifying shoes. She had thirty-seven doubles ringers, fourteen of the doubles in succession, all for world records.

Miss Caroline Schultz, the defending champion of Harvey, Illinois, qualified in second position with 256 points and 82 percent ringers. Her sister, Charlotte, was third with 243, piling up 76 ringers.

The qualifying scores and percentages follow:

	Score	%
Mrs. Esther James, Hastings, Mich.	266	86
Miss Caroline Schultz, Harvey, Ill.	256	82
Miss Charlotte Schultz, Harvey, Ill.	243	76
Miss Bettie Davis, Detroit, Mich.	212	61
Mrs. Guy Zimmerman, Sac City, Iowa	206	65
Mrs. Charles Johnson, Milwaukee, Wisc.	191	56
Mrs. Glenn Rust, Milwaukee, Wisc.	187	51
Mrs. Lee Rose, Detroit, Michigan	153	36

- - - - - - -

And throughout, our hero is contending for the winning share of the prize.

- - - - - - -

Bales, Henson and Frye Beat Six Opponents
Mahoney Captures Four
Young New Jersey Star Still in Running
Caleo Among Chief Contenders

Three pitchers worked their way into the lead in the opening games of the Dispatch Invitational Horseshoe Tournament before about 100 shivering fans at Riverside Park last night, piling up a perfect record of six straight triumphs.

Raymond Frye of Orkney Springs, Va., Clayton Henson of Arlington, Va., and Robert Bales of Kansas City, Mo., bested all of their opponents in the firing for a portion of the $310 in cash prizes provided for the second twenty-four qualifiers in the national meet.

Close on the heels of that trio came three other pitchers with five wins and one loss each, Carl Hoff of Lewisburg, Ohio, Johnny Caleo, the young Chicagoan and Lee Rose, the Michigan champion from Detroit. Four others won four of their six games, including 15-year-old Larry Mahoney of Red Bank, N.J.

The nocturnal meet will be resumed at 7:30 tonight with six more games. The third set of six matches is scheduled for the same hour tomorrow night, with the final five games and ties to be run off Monday evening.

Player Becomes Ill

John Garvey of Boone, Iowa, withdrew from the tournament because of illness after pitching two games, leaving only twenty-three to continue the contest. Garvey will receive the cash award for the last place and each of his games will be forfeited to the other pitchers. He had lost both of the games he engaged in before being forced to call off further activity.

In spite of the fact that three pitchers enjoyed perfect records after six games of competition, it is more or less out of the question to name a favorite. All three of the leaders had one game of 80 percent ringers or more and all won by fairly comfortable margins. However, such players as Rose, Caleo and Hoff demonstrated remarkable ability to rally after setbacks and there may be a battle down to the wire before the honors are distributed.

Youngsters Get Gallery

As in the afternoon session of the national when almost all of the spectators flocked to whichever court was occupied by Casey Jones, so was Larry Mahoney the center of attraction at night. The tiny New Jersey star was off to a good start, but he dropped his second game to Temple Jerrell of Hyattsville, Md., 50 to 46 and was defeated again in his fourth attempt. Victories in the third, fifth and sixth games gave him a .667 standing for the night and his followers are hopeful that the lad will hit an unbeatable stride tonight.

One of the major surprises of the play was the frequent defeat of Lloyd Woodard of Columbus, Ks., leading qualifier in the division. Lloyd dropped five of his six games to tumble almost out of the running.

John Simon, the Canadian Indian, likewise was in the one victory class, finding the competition tough at all stages. Fred Harburn, last year's dominion champion, managed to break even in his games and to stay within striking distance of the top.

Dean Brown of Riverside, Cal., who lost two of his six games, was one of the boys marked for observation tonight since he took several of his matches in convincing fashion and showed signs of becoming a real threat to Frye, Henson, and Bales before the event is finished Labor Day evening.

Fine Points of the Game

One of the finest hairline decisions ever recorded in horseshoe history was made by L. E. Tanner of Anchor, Ill., newly elected president of the national association, yesterday afternoon during the running off of matches in the national. Ellis Griggs, the Illinois champion had one shoe in a position, which to the eye, appeared to be a complete "Stymie." Use of the rule *(straightedge)*, to determine whether or not he had a ringer failed to solve the problem. It was so close to missing that a piece of ordinary paper would not fit between the rule and the peg. Mr. Tanner secured a cigarette paper and slipped it into the narrow opening, satisfying both pitchers that the shoe was far enough past the peg to count a ringer.

Veterans Stop Winning March of Young Aces
Jackson Trips Champion Ted Allen
and Davis Beats Casey Jones

When yesterday's steady rainfall washed out the third day's pitching in the national horseshoe tournament at Riverside Park the delegates to the national convention took advantage of the layoff to thrash out a multitude of questions pertaining to the future of the organization and to hope for fair skies today so that the delayed program might be crowded into one day and night of concentrated play.

With the day's show went Moline's chief hope of breaking even on the tournament, for the men who have worked for weeks to bring about the event, had been counting on Sunday and today for their largest crowds of the 5-day meet. Finances for the show were assured long ago, of course, but the Plow City club had hoped to be able to realize enough from gate receipts to make up the entire amount of the prize lists and cost of the tourney.

Saturday's happenings on the courts presented an ideal situation for the holiday weekend but for the dismal rain. Both leaders in the championship flight were defeated and would have met in the afternoon Sunday. A new title threat had arisen among the women who were slated to begin their tourney yesterday and two of the leaders in the dispatch tourney had been eliminated from the undefeated list. One of those was to have met the only unbeaten player Sunday and the other today. All in all, a great show had been built up for the fans.

Oldtimers Turn Trick

It took a pair of oldtimers to hand the young leaders their first setbacks in the national men's championship flight. Frank Jackson of Blue Mound, Kansas, who used to dominate the sport, turned the trick against champion Ted Allen after the latter had hung up nine straight triumphs. C. C. Davis of Kansas City, Missouri, who succeeded Jackson on the horseshoe throne a few years ago, stopped the streak of the sensational young Casey Jones at ten straight.

Those reversals left Casey and Ted tied for the lead, only one game ahead of Davis and Jackson. The latter breezed through Saturday's schedule of six games without a defeat, climbing into the contender class with a string of victories that stamped him as more than an ordinary threat to the title hopes of the youngsters.

Davis faltered at the start of the day's shooting, losing his important match with Allen, but he came back with five straight to remain in the running.

Elmerson Surprises

One notch back of the leading four came Guy Zimmerman, Sac City, Iowa, and Harvey Elmerson of Milwaukee with nine wins and three losses. Elmerson surprised the experts by winning five out of his six games Saturday, while the Iowan, bothered by illness which kept him in bed all Saturday morning managed five straight victories before he finally was defeated by Howard Collier of Cuba, Illinois.

Jimmy Risk of Montpellier, Ind., dropped two more games to finish in a tie for seventh place with Joe Bennett of Moline, who could do no better than break even. The latter pair virtually was eliminated from title consideration by those losses.

In the feature matches of the day Jackson and Allen were deadlocked most of the way and the veteran won because he could take advantage of a couple of openings in the crucial stages of the game. Jones had Davis almost beaten twice but blew a lead late in the game to permit Charley to go ahead and win. Jackson's score over Allen was 51 to 41, while Davis beat Casey 51 to 46.

Mrs. James Shines

The new sensation of the women's division of the tournament was Esther James of Hastings, Michigan, who not only established three world records for her sex, but also broke two men's marks and tied another. Of course, she was pitching the 30-foot distance standard for women and her feats could not be compared to those of the men, but her 266 qualifying score and 86 ringers percentage were brilliant accomplishments.

Robert Bales remained the lone undefeated participant in the Dispatch tourney after Saturday night's battles. Raymond Frye fell before the expert pitching of Dean Brown and Clayton Henson was removed from the perfect class by Myron Ferguson of Columbus, Ohio.

Frye and Henson were tied for second, one game behind Bales, while Brown of California moved up into a contending position with six straight wins, which gave him ten victories and two losses.

Other threats included Johnny Caleo, Larry Mahoney and Lee Rose, all with nine wins and three losses.

- - - - - - -

The media coverage even gave some notice to the convention activities. This next article mentions L. E. Tanner's election as NHPA president. That the convention was being held in Tanner's home state may have heavily influences the election results. Of the people named in this article, six are members of the NHPA Hall of Fame, including Tanner, who was inducted in 1991.

- - - - - - -

Horseshoe Men Select Tanner as New Leader

L. E. Tanner of Anchor, Illinois, was elected president of the National Horseshoe Pitchers' Association this morning during a session of the annual convention in the Moline City Hall. Mr. Tanner, who is president of the Illinois state association, succeeds Alex Cumming of Minneapolis.

P. V. Harris of Holden, Mass., was elevated from second vice president to the position of first vice president to succeed Mr. Tanner. Dr. Alan R. Pottle of Dayton, Ohio, was named second vice president and L. R. Bates of Los Angeles was elected third vice president.

R. B. Howard of London, Ohio, publisher of the *Horseshoe World* magazine, was reelected secretary-treasurer of the association.

Committees Named

Committees were named at a session of the convention last night and there was considerable discussion of ways to finance the organization. No definite action was taken on any of the problems.

Here is a list of persons chosen for the committee work:

Constitution and rules – Jack Claves, St. Louis; Frank Jackson, Blue Mound, Kansas.

Auditing committee – James Risk, Montpelier, Indiana; Gaylord Peterson, Varna, Illinois.

Grievance committee – Jack Claves and C. C. Davis, Kansas City, Mo.

Publicity committee – R. B. Howard, Dave Swanson, Moline; Andrew Peterson, Moline.

Resolutions committee – Rev. E. V. Stevens, Marlboro, Mass.

Nominations committee – Andrew Peterson, Moline; Mrs. Glen Rust, Milwaukee; W. E. Santoro, Newark, N.J.

Special committee to confer with manufacturers – R. B. Howard; Bert Duryee, Wichita, Kansas; P. V. Harris.

- - - - - - -

The next article is rather historic because it announces the start of the NHPA Stamp Program. This novel creation was not just a whim of the association to raise some much-needed operating capital; it was a program that existed well into the 1960s. The article doesn't delve into whose suggestion it was or who made the presentation of the proposed plan, but for those of you interested in trivia, the idea came from Harry Duncan of Denver, Colorado, and Ted Allen made the presentation. Duncan was inducted to the NHPA Hall of Fame in 1992.

- - - - - - -

National Shoe Leaders Make Many Changes
Establish Methods of Raising Funds To Operate Association

Drastic revision of the National Horseshoe Pitchers' Association was made yesterday afternoon at a special session in the city hall. Complete change of the state charter system, effective June 1, 1936, and provision for the financing of the association were negotiated by the delegates.

It also was decided that the nation or world champions in both men's and women's divisions should be exempt from qualifying in national tournaments in the future.

The meeting was presided over by L. E. Tanner, new national president, who was assisted by R. B. Howard, secretary-treasurer and Jack Claves, chairman of the rules and constitution committee. The convention voted to make all committees serve for a full year instead of for the duration of the convention.

Reduce Member Fees

In connection with the state charter system it was voted to abolish the present plan of charging state organizations a yearly fee of $25.00 for membership in the national and to grant charters free of charge to all states. It also was voted to abolish the present system of charging individual members of national association $1.00 per year and to require all members to pay an annual fee of 25 cents. It was agreed that that [the 25-cent] fee was to be divided, 15 cents to the national and 10 cents to the state association.

All tournaments are to be sanctioned by the national group through state organizations, whether county, city or state meets and only national association members will be permitted to compete in sanctioned tournaments. Moreover, national association members who to take part in unsanctioned tournaments are to be suspended for one year from membership in the organization and barred from all competition in sanctioned meets.

Another method of raising funds for the association was adopted in cooperation with manufacturers of horseshoes. The manufacturers agreed to purchase 1-cent stamps to be provided by the national association and to place one of those stamps on each horseshoe manufactured and sold to pitchers throughout the world. In return for that extra revenue, the national association agreed to sanction only those shoes manufactured by companies participating in the new "tax" scheme.

Pleased with Results

There was discussion of many other things, mostly technical and more or less uninteresting to the average person not closely connected with the sport. No action was taken on any of the measures because it was believed that the permanent committees should investigate in detail and report back later in the year.

Leaders of the organization stated after the meeting that they are happier about the results of the convention than they ever have been in the history of the sport. They eventually hope to provide enough funds to permit the association to stage its own national tournament without the aid of cities in which they are held and to provide one or more class flights similar to the Dispatch Tournament this year in order to attract more men and women to the national meet.

- - - - - - -

Robert Bales of Kansas City Wins Dispatch Tournament

Robert of Kansas City captured first money in the Dispatch Horseshoe Pitching Tournament last night at Riverside Park as sixteen of the twenty-four pitchers in the second flight of the national meet battled until after midnight in a steady drizzle of rain to complete the event.

Seven of the pitchers either went home or gave up the struggle when the weather turned damp late in the afternoon, so a large number of forfeits entered into the race for the $310 in cash prizes.

Bales breezed through 24 games before he finally was beaten by Bill Garvey of Boone, Iowa, 52 to 49. That victory climaxed a sensational drive, which landed the Iowan in a tie for fourth place in the standing.

Raymond Frye dropped two of his games and fell back into a tie with Dean Brown for runner-up honors. Clayton Henson, who had been tied with Frye for second place, lost six games in a series of upsets to tumble back into a tie for seventh place with two others.

- - - - - - -

As the following article relates, Esther James became the new women's champion. The article also discusses the next-to-final round for the men. Rose's journal doesn't contain an article that reports the results of the men's final round. The Roses started traveling back home to Michigan before that paper was on the newsstands. The men's final standings chart is copied from an old *Horseshoe World* magazine.

Mrs. Esther James Wins Women's Horseshoe Championship
Caroline Schultz, Defending Champion, Quits Meet Because of Weather

Mrs. Esther James of Hastings, Michigan, the pretty young matron who startled the Schultz sisters and all the game's followers Saturday by breaking three world records in the qualifying rounds, ascended to the throne left unguarded by the Harvey girl. Mrs. James trimmed five other rivals to garner the coveted crown.

Caroline Schultz did not defend her title, withdrawing from the tournament along with her sister, Charlotte, declaring that the weather was not fit for competition. Had she taken part in the games along with the women who did brave the weather, it is doubtful if even the champion of 1934 could have stopped the sensational march of the new title-holder.

Woman's Championship Class 1935 World Tournament

The article doesn't make much out of Caroline Schultz's withdrawal from the tournament, but at the time—and even still today—that kind of decision is shocking news. In 1933, Schultz hit the horseshoe scene with stunning skills and performances, setting new world records in qualifying and then averaging 73.8 percent in winning her first World Championship. (The previous record women's tournament average was set by Laura Lanham at 58.9 percent.) Then in 1934, Schultz pitched an unbelievable 81.3 percent, a record that stood for 44 years. Many didn't really believe it was the weather that scared Schultz off, but rather a decision made by her father. Here is an excerpt from *World Champions of Horseshoe Pitching*.

> At this late date, it would be impossible to ever confirm the exact reasoning behind the pulling out by both Schultz sisters, except for the fact that one of our "elder statesmen," Ottie Reno spent time visiting with the Schultz sisters and in an article he wrote of that experience for the July 1977 *News Digest*. It is as simple as, Mr. Schultz was the boss of the family, he ran things and what he said is what took place. We can be assured that any decision made to withdraw from the competition for whatever reason was made by Mr. Schultz. It would not have been a decision made by Caroline. So if it was the weather, or competition, or something else that sent the Schultz family home, we can be comfortable knowing that Caroline did not make the decision to withdraw but merely responded to her dad's direction.

Finish Meet Today

Men in the championship flight were to finish up their division this afternoon with five games scheduled for all contestants. Champion Ted Allen appeared in a good position to retain his title, one full game ahead of the field, although he had to meet Harvey Elmerson, a young ringer tosser who came up with a burst the second and third days of the meet and who climaxed his drive for honors yesterday by tripping Casey Jones.

Young Jones conquered Allen in the final match of the day but the win failed to have the drama, which had been expected when the two rivals still were tied for the leadership.

While Allen was plugging along, showing remarkable consistency against all opponents, the Waukesha flash was having his troubles. The rain made the concrete slabs slippery for all pitchers and especially so for Jones, who stretches out more than any other entrant in the tournament when delivering the shoe.

After Elmerson had handed the 16-year-old a beating 53 to 33, another Waukesha pitcher, Harold Scheets, stepped up from far down the list of players in the standing and defeated Casey, 50 to 42.

Casey Had to Win

Jones rallied to win three straight games before he hooked up with Allen who had garnered five in succession. Ted was two full games ahead of the youngster and Casey had to win their game or drop out of the title class for keeps.

The slender little fellow returned to form against the champion, gaining a 16 to 0 lead before Allen started his usual comeback. Three times the score was tied before Casey pulled out a flock of doubles.

Ted started today's final games with sixteen wins and two losses, while Jones, C. C. Davis, Guy Zimmerman and Elmerson were deadlocked in second place with fifteen victories and three defeats.

Frank Jackson had his toughest day of the tournament, dropping three of his six games and slipping back to sixth place.

Joe Bennett of Moline copped four games and climbed ahead of Jimmy Risk and W. O. Maxwell into seventh place. Joe has a dozen wins and six losses, while Risk and Maxwell finished with eleven victories.

Ted Puts on Heat

Allen staged a succession of rallies to win his five games yesterday. Risk had him beaten, 40 to 20, in the first game but the champion put on pressure and steamed through with a victory, laying on the double ringers with monotonous regularity when they counted most. Risk cracked under the steady firing.

Against Howard Collier of Cuba, Illinois, the steady Allen had to rally in order to win, 52 to 43. Roy Addington, of Dunkirk, NY, was beating Ted 21 to 7 in the early stages of their game but the champ blanked the tall easterner for a series of frames during which he gained a tie and then took command of the situation by scoring 12 points on four shoes. Addington missed one golden opportunity when Allen left the both shoes off the peg in one frame and the best Roy could de was get a point.

Mrs. Johnson Second

In the women's tournament, Mrs. Charles Johnson of Milwaukee finished in second place with four wins out of five games. None of the five women seriously threatened Mrs. James, although she did engage in one or two close contests.

The Michigan star's triumph was worth $75 in cash to her, while second place drew $50 and third $25. Each of the other contestants received $10. The tournament committee had not decided what to do with the Schultz girl's share of the prize money early today.

1935 Men's World Championship Finals

Name	W	L	Pts	R	SP	Pct.	Prize
1. Ted Allen	21	2	1144	1222	1618	76.5	$200
2. Harvey Elmerson	19	4	1043	1256	1740	72.1	240
3. Guy Zimmerman	18	5	1085	1213	1654	73.3	200
4. C. C. Davis	18	5	1103	1198	1626	73.6	150
5. Frank Jackson	17	6	1111	1285	1762	72.9	100
6. Casey Jones	17	6	1125	1244	1712	72.6	75
7. Jimmy Risk	15	8	1115	1225	1720	71.2	50
8. Joe Bennett	14	9	974	1114	1612	69.1	45
9. W. O. Maxwell	14	9	973	1059	1524	69.3	40
10. Ellis Griggs	13	10	1038	1232	1728	71.2	35
11. Alvin Dahlene	12	11	920	987	1482	66.5	30
12. L. F. Gray	12	11	896	1205	1734	69.4	20
13. James O'Shea	12	11	1365	1003	1492	67.2	15
14. Earl Bomke	10	13	929	932	1470	36.4	10
15. Howard Collier	10	13	879	991	1490	66.5	10
16. Leo Lattore	9	14	945	1068	1646	64.8	10
17. Oscar Bozich	8	15	892	1011	1580	63.9	10
18. Leo Rollick	8	15	668	794	1231	64.5	10
19. Harold Scheets	7	16	747	793	1414	56.0	10
20. Aden Swinehammer	7	16	675	910	1376	65.9	10
21. Roy Addington	5	18	784	1014	1561	64.9	10
22. Glenn Rust	5	18	790	871	1510	57.6	10
23. Gaylord Peterson	4	19	717	849	1492	56.2	10
24. E. R. Baker	1	23	485	628	1116	56.2	10

Women's Championship Finals – 1935

Prize	Name	W	L	P	R	DR	SP	%
$75	Esther James	5	0	257	178	61	268	63.6
$50	Mrs. Chas. Johnson	4	1	242	176	55	308	59.3
$25	Betty Davis	3	2	220	159	40	290	58.3
$10	Grace Zimmerman	2	3	212	161	50	296	55.5
$10	Ann Rust	1	4	139	110	21	268	41.0
$10	Helen Rose	0	5	51	52	6	206	25.3

Summary of Dispatch Tournament

Name	W	L	Pts	R	SP	Pct.	Prize
1. Bob Bales	22	1	1033	894	1336	68.3	$60
2. Ray Frye	20	3	1036	905	1324	68.3	50
3. Dean Brown	20	3	1046	693	1086	64.0	40
4. Bill Garvey	17	6	1006	863	1402	62.9	30
5. Myron Ferguson	17	6	939	784	1208	63.8	20
6. Carl Hoff	16	7	1022	902	1436	62.1	10
7. John Caleo	16	7	997	821	1442	59.3	9
8. Clay Henson	16	7	1040	924	1458	60.6	8
9. F. Harburn	15	8	739	644	1066	60.0	7
10. Larry Mahoney	14	9	864	815	1374	57.1	6
11. Lee Rose	14	9	915	820	1418	58.5	5
12. John Simon	10	13	578	524	1090	48.4	5
13. T. Jarrell	10	13	634	640	1040	61.2	5
14. L. Steinmann	10	13	838	723	1380	51.5	5
15. John Paxton	8	15	825	763	1308	59.3	5
16. Ray Wilson	6	17	528	475	1018	50.0	5
17. H. Rizor	6	17	726	623	1308	50.0	5
18. Joe Clayton	5	18	464	464	752	61.7	5
19. A. Terry	4	19	427	375	718	53.4	5
20. Carey Davis	3	20	418	421	756	56.4	5
21. D. Terry	3	20	359	351	702	50.0	5
22. Alton Woods	2	21	297	327	654	50.0	5
23. L. Woodard	2	21	403	416	832	50.0	5
24. J. Garvey	0	23	32	43	128	34.3	5

———————

The Moline newspapers' coverage of the 1935 World Tournament was impressively complete, which is fortunate since the 1935 tournament saw some historic moments. It was the final World Tournament appearance for four of the biggest names in the game: Frank Jackson and C. C. Davis, the top two players of the initial decades of the sport; Jimmy Risk, one of great showmen of the game, who conducted pitching exhibitions all over the world and even at the White House; and Burt Duryee, the great player from Kansas. All four are members of the NHPA Hall of Fame.

The 1935 event also shined a spotlight on several newer players whose careers were highlights of the fabulous 1950s at Murray, Utah. This tournament, more than any other, was a true changing of the guard. Most of the major accomplishments for these young players would come after this event. Here is a rundown on what some of them accomplished.

Ted Allen of Alhambra, California. This was just Allen's third World Tournament and of course his third title. In 1935, no one could have foreseen that Allen would go on to qualify for the men's finals 31 times and then win 10 championships altogether. His record stood for many years until contemporary phenom Alan Francis surpassed the mark. Allen won nine Colorado state titles, two California titles (1934 and 1935), and one in Oregon (1932).

Casey Jones of Waukesha, Wisconsin. Jones was only 16 when he entered the 1935 tournament, but he was already the Wisconsin state champion. He became known as the greatest pitcher who never won a World Championship. In 1948, Jones set a new record by averaging 87.5 percent for the tournament; he lost three games and ended up in second place, one win short of winning the title. He finished second in World Tournaments five times. His 298 career wins still ranks 22nd on the World Tournament All-Time Wins List.

Harvey Elmerson of Milwaukee, Wisconsin. Elmerson won his first Wisconsin championship in 1926. By 1935 he won seven state championships, and he went on to win two more in the 1940s. Elmerson qualified for the men's finals at four World Tournaments (1928, 1929, 1935 and 1940) and earned 68 wins in those events.

Guy Zimmerman of Sac City, Iowa. There were two big events in his career. First, he was the first player to pitch a perfect game in a World Tournament.

That game was 44 shoes against Henry Pergal in 1948. In a twenty-six-year span, from 1933 through 1959, 19 World Tournaments were held. Two players dominated the tournaments during that span—Ted Allen won 10 titles and Fernando Isais won eight. Except in 1954, when Zimmerman averaged 84.2 percent and went undefeated in 20 games to win his only World Championship. Zimmerman won 10 California state championships between 1942 and 1954, and nine of these were consecutive. From 1934 to 1940, he won five Iowa state titles. Zimmerman was elected to the NHPA Hall of fame in 1967.

C. C. Davis of Kansas City, Missouri. The 1935 World Tournament was Charles C. Davis's last. During his career he racked up five World titles and was probably the best overall player of his time. He designed and manufactured his own brand of pitching shoes in 1932. He earned the Missouri state championship in 1934 and 1935. Davis won 274 games in his World Tournament career. Remarkably, 75 years later, he still ranks 25th on the World Tournament All-Time Wins List. Davis was elected to the NHPA Hall of Fame in 1968.

Frank Jackson of Blue Mound, Kansas. Jackson hailed from both Iowa and Kansas. The 1935 tournament was also his final World Tournament. He was a star of stars in the game during a career in which he won seven World Championships, the first in 1909. His 328 career wins still ranks 18th on the World Tournament All-Time Wins List.

Joe Bennett of Moline, Illinois. Bennett was the Illinois state champion in 1932.

Jimmy Risk of Montpelier, Indiana. Just 22 years old in 1935, this was his last World Tournament. He played in six World events and was a runner-up in the 1927 World Tournament. He earned the Indiana state championship an impressive seven times—in 1927, 1928, 1930, 1932, 1933, 1935, and 1939. Risk was elected to the NHPA Hall of Fame in 1971.

W. O. Maxwell of Hicksville, Ohio. Maxwell entered this event, his first World Tournament, at the age of 55. Twenty-five years later, in 1960 at age 80, he won the first Senior Men's World Championship, in a playoff, and averaged 62.4 percent. The following year he retained his title, averaging 69.2 percent.

Howard Collier. Collier was the 1936 Illinois state champion.

James O'Shea. O'Shea entered this event at age 21. He went on to win the Massachusetts state championship 13 times.

L. F. Gray. Gray was the 1935 California state champion.

Alvin Dahlene. Dahlene was a 60-year veteran of the sport. He qualified for the men's championship finals four times, and 1935 was the first. He played in 42 Kansas state tournaments, winning the state title twice—in 1941 and 1942. Dahlene was elected NHPA vice president in 1939, and was appointed as one of the seven original regional directors in 1955. His region consisted of nine states.

Leo Rollick. Rollick earned the 1943 Utah state title.

Ellis Griggs. Griggs was just 24 year old in 1935. He won the Illinois state championship that year and distinguished himself by winning 10 state titles in five different decades: 1935, 1940, 1952, 1957, 1959, 1961, 1966, 1967, 1968, and 1970.

Earl Bomke. He entered the 1935 tournament at age 22. He went on to win Illinois state championships in 1946, 1947, and 1951.

Harold Scheets. This was the second time Scheets qualified for the men's finals. He was the Wisconsin state champion in 1932 and 1933.

Aden Swinehammer. Swinehammer was the 1939 Illinois state champion.

Oscar Bozick. This was his only World Tournament appearance. He was 19 years old at the time, and four years later he was the 1939 Missouri state champion.

Glenn Rust of Wisconsin. The 1935 World Tournament marked the only time Rust appeared in the finals, but his wife Ann Rust qualified for the Women's Championship finals in 1935 and 1947.

Gaylord Peterson. Peterson won the Illinois state championship in 1928 and 1934.

The 1935 World Tournament was the first to conduct a Class B competition, which at the time was called the Dispatch Tournament. Several remarkable pitchers participated.

Robert Bales. Bale was 26 years old in 1935. Pitched the first perfect game on record, a 22-shoe effort in 1941 state tournament held at the Missouri State Fair. Bales won the Missouri state championship in 1940, 1942, and 1961.

Raymond Frye. He was the Virginia state champion in 1934, 1935, 1937, and 1950.

Clayton Henson. Henson was the Virginia state champion an impressive 15 times (1930, 1932, and 1938–1949).

Dean Brown. He was the California state champion in 1926, 1928, 1938, and 1939. Between 1934 and 1958, Brown qualified for the men's championship finals in World Tournament play 13 times, winning 259 games, an achievement that still ranks 27th on the All-Time Wins List. Brown was elected to the NHPA Hall of Fame in 2000.

John Calao of Illinois. Calao qualified for the men's Championship Class in 1933.

Larry Mahoney. Mahoney was just 15 years old at the time of the 1935 World Tournament. He was a nine-time New Jersey state champion, with seven consecutive titles from 1934 to 1940, and wins again in 1947 and 1948. In 1937, Mahoney captained a U.S. team that defeated a Canadian team before 6,000 people in Exposition Stadium in Toronto.

John Paxton of Ottumwa, Iowa. Paxton was a long-time championship-class player. He qualified for nine men's championship finals between 1940 and 1959, but he didn't reach his peak for another 30 years, when he won five straight Senior Men's World Championships beginning in 1966. Paxton was inducted to the NHPA Hall of Fame in 1982.

Lefty Steinmann. He qualified for the finals in 1933, but missed the cutoff in 1935. Steinmann was the Missouri state champion in 1931.

Myron Ferguson. He was the Ohio state champion in 1942.

Fred Harburn of Canada. Harburn was the Canadian national champion in 1936, 1937, and 1939.

Temple Jerrell. Jerrell was the Maryland state champion in 1935 and 1936, and the Tennessee state champion in 1945.

Dale Terry of Illinois. Terry didn't play in a World Tournament again until 1952, when qualified for the finals and and placed 26th overall, shooting a 65.0 percent average.

Lloyd Woodard. Woodard qualified for the men's finals at the 1933 World Tournament. He was the 1928 Kansas state champion.

John Garvey. He won the 1935 state title in Iowa.

There are a several notables at the 1935 World Tournament who missed the cut for the Class B event.

Nelson Vogel of Illinois. Vogel never won an Illinois championship, but qualified for the men's finals in World Tournament play six times between 1950 and 1964. He is part of the only three-generation family to qualify for the men's finals. His son Roger qualified 11 times and his grandson Bret qualified in 2004 and 2010.

Arlo Harris. Harris was 25 years old in 1935. He went on to win the Indiana state championship in 1937 and 1948. In 1949, Harris was elected president of NHPA. He was one of the organization's most controversial officers. He served for just one year, then formed the American Horseshoe Pitchers Association (AHPA) in his home state, which still is active. Harris was the Indiana AHPA champ in 1950, 1952, and 1958. Harris is also known for designing the Harris Profession Pitching Shoe, which was manufactured by Giant Grip in Oshkosh, Wisconsin.

James Denny. Denny claimed the Missouri state championship in 1937.

Hubert Trinkle. Trinkle was the Indiana state champ in 1934, 1936, and 1941 and the National Amateur Athletic Union (AAU) champion in 1938 and 1939. He teamed up with Walter Lane Sr. to win the 1937, 1938, and 1940 national doubles title.

Henry Harper of Monterey, California. Harper had qualified for the finals in 1934, and he did again in 1946, 1947, 1949, 1950, 1952, 1959, and 1963.

William Isaacs of Hamilton, Ohio. He was the designer and manufacturer of the Isaacs AIR-FLO pitching shoe.

Carl Von Der Lancken. He was one of the nation's greatest promoters in the 1930s and 1940s. In 1936, Von Der Lancken gave pitching exhibitions in England, France, and Spain. He was elected NHPA vice president in 1941 and was inducted into the NHPA Hall of Fame in 1972.

Lee Rose noted his personal games played in the Dispatch Tournament.

Friday, August 30th

Harburn	50	59.2	Rose	50	50.5
Rose	35	56.3	Woodard	21	44.4
Rose	50	59.6	Rose	50	75.9
D. Terry	30	50.0	Jerrell	41	69.1
Rose	50	54.4			
J. Simon	40	48.5			

Saturday, August 31st

Dean Brown defeated Rose 50–41

Rose defeated Roy Wilson 50–37

Rose defeated A. Terry 50–41

Rose defeated Carey Davis 50–43

Rose defeated Joe Clayton 50–49

Ferguson defeated Rose 53–37

Monday, September 2 – Rain, but we played anyhow.

Rose defeated Rizor 50–49

Rose defeated Mahoney 50–27

Rose beat Steinmann 50–28

Rose defeated J. Harvey(default)

Rose beat Paxton (default)

Then the deluge!

Henson defeated Rose 50–49

Frye defeated Rose 50–35

W. Garvey defeated Rose 50–44

Bales defeated Rose 50–36

Hoff defeated Rose 50–41

Calao defeated Rose 50–24

Rose tied for 10th with Larry Mahoney, champion of New Jersey, and they split the purse, each taking $5.50.

Bertie, Rizor and I started for home on Tuesday, 5 p.m. and arrived home on Wednesday, 10:00 a.m.

So much for Moline!!!

- - - - - - -

Now to close out his record of 1935, Rose's journal includes a number of pages dedicated to the 1935 state tournament in Michigan. Notice that his record is as nearly as engaging and complete as the newspaper coverage of the World Tournament. But this account comes from the hand of the defending Michigan state champion.

- - - - - - -

My Twelfth State Tournament

Held at Dearborn, Monroe & Park Streets, Saturday and Sunday, September 21 & 22. There were 20 entries and they played a single round robin to decide the title. Ed Walls was forced to cop the title off my brow, while Bobby Hitt, Lattore and Lundgren were given chances. I used Gordon shoes and pitched bare handed.

In the first round, I met C. H. Davis. He got off in the lead, 10–0 and kept right on adding up, leading 21–9 and later 26–12. It looked bad for the title-holder at this point, but I rallied nicely with 16 ringers in 20 shoes to shoot ahead of him, 40–32. I held onto my lead to finally win 50–40.

	Pts	R	DR	SP	Pct	4-On
Rose	50	38	11	64	.593	1
Davis	40	34	8	64	.531	1

In other games, Skinner beat Getz; Lattore swamped Valleau; Walls downed Armstrong; Hitt made a sensational start, beating Goodell 50–1 with 77%; Lundgren downed a tough customer in Brown; Stephens turned back the Upper Peninsula Champion, Lynford Norton; Burt nosed out Gorsline; Field edged out Rizor; Koppitsch slaughtered Wrobble and all the favorites were to a good start with no upsets registered.

In the second round I met Valleau. I got the first six and then stayed there until Orville had run up 11. I then went ahead 27–14. Valleau rallied with the help of 3 straight doubles to make it 27–24, but he fell off as I shot ahead 38–24. I later led 45–28 and was trying to coast out, but Valleau smashed out 13 points to get up to 41. I rallied in the pinch to eke out a 50–44 victory.

	Pts	R	DR	SP	Pct	4-On
Rose	50	37	10	70	.530	2
Valleau	44	34	8	70	.485	2

In other games, Walls came from behind to down Lattore and establish himself more firmly as favorite; Norton defeated Field; Lundgren, Koppitsch, Stephens and Burt all won to stay in the undefeated class; Hitt stepped up his sensational pace a trifle to smatter Getz down 50–6 with 78%; while Skinner repeated with a fine performance to beat Davis and draw some of the attention of the crowd to him as a possible potential champion.

In the third round, I was called up to play Lattore and the crowd gathered around to witness the downfall of an unpopular champion. Lattore did not disappoint them at the start, for he hung on seven out of eight to jump ahead 13–0. But he missed a couple of times and I got to 11 while he was only getting 1 more. He then went further ahead, 20–11. I made it 20–18; he made it 27–18; I made a pointy and he went ahead again 33–19 with a double on. However, I topped his double, picked up three points on a single, six more on 2 doubles and then got away with six on another double to shoot ahead 34–33. Another single scored me three more and I led 37–33. Lattore, incensed, responded to the cheers of the crowd and rallied with 7 out of 8 to go ahead 43–37. I got a point, then threw a double and he missed both shoes to allow me to go ahead again 44–43. I threw a single and had the other shoe two feet away. He missed his first shoe and then his second shoe missed, landed on mine and my shoe leaped into the air and fell on the stake and that six put me out 50–43, much to the chagrin of my enemies.

	Pts	R	DR	SP	Pct	4-On
Rose	50	38	10	64	.594	3
Lattore	43	36	12	64	.564	3

In the other games, Bobby Hitt crashed Lundgren out of the unbeaten class with a 50–25 victory, pitching 68%; Koppitsch took his first beating from Getz;

Rizor led Stephens all the way to defeat him and Walls, Skinner and Burt each hung up their 3rd consecutive win to remain tied with Rose and Hitt for 1st. A halt was then made for lunch.

In the fourth round I was expected to have a tough battle with Lundgren, but he blew up and I had an easy time smearing him.

	Pts	R	DR	SP	Pct	4-On
Rose	50	29	7	46	.630	0
Lundgren	12	16	3	46	.348	0

Skinner defeated Burt in their battle of undefeated players; Walls easily defeated Rizor and Hitt out-lasted Al Field.

In the fifth round I met Don Stephens. I took a lead of 10–7 and then suddenly slumped off badly, throwing only 3 ringers in 12 shoes and he ran ahead 26–10. I then gritted my teeth and dug in to catch him. I got up to 26–15 before he got another three. I then got up to 22, but here he got two 3's to lead again 35–22. I got up to 28 on a double, but he got three right back on a double and then got six more when my second shoe knocked my first ringer off. He led 44–28 and my defeat seemed sure. But again I rallied, crashing out 13 points to his one to make it 45–42. Here, two doubles in a row put him out as the crowd cheered.

	Pts	R	DR	SP	Pct	4-On
Rose	42	37	9	72	.525	2
Stephens	50	42	11	72	.585	2

Walls hung up his 5th straight and by beating one of his most dangerous rivals when he turned back Bobby Hitt 50-38. Skinner remained tied with him by beating Koppitsch.

In the 6th round, I met — — Ed Walls!!! The spectators jammed around to see this game, expecting a red-hot fight. None were prepared to witness what happened. Smashing 15 ringers in my first 20 shoes while the white-faced, shaking Walls could fling on only six. I romped away into a 31–5 lead. That sealed Walls doom, as I merely played along even with him after that to win.

	Pts	R	DR	SP	Pct	4-On
Rose	50	29	10	48	.605	2
Walls	26	22	6	48	.460	2

Skinner trimmed Valleau 50–17 to become the only undefeated player and the crowd, disgusted at Walls blowing up against me, began to "pull" for the ancient rustic with the whip-like flipper to come through. Burt defeated Norton and Hitt out-fought Davis to stay in the running with one defeat each.

In the 7th round, I had a breather against Goodell.

	Pts	R	DR	SP	Pct	4-On
Rose	50	31	10	52	.595	3
Goodell	16	20	5	52	.385	3

Skinner took another stride forward by nosing out Lundgren in a ding-dong battle, 50–46, with each man hurling 50 ringers in 82 shoes. Walls trampled over Norton and Burt caused a mild sensation by squelching Hitt 50–25. Hitt was tiring badly.

My eighth game was a romp:

	Pts	R	DR	SP	Pct	4-On
Rose	50	34	11	50	.680	2
Koppitsch	12	21	3	50	.420	2

Skinner "brought down the house" by slamming Walls down 50–40 with a 69% to stay in first place. Burt stayed in a tie with me for 2nd by beating Wrobbel.

I met Al Field in the ninth round. After I had scored the first eight points, I slumped slightly and Field rolled up 19 points. I tied it up at 26 all, then with 7 out of 8, Al shot ahead, 33–26. But, flinging on 11 out of 14, I tore ahead of Field, 43–33 and held my lead to win 50–40.

	Pts	R	DR	SP	Pct	4-On
Rose	50	35	10	68	.516	3
Field	40	32	8	68	.470	3

The "in and out" Stephens had one of his "ins" against Skinner and the old fellow "bit the dust" 50–23 as Don smashed out 75%. Lattore lit on Burt with

68% to keep him in a tie for 2nd with Walls and Hitt. So, once more, Rose was tied for 1st.

In the 10th round, which wound up Saturday's games, I met Burt. We had a nip and tuck game until the score stood 17–16 in my favor, then I walked over him with 18 out of 24 to triumph 50–21.

	Pts	R	DR	SP	Pct	4-On
Rose	50	32	10	48	.667	0
Burt	21	22	4	48	.460	0

Skinner remained tied with me by coming from behind to defeat Field 50–42. Walls hung up the highest percentage of the tournament in beating Gorsline 50–7, throwing 30 in 36 for 84%. Lattore stayed in a tie for 3rd by beating Lundgren, but Bobby Hitt was nosed out by Stephens' late rally 50–48. The leaders:

Rose	9–1	Lattore	8–2	Burt	7–3
Skinner	9–1	Hitt	7–3	Brown	6–4
Wall	8–2	Stephens	7–3	Rizor	6–4

Starting out against Getz, I traveled until it stood 15–13, then fell into a terrific slump and Getz shot all the way to 40 while I languished on 13. I could only get up to 28 before he went out.

Skinner again was alone in 1st as he beat Gorsline. Walls won from Goodell and Lattore bested Norton as they rode into a tie for 2nd with me.

I met Brown next. There were four-dead five times in the first 10 innings. At the end of the 11th, I led 7–3, but again fell into a poor streak and Brown went ahead 18–7. I brought it up to 22–16 but I faded badly again and I lost the game 50–22.

	Pts	R	DR	SP	Pct	4-On
Rose	22	37	11	78	.475	9
Brown	50	47	16	78	.604	9

Skinner, Walls Lattore and Hitt all won their games.

I sailed into Hitt in an ugly frame of mind as I could see my title slipping. He got 6; I rang up 13; he got 3; I got 3; he got 6; I got 1; he got 6 more and he led

21–17. I got ahead 29–24; he went ahead 33–29; I tied at 33 and he went ahead 34–33. I went in front again 37–34 but again he took the lead 40–37. I then skipped ahead 45–40 and held my lead over a desperate finish to win 50–46.

	Pts	R	DR	SP	Pct	4-On
Rose	50	45	14	68	.662	4
Hitt	46	47	14	68	.692	4

Skinner, Walls and Lattore each won.

I toyed with Armstrong for half our game and then stepped on the gas to win 50–28.

	Pts	R	DR	SP	Pct	4-On
Rose	50	35	8	70	.500	1
Armstrong	28	27	4	70	.385	1

Skinner turned back the challenge of Lattore with 74.4%. Davis came into the limelight by smearing Walls 50–40. I was again back in a tie for 2nd.

I easily squelched Rizor in the last game before dinner.

	Pts	R	DR	SP	Pct	4-On
Rose	50	34	10	54	.630	2
Rizor	17	24	5	54	.445	2

Skinner, Walls and Lattore all won very easily.

I defeated Gorsline 50–7.

	Pts	R	DR	SP	Pct	4-On
Rose	50	25	8	36	.695	0
Gorsline	7	9	0	36	.250	0

Rizor battled Skinner furiously but after 39–36, Harley got stuck on 39 and lost 50–39. Lattore came from behind in the dying moments to overcome Hitt 50–48. Walls won.

I marked time for my game with Skinner by beating Norton 50–29.

	Pts	R	DR	SP	Pct	4-On
Rose	50	33	9	62	.534	3
Norton	29	26	8	62	.420	3

Wrobbel gave Skinner a stubborn battle but old Jim won 50–32. Lattore beat Davis and Wall downed Getz. The leaders: Skinner 16–1, Walls 14–3, Lattore 14–3 and Rose 14–3.

Skinner still had to play Rose and Hitt and I knew that if I could only defeat him, it might upset him so that Hitt might beat him also and I could tie for first place.

Rose vs. Skinner

The crowd surged close around the courts. I scored 3, then 6 and had leaped ahead of Jim 13–0 as the spectators shook their heads. I threw another double but Skinner topped it. Skinner shot a double and got his first 3 as the crowd cheered. I threw a double over his single to go ahead 16–3. Then I missed and Skinner climbed on for 6 points to the tune of a loud applause. Jim got 4 more to make it 16–13 and then tossed on another double. I topped his double to remain in the lead. I got a point with a ringer each and then threw a double. Skinner slammed a double on top and came back with another double. Again I held my lead by topping his double. Then I missed and Skinner rammed on a double to go ahead 19–17. He threw a single and scored 3 and then threw another double. I stopped his double with one of my own and then he scored 3 more on a double to lead 25–17. Here he missed and I picked up 4. He scored 3 more on a double then missed and I got 3 on a single and another 3 on a double to tie the score 28–28. He scored 3 more on a double then threw a double, which I covered. I slammed on a double but Skinner topped it. I picked up a point, then scored 3 more on a double to go ahead 32–31. I got another point, then Jim got 3 on a double to lead 34–33. I picked up a point, he picked up a point and I again got a point to tie it 35–35. Sweat streamed down our faces, the young one determined to fight for his title to the bitter end. The old gnarled one fired with inspiration to keep on the high road to fame. I missed; Jim got 3 on a single. In the next inning there was no count then I threw a double. Skinner topped it. Skinner missed and the crowd groaned but broke into renewed cheers as I could only get one point.

Then the champion made his final bid. Three times in a row I plowed on a double and three times in a row, Skinner could only get on a single. I led 45–38. I threw a single and Skinner bored in with a double to make it 45–41. Two more doubles he threw as the crowd screamed approval and each time I could only get a single and Skinner led 48–45. He threw a single and I took careful aim and dropped on a double to tie the score at 48 all. I stepped up, threw a single and a close one. Skinner stepped up slammed on one ringer then slapped on the other one and to the tune of a riotous yell; a new Michigan Champion came into being.

	Pts	R	DR	SP	Pct	4-On
Rose	48	53	16	86	.617	8
Skinner	50	56	18	86	.658	8

Walls beat Field and Lattore beat Brown to remain in a tie for 2nd. In my last game I defeated Ray Wrobbel.

	Pts	R	DR	SP	Pct	4-On
Rose	50	39	11	72	.542	1
Wrobbel	35	34	4	72	.472	1

Skinner celebrated his winning of the title by slaughtering Bobby Hitt 50–33 with 73%. Walls and Lattore tied for 2nd place by beating Stephens and Armstrong respectively. They refused to play off for 2nd and 3rd. I took 4th and Hitt defeated Lundgren in a single game playoff for 5th.

1935 Michigan State Championship Final Results

Place	Name	W	L	Pts	R	DR	SP	Pct	4-On	Prize
1.	James Skinner, Athens	18	1	923	768	240	1226	.626	63	$25.00
2.	Edward Walls, Detroit	16	3	906	730	229	1128	.647	64	17.50
3.	Leo Lattorre, Dearborn	16	3	909	706	230	1122	.629	50	17.50
4.	Lee Rose, Detroit	15	4	890	670	189	1170	.570	46	10.00
5.	Robert Hitt, Plymouth	13	6	881	742	210	1226	.605	62	7.50
6.	Charles Lundgren	13	6	811	691	199	1158	.596	54	5.00
7.	Charles Davis, Detroit	12	7	822	617	169	1116	.552	43	2.50
8.	Donald Stephens, Highland	12	7	818	654	162	1184	.552	38	1.00
9.	Curtis Brown, Kalamazoo	11	8	775	637	180	1158	.559	52	1.00
10.	Albert Field, Detroit	10	9	844	733	198	1316	.557	48	1.00
11.	James Burt, Detroit	10	9	824	679	187	1244	.545	50	1.00
12.	Orville Valleau, Dearborn	8	11	723	598	126	1198	.499	28	1.00
13.	M. B. Getz, Ferndale	6	13	715	648	170	1188	.546	40	1.00
14.	R. Harley Rizor, Detroit	6	13	682	585	149	1180	.496	38	1.00
15.	Frank Koppitsch, Dearborn	6	13	635	556	138	1122	.495	35	1.00
16.	Lynford Norton, S. St. Marie	6	13	727	579	151	1194	.484	35	1.00
17.	Ray Wrobbel, Detroit	5	14	646	570	136	1240	.459	44	1.00
18.	Kenneth Armstrong, Dearborn	5	14	677	542	123	1186	.457	33	1.00
19.	Ray Gorsline, Fulton	2	17	434	384	81	1150	.334	20	1.00
20.	Mark Good, Dearborn	0	19	337	281	41	914	.306	13	1.00
	Totals				12,390		23,420	.529		$98.00

Hitt Is State Champ at Age 14

R ose did not write throw-by-throw coverage of the 1936 state tournament, but his detailed recording of statistics is just plain incredible. No state association today keeps such detailed records, although it would be a good practice for future generations to see. The full display of record keeping is presented here, not because the numbers are so impressive but to demonstrate Lee's admirable ability to dedicate himself to detail.

- - - - - - -

Michigan State Championship Tournament
At Shiras Park Courts, Marquette
August 21,22,23, 1936
The Round Robin Game by Game – 16 High Players

Player	Pts	R	DR	SP	Pct	Player	Pts	R	DR	Pct
R. Hitt	50	30	9	50	.660	Tonn	18	19	3	.380
	50	25	8	36	.694	Koppitsch	10	13	4	.361
	50	23	9	30	.766	Medosh	1	7	0	.233
	50	37	12	54	.685	Egan	9	23	4	.426
	50	22	9	26	.846	Grobar	1	6	1	.231
	50	47	18	62	.758	Rose	21	39	11	.629
	50	25	9	36	.694	Nyman	3	10	1	.278
	50	23	7	34	.676	Pearson	7	9	1	.265
	50	47	13	66	.712	V. Hitt	39	36	8	.545
	50	39	11	64	.609	Lundgren	40	34	10	.531
	50	22	8	30	.733	Norman	6	7	1	.233
	47	41	12	74	.554	Davis	50	43	13	.581
	50	23	9	30	.766	R. Olson	3	8	0	.267
	50	20	4	36	.555	E. Olson	10	8	1	.222
	50	30	9	44	.681	Aho	5	15	0	.341

Player	Pts	R	DR	SP	Pct
Rose	50	27	7	50	.540
	50	36	9	64	.563
	50	43	14	74	.581
	50	24	7	42	.571
	50	27	6	64	.422
	50	37	8	72	.514
	50	24	7	46	.522
	50	32	10	62	.516
	50	38	11	74	.514
	50	24	6	42	.571
	50	19	4	44	.432
	50	29	9	50	.580
	50	18	5	36	.500
	50	45	13	78	.577

Player	Pts	R	DR	Pct
Medosh	18	16	1	.320
Egan	45	36	12	.563
Grobar	32	35	9	.473
Pearson	16	12	2	.286
Nyman	42	28	6	.438
V. Hitt	38	33	11	.458
Lundgren	18	15	2	.326
Norman	38	32	8	.516
Davis	37	35	9	.473
R. Olson	13	12	1	.286
E. Olson	18	12	4	.273
Tonn	11	18	3	.360
Aho	13	6	1	.167
Koppitsch	34	41	10	.526

Player	Pts	R	DR	SP	Pct
Lundgren	50	20	3	40	.500
	50	18	6	24	.750
	50	20	4	38	.526
	50	39	13	54	.722
	50	26	8	44	.591
	50	53	9	100	.530
	50	26	12	30	.866
	50	28	9	42	.667
	50	31	12	42	.738
	50	18	4	34	.529
	50	33	11	62	.532
	50	41	13	62	.661
	50	28	8	50	.560

Player	Pts	R	DR	Pct
E. Olson	10	9	0	.225
Aho	0	2	0	.086
Tonn	7	6	0	.158
Koppitsch	12	27	5	.500
Medosh	17	16	2	.364
Egan	49	55	15	.550
Grobar	4	11	1	.367
Nyman	18	17	4	.405
V. Hitt	11	20	6	.476
Pearson	8	6	1	.176
Norman	33	27	3	.435
Davis	29	31	6	.500
R. Olson	23	21	4	.420

Player	Pts	R	DR	SP	Pct
Davis	50	28	8	50	.560
	48	38	10	76	.487
	50	27	7	54	.500
	48	47	12	86	.547
	50	40	7	82	.488
	50	37	9	68	.544
	50	37	9	64	.578
	50	26	6	44	.591
	50	32	10	56	.571
	50	30	9	60	.500
	50	25	6	60	.417
	50	26	5	54	.481

Player	Pts	R	DR	Pct
Pearson	9	12	1	.240
R. Olson	50	39	11	.513
E. Olson	25	19	1	.352
Koppitsch	50	49	14	.570
Medosh	39	34	7	.415
Egan	35	32	6	.471
Tonn	22	30	3	.468
Aho	8	14	2	.318
Grobar	17	17	1	.304
Nyman	33	25	3	.417
V. Hitt	41	24	3	.400
Norman	24	17	4	.315

Player	Pts	R	DR	SP	Pct
Koppitsch	50	31	8	66	.470
	50	28	6	46	.609
	50	24	6	48	.500
	50	23	5	40	.575

Player	Pts	R	DR	Pct
Egan	38	27	5	.409
Medosh	3	12	0	.261
Pearson	23	14	2	.292
Tonn	6	8	1	.200

					Player	Pts	R	DR	Pct
50	20	6	30	.667	Aho	1	5	0	.166
50	26	4	60	.433	E. Olson	28	17	3	.283
50	23	6	48	.479	R. Olson	28	12	2	.250
50	32	7	52	.596	Norman	24	21	6	.404
47	31	6	66	.470	V. Hitt	50	33	8	.500
50	33	7	64	.516	Nyman	36	26	6	.406
50	35	10	72	.486	Grobar	39	31	6	.431

Player	Pts	R	DR	SP	Pct	Player	Pts	R	DR	Pct
V. Hitt	50	20	7	34	.588	Aho	12	7	1	.206
	50	19	6	28	.679	Tonn	3	3	0	.107
	50	19	3	34	.559	E. Olson	6	5	1	.147
	50	26	7	52	.500	Medosh	18	17	2	.327
	34	36	7	76	.474	Egan	50	43	12	.566
	50	24	4	48	.500	Gorbar	16	15	2	.313
	50	34	8	66	.515	Nyman	34	28	4	.424
	50	41	11	74	.554	Pearson	30	34	6	.459
	50	31	7	70	.443	Norman	46	27	3	.386
	50	22	3	46	.478	R. Olson	13	12	2	.261

Player	Pts	R	DR	SP	Pct	Player	Pts	R	DR	Pct
Norman	39	24	5	74	.324	R. Olson	50	28	44	.378
	50	21	4	62	.339	E. Olson	41	19	2	.306
	50	23	2	54	.426	Aho	9	12	0	.222
	50	28	6	60	.467	Egan	30	21	4	.350
	50	23	5	48	.479	Grobar	23	13	4	.271
	50	25	2	58	.431	Pearson	19	17	4	.293
	50	23	4	56	.411	Tonn	21	12	3	.214
	50	27	6	68	.397	Medosh	49	27	4	.397
	50	25	3	70	.357	Nyman	44	19	2	.271

Player	Pts	R	DR	SP	Pct	Player	Pts	R	DR	Pct
R. Olson	50	25	6	58	.431	Pearson	24	14	3	.241
	50	16	3	46	.348	E. Olson	12	4	0	.087
	50	23	3	78	.295	Aho	41	17	2	.218
	41	28	5	70	.400	Tonn	50	29	6	.414
	50	26	6	56	.464	Medosh	39	23	5	.411
	31	28	2	74	.378	Egan	50	32	6	.432
	50	39	7	78	.500	Grobar	44	35	6	.449
	50	25	8	56	.446	Nyman	28	16	0	.286

Player	Pts	R	DR	SP	Pct	Player	Pts	R	DR	Pct
Egan	44	34	10	76	.447	Grobar	50	32	4	.421
	36	28	5	64	.438	Nyman	50	34	8	.531
	50	21	4	48	.438	E. Olson	19	12	1	.250
	50	24	3	60	.400	Aho	30	17	2	.283
	50	33	10	62	.532	Tonn	35	30	7	.484
	50	18	3	68	.265	Medosh	36	16	1	.235
	50	20	4	50	.400	Pearson	21	11	1	.220

Player	Pts	R	DR	SP	Pct		Player	Pts	R	DR	Pct
Nyman	50	16	1	56	.286		E. Olson	17	8	0	.143
	50	24	5	56	.429		Pearson	19	13	2	.232
	50	32	5	72	.444		Grobar	40	29	3	.403
	32	19	4	64	.297		Medosh	50	23	5	.359
	50	16	1	50	.320		Aho	14	5	0	.100
	50	28	5	68	.412		Tonn	34	26	4	.382

Player	Pts	R	DR	SP	Pct		Player	Pts	R	DR	Pct
Grobar	50	25	3	84	.298		Medosh	45	27	3	.321
	45	19	3	67	.279		Pearson	50	21	1	.309
	50	23	3	72	.319		E. Olson	36	19	2	.264
	50	18	2	64	.291		Aho	32	13	2	.203
	50	13	0	66	.197		Tonn	44	15	2	.227

Player	Pts	R	DR	SP	Pct		Player	Pts	R	DR	Pct
Tonn	50	26	2	62	.419		E. Olson	20	15	4	.242
	50	24	0	66	.364		Aho	27	18	4	.273
	50	25	6	64	.319		Pearson	33	19	1	.297
	14	9	1	46	.196		Medosh	50	19	3	.413

Player	Pts	R	DR	SP	Pct		Player	Pts	R	DR	Pct
Pearson	50	23	6	56	.411		Medosh	18	19	3	.286
	50	22	2	72	.306		E. Olson	40	20	3	.278
	50	24	0	86	.279		Aho	31	20	2	.233

Player	Pts	R	DR	SP	Pct		Player	Pts	R	DR	Pct
Medosh	50	17	2	40	.422		Aho	2	4	0	.100
	50	22	4	52	.423		E. Olson	19	13	1	.250

Player	Pts	R	DR	SP	Pct		Player	Pts	R	DR	Pct
Aho	50	16	0	64	.250		E. Olson	21	10	0	.156

Round Robin Final Standings

Player – City	W	L	Pts	R	DR	SP	Pct	4-On
1. Robert Hitt – Plymouth	14	1	747	454	97	672	.675	23
2. Lee Rose – Detroit	14	1	721	455	127	860	.529	28
3. Chas. Lundgren – Detroit	13	2	718	433	124	732	.591	20
4. C. H. Davis – Detroit	11	4	712	502	125	964	.521	25
5. Frank Koppitsch – Dearborn	11	4	653	434	104	846	.513	17
6. Verna Hitt – Plymouth	10	5	663	418	99	834	.501	18
7. Harry Norman – Marquette	8	7	610	351	62	880	.399	6
8. Roy Olson – Marquette	8	7	552	342	65	852	.401	8
9. John Egan – Thompsonville	7	8	636	447	103	990	.451	18
10. Matt Nyman – Palmer	6	9	570	338	55	888	.382	7
11. Martin Grobar – Marquette	5	10	509	322	48	934	.344	14
12. Robert Tonn – Marquette	4	11	420	267	36	822	.325	6
13. Rich Medosh – Marquette	4	11	497	292	40	838	.348	4
14. John Pearson – Marquette	4	11	409	251	33	850	.295	5
15. Toivo Aho – Marquette	1	14	275	171	16	771	.221	1
16. Edward Olson – Marquette	0	15	322	190	24	802	.237	4
Totals	120	120	8,714	5,667	1,158	14,538	.390	204

Playoff For 1st Place in Finals

Player	Pts	R	DR	SP	Pct	4-On
Hitt	50	36	11	52	.692	2
Rose	18	24	6	52	.491	2

Finals – Round 1

R. Hitt vs. R. Olson

Game	Player	Pts	R	DR	SP	Pct	4-On
1.	R. Hitt	50	29	12	36	.806	1
	R. Olson	1	13	1	36	.361	
2.	R. Hitt	50	25	6	46	.695	0
	R. Olson	13	14	3	46	.304	
3.	R. Hitt	50	25	7	36	.669	0
	R. Olson	4	10	2	36	.278	
Totals	R. Hitt	150	79	25	118	.669	2
R	Olson	18	37	6	118	.313	2

Rose vs. Norman

Game	Player	Pts	R	DR	SP	Pct	4-On
1.	Rose	50	27	7	52	.519	0
	Norman	26	22	3	52	.423	
2.	Rose	50	21	5	36	.583	0
	Norman	5	7	0	36	.194	
3.	Rose	50	32	6	64	.500	1
	Norman	23	24	3	64	.375	
Totals	Rose	150	80	18	152	.526	1
	Norman	54	53	6	152	.349	1

Lundgren vs. V. Hitt

Game	Player	Pts	R	DR	SP	Pct	4-On
1.	Lundgren	50	38	10	64	.594	0
	V. Hitt	34	29	5	64	.453	
2.	Lundgren	50	47	16	68	.691	5
	V. Hitt	37	42	13	38	.617	
3.	Lundgren	46	34	9	62	.548	3
	V. Hitt	50	35	11	62	.564	
4.	Lundgren	50	40	12	68	.588	5
	V. Hitt	28	32	8	68	.471	
Totals	Lundgren	196	159	47	262	.607	13
	V. Hitt	149	138	37	262	.527	13

Davis vs. Koppitsch

Game	Player	Pts	R	DR	SP	Pct	4-On
1.	Davis	50	33	11	66	.500	2
	Koppitsch	34	30	6	66	.455	
2.	Davis	50	33	9	60	.550	3
	Koppitsch	28	27	7	60	.450	
3.	Davis	50	33	9	70	.471	0
	Koppitsch	34	29	3	70	.414	
Totals	Davis	150	99	29	196	.505	5
	Koppitsch	96	86	16	196	.438	5

Second Round – Championship Flight

R. Hitt vs. Davis

Game	Player	Pts	R	DR	SP	Pct	4-On
1.	R. Hitt	50	32	15	42	.761	3
	Davis	5	17	5	42	.404	3
2	R. Hitt	50	33	12	44	.750	3
	Davis	9	21	4	44	.477	3
3	R. Hitt	50	43	17	68	.632	7
	Davis	39	38	11	68	.558	7
Totals	R. Hitt	150	108	41	154	.701	13
	Davis	53	76	20	154	.493	13

Rose vs. Lundgren

Game	Player	Pts	R	DR	SP	Pct	4-On
1.	Rose	50	45	13	66	.682	6
	Lundgren	22	37	10	66	.561	
2.	Rose	33	29	8	56	.518	1
	Lundgren	50	34	9	56	.617	
3.	Rose	50	36	13	54	.666	2
	Lundgren	28	26	5	54	.481	
4.	Rose	34	42	9	72	.583	2
	Lundgren	50	48	14	72	.666	
5.	Rose	50	40	15	62	.645	4
	Lundgren	27	36	9	62	.581	
Totals	Rose	217	192	58	310	.619	15
	Lundgren	177	181	47	310	.584	15

Fifth Place Flight

Koppitsch vs. R. Olson

Game	Player	Pts	R	DR	SP	Pct	4-On
1.	Koppitsch	50	28	4	62	.452	0
	R. Olson	23	21	4	62	.339	
2.	Koppitsch	49	35	7	88	.397	2
	R. Olson	50	36	6	88	.409	
3.	Koppitsch	50	28	9	62	.452	2
	R. Olson	33	22	2	62	.354	
Totals	Koppitsch	149	91	20	212	.429	4
	R. Olson	106	79	12	212	.372	4

V. Hitt vs. Norman

Game	Player	Pts	R	DR	SP	Pct	4-On
1.	V. Hitt	43	35	7	82	.427	1
	Norman	50	35	6	82	.427	
2.	V. Hitt	50	37	9	68	.544	3
	Norman	36	32	9	68	.471	
3.	V. Hitt	50	24	10	36	.666	0
	Norman	13	12	1	36	.333	
Totals	V. Hitt	143	96	26	186	.515	4
	Norman	99	79	16	186	.424	4

Seventh Place

R. Olson vs. Norman – 1 Game

Player	Pts	R	DR	SP	Pct	4-On
R. Olson	50	28	7	56	.500	1
Norman	22	16	2	56	.285	1

Fifth Place

Koppitsch vs. V. Hitt – 2 out of 3

Game	Player	Pts	R	DR	SP	Pct	4-On
1.	Koppitsch	50	29	7	72	.403	1
	V. Hitt	49	27	6	72	.375	
2.	Koppitsch	15	12	2	42	.286	0
	V. Hitt	50	23	7	42	.547	
3.	Koppitsch	50	36	11	64	.562	2
	V. Hitt	45	29	8	64	.451	
Totals	Koppitsch	115	77	20	178	.432	3
	V. Hitt	144	79	21	178	.443	3

Finals – 3rd Place

Lundgren vs. Davis – Series 3 out of 5

Game	Player	Pts	R	DR	SP	Pct	4-On
1.	Lundgren	50	42	16	70	.600	5
	Davis	49	38	10	70	.542	
2.	Lundgren	50	30	10	50	.600	2
	Davis	32	24	7	50	.480	
3.	Lundgren	42	52	15	86	.605	8
	Davis	50	56	19	86	.651	
4.	Lundgren	48	44	14	78	.564	6
	Davis	50	45	12	78	.577	
5.	Lundgren	50	37	9	62	.597	1
	Davis	34	31	8	62	.500	
Totals	Lundgren	240	205	64	346	.592	22
	Davis	215	194	56	346	.561	22

Championship Finals

Rose vs. R. Hitt – Best 4 out of 7 games

Game	Player	Pts	R	DR	SP	Pct	4-On
1.	R. Hitt	50	32	13	42	.761	3
	Rose	10	17	5	42	.404	
2.	R. Hitt	50	45	15	66	.682	4
	Rose	35	39	13	66	.591	
3.	R. Hitt	46	64	19	94	.681	10
	Rose	50	65	20	94	.691	
4.	R. Hitt	50	41	14	56	.732	2
	Rose	24	31	8	56	.554	
5.	R. Hitt	50	50	18	72	.694	9
	Rose	32	43	14	72	.597	
Totals	R. Hitt	246	232	79	330	.703	28
	Rose	151	195	60	330	.591	28

Standings for All Games in Finals

Place	Player	W	L	Pts	R	DR	SP	Pct	Prize
1.	R. Hitt	10	1	546	419	145	602	.696	$40.00
2.	Rose	7	6	518	467	136	792	.589	32.00
3.	Lundgren	8	6	613	545	158	918	.594	25.00
4.	Davis	5	6	418	369	105	696	.530	17.50
5.	Koppitsch	4	5	360	254	56	586	.433	12.50
6	V. Hitt	4	6	436	313	84	626	.500	10.00
7.	R. Olson	2	5	174	144	25	386	.372	7.50
8.	Norman	1	6	175	148	24	394	.375	5.00
	Totals	41	41	3,240	2,659	733	5,000	.532	$150.00

- - - - - - -

After his extraordinary report of the 1936 Michigan state tournament, the next journal page in Lee Rose's journal records the results of the ladies state tournament! A women's state competition was a bit unusual for the times; few if any states were holding women's events. Although women's world champions were crowned in 1933, 1934, and 1935, no women's world competition was held in 1936, when there was also no men's World Tournament. Incidentally, the 1935 women's world champion was from Lee's home state— Esther James of Hastings, Michigan.

The Michigan women's tournament in 1936 was probably set up rather impromptu as there were a couple of lady pitchers on the grounds and their spouses may have sensed the possibility that one of them would be a state champion and earn a few bucks. If the competition had been planned in advance and advertised prior to event dates, one imagines Esther James would have been on hand.

Take note also of the $50.00 purse for the women's event. That was a fairly handsome purse for just four competitors. As a comparison, the 1955 women's world champion earned $25.00. In 1936, a $20.00 prize for first place was very generous. Records show that Esther James earned $75.00 for winning the 1935 world crown.

Ladies 1936 State Championship Tournament

Round Robin Games

Player	Pts	R	DR	SP	Pct	Player	Pts	R	DR	Pct
Mrs. Davis	50	16	5	28	.571	Miss Kalmer	3	3	0	.107
''	50	18	4	36	.500	Miss Hult	1	3	0	.083
''	50	25	6	52	.481	Mrs. Rose	25	16	3	.307
Mrs. Rose	50	26	1	54	.481	Miss Kalmer	21	7	0	.129
''	50	17	2	50	.340	Miss Hult	13	6	0	.120
Miss Hult	50	15	1	92	.163	Miss Kalmer	26	7	0	.076

Finals – Round 1

Player	Pts	R	DR	SP	Pct	Player	Pts	R	DR	Pct
Mrs. Davis	50	17	5	28	.607	Miss Kalmer	3	2	0	.071
''	50	19	5	34	.559	''	2	3	1	.088
Totals	100	36	10	62	.581		5	5	1	.081

Player	Pts	R	DR	SP	Pct	Player	Pts	R	DR	Pct
Mrs. Rose	50	25	4	56	.446	Miss Hult	14	12	1	.214
''	50	17	5	42	.405	''	14	4	0	.095
Totals	100	42	9	98	.429		28	16	1	.163

Championship Series

Player	Pts	R	DR	SP	Pct	Player	Pts	R	DR	Pct
Mrs Davis	50	29	9	48	.604	Mrs. Rose	14	17	4	.351
''	50	32	8	70	.457	''	38	28	4	.400
''	50	34	10	50	.680		2	19	2	.380
Totals	150	95	27	168	.565		54	64	10	.381

3rd Place Series

Player	Pts	R	DR	SP	Pct	Player	Pts	R	DR	Pct
Miss Hult	50	10	0	76	.013	Miss Kalmer	26	4	0	.053
	45	14	0	84	.166		50	15	2	.178
	50	19	2	82	.237		31	9	0	.109
Totals	145	43	2	242	.178		107	28	2	.116

Ladies Standings for Entire Tournament

Place	Player	W	L	Pts	R	DR	SP	Pct	Prize
1.	Mrs. Davis	8	0	400	190	52	346	.548	$20.00
2.	Mrs. Rose	4	4	279	155	25	422	.367	15.00
3.	Miss Hult	3	5	237	83	4	518	.160	10.00
4.	Miss Kalmer	1	7	162	50	3	478	.105	5.00
								.271	$50.00

Hitt Wins State Title Again

The 1937 Michigan state tournament was also reported in the Lee Rose journals, with the same level of detail as the 1936 event. His account of the 1937 tournament aren't reprinted in full, but because Lee was participating, it is only proper to share some of the stats and, of course, the final standings.

- - - - - - -

**Michigan State Championship
Horseshoe Tournament
Iron River, Michigan
August 30, 31–September 1, 1937**

Qualifying Scores – 350 Shoes Pitched

Place	Player	City	R	Pct
1.	Robert Hitt	Plymouth	242	.681
2.	Carl Lundgren	Detroit	232	.663
3.	Lee Rose	Detroit	208	.594
4.	R. H. Rizor	Detroit	185	.528
5.	Verne Hitt	Plymouth	170	.485
6.	August Larson	Stambaugh	163	.465
7.	K. D. Campbell Sr.	Stambaugh	160	.457
8.	K. D. Campbell Jr.	Stambaugh	160	.431
9.	Charles Hager	Mineral Sps.	146	.417
10.	Fred Hutchison	Eaton Rapids	133	.380
11.	Lyle Brazell	Iron River	128	.366
12.	William Cook	Iron River	110	.314
13.	Eskil Erickson	Iron River	Did Not Qualify	

Final Standings for All Games

Place	Player	W	L	Pts	R	DR	Sp	Pct	$
1.	R. Hitt	22	3	1218	980	323	1488	.658	$50.00
2.	Lundgren	19	7	1206	969	312	1568	.618	40.00
3.	Rose	17	5	1025	748	208	1298	.576	30.00
4.	Rizor	12	9	854	633	145	1216	.520	22.50
5.	Erickson	10	11	783	496	109	1180	.420	17.50
6.	Brazell	9	11	727	477	81	1222	.390	12.50
7.	Hager	8	12	627	383	57	1132	.330	10.00
8.	Larson	6	13	616	380	66	1084	.350	7.50
9.	Hutchison	5	9	488	340	79	844	.403	
10.	V. Hitt	4	8	386	370	92	640	.515	
11.	Campbell Jr.	4	8	313	304	57	602	.490	
12.	Campbell Sr.	2	10	422	308	63	740	.416	
13.	Cook	0	12	257	168	26	560	.300	
				6,556			13,592	.481	$190.00

A Third Title for Hitt

Rose used eleven pages of his journal to report on the 1938 Michigan state championships. This is an abbreviated version.

- - - - - - -

1938 Michigan State Championship Tournament
Held at Riverside Park in Plymouth
August 6, 7, 8

Preliminary Scores – 400 Shoes

Place	Player	City	R	Pct.
1.	Robert Hitt	Plymouth	DefendingChampion	
2.	Joe Latzko	Flint	299	.747
3.	Ed Walls	Detroit	290	.725
4.	R. H. Rizor	Detroit	265	.662
5.	James Burt	Detroit	257	.642
6.	Harold Arnold	Detroit	243	.607
7.	Albert Field	Detroit	239	.597
8.	M. B. Getz	Ferndale	238	.595
9.	Lee Rose	Detroit	233	.582
10.	Karl Lundgren	Detroit	233	.580
11.	Earl Graves	Highland Pk.	232	.580
12.	Ray Gorsline	Fulton	229	.572
13.	Phillip Carl	Kalamazoo	224	.560
14.	Frank Koppitsch	Dearborn	221	.552
15.	L. Hammerschmidt	Detroit	217	.542
16.	Steve Pinter	Flint	216	.540
17.	James Skinner	Athens	212	.530
18.	William Miller	Flint	208	.520
19.	John Carlson	Negaunee	204	.510

(Continued on next page)

(Continued from previous page)

Place	Player	City	R	Pct.
20.	Don Walls	Detroit	203	.507
21.	C. H. Davis	Detroit	198	.495
22.	C. C. Williams	Detroit	186	.465
23.	Charles. Pinkstaff	Flint	173	.432
24.	Joe Kelly	Highland Pk.	170	.425
25.	Clarence Wood	Flint	162	.405
26.	Charles Karhu	Detroit	160	.400

Top 16 Advance to Semi-Finals Round Robin

- - - - - - -

After a 15-game round robin of 50-point games, the top eight players advanced to the match-play finals. Rose made the qualifying cut and also advanced out of the semifinals round robin, but barely. He was the 7th seed and ended up in 8th place in the tournament.

Below are the stats for the final match between Hitt and Latzko and the results for the final eight pitchers. Rose did not note the prize money that the players earned.

- - - - - - -

Championship Finals

Hitt vs. J. Latzko – Best 4 out of 7 games

Game	Player	Pts	R	DR	SP	Pct	4-On
1.	R. Hitt	50	66	24	90	.733	12
	Latzko	42	63	22		.700	
2.	R. Hitt	50	73	30	90	.811	17
	Latzko	42	69	28		.766	
3.	R. Hitt	50	63	24	82	.768	9
	Latzko	35	56	17		.680	
4.	R. Hitt	28	56	18	78	.717	10
	Latzko	50	61	23		.782	
5.	R. Hitt	49	75	26	102	.735	12
	Latzko	50	74	25		.725	
6.	R. Hitt	50	52	20	68	.764	10
	Latzko	33	47	19		.692	
Totals	R. Hitt	277	385	142	510	.754	70
	Latzko	252	370	134	510	.725	70

Final Standings For All Games – Top Eight

Place	Player	W	L	Pts	R	DR	Sp	Pct
1.	Hitt	24	3	1321	1367	501	1842	.742
2.	Latzko	22	6	1337	1478	541	2022	.731
3.	Walls	19	6	1159	1155	384	1674	.689
4.	Field	13	11	960	973	296	1598	.609
5.	Getz	13	12	994	964	284	1602	.602
6.	Graves	13	13	1000	998	295	1630	.612
7.	Lundgren	10	12	876	827	237	1434	.577
8.	Rose	9	13	773	865	242	1476	.586

Rose's 16th State Tournament

The year of 1939 does not hold much promise for horseshoe pitching. The National Association is not very active and while there will be a World Tournament at San Francisco, it will be too far away to have any effect on Michigan.

The outlook in Michigan is none too bright. There is only a remote possibility of a financially successful state tournament and that is at Iron River. The only other chance is Ann Arbor and very little money can be expected there.

As for the local outlook, I have washed my hands of anything that goes on in the Detroit District other than to do my best to enforce the National rules.

As for my home club, Dearborn, I am going to try to form a team ladder league and if by any chance a team league is formed in Detroit, I will have a team in it, but it will be only local talent.

- - - - - - -

Allowing Lee Rose's own ledger comments to introduce the 1939 chapter is more fitting than what any other writer could provide. Obviously he anticipated a bleak year and his comments regarding the national association were direct and accurate. A World Tournament had not been held since 1935, and his mention of a tournament in California was likely a rumor, because there no 1939 World Tournament held in San Francisco, or anywhere else in the U.S. for that matter. Perhaps, though, plan were being made. Regardless, Rose doesn't suggest where his information came from; that would have a filled a gap in our knowledge.

Dismal times or not, Lee Rose was still a promoter of the sport and he was very involved in the Detroit area.

- - - - - - -

On April 23, I managed to get the Dearborn Ladder League started with 8 original entrants. The weakest players were put on top. I was 8th. Four more were added after initial roster was drafted.

Ladder Standings

1. Wright	7. Swango
2. Sheridan	8. Rose
3. Meghan	Added Later
4. Himelberger	9. Ozark
5. Mierzwa	10. Wensko
6. Craig	11. Valleau
12. Burkheimer	

April 23 – I immediately challenged Craig for sixth and won as follows:

Rose	26	50	50
Craig	50	43	26

Then after Craig had turned back the challenge of Ozark, he in turn, challenged me. I retained 6th place as follows:

Rose	50	50
Craig	30	11

April 24 – Challenged Himelberger for 4th place and won it as follows:

Rose	50	50
Himelberger	25	10

Craig also defeated Himelberger and promptly challenged me. I held 4th as follows:

Rose	50	50
Craig	38	28

April 25 – Challenged and beat Sheridan for 2nd:

Rose	50	50
Sheridan	6	6

Valleau had beaten Ozark for 9th and the ladder standings were:

1. Wright	0–0		7. Mierzwa	0–0
2. Rose	5–0		8. Swango	0–0
3. Sheridan	0–1		9. Valleau	1–0
4. Meghan	0–0		10. Ozark	0–2
5. Craig	2–3		11. Wensko	0–0
6. Himelberger	0–2		12. Burkheimer	0–0

May 7 – Defeated Meghan for 2nd place:

Rose	50	50
Meghan	2	10

Then moved into 1st place against Wright:

Rose	50	50
Wright	9	14

Ladder standings as of May 7:

1. Rose	7–0		8. Swango	0–0
2. Wright	1–1		9. Valleau	1–0
3. Craig	3–3		10. Ozark	0–2
4. Sheridan	0–2		11. Wensko	0–0
5. Meghan	0–1		12. Raymo	1–0
6. Himelberger	0–2		13. L. Burkheimer	0–1
7. Mierzwa	0–0		14. E. Burkheimer	0–0

- - - - - - -

The ladder-league format Rose set up was unique arrangement. He had to be a master of promotion and very creative in establishing a league under that format. He is likely the only director to implement a ladder schedule for league play. Ladder playoffs are well known in the sport of bowling and sometimes in other sports tournaments. Rarely, however, is a ladder playoff or schedule used in horseshoe pitching. The two prominent exceptions to that general rule were the 1989 and 1994 World Tournaments. Yet, here is evidence that Rose was able to use the ladder format successfully in a league setting. Rose was not only a creative promoter but a determined worker for the sport as demonstrated by his next effort to put together a team four-team league.

- - - - - - -

The ladder league was disbanded at this point and a four-team league was formed. Entries were Nighthawks, Tigers, Bats and Eagles. On May 9 play opened with the Tigers meeting the Bats:

Tigers			Bats	
1. A. Mierzwa	4–1		1. Valleau	5–0
2. Raymo*	4–1		2. Perkins	3–2
3. R. Craig	3–2		3. Romanelli	1–4
4. J. Mierzwa	2–3		4. Cudzik*	1–4
5. Bagozzi	1–4		5. Butzke*	1–3
6. Sheridan*	0–4			

Tigers   3–3–3–3–2 = 14
Bats   2–2–2–2–3 = 11
*Pickups, not regulars

May 11 –	Nighthawks			Eagles	
	1. Raymo	4–1		1. Rose	5–0
	2. Perkins	3–1		2. Grant	2–2
	3. Trudeau	2–1		3. Himelberger	1–4
	4. J. Mierzwa	2–2		4. Wright	0–1
	5. Sheridan	2–3		5. Maybury	0–1
	6. Wensko	1–0		6. Romanelli	0–4
	7. Swango	2–0		7. Gertz	0–4
	8. Lemon	0–1		8. Meghan	1–0

Nighthawks   2–4–2–4–4 = 16
Eagles   3–1–3–1–1 = 9

Rose's Scores:

Rose–50	Rose–50	Rose–50	Rose–50	Rose–50
Raymo–25	J. Mierzwa–16	Trudeau–9	Sheridan–36	Perkins–23

Dearborn defeated by Clark Park, 13–12

On May 14, at Dearborn, the Dearborn horseshoe team made their first start of the season against an outside team and were nosed out by Clark Park 13–12.

It was a very windy day, rendering pitching very difficult and no good ringer averages were made.

Manager Rose of Dearborn topped the win column for the day by hanging up five victories, but on account of the strong wind, his ringer percentage was low, under 50%.

But as Rose was edging out wins, his teammates were wallowing badly; losing to players they hadn't any right to lose to. Valleau, slaughtered by Gothard in the first game, came back to win 3 out of 4, but the one he lost was to Miller and Miller should have been easy for Orville. Joe Rayco was distinctly a flop; winning only one game in 5 and especially the game he lost to Goodwell hurt Dearborn's chances. Nick Wensko also played badly and after dropping his first 3 games, was removed in favor of Craig who won 1 game out of his 2. Perkins did fairly well, winning 2.

Clark Park		Dearborn	
1. Gothard	4–1	1. Rose	5–0
2. Miller	4–1	2. Valleau	3–2
3. Ingram	2–3	3. Craig	1–1
4. Mielbeck	2–3	4. Perkins	2–3
5. Goodell	1–4	5. Raymo	1–4
6. Wensko	0–3		

Clark Park – 4–3–2–2–2 = 13
Dearborn – 1–2–3–3–3 = 12

Rose's Scores:

Rose–50	Rose–50	Rose–50	Rose–50	Rose–50
Miller–19	Mielbeck–39	Gothard–44	Goodell–37	Ingram–37

May 16 –

Tigers		Nighthawks	
1. R. Craig	5–0	1. Raymo	4–1
2. A. Mierzwa	4–1	2. Swango	3–2
3. Cudzik	3–2	3. Sheridan	2–3
4. J. Mierzwa	1–4	4. Ozark	2–3
5. Bagozzi	1–4	5. E. Burkheimer	0–2
6. Grell	0–3		

Tigers – 3–2–2–3–4 = 14
Nighthawks –2–3–3–2–1 = 11

May 18 – The Bats and the Eagles played their game with three men a side because of the lack of players.

Eagles
1. Rose   3–0
2. Cudzik   2–1
3. Gertz   0–3
4. Sheridan   0–1

Bats
1. Valleau   2–1
2. Perkins   1–1
3. Romanelli   1–2

Eagles –   1–2–2 = 5
Bats –   2–1–1 = 4

Rose's Scores:

Rose–50   Rose–50   Rose–50
Sheridan–9   Romanelli–5 Valleau–44

League Standings:

1. Tigers   2–0
3. Nighthawks   1–1
2. Eagles   1–1
4. Bats   0–2

Top Ten Individual Leaders:

1. Rose   8–0
2. Wensko   1–0
3. Meghan   1–0
4. Valleau   7–1
5. Raymo   12–3
6. A. Mierzwa   8–2
7. R. Craig   8–2
8. Swango   5–2
9. Trudeau   2–1
10. Perkins   7–4

May 23 –

Bats
1. Valleau   5–0
2. A. Mierzwa   3–2
3. Perkins   2–3
4. Ozark   2–3
5. Wensko   2–3
6. Sheridan   1–4
7. Thomas   0–1
8. Bagozzi   0–1
9. Raymo   0–2

Nighthawks
1. Williams   3–1
2. Craig   2–1
3. Swanko   3–2
4. L. Burkheimer 1–1
5. Meghan   1–1

Bats –   3–4–2–3–2 = 14
Nighthawks – 2–1–3–2–3 = 11

Dearborn Topples Tip-Top Tossers

On May 25, Dearborn invaded the domain of the Tip-Top Club on Harker & Iroquois and won 8–4. The home team had only 2 courts and so only 12 games were played. Here are the results:

Dearborn	W	L	Pts	OP	R	DR	SP	Pct
1. Valleau	2	0	100	42	71	20	114	.623
2. Raymo	2	0	100	69	65	18	122	.532
3. Craig	2	0	100	86	62	15	132	.469
4. Rose	1	1	97	84	85	22	154	.552
5. A. Mierzwa	1	1	81	93	57	14	132	.432
6. Ozark	0	2	58	100	40	8	122	.328
Totals	8	4	536	474	380	99	776	.489

Tip-Top	W	L	Pts	OP	R	DR	SP	Pct
1. Miller	2	1	128	119	68	14	190	.358
2. Allagreen	1	1	93	70	62	19	124	.500
3. Rome	1	2	118	147	108	26	216	.500
4. Godfrey	0	2	75	100	57	15	126	.452
5. Turner	0	2	60	100	50	9	120	.417
Totals	4	8	474	536	345	83	776	.444

Dearborn Nosed Out by Plymouth Tossers

Dearborn was nosed out by Plymouth on Riverside Park. It was a six-man match and outside of Rose and Valleau, the Dearborn pitchers were not used to pitching in sand.

Dearborn		Plymouth	
1. Rose	5–1	1. R. Hitt	6–0
2. Valleau	5–1	2. V. Hitt	4–2
3. Raymo	2–4	3. W. Hitt	3–3
4. Craig	2–4	4. Burton	3–3
5. Swango	1–5	5. Lute	2–4
6. Ozark	1–5	6. Schultz	2–4

Dearborn is to be host to Plymouth on June 10.

1. Rose	11–2		6. Perkins	2–3
2. Valleau	10–3		7. Swango	1–5
3. Craig	5–5		8. Ozark	1–7
4. A. Mierzwa	1–1		9. Wensko	0–3
5. Raymo	5–9			

Dearborn Trounces Plymouth 16–9

Dearborn easily whipped Plymouth, 16–9 in a return game played at Dearborn on June 10. Dearborn's victory was due to the poor pitching of the visitors who were out of their element – – sand. State champion Bobby Hitt again won all 5 games, but his ringer average of only .615 doesn't look too good. It is to be remembered that his three state titles have all been won in sand.

Plymouth	W	L	P	OP	R	DR	SP	Pct
1. R. Hitt	5	0	250	122	176	60	286	.615
2. V. Hitt	3	2	185	234	116	21	330	.351
3. W. Hitt	1	4	159	236	107	13	336	.318
4. Lute	0	3	117	150	62	10	194	.319
5. Burden	0	5	118	250	63	8	264	.238
6. Brown	0	2	28	100	16	1	108	.148
Totals	9	16	857	1092	540	113	1518	.355

Dearborn	W	L	P	OP	R	DR	SP	Pct
1. Rose	4	1	226	145	144	40	286	.503
2. Valleau	4	1	238	144	137	35	294	.466
3. Raymo	3	2	225	164	137	23	328	.417
4. R. Craig	3	2	206	196	94	13	312	.301
5. Ozark	2	3	197	208	105	19	298	.352
Totals	16	9	1092	857	617	130	1518	.406

Plymouth 2–2–2–2–1 = 9
Dearborn 3–3–3–3–4 = 16

Clark Park Noses Out Dearborn Again

Clark Park again defeated Dearborn by a 13–12 score at the Clark Park courts. The Dearborn team twice went into the lead. 3–2 and 8–7, but could not quite produce a victory. Notable in the Park's victory was the showing of Mark Goodell who has been always a "push-over," but who won his first 4 games before being flattened by Rose. Rose after beating Al Field and smothering Stevens and Gothard, was nosed out by Ingraham 50–48.

Clark Park	W	L	P	R	OP	DR	SP	Pct.
1. Field	4	1	246	161	175	54	294	.595
2. Ingraham	4	1	238	212	166	45	338	.491
3. Goodell	4	1	241	203	149	29	322	.462
4. Miller	1	1	95	90	58	8	156	.371
5. Mielbeack	0	2	77	100	59	15	126	.468
6. Gothard	0	3	79	150	69	9	186	.371
7. Stevens	0	3	61	150	47	7	164	.286
Totals	13	12	1037	1046	723	167	1586	.456

Dearborn	W	L	P	R	OP	DR	SP	Pct
1. Rose	4	1	248	168	157	43	292	.536
2. Valleau	3	2	232	185	150	36	300	.500
3. Craig	2	3	202	231	150	33	340	.441
4. Raymo	2	3	198	222	125	20	336	.372
5. Ozark	1	4	166	231	124	21	318	.389
Totals	12	13	1046	1037	706	153	1586	.445

Standings of the Dearborn Players:

1. Rose	19–4	2. Valleau	17–6	3. Craig	10–10
4. Perkins	2–3	5. Raymo	10–14	6. Ozark	4–14
7. A. Mierzwa	1–1	8. Swango	1–5	9. Wensko	0–3

June 16 – At Clark Park Class "B" Game

Clark Park – 13		Dearborn – 12	
1. Miller	5–0	1. Himelberger	3–1
2. Lundin	5–0	2. Swango	3–2
3. Stevens	2–3	3. Ozark	3–2
4. Whitmeyer	1–4	4. Romanelli	1–1
5. Logan	0–5	5. Wright	1–2
		6. Cudzik	1–4
		7. Valleau	0–1

June 20 – At Dearborn Class "B" Game

Dearborn 21
1. Himelberger   5–0
2. L. Burkheimer 5–0
3. Swanko   3–0
4. Romanelli   2–0
5. ???   1–0
6. Ozark   2–2
7. McClung   2–2
8. E. Burkheimer 1–1

Clark Park 4
1. Clark   2–3
2. Jensen   1–3
3. G. Kinsman   1–4
4. L. Kinsman   0–2
5. Whitmeyer   0–3
6. Logan   0–3
7. M. Ingraham   0–3

June 21 at Dearborn:

Clark Park 14	W	L	Pts	OP	R	DR	SP	Pct
1. Field	5	0	250	141	194	54	322	.602
2. Gothard	3	2	238	197	180	43	348	.517
3. Miller	3	2	226	162	151	38	318	.474
4. Ingraham	2	3	183	227	136	31	298	.456
5. Goodell	1	4	152	234	100	22	262	.381
Totals	14	11	1049	961	761	188	1548	.491

Dearborn 11	W	L	Pts	OP	R	DR	SP	Pct
1. Rose	4	1	237	139	167	50	288	.580
2. Ozark	3	2	206	226	147	30	354	.415
3. Lundgren	2	2	166	172	123	32	252	.488
4. Valleau	1	4	215	213	183	46	342	.535
5. Craig	1	4	130	249	89	12	272	.327
6. Raymo	0	1	7	50	12	1	40	.300
Totals	11	14	961	1049	721	171	1548	.465

I have won 57 and lost 7 so far this year.

June 27 at Clark Park

Clark Park 13	W	L	Pts	OP	R	DR	SP	Pct
1. Field	4	1	247	125	172	56	272	.632
2. Ingraham	4	1	228	151	192	61	320	.600
3. Goodell	3	2	217	199	151	40	304	.497
4. Miller	1	3	150	177	115	28	240	.479
5. Gothard	1	4	122	241	110	24	276	.398
6. Jensen	0	1	27	50	10	1	66	.151
Totals	13	12	991	943	750	210	1480	.507

Dearborn 12

	W	L	Pts	OP	R	DR	SP	Pct
1. Rose	5	0	250	157	163	43	290	.562
2. Lundgren	2	1	143	90	114	35	184	.619
3. Valleau	2	3	195	203	175	49	324	.540
4. Raymo	2	3	143	214	128	26	280	.457
5. Ozark	1	4	163	227	111	20	298	.372
6. Craig	0	2	49	100	38	10	104	.365
Totals	12	13	943	991	729	183	1480	.492

July 23, 1939 – At N.W. Field

Detroit – 51

Player	W	L	Pts	OP	R	DR	SP	Pct
1. Goodell	5	0	250	135	155	48	278	.557
2. Field	7	1	374	150	221	68	364	.607
3. Galesky	7	1	380	194	355	71	436	.584
4. Rose	7	1	366	194	243	68	422	.576
5. Rizor	6	1	317	204	213	49	400	.532
6. Lundgren	5	1	285	152	201	56	352	.571
7. Arnold	3	1	178	86	105	30	190	.552
8. Williams	3	1	171	147	121	25	252	.480
9. Kelly	2	1	134	95	79	15	182	.434
10. Wolfe	5	3	311	240	218	54	434	.502
11. Malison	1	1	90	99	60	12	156	.385
12. Keseric	0	1	22	50	13	2	48	.271
Total	51	13	2878	1746	1884	498	3494	.539

Flint – 13

Player	W	L	Pts	OP	R	DR	SP	Pct
1. J. Latzko	7	1	394	210	360	127	524	.687
2. R. Middleton	3	5	284	330	228	56	478	.477
3. Toms	1	7	221	376	204	43	450	.453
4. B. Wood	1	7	228	372	179	34	470	.381
5. Patterson	1	7	162	390	141	21	438	.322
6. Miller	0	8	210	400	187	42	446	.419
7. Shepard	0	8	144	400	113	23	376	.301
8. Kelling	0	8	103	400	81	8	332	.244
Totals	13	51	1746	2878	1493	354	3494	.427

July 30, 1939 – At N.W. Field

Flint – 14

Player	W	L	Pts	OP	R	DR	SP	Pct
1. Latzko	5	0	250	92	199	70	278	.715
2. Miller	2	1	139	116	122	25	224	.544
3. Toms	2	1	103	121	69	17	160	.431
4. Loney	3	2	216	198	186	44	344	.541
5. E. Middleton	1	2	83	149	77	13	178	.432
6. Kazer	1	2	97	1341	69	12	162	.426
7. Pinkstaff	0	1	43	50	40	8	76	.526
8. Frank	0	1	43	50	30	3	78	.384
9. Patterson	0	1	25	50	17	3	46	.369
Totals	14	11	999	960	809	195	1546	.523

Detroit – 11

Player	W	L	Pts	OP	R	DR	SP	Pct
1. Rose	4	1	226	149	150	43	266	.560
2. Field	3	2	221	202	199	61	342	.582
3. Gothard	3	2	197	155	162	48	280	.578
4. Swango	1	2	81	143	74	13	182	.409
5. Goodell	0	5	183	250	186	46	362	.514
6. Bennett	W	L	Pts	OP	R	DR	SP	Pct
6. Bennett	0	2	52	100	39	7	114	.342
Totals	11	14	960	999	810	218	1546	.524

August 3 – I won one exhibition game against Valleau just after he had won the Dearborn Tournament. 50–39.

August 4 – Played Getz in a exhibition match at Cass Field in Royal Oak. Defeated him 2 games, 50–43, 50–40.

The State Tournament is set for Iron River on August 16, 17, 18 and perhaps 19th. $350.00 in prize money.

City Meet starts September 9 at N.W. Field.

- - - - - - -

A number of team matches have been recorded in incredible detail in the last few pages. There were no calculators and desktop computers in Rose's day, but he took the time and effort to keep track of all the data and then manually calculated totals. In the "old days" a percentage booklet was available so a league secretary or tournament director could save considerable time by looking up players' ringer averages up to several hundred shoes pitched.

Diamond Tool in Duluth, Minnesota, was one of the companies that produced a ringer percentage chart. Now and then one of their books shows up in an antique shop.

- - - - - - -

Dearborn Trounces Clark Park 18–7

Dearborn's tossers won a very sweet victory over Clark Park when at Dearborn on August 9 they overwhelmed the Parkers, 19–7 and gained partial revenge for the four close matches that have lost to Clark Park this year.

Led by manager Lee Rose, who was tuning up for the State Tournament, the Dearborn boys waded thru their rivals and left no doubt as to their superiority, sweeping all 5 games in the first round. Weakened by the loss of Al Field, who was out with a boil on his arm, Clark Park died without much of a struggle. Rose served notice on the state meet rivals that he was ready by easily squelching 5 opponents, hanging up a .685 average. He defeated Gothard 50–36, with a .656 and then landed on Miller with .806 to win 50–8. Goodell battled him hard the next game, but Rose hurled 52 ringers in 76 shoes for .684 to win 50–34. After blasting Mielbeck 50–9 with .725, Rose fell down slightly against Ingraham, winning 50–26 with .617. Match scores:

Dearborn	W	L	Pts	OP	R	DR	SP	Pct
1. Rose	5	0	250	113	189	66	276	.685
2. Lundgren	3	0	150	22	85	28	120	.708
3. Valleau	4	1	217	162	142	36	280	.501
4. Mierzwa	3	2	227	212	157	39	334	.470
5. Raymo	1	1	66	95	50	11	130	.384
6. Craig	2	3	219	210	131	24	326	.402
Totals	18	7	1129	814	754	204	1466	.514

Clark Park	W	L	Pts	OP	R	DR	SP	Pct
1. Goodell	3	2	222	170	153	45	284	.538
2. Gothard	2	3	179	236	158	46	318	.497
3. Mielbeck	1	4	146	249	116	21	282	.411
4. Ingraham	1	4	130	224	113	25	276	.409
5. Miller	0	4	115	200	113	20	258	.438
6. Jensen	0	1	25	50	14	2	46	.304
Totals	7	18	814	1129	667	159	1466	.455

The next item in the Rose journals is an amazing accounting of the 1939 Michigan state tournament. It's exciting to be able to look back through the years thanks to the incredible detail Rose uses to record his experience. Some 70 years later, is a real treat to anyone who appreciates our sport's history. It's especially remarkable to see how competitive Michigan was back in Rose's era. There are many other historical horseshoe-pitching events that would be interesting to read about, but no one took the time to write them up. But Lee Rose did so for this event.

- - - - - - -

My Sixteenth State Tournament
Held at Iron County Fair Grounds, Iron River

August 16, 17, 18, 1939

On the evening of Aug. 14 at 7:00 p.m., I started off in my car, the "Escritoire." With me was Bertie, of course, Frank Koppitsch, Carl Lundgren and Jim Burt. We went via Chicago, Milwaukee and Green Bay and arrived in Iron River at 4:30 p.m. on Aug. 15. Bad news greeted us on our arrival! The courts were not even touched, weeds growing all over, no stakes and only gravel available. Very, very disconcerting. Next, after finally finding Mr. Campbell, it was disclosed that there would be no prizes even close to the $350.00 promised!

Many of the pitchers worked out that night at Stambaugh. [17-year-old] Bobby Hitt was there, of course, and his chief rival, Joe Latzko. Jack Hoeksema, Jim Skinner, Phillip Carl, Louis Craft, Ray Middleton, Dan Latzko, Bruce Getz and others were also there, attracted by the $350 advertised!

August 16

Play did not get going until 3:00 p.m. Before that, the courts were filled in with gravel, stakes were just driven into the ground and a terribly mixed-up tournament finally got off to a latent start. There were 24 entries.

ROUND ONE

Joe Latzko seized the spotlight by trouncing Art Norlin, U.P. Champion 50–3, throwing .875. Hitt followed close, hurling .775 to wallop Eldred Erickson 50–10. Hoeksema fell into step, beating Joe Kelly 50–12 with .688, while Skinner ploughed Campbell under 50–10, hurling .639. Getz threw .612 to wallop Eskil Erickson 50–36; Koppitsch threw the same to beat Dan Latzko 50–30; Carl beat Larsen 50–33 with .592; Craft hit .569 to nose out Salvatore Ferrigno 50–47; Rose eked out a win over John Egan 50–42, with .555 and Burt beat Hollingsworth 50–30, throwing .548. Middleton won from Walter Juneua by default, while the Lundgren–Rizor game was postponed by mutual consent. In fact, it was never played. All the favorites were off to a good start.

ROUND TWO

Hitt was high man in this round, turning in .742 to beat Carl 50–23. Carl hit .581. Hoeksema stepped right along, snubbing Rose 50–26, shooting .717 to Rose's .550. "Old Man" Skinner crashed out .700 to slaughter Dan Latzko 50–7 and the U.P. champ Norlin walloped Eskil Erickson 50–10 with .684. Lundgren, making his first start, pitched .672 to flatten Middleton 50–23; Egan threw .660 to beat Kelly 50–7; Joe Latzko went only .619 against Getz but won 50–40; Burt threw .615 to defeat Craft 50–19 and Ferrigno walloped Hollingsworth 50–27 with .534. Koppitsch remained in the unbeaten class by trouncing Campbell 50–22, throwing .534 and Eldred Erickson won from Larsen. Rizor, although not even present, won from Juneau by default. Juneau never did show up and defaulted ALL his games!! Leaders—Hitt 2–0, Hoeksema 2–0, Skinner 2–0, J. Latzko 2–0, Burt 2–0, Koppitsch 2–0, Lundgren 1–0, Rizor 1–0 (high eight go to finals).

ROUND THREE

Joe Latzko really scorched Kelly when he threw 30 out of 34 for .882 to win 50–4. Hitt easily toped Hollingsworth in a good game 50–20, throwing 46 in 62 for .742. Lundgren, warming to his work, squelched Larsen 50–14, shooting .666; Carl nosed out Ferrigno in a good game 50–45, shooting 49 out of 76 for .645, while Salvatore had 46 R's for .605. Getz pitched .640 to beat Egan 50–20; Hoeksema pushed Koppitsch out of the unbeaten class 50–33, throwing .611; Skinner kept on his way with a 50–28 win over Norlin, shooting only .536

however; Rose fiddled a win away from Campbell 50–33 with only .531; Burt stayed unbeaten by winning from Rizor 50–33. (This game was really played on August 17, but is placed in here.) Middleton won from Eldred Erickson and Craft got a default from Juneau. The leaders: Hitt 3–0, J. Latzko 3–0, Hoeksema 3–0, Skinner 3–0, Burt 3–0, Lundgren 2–0, Rose 2–1, Getz 2–1, Carl 2–1, Middleton 2–1, Craft 2–1, Koppitsch 2–1.

ROUND FOUR

J. Latzko pounded out .700, 40 out of 70 to beat Rose 50–30. Rose threw 42 R's for .600. Skinner trampled Getz 50–39, shooting 50 R's in 72 shoes for .695 while Getz shot 46 R's for .640. A nice game. Egan poured on a .690 in beating Norlin 50–14. In another fine game, Lundgren beat Carl 50–46. Lundgren had 56 R's in 84 shoes for .667, while Carl had 52 ringers for .619. Hoeksema slapped on .661 in disposing of D. Latzko 50–22. Hitt walloped Craft 50–13 with .661 and Burt trimmed Middleton 50–11 with .630. Koppitsch remained with the leaders by thumping Kelly 50–11 with .592. Ferrigno beat Eldred Erickson and Rizor took a forfeit from Larsen. The leaders:

Hitt	4–0	Burt	4–0	Koppitsch	3–1
J. Latzko	4–0	Skinner	4–0	Rizor	2–1
Hoeksema	4–0	Lundgren	3–0		

ROUND FIVE

Lundgren hit the high spot in this round by throwing .786 against Ferrigno's .553 to win 50–13. L. Latzko crashed out .780 to trim Koppitsch who threw .648 50–25. Hoeksema sailed right along with .736 in beating Eskil Erickson 50–11 and Hitt whipped on .690 to smother Rizor 50–11. Egan hurled .679 to beat Latzko 50–36; Skinner squelched Kelly 50–27 with .651; Getz and Burt won and Rose beat Norlin 50–46 with only .485. Carl & Craft won defaults. The leaders:

Hitt	5–0	Skinner	5–0	Carl	3–2
J. Latzko	5–0	Lundgren	4–0	Egan	3–2
Hoeksema	5–0	Rose	3–2	Craft	3–2
Burt	5–0	Getz	3–2	Koppitsch	3–2

Bobby Hitt broke the Michigan state record for high single game by landing on Middleton with 38 ringers out of 42 shoes for .905. The score was 50–8. Hitt held the former record of .900 also. The Latzko brothers put up a fine brotherly fight with Joe beating Dan 50–29. Joe had 56 ringers in 72 shoes for .778 and Dan had 50 ringers for .695. Lundgren beat Craft 50–12, hurling .761; Burt shot .741 to beat down Carl 50–19 and Hoeksema rolled along nicely to beat Getz 50–19 with .704. Rose finally took a round out of the "big guns," picking on Skinner to win 50–40, though only throwing .616. Ferrigno downed Rizor, Koppitsch walloped Norlin and Egan and Kelly won. This completed the day's play. The leaders:

Hitt	6–0	Burt	6–0	Rose	4–2
J. Latzko	6–0	Lundgren	5–0	Koppitsch	4–2
Hoeksema	6–0	Skinner	5–1	Egan	4–2

August 17

Today was just a nightmare! Players got mixed up on their schedules, seven players dropped out during the day and everything was in terrific confusion throughout. Here's the way it ran:

J. Latzko mowed on .781 in beating Eskil Erickson 50–6; Hitt slammed on .718 to beat Larson 50–4; Hoeksema banged on .705 to down a hard fighting Egan 50–30. Rose stepped along with .635 to whip Kelly 50–19. Getz beat Norlin and Burt beat Ferrigno; Rizor and Carl won and Skinner nosed out Koppitsch. Lundgren got a forfeit. The leaders:

Hitt	7–0	Skinner	6–1	Carl	4–3
J. Latzko	7–0	Rose	5–2	Rizor	3–3
Hoeksema	7–0	Getz	4–3	Ferrigno	3–4
Burt	7–0	Koppitsch	4–3		
Lundgren	6–0	Egan	4–3		

ROUND EIGHT

The five undefeated leaders stayed unbeaten. Hitt pounding out .780 to wallop Ferrigno 50–13; Latzko hitting .732 to trounce Egan 50–7; Lundgren going only .571 to best Eldred Erickson in "the battle of Copenhagen," and Burt and Hoeksema getting defaults. Skinner trailed on in 6th place, beating Eskil Erickson 50–31 and Rose stayed in 7th by downing Koppitsch 50–25 with .587. Carl grabbed 8th place all alone by beating Hollingsworth while Getz was being upset by Kelly. The leaders:

Hitt	8–0	Lundgren	7–0	Koppitsch	4–4
J. Latzko	8–0	Skinner	7–1	Egan	4–4
Hoeksema	8–0	Rose	6–2	Getz	4–4
Burt	8–0	Carl	5–3	Rizor	4–3

ROUND NINE

Hoeksema stole the show this round by hanging up .844 in beating Middleton 50–4. Hitt rolled up .750 to beat Getz. Latzko had .706 to beat Craft. Lundgren got a default, but the other undefeated man, Burt, fell by the wayside when he was ambushed by Rose and beaten 50–10. Rose hanging up a .666. Skinner was upset by Carl, who was now going places 50–44. Rizor defeated the fading Koppitsch and Egan won. The leaders:

Hitt	9–0	Burt	8–1	Carl	6–3
J. Latzko	9–0	Skinner	7–2	Egan	5–4
Hoeksema	9–0	Rose	7–2	Rizor	5–3
Lundgren	8–0				

ROUND TEN

Hitt and Latzko won defaults; Lundgren hung up .712 to beat Hollingsworth 50–12; Hoeksema beat Norlin; Getz beat Koppitsch; Rose beat Eskil Erickson and Skinner defeated Egan. Rizor outlasted Carl to put a crimp in Phillips aspirations and Eldred Erickson stepped up from the cellar and knocked Burt off 50–32 with only .484. The leaders:

Hitt	10–0	Burt	8–2	Carl	6–4
J. Latzko	10–0	Skinner	8–2	Egan	5–5
Hoeksema	10–0	Rose	8–2	Ferrigno	5–5
Lundgren	9–0	Rizor	6–3	Getz	5–5

The three leaders kept on their way, Latzko smothering Middleton 50–11 with .730; Hoeksema downing Carl 50–18 with .730 and Hitt stopping Rose's six game winning streak 50–32. Lundgren was toppled from his unbeaten perch by Getz 50–41; Burt won by default, Skinner beat Craft; Rizor hung up his 5th straight by beating Eskil Erickson and Ferrigno, Egan and Kelly won defaults. The leaders:

Hitt	11–0	Skinner	9–2	Getz	6–5
J. Latzko	11–0	Rose	8–3	Egan	6–5
Hoeksema	11–0	Rizor	7–3	Koppitsch	5–6
Lundgren	9–1	Carl	6–5	Kelly	5–6
Burt	9–2	Ferrigno	6–5		

Round Twelve

Latzko hit .740 to sting Hollingsworth 50–7; Hitt beat Norlin and Hoeksema downed Rizor in a long slow fight 50–45. Lundgren resumed his winning ways with a win over Koppitsch, Skinner won, but Burt tumbled before Kelly who thus hung up his 5th straight win. Rose got a default, Getz won from Ferrigno and Egan & Carl both won. The leaders:

Hitt	12–0	Burt	9–3	Egan	7–5
J. Latzko	12–0	Rose	9–3	Kelly	6–6
Hoeksema	12–0	Rizor	7–4	Ferrigno	6–6
Lundgren	10–1	Carl	7–5		
Skinner	10–2	Getz	7–5		

The "Three Musketeers" marched on, Athos Latzko nosing out a close touch over Rizor 50–47; Porthos Hoeksema getting a default and Aramis Hitt hanging up .764 to stop Kelly's streak 50–4. D'Artagnan Lundgren parked in a .714 game to down Eskil Erickson in the "Battle of the Swedes in the Weeds" 50–6 and King Louie Skinner drubbed Hollingsworth 50–19. Burt nosed out Koppitsch 50–49 and Rose got another default. Getz slipped ahead into 8th with a default and Egan nosed out Carl 50–47 in their critical game. The leaders:

Hitt	13–0	Burt	10–3	Rizor	7–5
J. Latzko	13–0	Rose	10–3	Carl	7–6
Hoeksema	13–0	Egan	8–5	Ferrigno	7–6
Lundgren	11–1	Getz	8–5	Kelly	6–7
Skinner	11–2				

ROUND FOURTEEN

On they went — — — Latzko plastered Carl 50–18, Hoeksema smothered Craft 50–7 and Hitt taking a default. Lundgren staved off a late rally to defeat Rose 50–36, hurling .660 to Rose's .565 and Skinner stormed over Middleton in a late rally to win 50–47. Burt beat Getz and Egan took a reef on 8th place by defeating Rizor 50–43. The leaders:

Hitt	14–0	Skinner	12–2	Getz	8–6
J. Latzko	14–0	Burt	11–3	Ferrigno	8–6
Hoeksema	14–0	Rose	10–4	Rizor	7–6
Lundgren	12–1	Egan	9–5	Carl	7–7

Round Fifteen

Hitt rang up .764 to beat Koppitsch 50–7, Hoeksema shoved in .719 to whip Ferrigno 50–3 and Latzko got a forfeit. A .760 game by Lundgren stopped Egan's four game splurge 50–13 and Skinner's .780 easily murdered Rizor 50–13. Burt won a default but Rose pitching only .460 was nipped by Hollingsworth 50–43. Getz and Carl won by defaults to close in on Egan. The leaders:

Hitt	15–0	Skinner	13–2	Getz	9–6
J. Latzko	15–0	Burt	12–3	Carl	8–7
Hoeksema	15–0	Rose	10–5	Ferrigno	8–7
Lundgren	13–1	Egan	9–6		

ROUND SIXTEEN

Hitt crashed Hoeksema out of the top place 50–23 with .712. Latzko hung up .750 to slam Burt down 50–8. Skinner stepped up and took Lundgren's measure 50–30 hurling .713. Rose won a very sweet victory when he overcame a long lead to drag Getz to a 50–42 defeat. It was the first time Rose had even beaten Getz in a state tournament. Egan and Carl each won by default. The leaders:

Hitt	16–0	Skinner	14–2	Getz	9–7
J. Latzko	16–0	Burt	12–4	Carl	9–7
Hoeksema	15–1	Rose	11–5	Ferrigno	9–7
Lundgren	13–2	Egan	10–6		

ROUND SEVENTEEN

Latzko dashed Ferrigno's hopes somewhat with a 50–9 win hurling .772. Hitt & Hoeksema drew forfeits, as did Skinner & Lundgren. Burt beat Egan 50–36 and Rose beat Rizor 50–37. Getz won from Hollingsworth and Carl got a default. The leaders:

Hitt	17–0	Skinner	15–2	Getz	10–7
J. Latzko	17–0	Burt	13–4	Carl	10–7
Hoeksema	16–1	Rose	12–5	Ferrigno	9–8
Lundgren	14–2	Egan	10–7		

ROUND EIGHTEEN

Hitt landed on Burt with .850 to win 50–5. Latzko defeated Lundgren 50–35 throwing 59 out of 80 for .737 to Lundgren's 554 ringers for .675. Hoeksema whipped Skinner 50–40 and Rose crept up with a 50–37 win over raft. The battle for 8th place went on with Egan practically eliminating Ferrigno, Carl beating Middleton and Getz winning by default. The leaders:

Hitt	18–0	Lundgren	14–3	Getz	11–7
J. Latzko	18–0	Burt	13–5	Carl	11–7
Hoeksema	17–1	Rose	13–5	Ferrigno	9–9
Skinner	15–3	Egan	11–7		

ROUND NINETEEN

Favorites came through in this round. Hitt beat Egan, Latzko got a default, Hoeksema won a forfeit, Skinner defeated Ferrigno, Lundgren won a default, Burt got a forfeit and so did Rose. Kelly upset Carl 50–40 and Getz took undisputed possession of 8th by beating Rizor. The leaders:

Hitt	19–0	Lundgren	15–3	Getz	12–7
J. Latzko	19–0	Burt	14–5	Carl	11–8
Hoeksema	18–1	Rose	14–5	Egan	11–8
Skinner	16–3				

ROUND TWENTY

Lundgren fired the big shot in this round by upsetting Bobbie Hitt 50–36. Lundgren pitched 41 ringers in 60 shoes for .683 while Hitt had 36 ringers for .634. Latzko moved into first with a 50–27 win over Skinner, hitting .690. Hoeksema splattered Burt down 50–44. Rose sneaked up closer with a win over Middleton. Carl helped his cause with a nice win over Getz 50–28 shooting .697, while Egan got a default. The leaders:

J. Latzko	20–0	Skinner	16–4	Getz	12–8
Hitt	19–1	Rose	15–5	Carl	12–8
Hoeksema	19–1	Burt	14–6	Egan	12–8
Lundgren	16–3				

ROUND TWENTY-ONE

Latzko and Hitt both won by default and Hoeksema nosed out Lundgren in a poor game 50–48. Skinner got a default and Rose clicked in a .660 game to wallop Ferrigno 50–16. Burt won a default, as did Getz. Carl rapped out .713 to beat Koppitsch 50–14, but Egan's chances drooped when he lost a 50–44 game to Middleton. The leaders:

J. Latzko	21–0	Lundgren	16–4	Getz	13–8
Hitt	20–1	Rose	16–5	Carl	13–8
Hoeksema	20–1	Burt	15–6	Egan	12–9
Skinner	17–4				

ROUND TWENTY-TWO

In the clash of the Titans, Hitt dropped Latzko off his perch 50–46. Hitt whipped on 81 ringers in 104 shoes for .778 and Joe had 76 ringers for .731. Hoeksema and Lundgren won. Burt defeated Skinner and Rose won a default. Getz won from Middleton and Carl beat Craft. Koppitsch eliminated Egan with a 50–32 win. The leaders:

J. Latzko	21–1	Lundgren	17–4	Burt	16–6
Hitt	21–1	Skinner	17–5	Getz	14–8
Hoeksema	21–1	Rose	17–5	Carl	14–8

ROUND TWENTY-THREE

Hoeksema surprised all by smearing Latzko 50–19 with 52 ringers in 62 shoes for .842, while Joe had 43 ringers for .674. Hitt stayed in a tie for 1st by beating Skinner 50–34 with 59 ringers in 80 shoes for .737 to old Jim's 49 ringers for .612. Lundgren wound up in 4th place by beating Burt and Rose came in 5th by beating Carl 50–47. This game was a bitter struggle all the way, for Carl needed this game. The loss eliminated him from the finals, as Getz walloped Craft. The final eight:

Hitt	22–1	Rose	18–5
Hoeksema	22–1	Skinner	17–6
Latzko	21–2	Burt	16–7
Lundgren	18–4	Getz	15–8

The banquet was held that night at the Iron Inn, followed by a short meeting which was all the convention we had. Officers elected were:

President –	Ray Middleton
U.P. Vice President –	K. D. Campbell
West Vice President –	Jack Hoeksema
East Vice President –	Joe Latzko
Secretary-Treasurer–	Lee Rose

Next year's tournament was awarded to Flint.

– – – – – – –

Here the tournament veered away from the norm of how most state and major tournaments were being held. Play up to this point was a large round robin that determined the top eight players to enter the finals. The usual continuation would be another round robin among those eight finalists. Instead, though, the finals were a single-elimination or match play.

In an additional twist, each match was not a single contest but was the best of five games. So to advance, each player had to win three games over his opponent. Since the games were played to fifty points and the players were at a high skill level, these finals were something of an endurance test—if not a pitching marathon.

- - - - - - -

August 18 – Finals

Hitt defeated Hoeksema 50–34, in a single game to decide the No. 1 playoff position.

Series One – Hitt vs. Getz

Hitt easily stowed Getz away in 3 straight games; 50–21, 50–19 and 50–14, hurling .692, .767 and .815 for a 3-game average of .759. Getz averaged only .543.

Series Two – Hoeksema vs. Burt

The Grand Rapids giant had little trouble in beating Burt 50–24, 50–26 and 50–17, averaging .668 to Burt's .476.

Series Three – Latzko vs. Skinner

Old Jim tore into Latzko and upset 50–40 in the first game, hurling 55 ringers in 80 shoes for .687 to Joe's 52 ringers for .650. But Latzko, unaffected, wheeled around and crashed Skinner down the next three games 50–12, 50–15 and 50–31. Joe racked up .833, .794 and .678. Latzko had a four-game average of .723 to Skinner's .603.

Series 4 – Lundgren vs. Rose

Now, all figures pointed to a Lundgren win and very few gave the eccentric Rose a chance.

Game 1 – Rose started to pitch very slowly and deliberately, hoping to keep Lundgren bottled up and unable to strike his stride. Rose got 3 and after a no-count, missed and Lundgren piled in for 6. Carl missed, however Rose could only get a point. Rose slowly got one on, Lundgren missed again and Rose led 7–6. Rose hit one ringer, but Lundgren planked on 2 to lead 9–7. Again Carl missed and Rose very slowly fussed and fidgeted around and got in for 4 to go ahead 11–9. Rose then tossed a double but Lundgren topped it and came back with a double to get 3 and the lead at 12–11. Two close points made it 14–11 and then Lundgren missed. Rose aimed, balked, scraped his feet and finally tossed a double to lead, 17–14. Another double by Rose was voided and a double back by Lundgren tied it at 17 all. Carl got 4 and then 1 to lead 22–17. Rose picked up a point and Carl tossed on a double to go ahead 25–18. Rose's slow tactics kept up and in the next innings each man had a single and no count. Then Rose snaked in a double to make it 25–21 and another double that was topped. Lundgren picked up 4 more in the next inning and then missed. Then came another famous act. He walked around, stalled, aimed, scraped, filed and finally when all thought he would never pitch, he slapped in a double to make it 29–27. Lundgren got a point; Rose got a point, and then threw a double that Lundgren topped. Lundgren got 4 more to make it 34–28 and then tossed a double. Rose topped it, came back with a single to get a point, tossed a double, but Lundgren topped it. Again Lundgren missed and again came the fidgeting scene with Rose finally sliding in another double to leap ahead 35–34. Rose slipped on another double and got 3, then Carl chugged in a double to get 3 and make it 38–37. Rose banged in a double to get 3 more and a point made it 42–37. Lundgren dropped a double in to get 3 and Rose duplicated the feat to lead 45–40. Again Lundgren dropped in a double to score 3 and plastered another double back to score 3 more to lead 46–45. Here, however, he missed and after Rose got done with his two shoes, he had only thrown a single to lead 48–46. Another double over a single gave Lundgren 3 more to lead 49–48. Rose crawled in with a close point and in the next inning went out with a single ringer. Rose threw 54 in 92 shoes for .598. Lundgren threw 53 ringers for .576.

Game 2 – Rose "blew up" in this game and Lundgren had a walk-away. Rose was very careful, however, to keep things slowed down and while Carl won easily, he did not strike his high-powered stride. The score was 50–14, with Lundgren shooting .630 to Rose's .412.

Game 3 – Rose had slipped by the first game, but had been easily squelched the 2nd. The wheels were revolving again; Lundgren was just too good. It seemed that way, as Lundgren slammed in 7 out of the first 8 shoes to go ahead 7–0. Then came something that was inexplicable to the crowd, but quite understood by Rose. His system was now working with fiendish efficiency and

Lundgren was off his game. During the next 12 innings, Rose slowly pitched 15 ringers, which is not good, but Lundgren was so far off that he threw only 8 ringers. Rose rolled up 26 points to Lundgren's none in this interval. Lundgren got up a little steam and after picking up a point, banged on 4 doubles in a row to come up to 23 points. Here Rose got 3 on a double as Carl missed and than Lundgren got a point on a single, and shot 2 more doubles. The first put him ahead 30–29 and the second Rose topped. Lundgren got a point with a single and ploughed on 2 more doubles, getting 3 on each to lead 37–29. Here Carl missed and Rose enacted his ritual but could only slide in 2 points. Coming slowly back with a single, Rose picked up 3 more as Lundgren again missed. Rose pumped on a double, but Lundgren topped it and came back with another double that put him ahead 40–34. Rose drove in a point on a single and came back with a double, which Carl topped. Lundgren, much to his registered disgust, then missed and walked away to get a drink as Rose scraped around and coaxed both shoes to slide on and put him ahead 41–40. Rose got 2 points on 2 singles, then missed, but Carl could only get a single to tie it at 43. There was a ringer each and no count, then Lundgren draped a double over Rose's single to in front 46–43. Rose duplicated to tie it at 46 and then got away with a single to go to 49. A double by Lee put him out as Carl missed his 2nd shoe. Each man threw 50 ringers in 86 shoes for an average of .582.

Game 4 – With 2 games tucked under his belt, Rose now enjoyed a psychological advantage. However, his grim determination to never allow Lundgren to get up steam never wavered. With only 4 out 10, Lundgren ran ahead 9–3, but Rose tied it up with 3 straight doubles. Lundgren fired back with 5 straight doubles but only picked up 6 points. Rose's slow-down system then began to function once more and in the next 8 innings Carl could only throw 6 out of 16 while Lee piled in 12 ringers and moved ahead 30–15. A double gave Carl 3 and he picked up 4 more on a single. Rose grabbed 3 on a double, then Lundgren chugged on 4 more doubles to make it 33–31. Here Carl missed and Rose, as usual, finally shoved in 6 points to lead 39–31. Carl got a point on a single and then scored six on a double when Rose's shoes both bounced off. A double over a single put Rose ahead 42–38, but 2 doubles gave Carl 6 points and another point put him ahead 45–42. Rose got in 2 points on singles and then Lundgren, in an inspired finish, drove on 3 straight doubles to win. And square the match. Lundgren had 53 ringers in 80 shoes for .663 and Rose had 50 ringers for .625.

Game 5 – Despite the tension and the long, weary struggle, Rose clung steadfast to his plan like a toy bulldog and kept his slow tactics up. Carl got the first point, but Rose rolled up 9 points before Lundgren got 2 more points singles. Two doubles gave Rose 6 more points and a single scored 3 more to make it 18–3. There was a ringer each and no count, then Carl threw a double but the "Tiger," who was a slow-motion "Tiger," topped it. A double gave Lundgren 3 to make it 18–6, but Carl missed and Rose got in for 4. Lee picked up a point on a single, then drove on 2 doubles to take 6 more to make it 29–6. Another Rose double was topped, then Carl got 4, scored 3 more on a double and another point on a single to make it 29–14. Rose coasted slowly along, keeping Lundgren from rallying and finally emerged the victor in this one-sided battle 50–25. Rose threw 46 ringers in 47 shoes for .622 but Lundgren threw 46 ringers for .514.

Rose averaged .579 in the series, while Lundgren averaged .589.

Semi–Finals

Latzko vs. Hoeksema

Hoeksema took a running jump at Joe and banged on 7 straight doubles to start and with 20 out of the first 22 shoes, Jack led 22–0. Then Hoeksema fell off some and Joe began to gain until it stood 33–21 when Latzko slammed on 8 straight doubles to go ahead 45–33 and finally win 50–39.

Hoeksema had a lead of 20–10 in the second game but a streak of 21 ringers in 22 shoes enabled Joe to win 50–33. Five doubles in a row enabled Hoeksema to go in front in the 3rd game 21–0, but Latzko's steady firing brought him out on top 50–32. Latzko hit 56 ringers in 78 shoes for .718, 50 ringers in 66 shoes for .758 and 47 ringers in 64 shoes for .735. Jack averaged .654, .651 and .656.

Hitt vs. Rose

Game 1 – Well, here it was—those three motions Hitt had to make to meet Latzko for the title. Rose had determined to try a slow, steady gait on Hitt; also knowing that it usually worried him. Hitt missed to start and Rose fiddled around and slipped in a double, but missed right back and Hitt tied it up with a double.

After a ringer each and no count, Rose missed again and Hitt slapped in another double to lead 12–6. After a single and no count again, Rose grabbed 4 on a single and then tossed a double, which Hitt canceled. Bob socked on another double and got away with six more to lead 18–10 and another 3 on a double made it 21–10. Hitt poured another double on and it looked like the parade was on, but Rose managed to top this one. Back came Rose with another double to pick up 3 and another double scored 6 as the "boy wonder" missed and the score stood 21–19!! After a single each for no count, Hitt threw a double and got 6; after a single each for no count, Rose threw a double and got 6. Hitt dropped a double over a single to make it 30–25 and Rose duplicated. Rose dropped on another double and Hitt went right over the stake with both shoes as Rose sprang ahead 34–30. Rose popped on another double, but Hitt poured 2 on top. Hitt got a single and Rose worked in for a point to make it 35–30. Hitt picked up a point on a single and then got away with a critical 6 on a double. Rose, tightening up as he saw a chance for victory, hit an off-streak as a result. Hitt finished the game with 11 out of 12 to win 50–38. Hitt threw 37 ringers in 56 shoes for .661 and Rose threw 32 ringers for .571.

Game 2 – Rose's sudden collapse looked like his finish. After 2 single with the score 1–1, Hitt looked on seven straight doubles to run up the score up to 13–1. Rose got 3 on a double and Bobbie picked up a point on a single. Again Rose dropped a double over a single to make it 14–7. Lee picked up a point on a single and then there was a single each and no count. Again Rose picked up a point on a single and then Hitt banged a double over a single to make it 17–9. Then Hitt missed and Rose slid in a double and scored 3 on a single back as Hitt missed again. Rose led 18–17. Rose missed much to his disgust and Hitt pounded in a double to lead 23–18. Bob tossed another double, but Rose topped it. Hitt picked up another point on a single and slammed on another double. It was here that Rose suddenly speeded up his game and began to run up and down. He banged a double on top of Hitt's and came back with another. Hitt topped it and doubled again. Rose promptly topped that and swarmed back with another double. Hitt, however, socked another double on top. Bob missed one and Rose did also, but got one point to make it 24–19. Lee then missed with both shoes and Hitt slammed in a double to go ahead 30–19. A grin of triumph lighted Hitt's face as he laid on another double and a snarling, teeth-gnashing Rose crashed a double on top. Rose came back with a double, but Hitt slashed another on top. Hitt missed one shoe and Rose climbed in for 3 more on a double to make it 30–22. "A stubborn guy!" quoth the hundreds of spectators jammed around the court, "but he may as well give up — — he has no show with Bobbie Hitt!" It seemed so as Rose up and missed and the kid ripped in another 6 points. There was a single each for no count and Hitt again plopped a double in to score 3 more to make it 39–22.

All seemed over, but stark drama was striding into the scene in the person of a fire-spitting, snarling "Tiger" Rose. Hitt pounded on another double but Rose, with venom dripping from every pore, was off on a rush that marked not time or score. Hitt's double was stopped and Rose next double scored 3. Rose's 3rd and 4th doubles were voided but his 5th, 6th and 7th each scored 3 and the score stood 39–34. "A stubborn guy," quoth the spectators, "and he's sure makin' Bobbie work!" Bob picked up a point on a single and then Rose started in again. For 8 more innings the crowd watched amazed as Rose drove on double after double and Hitt tried in vain to stem the tide. Rose had gone into the lead 43–40 before finally having a shoe bounce off. But Bobbie, his nerves a little shaken and cursing roundly and audibly, only got in for a point. Again Bobbie could only throw a single, but Rose, spent badly by his 31 out of 32 streak, could only muster up a killing double and could only get a point to make it 44–41. Rose again could only coax on a single and Hitt with his courage returning draped on a double to tie it at 44–44. Here Bobby missed one and Rose, calling forth all his reserve, planked a double on top to go ahead 47–44. Again Rose could only manage a single and Hitt tied it with a double. Again, Hitt banged on a double and Rose missed his and the long battle was over. Rose's sensational streak had not succeeded. There is every reason to believe that had Rose nipped Hitt in this game, he would have won the series for it would have been all squared up and Hitt would have been left with the knowledge that he couldn't hold a 17-point lead.

Score –	Pts	R	DR	SP	Pct
Hitt	50	83	30	110	.756
Rose	47	81	31	110	.736

Game 3 – There still remained another game, but it seemed just a formality. Rose had "fired and fled" and his chances were gone. Hitt quickly rolled up a 13–0 lead, but Rose here hit 5 doubles in a row. He could only score 3 points on this string and it certainly was discouraging. The fighting deteriorated some here with Rose getting a point on a single, a four-dead, a two-dead twice, a point for Rose on a single, a miss for Rose and 6 for Hitt to make it 19–5. Two doubles by Rose scored nothing, Hitt got a point on a single and Lee scored 3 on a double. Rose brought it to 23–12 and here he missed and Hitt pounded in 6. It was all over after that, with Rose just banging away to play out the string. Hitt finally won 50–24, hurling 65 ringers in 84 shoes for .774 and Rose shooting 55 for .655. In the three games, Hitt averaged .740 while Rose had .672.

In the fifth place flight, Lundgren was not held off stride by Getz and his pent-up flood of ringers poured over Getz to win 50–11, 50–1. Carl hit .750 the first game and .893 the second.

Skinner hit .654 to wallop Burt 50–25, but Burt nosed him out in the second 50–43. Old Jim fell before Older Jim [who was 72 years old] in the three as Skinner hit .600 to win 50–38. Burt took 7th from Getz 50–20. Lundgren beat Skinner 50–35 and 50–49 to take 5th place. Hoeksema and Rose agreed to shorten their match to 2 out of 3 and Hoeksema had no trouble winning the first from a listless Rose 50–15. Rose made a fight of it in the second game but was in no mood for a long, slow game and finally lost 50–38.

All was set for the big show between Hitt and Latzko, which was played at night inside the arena before a densely packed crowd. The match was preceded by an exhibition by Guy Zimmerman and wife.

Finals – Joe Latzko vs. Bobbie Hitt

Game 1 – With 3 doubles, Latzko took a 6–0 lead in the first game, but Hitt crept up until it stood 10–9 in favor of Joe. Here Hitt plopped on 17 out of 18 to go ahead 30–10. Joe could not stop Bobby in this game and the "kid" aided by another run of 7 doubles and 22 out of 24, won out 50–23. Hitt rammed on 62 out of 74 for .815 to Latzko's 53 for .697.

Game 2 – Between games, Latzko entered a protest because the stakes were too high, having been left high from Zimmerman's exhibition. The protest was upheld and the stakes were lowered to 12 inches over the indignant shouts of the Hitt family. The lower stakes handicapped Bobby who was steaming his shoes in low and hard [while Latzko was] pitching slowly and deliberately;

much to Bobby's chagrin and surprise, he arched his shoes neatly and trimmed Hitt 50–18. Joe threw .712 and Bobby could only negotiate .538.

Game 3 – With 25 out of the first 30, Joe took a 20–6 lead. He was never headed after that and rounded Hitt up again 50–26, throwing .744 to Hitt's .659.

Game 4 – Latzko hit a slump after taking a 9–3 dead and Hitt commenced to finally get the range on the stakes and trimmed Joe 50–30, shooting .708 to Joe's .597.

Game 5 – With the series even, each pitcher went after the critical 5th game with fervor. Latzko, with 8 out of 10, took the lead 10–1, but Hitt, with 7 out of 8, tied it up at 10–10. Joe got a point, but Bobby grabbed 9 on 2 doubles to go ahead 19–10. After Joe had scored 3, Bobby banged on 4 doubles to step farther ahead, 25–14. Then, just as things were going his way, Bobby hit only 1 ringer in 6 shoes and the alert Joe had slipped into the lead 26–25! After a couple of 4-deads, Joe got a point, then piled on 5 doubles more to increase his lead to 33–25. After a single no-count, Bob got two 3's on 2 doubles, Joe got a point on a single, and after 3 times 4-dead, Bobby got a point on a single, 3 more on a single as Joe missed and 3 more on a double to lead 38–34. Joe here got in a point and then Hitt banged on 3 doubles and scored 3 on each one to lead 47–35. All seemed over for Joe. Bobby threw a single and Latzko could only get in for a point to make it 47–36. Saved for a moment, Joe then whacked on 4 doubles in a row and sailed to 46. Here he threw only a single, but Hitt again missed one and Joe had tied the score 47–47. Again Latzko fired only a single but for the 3rd time, Hitt allowed Joe to get a point. Latzko then hit a double, but Hitt came through with a double on top. The unnerved Bobby then missed one and the confident Latzko banged in a double to win 50–47! Joe had 76 ringers in 108 shoes for .703, while Hitt had 77 ringers for .712.

Game 6 – With Latzko holding the whip-hand, Hitt was in a spot new to him, especially as the hundreds of spectators contained plenty of Latzko rooters and dissenting voices were new for Bobby, who was used to having everyone for him. The old story—a "boy wonder" growing up and a fickle public going over to a winner. Latzko steamed on 7 out of 8 to take a 7–0 lead and led later 11–3. Hitt brought it up to 7 but Joe made it 14–7. Here Hitt made a run of 6 doubles to slide ahead 16–14 but with 5 doubles right back, the relentless machine from Flint went back in front 26–16. Hitt made it 26–25 and that was as close as he got! Latzko went ahead 33–25; Hitt made it 33–28, then Joe made it 42–28. Bobby got 3 on a double then missed. Joe only got a single but picked up another point to make it 46–31. The fading champion made one last pitiful effort. Hitt threw 3 doubles and scored 6 more to make it 46–40 but Latzko tossed 2 doubles back and went out as Hitt only threw 2 singles. Joe threw .708 to Hitt's .667.

Latzko received the Lattore Trophy and the congratulations of the crowd and he certainly was a happy boy.

It was after 11:00 p.m. when the battle was over and everyone returned to the Legion rooms at the town hall for distribution of the prizes and a big general party.

The Iron River Club had lowered the prizes from $350.00 to $227.50 and after counting up the cash on hand only $97.00 was forthcoming. Each prize-winner was paid approximately 42% of his money and the rest was promised to be mailed at a later date.

A great party [that lasted] all night until 6:00 a.m. was now underway. Whiskey, gin, beer and wine was consumed copiously (especially by Koppitsch) and a big parade around town at 4:00 a.m. was the highlight of the proceedings! The parade was led by that beautiful blond drum majorette, Mrs. Lee Rose, and she really "went to town" with a baton, whistle and tin helmet.

At 6:00 a.m. we set out for home and arrived after a nightmare trip lasting for 26 1/2 hours! WHEWEE!!!!

– – – – – – –

Few states then or now could field as competitive a group of skilled players as Michigan boasted in 1939. Today the competition would be a simpler round robin of 40-point games, not the grueling finals playoff Lee describes—the pinnacle of which was the final match for the championship, a best of five series with 50-point games.

Entire Tournament Final Standing (High Eight)
(Includes Round Robin, Play-offs and Finals)

Place	Player	W	L	Pts	R	DR	Sp	Pct
1.	Latzko	31	5	1508	1466	523	2028	.723
2.	Hitt	31	5	1517	1448	526	2000	.724
3.	Hoeksema	27	5	1311	1102	363	1660	.665
4.	Rose	21	12	1237	1113	314	1938	.574
5.	Lundgren	24	7	1274	1077	347	1668	.646
6.	Skinner	20	12	1302	1068	313	1838	.581
7.	Burt	18	12	956	790	206	1500	.528
8.	Getz	15	14	903	806	233	1472	.547

Here Lee's journals show a change in format. The journals record more of the national aspect of the sport, with newspaper clippings affixed to the journal pages. Of course, Rose was still part of the intense league action and Michigan and local activity.

During the late half of the 1930s, while no World Tournament was being hosted by NHPA, some solid promoters were hosting the Midwest National Tournaments, which were held in Iowa. Rose was there among the notables for the 1939 tournament. It was a highlight of his pitching career when he was elected the national secretary-treasurer of NHPA at the 1939 convention.

The 1939 Midwest National Tournaments could have been sanctioned as a World Tournament, since all the top players were there. Reading Lee's account of this event is something of a Who's Who of horseshoe pitching at the time.

- - - - - - -

On August 26 was to begin the Midwest meet and National Convention at Des Moines, Iowa, and I managed to catch a ride out there with Lattore & Levagood. Following are clippings from the Des Moines papers:

Jones Betters World Record

Wisconsin Shoe Ace Tops Fair Field

Casey Jones, Waukesha, Wis., barnyard slipper champ from the Badger State, set an unofficial world record in leading a field of 38 challengers at the halfway mark in the Midwest National Horseshoe Pitching Tournament at the Iowa State Fair Saturday.

Meeting Roy Parr, Comfrey, Minn., Jones laid on 22 consecutive double ringers, 4 more than the official mark held jointly by Ted Allen, world champion and Eddie Packham, Los Angeles, to trounce his rival 35–0.

Posts 18 Victories

Jones, who lost only one match during the opening day's qualifying round to determine the final 16 in the $500 purse division, posted 18 victories.

Ted Allen, who makes his Bolder, Colo., his home and defending champion of the current tournament, suffered his first 2 defeats in several seasons when he dropped matches to Packham, Los Angeles, Cal., aviation mechanic and Sam Somerhalder, Guide Rock, Neb., high school coach. He was in second place with 16 victories.

Ira Allen Third

Brother Ira Allen held third position with 15 victories and three defeats, one of them administered by Alvin Gandy, Kansas champion and another one by Leon Rodda, Newell, Iowa, who caught Allen napping to toss a 35 to 9 victory.

Guy Zimmerman, newly crowned Iowa champion from Sac City, was in fourth place with 13 victories and 3 defeats, one of them coming at the hands of Ray Frye, Virginia state title holder from Richmond, Va.

The field finishes late today with the top 16 going into the final two-day round robin to determine the distribution of medals and cash.

Shoe Field Led by Zimmerman

Ted Allen Second in Qualifying Round

Guy Zimmerman, Sac City, Iowa, newly crowned state champion, led a field of 38 challengers into the $500 table of the Midwest National Horseshoe Pitching Tournament at the Iowa State Fair Sunday.

Zimmerman collected 35 victories in his 37 matches, with Ted Allen, Boulder, Colo., world and defending champion of the present meet, trailing in second place with 33 victories and four defeats.

At the end of the qualifying matches to determine the top 16 contenders for the crown and prize money distribution, four were tied for fourteenth place with 24 victories and 13 defeats.

Leland Mortenson, tournament director, announced the four, Robert Tompkins of Dysart, Ia., Aden Swinehammer, Aurora, Ill., Sam Somerhalder, Guide Rock, Neb., and Ellis Griggs, Plainville, Ill., would participate in a 100-shoe pitch-off early today to decide which three of the quartet remain in the running.

The qualifiers, including the ties and their scores at the end of the preliminary round follow:

Player, City, State	W	L
1. Guy Zimmerman, Sac City, Ia.	35	2
2. Ted Allen, Boulder, Colo.	33	4
3. Charles Jones, Waukesa, Wis.	31	6
4. Ira Allen, Fresno, Cal.	29	8
5. Dean Brown, Oakland, Cal.	29	8
6. Bob Bales, Kansas City, Kan.	28	9
7. Grover Hawley, Bridgeport, Ohio	27	10
8. Alvin Gandy, Topeka, Kan.	26	11
9. Dale Dixon, Des Moines, Iowa	26	11
10. Roland Kraft, LeComton, Kan.	25	12
11. Ray Frye, Richmond, Va.	25	12
12. Sidney, Minden, Neb.	25	12
13. Lyle Brown, Des Moines, Iowa	25	12
14. Robert Tompkins, Dysart, Iowa	24	13
15. Aden Swinehammer, Aurora, Ill.	24	13
16. S. Somerhalder, Guide Rock, Neb.	24	13
17. Ellis Griggs, Plainville, Ill.	24	13

Standings of those who failed to qualify

Alvin Dahlene, Lawrence, Kan.	23	14
John Paxton, Fairfield, Iowa	21	16
Eddie Packham, Los Angeles, Ca.	21	16
Nels Peterson, Jeffers, Minn.	17	20
Herbert Patrick, Fairbury, Ill.	17	20
Leon Rodda, Newell, Iowa	16	21
Gaylord Peterson, Varna, Ill.	15	22
Harry Reese, Lake City, Iowa	13	24
E. R. Lee, Omaha, Neb.	12	24
Howard Robin, Nebraska City, Neb.	12	25
Russell Sheetz, Cedar Rapids, Iowa	12	25
T. Madsen, Good Thunder, Minn.	11	26
Virgil Murphy, West Point, Iowa	10	27
Glenn Hartz, Blairstown, Iowa	10	27
Lee Rose, Detroit, Mich.	9	28
Roy Parr, Comfrey, Minn.	6	31
Vernor Drager, Graymont, Ill.	0	37
Glenn Tasse, Rippey, Iowa	0	37
W.F. Johnston, Stockport, Iowa	0	37
W. F. Curtx, Worthing, S.D.	0	37
Toe Harlan, Des Moines, Iowa	0	37

- - - - - - -

The qualifying games were played to 35 points, which was very unusual at that time. It makes good sense, though, to shorten the games and avoid wearing out all the players before the meaningful games take place if there will be a 2-day, 37-game round robin just as a qualifying round. In the 1930s,

1940s and 1950s, 50-point games were the rule. The sport finally adopted a 40-point game for World Tournaments starting in 1982.

There are a number of players at the bottom of the list that all have 0–37 records. One would think that some of these five players would have won a game or two as they played against each other. That might have been the case or they might have even won a game or more against other players, but then at some point before the conclusion of the qualifying round they withdrew from the competition. In that case, the withdrawing player would forfeit all games and be granted no wins. That rule used to raise havoc in many major events for players who had earned wins against a player who withdrew because they would lose credit for their win and all the stats associated with their game against the withdrawing player. The rule has been changed so players retain wins and any stats for games actually played.

Lee Rose did compete in the qualifying, but ended up far down the list and did not advance to the finals. There are more clippings included in the journal, including this shoe-pitching stopper.

Halt Horseshoes for Church

The Midwest National Horseshoe Tournament at the Iowa State Fair was stopped for two hours Sunday when the noise made by the iron shoes interfered with church services in the nearby assembly tent.

LeRoy Page, president of the National Association of Horseshoe Pitchers and superintendent of the tournament, said Monday that Dr. John B. Magee, new president of Cornell College, Mount Vernon, Iowa, came to the courts just before the service opened. He asked the players to "stop immediately — we can't hear a thing in there," Page said.

According to Page, A. R. Corey, fair secretary, had come to the courts a short time before and told contestants they could pitch shoes between 10 and 11 a.m., the hour the service started.

Ted Allen Tops Fair Shoe Field

Wins All 8 Matches for Halfway Lead

Averaging 81.1 per cent ringers, Ted Allen, world champion and the defending champion, led the field at the halfway mark in the $500 Midwest National Horseshoe Pitching Tournament at the Iowa State Fair Monday.

Ending today, with the championship worth $125 in additional to a gold medal, the tournament saw a new world record created when Dean Brown, Oakland, Cal., threw 20 consecutive double ringers.

His performance, while not as good as the 22 mark set by Charles Jones in the preliminary round last week, nevertheless stood as an official record since his game was scrutinized by an official scorer. Jones unfortunately, tossed his 22 without benefit of a goggling official.

The defending titleholder wan all eight of his matches. Jones and Guy Zimmerman each took six and lost two to place second on the opening round.

Most exciting match of the day came when Ira Allen, northern California champion of Fresno, Cal., tangled with Roland Kraft, Lecompton, Kan. Allen led Kraft 19 to 1 at the end of 30 shoes but the latter hit a hot streak to come up to 48–47 at 104 shoes. In the next frame, Allen tossed a double and Kraft apparently duplicated it but his second shoe fell back off the peg.

Play is resumed at 9 a.m. today, with finals scheduled shortly after 12 o'clock noon.

- - - - - - -

The final account of the tournament and meeting are actually taken from an article that appeared in the NHPA's August–September 1939 *Horseshoe World* magazine, not from Rose's journal. The article may duplicate some of the qualifying rounds and the Iowa state tournament information conveyed in previous clippings, but is written by NHPA Hall of Fame member Leland Mortenson, who always also gives us some interesting and enjoyable background stories and folklore of the sport's history.

Allen is Still World's Greatest Horseshoe Pitcher

Zimmerman Regains Iowa State Title

By Leland Mortenson

Ted Allen, businesslike, considerate of others, healthy, hard-working, good looking, single and 31 years old, has decisively demonstrated that he is still the world's greatest horseshoe pitcher. He did this by winning 15 successive games in the finals of the Iowa State Fair Mid-West National Horseshoe Pitching Tournament.

Before the Mid-West National Tournament, Guy Zimmerman, also 31 years old and a real professional from Sac City, Iowa, easily captured the Iowa title by winning all games in the finals of that tournament. He averaged 77.5 per cent in all nine final games.

Along with the two tournaments, was the important National Horseshoe Pitchers Association at Hotel Fort Des Moines; the covering of the tournament by *Life* magazine; the radio broadcast of a picture of a great horseshoe pitcher; and many other interesting events. Since they are all interlocked, I shall write about them chronologically.

During the past few years several manufacturers have been deviating from the National rules in respect to the measurements of the horseshoes. The deviation had been in violation of the rules that no projection [the hooks] shall extend from the inner circle of the shoe; and that the slant of the pitch shall not be more than one-half inch. The violations had gone to such seriousness that this spring President L. E. Tanner, of Anchor, Illinois, issued an order that sanctioned tournaments must absolutely enforce the rules of section 6.

As superintendent of the Iowa State Fair horseshoe contests, I agreed to obey Mr. Tanner's order. Mr. Tanner then attempted to enforce the rules in the Illinois tournament but was unable to do so because of the violent opposition from the pitchers. He then ordered me not to enforce Rule 6 at Des Moines.

Meanwhile, President Tanner had ordered a National convention to be held in Des Moines.

In preparing for our horseshoe events, I hired my assistants, chief of which was LeRoy Page, popular, nervy and in my opinion, the best public address man the Iowa State Fair ever had. He assisted me ably at the State Fair in '32, '35, '36, '37 and '38. Part of his task that year was to line up the radio stations.

On the morning of August 24, 22 Iowa pitchers entered the Iowa State Championship Tournament. A half dozen Iowa tossers protested the entry of Guy Zimmerman of Sac City, upon the grounds that he was not a state resident, but it was found that by law Zimmerman did not lose his residence by barnstorming about the country. The protesting players, headed by Lyle Brown and Dale Dixon, of Des Moines, were defining residence by the popular definition, while the committee merely judged it by the law.

The 22 entries were divided into two groups of 11, with the known best players [seeded]. The best five of each group was to go into the finals on the following day. Zimmerman lead his group with ten consecutive victories, while Lyle Brown, defending champion, headed his group with nine victories and one defeat.

The finals of ten pitchers were held on Friday, August 25, in a round robin. Zimmerman won and was not forced to any great extent. Today, Guy Zimmerman is Iowa champion and apparently he can easily hold it for several years.

By Friday afternoon, several of the nation's best pitchers, including Ted Allen, were at the courts. Shoe manufacturers, including Harry Duncan, of Denver and manager of the Allen Co.; John Gordon, of Los Angeles; and Mr. Lattore and Mr. Levagood of Dearborn, Michigan were also on hand.

During Friday and the next two days there was considerable discussion about the rules, etc., and this man and that man was busy grooming his favorite for an office. The most effective campaigning, however, must have been done very quietly for of those elected, I heard nothing beforehand of their being prospective nominees.

Thirty-eight entries started off on a round robin of 35-point games, which was finished Sunday evening. Guy Zimmerman topped the field, defeating Allen. He also beat Allen in a 50-point exhibition match broadcast play-by-play by radio station KRNT. Zimmerman had previously, during this year's fair, received his state championship trophy in a radio studio.

All Saturday, Wallace Kirkland, ace photographer for *Life* magazine, was on the courts snapping about 400 photos of every conceivable thing pertaining to the tournament. *Life* magazine was interested in sending Mr. Kirkland for this special assignment because of Ted Allen. One of the early editions will have pictures.

Also on Saturday, we took several pictures, one of which, Dean Brown, was chosen to be broadcast by the WHO radio-photo machine. Dean Brown, thus I believe, becomes the first horseshoe pitcher to have his picture radioed. (Understand this is wireless radio, not wire photo.)

At the convention meeting at Hotel Fort Des Moines, Sunday evening, August 27, President Tanner appointed LeRoy Page as chairman, Lee Rose as temporary secretary and myself as reporter to *Horseshoe World*. Unfortunately, there was no shorthand reporter.

A Credentials Committee composed of Gaylord Peterson, Sidney Harris and Robert Tompkins was appointed to pass upon qualifications of delegates.

The following rules were changed or made: National dues to be 25 cents with 10 cents returned to the state of residence if the player joins in another state than were he resides.

The delegates voted to require the manufacturers to place a 5-cent stamp on every pair of shoes after January 1, 1940, and this rule is to be effect for 3 years and the funds to be used solely as prizes for world championship tournaments. It shall be the business of the rules committee to enforce this rule.

The question of shoe measurement was then brought up and I was called upon to tell the history of the argument about unofficial shoes, but later the delegates voted to have that information made available only to the committee. It was moved and seconded that 3 members of the rules committee shall constitute a quorum, and it carried. The motion was made by John Gordon.

Election of officers came up. LeRoy Page and L. E. Tanner were nominated for president, with Page winning by a narrow margin.

The following men were elected without opposition: First Vice-President, Jack Claves, of St. Louis; Second Vice-President, Sam Somerhalder, of Guide Rock, Neb.; Third Vice-President, Alvin Dahlene, of Lawrence, Kansas; Secretary-Treasurer, Lee Rose, of Detroit, Mich.

It was stated in the meeting that anyone wishing to protest the appointment of Claves, Rose, Somerhalder, Aden Swinehammer and Tompkins to the rules committee, let him do so then. No one protested. Al agreed to accept the decision of this committee without protesting. The rules committee had been appointed early in the evening by President Tanner. The meeting was adorned and the rules committee was to report Tuesday afternoon.

The finals began on Monday morning, 8 games on Monday and 7 on Tuesday.

Allen averaged 82.77 for the fifteen games. In 1938, he averaged 84.1. Allen was so decisive in victory that a bystander was heard to state that he shouldn't be allowed to play against the others because he was far too good. That is the situation today. Allen is in a class by himself.

In the finals, Dean Brown broke an official world's record by connecting with 20 consecutive double ringers; and in a playoff game between Dean Brown and Lyle Brown, ten successive times there were four dead ringers, an unofficial world's record. This ties an unofficial record made by Davis and Risk here in 1935. Allen had a game in which he tossed 17 successive double ringers.

After the tournament was finished, the rules committee reported: 1. A shoe is delivered when it lands on the opposite end of the court, 2. No change in rules on shoe measurement.

The number 2 report brought up a howl of protest from Glover Hawley, Dale Dixon and John Gordon. [All three of whom, at some point in their careers, manufactured pitching shoes bearing their names.]

John Gordon threatened to form an international association unless the rule on shoe pitch was changed to three-quarter inches. The rules committee went into further session and delayed a further report until a later date.

John Gordon later claimed that since it was Mr. Tanner who appointed the rules committee, the new president had the duty of appointing a new committee. If this is the case, in this writer's opinion, since the delegates did not object to the committee members at first, Mr. Page should reappoint the same members.

1939 Midwest National Final Results

Place	Player	W	L	Pct.
1.	Ted Allen	15	0	82.77
2.	Guy Zimmerman	13	2	80.01
3.	Charles Jones	12	3	80.95
4.	Alvin Gandy	10	5	76.70
5.	Lyle Brown	9	6	75.54
6.	Dean Brown	9	6	80.16
7.	Grover Hawley	7	8	77.21
8.	Aden Swinehammer	7	8	73.75
9.	Ira Allen	7	8	77.40
10.	Ellis Griggs	7	8	74.66
11.	Ray Frye	7	9	70.86
12.	Roland Kraft	6	9	70.84
13.	Dale Dixon	5	10	72.60
14.	Sidney Harris	4	11	69.23
15.	Robert Tompkins	2	13	65.06
16.	Robert Bales	2	13	73.73

- - - - - - -

Now Lee Rose is a national officer! Rose was extremely proud of this achievement. In his journal, he wrote: "SPECIAL, EXTRA, LOOK!!! LOOK !!! LOOK!!! ROSE ELECTED NATIONAL SEC-TREAS!!!"

Beside his emphatic headline, he pasted in a short announcement that appeared on the inside cover page of *Horseshoe World*. It was written by Raymond Howard, who was the editor and publisher of *Horseshoe World* during its entire existence (1924–44). Howard was Rose's predecessor in the position; he had served as the national secretary-treasurer since 1933.

- - - - - - -

Newly Elected National Officers: (L–R) Lee Rose, Alvin Dahlene, Sam Somerhalder, and LeRoy Page.

Our Good Wishes

The good wishes of the *Horseshoe World* go to the newly elected officers of the National Horseshoe Pitchers Association. We believe that they are all endowed with special qualifications for their positions and that they are earnest in their desire to further the interests of the National Association.

Especially do we offer our cooperation to Lee Rose, new secretary, who succeeds the editor of this magazine. Let it be said that no one knows better than the editor of this publication the work that faces this young man in his new job. Bear with him, help him and do all you can to make his path easier and your game a bigger success.

Now a National Officer

In addition to pride at his recent appointment, Rose also had a strong ambition to get some things accomplished and as goes the saying "he hit the ground running." He quickly set up his own agenda of issues to pursue, which included:

1. Allowing states to chose their own scoring methods, which boils down to allowing states to use count-all scoring if they so chose.
2. Addressing the issues of membership dues and membership complaints about paying dues to a national association.
3. Having a World Tournament in 1940; he favored Toronto, Canada, to host the event.
4. Establishing a national team league.
5. And finally, his greatest contribution to NHPA, publishing *Horseshoe Compendium*.

- - - - - - -

I was extremely busy in my new office and one of the first things I did was to clarify the national rules and then get the Rules & By-laws Committee to pass on my idea, Art. V of the By-laws, as follows:

Article V

Section 1. Beginning with the year of 1940 and each year thereafter, the National Association shall conduct a National Team League under the following rules:

Rule 1. Eligibility. Any member in good standing is eligible to compete as a player or hold position as manager, coach, director, owner or some such office on or in connection with any team in this league.

Rule 2. Source of Team. Any source, such as a horseshoe club, county, district or state association, city, town, village, fraternal organization may enter a team in this league.

Rule 3. Registration. Each source desiring to enter a team shall file notice of prospective entry with the National Secretary before April 1st. Each prospective entry shall be sent a team contract, which shall be filled in and returned no later than May 1. This contract will simply affirm that team's willingness to participate in the leagues play and accept the schedule and rules as given and will be signed by no more than ten players and such other officials connected with that team.

Rule 4. General Plan of Schedule. On or before May 15, each team will receive its official schedule for the year. The entries to this league will be divided into divisions according to geographic locations and each team will play a home-and-home series of at least two matches with each other team in its division. After division champions have been decided, a plan for play-offs between them to decide the National Championship team will be drawn up and played.

Rule 5. Method of Deciding Winners. The team matches shall be decided on the basis of seven-men-a-side. There will be seven games rounds of play and seven games per round. The team winning 25 or more games is the winner of the match. Matches won and lost shall decide the team's standing in the league.

Rule 6. Rosters. Each team will be allowed to sign ten players. There will be no limitations placed upon their ability or distance of residence from the home courts of the team they represent.

Rule 7. Uniforms. Each team will be required to be uniformed and it is recommended that each player's name be engraved on his uniform.

Rule 8. Method of Conducting Team Match. The home team manager shall be responsible for having the courts in perfect shape and shall also make arrangements for groundskeepers, scorers, judges, ushers, etc. They shall also furnish score sheets. Just before the match is to begin, each manager shall write out his line-up, numbering his players from one to seven, the number indicating the court on which that player will start. Neither manager shall see the opponent's line-up until both have turned it in to the official referee or announcer.

After each round of play, the members of the visiting team shall move one court to their right and the home team, one court to their left. Each manager may make substitutions before each of the last six rounds, providing that such substitution does not place a man upon a court where he has already played one game or bring together two men who have already played each other. If both managers substitute simultaneously, bringing up such a case, the home team must withdraw or change its substitution.

Rule 9. The home team shall send either score sheets or a compiled result of each match to the National Secretary. If a compiled result is sent, it should include each player's games, won and lost, his points and opponent's points, his ringers, double ringers, shoes pitched and ringer percentage. The National Secretary shall have all the results and standings published in the *Horseshoe World*.

Rule 10. Financial Arrangements. A team entry form of ten ($10.00) dollars shall accompany each team's entry into the league. Each team shall defray its own expenses for uniforms, travel, etc. (It is to be left up to each team to obtain its own commercial sponsor for these things.) Each team shall be at liberty to charge admission to the general public for its home games or take up a collection, or hold raffles or drawings and is not under any obligations to share receipts with the visiting team unless a special pact between the two has been previously agreed upon.

Rule 11. Any point not fully covered by these foregoing rules may be decided upon by the National Secretary or if demanded by the Executive Committee.

Rule 12. It is desired by the National Association that each state association form within its own state, a league similar to the National League, using the same general rules and that results of these leagues be also sent to the National Secretary. It is requested, however, that no member of a National League team shall play on a state league team.

It is further desired by the National Association that each district or locality with enough players to form a league shall form local leagues on the same patterns as the National League, with the understanding that no player from either a National League or state league be allowed to play in this local league.

- - - - - - -

Lee Rose had a long-time passion for league play. While that may not seem unusual today, it certainly was back in 1940. At that time, NHPA was a tournament-oriented organization and Rose's efforts to set up a national-league competition hit some nerves. There certainly were horseshoe leagues in that day and Rose lived in a unique area with an abundance of highly skilled pitchers and league players, but that was not the focus of NHPA.

From one perspective, Rose may have been trying to set up an opportunity to pick up a national championship. It isn't a reach to consider that his efforts could have been a bit self-serving, since he knew his Detroit area likely had the best league players in the nation. That is probably why he designed the national league teams to have seven players, which exceeds the traditional four to five players most leagues used per team. Other cities may have had four or five pitchers who could complete with the Detroiters, but probably not seven.

Rose's efforts to foster league play lasted just one year. The league issue and debates surrounding it would not come up again until later in the decade, at which point the conflict was so serious that it divided some states into setting up separate associations. Not until Donnie Roberts established the NHPA Sanctioned League Program in the late 1970s did league play earn its deserved prominence in the NHPA.

In his journal following his national league rules article for the bylaws, Rose wrote this comment.

- - - - - - -

This completed, I began gathering and writing material for a horseshoe book to be called "HORSESHOE COMPENDIUM." By February 9, 1940, I had the bulk of it ready for setting up and I took a trip to London, Ohio, for the purpose of arranging everything. I stopped in Columbus to see Fred Brust, also.

- - - - - - -

That is one of the more historic notations in the Lee Rose journals. Given the impressive accomplishment for NHPA that *Horseshoe Compendium* represents, it's surprising that he didn't devote more journal space to explaining his project. It's likely he didn't realize the magnitude of his project and its ripple effect. He doesn't mention the book again in his journal, but this book reprints some endorsements on the book by other NHPA notables.

Until Rose embarked on his *Compendium*, there were only two history books written on the sport of horseshoe pitching. Art Headlough, secretary of the Buckeye Horseshoe Pitching Association, wrote the *Official Horseshoe Pitching Guide* in 1920, which became the blueprint for establishing the NHPA in 1921, and D. D. Cottrell wrote *Horseshoe Pitching: How to Play the Game* in 1928. Those were supported by the NHPA periodical, *Horseshoe World*.

Rose's *Horseshoe Compendium* was mostly a historical account of the sport from its beginnings right up to 1940. It's one of two official histories. The other is Gary Kline's *Official N.H.P.A. History of the World Tournament 1909 to 1980*, which was published in 1980. So you can see that Rose's effort filled a major gap in the sequence. His book is considered a precious document of the NHPA and is on display at the National Hall of Fame Museum in Wentzville, Missouri. *Horseshoe Compendium* is still a gem to read and is reprinted in its entirety at the end of this book.

Soon he was writing some journal notes about his next big historic project.

- - - - - - -

January and February were spent in first coaxing a bid for the World Tournament out of the Canadian National Exhibition and then having received the bid, trying to get the other members of the Executive Committee to okay it.

They absolutely refused to do so!!!

I tried to coax them — — I pleaded with them, I stormed at them, but I finally realized that I am up against a mid-west coalition that will leave no stone unturned to bring the tournament to Des Moines regardless of any other bids or regardless of whatever may be the best for horseshoes as a whole.

At this writing, March 5, 1940, I have about given up hope of ever accomplishing anything with this set of working-mates.

- - - - - - -

So what was the big deal with holding a World Tournament in Canada? Wouldn't that be good for the sport? The real problem was timing. A World Tournament hadn't been held for four years, so holding the 1940 event somewhere in the States, and more specifically somewhere mid-country, would probably serve the most and the best pitchers.

Rose was onto something big in promotion, it was just lousy timing. A World Tournament in Canada at that time would have been too historic, too bold, and maybe too radical.

Ultimately, the 1940 tournament was held in Des Moines. Almost 60 years later, the 1997 World Horseshoe Tournament was held in Canada for the first time—in Kitchener, Ontario. A second Canadian-hosted event was held just five years later, in Red Deer, Alberta, in 2002.

Next we take a step back in time with a real page out of NHPA's history, Raymond Howard's article from the March 1940 edition of *Horseshoe World*.

– – – – – – –

Rose Favors Canadian City for 1940 Meet

Age-Old Question of Where to Hold the Tourney Springs Up Again — Toronto Makes Bid

The annual question of where to hold a National Convention and Tournament come up again in 1940.

Former Secretary R. B. Howard did not become a candidate for election in 1939 because of the criticism directed at him for not holding a National Tournament and because of more pressing duties in other lines of endeavor. The tournament question is a tough one.

It was disagreement over the holding of the 1933 World's Fair Tournament that led to the selection of a new secretary — or at least that was one of the reasons. The late D. D. Cottrell held many successful tournaments in Florida, but failed to find a sponsor for one in the North.

In 1933, the World's Fair management offered a proposition that met with the approval of many pitchers but did not meet the specifications of the Association or the secretary. Howard, then vice president, assumed the responsibility of scheduling a tournament and it was a success. Another was held in 1935 and it was a success, as those who visited Moline that year well know.

In 1939, it looked for a time like a meet might be held at the World's Fair in San Francisco, but this did not materialize, nor did efforts to secure enough money from the Iowa State Fair Board. In desperation, the officers called a convention in connection with the Mid-West Tournament at Des Moines. L. E.

Tanner, then president, and Mr. Howard, then secretary, felt this was the best thing that could be done.

Now the new secretary, Mr. Rose, is confronted with the same question and in a letter to Vice President Jack Claves and Alvin Dahlene, he indicates that he will accept the tourney offer of Toronto, Canada.

If it goes to Canada this will be the first time it has ever been held outside of the United States.

Mr. Rose states that he has been told the Iowa State Fair will bid $800, but that he hasn't received that bid officially.

As this is being written the facts are not all known, but Secretary Rose requests that his letter to certain officials of the National Association be printed in the magazine. In it, he "raps" those who didn't reply to his request for a vote on the Canadian offer.

The *Horseshoe World* wants to be neutral in the matter, but prints Mr. Rose's letter in order that our readers may know his views. These columns will be open to those who may oppose taking the tournament to Toronto. The Rose letter reads as follows:

Dear Sirs:

You are familiar with the offer from Toronto regarding the World Tournament. To date I have received only a post card from Mortenson and a letter from Gordon.

Mr. Gordon declares he is completely for a tournament at Des Moines. Before going on [about] this any further I might say that I HAVE NOT RECEIVED ANY OFFER FROM DES MOINES. The only notice I have is contained in a letter from Leland Mortenson in these words: quote "The State Fair Board is going to make an $800 bid for the World Tournament. To date I have Mr. Corey's promise, but of course, not official until the Fair Board meets," unquote. That is all the offer I have from Des Moines.

On the other hand, I have an officially guaranteed offer from Toronto, but this offer MUST be accepted BEFORE the 18th of February. To make it official in every way it is necessary to obtain the consent of at least two more of the Executive Committee. I dispatched each of them telegrams and airmail letters last Saturday. As I write this I have received only one answer, from Sam Somerhalder. Since the time for accepting the Toronto bid is growing short it seems that the matter is to be left entirely up to me, and here is my decision:

Since I have received only ONE offer for a tournament and since that offer MUST be accepted quickly and since other offers are yet on the doubtful side, I cannot turn down a fine opportunity such as this for something not yet known, so I am writing Toronto that they will have the official World Tournament.

There are many items in connection with the tournament, which prompts my acceptance. Toronto is much closer to the majority of National Association members. Eastern players who went to Toronto last year returned home with nothing but praise for the way they were treated and will be anxious to go again. A tournament at the world's largest permanent fair would elevate the game to a position of greater dignity. The possibility of opening the entire Dominion of Canada for a field for American-made pitching shoes is certain to appeal to and receive the support of a majority of manufacturers who are now paying stamp money for prizes. The bringing of the National Association and the Dominion Association into closer relationship cannot help but result in a gigantic boost for the game.

Let us sincerely hope that now that the tournament question is settled all parties will attend without offering opposition that can only do the game irreparable harm. Any differences can be settled in an open meeting at the convention.

Yours sincerely,

Lee Rose

- - - - - - -

Horseshoe World carried several letters from other NHPA officers and it appears Lee Rose was the only one of the Executive Committee in favor of the 1940 World Tournament being held in Canada—or even the possibility of looking in the direction.

- - - - - - -

The Lee Rose Story

Tournament "Scrap" Continues

There are times when a publication may be justified in "suppressing" news. The *Horseshoe World* may have erred when it offered a page to the secretary and other officers of the National Association for such use as they cared to make of it. The page has been used to air differences of opinion over the 1940 tournament. But good may result after all—at least we hope so. It may be that in giving both sides a chance to "say their piece" the atmosphere has been cleared and that this magazine may have had a part in bringing about the friendliness and peace that now seems to prevail. The last letters on the subject are printed this month and it should be borne in mind that they were written before the affair was settled—we only print them in order that all concerned be treated fairly and given equal space. But we are through.

It is time now—and all concerned are fully agreed—that we put our shoulders to the wheel and make the 1940 meet at Des Moines the best ever. We can also lend our support to the open tournament that Canada will stage. I am sure that the United States and Canada can be just as good neighbors in the horseshoe sport as they have been in everything else. If any misunderstanding has arisen, the same good sportsmanship that always makes horseshoe pitching a pleasure has quickly erased it. It looks like a big year for horseshoe pitching on the North American continent!

- - - - - - -

But Lee Rose did not give up easily. Apparently he couldn't see that he was fighting a losing battle when it might be best to "give up the ship"! What he was attempting to do was innovative and just might be a great event, but it was not going to be accomplished in 1940. The next issue of *Horseshoe World* printed the following letter from Rose.

- - - - - - -

The Secretary says:

> In the last issue of this magazine it was stated that the official National or World Tournament would go to the Canadian National Exhibition in Toronto, Ontario. Since that time the Executive Committee has

overruled the decision of the National Secretary and has just about decided to award the meet to the Iowa State Fair for the sum of $800.00.

Toronto, however, has not yet given up hope and has stated that they will stage a world tournament regardless and will endeavor to raise $2,000.00 in prize money for it. If this happens the Executive Committee will have a lot of explaining to do.

The best policy in a case of this kind should be to wait and see if the C.N.E. will really guarantee this amount and if such a guarantee is forthcoming it would only seem just that they should get the official world tournament and that the stamp money raised by the National Association should go toward increasing the prize money.

After all, the American pitchers stand a good chance of carrying away the lion's share of the prize money and since the Iowa Fair has stated that they would still hold the Mid-West Meet for $500.00, it seems that the horseshoe pitchers would benefit more if Toronto landed the big meet.

The National Secretary is endeavoring to get a guarantee from the C.N.E., and if same is received, one more attempt to persuade the Executive Committee will be made and it is hoped that the meet will go to the place making the best offer and that the offer will be judged on its merits alone.

Lee Rose, National Secretary

- - - - - - -

The exchange of barbs and subtle infighting continued some through the Horseshoe World. The exchange that took place was acknowledged by editor Ray Howard and he took steps to promote the 1940 Des Moines tournament, once it was clear that that decision had been made. One point that remains a question is that all the NHPA officers except for Lee Rose that wrote on the matter, called the 1940 event a National Tournament, while the Canadian input referenced their proposal for a World Tournament. Later on the 1940 event is called a World Tournament but not why in this published exchange. This maybe the most volatile public exchange other than later in 1948 and 1949 when the NHPA had to endure the debate of the expansion of league involvement in the NHPA. Here are a couple of the other NHPA officers responding to the issue...

- - - - - - -

The President says:

To All Members: N.H.P.A. of America

I had hoped at this writing to be able to announce the site and all details in connection with the 1940 National Tournament. A few minor points remain to be decided upon at this time. The next issue of the *Horseshoe World* should carry the official announcement.

Regarding Mr. Rose's statement in the last issue: At present the committee has come to an agreement on the issue involved, but there remain a few statements [that] need clarification. In the first place, no one had the authority to set February 18 as the last day on which bids would be accepted for the 1940 National Tournament. In the second place, I have written proof that each member of the Executive Committee either wrote or wired Mr. Rose in negative, so that the votes would reach the secretary's office not later than February 17. Thirdly, although Toronto may be nearer to the majority of members of the National Association, we of the executive must remember that this Association has members from coast to coast and border to border and to place a National Tournament nearer to one section of the country than another, would be unfair to the prospective entrants in the far sections. It would be very unjust to force an entrant from California to travel over 3,000 miles each way to the tournament, while the New York entrant traveled less than 1,500 miles both ways. A central location is fairest to all; therefore, we of the Executive Committee have rejected the Toronto proposal of $500. We have however suggested that the Canadian National Exhibition conduct a Canadian-American meet for which we will be very glad to grant a sanction.

At present we have the bid of the Iowa State Fair for $800. To this we propose to add $300 of stamp funds, making a total of $1,100 for the 1940 National Tournament. Des Moines is centrally located and the

Iowa State Fair Association has consistently offered high cash prizes for a horseshoe tournament each year since 1923.

Mr. A. R. Corey, the Fair Secretary, is an ardent supporter of the game and certainly deserves fair consideration for the first National Tournament since 1935. The Fair Ground courts hold practically all world records, each year bringing some new record achievement on the pegs. All who have attended the Fair Tournaments in the past have commented on the fine quality of the show, the newspaper and radio publicity in connection therewith and the fair and just manner in which the tournaments were conducted and the entrants treated.

Your President and Secretary are in accord that the Association for 1940 shall establish a precedent for achievement and cooperation. The Executive Committee are a group of two-fisted square shooters, insisting on justice, honesty and equality. What more is there to ask?

With your enthusiasm and cooperation, we can go places in 1940. Let's do it!

Yours very sincerely,
C. LeRoy Page, President

- - - - - - -

Jack Claves, NHPA Hall of Fame member who was NHPA's vice president at the time, also took exception to Lee Rose's attitude. Claves took his turn on the soapbox provided by *Horseshoe World*.

- - - - - - -

In the February issue, under the caption of "Rose Favors Canadian City for 1940 Meet," the old proverb of "every story has two sides" was grossly abused.

I do not care to air either side but as the opinion was given that all the other National Association officers, except Mr. Rose, were not only incompetent, but also lacking in their duties and loyalty, I wish to give those who read the letter some additional light.

I do not take exception that Mr. Page, the president of the National Association was entirely ignored, as was Mr. Somerhalder. Neither do I condemn Mr. Rose for thinking his opinion was superior to all others and that he alone is qualified to guide the association's affairs. Every man has the right to place his own value on himself; that is a human privilege.

My objection is that the date of the letter was not printed. The date was all important. Had that been mentioned everyone would have realized that Mr. Rose was suffering with "Ants in the Pants" and had "Jumped the Gun" and had not given his brother officers the courtesy of giving their opinions before the deadline of Sunday, February 18.

Mr. Rose's letter was dated February 16, 1940. Had that been printed, no false impressions would have been given. The truth is that all officers were very efficient and all had voted before the deadline. The Western Union had a record of my telegram dated February 16, 1940.

I do not blame Mr. Rose for the omitted date, that may have been the printer's mistake, but I do resent his giving the Canadian officials and our members the impression that he has more powers in our game than Judge Landis has in baseball. It spells chaos to our great game and our National Association.

Yes, there are two sides to every story—the right one and the wrong one.

Jack H. Claves
Vice President

- - - - - - -

Even though it was announced that the 1940 World Tournament was to be held in Iowa, Canada wanted to be heard in the matter, which led to more intriguing comments.

- - - - - - -

Dear Mr. Howard,   March 18, 1940

I am writing you to clear up a few points regarding the Canadian bid for the world championship to be held in Toronto that seems to have been in some way distorted in the United States.

To sum up the Canadian offer: The Canadian National Exhibition, the world's largest annual fair, through an interview with myself on the offer, said that they would put up for a world tourney in Toronto, an indoor arena, which would hold about twenty courts and seat about 5,000 people, plus all amplifying equipment, $500.00, trophies and a banquet for all visiting players.

Add to this, on the suggestion of the National Association, the sum of $500 from the stamp tax and the sum of $1,000, which the Dominion Association of Canada said they would raise and I think it adds up to $2,000, which is not too bad an amount for prize money, although we may not have reached the peak that the National Association once raised.

Also the impression has been conveyed that because Canada is now at war, that anyone coming over here is liable, etc. At this point I would like to state that the borders of Canada are wide open to any United States visitor, with conditions the same as they were before the war and that our sport and living conditions are also the same. Then again, when the United States dollar is tendered here, one dollar and ten cents is paid back, which is an advantage to all visitors.

Apparently Mr. Leroy Page, through correspondence with Lee Rose, was not satisfied with the version that Mr. Rose had given to him on this bid, so he wrote to the C.N.E. asking for confirmation of it. The C.N.E. gave me full authority to act for them in the absence of Mr. Duthie, sports director, and I wrote Mr. Page, giving him all details and to date I have not yet heard from Mr. Page, one month ago.

In my letter to Mr. Page and on behalf of the Dominion Association, we held out the hand of friendship to the National Association and stated that it may be the beginning of affiliation between the two countries and be of great benefit to horseshoe pitching.

Canada from now on will be pitching hooked shoes with the longer and softer pegs and all arrangements had been made to conform to National rules, regulations, with soft pegs to suit your style of shoes, so you may see that we were trying to make everything for the convenience of visitors and were willing to let Canadian pitchers take their chances on the change of their orthodox playing equipment.

It was merely the fact that we were willing to try to put the game on a higher level here and the thought that with affiliation in view, we may make the game on a comparable level to other sports.

In previous years, the Dominion Association has been as a ruling body, a dead issue, but very recently a group of men, with the thought of the game only at heart, have been taking control and are tying to modernize the game, make a bigger appeal to the public and are now introducing the game into the army, even to the extent of giving the soldiers all horseshoe equipment to take overseas with them, with the idea of keeping the game alive and built up when the war is over. The only way that we can make horseshoes go is for all players and officials alike, to forget their selfishness and work together to one end.

To my many friends in the United States I have written this letter to clear up a point that may have caused considerable controversy and to say that, while we may not put on as big a show as the United States, it is our first real chance to try and we ourselves would not think of calling a mere $500 a prize for a world tournament and we have done our best to work with the National Association.

I trust that this letter will be published in the Horseshoe World, worthy issue, which is gaining much popularity in Canada.

Yours sincerely,

E C. Steadman

- - - - - - -

After a five-year gap in which there were no World Tournaments, the NHPA was obligated to present a World Tournament for its members—and do it in the U.S. Des Moines was an excellent and obvious choice with a track record of holding meets on a national scale that could draw premier pitchers.

Jacobs's efforts to arrange a World Tournament in Canada came at an inopportune time—it boiled down to lousy timing. Lee was thinking outside the box. A Canadian-hosted World Tournament would have given the sport an international flair and may have served both countries well in promoting the sport. But World War II may have eroded any progress gained since it caused another five-year gap between World Tournaments.

Once 1947 came around, though, there were no more gaps. Horseshoe pitching was an active sport in both Canada and the U.S. and Canadian players were participating in NHPA World Tournaments. It wasn't until 1965 that a Canadian won a world championship: Elmer Hohl won six men's world championships (1965, 1968, 1972, 1973, 1975, and 1977). Hohl was one of the best pitchers of all time and arguably the sport's fiercest competitor.

Canada produced an exceptional Women's champion in Sylvianne Moisan, who won four consecutive world titles starting in 2000. She was not the first Canadian women's world champion, however. In 1987 Sandy McLachlin (now Sandy Janssens) won the women's world title in one of the most spectacular performances of all time, averaging 88.24 percent ringers for the entire tournament. In the process of winning that championship, Janssens bested another talented Canadian star, Diane Cantin, in a playoff game.

In 1986, Janssens won the junior girls' world championship while pitching a respectable 67.33 percent. So in 1987, she passed up her final year of junior eligibility to enter the women's division, a rather daring effort that certainly paid off. Crystal Curtis is the only other Canadian junior to win a girls' world title, which she did in 1993.

Three Canadians have won junior boys' titles: Steve Hohl in 1978, Ed Neeb in 1988, and Drew Becker in 2002 (and again in 2003).

It's tantalizing to wonder if earlier Canadian players might have earned world titles if the 1940 World Tournament had been held in Toronto. Nonetheless, Rose's efforts to advocate for were in vain and just may have caused him to lose interest in being a national officer. He served only one year as the NHPA secretary-treasurer.

Now his journals return to his own heavy involvement in the pitching scene in the Detroit area. But before going into those records, it's important to note that despite his contentious bout with the NHPA officers about planning the 1940 World Tournament, those officers must have retained a great deal of respect for Rose's efforts.

It is not clear just when Rose's *Horseshoe Compendium* was released or exactly what month the following articles appeared in the *Horseshoe World*, but the leaders of the NHPA clearly appreciated his efforts and gave great plugs for the book.

- - - - - - -

Every month I have about ten persons who either drop around and read or borrow my *Horse World*.... Now they are coming to read that new book *The Horse Compendium*, put out by Lee Rose. And by the way, Harry Woodfield, of Washington, D.C., says, "Every library in the United States should have a copy of that book."

Since Lee Rose's book has come off the press, two Iowa pitchers have announced that they will write books. One of these, Eddie Packham, has already written twenty pages of what he plans to be a cloth-bound edition of several hundred pages. It is quite possible that the Iowa Horseshoe Pitchers Association will publish a book on its own.

Leland Mortenson

I recently received a copy of the *Horseshoe Compendium* from secretary-treasurer Lee Rose and spent many pleasant minutes reading various articles therein. One of the articles alone, Leland Mortenson's "History of Horseshoes in Iowa," is well worth the price of the entire book. Although I cannot entirely agree with Rose's "Michigan Plan" of conducting tournaments, his idea has its points but beyond that I most heartily recommend the *Compendium* to everyone who has any interest whatever in the horseshoe game. It is well worth many times the nominal 50-cent fee. If your copy isn't ordered already, don't fail to do so at once. You'll be sorry if you don't.

C. LeRoy Page, President

- - - - - - -

Now Lee's journals return to coverage of the horseshoe leagues of Michigan. Rose remains, for the moment, a national officer, but it's summertime and the shoes are flying.

- - - - - - -

Detroit Captures First Match

On Sunday, May 26, at Northwestern Field, the powerful Detroit team easily bested Flint's tossers 21–9 in a match cut short by showers and wind.

The team placed on the field by Detroit was a far cry from their best, but sufficiently strong to stow away the visitors easily. Four of Flint's wins were gathered in by Carl Gothard and Jimmy Field who was loaned to Flint when two of their players failed to show up on time.

Rizor supplied the feature of the day by coming from behind with seven straight doubles to down State Champion Joe Latzko 50–47. Rizor has previously lost to J. Field. Al Field and Harold Arold each pitched well, each losing only to Latzko. Field's game with the champ was a real ringerfull battle. Summary: (No ringer averages were kept)

Detroit – 21		Flint – 9	
Lee Rose	2–0	Joe Latzko	4–1
R. H. Rizor	4–1	C. Gothard	2–3
Al Field	4–1	J. Field	2–3
H. Arold	4–1	W. Miller	1–4
J. Galesky	3–2	R. Middleton	0–5
M. Goodell	3–2	W. Heddy	0–5
F. Koppitsch	1–2		

~Bulletin~

The Michigan State Championship Tournament will be played at Berston Field in Flint, August 16-17-18.

Detroit's Teams Wallop Toledo

Two five-man teams from Toledo invaded Detroit on June 16 and both went home defeated. The best five took a 22–3 lacing from the powerful Detroiters, but the second team held Detroit's seconds to a 14–11 score.

Al Field led the way for Detroit with five wins and Carl Gothard won four out of four. Al averaged .632 and Carl only made .559. Rose hung up the highest average for the day with .637, but dropped a close game to Bill Konz.

Konz, by the way, won 3 out of five and was the only Toledo player to win a game. He won his other games from Koppitsch and Lattore and lost to Field and Lundgren. The latter also went undefeated in 4 games. Detroit hit .595 for a team average and some of their best men were absent.

Jimmy Herbert loped through the Toledo boys for five wins in the second team match and Williams and J. Field each took three out of five.

For Toledo, Stefel won four and Schotherman won 3. Summaries:

Detroit – 22

Player	W	L	Pts	OP	R	DR	SP	Pct
A. Field	5	0	250	124	196	58	310	.632
Lundgren	4	0	200	97	133	37	232	.573
Gothard	4	0	200	96	123	32	220	.559
Goodell	1	0	50	17	30	9	56	.553
Rose	4	1	244	136	200	61	314	.637
Koppitsch	4	1	230	173	165	47	300	.550
Lattore	0	1	40	50	53	15	82	.646
Total	22	3	1214	693	901	259	1514	.595

Toledo – 3

Player	W	L	Pts	OP	R	DR	SP	Pct
Konz	3	2	218	214	223	64	370	.603
Stewart	0	5	151	250	140	33	300	.466
Antill	0	5	120	250	136	29	294	.462
FitzGerald	0	5	124	250	108	11	290	.372
Schroeder	0	5	80	250	107	21	260	.412
Total	3	22	693	1214	714	159	1514	.465

Toledo 1st – 1 1 0 0 1 = 3
Detroit 1st – 4 4 5 5 4 = 22

Team 2 – Summary

Detroit – 14

Player	W	L
Herbert	5	0
Williams	3	2
J. Field	3	2
Craig	2	3
Giesey	1	3
Skelly	0	1
	14	11

Toledo – 11

Player	W	L
Steffel	1	4
Schotherman	3	2
Helser	2	3
Worline	2	3
Heinye	0	5
	11	14

Toledo 2nd – 1 2 2 3 3 = 11
Detroit 2nd – 4 3 3 2 2 = 14

Note – Detroit is to play their first match in the National League on June 23 when they go to Canton, Ohio. Bill Konz of Toledo, is to be added to the (Detroit) team, which lines up as follows: Joe Latzko, Al Field, Leo Lattore, R. H. Rizor, F. Koppitsch, Carl Lundgren, Lee Rose, Carl Gothard, W. Konz and Orville Valleau.

Rose's pet project, a national league, is still alive, however faintly. Here is a clipping from the *Horseshoe World* of a column written by Rose.

League News

The somewhat doubtful adventure of the National Association into the realm of league promoting will begin soon and the outlook is at best only fair. The response of the so called "big time" clubs or teams to this league has not been quite as good as was expected. Mind you, the expectations for this enterprise were not very high, for it is something new and needs a while to get a good start and it was to be expected that many possible entries would hold back to see what the other entries looked like before joining. Only a few of the hardier teams willing to take a chance to further a cause were expected to join and it seems that these hardy ones are fewer than supposed.

To date, there are three bona fide entries and three other probable ones. The three cities already in are Indianapolis, Canton and Detroit. The other three who are still making up their minds are Pittsburgh, Fort Wayne and Terre Haute.

These teams are really too far apart to allow them to play a regular home-and-home schedule between each of the teams, but after all entries are definitely in, a schedule will be drawn to form three teams in a division and this will give those teams four games. Then each will play a match or two with teams from the other division and the two division winners will play at the end of the season to decide a national champion. The national champion can then play the Canadian winner for a world title.

The entry list to the league will be held open until a week from the day this issue of the *Horseshoe World* is out and at that time a schedule will be sent out to start play with whatever teams have entered.

Any team who still desires to enter this league is urged to get in touch with Secretary Lee Rose immediately and your teams will be included in the schedule. Don't delay, for the time is growing short and the league is late in starting.

The complete schedule and team rosters are expected to be printed in the June issue of this magazine. More news then.

And so the new national league was about to begin. It was Lee Rose's baby and an energetic enterprise that was in many ways both creative and extraordinary. But we should not forget that this program is very self-serving to Rose.

One imagines this must have been a rebuilding time for Rose after his winter battle over the 1940 World Tournament site. With that behind him, he could get out on the courts and put his energies into doing battle there.

There were national-league contests between teams from different states, but they were all border states and the teams involved were from towns that were rather close together. While those circumstances were generally true, there was an expansion to the sport's competition that drew out some tremendous pitchers. Rose recorded this first-round match great description in his journals.

- - - - - - -

Detroit Captures League Opener
Subdues Canton's Tossers

Detroit's aspiring horseshoe team made its first start in the National Horseshoe League a winning one by defeating the Canton, Ohio, team, 27–22, in a game played June 23 in the City Park in Canton.

A gusty, swirling wind rendered pitching difficult.

Canton presented two star pitchers in John Sebek and Andrew Stolarik, but the balanced power of Detroit roaring strongly along from the 3rd round to the 7th rolled up enough points to assure themselves of a victory. The match, round by round:

Line ups: Detroit – Carl Gothard, Bill Kong, Al Field, Jim Burt, Frank Koppitsch, Lee Rose, Leo Lattore and Orville Valleau.

Canton – Hunt, Kovacs, Miller, Andy Stolarik, Elmer Stuckey, John Sebek and Wheeler.

Round One

Carl Gothard started like a house a-fire by drubbing Hunt 50–8, hurling 38 out of 48 for .792. Bill Kong, in his first start for Detroit, made it a winning one by beating Kovacs 50–13. Field walloped Miller 50–7. Jim Burt, in his first competitive match after not doing much pitching so far this year, lost to Stolarik 50–25. Rose defeated Stuckey 50–35, hurling 52 out of 80 for .650. Sebek landed on Lattore with 42 out of 52 for .778, beating Leo 50–8 and Wheeler hit .685 to down Valleau 50–27. Detroit led 4–3.

Round Two

Wheeler defeated Kong 50–39, but Field walloped Hunt 50–8 with 36 out of 46 for .783. Burt, pitching only .333 was beaten by Kovacs 50–32. Rose won his 2nd game by beating Miller 50–16, shooting 38 out of 56 for .679. Lattore fell victim to Stolarik's .712, 50–31, but Valleau turned in a win over Stuckey 50–38. Gothard dropped to .558 in his game with Canton's star Sebek and lost 50–16, Sebek shooting .750. This tied the match at 7-all, and a tight battle was in prospect.

Round Three

Detroit's "bull-dog", Field, battled nip and tuck with Sebek and after losing a 36–26 lead, came from behind to finally nose out Johnny 50–49. Each man threw 67 out of 94 for .713. Burt dropped his third straight game, this time losing to Wheeler 50–28. It was Wheeler's 3rd straight win. Rose easily trounced Pettit (subbing for Hunt) 50–5, throwing 25 out of 36 for .695. Lattore gathered in his first win, beating Kovacs 50–22 and Valleau hung up another win by beating Miller 50–44, throwing 53 out of 88 for .602. Gothard was nosed out by Stolarik 50–48, with Andy hitting 60 out of 90 and Carl hitting 58. Kong turned in another win, beating Stuckey 50–15. This was the round that sent Canton on the road to defeat, for Detroit was now in front 12–9 and destined to remain there.

Round Four

Burt, facing almost certain defeat at the hands of Stuckey, was removed from the match in favor of Koppitsch and it was Frank who was drubbed 50–6 but was just warming up for the next one. Rose tumbled before Sebek 50–34, shooting 41 out of 68 for .602 to Sebek's 45 for .676. Lattore stopped Wheeler's winning streak, taking the chubby Canton tosser 50–28, hitting .692. Valleau racked up his 3rd straight win, beating Pettit 50–23. Gothard resumed winning ways with a win over Kovacs 50–13 and Kong hung up a win over Miller 50–44.

Field and Stolarik engaged in a ding-dong battle, but Andy nosed Al out at the finish 50–49, throwing 55 out of 88 for .625, while Al had 53 for .602. Score: Detroit 16, Canton 12.

Round Five

Rose flopped completely against Stolarik and lost 50–8, with Andy hitting .760 to Rose's .480. Lattore was nipped by Stuckey 50–39, Elmer hitting .708. Valleau was left on 9 by Sebek who hit .800, 40 in 50, but on the back four courts it was all Detroit. Gothard beat Wheeler 50–38 with .645; Kong won from Pettit 50–39, Field trounced Klink (substituting for Kovacs) 50–18, hitting .709 and Koppitsch nicked Miller 50–42. Score: Detroit 20, Canton 15.

Round Six

Lattore walloped Miller 50–26 and Valleau bowed to Stolarik 50–29. Gothard was nosed out by the aroused Stuckey 50–46 and Kong was polished off by Sebek 50–38. Sebek had 59 out 82 for .720 and Kong had 56 for .688. A nice game. Field went .662 to dispose of Wheeler 50–44, a great rally by Wheeler almost pulling the game out of the fire. Koppitsch eked a 50–45 win over Pettit and Rose walked away from Klink, 50–17 with 31 out 50 for .620. Score: Detroit 24, Canton 18.

Round Seven

Valleau finished a nice performance with a 50–22 win over Klink. Orville shot 42 out of 60 for .700. Gothard dropped a 50–48 game to Miller and Kong lost to Stolarik 50–30. Andy shot .735 to complete a perfect day of 7 wins. Field was surprised by Stuckey and lost to Elmer 50–31. Stuckey has 66 out of 94 for .702. Koppitsch was slaughtered by Sebek 50–5, but Rose although having to pitch 32 shoes to score the 50th point, beat Wheeler 50–42. Rose has 52 out of 82 for .634. Lattore won from Pettit 50–9. Canton promised to return the visit on July 7. The game is slated for Clark Park.

Final scores:
Detroit – 4 3 5 4 4 4 3 = 27
Canton – 3 4 2 3 3 3 4 = 22

Detroit – 27

Player	W	L	Pts	R	DR	SP	Pct
Field	5	2	330	328	106	496	.641
Rose	5	2	292	263	79	422	.623
Lattore	4	3	278	237	72	390	.608
Valleau	4	3	265	247	71	424	.582
Konz	4	3	307	271	75	474	.571
Gothard	3	4	308	298	94	488	.610
Koppitsch	2	2	111	82	18	210	.390
Burt	0	3	85	71	11	178	.398
Totals	27	22	1976	1797	526	3082	.583

Canton – 22

Player	W	L	Pts	R	DR	SP	Pct
Stolarik	7	0	350	313	104	464	.674
Sebek	6	1	349	325	114	442	.735
Stuckey	4	3	288	290	92	480	.604
Wheeler	3	4	302	279	87	468	.596
Kovacs	1	3	101	88	16	226	.389
Miller	1	6	229	243	58	488	.497
Hunt	0	2	16	46	8	94	.489
Klink	0	3	57	78	22	158	.498
Pettit	0	5	121	92	12	262	.351
Totals	22	27	1813	1754	513	3082	.569

– – – – – – –

So the "big" league was on the way. Rose's dream league was in process and his in-depth records offer us some historic moments. One of those was in this first match with the appearance of John Sebek. Sebek was a championship-class pitcher. He had three World Tournament appearances that featured two top-ten finishes. It is not shabby to be ranked in the top-ten pitchers in the world. In 1940, Sebek qualified and placed 9th on a 21–10 record with a 77.7 percent ringer average. His highest finish came in 1946 when he placed on an 18–5 record and a 69.7 percent average. Sebek qualified again in 1949, placing 14th with a 14–16 record and a 69.7 percent average.

Johnny Sebek.

Not only was he a great pitching star, Sebek was a tremendous promoter of the game. He was elected NHPA vice president in 1948 and at about that same time joined NHPA president Arlo Harris's efforts to promote league play in the NHPA and the count-all scoring method. At the time there were many leagues across the country, but the NHPA emphasized tournament play and tournament pitchers.

Next from Lee's journal, a special announcement.

- - - - - - -

The next match for Detroit is scheduled for Northwestern Field on June 29–30. The visitors are to be the Canadian players from all over Ontario and will play under the banner of Toronto.

Weak Canadian Team Easily
Drubbed by Detroit as McLaughlin Stars

The long-awaited clash between Detroit stars and Toronto stars came at Northwestern Field on June 29, but the 6-man team presented by Canada was far too weak to cope with the Americans and took a 28–8 lacing. The best players from Ontario were unable to make the trip, so these six came anyway as a sporting gesture. Manager Rose used 11 players in order to ease the blow. Dean McLaughlin, Dominion Champion, showed his class by winning all his six games.

The visitors were treated to a banquet and later to a party at Rose's home where they stayed all night. Summary:

Detroit – 28

Player	W	L	Pts	R	DR	SP	Pct
Getz	3	0	150	103	27	176	.585
Rizor	3	0	150	82	20	170	.482
Herbert	2	0	100	45	9	108	.416
Arold	1	0	50	32	8	66	.484
Koppitsch	5	1	284	188	55	356	.528
Lundgren	4	1	228	153	47	262	.584
Rose	3	1	181	116	27	238	.487
A. Field	2	1	126	106	35	154	.688
Burt	2	1	138	109	25	202	.539
Gothard	2	1	120	87	21	178	.488
J. Field	1	2	138	84	17	182	.461
Total	**28**	**8**	**1655**	**1105**	**291**	**2092**	**.528**

Toronto – 8

Player	W	L	Pts	R	DR	SP	Pct
McLaughlin	6	0	300	260	89	400	.650
Liston	1	5	205	176	36	380	.463
Morris	1	5	153	135	24	340	.397
Stamper	0	6	126	124	23	308	.402
Lawrence	0	6	145	117	13	360	.325
Aiken	0	6	122	88	9	304	.289
Total	8	28	1048	900	194	2092	.430

- - - - - - -

Indeed Dean McLaughlin was a star in this match and he was a star of the sport throughout Canada and the United States. In recognition of his achievements, he was inducted to the NHPA National Hall of Fame in 1974. He won 13 Canadian national championships, the first in 1937 at age 17 and his last in 1974. He entered two World Tournaments and qualified both times; in 1951 he finished 16th, averaging 73.5 percent ringers, and in 1956 he finished 7th on a 26–9 record with a 74.5 percent ringer average.

- - - - - - -

Ann Arbor Yields Before Detroit's Ringers

Ann Arbor visited Northwestern Field on the evening of July 5th and was walloped 19–6 by the great Detroit team. The visitors, however, exhibited unexpected ability and put up a hard fight and the Detroit powerhouse had to keep in high gear all the way to win.

Al Field led the way for Detroit, winning all five and hanging up an average of .672. Rizor and Koppitsch each took 4 out of 5, Rizor losing to Otto in the 4th round and Frank being nipped by Raab in the last round. Rose played only 3 games, beating Otto and Fisher and losing a close one to the inspired Raab.

Summary:

Detroit - 19

Player	W	L	Pts	OP	R	DR	SP	Pct
Field	5	0	250	100	204	64	302	.672
Rizor	4	1	244	139	189	61	306	.617
Koppitsch	4	1	232	166	176	49	322	.552
Rose	2	1	141	97	131	40	204	.642
Gothard	3	2	204	191	155	36	306	.506
Hammerschmidt	1	1	81	81	57	12	134	.425
Total	19	6	1154	783	914	262	1574	.584

Ann Arbor – 6

Player	W	L	Pts	OP	R	DR	SP	Pct
Raab	3	2	217	203	190	58	316	.601
Otto	2	3	194	220	198	59	338	.586
MacGregor	1	4	133	231	112	24	382	.397
Weinkauf	0	5	140	250	169	40	334	.506
Fisher	0	5	99	250	133	27	304	.437
Total	4	19	783	1154	799	208	1574	.507

- - - - - - -

The Detroit team had a couple of invitational matches and then it was back to national-league competition and a rematch with the Canton team. The Detroit team was made up of a number of talented players, but we are about to see that the other teams in this newly formed league were also highly talented.

Canton Again Loses To Detroit
Victors Qualify to Play for National Title

The return match between Detroit and Canton was played on July 7 at Clark Park and Detroit made it two straight by besting the visitors 26–23.

The Canton boys put up a stiff battle and the result was in doubt until the last round was almost over. Three men led the way for Detroit with 5 wins out of 7 starts, the highest percentage being racked up by Joe Latzko who hit .712. Bill Kong pitched .589 and Lundgren squeezed by with .545.

For Canton, Sebek led the way with .664 but almost on top of him was Stolarik with .661. Each hung up 6 wins in 7 games. Stuckey turned in 5 wins with .591.

A large crowd was on hand to witness this classic match and they were rewarded by a close contest. Detroit took four of seven in each of the first 2 rounds but Canton turned in a surprise by sweeping to victory in 5 games of the third round to take an 11–10 lead. Detroit took 4 games in the fourth round to square the match at 14-all and continued to take 4 games in each succeeding round.

Detroit qualified to meet the winner of the Indianapolis–Fort Wayne series for the national league championship. Summary:

Detroit – 26

Player	W	L	Pts	OP	R	DR	SP	Pct
Latzko	5	2	324	173	298	110	418	.712
Konz	5	2	291	257	271	80	460	.589
Lundgren	5	2	306	240	229	63	420	.545
A. Field	4	3	303	2647	274	88	452	.606
Rose	3	4	258	253	223	61	394	.566
Gothard	1	2	95	119	99	23	186	.532
Rizor	2	5	141	310	195	49	392	.497
Koppitsch	1	3	110	198	79	22	104	.382
Total	26	23	1928	1817	1668	496	2926	.570

Canton – 23

Player	W	L	Pts	OP	R	DR	SP	Pct
Sebeck	6	1	323	209	274	87	412	.664
Stolarik	6	1	341	184	274	92	414	.661
Stuckey	5	2	298	254	266	82	450	.591
Miller	2	5	224	327	234	57	434	.539
Wheeler	2	5	244	312	220	54	438	.502
Hunt	1	6	225	335	215	55	424	.507
Kovacs	1	6	162	315	143	33	354	.402
Total	23	26	1817	1928	1626	460	2926	.555

- - - - - - -

Note: Joe Latzko of Flint, Michigan, was a prime foe and competitor to Lee Rose for years. But for this competition, Rose brought in Latzko as a "ringer" to participate on the Detroit team.

- - - - - - -

~Bulletin~

On July 7, Fort Wayne played at Indianapolis and Indianapolis won by the score of 30–19. Indianapolis averaged .552 and Fort Wayne .540.

Detroit plays at Flint on July 14 and at Ann Arbor on the evening of August 2.

On July 21st, the Indianapolis Moose made it 2 straight wins over Fort Wayne by beating them 25–24 in a match played at Anderson, Indiana. Indianapolis averaged .581 and Fort Wayne .597.

- - - - - - -

The ringer averages turned in by the Detroit players were very impressive, but the other teams were also displaying admirable skills. Next Detroit had a match with another competitive team in the state of Michigan.

July 14 – Berston Field, Flint, Michigan
Detroit 38 – Flint 26

Detroit – 38

Player	W	L	Pts	OP	R	DR	SP	Pct
A. Field	7	1	373	372	309	101	482	.641
Lattore	6	2	379	227	281	83	460	.611
Koppitsch	6	2	334	269	254	74	452	.561
Rose	5	3	381	272	273	73	476	.574
Gothard	5	3	355	297	262	76	482	.514
Rizor	3	5	340	334	277	75	504	.549
Galesky	3	5	313	285	222	53	414	.536
Goodell	3	5	287	346	231	58	480	.481
Total	38	26	2762	2302	2109	593	3750	.562

Flint – 26

Player	W	L	Pts	OP	R	DR	SP	Pct
Latzko	8	0	400	210	361	125	522	.691
Miller	4	4	341	342	289	78	522	.522
Middleton	4	4	328	330	272	74	500	.544
Loney	3	5	296	366	278	67	528	.526
Jones	3	5	289	310	251	60	490	.516
Pinkstaff	3	5	261	386	235	62	492	.458
Pinter	1	7	273	391	220	54	490	.449
Kizer	0	4	86	200	68	17	160	.431
Posadecki*	0	4	28	200	17	5	42	.404
Totals	26	38	2302	2762	1991	542	3750	.531

*forfeited 3 games

The courts were very poor, for altho' they were concrete was outside of a 3 foot radius of the stake and the courts were sand. Flint promised to have the concrete and clay put in for the stake tournament.

- - - - - - -

Rose's description of this next event makes apparent that he was rather proud of his performance— and he certainly should have been. He achieved a career-high ringer average while beating a couple of big-name players and area competitors who year after year stood between him and winning

Michigan state championships. This event was held in 1940, and while Rose was getting older, he was still only 34 years old at the time and a rather young man by pitching standards.

- - - - - - -

Rose Shocks Hitt & Latzko
As Detroit Beats All-Stars

Lee Rose fired a devastating broadside at his two main obstacles to a state title when at Wines Field in Ann Arbor on August 2 he managed both Joe Latzko and Bobby Hitt, who were members of an all-star team which was pitching against Detroit. Rose's win over Latzko came in the second round. Rose had blasted Bill Miller 50–13, with .792 and he waded right into Joe with the same stride. Latzko went right along in his usual confident way, but as Rose continued to pour on ringers, Joe began to look worried and finally with the score 36–33 in his favor, Joe reached his limit of his nerve and he suddenly cracked as Rose won out 50–39. Rose hurled 69 ringers in 88 shoes for .795.

Then, after coasting to 2 more wins over Raab and Weinkauf, Rose met the undefeated Hitt in the final round. Rose never gave him a chance, grabbing an 11–0 lead at the start. After Hitt made it 11–9, Lee went ahead to 21–9. Here Bobby got 3 more and Rose grabbed 6 more to make it 27–12. A little later it stood 37–15! Surprising and rude treatment to the confident Hitt! Hitt got to 30 before Rose went out hitting .764 to Bobby's .718.

Lundgren altho' winning only 2 games, made one of his victims Joe Latzko. Rose averaged .731, his best lifetime total!

Oh yes! Detroit won the match 14 to 11.

Detroit – 14

Player	W	L	Pts	OP	R	DR	SP	Pct
Rose	5	0	250	150	262	90	358	.731
Konz	3	2	225	222	213	64	356	.603
A. Field	2	3	225	190	2638	92	390	.686
Lundgren	2	3	208	214	215	69	336	.640
Middleton	2	3	189	231	204	55	344	.592
Total	14	11	1097	1007	1162	370	1784	.650

Player	W	L	Pts	OP	R	DR	SP	Pct
Hitt	4	1	230	203	269	98	364	.739
Latzko	3	2	227	208	269	88	408	.659
Raab	2	3	182	194	192	54	316	.607
Miller	2	3	206	242	227	71	376	.600
Weinkauf	0	5	162	250	179	49	320	.560
Total	11	14	1007	1097	1136	360	1784	.636

- - - - - - -

Out of the 10 players in this match, eight had averages over 60 percent and one player was just three ringers short of that mark. Every state back in that era had a few great pitchers, but few states could boast of that many 60-percent players. Michigan was a hot bed for skilled horseshoe pitchers. Rose's journal included this newspaper clipping describing the same match—with a little less hype. On balance, though, Rose did get good press coverage before his next big achievement.

- - - - - - -

Unbeaten Detroit Horseshoe Squad Remains That Way

Lattore's unbeaten horseshoe team remained undefeated last night at Wines Field in a match with All-Stars from Flint, Plymouth and Ann Arbor. The Detroiters won the match 14 games to 11. In several of the games more than 70 percent ringers were pitched.

Lee Rose of Detroit was the star of the evening, winning five games with ringer percentages of 79.2, 79.5, 68.8, 64.8 and 76.4.

Bobby Hitt of Plymouth, former state champion, won four out of five for the All-Stars with percentages of 70, 79.7, 72.9, 75.7 and 71.8.

Joe Latzko of Flint, state champion, was able to win only three out of five games, losing to Rose and Carl Lundgren, the latter being the Detroit City Champion.

Rose Shatters Ringer Record
As He Wins City Title

Lee Rose took up on August 3 where he left off on August 2 and set up a new record for ringer average pitched in a city tournament round robin by hitting .715 for 11 games and on August 4, won 7 out of 8 in the finals to take the city title for the first time since 1929.

Round One – Lundgren

Lundgren pounced on Rose from the start and was never headed as he threw 43 out of 52 for .826 and won 50–12. Rose had 32 out of 52 for .615.

In other games, Arold defeated Rizor, J. Field beat Kelly, Gothard beat Williams, Herbert downed Galesky and Koppitsch upset Al Field.

Game Two – Kelly

There was not much to this game. With the score 10–9 in his favor, Rose pounded out a spurt of 14 out of 18 and was leading 36–9; finally winning 50–22, throwing 33 out of 50 for .660. Kelly hit .500.

Al Field broke into the win column by beating Williams; Arold won again beating J. Field; Gothard won from Galesky; Herbert beat Rizor and Lundgren won from Koppitsch.

Game Three – Arold

Spearing 35 out of 46 for .761, Rose easily knocked Arold out of the unbeaten class 50–21. Arold hit .565.

Lundgren defeated Williams and Herbert won from Gothard to stay unbeaten. Al Field came from behind to nose out Galesky, Koppitsch walloped Kelly and J. Field nosed out Rizor.

Game Four – J. Field

Jimmy gave it the "the old college try," but it wasn't enough. He got a 9–1 jump on Rose and held on very stubbornly until he led 30–21, but with 24 out of the last 32, Rose subdued him 50–36. Rose had 48 out of 74 for .648 and J. Field had 43 ringers for .582.

Lundgren kept on his unbeaten way by trimming Galesky, but Herbert fell before Al Field. Gothard whipped Rizor and Koppitsch bested Arold. Kelly beat Williams.

Game Five – Rizor

Rose quickly and mercifully slaughtered his old rival 50–23, piling on 41 out of 54 for .760. Rose had 31 out of the first 36, hitting 7 straight doubles.

Lundgren walloped Herbert to stay in the lead, as Al Field knocked Gothard off. Koppitsch won from J. Field, Williams upset Arold and Kelly defeated Galesky.

Game Six – Koppitsch

Koppitsch began with a weak rush, tossing on 10 out of 12 to take a 12–3 lead. Rose here got a point, then 6, and it was 12–10. Here Rose missed and Frank piled on 6 more. At this point, Rose strung on 8 consecutive doubles and ran ahead 37–18. Eight more out of 10 finished it 50–21. Rose threw 24 out of the last 26 shoes and 34 out of 44 for .772. Frank had 24 out of 44 for .545.

Lundgren won his 6th straight game by erasing 20–11 lead to beat Gothard. Al Field downed Rizor to stay in a tie for 2nd. J. Field beat Williams, Arold nosed out Galesky and Herbert won a close, very good game from Kelly. Each man had 50 out of 76 for .657.

Here, the tournament had a one hour break.

The leaders:

Lundgren	6–0	Rose	5–1
A. Field	5–1	Koppitsch	4–2
Herbert	4–2	Gothard	3–3
J. Field 3–3	Arold	3–3	

Game Seven – Williams

Williams took a 13–6 lead, but Rose with 9 out of 12 went ahead 23–16. Williams battled hard and kept the score to 35–28, with Rose still leading. Here he suddenly weakened and Rose ran out with 4 doubles. Rose threw 40 out of 60 for .666. Williams threw 34 ringers for .556.

Al Field pitched .710 to topple Lundgren from the top perch. Koppitsch nosed out Rizor and Herbert defeated Arold. Gothard beat Kelly and J. Field beat Galesky.

Game Eight – Galesky

This was over swiftly with Rose hitting 23 out of 30 for .776 and winning 50–10.

Lundgren squelched Rizor 50–5 and Al Field crunched Kelly. Koppitsch continued hitting well; beating Williams and Herbert won from J. Field. Gothard slaughtered Arold.

Game Nine – Herbert

The surprising Herbert put up a desperate battle but Rose poured a steady stream of ringers on the peg to steadily draw away. With the score 4–4, Rose got 8 out of 12 to go ahead 12–8. Three doubles by Rose added only 3 more points and then Red brought it up to 15–14. Here Rose hit 13 out of 14 to go ahead 28–14. After a point for Lee, Herbert shot 4 doubles to make it 29–20, but Rose added 9 more points on 3 doubles. After a single which allowed Herbert to pick up 3 on a double, Rose scored 6 on 2 more doubles. Herbert picked up 6 more on a Rose miss and then Lee went out with 3 more doubles, winning 50–29. Rose shot 54 out of 72 for .750 and Herbert had 48 ringers for .667.

Lundgren trounced Kelly and Al Field murdered Arold. Koppitsch won his 7th game in 9 starts in beating Galesky and took 4th place all alone. Gothard beat J. Field and Rizor finally won a game, beating Williams.

Game Ten – Gothard

Gothard was never in the running as Rose mauled over him. Rose won 50–11, shooting 37 out of 48 for .772. A. Field beat J. Field, but Lundgren allowed Arold to win from him purposely to help Arold make the finals. Herbert nosed out Koppitsch, Rizor beat Kelly and Williams won from Galesky.

Game Eleven – Al Field

First place was at stake! Each tossed a double to open and then Rose got a point on a single [ringer]. Rose missed and Al piled in for 6. Rose got another point on a single and then threw a double which Al topped. Field doubled back and scored 3 more. Then doubled again, but Rose covered it. Rose took 3 on a double, a point on a single and 3 more on a double to tie the score 9–9. Al got ahead 15–9 on 2 doubles and a single, but Rose tied it on a single and a double. Rose hit 4 more doubles and a single to 24–15. Field picked up a point on a single, then Rose got 6 more on a double and a single to make it 30–16. Al picked up a little until it stood 34–25, then Rose tossed 16 out of 18 to go out 50–25 and hold first place all alone. Rose shot 56 out of 76 for .737.

Lundgren pitched .809 to bash J. Field 50–1 and tie for second place. Herbert whipped Williams to take 4th place and Gothard trounced Koppitsch to tie him for 5th place. Arold beat Kelly to tie with J. Field for 7th. Rizor beat Galesky.

Rose set a new city tournament record by shooting 433 ringers in 606 shoes for an average of .715. The former record was set by Ed Walls in 1937 when he shot 460 ringers in 648 shoes for .709.

- - - - - - -

The preliminary round-robin stats were printed in *Horseshoe World*, likely because they were provided by Rose. These stats do not include the games played in the finals.

- - - - - - -

Lee Rose Winner of Detroit Title

Lee Rose, secretary of the National Horseshoe Pitchers Association of America and a Detroit, Michigan, resident, was the winner of the Greater Detroit championship August 3. Here are the statistics:

Player	W	L	Pts	R	DR	SP	Pct
Lee Rose	10	1	512	433	157	606	.715
Al Field	9	2	518	467	158	700	.667
Carl Lundgren	9	2	509	430	146	666	.645
Fred Herbert	8	3	501	457	136	760	.601
Carl Gothard	7	4	466	406	126	682	.595
Frank Koppitsch	7	4	455	441	120	758	.581
Harold Arold	4	7	394	308	68	682	.451
James Field	4	7	395	337	82	682	.493
R. H. Rizor	3	8	405	328	80	630	.520
Joe Kelly	3	8	404	330	87	636	.518
Joe Galesky	1	10	334	300	81	650	.461
C. C. Williams	1	10	343	296	75	678	.435
Totals			5246	4527	1314	7850	.576

Finals – August 4, 1940

First Round

Rose easily eliminated J. Field 50–18, 50–13, throwing 69 out of 102 for .676.

A. Field beat Arold 50–23, 50–21, averaging .627. Lundgren beat Koppitsch 50–43, 50–23, averaging .634. Gothard beat Herbert 50–34, 45–50, 50–20, averaging .665.

Second Round

Al Field eliminated Lundgren 50–47, 50–40 with .625 to Lundgren's .614. Rose trounced Gothard 50–40, 50–30, averaging only .607. A rainstorm held up the meet for a while between games and a very strong and swirling wind cut the percentages down.

The strong wind nearly ruined the meet but after an hour's wait, Al Field and Rose decided to play their 3 out of 5 games and get it over with. Meanwhile Lundgren beat Gothard for 3rd place.

Championship Series

Game One

Rose got three on a single and then there was a single each and no score. Field shot a double, but Rose topped it. Rose then missed and Field grabbed 6 points. Field got 3 on another double, 4 more on a single and 3 more on a double to go ahead 16–3. The game was more of a struggle against the wind than a struggle between 2 players. Ringers, misses and points passed along until it stood 33–26 in Al's favor. Here Field shot 5 doubles to get to 39–26 and finally went out 50–36. Field had 49 out of 84 .583 and Rose had only 43 ringers for .512.

Game Two

Field slowly worked ahead until he led 30–16 at the end of 54 shoes. Here Rose got 6 on a double and had another double voided. Field missed and so did Rose, Lee got a point. Rose doubled and Field topped it. Rose scored 6 more on a double and a single and then Al got 3 on a single. Rose got a point on a single and 3 more on a double tied the score at 33. Rose shot 2 more doubles and got 3 on each and managed to stay ahead through the wind to win 50–39 and even the match. Rose had 50 out of 88 for .569 and Field had 49 for .557.

Game Three

With 14 out of 20, Field seized a 17–2 lead. Rose was floundering around, trying to get his shoe to work in the wind. Suddenly he seemed to get the right height to make it ride the wind and hit 2 doubles to make it 17–8. Two doubles by Field scored 6 more to make it 23–8. Rose hit a double over a single to score 3 and a single scored 4 more as Field missed and it was 23–15. Rose picked up another point with a single and then got away for 6 on a double as Al missed. Rose shot another double, but Field topped it. Field came back with a single and Rose dropped on another double to go into the lead 25–23. Rose whipped on his 4th straight double but Field topped it and came back with a double which scored 3. Rose threw a double over a single to go ahead again 28–26, but Field duplicated to lead 29–28. Rose triplicated to lead 31–29. Rose doubled again but Field topped it and doubled back to score 3 more and go back in front 32–31. Rose doubled again over Al's single and again led 35–34. The terrific strain was telling on Field, while Rose had calmed down now and looked confident. Al missed his next two and Rose with this start whopped on five straight doubles to run the game out. Rose finished this game with 30 out 34. For the game, Rose had 50 out of 68 for .735 and Field had 46 ringers for .632.

Game Four

After Rose had pitched .735 to win that 3rd game, Al Field looked like a "dead bird." Al threw only 6 out of 16 to open the 4th game, but Rose did not play the part of a killer, for he only threw 9 out of 16 to take the lead 14–6. Field here hit 3 straight to go ahead 15–14. Field missed, but Rose only threw a single to lead 17–15. Field got a point on a single and then banged on 3 doubles to go ahead

22–17. Here he missed and Rose could only throw a single. Lee threw another single but Al hit a double to lead 25–20. Field shot another double, but Rose topped it. Rose got 3 on another double, but Field topped his third double and came back with another which scored 6 as Rose missed. Al led 31–23. Rose got 3 on each of 2 doubles and 2 points on 2 singles to tie the score at 31 all. Lee doubled and Al topped it. Al singled and Lee doubled to lead 34–31. Lee singled and Al doubled to tie it 34–34. Al singled and Lee doubled to lead 37–34.

Lee singled and Al doubled to tie it at 37–37. Again Al doubled and got 3, then singled and Lee doubled to tie the score at 40–40. Rose doubled again, but Field topped it. Rose got in for a point on a single then shot a double. Field missed with both shoes and Rose led 47–40. Then Rose missed! Field could only get 4, but shot in another double to tie it at 47–47. Al got his first one on but missed with the second. Rose very calmly dropped a double over the stake to end the struggle. Rose shot 51 out of 78 for .654 and Field had 50 for .633.

It was Rose's first city title since 1929 and his winning of the title, his record-breaking performance in the round robin and his trouncing of Hitt and Latzko the night before that certainly stamps him as a state title threat!

Lee Rose, 1940 Detroit City Champion.

- - - - - - -

The fascinating level of detail provided for the *Horseshoe World* account offers another amazing record-keeping feat by Rose. The fact that he set ringer percentage records in the preliminary round invites us to wonder who had been keeping track of the previous city tournaments. Most cities in the country held annual city-wide horseshoe-pitching tournaments, but not very many kept records from year to year. So who in Detroit was keeping such detailed records? The Rose journals offer enough evidence to make an educated guess.

The following article is an update that Rose, as NHPA secretary-treasurer, wrote on the national league standings for *Horseshoe World*.

- - - - - - -

National Team League Results

Indianapolis Moose horseshoe team took two straight matches from Fort Wayne to become the other finalist along with Detroit in the National Team League. The playoff between these two teams will probably take place in September.

In the first match, which was played at Indianapolis on July 7, the home team won by a score of 30–19. Indianapolis averaged .552 to Fort Wayne's .540. Arlo Harris, George Johnson and Lowell Edmonson each won six out of seven for Indianapolis, averaging .567, .618 and .600, respectively. For Fort Wayne, Glenn Rust, Henry Lemke, Elmo Polley and Honor Maxwell each took four out of seven.

The second match, played at Anderson, Ind., was a much closer battle with Indianapolis winning five games out of seven in the last round to win the match 25–24. Indianapolis averaged .581 and Fort Wayne hit .597. Arlo Harris and Lowell Edmonson each won five for Indianapolis with averages of .665 and .598 and for Fort Wayne, Guy Binkley, Honor Maxwell and Ernest Recht each captured six out of seven, with averages of .758, .658 and .647, respectively.

The series between Detroit and Indianapolis ought to be close. Indianapolis has thrown 3,408 ringers in 6,004 shoes for an average of .567, while Detroit has thrown 3,465 ringers in 6,008 shoes for an average of .573.

- - - - - - -

This next entry in the Lee Rose journals is another extensive, detailed account of one of his events. As usual, he keeps it interesting. Though the match he describes took place over 70 years ago, it's easy imagine being there as the shoes were pitched.

- - - - - - -

My Seventeenth State Tournament
Held at Berston Field, Flint
August 16 – September 1, 1940

August 16 – Qualifying

Twenty-six men entered the meet and 25 of them qualified today by pitching 8 fifty-shoe games for total points, Latzko, defending champion, was not required to qualify.

Hitt was high with 957 points and .750 average. Lundgren was 2nd with 904 points and .690 average, while I was third high with 896 points and .660 average. Others to qualify in the high 16 were: Carl Gothard, Phillip Carra, Al Field, Glen Portt, Ray Gorsline, James Skinner, Bill Miller, Fred Herbert, M. B. Getz, Jim Burt, Frank Koppitsch and John Egen.

Others who failed to qualify were: Ray Middleton, R. H. Rizor, Harold Arold, Steve Pinter, Charles Pinkstaff, Mark Goodell, N. E. Shepard, Joe Kelly, Louis Craft and Jim Davis.

August 17 – Round 1

Glenn Portt, of Mayville, hit the best game of the first round by beating Egan 50–20 with .740. Bobby Hitt ran .714 to dispose of old Jim Skinner 50–25 and Latzko nosed out Gorsline 50–44 with .690. Gothard trimmed Getz 50–35 with .680 and Bill Miller upset Lundgren 50–45 with .678 to Lundgren's .667. Phil Carra (formerly Carl) took Jim Burt 50–36, pitching .672. Rose trailed Fred Herbert 30–16 at the end of 50 shoes, but finished the game hurling 28 ringers in the last 36 shoes to win out 50–42. Rose hit .602. Field nosed out Koppitsch 50–48 with .597.

ROUND 2

Latzko got 'er into high gear against Gothard, beating him 50–23 with 55 out of 66 for .833 to Gothard's .697. Hitt stayed right along with Joe by trampling Carra 50–8 with .792. Rose opened his game with Portt by shooting 16 out of 18 to take a 23–0 lead and coasted to a 50–26 win, hitting .697. Field hit .666 to beat Lundgren 50–41 and Miller downed Koppitsch 50–44. Burt won from Skinner 50–14, pitching .750, Egan defeated Herbert 50–29 and Getz beat Gorsline 50–45.

ROUND 3

Latzko pounded out .737 to administer the initial defeat to Miller 50–26 and Hitt went .704 to down Herbert 50–21. Rose had no trouble in beating Burt 50–21, throwing only .634 to turn the trick. Field went down to his first defeat when Gorsline beat him 50–24. Carra beat Egan 50–45, Koppitsch upset Gothard 50–45, Portt won from Skinner 50–32 and Lundgren won his first game by beating Getz 50–46. The leaders: Latzko 3–0, Hitt 3–0, Rose 3–0, Miller 2–1, Field 2–1, Portt 2–1, Carra 2–1.

ROUND 4

Rose hit the high game in round four when he landed on Gothard with 51 out of 70 with .728 to win 50–30. Latzko had to go 114 shoes to down Field 50–37, throwing 78 ringers for .684 to Al's 77 ringers for .675. Hitt beat Portt 50–35 with .680. Lundgren went .708 to wallop Carra 50–21 and Skinner won his first game in beating Koppitsch 50–33. Gorsline downed Burt 50–36, Getz beat Herbert 50–43 and Egan defeated Miller 50–40. Leaders: Latzko 4–0, Hitt 4–0, Rose 4–0, Miller 2–2, Field 2–2, Portt 2–2, Carra 2–2, Lundgren 2–2, Gorsline 2–2, Getz 2–2, Egan 2–2.

ROUND 5

Getz fired the shot heard 'round the state by upsetting Joe Latzko 50–33 with .707 to Joe's .634. Hitt squelched Burt 50–17 and Rose remained in a tie for first place by angling to a 50–24 victory over Egan. Lundgren was the high percentage man in this round in beating Koppitsch 50–20 with .743. Gorsline nosed out

Gothard 50–46, Skinner won from Carra 50–23. Field topped Miller 50–33 and Herbert upset Portt 50–38. Leaders: Hitt 5–0, Rose 5–0, Latzko 4–1, Field 3–2, Lundgren 3–2, Gorsline 3–2, Getz 3–2.

ROUND 6

This round followed an hour halt for dinner and the fireworks started right in with Gothard jumping on Bobby Hitt and rounding him up 50–26 with .673.

Rose, with a chance to take the undisputed lead, flopped miserably against Field and lost 50–31, throwing only .446! Latzko jumped back into a tie for 1st by trouncing Carra 50–29. Gorsline continued his winning ways by beating Koppitsch 50–31, Lundgren walloped Portt 50–17 and Getz beat Miller 50–24. Burt won from Herbert 50–31 and Skinner hung up his third straight win on Egan 50–47. Leaders: Hitt 5–1, Latzko 5–1, Rose 5–1, Gorsline 4–2, Lundgren 4–2, Getz 4–2, Field 4–2.

ROUND 7

Rose rang up the highest percentage in this round when he pounced on Skinner with 39 out of 50 for .780 to win 50–13. Hitt trimmed Egan 50–27 and Latzko defeated Koppitsch 50–37. Lundgren and Field remained on the heels of the 3 leaders, Lundgren winning from Gorsline 50–37 and Field beating Getz 50–40. Portt beat Burt 50–18, Gothard walloped Miller and Herbert nicked Carra 50–44. Leaders: Rose 6–1, Hitt 6–1, Latzko 6–1, Lundgren 5–2, Field 5–2.

ROUND 8

Rose continued his super-power pitching on Carra. With Carra leading 15–14, Rose strung on 11 straight doubles to run up to a lead of 44–15 and finally won 50–24. Rose hurled 39 out of 52 for .750. Hitt and Latzko also won. Hitt won from Field 50–45 and Latzko from Portt 50–37. Lundgren was knocked off by the up and coming Gothard 50–38. Getz beat Skinner 50–42, Herbert won from Koppitsch 50–44, Burt defeated Miller 50–37 and Egan downed Gorsline 50–22. Leaders: Rose 7–1, Hitt 7–1, Latzko 7–1, Lundgren 5–2, Field 5–3, Getz 5–3.

ROUND 9

Latzko hit 51 out of 66 for .773 to slaughter Skinner 50–21, Hitt pitched .740 to trounce Miller 50–24, but Rose fell before his old jinx, Getz, 50–46. Lundgren beat Herbert 50–37, Field beat Egan 50–46, Carra won from Koppitsch 50–41, Gorsline nosed out Portt 50–49 and Gothard won his 4th straight by beating Burt 50–32. Leaders: Hitt 8–1, Latzko 8–1, Rose 7–2, Lundgren 6–3, Field 6–3, Getz 6–3.

ROUND 10

Lundgren got in the grove on Latzko and showered a terrific stream of ringers on the stake as he rolled farther and farther ahead. At the end of 50 shoes Lundgren had thrown 38 ringers and was ahead 24–15. With 37 out of the next 42, the stolid slinger rolled to a lead of 49–16, but had to pitch 22 more shoes before winning 50–27. Lundgren threw 91 ringers out of 114 for .798 and Latzko had 89 ringers for .772.

On the adjoining court, Hitt assumed the sole lead by defeating Rose 50–33. Rose threw 4 doubles to take a 6–0 lead and a point made it 7–0. With 11 out of 12, Hitt ran ahead 13–7, but Rose hit 9 out of 10 to go back in the lead 14–13. A point, a six and two 3 and 3's made it 26–14 for Bobby and a little later at the end of 60 shoes it stood 40–20. In the last 38 shoes of the game, Rose walloped on 31 ringers, but Hitt also threw 31 and Rose could only gain 3 points. Hitt had 76 out of 98 for .775 and Rose had 69 for .709.

Gothard crashed out .730 to smack Field 50–38, Miller tripped Gorsline 50–32, Burt beat Egan 50–35, Carra outlasted Portt 50–44, Herbert won from Skinner 50–42 and Koppitsch crimped Getz 50–40. Leaders: Hitt 9–1, Latzko 8–2, Rose 7–3, Lundgren 7–3.

ROUND 11

Latzko shattered Herbert 50–12 with .796, Gorsline rolled up .759 to beat Carra 50–20, Lundgren banged on .732 to slam down Burt 50–22, Hitt rolled on .720 to smother Getz 50–8, Field went .703 to beat Skinner 50–27, Portt beat Miller and Koppitsch nosed out Rose 50–46 as Lee fell down to .555. Leaders: Hitt 10–1, Latzko 9–2, Lundgren 8–3, Rose 7–4, Field 7–4, Gothard 7–4.

ROUND 12

Hitt nosed Lundgren out in a close game 50–46, pitching .680 to Charlie's .654. Latzko won from Rose 50–38, hitting .691 to Lee's .648. Field was nicked by Carra 50–34 and Gothard was tripped by Portt 50–42. Getz and Gorsline pulled into a 5-way tie for 4th as Getz beat Egan and Gorsline won over Herbert. Miller beat Skinner and Koppitsch beat Burt.

ROUND 13

Hitt beat Koppitsch 50–32 with .720, Latzko rapped out .772 to trounce Burt 50–15, Lundgren eased a win over Egan, Getz slapped on .788 to wallop Portt 50–11, Gothard rammed on .759 to whip Skinner 50–19, Field went .731 to defeat Herbert 50–23 and Rose finally got back on the bandwagon with a 50–21 win over Ray Gorsline, pitching .680. Miller also beat Carra. Leaders: Hitt 12–1, Latzko 11–2, Lundgren 9–4, Rose 8–5 , Field 8–5, Gothard 8–5, Getz 8–5, Gorsline 8–5.

ROUND 14

Rose hit the high game by jumping on Lundgren with 57 out of 78 for .744 to beat him 50–41 and go into a 5-way tie for 3rd. Latzko hit .712 to drag Hitt off his high perch 50–42. Field beat Portt 50–19, Gothard beat Carra 50–48 and Getz downed Burt 50–46. Egan beat Koppitsch, Herbert downed Miller and Gorsline dropped Skinner.

ROUND 15

Latzko trounced Egan and Hitt dittoed on Gorsline to remain tied for first. The 5-way tie for 3rd continued as Lundgren hit .834 (30 out of 36) to beat Skinner 50–8, Getz beat Carra, Field won from Burt, Rose trounced Miller and Gothard trimmed Herbert.

- - - - - - -

Before continuing with the August 18th competition, let's take a moment to examine what has just happened. This was a state tournament, not a World Tournament—though it was held in the competitive state of Michigan.

In one day, a fifteen round-robin eliminations of 50-point games were played; that's a grueling feat. Today's World Tournament (and most state tournaments) use 40-point games and generally a given day's competition is limited to five games.

Toward the end of the first day's competition at this 1940 Michigan state tournament, those players had to be nearing exhaustion. Still, they were turning in incredibly high percentage games.

Then on the second day, described below, several additional games were played as tie-breakers to establish the positioning for the finals. In today's competitions, those ties would have been broken by players' established ringer percentages. In my view, that would have been a fair choice back in 1940 as well—especially considering that the previous day's competition was basically a preliminary round to seed the eight qualifying players for the finals. They all must have loved the sport!

- - - - - - -

August 18

Hitt won 1st position from Latzko 50–29, hitting 61 out of 76 or .803. The 5-way for 3rd was decided by a round robin which resulted as follows: Rose and Lundgren each won 3 of 4 games to again tie for 3rd, Rose beating Lundgren, Field and Gothard and losing to his perennial jinx, Getz. Lundgren defeated Field, Getz and Gothard, Hitting .808 on Field. Field took 5th by beating Getz and Gothard, but Getz and Gothard tied for 6th. Rose and Lundgren decided 3rd on a toss of a coin and Rose won the toss. Gothard beat Getz for 6th. The top eight:

1. Hitt	5. Al Field
2. Latzko	6. Gothard
3. Rose	7. Getz
4. Lundgren	8. Gorsline

Finals

Hitt and Gorsline shortened their series to 2 out of 3 by agreement and Hitt easily won in two games 50–21 and 50–21, hitting .709 and .722. Latzko disposed of Getz in 3 straight games 50–41, 50–43 and 50–14. Lundgren whipped Field 3 straight games 50–40, 50–37 and 50–22.

Rose had little difficulty in beating Gothard 3 straight games 50–11, 50–28 and 50–33. In the middle of this series it grew dark and began to rain. A halt was made for a while before being able to finish. However, the sky remained dark and things did not look well for the finals. The 5th place flight went on first with Field beating Gorsline 50–11, 25–50 and 50–24. Getz won from Gothard 50–43, 36–50 and 50–24. Gothard defeated Gorsline and game 50–35 for 7th place.

Rose vs. Latzko

Rose won the toss and walloped on a double which was promptly topped by Latzko. Joe came right back with a double which Rose just as promptly topped. Rose fired another double but Latzko covered it and shot back with a double. But Rose, pitching just as fast as the speedy Joe, slapped a double right on top of Joe's. For the fifth time, Rose pounded on a double and Latzko suddenly missed with both shoes as the tension got to him. A state champion was about to fall!

Rose came back with a single and a close one which scored a point, then doubled to score 3 more and doubled again and scored 6! The score was now 16–0 and the surprising Rose had banged out 15 out 16.

The Flint rooters were aghast at this turn of events. Rose threw a single and Joe doubled to score his first 3 points, but missed both shoes to allow Lee 3 more on a single. Rose doubled, but Latzko topped it. Again the shaking champ missed both shoes and Rose came in for 4 to make it 23–3! Then Rose missed both shoes and Latzko climbed in for 6. Latzko singled back and Rose's high-dropping shoes picked up a point, then scored 3 more on a double and another point on a single to make it 28–9. Rose shot on another double which Latzko topped. Latzko doubled back, but Rose dropped the cancellers on top. Rose came back with a single but Joe could only get one on for no-count. Again, Joe could only throw a single and Rose picked up three more on a double to make the 31–9.

Then it suddenly began to rain, but not quite hard enough to halt play. Latzko got a point on a single, then 6 more on a double. Another Latzko double was topped by Rose. Rose then could only manage a single and Joe picked up 3 more on a double and another point on a single to make it 31–20. Joe's rooters were taking heart once more and it was raining a little harder. Rose got a point on a single and then three times in a row Joe doubled, scoring 3 points each time to make it 32–29. Here, however, Joe missed one and Rose bore down with a double to take 3 and then doubled again and scored 6 more as Latzko missed! Score: 41–29.

There was a single each for no count; Rose then topped a Latzko double and doubled back to score 3 more. Still another double by Rose scored three to make it 47–29, Latzko got 3 on a double and singled and Rose tossed on another double to go out. Game score:

	Pts	R	DR	Sp	Pct	4-On
Rose	50	54	19	74	.730	9
Latzko	32	49	17	74	.662	9

Rain began pelting down very hard, forcing spectators and players to scurry for shelter. For quite a while, the better part of an hour, it continued to drizzle and it was not a fitting time to play, but as it finally slackened to a fine misty drizzle, the courts were fixed and Rose and Latzko began their 2nd game. Rose was very anxious to continue, but Joe looked rather indifferent. Latzko opened with a single and Rose promptly dropped a double over it. Rose doubled back and scored 6 more as Joe missed. 9–0!

Two more singles brought in 2 more points to make it 11–0 and then Latzko suddenly threw down his shoes and remarked that he needed a different pair and walked away to get them. Rose felt that this was not the right way to act, but said nothing. Joe came back with another pair of shoes after several minutes and the game was resumed.

Latzko banged on 17 ringers in the next 20 shoes, but Rose was unable to get going and threw only 8 ringers, so Latzko had gone ahead 28–11. The rain began to fall harder again and some spectators began leaving. Rose rallied with 13 out of 14, to make the score 29–23, but hit another off streak of 6 out of 12 and Joe ran ahead 38–23. Rose then started a rally and banged on 15 out of 16, but could only score 6 while Joe with 14 out of 16, scored 3. A 3 and a 6 put Joe ahead 47–29. Rose threw 10 out of the next 12 to make it 48–41, but the slippery shoes missed here and Latzko went out. Score:

	Pts	R	DR	SP	Pct	4-On
Rose	41	60	22	88	.682	11
Latzko	50	62	20	88	.704	11

Blinding rain deluged everything and the rest of the meet for that day was completely washed out.

Hitt had won the first 2 games from Lundgren and Field had beaten Getz, the first game in their series for fifth.

A consultation was held in the field-house. By all odds, the meet should have continued the next day, but Latzko and Hitt had to work, while Rose needed to do several things before leaving for Des Moines on Tuesday.

I will always feel that if that tournament had finished that day without any rain to interfere, Lee Rose would have come out as the state champ!

To be continued ——— September 1!!!

- - - - - - -

In this next section, Lee Rose writes about his trip to the 1940 World Horseshoe Pitching Tournament. As with so many of his previous entries, it's unusual in its incredible game detail and description. There are very few personal accounts of attending and participating in a World Tournament from seven decades ago, much less a championship pitcher, hall of famer, and national officer.

In 1940, five years had passed since the last World Tournament. Ted Allen had won all three tournaments held in the 1930s and he was expected to win all the World Tournaments held in the next decade. This 1940 tournament, however, featured a couple of newer pitchers who helped raise the sport to a higher level of competitiveness. Fernando Isais of Mexico was making his third appearance, and Guy Zimmerman from Sac City, Iowa, won the Iowa state tournament (held at the same time and at the same venue) in record-breaking fashion to make everybody notice his presence.

Isais, now a hall of fame member and one of the all-time great pitchers, went on to win eight world championships, six of which were in consecutive years. Zimmerman, made a mark in the sport as well. He was a great exhibition pitcher and earned the 1954 men's world champion before being elected to the NHPA Hall of Fame.

Lee Rose was there for it all, and his writing puts us right in the stands.

- - - - - - -

On Tuesday morning, August 20, Bertie, Koppitsch and I started for the west in the "Escritoire." We rolled out to Coldwater and then dipped south into Indiana, passing through Goshen, Peru, Logansport, Decatur and finally reached Springfield, Ill. We arrived there in time to get into the fair and meet met a few of the horseshoe pitchers who were gathering for the Illinois state meet which opened on the 21st. After pitching for a while on the 12 splendid courts which are covered by a huge tent, we drove out to Williamsville where we got beds for the night.

The next morning we went back to the fair and met all the Illinois boys. Mr. Tanner was there, of course, as was Earl Graves, Aden Swinehammer, Ellis Griggs, Joe Dubie, Gaylord Peterson, and many others, including Dave Swanson and Joe Bennett. During the morning, Mr. W. A. Banta of Indianapolis stopped by on his way to Des Moines.

I pitched some more, but could only entice one player to play me, the famous left-hander Greenberg of Chicago and I rewarded his kindness by slaughtering him one game. I was starting another game with Herbert Patrick of Fairbury when the courts were ordered cleared for the finals. So we watched a couple of rounds and with several handshakes we left. It was then about 3:00 p.m.

We headed northwest through Beardstown, Macomb and crossed the Mississippi into Burlington, Iowa, just before dark.

We continued on through Mt. Pleasant, Fairfield and into Ottumwa. From then on we watched for a good place to stop for the night but found none.

We passed through Albia and Knoxville and having found no place to stay, continued on into Des Moines, arriving about 2:00 a.m. E.S.T. We got cabins at an auto camp, but found better rooms in a house the next morning for the balance of out stay.

[The next day] we entered the fairgrounds and went to the horseshoe courts to meet whoever was there. The Iowa State Tournament was going on when we arrived and we slipped into the stands and watched for a while. Then I was discovered sitting there and the whirl started.

I got some practice and went pretty well. I also got to make an announcement about the *Horseshoe Compendium* on the P.A. system.

My PAL, Mr. Page (NHPA president) came around after a while and we shook hands.

The courts gradually filled up with the "greats" who were steadily pouring in from all points.

The "Constitutional Meeting" was held that evening in the cow barn.

- - - - - - -

Rose tacked in some clippings covering the World Tournament, including this article on the Iowa state tournament and how Zimmerman won the title to suddenly become the state's favorite son.

- - - - - - -

Zimmerman Shoe Champ
Guy Shatters World Record

Guy Zimmerman, Sac City, unofficially shattered a world record for ringer accuracy Friday as he won the Iowa State Horseshoe Tournament with 16 straight victories.

Pitching against Walt Miller of Marshalltown, he threw 51 ringers in 52 shoes for a percentage of 98.07. He won 50–0. The present world record for accuracy in tournament play is 97.5, set by Ted Allen, Boulder, Colo., in 1935. Zimmerman's mark was unofficial because no scorekeeper was on duty for the game.

Second in the meet was Lyle Brown, Des Moines, whose only loss was a heartbreaker to Zimmerman. Zimmerman took the game 50–49 after Brown had taken a 49–48 lead. [In that game, Harry Henn of Kentucky served as a special referee for this game. He called one foul shoe on Brown and threw out the shoe, claiming Brown had stepped across the foul line as he made his delivery.]

Third money went to Dale Dixon of Des Moines with a playoff victory over Eddie Packham and Ted Harlan, two other Des Moines stars. Dixon gathered 250 points in the playoff, Packham 247 and Harlan 191.

Zimmerman's brilliant performance stamped him as one of the favorites for the World Tournament, opening at the fairground this morning. The final standings:

	W	L
Guy Zimmerman, Sac City	16	0
Lyle Brown, Des Moines	15	1
Dale Dixon, Des Moines	12	4
Eddie Packham, Des Moines	12	4
Ted Harlan, Des Moines	12	4
Glen Tassel, Rippey	10	6
John Paxton, Fairfield	10	6
W. F. Johnson, Stockport	7	9
Cliff Hanson, Gilbert	7	9
Russ Butterfield, Des Moines	7	9
Wellington Taylor, Grand River	7	9
Virgil Murphy, West Point	7	9
Walt Miller, Marshalltown	3	11
Bud Fisher, Des Moines	2	14
C. L. McGinnis, Ade	2	14
Homer Lippencott, Grinnell	Withdrew	
J.F. Fisher, Titonka	Withdrew	

- - - - - - -

Then Rose gets back to describing his participation at the 1940 World Tournament.

- - - - - - -

My Fifth World Tournament

I shall pass over quickly the hour of living hell and agony it required to throw my qualifying shoes and simply state that I qualified easily.

Thirty-two men faced the barrier as play began on the morning of August 24, or rather, just after dinner, due to rain having fallen the night before.

My 32-man schedule as appearing in the *Horseshoe Compendium* was used. I was No. 20.

- - - - - - -

The qualifying round must have been "hell and agony" since he didn't mention much about his accomplishment in making the Championship Class. We can detour a bit from the journals and print out the list of qualifying pitchers.

Ted Allen's name is not among the qualifiers since the defending champion is not required to qualify, even if five years have passed since the previous

World Tournament. That makes 33 qualified players, which is strange because now a bye is required due to the odd number of players. One might expect that the top 31 qualifiers would be selected to avoid that complication.

Many notable pitchers, including ten hall of fame members, are included on this list:

– – – – – – –

32 Qualifiers

Player City	Qual	Pct.
Fernando Isais, Mexico City, Mexico	532	.830
Ira Allen, Fresno, California	526	.835
Casey Jones, Waukesha, Wisconsin	523	.825
Guy Zimmerman, Sac City, Iowa	521	.815
Dale Dixon, Des Moines, Iowa	515	.805
C. C. Henson, Arlington, Virginia	813	.800
Dean Brown, Oakley, California	510	.810
Roland Kraft, Lecompton, Kansas	505	.790
Johnny Sebek, Canton, Ohio	504	.785
Ellis Griggs, Plainville, Illinois	504	.780
Syndey Harris, Minden, Kansas	498	.775
Robert Bales, Kansas City, Kansas	496	.765
John Paxton, Fairfield, Iowa	491	.735
Sam Somerhalder, Guide Rock, Ks.	492	.765
Alvin Dahlene, Lawrence, Kansas	490	.755
Lyle Brown, Des Moines, Iowa	480	.770
Harvey Elmerson, Milwaukee, Wis.	488	.745
Edward Packham, Des Moines, Iowa	486	.735
Lee Rose, Detroit, Michigan	486	.735
Alvin Gandy, Topeka, Kansas	485	.720
Wilbert Steinkamp, St. Louis, Mo.	482	.766
Howard Robinson, Nebraska City, Ne.	476	.730
Gaylord Peterson, Varna, Illinois	475	.705
Thorsten Madsen, Good Thunder, Mn.	474	.715
Joe Bennett, Deer Creek, Illinois	471	.680
Ervin Hosier, South Gate, Cal.	469	.710
Wellington Taylor, Grand River,Ia.	465	.675
Nels Peterson. Jeffers, Minnesota	464	.675
W. O. Maxwell, Hicksville, Ohio	464	.675
Lefty Steinman, St. Louis, Mo.	461	.700
W. F. Johnson, Stockport, Iowa	452	.645
Joe Dubie, Peoria, Illinois	452	.685

My first opponent was the famous Wisconsin state champion, Charles "Casey" Jones. I started out bravely enough, shooting a double over his single to score three points. I doubled back and he covered me and he doubled back and I covered him. I missed one, [and] he missed one also, but he got a point, 3–1. Jones then hit 2 doubles and to my discomfort, I missed completely both times and he was out in the lead 13–3. Here he missed one and I hit a double to score 3 more and with only a single in the next inning, I picked up another point to make it 13–7.

I fired on another double, but the slow machine-like pretzeling Jones laid a pair on top. Jones hit another double and scored 3, picked up a point on a single, got 3 more on a double and 6 more on another double to lead 26–7. Here he threw a single and I managed to lay on a double to score 3. Then I missed with both shoes, but Casey let me off easy by throwing a single. Jones doubled and I topped. I doubled again and scored 3 more to make it 29–13.

I singled and Casey doubled and came back with another double which scored 6 as I missed. Score: 38–13. Jones doubled again, but I covered him this time. I could only throw a single back but Jones only took a point. Jones doubled and again I topped him and came back with a double which he topped. Again Casey doubled and scored 3, but on the next pitch he missed the stake with both shoes for the first time and I climbed in for 6 to make it 42–19.

I doubled and Jones topped. Jones missed one, but I also missed one, but took a point. Then I missed both shoes, but Casey missed both his also! Jones doubled, but I dropped two on. I doubled back and Jones topped me. Again Casey doubled, but I banged two on top and came back with my fourth double only to have Jones drape two more over mine. Jones drove on another double and scored 3, but I scored 1 on a single on the next throw [...] but Casey missed both shoes! Again I only singled and Casey doubled to go out. Score:

	Pts	R	DR	SP	Pct	4-On
Rose	24	47	17	72	.653	12
Jones	50	55	22	72	.764	2

Lyle Brown dropped Ted Allen 50–41 with 78 out of 94 for .829 to Allen's 74 ringers for .787. Isais hit the high game by beating Elmerson 50–23 with 73 out of 84 for .869. Zimmerman beat Gandy 50–27 with 71 out of 82 for .865; Sebek beat Bennett 50–33 with 68 out of 82 for .829 and Ira Allen beat Packham 50–23 with 52 out of 64 for .813. Other winners were: Dean Brown, Somerhalder, Kraft, Griggs (who won the Illinois tournament) Henson, Bales, Dixon, Paxton and Dahlene. Taylor dropped out entirely, so Sid Harris drew a bye.

ROUND TWO

In the second round, I drew the bye. Isais again hit the highest game, this time beating Sebek 50–26, throwing 79 out of 94 for .840. Ted Allen defeated Roland Kraft, the one-armed star from Kansas, 50–25, throwing 67 out of 80 for .837. Zimmerman beat Bales 50–22 with 59 out of 72 for .820. Other winners were Elmerson, Jones, Paxton, L. Brown, Dubie, I. Allen, Robinson, Somerhalder, Nels Peterson, Gandy and Hosier.

ROUND THREE

I was called upon to face — Fernando Isais!!! Isais opened with a double to score 3, but I topped his second double. I doubled back again and tied the score at 3-all. I singled, but Isais only picked up a point. He doubled, but I covered him. Again I singled and Isais hit a double for 3 to make it 7–3.

Here he missed one, but I could only get one also and he scored a point. Then a double gave him 3 more in the following inning. Again he doubled but I topped it. Again, I only singled but again Isais only took a point. Isais doubled twice more and scored 3 on each one, but his next double was topped. I shot a double back and picked up 3 to make it 18–6.

Again I doubled but Isais topped. He singled and I hit my fourth straight double to make it 18–9. Here I missed both shoes and Fernando whopped in a double to go to 24. Isais doubled again, but I topped him. I missed one and Isais doubled to reach 27. He missed one here and I climbed in for 3 on a double to make it 27–12.

He got 3 more on a double and dittoed, score 30–15. I doubled and he topped. He scored 3 on another double and I topped him next double. He got 3 on each of his next two doubles and I topped his next and doubled again only to have him take me with his 7th double. Score now 39–15.

Then he missed both shoes, but I could only score 3. I doubled twice more and picked up 3 on each to make it 39–24. I singled and he hit a double, scored 3 on another double and I topped his next. Score was 45–24. I singled and he doubled to make it 48–24. He doubled again and I kept the game going by topping it. I doubled again but he topped and his 7th straight double put him out as I missed one. Score:

	Pts	R	DR	SP	Pct	4-On
Rose	24	58	20	78	.743	13
Isais	50	66	28	78	.846	13

Zimmerman slaughtered Robinson 50–4 with 54 out of 58 for .931. Sid Harris beat Nels Peterson 50–13 with 49 out of 56 for .875. Ted Allen beat Packham 50–19 with 69 out of 80 for .862. Jones rapped Steinkamp 50–10 with 42 out 50 for .840. Somerhalder downed Dubie 50–18 with 72 out of 88 for .818 and Gandy nosed out Ira Allen 50–46 with 82 out of 102 for .803 to Ira's 81 ringers for .794. Dean Brown neat Bennett, Paxton won his 3rd straight by upsetting Lyle Brown. Other winners were: Griggs, Steinmann, Kraft, Dixon and Madsen. Sebek drew the bye.

ROUND FOUR

I met Nels Peterson of Jeffers, Minnesota, starting right out by slamming out six straight doubles and had him 15–0 before missing one shoe to let him score 3. Two more doubles gave me 6 more and a single gave me another point.

He topped my next double and scored 3 on another double to make it 22–6. Again I hit a I hit a streak of six straight doubles to make it 31–6. I missed one here and he picked up 3. I got a point on a single and he did the same, now 32–10.

He missed here, but I only got 3. I doubled but he topped and he got 1 more on a single. I wound up the game with four more doubles. Score:

	Pts	R	DR	SP	Pct	4-On
Rose	50	48	20	56	.857	9
Peterson	11	35	12	56	.625	9

The Lee Rose Story

This was the high game of the 4th round. I was now tied for 12th place with Dubie, Harris, Kraft, Henson and Madsen.

Zimmerman beat Paxton 50–20 with 58 out of 68 for .853; Ira Allen beat Bales 50–25 with 75 out of 88 for .852; Jones defeated Somerhalder 50–37 with 84 out of 102 for .823; Lyle Brown won from Hosier 50–30 with 73 out 90 for .811 and Dixon downed Dahlene 50–26 with 61 out of 76 for .802. Gandy beat Steinmann and Sebek nosed out Dean Brown 50–48, with each player shooting 82 out 106 for .773. Isais beat Harris. Other winners: Packham, Ted Allen (beating Griggs), Madsen, Henson, Dubie and Bennett. Elmerson drew the bye.

ROUND FIVE

I met Alvin Dahlene of Lawrence, Kansas. Dahlene opened with a double and scored 3 and I doubled back over his single to tie it. I picked up a point on a single and 3 more on a double. He grabbed 3 on a double, then I topped his double and he topped mine. He doubled again and scored six as I missed, Dahlene led 12–7.

We then had consecutive four-deads. Then he missed both shoes and I grabbed 6 to go ahead 13–12. Again I doubled and picked up 3, but he topped my next double. He scored a point on a single and then I doubled over his single to lead 20–13.

He grabbed 3 on a double and then we had three consecutive 4-on. I took a point on a single, then I scored 3 on each of two doubles to go ahead 27–16. I singled and he hit for a double for 3. He singled but I missed with both shoes and Alvin scored 3 more to make it 27–22.

Here he missed and I dropped in for 6. He picked up 3 on a double and I did the same. Rose led 36–25. I doubled and he topped. I got a point on a single, then missed and he scored 4 to make it 37–29. I got 3 on a double and he dittoed. I took 3 more on each of two more doubles to make it 46–32. Dahlene got to 38 on 3 doubles before missing one shoe and letting me go out with a double. Score:

	Pts	R	DR	SP	Pct	4-On
Rose	50	61	24	80	.762	11
Dahlene	38	58	20	80	.725	11

I am still tied for 12th with Lyle Brown, Harris, Somerhalder, Gandy and Henson.

Ted Allen slammed Gandy 50–24 with 79 out of 88 for .897 to Gandy's 70 ringers for .795; Jones beat Gaylord Peterson 50–18 with 57 out of 66 for .864; Isais trounced Steinkamp 50–8 with 43 out of 52 for .826 and Zimmerman beat Madsen 50–27 with 48 out of 60 for .800. Other winners were: Griggs, Ira Allen, Sebek, Harris, Henson, Bales, Maxwell, Dixon, Paxton, and Elmerson. D. Brown had the bye.

ROUND SIX

I met Joe Dubie of Peoria, Illinois. I doubled to open and scored 3. Dubie gained a point on a single, then doubled and I topped. There was a single for each for no-count, then Dubie scored 3 on a double and led 4–3.

I picked up a point on a single, 3 more on a double, had a double topped by Dubie and scored 3 more on another double to lead 10–4. Joe got a point on a single then missed and I piled on for 6. I got 3 on another double, then had a double topped. Joe got 3 on a double, then doubled again and I topped it. I scored 4 on a single to make it 23–8.

Dubie took 3 on a double, then repeated this twice more to come up to 17 before I topped his 4th double. Then I grabbed two 3's on two doubles before Dubie topped my fourth double, I led 29–17. My fifth double took 3 more, then I got away with 4 more on a single. Score: 36–17.

Dubie got 3 on each of two doubles, then I took 3 on a double. Again Dubie got 3 on a double and then threw another double which I topped. I grabbed 3 more on another double to lead 42–26. Dubie got 3 on each of two more doubles and I dittoed with the same to make it 48–32.

Dubie topped my 3rd double and came back with another double which I topped. Dubie topped my 5th double and came back with another double, but I hit my 6th double on top. Here I missed one, but got a point as Joe missed one. I missed both shoes next turn and Dubie banged on two for 6 points and came back with another double, which gave him 13 out of his last 14. I topped his double and came back with a double and finally went out as Dubie missed one. Score:

Pts	R	DR	SP	Pct	4-On
Rose	50	67	25	86	.779	12
Dubie	38	63	23	86	.732	12

Jones trounced Dahlene 50–13 with 54 out of 60 for .900; Harris landed on Dean Brown and banged him down 50–16 with 70 out of 78 for .897; Ted Allen beat Bales 50–27 with 94 out of 110 for .854 to Bales 85 ringers for .772; Isais beat Somerhalder 50–31 with 85 out of 102 for .833; Kraft lost to Zimmerman 50–23 who had 75 out of 92 for .815. Other winners were: Gandy, Hosier, Elmerson, Griggs, Dixon, Bennett, Lyle Brown, Packham, Ira Allen and G. Peterson

This was all for the first day, with the standings:

1.	Zimmerman	6 0	12.	Harris	4 2	23.	Hosier	2 4
2.	Isais	6 0	13.	D. Brown	4 2	24.	Madsen	2 4
3.	Jones	6 0	14.	Gandy	4 2	25.	Dahlene	1 5
4.	Ted Allen	5 1	15.	Paxton	4 2	26.	N. Peterson	1 5
5.	Ira Allen	5 1	16.	Somerhalder	3 3	27.	G. Peterson	1 5
6.	Elmerson	5 1	17.	Henson	3 3	28.	Robinson	1 5
7.	Griggs	5 1	18.	Bales	2 4	29.	Maxwell	1 5
8.	Dixon	5 1	19.	Kraft	2 4	30.	Steinman	1 5
9.	Rose	4 2	20.	Packham	2 4	31.	Steinkamp	0 6
10.	L. Brown	4 2	21.	Dubie	2 4	32.	Taylor	0 6
11.	Sebek	4 2	22.	Bennett	2 4			

[This list is down to 32 players because F. W. Johnson was qualified in error by tournament officials.]

In this first day of the tournament I had played 5 games. I had thrown 281 ringers out of 372 shoes for an average of .755!! Probably the best day of pitching I had ever done! I had scored only 198 points and had thrown 106 doubles. I had "four-deads" 57 times.

Second Day – August 25

ROUND SEVEN

I met Sam Somerhalder of Guide Rock, Nebraska. I hit a double over a single to score 3 and threw another double which he covered. He doubled again and scored 3 and scored 3 more on another double. Again he doubled, but I topped him. I singled back, but he hit his fifth double to go ahead 9–3. Sam singled and

I got in for a point. I doubled and scored 3 and he topped the next double. Sam singled again and I dropped on for two more ringers to go ahead 10–9.

Again I doubled and scored 3 more and hit a fifth double which he topped. Sam picked up a point on a single and then doubled, but I banged two ringers on top. This was 23 out of 28 for me. Then I missed both shoes and Sam shot ahead with a double. I picked up a point on a single, but Somerhalder grabbed two 3's on two doubles to lead 22–14.

We then had two four-deads. Sam scored 3 more on each of his next two doubles and his seventh double scored 6 to make it 34–14. He scored his last 16 while I was getting 6. Score:

	Pts	R	DR	SP	Pct	4-On
Lee Rose	20	43	15	64	.672	9
Somerhalder	50	53	21	64	.828	9

Zimmerman, Isais and Jones each won their 7th straight game and Ted Allen, Ira Allen, Elmerson, Griggs and Dixon each won their 6th in 7 starts.

ROUND EIGHT

I met Joe Bennett of Deer Creek, Illinois. Bennett scored 3 on double, then I scored 3 on each of two doubles and four more on a single. Joe picked up a point on a single and 3 more on each of two doubles to tie it at 10-all. Joe then missed and I grabbed 6. I led 16–10.

I doubled again but he topped it. Joe got a point on a single and I picked up 3 on a double. 19-11. I hit another which Bennett topped it. Again Joe got a point on a single and 3 on a double, then I covered his double and came back with a double which scored 3 to make it 22–15.

I singled and he doubled to take 3 and the next two times were four-on. Then he missed one and I doubled to score 3. My next double was topped. Bennett scored 3 on a double, then I covered his next double. My next 3 doubles each scored 3 points and I led 34–21.

Joe got 3 more on a doubled and again I dittoed for 40–27. I missed for the first time and Bennett scored 4. I grabbed 3 more on a double. It was 46–32. I missed again with both shoes and Bennett got in for 4. He singled back and scored 4 more as I whopped over the stake with both shoes. It was 46–40!

Then — — three times in a row Joe doubled and scored 3 points each time to go ahead 49–46. Joe singled here and I tied it up with a double and another double put me out as Bennett missed his second shoe. Score:

	Pts	R	DR	SP	Pct	4-On
Rose	50	60	22	82	.732	7
Bennett	49	57	18	82	.695	7

Casey Jones was dropped from the ranks of the unbeaten by Johnny Sebek 50–45. Each threw 66 ringers out of 84 shoes for .785. Zimmerman, Isais, Ted Allen and Elmerson all won, but Ira Allen was upset by Kraft. I was tied for 11th place with L. Brown, Harris, D. Brown and Somerhalder.

ROUND NINE

I met the Nebraska state champion Sidney Harris, of Minden. It was short—but to me—not sweet!! There was a four-dead to open, then Harris got 4 on a single and 3 on a double, another four-dead and he scored 3 more on a double. I topped his next double then missed and he got 6 more to make 16–0.

Then he missed one and I got my first 3 on a double. It was just one of those things and I could not cope with the flying Harris. Score:

	Pts	R	DR	SP	Pct	4-On
Rose	13	30	10	50	.600	7
Harris	50	42	18	50	.840	7

Zimmerman and Isais continued undefeated and Ted Allen, Jones, and Elmerson trailed closely with just one loss each. Sebek, Harris, Dean Brown, Somerhalder and Griggs stood 6–3. I was tied for 15th.

ROUND TEN

I met W. O. Maxwell of Hicksville, Ohio. Maxwell got off to an 8–0 lead as he scored points on 2 singles and 3 each on two doubles. Here however, I hit six straight doubles and went ahead 12–8. Maxwell got a point on a single and 3 on a double to tie it at 12. I got 3 on a double and after a 4-on, Maxwell got two 3's on two doubles to go ahead 18–15.

I topped a double and tied it with another double. My next double scored 6, then Maxwell topped my fourth double and my 5th double over his. I picked up a point on a single to lead 25–18, then missed both shoes and Maxwell shot in for 6. I moved along after that with 12 out of the next 14 to lead 39–24 and after Maxwell had scored 3 on a double, I went on out with 15 out 18. Score:

	Pts	R	DR	SP	Pct	4-On
Rose	50	63	24	80	.787	11
Maxwell	31	56	19	80	.700	11

Standings: Zimmerman and Isais 10–0; Ted Allen, Elmerson 9–1; Bales upset Jones 50–47 with 91 out of 114 for .797; Jones 8–2; Ira Allen 8–2; Gandy 8–2; Dixon 8–2; Lyle Brown 7–3; Dean Brown 7–3; Sebek 6–4; Harris 6–4 Somerhalder 6–4; Griggs 6–4; Rose 6–4.

I was tied for 11th. I had 331 points, 477 ringers, 177 doubles, 648 shoes pitched for .736.

ROUND ELEVEN

I met Jonny Sebek of Canton, Ohio. Sebek scored 3 on a double to open and followed with 3 more on a single. Then I wheeled on 3 doubles and scored 3 on each one to lead 9–6. I added another point on a single and 3 more on a double to make it 13–6. Johnny then strung on 7 doubles in a row, but I had 12 out of the same 14 and still led 13–12.

I added 3 on a double and 3 more on a single to lead 19–12. Then I really "got hot"! Ten consecutive times I poured on a double against the perspiring Sebek. At the end of the first 52 shoes, I had thrown 45 ringers and was in front 34–12. But the fighting Canton boy was far from beaten. After picking up 3 on a single, I missed both shoes, Sebek hit four doubles but only scored 3 points to still trail 34–18.

I got a point on a single, then Johnny whammed on six more doubles to pick up 6 more points to creep up to 35–24. I took 3 on a double and two four-deads followed. Sebek got a point on a single, then scored 3 each time on 3 more doubles and 4 more on a single to tie it at 38–all.

Here he missed one and I got a point. I scored 3 on a double and he topped my next double. Sebek picked up 3 on a double and at 100 shoes I led 42–41. I had 79 ringers to Sebek's 78. Sebek then missed both shoes and what did I do but miss both of mine also. I got 1 point, however. I singled back, but Johnny could only get in for a point. Then Sebek doubled but I hung two on top. I finished the game with three doubles which each scored 3! Score:

	Pts	R	DR	SP	Pct	4-On
Rose	50	88	36	112	.785	22
Sebek	42	84	332	112	.750	22

Zimmerman 11–0; Isais 11–0; Ted Allen 10–1; Jones 9–2; Ira Allen 9–2; Dixon 9–2; Elmerson 9–2; Lyle Brown 8–3; Dean Brown 8–3; Gandy 8–3; Harris 7–4; Somerhalder 7–4; Griggs 7–4; Rose 7–4; Bales 6–5; Sebek 6–5.

This was a record game for me! I was still tied for 11th, averaging .743.

ROUND TWELVE

I met Lefty Steinman of St. Louis, Missouri. After a four-dead to open, Lefty took 3 on a single and I came back with the same. Then I scored 6 on a double to take a 9–3 lead. My next double was topped, but then Steinman missed and I got 3 more on a single. Then I missed and Lefty grabbed 3 on a single. He picked up 3 more on a double, a point on a single, six on a double and 4 on a single as I labored in an off-streak. Lefty led 20–12.

Then I suddenly started to click and reeled off 8 consecutive doubles. Four of them scored 3 each and the other four were voided. I led 24–20.

Steinman again took 3 on a double and threw another double which I topped. I picked up a point on a single and hit four more doubles, one of which scored 3 and one scoring 6. I added 3 more on a single and led 40–26. Lefty got a point on a single, but remained behind as I hooked on seventeen out of twenty to end the game. Score:

	Pts	R	DR	SP	Pct	4-On
Rose	50	60	24	80	.750	12
Steinman	37	53	19	80	.663	12

Standings: Zimmerman 12–0; Isais 12–0; Ted Allen 11–1; Jones 10–2; Ira Allen 10–2; Elmerson 10–2; Lyle Brown 9–3; Dixon 9–3; Rose 8–4; Dean Brown 8–4, Griggs 8–4.

I was tied for 9th place.

I met Dean Brown, Southern California champion. After two four-deads, I took 3 on a double then missed one and Brown took a point. Brown doubled and I topped him. I missed one again, but Brown again only got a point. Dean threw a single and I doubled to go ahead 6–2. I singled again and this time Brown doubled to make it 6–5.

Brown doubled and I missed both shoes! He was up 11–6. I chugged on four doubles but the first one was the only one which scored 3. Then with a Brown double on, I missed both shoes again and Dean led 17–9.

He took 3 more on a double, then I hit three more doubles and picked up 6 points to make it 20–15. Dean got 3 on a double and doubled back but I topped him. I missed both shoes again, but Dean caught the fever and missed both of his. He did get a point however, and grabbed 3 more on a double to lead 27–15.

I picked up 3 on a double and had next double topped. Brown missed one and I got in for 1 point and at 50 shoes, Brown led 27–19. Again I took 3 on a double and shot another double which was covered. Brown doubled again and scored 3, but I grabbed 3 more on a double to make it 30–25. I doubled again, but Brown topped and doubled back, but I also topped. I could only single and Brown looped on a double. He doubled again which I topped. Again I could only single and Brown hit another double to lead 36–25.

I got in for 3 on a double and doubled again but Brown topped. Brown singled, but I could not get in there in the clutch and he got a point. Again he doubled but I topped him. The next three innings definitely decided the contest, for Brown threw three doubles in a row and picked up 3 points on each to lead 46–28. I picked up 6 on two doubles, but Brown whopped on three more doubles to go out. Score:

	Pts	R	DR	SP	Pct	4-On
Rose	34	69	27	92	.750	16
Brown	50	75	30	92	.815	16

Standings: Zimmerman 13–0; Isais 13–0; Ted Allen 12–1; Jones 11–2; Ira Allen 11-2; Elmerson 10–3; Dixon 10–3; Lyle Brown 9–4; Dean Brown 9–4; Gandy 9–4, Rose 8–2; Sebek 8–5; Harris 8–5; Somerhalder 8–5; Griggs 8–5.

I met Thorsten Madsen of Good Thunder, Minnesota. This game was featured on the P.A. system with Vincent Dearing of San Francisco doing the announcing. After a four-dead, I got a point on a single. Madsen then scored 3 on a double and point on a single. Then he missed and I piled in for 6.

The next three innings saw four-dead, then Madsen missed one and I took 3 on my fifth double. My sixth double was topped. Madsen got a point on a single, then he missed and I piled in for another 6 to put me in the lead 16–5.

I hit two more doubles, scoring 3 more on the second one and from there on out I was never threatened. Score:

	Pts	R	DR	SP	Pct	4-On
Rose	50	48	18	60	.800	6
Madsen	22	38	12	60	.634	6

Standings: Zimmerman 14–0; Isais 14–0; Ted Allen 13–1; Jones 12–2; Ira Allen 12–2; Elmerson 11–3; Dixon 11–3; Lyle Brown 10–4; Gandy 10–4; Rose 9–5; Dean Brown 9–5; Bales 8–6; Sebek 8–6; Harris 8–6; Somerhalder 8–6; Griggs 8–6.

I was tied for 10th place.

I met Dale Dixon of Des Moines, Iowa. Dixon started the game in a red-hot mood by slamming ten consecutive doubles on the stake and had me 18–0. He threw 27 out of the 28 shoes and had me 24–1.

I never had a chance after that, but fired away in an effort to go places. With 19 out of my next 22 shoes, I had pulled up to 24–18 and had Dixon looking worried. With three doubles, however, Dale made it 30–18 and after I had scored 3 on a single, Dixon threw 5 more doubles and it stood 36–21. I took 3 on a double, then with seven out of eight he stood in the lead 46–24. Dixon had to throw fourteen out of sixteen before going out. Score:

	Pts	R	DR	SP	Pct	4-On
Rose	27	69	25	92	.750	18
Dixon	50	77	33	92	.836	18

Standings: Zimmerman 15–0; Isais 15–0; Ted Allen 14–1; Jones 13–2; Ira Allen 13–2; Dixon 12–3; Elmerson 11–4; Gandy 11–4; Lyle Brown 10–5; Rose 9–6; Bales 9–6; Sebek 9–6; Harris 9–6; Somerhalder 9–6; Griggs 9–6.

I was still tied for 10th.

ROUND SIXTEEN

I met Ervin Hosier of South Gate, California. This game will always haunt me as "one of those things." I scored 3 on a double to open and he dittoed. There were four ringers on in the next two innings, then I scored 3 more on a double. A four-dead followed and he then scored 3 on a double to tie it at 6–6. We each had 12 ringers out of the first 14 shoes at this point.

Hosier got a point on a single, then two more four-deads followed. I took 3 on a double and he dittoed to lead 10–9. He grabbed 6 on another double, then I topped another double. Hosier, who had only won three games so far, certainly was going strong. I picked up 3 on a double and he got a point on a single to make it 17–12. Then I began to bear down and whacked on four doubles to go ahead 21–17.

I got another point on a single, 3 on a double and six on another double. Another point on a single made it 32–17 and it looked as if I were on my way to a victory. I doubled again but he topped it and came back with another double, but I topped that one. He got a point on a single, then got 6 on two more doubles to close in and trail by 8 points. I grabbed 3 on a double and Hosier took a point on a single. I got a point on a single, then he topped my double. There was a ringer each for no count, then I grabbed 3 more on a double and a point to lead 40–25.

Here I missed and he got 3 on a single. Then he missed and I missed too, but I got a point. I doubled and he topped and he doubled and I topped. He got 3 on a double, then 4 on a single and 3 more on a double to tie it at 41–41. He doubled and I topped and I doubled back and he topped. Hosier doubled again and got 3, then I dittoed. I got a point on a single to go ahead 45–44.

I doubled and he topped. This was 100 shoes pitched. Then I missed and with a chance to go out, Hosier only threw a single to lead 47–45. He doubled, but I topped. I doubled again and got 3 to lead 48–47. I singled, but Hosier only got in for a point as the strain was too much. Hosier doubled again, but once more I dropped two on top. I missed one and Hosier finally hit a double to go out. Score:

	Pts	R	DR	SP	Pct	4-On
Rose	48	81	30	112	.723	17
Hosier	50	80	27	112	.714	17

Standings: Zimmerman 16–0; Isais 16–0; Ted Allen 15–1; Jones 14–2; Ira Allen 14–2; Dixon 13–3; Gandy 12–4; Lyle Brown 11–5; Dean Brown 11–5; Elmerson 11–5; Somerhalder 10–6, Rose 9–7; Bales 9–7; Sebek 9–7; Harris 9–7; Griggs 9–7. I was tied for 12th.

ROUND SEVENTEEN

I met Ira Allen of Fresno, California. Three doubles and a single gave Allen a lead of 10–0, but I picked up a point on a single and 3 on a double to make it 10–4. Allen got a point on a single, then I hit into him with five straight doubles and rolled ahead 13–11.

Here I missed, but Ira only took 4. Two doubles put me ahead again 16–15, but here Allen streamed on nine straight doubles and ran up a lead of 33–16. I piled on six straight doubles and came up to 25 and then Allen hit 10 out of 12 to lead 43–26. Three doubles brought me up to 35 before Ira scored 3 on a double. I then hit four more doubles, scoring 3 on each of the first three to make it 46–44. But Allen topped my fourth double and came back with a double which put him out as I missed. Score:

	Pts	R	DR	SP	Pct	4-On
Rose	44	64	25	86	.744	11
Ira Allen	50	66	23	86	.767	11

Standings: Zimmerman 17–0; Isais 17–0; Ted Allen 16–1; Jones 15–2; Ira Allen 15–2; Dixon 14–3; Gandy 12–5; Lyle Brown 12–5; Dean Brown 12–5; Elmerson 11–6; Somerhalder 11–6; Bales 10–7; Sebek 10–7; Harris 10–7; Griggs 10–7; Rose 9–8. I was now in 16th place.

This was the last round on August 25th. I met Gaylord Peterson of Varna, Illinois. Peterson opened with 10 out of 12 and led 8–0, but four doubles put me up to 18. Peterson worked ahead again 23–19. Then 13 ringers out of my next 16 put me ahead again 37–33. I was never threatened after that. Score:

	Pts	R	DR	SP	Pct	4-On
Rose	50	48	16	68	.705	5
Peterson	41	46	16	68	.676	5

The greatest game of horseshoe ever pitched occurred in this round when Zimmerman's 17-game winning streak was snapped by Ted Allen. Zimmerman opened the game by tossing 18 straight doubles ringers and had Allen down 21–0. At 48 shoes, Guy had Allen down 24–12 and through the next 46 shoes held his advantage, leading 39–25 at the end of 94 shoes.

Allen here hit 12 doubles in a row to come up to only 28 as they had four-on in nine consecutive innings. Allen got a point on a single, then laid on 10 more doubles and crawled ahead of Guy 41–39. Allen had just thrown 61 ringers out of his last 64 shoes and Zimmerman had pitched 40 out of 46 and failed to move off 39. However, Guy moved to 48 with 6 doubles then the champ fired 6 doubles back and went out. Score:

	Pts	R	DR	SP	Pct	4-On
Ted Allen	50	145	65	164	.884	50
Zimmerman	48	145	64	164	.884	50

Standings: Isais 18–0; Zimmerman 17–1; Ted Allen 17–1; Jones 16–2; Ira Allen 16–2; Dixon 14–4; Lyle Brown 13–5; Dean Brown 12–6; Elmerson 12–6; Gandy 12–6; Bales 11–7; Sebek 11–7; Harris 11–7; Griggs 11–7; Somerhalder 11–7; Rose 10–8. I was 16th.

August 26th – Round Nineteen

I met — — — Ted Allen, World's Champion! Ted opened with two doubles, scored 3 on each and led 6–0. Then he missed one and I hit a double to score 3. I doubled again and to my surprise, Allen missed both shoes and I led 9–6! I suddenly realized that Ted was not fully warmed up as yet and I began to pitch very, very slowly to keep him cold. I scored a point on a single and dittoed in the next inning to lead 11–6.

Slowly and to Ted's chagrin, I reeled off six straight doubles to roll up to 20. Allen scored 3 on each of two doubles, then we had three straight four-deads. My fourth double scored 3 and my fifth double was topped. I led 23–12. Ted then picked up 3 on each of three doubles and a point on a single to make it 23–22.

Four times in a row I scored 3 points on a double and was out in front 35–22! I continued to throw doubles, running my string up to nine, but the last five did not score, for the sweating Allen voided them with the first five of a string of 11 doubles which put him ahead 40–35.

I got 3 on a double to make it 40–38. Allen got a point on a single, then doubled, but I topped. I singled back and Allen took 3 on another double to lead 44–38. I doubled over his single to make it 44–41 and he doubled over my single to lead 47–41.

Allen doubled again, but I topped it and came back with another double which scored 3 to make it 47–44. I hit another double, but Ted topped it and came back with another double which put him out. Score:

	Pts	R	DR	SP	Pct	4-On
Rose	44	76	28	96	.791	15
Allen	50	78	31	96	.812	15

Zimmerman hit 41 out of 44 for .932 to beat Gaylord Peterson 50–0 and Alvin Gandy upset Fernando Isais 50–28 with 74 ringers out of 86 for .860 to halt his string of wins at 18 and create a triple tie for the tournament lead.

Standings: Ted Allen 18–1; Fernando Isais 18–1; Guy Zimmerman 18–1; Jones 17–2; Ira Allen 17–2; Dixon 15–4. Lyle Brown 13–6; Gandy 13–6; Bales 12–7; Sebek 12–7; Harris 12–7; Dean Brown 12–7; Somerhalder 12–7; Elmerson 152–7; Griggs 12–7; Rose 10–9. I was still 16th!

ROUND TWENTY

I met Alvin Gandy of Topeka, Kansas, fresh from his win over Isais and he was "too hot to handle." He scored 3 on a double and 4 on a single, then we had "four-on" six consecutive innings before I got 4 on a single to make it 7–4. A little later it stood 13 to 7 in favor of Gandy and after that it ceased to be a game.

Gandy banged on six doubles to run up to 28, and continued right on to win 50–11. Score:

	Pts	R	DR	SP	Pct	4-On
Rose	11	45	145	66	.682	13
Gandy	50	58	26	66	.879	13

Standings: Ted Allen 19–1; Zimmerman 19–1; Isais 19–1; Ira Allen 18–2; Jones 17–3; Dixon 15–5; Lyle Brown 14–6; Gandy 14–6; Bales 13–7; Sebek 13–7; Elmerson 13–7; Harris 12–8; Dean Brown 12–8; Somerhalder 12–8; Griggs 12–8; Rose 10–10, Kraft 9–11; Dahlene 8–12; Packham 8–12.

ROUND TWENTY-ONE

I met John Paxton of Fairfield, Iowa. With four out of six, I led 4–3, but Paxton here hit six doubles to go ahead 12–4. I never caught him after that through a heart-breaking game. I got up to 12–10 and he shot ahead 18–10.

I brought it up to 19–17, he went ahead 23–17 and I made it 23–20. He went ahead 30–20 and later led 37–25. Five doubles aided me to make it 37–34, then after he had reached 41, I rallied to bring it to 41–40, but faltered here and he won out. Score:

	Pts	R	DR	SP	Pct	4-On
Rose	40	69	25	98	.704	14
Paxton	50	72	24	98	.734	14

Standings: Ted Allen 20–1; Zimmerman 20–1; Isais 20–1; Ira Allen 19–2; Jones 18–3; Dixon 16–5; Lyle Brown 15–6; Gandy 15–6; Bales 14–7; Sebek 14–7; Dean Brown 13–8; Somerhalder 13–8; Elmerson 13–8; Griggs 13–8; Harris 12–9; Rose 10–11; Kraft 10–11; Dahlene 8–13; Paxton 8–13; Packham 8–13; Henson 8–13. Still in 16th place.

ROUND TWENTY-TWO

I met Howard Robinson of Nebraska City, Nebraska. He scored 4, then we had four-on five straight times before my 6th double scored 6. After he made it 6–6, I whacked on five doubles to shoot ahead 24–6. I kept ahead to the finish after that. Score:

	Pts	R	DR	SP	Pct	4-On
Rose	50	50	20	66	.758	8
Robinson	33	42	14	66	.636	8

Isais came from behind to nick Guy Zimmerman 50–48. With the score 7–6 in favor of Isais, the two pitchers had "four-dead" eight times in a row before Isais got a point. Isais led 11–6, but at the end of 50 shoes, Zimmerman was ahead 12–11 and was in the midst of a string of doubles which he ran up to 17 straight to lead Fernando 33–11.

After a single, Zimmerman hit 6 more doubles to lead 42–14. No one conceded Isais a chance at this point, but the great Mexican never batted an eye. He plopped on five doubles to make it 42–30, then Guy got 3 more on a double to reach 45–20. Isais strung on six more doubles to make it 45–26, then missed one and Guy made it 48–26. Guy doubled and Isais covered and shot another double which scored 6 as Zimmerman missed and it was 48–32.

Isais doubled again but Guy topped. Zimmerman got only two singles as Isais scored two 3's to make it 48–38, then Zimmerman "blew" completely as Isais scored 6 more to reach 44 and another 6 to go out!!! Score:

	Pts	R	DR	SP	Pct	4-On
Isais	50	109	48	128	.851	35
Zimmerman	48	109	48	128	.851	35

Clayton Henson also surprised by upsetting Casey Jones. Standings: Ted Allen 21–1; Isais 21–1; Ira Allen 20–2; Zimmerman 20–2; Jones 18–4; Lyle Brown 16–6; Gandy 16–6; Dixon 16–6; Bales 15–7; Sebek 15–7; Harris 13–9; Dean Brown 13–9; Somerhalder 13–9; Elmerson 13–9; Griggs 13–9; Rose 11–11; Kraft 10–12.

ROUND TWENTY-THREE

I met Bob Bales, the Missouri champion from Kansas City. Bales was in the midst of a great winning streak and things looked bleak for me. We started out with two "four-deads," then Bales got a point on a single, 6 on a double and 3 more on a double to have me 10–0. I got 3 on a double and he dittoed. I got a point on a single, then missed and saw him grab 6 and another point on a single made it 20–4.

I hit four doubles, a single and two more doubles, but Bales still was ahead 23–10. Here I seemed to crumble up and Bales got 6 on a double, 3 on a double, 3 on a double and 6 more on a double, and was ahead 42–10! What happened after that just plain broke Bob Bales' heart.

He doubled and I topped it. I doubled and got 3 to make it 42–13. I doubled again and he topped it. He singled and I dropped on a double to make 42–16. My fifth double scored 3 more to make it 42–19 and my sixth double was stopped by Bales. Bales got a point on a single and led 43–19. Bales doubled back, but I topped him. I doubled again and grabbed 3 and scored 3 more in the next inning to make it 43–25. I hit my fourth double, but Bales voided it. However, my fifth, sixth and seventh doubles each scored 3 points to make the score 43–34 as Bales began to look worried.

Here I missed one and Bob climbed in for 3 to move to 46–34. I started inexorably forward again, taking 3 on a double as Bales missed one and the score was 46–37. I hit another double, but Bales topped it. He could only single back and again I doubled to reach 40.

Again I doubled and Bales, shaking with worry, missed both shoes! It was 46–46! Again I doubled and took 3 more to go ahead 49–46. Here I missed one and Bales tied it with a double. Then Bales missed one and I wound it up with another double!! I shot 41 out of the last 44! Score:

	Pts	R	DR	SP	Pct	4-On
Rose	50	68	28	88	.772	12
Bales	49	66	23	88	.750	12

Standings: Ted Allen 22–1; Isais 22–1; Zimmerman 21–2; Ira Allen 21–2; Jones 19–4; Gandy 17–6; Lyle Brown 16–7; Sebek 16–7; Dixon 16–7; Bales 15–8; Harris 14–9; Dean Brown 14–9; Griggs 14–9; Somerhalder 13–10; Elmerson 13–10; Rose 12–11; Kraft 11–12; Paxton 10–13; Henson 10–13.

ROUND TWENTY-FOUR

I met Wilbert Steinkamp of St. Louis, Missouri. Wilbert started with a double and got 3 and then for a while the "Tiger" stalked the courts in Des Moines!! Eleven consecutive times I poured a double on the stake and ran ahead 30–3.

This was 23 out of 24 and added to the string in the game before, it was a streak of 64 out of 68! This was the greatest streak of my career to date! A percentage of .941! I beat Steinkamp. Score:

	Pts	R	DR	SP	Pct	4-On
Rose	50	45	18	52	.865	3
Steinkamp	21	34	9	52	.654	3

I was high man in this round! And still in 16th place. Standings: Ted Allen 23–1; Isais 23–1; Zimmerman 22–2; Ira Allen 21–3; Jones 20–4; Gandy 18–6; Lyle Brown 17–7; Bales 16–8; Sebek 16–8; Dixon 16–8; Harris 14–10; Dean Brown 14–10; Somerhalder 14–10; Elmerson 14–10; Griggs 14–10; Rose 13–11; Kraft 12–12; Paxton 11–13; Henson 10–14; Dahlene 9–15; Packham 9–15.

ROUND TWENTY-FIVE

I met Ellis Griggs, Illinois state champ from Plainville. We really had a good game! Griggs opened up strongly and put me in the hole at the start by flinging on nine consecutive doubles. He only scored 12 points on this string, however. I scored 3 as he missed one shoe, then he hit three more doubles to make it 18–3.

I scored 3 more as he missed one, then he hit three more doubles to reach a score of 24–6. Again he missed one, but got the extra point and then strung on four more doubles! He had 41 ringers out of 44 shoes and led 37–6.

Then out of the midst of ruin I launched out with a nice string of eight consecutive doubles which brought the score to 37–24. Griggs, however, was not shaken in the least, but pounded back with six straight doubles to run it to 49–24. I staved off inevitable defeat for a while with another run of six doubles which brought it to 49–36 before I missed one and allowed him to go out. Score:

	Pts	R	DR	SP	Pct	4-On
Rose	36	64	25	82	.780	14
Griggs	50	69	29	82	.841	14

Standings: Ted Allen 24–1; Isais 24–1; Zimmerman 23–2; Ira Allen 22–3; Jones 21–4; Gandy 19–6; Lyle Brown 18–7; Bales 17–8; Dixon 17–8; Sebek 16–9;

Somerhalder 15–10; Elmerson 15–10; Griggs 15–10; Harris 14–11; Dean Brown 14–11; Rose 13–12; Kraft 12–13; Paxton 12–13; Henson 11–14.

This was the last round of August 26th. I met Harvey Elmerson of Milwaukee, Wisconsin. Elmerson pitched a strong steady game and led throughout. He led 18–7 and I rallied to make it 18–15. He shot ahead to 30–16, but a 13 out of 14 spurt enabled me to bring it up to 30–28. He moved away again to 37–28 and I never threatened after that. Score:

	Pts	R	DR	SP	Pct	4-On
Rose	37	62	41	86	.721	10
Elmerson	50	68	24	86	.779	10

Casey Jones nicked Fernando Isais 50–48 to allow Ted Allen to hold the lead all along. Standings:

Ted Allen	25–1	Griggs	16–10	Bennett	8–19
Isais	24–2	Somerhalder	15–11	Hosier	8–18
Zimmerman	24–2	Dean Brown	15–11	N.Peterson	7–19
Ira Allen	22–4	Harris	14–12	Madsen	7–19
Jones	22–4	Rose	13–13	Maxwell	6–20
Gandy	20–6	Kraft	12–14	Robinson	6–20
L. Brown	19–7	Paxton	12–14	Steinkamp	5–21
Bales	18–8	Dahlene	11–15	Steinmann	5–21
Dixon	17–9	Henson	11–15	G. Peterson	4–22
Sebek	17–9	Packham	10–16	Taylor	0–26
Elmerson	16–10	Dubie	9–17		

August 27

It had rained all night and it was a miserable day all the way around. I did not feel like even pitching at all. I met Roland Kraft, the one-armed man from LeCompton, Kansas. I did not offer much resistance to Kraft's strong game and was quickly beaten. Score:

	Pts	R	DR	SP	Pct	4-On
Rose	22	26	9	48	.542	3
Kraft	50	36	13	48	.750	3

Standings: Ted Allen 26–1; Isais 25–2; Zimmerman 25–2; Jones 23–4; Ira Allen 23–4; Gandy 21–6; Lyle Brown 20–7; Bales 19–8; Dixon 17–10; Elmerson 17–10; Griggs 17–10; Sebek 17–10; Dean Brown 16–11; Somerhalder 16–11; Harris 15–12; Rose 13–14; Kraft 13–14; Paxton 12–15.

ROUND TWENTY-EIGHT

I met Lyle Brown of Des Moines. Five out of six put me ahead of Brown at the start 9–1. He got a point on a single; there was a "four-dead" and I got a point to stand 10–2. Here I fired four more doubles at him and scored 3 more to lead 13–2. Six doubles by Brown made it 13–8.

I here got 3 on a double and Lyle got a point on a single. Two more doubles by Brown made it 16–12. Nine out of my next ten put me in the lead 23–12, but I couldn't keep up the pace. Brown strung on five doubles and ran ahead 27–23, and I never caught him after that. He led 37–26 and four doubles helped me make it 37–35, but with 15 out of 16, Brown ended up the game. Score:

	Pts	R	DR	SP	Pct	4-On
Rose	35	64	23	86	.744	13
Brown	50	68	26	86	.791	13

Ted Allen's crown almost slid off his head in his game with Casey Jones! Ted led off with a 10–1 lead, but by the end of 50 shoes Jones had tied it at 25-all. Ten straight doubles helped Allen go ahead to 37–28, but a 23 out of 24 spurt put Jones ahead 46–37! Jones led at 100 shoes 46–40. Allen made it 46–43 and Jones made it 49–43 at 108 shoes.

Casey singled and Ted doubled to make it 49–46. Allen then missed one, but so did Jones! A long measurement followed to determine the point and it was finally awarded to Allen, making it 49–47, then the almost unbelievable happened. Allen missed both shoes! Then for an anti-climax, Jones also missed both shoes! Allen scored 2 points and the score was 49–49. Allen threw a double and went out.

Standings: Ted Allen 27–1; Zimmerman 26–2; Isais 26–2; Jones 23–5; Ira Allen 23–5; Lyle Brown 21–7; Gandy 21–7; Bales 20–8; Sebek 18–10; Dixon 18–10; Elmerson 18–10; Griggs 17–11; Somerhalder 17–11; Dean Brown 16–12; Harris 16–12; Rose 13–15; Kraft 13–15; Paxton 12–16.

ROUND TWENTY-NINE

I met Clayton Henson of Arlington, Virginia. I started this game with only two out of the first 10 and Henson had me 14–0. Five doubles brought me up to 14–9 and we played along, scoring evenly back and forth until it stood 21–16 in Henson's favor. Three doubles put me ahead 25–21. A little later I led 31–30 and then I put a finishing rush of 21 out of 24 and went out. Score:

	Pts	R	DR	SP	Pct	4-On
Rose	50	60	24	78	.769	8
Henson	37	54	16	78	.692	8

Standings: Ted Allen 28–1; Zimmerman 27–2; Isais 27–2; Jones 23–6; Ira Allen 23–6; Lyle Brown 22–7; Gandy 21–8; Bales 21–8; Sebek 19–10; Dixon 18–11; Elmerson 18–11; Griggs 18–11; Somerhalder 18–11; Dean Brown 17–12; Harris 17–12; Rose 14–15; Kraft 14–15; Paxton 13–16.

ROUND THIRTY

I met Eddie Packham of Des Moines, Iowa. It was over quickly! Score:

	Pts	R	DR	SP	Pct	4-On
Rose	7	23	6	42	.547	4
Packham	50	37	16	42	.880	4

This round featured Isais vs. Ted Allen. Isais jumped upon Allen and led the game all the way to easily beat him 50–38, and create a triple tie for first place.

LAST ROUND — ROUND THIRTY-ONE

I met — — — Guy Zimmerman! Zimmerman opened it by hurling eleven straight doubles to lead 18–0. Here I scored 3 on a double, then threw only five out of twelve and Guy was leading 35–3. Here I hit five doubles to make it 35–6 and a little later four more doubles helped make it 36–12. Then, after Zimmerman had gotten a point on a single, he hit eleven more doubles to go out. Score:

	Pts	R	DR	SP	Pct	4-On
Rose	12	60	21	80	.750	17
Zimmerman	50	72	32	80	.900	17

Final Standings:

Ted Allen	29–2	D. Brown	19–17	Bennett	11–20
Zimmerman	29–2	Somerhalder	19–12	Hosier	10–21
Isais	29–2	Elmerson	19–12	N. Peterson	10–21
Jones	25–6	Griggs	18–31	Madsen	8–23
L. Brown	23–8	Dixon	18–13	Steinkamp	7–24
Bales	23–8	Rose	14–17	G. Peterson	7–24
Ira Allen	23–8	Kraft	14–17	Robinson	6–25
Gandy	23–8	Dahlene	14–17	Maxwell	6–25
Sebek	21–10	Dubie	11–20	Steinmann	5–26
Harris	19–12	Henson	11–20	Taylor	0–31

There were some 100-shoe pitch playoffs to decide place ties and then Allen, Zimmerman and Isais started their playoff. Allen defeated Zimmerman two straight games and Zimmerman, in turn, beat Isais two straight. The Allen–Isais [playoff] had to be postponed until the next day [due to] rain. After hanging around the fair-grounds until mid-night, Koppitsch, Bertie and I suddenly decided to start for home and in the dead of night we rolled out of the state of Iowa, breakfasting in Moline, Illinois, and arriving home about 8:00 p.m. on Wednesday, August 28.

- - - - - - -

Because Rose had left the tournament site, he didn't write any more about the playoff for the world title or mention the prize money amount he might have earned. He did supplement his account of the tournament with in some clippings from *Horseshoe World* magazines, which report that Allen beat Isais two straight games to win the title.

The playoff format remains difficult to comprehend, and I could find no explanation of it. Ted Allen was paid $210 for first place, second place earned Zimmerman $135, and Isais was given $110 for third place.

One of the clippings Rose saved included coverage of the two-session NHPA member convention. This was a newsworthy convention that included political fireworks around issues that hung around for a number of years to be dealt with several times.

Here we can read about the fate of the NHPA secretary-treasurer Lee Rose. We might learn if Rose re-ran for his office, or not run again or whatever. This article was expertly written by NHPA Hall of Fame member Leland Mortenson.

- - - - - - -

The association met for its constitutional and rules convention August 22 at 7 p.m. at the Livestock Sales Ring, State Fair Grounds. This room is arranged in a curve with seats rising to a height of about 25 feet in a space of about 50 rows. The chairman was below the audience and somewhat in the center.

The general atmosphere was of such a nature as to remove any shells of timidness about expressing oneself. The smell of straw permeated the air and the pitchers took their seats dressed as they had left the courts, a little clay on their shoes. Some kept their hats on. President Page was dressed in a sweater, no necktie, clay on his shoes. Now and then a member dropped out to bring in two or three bottles of refreshment. There was nothing at all dignified about the meeting.

Why do I mention such things? Because at the convention in 1939, at the expensive air-cooled hotel room, with the pitchers and officers dressed in near tuxedo fashion, choked with stiff collars, and feet cramped in tight shoes, nothing of importance took place except the passage of the five-cent stamp rule. But here in this informal meeting things really happened.

LeRoy Page opened the meeting at 7 o'clock and read his prepared speech. It showed that he had spent several hours preparing it. He raised and lowered his voice and at times shouted in order to put over his point. He recommended an easy method to impeach officers; he urged that the president and secretary live near each other. He made a complaint because the secretary had not [prepared] reports on how the association's money was being spent. He recommended $2.50 as dues for membership: called 25 cents ridiculous; he suggested that secretary-treasurer be required to make complete business reports in the *Horseshoe World* each month, that the members were entitled to know the status of conditions. He also made the following recommendations: That the secretary-treasurer's office be separated and made two offices; that the five-cent stamp rule remain in force another year (it was passed in 1939 for a three-year duration); that the president be permitted expense money.

Page painted a rosy picture of the wonderful possibilities that would result if dues were increased to $2.50 a year, a suggestion which failed to make much impression.

The delegates voted that a shoe is delivered when it leaves the hand, and they voted to throw out the constitution the clause relating to a sanction fee.

I personally brought to the attention of the delegates the fact that Section 3 of Article 3 and Section 4 of Article 4 were missing. Other criticisms of the old constitution were made. I argued the point that the Rules Committee had never had the power to change the constitution, a point which Robert Tompkins later brought up Sunday evening. The point involved was in regard to the article calling for team championship tournaments. Secretary Rose took this as an attack upon team leagues, which was not the case. My point was that if the committee could change or add to the constitution at all, then they could change the constitution completely.

Lee Rose read a prepared speech in which he defended the Rules Committee and he made several recommendations: That the nation be divided into geographical sections, no two officers to be permitted to come from any one section; that proxies be permitted to vote for absent delegates; that states be permitted delegates in proportion to membership.

(This meeting was then adjourned and reconvened on the evening of August 25th, back in the cattle barn.)

J. Robert Tompkins, brilliant young lawyer from Dysart, Iowa, was presented to the convention to present a new constitution which he, as an appointee of one to a special Constitutional Committee, had written. Tompkins, with his pleasing personality, immediately won confidence with two-thirds of the members present. Tompkins proceeded to read his constitution, section by section and almost as fast as he read them they passed. But as Tompkins reached Article III, Johnny Sebek, of Ohio, demanded that the delegates all show their credentials, which they did.

Delegate Koppitsch of Michigan, evidently knowing that one of the officers had failed to pay his dues and thus technically was not a member of the Association, demanded that the officers show their membership cards.

President Page snapped Koppitsch off with his remark, "Unfortunately, the officers aren't voting." Laughter ensued.

Delegate Banta, of Indiana, made a motion to adopt the Chess non-cancel scoring system [later known as the count-all scoring method]. Benedict, from Ohio, supported him. The motion was rejected by all but three or four delegates.

The election of officers came up. Andrew Stolarik, from Canton, Ohio, was unopposed for third vice president, as was Sam Somerhalder for second vice president.

Wilbert Steinkamp and Jack Claves, both from St. Louis, received nominations for first vice president, with Steinkamp refusing. Claves was then elected.

Mrs. Archie Gregson of California and L. E. Tanner of Anchor, Illinois were nominated for treasurer. Mrs. Gregson won, although her husband, Archie, voted for Tanner.

Rose and Tompkins were nominated for the much desired secretary's job, a position that pays $600 a year. Tompkins won 27–17. Tompkins can be proud of the fact that his nomination came from that great eastern leader, Harry Woodfield.

Page, Rose, Tanner and D. O. Chess, of Ohio, were nominated for president, with Page winning more than a majority on the first ballot.

Sidelights of the Tournament

Mrs. Lee Rose served as chief statistician of the National tourney. She was as efficient and accurate as could be expected of anyone.

Late Sunday afternoon came the big thriller. Suddenly came the announcement "the game you all have been waiting for; on court 4, Allen and Zimmerman." There were about 2,000 people in the stands and they made a grand rush for choice seats. The audience for that game grew to over 3,000 spectators.

On August 24, and every remaining day of the National meet, rain soaked the courts in the morning, making it necessary to burn them with gasoline. Archie Gregson with his movie camera and several others with ordinary Kodaks, took advantage to record these scenes.

Pre-tournament plans had called for the National Association to add $300 to the $800 put up by the Iowa State Fair Board, however, as the tournament time neared, most of the pitchers as well the manufacturers present demanded that the Association add $300 more, which was done. With the addition of more money it was decided to have 32 in the finals.

- - - - - - -

It's uncommon for Rose to neglect writing about his accomplishments. This was a tremendous tournament for him—he averaged 74.0 percent for the tournament and had 18 games of 75 percent or better. Generally he is quick to point out his career highlights, but not this event. He did not post the final results in his journals. He may have had higher expectations about his performance, but this writer thinks Rose was disillusioned after failing to be reelected as an NHPA officer.

Since it was deemed by some the greatest World Tournament, the full final standings are printed in Gary Kline's *Official N.H.P.A. History of the World Tournament 1909 to 1980*. Kline points out that this event marked the emergence of the 80-percent pitcher.

- - - - - - -

1940 World Tournament Final Results

Player	W	L	R	SP	Pct
1. Ted Allen	29	2	2187	2642	82.8
2. Guy Zimmerman	29	2	1884	2188	86.1
3. Fernando Isais	29	2	1923	2330	82.5
4. "Casey" Jones	25	6	2043	2538	80.5
5. Alvin Gandy	23	8	1929	2664	78.3
6. Ira Allen	23	8	1896	2438	77.8
7. Robert Bales	23	8	1933	2510	77.0
8. Lyle Brown	23	8	1873	2454	76.3
9. John Sebek	21	10	1992	2574	77.4
10. Dean Brown	19	12	1994	2522	79.1
11. Sydney Harris	19	12	1765	2284	77.3
12. Sam Somerhalder	19	12	1858	2444	76.0
13. Harvey Elmerson	19	12	1704	2308	73.8
14. Ellis Griggs	18	13	1836	2472	74.3
15. Dale Dixon	18	13	1665	2308	72.1
16. Lee Rose	14	17	1716	2318	74.0
17. Alvin Dahlene	14	17	1704	2372	71.8
18. Roland Kraft	14	17	1638	2290	71.5
19. John Paxton	13	18	1514	2272	66.6
20. Eddie Packham	12	19	1531	2198	70.0
21. Joe Bennett	11	20	1608	2314	69.4
22. Clayton Henson	11	20	1500	2166	69.3
23. Joe Dubie	11	20	1433	2152	66.6
24. Ervin Hosier	10	21	1645	2388	68.9
25. Nels Peterson	10	21	1333	2004	66.5
26. Thorsten Madsen	8	23	1338	2046	65.4
27. Gaylord Peterson	7	24	1405	2148	65.4

(Continued on next page)

(Continued from previous page)

Player	W	L	R	SP	Pct
28. Wilfred Steinkamp	7	24	1158	1874	61.8
29. Howard Robinson	6	25	1408	2146	65.6
30. W. O. Maxwell	6	25	1296	2040	63.5
31. "Lefty" Steinmann	5	26	1201	1950	61.5
32. Wellington Taylor	Forfeited All Games				

- - - - - - -

Rose had a tremendous tournament. Against the best pitchers in the world, he logged 18 games with over 75 percent ringers, including five over 80 percent, and he averaged 74 percent for the entire event.

One additional sidebar from Leland Mortenson fits here. In my estimation, Mortenson is the best reporter the sport has ever had. He produced more historic articles than any other writer or NHPA historian. Though he was never named or appointed as the official NHPA historian, he was the best there ever was. Mortenson wrote:

> Before the finals started, the officers decided to have games won and lost decide. All ties to be played off. They came very near deciding to settle ties by giving top position to the player with the higher ringer percentage, an act which later would have given Guy Zimmerman the world's title. Luck No. 1 for Ted Allen.

Now, back to Rose's journal and his description of heading to the Canadian National Exhibition in Toronto and then the postponed 1940 Michigan state tournament.

- - - - - - -

At noon the next day, Thursday, August 29, Koppitsch and I crossed the Ambassador Bridge and headed for Toronto, arriving there at dusk. We went directly to the Canadian National Exhibition and entered, found the small arena and went in to see the horseshoe tournament.

Ted Steadman soon spotted us and we met the rest of the players, James O'Shea, Larry Mahoney, Vito Fellecia, etc.

We were given passes to the grounds, official badges to wear and free banquet tickets.

I was asked to make an address over the P.A. system and I complied with a brief account of the Des Moines meet. After the evening's play we sat out a while in a tap-room at a big hotel and then Frank and I obtained a room and stayed up all night.

The next day it rained! A 25-year record was set for precipitation!! Boy, it really poured all day and we had to duck from building to building.

We saw the finish of the tournament and had a long talk with the Eastern and Canadian people. We stayed all night in the hotel and drove home the next morning, Saturday, August 31.

The Finish of my Seventeenth State Tournament

The next morning, September 1, we drove to Flint to finish the Michigan State Tournament.

You can well imagine the physical condition I was in from my two weeks of pitching, driving and sleeping infrequently and eating at all hours.

I didn't even warm up enough to get going right and then Latzko and I took up our series where it had stopped two weeks before. (It seemed like two years).

Latzko was all in trim, having had two weeks to practice on these courts. It was soon 25–0 in his favor and he won the game 50–11, shooting 48 out of 60 for .800 to my 36 ringers for .600.

Latzko took a lead of 18 to 9, but I rallied to go ahead 19–18. He shot ahead 27–19 and I made it 27–25. Latzko made it 30–25, but I surged ahead 32–30. Latzko jumped ahead 33–32, but two points on singles put me ahead again 34–33. Latzko streamed on 16 out of 18 to wind it up 50–40. He had 55 out of 74 for .744 and I had 50 ringers for .676.

Thus, my 1940 season was ruined by rain!!! RAIN on the last day of the city tournament! Rain in the finals of the state tournament when I had the title in the hollow of my hand. RAIN all through the World Tournament.

Lundgren had lost his game to Hitt, so he and I started our three out five games series for third place.

Lundgren beat me easily the first two games 50–26 and 50–15, hitting .734 and .750 to my .617 and .553.

The third game was more even and after battling to 44 shoes, Lundgren led 28–19. Here I piled in 10 straight doubles and went right out 50–28. I hit .750 to his .640.

1940 Michigan State Tournament Top row L–R: Frank Koppitsch, R. H. Rizor, Albert Field, Carl Gothard, Carl Lundgren, Joe Latzko. Front row: Lee Rose, William Konz.

The last game was even to 11–11 and then Lundgren went ahead to stay and won 50–37, hitting .751 to my .670.

The title series was won by Latzko, beating Bobby Hitt four games to two. Latzko won the first game 50–48 and the second game 50–49. Hitt defeated him the third game 50–45 with 88 out of 110 shoes for .800 to Joe's 85 ringers for .772.

Hitt threw 49 out of 56 in the fourth game for .875 to win 50–13 and even the series at two wins each.

Latzko won the fifth game 50–42 with .767 and retained his title by winning the sixth game 50–22 with .787.

- - - - - - -

Next the Rose journals give an account of the national league championships that calls a world championship. It's difficult to imagine a world championship in which only four teams are involved.

Rose's concept to set up major team competition on a league level was a great notion, but it was contrary to NHPA's focus on individual tournament play at that time. Unfortunately, horseshoe pitchers in the U.S. didn't step up to plate on this endeavor. But at least Rose found three other teams to participate.

- - - - - - -

Detroit Wins Opening Match of Title Series

The Detroit Lattores moved to within one notch of a world championship by defeating the Indianapolis Moose team 28–21 in a match played September 8 at Athletic Park in Anderson, Indiana.

The Detroit team, cramped by a six-hour ride, lost the first round 4–3, but the next four rounds found them grabbing four wins out of each seven games to take a 19–16 lead. The match sealed in the sixth round when Detroit won six out of seven.

Manager Lee Rose led the Detroit team to its victory by taking six out of seven games. He defeated Orville Harris, Johnson, Edmonson, Deer, Radcliff and Newbold and lost only to Arlo Harris, former state champion [1937], who went undefeated on the day.

Carl Gothard did well, winning five games in seven starts and hanging up the highest Detroit percentage .599. A very strong wind held the percentages down.

Indianapolis will meet Detroit in the second game of this two out of three series on September 22. The game will be played at Wines Field in Ann Arbor, Michigan.

Detroit – 28

Player	W	L	Pts	R	DR	SP	Pct
Rose	6	1	334	277	79	470	.589
Gothard	5	2	336	277	91	462	.599
Lundgren	4	3	318	265	75	456	.581
Lattore	4	3	286	280	79	482	.581
Konz	3	4	307	279	74	480	.575
Field	3	4	313	263	77	470	.559
Koppitsch	3	4	309	266	64	504	.528
Total	28	21	2203	1904	539	3324	.573

Indianapolis – 21

Player	W	L	Pts	R	DR	SP	Pct
A. Harris	7	0	350	322	102	518	.622
O. Harris	4	3	319	286	80	492	.581
Johnson	3	4	313	303	88	502	.604
Edmonson	3	4	305	272	77	472	.576
Deer	.	4	249	225	68	440	.511
Templeton	1	3	143	155	41	282	.549
Radcliff	0	2	66	56	14	126	.444
Van Sickle	0	3	99	83	19	188	.441
Newbold	0	3	83	78	14	180	.433
Speece	0	4	56	52	9	124	.419
Total	21	28	1983	1832	512	3324	.551

Games Won by Rounds :
Detroit – 3 4 4 4 4 6 3 = 28
Indianapolis – 4 3 3 3 3 1 4 = 21

- - - - - - -

So enters the name Arlo Harris, a prominent name in the sport of horseshoes and the NHPA. We meet him here as a league horseshoe pitcher who found his way to a notable team participating in the national league. He had not yet reached his peak.

Arlo was elected NHPA president in 1947. Much of his platform and activity was to promote the chess scoring system, an issue that was raised and overwhelmingly defeated at the 1940 NHPA convention. The system was strongly and actively supported by Johnny Sebek, another star pitcher on the Canton team. The NHPA still was not ready to invest in a league pitching alongside tournament involvement—and they also weren't prepared to convert to the chess scoring system, a count-all method versus a collation system.

During the year of his NHPA presidency, Harris paid a tremendous toll as a result of his active promotion of the league aspect of the sport and his administration ended in ruins. The other NHPA officers fought him tooth and nail, creating such discord that he didn't even conduct the 1948 membership convention after failing to qualify for the Championship Class; he just resigned and went home. Most of his supporters did the same, including Johnny Sebek, who was not reelected to his post of vice president.

But Harris was not finished with his promotion of the sport. He established the American Horseshoe Pitchers Association (AHPA) in 1948, an organization that still exists in Ohio and Indiana. This association employed count-all scoring, of course, and today the method Harris advocated is used in 90 percent of the leagues throughout the NHPA.

In addition to his leadership in AHPA, Harris won a number of Indiana state championships and designed and developed his own pitching shoe—the Harris Professional Shoe that was manufactured by Giant Grip Manufacturing in Oshkosh, Wisconsin.

Next, a somewhat humorous page out of the Lee Rose journals. The competition wasn't a joke, but the circumstances were. Then on to the all-important national league competition that Rose referred to as the world championship.

- - - - - - -

New Castle!!!

On the morning of Saturday, September 14, four aspiring horseshoe pitchers left Detroit for New Castle, Indiana, for a tournament billed as the Mid-West Open. The four were Rose, Lundgren, Field and Goodell.

Seven hours of driving brought them to Memorial Park in New Castle. Ten courts were there. Five of them, down in a veritable "hole-in-the-wall" were just fair and five more, way up a steep hill, the "balcony," were terrible!

All four [players from Detroit] qualified for the first twenty who were to play in class A and all stayed overnight in a New Castle hotel. The next day some more pitchers qualified and then the 10 in Class B played first. It was late in the afternoon before they finished and the Class A started. They were divided into two squads of ten each and the two highest in each squad were to play in the finals.

All four Detroit men drew to play in the squad on the "balcony." Casey Jones won all his nine games and Lundgren won eight to take 2nd and qualify for the finals. (The first four games were 50-point games and the last five games were cut to 25 points as darkness approached.) All 20 finished their last two games downstairs after dark, there being no lights on the "balcony."

Field won seven and lost two. Rose won five and lost four, beating Overholger, Goodell, Van Sickle and two others, and losing to Lundgren, Field, Jones and O. Harris.

The finals started late at night and the final four were Jones, Lundgren, A. Harris and the Indiana champ Neilson. Jones won three games to take 1st, Neilson won two games to place 2nd and Orville Harris beat Lundgren for 3rd.

Prizes!! Lundgren got $3.00, Field got a HAM, and Rose got 75 cents.

It was after 11:30 p.m. as the four started for home and all arrived at 6:00 a.m. on Monday just in time to go to work. So four adventurers returned, saddened and wiser!

New Castle — — Phooey!!!!

Detroit Wins World Championship
Ringer Powerhouse Proves
Too Much for Indianapolis
Ringer Record Set

Detroit's horseshoe team won the world's team championship on September 22 when they defeated the Indianapolis team 29–20 at Wines Field in Ann Arbor, Michigan.

It was a very good match, played in good weather on good courts. Both line-ups were replete with star players and Detroit was forced to shatter all records to come out on top.

Indianapolis was without the services of the Harris brothers or Johnson, but picked up the Indiana state champion, Neilson, a star player in brochures, ex-National A.A.U. champ Trinkle and a good player in England.

Bobby Hitt and Carl Lundgren led Detroit to their victory by winning 6 out 7 each. Joe Latzko arriving late, won 4 out of 5.

Detroit hit a team average of .646, which beats the .620 set by Dearborn in 1933 and closely neared the .650 made by Detroit this year. This latter record is for five men, whereas the .646 is for seven men. Summary:

Detroit – 29

Player	W	L	Pts	R	DR	SP	Pct
Hitt	6	1	349	311	109	434	.716
Lundgren	6	1	333	329	121	464	.711
Latzko	4	1	242	263	94	372	.708
Konz	2	0	100	86	27	140	.614
Rose	4	3	288	280	90	436	.642
Field	2	2	139	151	48	238	.634
Raab	3	4	245	287	81	478	.600
Lattore	1	2	119	146	44	238	.613
Koppitsch	1	6	210	251	74	454	.553
Total	**29**	**20**	**2025**	**2104**	**688**	**3254**	**.646**

Score by Rounds:

Indianapolis –	3	3	4	2	3	2	3
Detroit –	4	4	3	5	4	5	4

Indianapolis – 20

Player	W	L	Pts	R	DR	SP	Pct
Neilson	6	1	323	345	124	480	.718
Broschears	5	2	324	367	125	520	.708
Trinkle	4	3	298	325	105	490	.663
England	3	4	296	310	98	480	.645
Deer	1	6	203	230	86	410	.561
Van Sickle	1	6	223	253	65	456	.554
Radcliff	0	7	192	208	52	418	.499
Total	**20**	**29**	**1859**	**2038**	**655**	**3254**	**.626**

- - - - - - -

Rose wrote very little on the national league championship game. Not only did he load up his Detroit team with Joe Latzko, a resident of Flint, but he also had Bobby Hitt pitching. They are two of the greatest players in Michigan history—and all of a sudden they were on the Detroit. The league rules do not prohibit that kind of thing, and one can only imagine other teams brought in some ringers also. Detroit very well could have won the championship match without Hitt and Latzko. Their presence on the roster meant two other members of the Detroit team who had practiced and dedicated time to the team were slighted playing time in the championship match.

The two substitute players for Indianapolis were pitching stars of Indiana. Bill Neilson's career began with winning the AAU junior national championship in 1938. He was also on the doubles national championship team in 1938. Neilson won the 1940 Indiana state men's title and was a follower of Arlo Harris and a member of the AHPA.

Hubert Trinkle also earned fame in AAU amateur competitions as the AAU men's national champion in 1938 and 1939. Trinkle was on the national doubles championship team in 1937, 1938, and 1939, and he won Indiana state championships in 1934, 1936, and 1941.

The next several pages contain reprints of articles from 1940 editions of *Horseshoe World* that Rose clipped and included in his journals. The articles are lengthy, but the purpose in reprinting them is to present the case that Rose was railroaded out of his NHPA post as secretary-treasurer—and perhaps unjustly, since he was on a track that could have improved the sport. His articles indicate that he certainly felt that was the case, and the accompanying articles offer important context.

The efforts to have him voted out of office were incited by an NHPA president who hadn't even bothered to pay his organizational dues. NHPA administration in the 1940s can only be described as inept—and that was probably the case during the 1930s too. This exchange of articles by the national officers themselves demonstrates the unfortunate state of NHPA's leadership team.

First is an article written by Rose when he was still in office. As a whole, it summarizes the World Tournament and summarizes the convention in his own words. Just the latter section is included here.

- - - - - - -

The National Convention was held in conjunction with the tournament and consisted of two meetings. The meetings were held in the cattle barn on August 22 and August 25.

At the first meeting it was decided not to collect thee $100 sanction fee due the Association for sanctioning the tournament at the Iowa Fair, though it was stated the fair was willing to pay it.

Rule 9 of the horseshoe rules was changed to read, "Both contestants must remain behind the foul line until the last of the inning is delivered. A shoe shall be considered delivered when it leaves the player's hand."

These two items were voted on upon by 34 delegates, many of whom held no membership in the Association at the time.

At the second [meeting] the main business accomplished was the adoption of a new constitution for the Association. The reason given by Mr. Page for the adoption was that the old one had become outdated and needed "streamlining."

The passing of this document was begun article by article, but so many arguments arose that it was finally decreed that it would be read in its entirety and passed and changes would be made afterward. The new constitution was then read quickly and passed. With only a few minor changes, it reads exactly the same as the old one, so only a few changes in the old one would have sufficed. The main thing accomplished by it all this was to bring up an election of officers which would not have held any election.

At one time, Johnny Sebek of Canton, Ohio, demanded to see the delegate's credentials and membership cards and while all had cards, few had credentials and it was revealed that Mr. Page, the president, had no card and therefore was not a member of the association, yet he was conducting the meeting and was later re-elected to office.

A motion by Mr. Sebek to raise the membership dues enough to include a subscription to the *Horseshoe World* was voted down and a statement by Mr. Tompkins that he would undertake to print a magazine to be the official organ of the association was received favorably. Over the protests of several delegates that officers elected to an office should serve full terms, an election was held.

New Secretary Outlines Association's Hopes

The *Horseshoe World* is pleased to report that the new secretary of the National Horseshoe Pitcher's Association has given this publication assurances that he is vitally interested in making the Association of benefit to all classes of pitchers.

J. Tompkin, who lives Ames, Iowa, is new secretary of the National Association. Iowa has produced some of the world's best horseshoe champions. This state can now boast of having both the National Association president [LeRoy Page] and the secretary.

In a message to this magazine, Mr. Tompkin has given us some of his ideas. His letter, reprinted in its entirely will speak for itself. Here it is:

Dear Mr. Howard:

Mr. Page has just turned over to me some correspondence which he received from you. These letters, together with certain excerpts from the September *Horseshoe World*, lead me to believe that a terrible misunderstanding exists. I am anxious to preserve harmony within the Association and when misunderstandings occur, that harmony is endangered. For this reason I am writing you this letter. I should like to have you print this in the *Horseshoe World*, if you see fit, to acquaint you and the readers with the actual facts of the Convention and the future policy of the officers.

Several statements in the article [written] by Mr. Rose convince me he has gained a wrong impression of the set-up. In the first place, all officers of the National Association are members of the Association. In a letter to me Rose said that the president was not a member. I can personally vouch for Page's membership. Another statement was made that the new constitution had only a few minor changes from the old one. I wrote the new document and completely deleted entire sections which had hitherto been obsolete. When we have a few more new ones printed I shall send you a copy that you may judge for yourself.

Since my election to the office of secretary, I have formulated a general outline of what I consider important moves. There has been a fairly widespread feeling of discontent among those players who are qualified to compete with 75 and 80 per cent pitchers. These players feel that the National Association has nothing to offer them. They are partially right, but only partially. A true lover of the game will support it for the satisfaction he derives from seeing it take place among the leading sport of the world.

There are 2,000,000 horseshoe pitchers in American and 1,700 of them are interested enough to pay 25 cents a year. Certainly the dues are not exorbitant. What, then, is the reason for such a horrible lack of support?

I made a statement that a certain group of lower-average pitchers were partially right in their contention that the National Association has nothing to offer them. There are two sides to this. Let us examine both of them.

In the first place, a 50 per cent pitcher seems to feel that because he does not throw 80 per cent, he has no place in tournament play. We must remember that any world champion, at one time in his life shot definitely under 50 per cent.

It is generally conceded that practice, competition and experience are three great factors in improving a player's game. With an association of a million or even a half a million members, we could stage state and county tournaments which would be available to everyone. These could be closed tournaments so that outside "big name" pitchers could not compete.

There are not enough 75 per cent pitchers in the United States that a county tournament could be monopolized by them. These local meets would provide the competition and experience necessary for rapid improvement.

Another factor to consider is the spectator's interest in the game. From experience and observation, I have found that an audience is interested in high-percentage games. However, we cannot assume that human nature is such that a normal person wants thrillingly close games, and feels that there is more likelihood of this in a game between two top-ranking players because they will shoot about the same percentage.

The Allen-Zimmerman National tournament game ending in a 50–48 score was as exciting a game as I've ever seen. The spectators enjoyed it immensely. But I believe that two players, evenly matched, who shoot 40 per cent can also stage an exciting game when pitted against each other. Therefore I propose to attempt three classes of horseshoe tournament competition.

Those pitchers qualifying over 70 per cent compete in Class A; those qualifying between 50 and 70 per cent will be Class B and those who pitch less than 50 per cent will comprise Class C. This would give a Class A National Champion, a Class B National Champion and a Class C National Champion. This would correspond to boxing, for example. A lightweight champion is the best in his class, although we know he cannot beat the heavyweight title holder. The middleweight title champion is king in his class. He can beat the lightweight but must in turn lose to the heavyweight ruler. Yet the lightweight or the middleweight may be as good a champion in his class as the heavyweight is in his. Such would be the status of horseshoe, if the horseshoe pitchers in American will back me in trying to put it across.

The backing that I need is letters containing ideas, suggestions, approval or disapproval to help me shape the best possible plan. The next step is to gain enough members so that we can make possible this plan. If every member now in the organization would add three more we could do it. If we could get 8,000 members from the two million players, I could guarantee a national tournament with fine prizes in all three classes. Believe me, it can be done.

Mr. Chess of the Ohio Association, writes that there are 2,000 active players in that state alone; Mr. Banta, of Indiana, writes in the same vein. I've had letters from several associations stating the same thing. All the players want an association which includes all the players.

I have informed President Page of my plans and he has given me his hearty endorsement. I might say here that he is spending time, without pay, toward the publication of our forthcoming booklet. I'd like to lead a rousing cheer for LeRoy.

Another cheer better go to Harry Woodfield, of Washington, D.C., Harry was appointed publicity chairman at the convention. The ensuing two months have proven the wisdom of the choice. He has written me two long letters outlining a publicity program which included a central information bureau, a progress exhibit showing the advancement of horseshoe and a nation-wide publicity drive to acquaint sports-minded people with the fact that we have a topnotch sport in horseshoe pitching. Woodfield is another man who is devoting hours and hours of his time for no remuneration except sheer love of the game. With a hundred men like him the association would number 100,000 in two or three years.

Yours very truly,
J. Robert Tompkin
National Secretary

- - - - - - -

The association (in this case, the members themselves) saw fit to vote out a knowledgeable, ambitious, and capable Rose, in favor of the unproven Tompkins who thinks he is capable and has all the answers. The move was probably solely at the request of a president who had issues with the incumbent.

One members who did have one answer to an improved association was Johnny Sebek. He suggested that the membership dues be raised a small amount, enough to allow the annual membership dues to include a subscription to the association's magazine. No other single issue or suggestion could have done more to improve the overall situation of the sport Sebek's proposal. Unfortunately, when the NHPA was originally formed, that step was not taken. Even today, some 70 years later, the NHPA has failed to implement this change, and the sport is still paying a penalty for that. The fact remains that the officers, the leaders, the administrators of the sport cannot speak directly to each and every member of the association. That's the main benefit of an association-wide publication.

In the 1940s *Horseshoe World*, the NHPA magazine at the time, was a magnificent effort on the part of a talented and capable Raymond Howard. But only a fraction of NHPA's pitchers received it. Now the NHPA has *Newsline*, which is also a very good magazine—but of nearly 10,000 members, it has a mere 1,700 subscribers. So over 7,000 (or 83 percent) of the association members have little knowledge of the needs of the sport or of the direction and advice of the administration. One can just imagine Lee Rose and Johnny Sebek shaking their heads and saying, "I told you so."

Note that Tompkins was proposing a class system for tournaments. Remember that Tompkins is not the first to think of the class system; the 1935 World Tournament included a Class B tournament alongside the

Championship Class. As we follow the evolution of the sport through the Rose journals, there will another fifteen years before the World Tournaments woke up to the extended class system and other divisions, such as the "old timers division" (presently called the senior division). It seems strange that Tompkins makes no mention of providing a junior boys or junior girls divisions, or reestablishing the women's division. Surely those would also be improvements to the sport at large. Nor was there any mention of the AAU involvement in the sport by holding many amateur state championship events and a national amateur championship tournament since 1937. (The AAU program was actually set up by Raymond Howard when he held the position of NHPA secretary for six years just prior to Rose's tenure.)

But enough of Tompkin's ramblings—and this writer's editorializing for that matter. Here's what Rose shot back in the pages of *Horseshoe World*.

- - - - - - -

Former Secretary Comments on National Affairs
By Lee Rose

I have just finished re-reading Mr. Tompkin's rather long, but interesting letter printed in the November issue of the *Horseshoe World* and I take note that my name was mentioned a few times in connection with "wrong impressions," "ridiculous statements," etc. It is not my intention to write this letter to quibble with anything Mr. Tompkins says, for I believe he is very much in earnest in his endeavors and statements and I think he actually believes in everything he says. It is probably true that Mr. Page is now a member of the association, but it is also true that he was NOT a member when reelected to office.

Mr. Tompkins says that the new constitution differs a great deal from the old one. I would like to say here that when the new constitution was read before the convention I listened intently to every word of it and at the same time I sat with the *Horseshoe Compendium* in my hand noting the old constitution. I say again that only a few minor changes had been made in the document. If it differs a great deal it is only in the wording and certainly not in the meaning. Of course, a great deal of time has elapsed between then and now and since

I know and the Western boys know, it is only fair to tell the rest of the pitchers everywhere EXACTLY why a new constitution was introduced and passed.

Many of your readers probably already know something about the battle I had with the balance of the executive committee over the awarding of the [1940] tournament. During this heated engagement I took occasion to inform the *Horseshoe World* at large just what was happening behind the scenes and thus aroused the ire of Mr. Page to the point where he sent out a petition to the other officers to have me put out of office. This was told to me by Mr. Claves on a visit he paid me in August. Mr. Claves also said he had informed Mr. Page that such a move was altogether unwise and to forget it. During the course of Mr. Claves' visit it was also brought out that since the constitution called for an election of officers only every two years, the brotherhood in the West would get around the difficulty of getting me out of office by writing a new constitution and putting it into effect immediately and thus bring about an election. The plan of their campaign is the story of it. It is not without some pride, therefore, that I can point to myself as the man for whom a constitution was changed.

Mr. Tompkin says in his letter that I have "gained a wrong impression of the set-up." Quite the contrary, Mr. Tompkin, I have too good of an impression of the present set-up.

But enough of this kind of talk. I did not start out to argue, but felt it necessary to again tell the other side of the story lest the National officers succeed in drawing too many red herrings across the trail. What I really wrote this letter for was to discuss frankly the situation which confronts the horseshoe game today.

Mr. Tompkin set forth his ideas concerning the running of a national tournament in three classes. On the face of it, this sounds good and certainly would be an improvement over any past tournament, but is it possible? Could enough prize money be raised to enable Class B and C players to travel several hundred miles to compete? I frankly do not think so. It seems that all plans which deal with the future of horseshoe pitching are based on the one idea that IF we get 8,000 members, or IF we could get 25,000 members or IF we could this or that, we would be a success.

Why should people try to kid themselves along such lines as these? The association records show that the best year for membership was the first year the new individual plan went into effect and these same records will show that there has been a steady decline ever since. No plan based on the supposition that we will get thousands of members should even be considered, for it is clearly a waste of time.

The National Association cannot hope to obtain members when it provides nothing for them—no inducement to join. The whole problem boils down to ONE BASIC FACT—provide inducement for the "run-of-the-mine" pitcher to join; provide something for him that he wants and he'll be eager to join. The only problem, therefore, is to find that SOMETHING. I can tell you what that something is and rest assured it is not running tournaments in several classes. That only adds a few more members and does not bring the sweeping and all-enveloping success each dreamer is looking for.

No, my friends, the future success of horseshoes is going to come from a complete change of basic ideas and principles. This change is much too involved to set down here, but I am going to set my ideas down on paper and present them to the pitchers at the next convention if a really representative group is present to whom to propound them. In the meantime, I am going to work toward the ultimate goal in my own way and I may have something very important to bring to the convention at Des Moines in 1941. (It will be at Des Moines; of that I am sure.)

I trust, Mr. Howard, that this letter can be printed in the *Horseshoe World* that all my friends may know that I am getting ready for a big season ahead.

- - - - - - -

Rose's claim that he was railroaded out of his office becomes ever more plausible. What is even more concerning is that the convention membership selected a candidate to oppose Rose who wasn't an experienced horseshoe promoter—and it turned out he wasn't destined to be an ongoing force in helping to shape the future of the sport. They elected Tompkins, who was nothing more than a flash in the pan, and his term of office lasted merely one year. He was just a part of LeRoy Page's plan to get Rose out of his way.

Former secretary Raymond Howard used his position as editor of *Horseshoe World*, to speak his mind on the matter.

- - - - - - -

The Lee Rose Story

INVENTORY TIME

Now that tournament time is about over it is time to give some serious thought to where we have been and where we are going. By and large 1940 was a successful year. We were fortunate enough to have a National Tournament and that always stimulates interest. We had a rather drastic upheaval in the management and that provokes interest and we hope new activity. New blood should engender new activity. It is time to take "inventory" of just how well we have succeeded in the National Association. Let's go back when B. G. Leighton, the writer, and the late D. D. Cottrell were the men behind the game. National Tournaments were held twice per year—once in the North in the summer and once in the winter in the South—those were the good old days. And the association had more money then than it has now, since changes were made not alone for individual memberships, but for club charters and tournament sanctions. State, district and even local clubs paid dues and county fairs and unaffiliated organizations paid for the privilege of holding tournaments under the sanction and rules of the Association. It wasn't big money but it was pretty certain income.

A NEW DEAL

Then came a change—a new deal, so to speak. We began to place emphasis on numbers. We wanted more individual members and a plan was evolved whereby the local club could belong to the state and to the National, with one set of dues, all exclusive, making the local club member automatically a member of the National. That worked out pretty well for a few years and brought in good revenue, along with the manufacturers stamp money, but not enough to put on tournaments. The dues were too small to expect much unless thousands and thousands were enrolled. So the treasury has been pretty lean.

Finances were discussed at Des Moines, but we don't know much about just what is to be the program. The *Horseshoe World* usually prints minutes of the convention, but these have not been sent to us—we understand they are to be printed by the new secretary in a paper he is to edit and send to each member. Reports say it isn't to be a regular monthly affair—just one issue. Rumors and more rumors come to us on the subject, but no statement from either the President or Secretary. As an old friend of the Association, the *Horseshoe World* feels it deserves the courtesy of the privilege of printing official proceedings, as usual, but if there is any reason why our readers should be denied this we will have to tell the story as best we can from the outside.

We offered Mr. Page the use of a column this month, but haven't a word from him.

But to get back to our editorial: Finances are the lifeblood of the Association. Maybe a combination of the old plan and the new one is the thing—membership dues, plus fees for charters and sanctions. We advocated the appointment at Des Moines of a "commission" or committee to study such things. We hope that such a committee was named and that it will give Mr. Page and his co-workers the answer to the problems that must be as perplexing to them as they were to the writer when he was secretary on two occasions in the past.

- - - - - - -

The next to stand on the soapbox was Jack Claves. He didn't whine or make excuses, but used his opportunity to step up to the plate and admit the NHPA administration had failed. He made a plea to all to step up and assist in potential improvements. Claves was a distinguished member of the association and a star pitcher from the state of Missouri. He was first elected as NHPA vice president in 1939, and after a distinguished career was inducted to the NHPA Hall of Fame in 1991. His claim to fame, known by all in his day and only by a few today, is that he coined the term "four-dead."

- - - - - - -

The National Association Has Failed
Let's Get Down to Brass Tacks
(Guest Editorial by Jack Claves)

If there ever was a challenge to the horseshoe pitchers of these United States, Mr. R. B. Howard's editorial of the January issue was it.

If any article shocked me it was that one and it hurt. What hurt most was that he was absolutely right and I congratulate him.

Who is to blame for its failure? "Let him who is partly responsible cast a few chestnuts." Your National officers failed and failed badly too. Our failure was our inability to awaken the millions of horseshoe pitchers throughout the country that this is their association and that they must help build it up by selling membership cards. These memberships mean money and the association will never get ahead without it. The officers, no matter how capable or diligent they may be, cannot accomplish anything worthwhile without money. Don't confuse the money derived from the shoe stamps—that is for the prize money only.

One of the worst failures of our officers and pitchers all over this country is that they failed to abide by the rules adopted at the Moline Convention. If that rule was recognized throughout the country, our association would get some-place because we would have those 10,000 members we need.

However, I doubt if the National Association's officers had enforced it, if there would have been six really eligible entries in the Midwest and the National Tournaments in the last four years. It was plainly explained to all attending the Moline Convention and published on page five, September 1935 edition of the *Horseshoe World*. In everyday language it meant that every member of a club, league and all tournament entries must hold a National card. To participate in any tournament not sanctioned and in which some did not have a membership card or used unsanctioned shoes, called for a one year's suspension. That meant that every tournament a member entered had to run under National rules. If he pitched in one unsanctioned tournament he was not eligible to pitch in another because he had violated the rules and was subject to suspension even though he had a membership card.

An example of how our "big league" pitchers fail our association is shown by the report I received from an authoritative source at the great Mid-West meet in 1939, 1938 and 1940. In 1938, 85%, or 28 out of 33 entries, were not members of the National until they entered and were forced to join by purchasing a 25-cent membership card. In 1939 and 1940, 75% had to buy their cards in order to pitch in the tournament. In other words, it seems our leading pitchers to whom the millions of lesser look up to for guidance, show they do not care "two bits worth" for the Association's welfare, which also mean the game unless they are assured a chance to win fame and fortune.

I personally know most of them do not think along those lines; the big problem is they do not even think. They all want to be champion, but they little realize there would be no champion without an association to promote a championship match. There is too much selfishness shown and too little desire to help the game and the Association's welfare.

As an example: Last year, the Association added $300 in cash to the Iowa State Fair's $800 cash prize list at Des Moines, making a total of $1,100. Were the majority of entrants satisfied? No! Someone, knowing the Association had a little money left, got a few others together and after a little campaigning put a motion upon the floor that the Association throw $300 additional into the prize fund so that they might cash in on more money. It passed, of course. Did the boys appreciate the Association that had made that fund possible? Did they turn around and show they believed in reciprocation? Let's look at the names listed in this issue, in which D. O. Chess is trying to solicit $1.00 donations from the lovers of the game to be put in the National Championship Prize Fund. How many names of those who cashed in at Des Moines do you find? Lefty Steinmann, of St. Louis, who finished 31st, is among the list.

Yes, we have failed, but only to an extent. Come on you leaders, appoint your key men, get them busy selling those membership cards. Sell them to your friends, the grocer, the baker, the filling station man—he doesn't have to be a pitcher. Let's resolve to get busy and make 1941 our best year ever and remember, you tournament managers, make every championship a National Sanctioned Tournament. Give the winner, in addition to the first cash or medal prize, a beautifully scrolled National Association Certificate of Championship. That certificate will be cherished a lifetime.

If I have hurt anyone's feelings without doing them some good, I am sorry and I apologize, but if some of you will put forth a little more effort to help the game of horseshoes, I'll feel repaid for writing this. I'll appreciate comments, good or bad.

Jack H. Claves

- - - - - - -

As a conclusion for the year 1940, Rose summarized his record against his opponents for the year. We've already discovered Rose's singular and unrivaled efforts to maintain a complete record of his involvement in the sport. But now consider that his journal also so contains an amazing list that compiles 15 years of statistics. Yes, a fifteen-year list.

Most of his opponents are pitchers from the Michigan area who Rose played in league play or state tournaments. A couple of the players are from out of the region, but Rose felt were good enough to include in his report:

Ted Allen, at the time, the greatest player ever, whom Rose had a win against; Johnny Sebek, a national ranked pitcher that Rose broke even with; and Bob Bales, a notable pitcher from Missouri. Rose kept incredible records and apparently retained a score sheet for any and every horseshoe game he ever played.

- - - - - - -

Won & Lost Record Against Leading Lifetime Opponents

Opponent	Years	Rose's Wins	Opponent Wins
R. H. Rizor	15	50	9
James Skinner	14	15	11
James Burt	12	48	29
Ed Walls	12	16	30
F. Koppitsch	10	12	7
Al Field	9	23	15
M. G. Getz	9	14	7
Ray Gorsline	9	9	1
Joe Latzko	9	4	18
Jack Hoeksema	9	6	5
D. Latzko	8	7	3
C. H. Davis	8	17	4
Lou Harrison	8	10	3
Leo Lattore	7	11	6
Ray Wrobbel	6	9	0
Richard Prediger	6	19	11
Harold Arold	6	15	2
Carl Lundgren	6	21	21
Robert Hitt	6	3	24
Mark Goodell	6	10	0
K. E. Armstrong	5	9	3
Ben Emmerson	5	6	5
Ray Middleton	5	5	1
Orville Valleau	4	7	0
Joe Kelly	4	4	1
Phillip Carra	4	3	1
Jimmy Field	3	10	0
Bill Miller	3	9	0
John Egan	3	3	0
Bob Bales	3	1	2
Ted Allen	3	1	4
Carl Gothard	2	13	0
Johnny Sebek	2	2	2
William Konz	2	1	1

The AAU Has a Presence in the Sport

Finally, we move on to another chapter, and what could be another interesting year. The fallout of the political activity in 1940 may not be over, but time marches on.

We begin with Lee's efforts to keep the league and team activity going. Without ever making any commitment, he sure is carrying on an effort to improve league activity within the sport—much in the same way Mr. Chess and Johnny Sebek of Ohio were promoting.

His journal entries for the year begin with notes about his ongoing efforts to create a league, including a clipping reporting on the plans for *Horseshoe World*.

- - - - - - -

I spent most of the spring pitching rather indifferently and writing letters and postcards no end in trying to get teams interested in joining my new International Horseshoe League.

We had a meeting in London, Ohio, on May 18th, and on the way home I became crippled in the legs and subsequently discovered I had a bad case of rheumatism.

Organize New Team League
(The following is by Lee Rose Former National Secretary)

A step toward bringing horseshoe pitching an organization devoted solely to the development of teams and team play was taken on May 18th when at London, Ohio, representatives of several large cities convened to draw up plans and rules for a new team organization called "The International Horseshoe League."

This organization is the continuation of the National Team League of last year, but decided to sever connections with the National Association owing to that body's apathetical attitude toward team play. Although it will not be necessary for a pitcher to belong to the National Association to pitch in this league, there will be nothing in the league rules to prevent any member from being a member of the National Association.

This league is being formed for the express purpose of conducting team play on a larger scale than ever before and the league hopes for a few more teams to take part this year. The league opener has been tentatively set to open on June 15 and any good horseshoe club who can load up a team that looks unbeatable is asked to join this league.

The territory included in the league is Michigan, Ohio, Indiana, Western Pennsylvania, West Virginia and Ontario. We would be glad to hear from teams in this locality, although we would consider entries from Illinois, Kentucky and even Western New York. Don't be bashful! If you want information concerning this league, write in for it. Address: Lee Rose, 5228 Shaw Ave., Detroit, Michigan.

By June 8, the International Horseshoe League shaped up in three divisions as follows:

Michigan–Ohio Division

1. Detroit – Will be ready
2. Flint – Say they're ready
3. Ann Arbor – A little wary, but will try to be ready
4. Toledo – Say they are ready

Indiana Division

1. Fort Wayne – Say they are ready
2. Indianapolis – Say they will be ready
3. Terre Haute – Still doubtful – but maybe

Ohio

1. Canton – Say they are ready, but no other teams to play them.

I still was crippled and unable to do hardly any pitching.

Schedule for Michigan–Ohio Division

June 15	Toledo at Ann Arbor, Flint at Detroit
June 29	Ann Arbor at Flint, Detroit at Toledo
July 13	Detroit at Ann Arbor, Toledo at Flint
July 20	Ann Arbor at Toledo, Detroit at Flint
August 3	Flint at Ann Arbor, Toledo at Detroit
August 10	Ann Arbor at Detroit, Flint at Toledo

Schedule for Indiana Division

June 22	Terre Haute at Indianapolis
June 29	Indianapolis at Fort Wayne
July 13	Fort Wayne at Terre Haute
July 20	Indianapolis at Terre Haute
July 27	Fort Wayne at Indianapolis
August 3	Terre Haute at Fort Wayne

Detroit vs. Flint Match Is Rained Out

The International Horseshoe League opening match between Flint and Detroit was rained out near the end of the third round on June 15 at Northwestern

Field. Both teams started a line-up sprinkled with subs. For Detroit, Field, Walls and Lundgren were not there as the match began, while Lattore was out with an injured toe. Rose, hardly able to hobble because of rheumatism, was not in condition [but played]. Fagan, Mierzwa, Kelly and Goodell filled in along with Ball and Gothard. Lundgren wandered along in time to enter the second round and Walls showed up as the third round was on. Detroit was ahead 13–7 with Rose and Latzko unfinished when a rainstorm burst suddenly and washed out the match. Ringer percentages for the Detroit players: Lundgren .580; Ball .573; Gothard .554; Fagan .424. Team average was .505.

Detroit is to go to Flint on June 22 and they are to return to Detroit on July 20.

Detroit Rained Out at Flint

Detroit's team was rained out at Flint on June 22, after four rounds of play. The score was 14–14 at the time, as Detroit played with only six players: Lattore, Gothard, Ball, Mierizwa, Lundgren and Rose. Flint promised to again come to Detroit on July 6th.

Detroit Beats Both Rain and Toledo

Detroit managed to squeeze an abbreviated victory in on June 29, when they met Toledo at Riverside Park in Toledo. Rain halted the match at the end of five rounds, but Detroit was leading 20–15 and seemed certain of victory and Toledo conceded the match. Detroit again had only six players, so five of Toledo's wins were forfeits. The score:

Detroit – 20

Player	W	L	Pts	R	DR	SP	Pct.
Field	5	0	250	178	51	294	.605
Lundgren	4	1	237	154	50	256	.601
Rose	4	1	245	192	52	332	.578
Fagan	4	1	232	151	32	336	.479
Mierzwa	2	3	158	113	21	276	.409
Goodell	1	4	134	132	23	316	.420
Totals	20	10	1256	920	229	1810	.508

Toledo – 15

Player	W	L	Pts	R	DR	SP	Pct.
Allison	3	2	217	190	51	328	.579
Konz	2	2	174	165	46	304	.543
Uberoth	2	2	142	101	20	220	.458
Fitzgerald	1	3	151	112	26	246	.455
Hart	1	3	140	98	20	218	.449
Garland	1	3	113	85	13	222	.387
Smotherman	0	5	116	102	14	272	.375
Totals	10	20	1053	853	190	1810	.471

Other League Scores

June 15:   Toledo 24 vs. Ann Arbor 11

Called at end of five rounds for rain

June 29:   Flint 34 vs. Ann Arbor 15

Division Standings

Team	W	L
Detroit	1	0
Flint	1	0
Toledo	1	1
Ann Arbor	0	2

Detroit Butchers Ann Arbor

Detroit easily squelched Ann Arbor on July 13, at Wines Field, 38–11. No score keepers were available, so no ringer percentages were kept.

Detroit			Ann Arbor		
Gothard	7	0	Raab	5	2
Rose	6	1	Otto	4	3
Field	6	1	Weinkauf	1	6
Ball	6	1	Fisher	1	6
Fagan	5	2	Godfrey	0	1
Mierzwa	4	3	Briton	0	6
Kelly	4	3	Fraser	0	7
			Curtis	0	7
Total	38	11	Total	11	38

Standings of the Detroit Players in League Matchers

	W	L		W	L
Gothard	7	0	Fagan	9	3
Field	11	1	Kelly	4	3
Ball	6	1	Mierzwa	6	6
Rose	10	2	Goodell	1	4
Lundgren	4	1			

HELP!!

Flint Slaughters Detroit

July 20 will go down as a black day for Detroit's horseshoe team, for they took a trip to Flint and came out on the short end of a 39–10 score. Detroit practically spotted Flint 21 games by being forced to use Ingraham, Hickman and Meirzwa, who each failed to win a game. Rose and Ball could only win one game each and Lundgren and Field managed to win four games each. No score sheets were kept so no ringer averages were known, but Flint really pitched in inspired fashion. Notable was the victory of Field over Latzko.

- - - - - - -

This is the second recent match record in which a lack of scorekeepers was mentioned. I believe this is the first mention of scorekeepers—present or absent—in the journals. One of the reasons for Lee's incredible level of detail in the journals must have been that score sheets were completed during the games he pitched. His specific mention of the lack of scorekeepers for these games leads one to assume that for most of his league and tournament matches a scorekeeper was on duty.

That is a bit strange by current standards. For at least the last few decades, in league play anyway, players fill out their own score sheets as the games are played. The same is sometimes true for smaller tournaments. And that practice is good for the sport. Spectators can visit and enjoy fellowship, observe the games, and buy concessions rather than being pressed into service as a scorekeeper.

It is puzzling then to figure out why, back in 1941, players couldn't keep score as they played—especially in this league, since Rose would have preferred to keep very precise statistics. Perhaps it's as simple as the players were spoiled and it never occurred to them to make the score keeping self-sufficient.

- - - - - - -

Revenge — Detroit Slaughters Flint

Detroit – 33

Player	W	L	Pts	OP	R	DR	SP	Pct.
Walls	7	0	350	171	273	110	380	.717
Field	7	0	350	130	258	81	378	.682
Lundgren	5	2	305	266	246	63	444	.554
Gothard	5	2	315	244	241	70	436	.552
Rose	4	3	320	239	263	76	444	.594
Ball	4	3	331	286	265	78	462	.573
Fagan	1	6	242	347	305	48	450	.455
Totals	33	16	2213	1683	1751	526	2994	.584

Flint – 16

Player	W	L	Pts	OP	R	DR	SP	Pct.
Latzko	4	3	295	278	256	75	432	.592
Miller	3	4	222	286	230	67	394	.583
Middleton	3	4	254	311	226	61	410	.505
Podsadecki	2	5	249	327	224	59	462	.485
Shepard	2	5	237	333	208	45	442	.470
Wood	1	6	204	331	206	45	422	.488
Jones	1	6	222	347	208	46	432	.481
Total	16	33	1683	2213	1558	398	2994	.520

Detroit Blasts Toledo

August 3 – Northwestern Field
Detroit – 36

Player	W	L	Pts	OP	R	DR	SP	Pct.
Lundgren	7	0	350	89	240	82	346	.693
Field	7	0	350	148	263	88	384	.684
Walls	7	0	350	157	268	82	404	.663
Ball	6	1	337	190	257	79	408	.629
Galesky	4	3	312	193	248	76	406	.610
Rose	4	3	322	196	223	63	384	.580
Goodell	1	3	185	194	132	33	286	.461
Hickman	0	3	25	150	31	2	120	.257
Totals	36	13	2231	1317	1662	505	2740	.606

Toledo – 13

Player	W	L	Pts	OP	R	DR	SP	Pct.
Konz	4	3	276	266	265	84	430	.616
Allison	2	5	271	277	269	83	456	.589
Ueberoth	2	5	212	341	233	52	446	.500
Hart	2	5	184	312	163	37	364	.447
Fitzgerald	1	6	148	346	171	44	362	.472
Becker	1	6	112	340	131	22	336	.389
Smotherman	1	6	114	349	124	22	346	.359
Totals	13	36	1317	2231	1345	344	2740	.491

Standing of Detroit Players

Player	W	L	Player	W	L
Walls	14	0	Galesky	4	3
Field	29	4	Kelly	4	3
Gothard	12	2	Fagan	10	9
Lundgren	20	6	Mierzwa	6	13
Ball	17	11	Goodell	2	7
Rose	19	14	Ingraham	0	7
Hickman	0	10			

Announcement: The greater Detroit Tournament is scheduled for August 16 and 17.

- - - - - - -

The journals contain a three-page article from *Horseshoe World* written by Rose. I was torn about whether or not to include the article. It's long and probably dull to most readers. But the article offers a great historic view of the sport—even if only from the standpoint that Lee Rose, out protagonist, wrote a brilliant piece that reviews the history of the sport as of 1940. He offers his opinion, which given his level of engagement should be viewed as an expert opinion, on what it will take to turn the sport around and improve its administration. In his previous article in *Horseshoe World* Rose claimed he had the answer to fixing the association's problems and would provide it later. Here it is.

– – – – – – –

Team Leagues

(Editor's note: This article does not necessary reflect the opinions of the *Horseshoe World* but it is written by Lee Rose, former secretary of the National Association and we feel we should accord space for him to present his views.)

The National Association was formed on May 10, 1921, and the rise of horseshoe pitching as a national sport can be truthfully dated from this event. The giving to the pitchers of this country a governing body and a uniform set of rules for all sections to use provided an impetus for the game's rapid development to the point at which it stands today. There is no doubt in anyone's mind and there should be no argument whatever to the assertion that the formation of this National Association made the game what it is today—a highly scientific sport which is both healthy and recreative.

When the National Association was first formed it was the intention of the leaders who formed it to form state associations patterned after the parent body, to whom charters would be issued denoting their affiliation. These charters were to cost a nominal sum of $25.00 and in return, the state association was given, complete control over all club and leagues, etc., in that state.

This system stayed in force until the Moline convention in 1935. By this time it had been proven that this system was not adequate to cope with the progress of the sport, so a new idea was incorporated by which the various states were given charters free and each individual member joined the National and State Association by the purchase of one membership card furnished by the National.

This system of membership is the one now in effect and it has been apparent for at least three years that this method of membership is not and can never be successful. To allow the Association sufficient funds for properly promoting the game, anywhere from 5,000 to 8,000 individual members must be secured. In five seasons, the highest figure reached in membership was 2,763 in the first year this system was tried. The next two years show membership of 1,893 and 1,847 and the fourth year showed 1,718. Figures of last season's membership are not available to me, but I notice by Lyle Brown's letter that it was 1,700.

Can there be any doubt in any one's mind that this plan is definitely a failure? Doesn't it appear that a drastic change is needed if the National Association is to continue as the governing body of horseshoes? It seems so to me.

I have from time to time, read various ideas submitted by horseshoe minds for the better organization of the sport, but none of them have, in my estimation, quite hit the right note. The letter in the May issue, written by Lyle Brown [which isn't included in Rose's journals or this book] and the letter by Jack Claves in the same issue are examples of the ideas I have seen.

These two letters and others I have read, all appeal to the horseshoe pitchers to "join the National." That is a noble thought, but it is a hopeless cause. Players have proven over a period of five years that they will not "join the National," at least under the present system. Any plan submitted for the betterment of the game must not simply ask players to join, but must go about the task of creating something which will make them join. The plan I am about to discuss here is one which I believe will do just that thing and I had intended to wait until a national convention was held to present it, but since no convention is in sight this year, or perhaps for several years, I have asked the *Horseshoe World* to print this plan just as I would have presented it at a convention.

Let's get down to plain facts. Who joins the National now? With a few notable exceptions, most states get their members around tournament time and those members join then mostly because they HAVE to join in order to participate in the meets. This statement can be borne out by the records of the last National Tournament and by records of several Mid-West meets in Des Moines. A good 75 per cent of the leading pitchers came to these meets without a membership card and had to obtain one before they could pitch.

Numerous state and city meets would disclose the same situation if the records could be obtained. The conclusion is that the leading pitchers would not join if they were not forced to do so.

Since the leading pitchers constitute only about ten per cent of the total number in this country and since most of them join only because they are forced to, how can the National Association hope to obtain the memberships of the other 90 per cent whose support they must have? Five years of experience has proven beyond question that under the present system, IT CANNOT BE DONE!

What is the basic reason for this failure? Just this: The National Association does not provide any reason or any inducement for the poorer pitcher to join. The better pitchers join when forced to, but the support of the "run-of-the-mine" pitcher can only be obtained by coaxing and this means is a failure—especially after he has been coaxed a few times.

Plainly speaking then, the only way for the National Association to become a body worthy of the same name is to be supported by the vast machine of the "run-of-the-mine" pitchers and the only way to obtain their support is to provide an inducement to make them WANT to join, or at least, MAKE them join. The whole problem boils down to one question. What can the National Association do to provide lower-average pitchers an incentive for supporting the National Association? The proper answer to this question if put into legislative effect, will solve the entire problem. And the answer to this question is so amazingly simple that I wonder that somebody else has not already thought about it.

What phase of the sport interests the "run-of-the-mine" pitcher? It cannot be tournaments, no matter how many classes it is divided into, for he would still not be good enough to take part. The "run-of-the-mine" pitcher is interested in seeing an event which carries through the entire season put into effect. He is interested in an event which will allow him steady participation and enjoyment over a whole season. Give him this and he'll join.

There is only one phase of the game which could answer to this description—team play and team leagues. The team league he is in must be only for pitchers of about his class [skill level], pitchers who won't beat him badly enough to humiliate him and pitchers whom he can figure on beating too. More than this, he wants something to look forward to when he develops into a better pitcher and this something can act as an added incentive for spurring him into action.

The National Association must give these pitchers team leagues and team play to get their support. I can hear the chorus now—"We already have leagues and teams like this this for these pitchers and they still don't join! They still ask what good they can derive from that national card." If they already have a league, how can it be bettered by simply giving membership dues to the National Association?

The Association cannot expect to simply step in, put out their hand and have money pour into it if they have done nothing toward helping these pitchers form their league. They cannot expect others to do the work of forming these leagues while they reap the harvest. If the Association wants to collect dues from players in leagues, it must do its part in getting leagues formed. It must place more emphasis on team leagues and team play than it does on individual play. The NATIONAL ASSOCIATION MUST CHANGE ITS MEMBERSHIP PLAN FROM INDIVIDUAL TO TEAMS.

I have thought about this problem for several years and each year has brought added knowledge which I have carefully stored away until such time as I would have a complete plan for this change. There are so many points to be considered that it provides quite a puzzle. For instance who would have the votes at a national convention? What would happen to state associations? What about players who couldn't or wouldn't play on teams? And many others.

I have the answers to all these questions and I am ready to present this plan to the pitchers of this country, believing sincerely that it will bring final success to the National Association. I have written this plan in the form of a constitution and by-laws to be adopted by the Association and a brief synopsis of this document follows:

There would be three classes of teams formed, A, B and C. The Class A teams would pay ten dollars a year in dues, the Class B teams would pay five dollars, and the Class C would pay two and one-half. Class A teams would be allowed one vote, Class B teams would be allowed one-half vote and Class C teams would be allowed one-fourth vote. Proxies shall be allowed, so each team could be sure of representation. Teams are to be divided into geographical divisions and one vice president shall come from each division, with the president and secretary-treasurer to come from any division.

Class A and B teams will play a regular season's schedule in much the same manner as provided now in Article V of the present By-laws and at the end of the regular season a National Team Tournament shall be held for the winners and runners-up in each division in both Class A and Class B. Class B teams will be allowed to enter the Class A meet if they wish. The team tournament will be awarded to bidders just as the individual tournament is awarded now.

The official national convention would be held at the time of the team tournament and elections would be held every year, with officers taking office at the beginning of the following year.

The national singles tournament would be held just the same as it always has been and its awarding and conduction will be solely in the hands of a five-man committee elected at the time of the tournament by pitchers participating in same. The rules concerning this singles meet will be made up only by those playing in it. In this tournament, or other sectional meets, a member of a Class A team can enter by paying his entrance fee, if any; a member of a Class B team will pay an additional 50 cents to enter and a Class C member must pay 75 cents. Anyone not a member of any team will pay $1.00 to enter. All other tournaments such as state, county and city meets can have their tournaments sanctioned by simply collecting the necessary dues from entries. Class B meets will be open only to members of Class B or C teams and Class C meets will be open to only members of Class C teams. Lists of eligible [players] will be furnished to any sponsors of sanctioned meets.

Horseshoes will be sanctioned just as they are now and only sanctioned shoes will be allowed in any team matches or individual meets. The stamp fund will be divided 50–50 between the team tournament and the individual tournament and the amount taken will be the fund as of August 15. The individual share will be apportioned into 16 graduated prizes and the team share into 12 graduated prizes with the last four going to the Class B teams.

All expenses of the Association shall be budgeted by the national convention.

This is only a very brief synopsis of this proposed constitution and by-laws, but it covers the salient points. There is nothing said about state associations, for they will have no place in the national scheme of organization by teams. The state associations can continue as always, collecting their own dues and keeping all of them and holding their own state tournaments, etc.

To sum up this plan and what it hopes to accomplish is our next step in presenting. The very good pitchers of the nation will soon find their way to a Class A team and will enjoy the season of play with their teammates, going on several short trips with them and meeting leading players in nearby cities. If the team they play on becomes eligible for the national team tournament they will have an opportunity to play for the world's team title. This is all in addition to having their regular individual meets as before. So the leading players of the nation gain something.

The next class of pitchers will be those on the Class B teams and I figure they will be those players from 40 to 55 per cent. They will be a group twice as numerous as the Class A group and will play in the same kind of matches and in the same kind of way as the Class A group. They too will have opportunities to develop and reach a Class A team the following year.

If a Class B meet is held, they can be sure no Class A player is going to sneak in and grab the prize because all players are now rated. This gives the secondary pitchers of the nation something more than they have now.

The Class C teams will be the local leagues which probably play under lights on week nights and I expect these teams to reach a figure greater than the other two classes combined. Each local league must be sponsored by a Class A or Class B team and the idea is that these bigger teams will be constantly on the outlook for talent to replace lagers on their teams and the Class C men will have the benefit of good coaching and advice from experts.

Not only will the Class C leagues be grounds for the developing of players, but will be political helps inasmuch as each Class C team is entitled to one-fourth vote, which can easily be swung to the will of the team sponsoring the league. The poorer pitcher, or the "run-of-the-mine" pitcher thus gets a league which is more or less directly provided for him by the National Association and will have pressure on him from start to finish to join the National Association.

Since, however, our idea is the building up of organized leagues which can, through their organization, more readily obtain commercial sponsors, we feel that it will be the sponsors who will pay the yearly dues of the various teams, just as it is in bowling, and the pitchers will not pay anything for their end. They can pay their own state association a yearly fee to keep their state tournament running, if they wish.

Added numbers of players using sanctioned shoes means a greatly increased stamp fund and, of course, added sales by the manufacturers of sanctioned shoes. So the horseshoe manufacturers gain something.

But of greatest importance of all will be the fact that for the first time in the history of horseshoe pitching the ruling body of the game will not be composed of pitchers who are not the leading champions of the sport, but will be instead a group of delegates from the bulk of horseshoe pitchers known sometimes as "scrubs." These are the ones who have always "paid the freight" and never had anything to say about running the game. But now, for the first time, they who "pay the freight" will have a chance to make out the bill of lading for it.

Will the National Association gain by this? I leave it to you.

- - - - - - -

So there is Lee Rose's proposal. The benefit of hindsight allows us to form some informed opinions about ut. His proposal never picked up steam, probably because of the reduced vote values for the proposed B and C classes and the danger of transitioning into an operation that didn't support state associations from the top.

Many aspects of his proposal have been implemented, such as equal competition opportunities for the various skill levels, which didn't stop at just three classes. League play really caught hold in the 1950s when the NHPA leadership got stronger and then again in the late 1970s when Donnie Roberts designed and developed the NHPA Sanctioned League Program.

Rose did not address handicap scoring as an option for some of the leagues, maybe that idea didn't exist back then, but it is a prevalent part of league play today.

Now Lee's journals return to the pitching season.

- - - - - - -

Rose Loses Detroit Title

Continuing in his slump, Lee Rose lost his Detroit District Championship in the annual tournament at Northwestern Field, August 16–17.

In the round robin on August 16, Rose placed in a tie for fifth with Jimmy Field, winning eight and losing five. He defeated Field in a playoff game for fifth place.

In the first round of the finals on August 17, Rose came from behind twice to down Galesky in a five game battle, but in the second round he was walloped three straight by Lundgren, who subsequently defeated A. Field in four straight games to win the meet.

- - - - - - -

Detroit beat Ann Arbor in the final league match to tie with Flint for 1st place.

- - - - - - -

Now comes some coverage of the 1941 World Tournament. The journal doesn't describe a trip to the tournament, or even indicate if Rose even attended it. There's just a newspaper clipping relating that Isais won followed by another from *Horseshoe World* that covers bits on the tournament, the convention, and a couple of other local items of interest.

- - - - - - -

Isais Takes Shoe Title

Senor Fernando Isais journeyed from his home in Mexico City, Mexico, to Des Moines last week and left Sunday with the 1941 world horseshoe pitching championship, gained at the expense of 23 of the leading pitchers of the nation at Birdland Park.

Isais turned in 23 consecutive victories without defeat, averaging 82.9 per cent ringers for the three-day tournament and defeated the defending titlist, Ted Allen of Boulder, Colorado, in the feature match Sunday.

Allen dropped his match to Isais by a 50 to 46 score after leading throughout the closing stages. He was beaten by Casey Jones of Waukesha, Wisconsin, Saturday to finish in second place with 21 victories against two setbacks.

Jones missed a chance to tie Allen for second when he was beaten in his last match of the meet by Sidney Harris of Minden, Nebraska. He lost also to Isais.

Almost 2,000 fans were present as Allen and Isais battled it out for the championship and saw Isais turn in an 87.8 ringer percentage to 87.1 for the defending champion. Isais threw 130 ringers and 57 doubles out of 148 shoes.

Harris placed fourth in the tournament with 19 victories and four defeats and Alvin Dahlene of Lawrence, Kansas, was fifth.

Iowa champion Dale Dixon of Des Moines headed the host state representatives with 14 games won and 9 lost for a ninth place tie.

Tournament ringer averages for the other leaders included 81.4 for Allen, 79.6 for Jones, 77.7 for Dahlene and 76.5 for Harris. Final Standings:

1941 World Tournament Finals
Des Moines, Iowa
August 22–24

Player	W	L	R	SP	Pct
1. Fernando Isais	23	0	1265	1526	82.9
2. Ted Allen	21	2	1262	1550	81.4
3. Casey Jones	20	3	1215	1522	77.7
4. Sidney Harris	19	4	1129	1514	74.6
5. Alvin Dahlene	18	5	1104	1530	72.2
6. Ervin Hosier	17	6	1171	1570	74.6
7. Roland Kraft	17	6	1013	1460	69.4
8. Earl Bomke	16	7	1177	1592	73.9
9. Dale Dixon	14	9	1019	1492	68.3
10. Clayton Henson	14	9	1119	1662	67.3
11. Eddie Packham	14	9	1052	1576	66.8
12. John Paxton	10	10	1119	1638	68.3
13. Theo. Harlan	12	11	919	1462	62.9
14. Well. Taylor	10	13	950	1476	64.4
15. Clarence Barton	9	14	665	1254	53.0
16. J. R. Tompkin	7	16	913	1572	58.1
17. Russell Sheetz	6	17	861	1488	57.9
18. Floyd Saffell	6	17	804	1396	57.6
19. Archie Gregson	5	18	802	1436	55.8
20. R. Butterfield	5	18	671	1276	52.6
21. Harold Darnold	4	19	835	1456	57.3
22. David Carter	2	21	572	1232	46.1
23. H. Kohlenberger	2	21	516	1218	42.4
24. Howard Robinson	2	21	420	1058	39.7

Convention Is Held

There was some objection to the short notice given for the tournament and convention.

However, a meet was held and a convention was held and it is the consensus of opinion that the officers elected will do everything they can to eliminate the bickering which has gone for some time. The *Horseshoe World* subscribes to this viewpoint and will do its best to support the new administration as long as it does reasonably well in its endeavors.

Harry "Pop" Woodfield, of Washington, D.C., is at the helm now. He has made quite a record in arousing interest in the East and he should make a good president. He has a big job on his hands, however, and needs support.

The office of secretary went to the other side of the country with Archie Gregson taking on that position, succeeding J. Robert Tompkin.

The report given in this issue of the *Horseshoe World* is as complete as can be given under the circumstances, since no representatives of this magazine could attend the meeting.

The Army Got Him

You might be interested in knowing that Frank Koppitsch, of Detroit, a good pitcher who stands 6 ft. 4 ins. and weighs about 240 lbs., is now in the Army at Camp Livingston, La. You remember him, I'm sure. His address is Company D, A.P.O., 32nd Division, 126th Inf.

Have New Baby

Mr. and Mrs. Lee Rose, of Detroit, have a new daughter, Diane Helene. They have two sons, Lee and Bob. The proud papa formerly was secretary of the National.

Movie Made

On September 16, a movie company filmed a horseshoe picture at Northwestern Field in Detroit for the Firestone Tire Company and Lee Rose acted as horseshoe adviser for the filming and also acted as "ghost" pitcher for the actors, throwing the ringers while the actors were filmed pitching. The picture, to be released in November, is known as the 1941 Farm Film of the Firestone Company.

- - - - - - -

Following these newsy tidbits is a tournament announcement that has been trimmed and tacked onto a journal page. Then Rose describes the event itself.

Michigan State Championship
Horseshoe Tournament
August 30, 31 – September 1
Wines Field – Ann Arbor
Plan to Attend this Tournament, Held on
Michigan's Finest Courts
CASH PRIZES   LEE ROSE, Sec.

- - - - - - -

My Eighteenth State Tournament

In the qualifying, on August 30, I hit 823 points, with .607, to finish number 12. Joe Latzko and Jim Skinner were not required to qualify and others to get in were: Carl Lundgren, Bobby Hitt, Carl Gothard, Elmer Raab, Bill Miller, Jonas Otto, Al Field, Ray Middleton, Dan Latzko, Ray Gorsline, Phil Carra, Norris Shepherd and Lincoln Greene.

August 31 – Round One

A very, very strong wind roared over the courts and made pitching for all entries difficult and for ME, practically impossible! I faced a tough enough situation with my feet still bad and my pitching still off form, but this wind, blowing as it was, practically precluded any possibility of me suddenly finding myself as I have often done in the past.

Carra took the opening spot-light by going .717 to wallop "Roundy" Raab 50–15 and the other favorites swung in behind him with Lundgren going 100 shoes to nose out Dan Latzko 50–47, as each pitched .650; Joe Latzko squelching Field 50–21; Hitt beating Rose 50–20, with Rose pitching only .342; Gothard beating Gorsline 50–39; Otto downed Greene 50–34; Miller trounced Shepard 50–33 and old Jim Skinner nosed out Middleton 50–49.

ROUND TWO

Joe Latzko hung up 60 out of 72 for .833 to trample Gothard 50–14; Hitt went .720 to best Otto 50–18; Raab walloped Skinner 50–12; Lundgren stayed with the two perennial leaders by trouncing his one-time jinx, Miller 50–33; Carra also stayed unbeaten by winning from Middleton 50–38; Field beat Gorsline; D. Latzko beat Shepard and Rose won a game from Greene, pitching only .448.

ROUND THREE

Hitt knocked Carra out of the unbeaten 50–17, hitting .750; Joe Latzko defeated D. Latzko; Lundgren smothered Gorsline to stay unbeaten; Field beat Miller; Gothard beat Shepard; Raab beat Greene. Rose won his second game by coming from behind in a late rally to trip Skinner 50–43, hurling just .558.

ROUND FOUR

Joe Latzko pitched .796 to slaughter Miller 50–14; Hitt pitched .796 to slaughter Gothard 50–15; Lundgren hit .689 to beat Raab 50–35; Field nicked Carra 50–44 and Rose nosed out Gorsline 50–43 with only .451 to stay in a tie for fourth place. In other games, D. Latzko beat Greene, Middleton beat Shepard and Otto won from Skinner.

ROUND FIVE

Joe Latzko went .700 to trounce Gorsline 50–13; Hitt easily beat Greene; Lundgren easily beat Shepard. Rose trailed Otto badly all the way, then put on a late rush to snatch the lead 48–47, then missed one shoe and saw Otto go out with a double. A very disheartening game to lose. Rose still remained in a tie for fourth, however as Gothard knocked Field off; Raab beat Middleton 50–40 with .650; Carra whipped Skinner and D. Latzko slaughtered Miller. An hour was taken for lunch. The leaders: Joe Latzko 5–0, Bobby Hitt 5–0, Lundgren 5–0, Rose 3–2, Gothard 3–2, Raab 3–2, Field 3–2, D. Latzko 3–2 and Carra 3–2.

ROUND SIX

Raab hit .662 to trip Joe Latzko 50–42; Hitt defeated Miller 50–20; Lundgren beat Otto 50–23; Carra beat Rose 50–31; Field trounced Shepard to stay tied for fourth with Raab; Gothard fell before Skinner; D. Latzko was tripped by Gorsline; Greene upset Middleton. Rose was now tied for seventh place.

ROUND SEVEN

Lundgren went .759 to whip Field 50–19; Hitt won from Middleton 50–40; Joe Latzko beat Shepard. Carra beat Otto; Raab won from Rose 50–28 to stay tied for fourth place; Gothard beat D. Latzko; Skinner beat Greene and Miller beat Gorsline. Leaders: Hitt 7–0, Lundgren 7–0, Joe Latzko 6–1, Carra 5–2, Raab 5–2, Gothard 4–3 and Field 4–3.

ROUND EIGHT

Lundgren pitched .857 to massacre Gothard 50–3; Hitt hit .761 to trample Raab 50–11; Joe Latzko smothered Otto 50–10; Carra fell before D. Latzko; Field beat Greene; Miller beat Skinner; Gorsline beat Ray Middleton and Rose managed to out-last Shepard 50–46. Leaders: Hitt 8–0, Lundgren 8–0, J. Latzko 7–1, Cara 5–3, Field 5–3, Rose 4–4, Gothard 4–4, D. Latzko 4–4.

ROUND NINE

Hitt and Lundgren continued to head the heap. Hitt pounding out a win over Gorsline; the "Swede" winning over Rose 50–24, the "Tiger" [Rose] was just simply without his claws; Joe Latzko easily stayed in third by plastering Middleton; Raab won over Shepard; Field won over Otto; Carr slipped before Gothard; Skinner nicked D. Latzko 50–47 and Miller beat Greene. Leaders: Hitt 9–0, Lundgren 9–0, Joe Latzko 8–1, Raab 6–3, Field 6–3, Gothard 5–4, Carra 5–4.

ROUND TEN

Joe Latzko smashed out .767 to down Lundgren 50–21, so Hitt stood all alone in first place by walloping Skinner 50–9. Field took D. Latzko; Raab beat his neighbor Otto to stay tied for fourth; Gothard beat Miller; Carra beat Greene; Gorsline beat Shepard. Rose picked up his heels a little for the first time, pitching .602 to whip Middleton 50–39 and now perched all alone in eighth place.

ROUND ELEVEN

Hitt remained at the top, beating Shepard and Joe Latzko and Lundgren kept on his heels by downing Rose and Carra, respectively. Raab beat Field to take over fourth all alone. Miller and D. Latzko won to move up to eighth place, while

Gothard was tripped up by Greene. Leaders: Hitt 11–0, Joe Latzko 10–1, Lundgren 10–1, Raab 8–3, Field 7–4, Gothard 6–5; Carra 6–5.

ROUND TWELVE

Joe Latzko knocked Hitt off 50–42 in a poor game; Lundgren made it a three-way tie for the lead by going .750 to thrash Skinner 50–8; Raab tumbled before Miller's .662; Field sneaked up to tie Raab by practically eliminating Rose 50–46 after Rose had led nearly all the way; Gothard mowed down Otto; D. Latzko won from Middleton and Carra beat Shepard.

ROUND THIRTEEN

Hitt trampled Field 50–11; Lundgren squelched Greene 50–6; Joe Latzko trounced Carra 50–25 to preserve the three-way tie for first place; Gothard flopped before Middleton .661; D. Latzko hit .743 to beat Raab and Miller definitely eliminated Rose 50–18.

ROUND FOURTEEN

Hitt took over 1st place all alone again by hitting .735 to beat Lundgren 50–34 as old Jim Skinner rose like a wraith from the past and walloped Joe Latzko 50–46 with .632. Middleton hit Field with .739 to crush him 50–10. Miller reeled off 63 out of 90 for .700 to beat Otto 50–34; D. Latzko and Carra both won with D. Latzko beating Rose.

FINAL ROUND – FIFTEEN

Hitt retained 1st place by beating D. Latzko; Joe Latzko hammered out .850 to beat Greene 50–3; Lundgren rang up .783 to butcher Middleton; Gothard won from Rose in a very good game wherein Rose hurled his best game of the day 56 out of 80 for .700, while Gothard had only 55 ringers for .687, but won 50–47. Field, Raab and Carra each won to create a four-way tie for fourth with Gothard; Miller and D. Latzko remained tied for eighth, both losing.

Field and Gothard defeated Raab and Carra in a play-off for fourth and fifth place and Carra beat Raab for 6th. D. Latzko beat Miller for 8th.

In the quarter-finals, Hitt averaged .791 to wallop D. Latzko three straight 50–18, 50–15 and 50–11. Joe Latzko defeated Raab three straight 50–36, 50–39 and 50–18, averaging .760. Lundgren stumbled over Carra in the first game, losing 50–44, but came back to win the next three, 50–38, 50–14 and 50–24. Carl averaged .690 for the four games.

Gothard surprised Field by averaging .672 to whip Al three straight games 50–36, 50–34 and 50–39.

SEMI-FINALS

The semi-finals were exciting. Gothard and Hitt played and Latzko played against Lundgren. The first game between Latzko and Lundgren was a record breaker. Each man tossed 16 ringers out of the first 22 shoes and the score was 10–10. Then Latzko hit four doubles, a single, four doubles and another single to run up a 26–13 lead. Lundgren got 4 on a single, then the ringers began to drop on and six consecutive times saw four ringers on the stake. Latzko broke first and Lundgren ran his string to eight doubles to make it 26–20. Ringers continued to fly on and it later stood 35–29 for Latzko, then Lundgren faded and Joe won out 50–29. Latzko threw 50 ringers in the last 54 shoes of the game. Score:

	Pts	R	DR	SP	Pct	4-On
Latzko	50	84	36	98	.857	23
Lundgren	29	76	31	98	.775	23

Lundgren came back to nick Joe in the second game 50–48, while Gothard, who had lost his first game to Hitt 50–43, turned the tables on Hitt 50–37.

Latzko defeated Lundgren 50–32 in the third game, but Hitt AGAIN fell before Gothard in their third game 50–41 and now stood facing elimination. Latzko eliminated Lundgren 50–15 and Hitt came back with games of .750 and .850 to beat Gothard 50–22 and 50–19.

Hitt rounded Latzko up 50–21, hitting .800 in the first game. Hitt led nearly all the way in the second game, but with the score 39–36 in his favor, Bobby suddenly hit only five out of ten and the alert Joe had won 50–39.

Latzko opened the third game with seven doubles to take a 12–0 lead which he maintained to 25–13. Here Hitt rallied long and, aided by 30 ringers out next 34 shoes, pulled ahead of Joe 32–30. Hitt was not headed after that and won 50–39 in 118 shoes, throwing 90 ringers to Latzko's 87.

Hitt took a lead 16–13 in the fourth game, but eight doubles by Latzko shot him ahead, where he stayed, winning 50–30 to square the series.

The "crucial fifth" then got underway with Hitt rolling up a 13–1 lead, but with Latzko tying it up at 22–22. Hitt then looped on 19 out of the next 20 to shoot ahead again 29–22, but Latzko tied it in two innings with a 4 and three ringers for 3 points. Latzko here missed and Hitt piled in for 6 and later led 42–33, but fell off at the final as Latzko came up to win 50–42.

The last game was 28–28 at 50 shoes, but Latzko pulled away after that to win 50–32 and retained his title.

- - - - - - -

Following Lee's characteristically thorough recounting of the action at the 1941 Michigan state tournament, he returns to chronicling international league concerns. First, with his summary of the Detroit team's final and unfortunate match of the season. Then, with a clipping from *Horseshoe World* announcing the National League's first championship team. I imagine it was much to Rose's dismay that the Detroit team was not at least part of the championship bout.

- - - - - - -

"Ragnarok"

Detroit came to the end of their championship trail on September 7, when they met Flint at Ann Arbor in a play-off match for the division title. Only four regulars showed up for the match, Lundgren, Rose, Walls and Gothard. Kelly and Goodell had to step in along with a pick-up scrub to round out a team.

The defeat of Detroit was almost certain even before the match began. Lundgren and Walls each won six games, Lundgren hitting .751 and Walls pitching .740. Gothard won five going .681. Rose pitching his best of a poor year, hit .605, but could win only two games. Kelly won two. The score was 28–21.

Indianapolis Moose Win League Championship

The Indianapolis Moose 17 horseshoe team, runners-up to Detroit in the 1940 competition for the National Horseshoe League team title, went a step further in 1941 by winning the International League crown, competition for which was open to the world.

In the seven-man team singles play the Moose defeated Fort Wayne twice in matches by scores of 30–19 and 33–15.

Then on September 21st at Fort Wayne, Indiana, the Indianapolis entry trimmed Flint, Michigan, the northern playoff winners by an overwhelming 31–18 margin. All games played by the new champions were on "foreign" courts. Sponsor of the winners was Lodge No. 17, Loyal Order of Moose, Indianapolis, Indiana.

Here are summaries of players' records for Indianapolis Moose No. 17; for all playoff matches played:

	W	L
George Johnson	18	3
Howard Deer	16	5
Lowell Gamendson	12	2
Arlo Harris	10	3
James Stringer	12	9
Orvil Harris	4	1
Charles McKinney	5	8
Glenn Austin	4	3
W. A. Banta	4	4
Paul Van Sickle	4	4
Clarence Ray	3	4
Robert Ross	2	4
John O'Brien	0	2

- - - - - - -

Then comes some interesting information about an AAU National Horseshoe Pitching Championship. Surprisingly, Rose hasn't made a previous mention in the journals before this entry, but in 1937 the NHPA joined into an agreement with the AAU to hold state and national amateur horseshoe pitching championships—under an agreement set up by then NHPA Secretary Raymond Howard, the editor of *Horseshoe World*.

The 1941 championship final standings are reprinted here as presented in *Horseshoe World*. This new program isn't particularly newsworthy at this point, but later a number of Michigan pitchers will have a significant involvement in AAU events.

- - - - - - -

John Lindmeier, Chicago
Wins National A.A.U.

The *Horseshoe World* is pleased to give the results of the 1941 National A.A.U. Senior Horseshoe Championship meet held in Chicago, September 19, 20 and 21.

John Lindmeier won the singles contest and did his share in upholding the honors with his teammate, Dorne Woodhouse, in the doubles meet.

1941 AAU National Championship
Senior Men's Singles

		W	L	Pct
1. John Lindmeier	Chicago, IL	14	1	67.01
2. Frank Breen	Elgin, IL	13	2	69.83
3. Dorne Woodhouse	Chicago, IL	12	3	67.56
4. Arner Lindquist	Morgantown, WV	9	6	61.23
5. Marion Morris	Pendleton, IN	9	6	60.30
6. Pete Markarian	Chicago, IL	8	7	60.30
7. Leonard Loerzel	Chicago, IL	8	7	61.22
8. Henry Fleming	Chicago, IL	7	8	57.54
9. Edward Babush	Chicago, IL	7	8	60.24
10. E. R. Zimmerman	Chicago, IL	7	8	57.76
11. Ralph Dykes	Lombard, IL	7	8	60.43
12. John Fleming	Chicago, IL	7	8	62.54
13. Tyler Loy	Chicago, IL	6	9	59.52
14. Lee Rollick	Chicago, IL	5	10	55.38
15. Gust Brock	Chicago, IL	2	13	49.41
16. Robert Pence	Chicago, IL	1	14	47.43

1941 AAU National Championship
Senior Men's Doubles

	W	L
1. Dorne Woodhouse–John Lindmeier	5	1
2. Frank Breen–Edgar Schmoldt	6	2
3. Tyler Loy–Robert Pence	5	3
4. H. Flemming–J. Fleming	4	4
5. Arner Lindquist–Lee Rollick	2	4
6. Leonard Loerzel–Wm. Danhauer	2	4
7. Walter Lane Sr.–Marion Morris	0	6

Teams 2, 3 and 4 played extra games because of a three-way tie.

- - - - - - -

A couple of names in this tournament require further mention because they both enjoyed distinguished horseshoe-pitching careers.

First, there is Ralph Dykes, who later in his career served as NHPA president from 1967–73, received the Stokes Memorial Award in 1968 and was inducted to the national hall of fame in 1973.

Then there is Bob Pence, who served the NHPA as its secretary-treasurer from 1958–72, received the Stokes Memorial Award in 1961, and was inducted to the national hall of fame in 1965.

Pence had first joined the NHPA in 1929, so he was in the sport prior to the A.A.U. involvement. It's not entirely clear, but it's possible that the AAU brought Ralph Dykes into the sport. Both men pitchers were skilled pitchers, but their careers were highlighted by their efforts to promote the sport.

The 1941 tournament was the fifth national championship held by the AAU and John Lindmeier, who earned the first AAU National title in 1937, won his second in 1940, and now won his third and final title. Lindmeier was indeed an amateur in those days, but later on (especially in the 1950s) Lindmeier was one of the leading pitchers in NHPA World Tournaments.

There is an engaging story in the AAU National Amateur Championships and that organization's involvement in the sport. For more information, find a copy of my book *AAU National Amateur Horseshoe-Pitching Championships 1937–1977*.

Rose didn't make previous mention of the AAU, probably because so far he was not directly engaged either as a participant or as a part of its development. That will change, though, for him and several of his Michigan pitching comrades, who will become very involved.

Rose Goes to the AAU Nationals

The 1942 section of the journal starts with final stats from a team match that isn't accompanied by Rose's customary colorful description. He goes on to mention a rematch with the Flint team, followed by a historic comment about the impact World War II was having on the sport, and then coverage of another Michigan state tournament.

June 28 – Northwestern Field

Detroit – 14

Player	W	L	Pts	OP	R	DR	SP	Pct
Rose	5	0	250	134	192	61	294	.653
Lundgren	4	1	218	129	189	60	298	.634
Walls	2	1	127	75	101	32	158	.639
J. Otto	1	1	83	84	72	20	132	.546
Gothard	2	2	147	167	132	32	244	.541
Fagan	0	5	132	250	107	24	266	.402
Goodell	0	1	23	50	17	2	50	.340
Total	14	11	980	889	810	231	1441	.564

Flint – 11

Player	W	L	Pts	OP	R	DR	SP	Pct
Latzko	4	1	241	123	199	70	282	.706
Miller	3	2	198	172	166	55	270	.615
Jones	2	3	161	222	127	28	278	.457
Shepard	1	4	143	240	155	39	314	.493
Wood	1	4	146	223	146	34	298	.489
Total	11	14	889	980	793	226	1442	.549

A return match, with 6-a-side was played at Flint on July 12. No score was kept, but Detroit won 21–15. Lundgren won all six games, while Rose could only win three, beating Wood, Shepard and Jones and losing to Latzko, Middleton and Miller.

Horseshoe pitching was already feeling the sting of the war, as many pitchers had gone to the armed forces and others were working different shifts, long hours and seven days a week and therefore found a few opportunities to get together.

Our 1942 State Tournament was held on August 15 and 16, at Wines Field, in Ann Arbor.

My Nineteenth
State Tournament

All entries except Skinner and Latzko qualified by four fifty-shoe games and I qualified easily in the no. 8 spot with 417 points [with an average of] .610.

The 16 high qualifiers were divided into 2 squads of 8 men each—Red and Blue—and they played a round robin in each squad. The 4 high in each division were to go to the finals.

Preliminary Round-Robins

ROUND ONE

BLUE Division – Louis Hirschman of Saginaw easily trounced Jonas Otto of Ann Arbor 50–11 with .750; Carl Gothard of Detroit defeated Ray Gorsline of Fulton 50–32, shooting .654; Lee Rose of Detroit coasted over Henry Zessin of Saginaw 50–22, hitting only .519; Joe Latzko of Flint opened his title defense by nosing out Norris Shepard of Flint 50–44, pitching only .486 to Shepard's .500.

RED Division – Carl Lundgren of Detroit easily squelched Jim Skinner of Athens 50–20 with .695; Ray Middleton of Flint trounced Jim Davis of Battle Creek 50–21 with .683; Elmer Raab of Ann Arbor defeated Louis Craft of Kalamazoo 50–21 and Bill Miller of Flint won from Joe Kelly of Highland Park 50–46.

ROUND TWO

BLUE Division – Rose flopped to only .409 against Gothard and was beaten 50–25; Latzko halted Hirschman 50–36; Gorsline slaughtered Zessin 50–8 and Shepard beat Otto 50–12.

RED Division – Raab turned Lundgren back 50–37 in a poor game; Miller defeated Middleton 50–33; Skinner beat Craft 50–13 and Kelly nicked Davis 50–36.

ROUND THREE

BLUE Division – Gothard and Latzko remained undefeated, Carl beating Otto 50–23 and Joe beating Gorsline 50–36. Rose and Hirschman remained tied for third, Rose beating Shepard 50–17, with .685 and Hirschman beating Zessin 50–19.

RED Division – Middleton and Lundgren got back in winning stride again, Ray hitting .767 to smash down Skinner 50–18 and Carl hitting .713 to trounce Kelly 50–34. Miller and Raab stayed unbeaten by beating Craft and Davis respectively.

ROUND FOUR

Lee Rose fired the big shot in this round by taking Mr. Latzko over the bumps!! With five out six, Rose went out in front 3–1, but Latzko tied it on two 1's, then shot on a streak of 11 out of 12 to go ahead of Rose 9–3. Three more 1 pointers made it 11–3. Rose got 3 on a double to make it 11–6 and Joe got a point on a single. There was four-dead twice and then Rose picked 3 more on a double to make it 12–9.

Joe got 3 on a double and 4 points more as Rose missed to make 19–9. Here Joe suddenly missed both shoes and Rose pounded in for 6, came back with another double and scored 6 more as Latzko again missed. Rose led 21–19 and 3 more on another double made it 24–19.

Joe got a point on a single and it stood 24–20 at 50 shoes. Latzko ripped three doubles and scored 3 on each to go ahead 29–24, but here he again missed with both shoes and the "Tiger" leaped in for 6 more to again lead 30–29. Rose picked up a point on a single, then hit two doubles which each scored 3.

It was 37–29 and the spectators began to believe that an upset was in the making. Latzko dug in with two doubles to make it 37–32, but Rose scored 3 on a double to lead 40–32. Joe got 3 on a double and followed with a double, but Rose topped to hold the lead and the score at 40–35.

Lee picked up a point on a single, and then doubled again, but Latzko topped. Joe got a point on a single and then doubled, but the toy bull-dog again topped. Now Rose led 41–36!!

Rose only shot a single, but Latzko missed! 44–36. Rose doubled and scored 3 more and doubled again, but Joe doggedly topped. Joe doubled and Rose up and missed both shoes. Now Rose led 47–42. Latzko doubled again and got 3 more, but Rose went out in the next inning by hanging a double over a ringer and leaner to win. Score:

Player	Pts	R	DR	SP	Pct
Rose	50	68	25	94	.723
Latzko	45	64	22	94	.681

Hirschman made it unanimous by tripping Gothard 50–24 with .688, Shepard beat Zessin and Otto defeated Gorsline.

Raab took over the only undefeated spot by turning back Miller 50–37, hitting .691 to Bill's .648; Lundgren went .718 to beat Middleton 50–31; Craft beat Kelly and Skinner beat Davis.

ROUND FIVE

Rose continued as high man again in this round and he had to do it to beat out Gorsline. The game started slowly with Rose going ahead 7–0 with three out four. Ray got 3 on a single and Rose dittoed to hold the lead 10–3. Rose then double missed and Gorsline took 4, then 6 more on a double as Rose missed again and Ray led 13–10.

Rose got a 3 and another 3, as did Gorsline, then Rose got 2 in a row to go ahead 19–16. Rose then missed and Gorsline banged in 6 to go out in front 22–19. Here, however, Gorsline missed and Rose jumped in for 6, had another double topped and doubled again over Ray's single to lead 28–22.

Ray got 2 points on 2 singles, then Rose got 1 point and then Ray scored 1 again. Gorsline doubled and picked up 3 to make it 29–28. Ray doubled again, but Rose preserved his one-point margin by topping. Rose doubled back but Gorsline topped it and came back with a double only to see Rose again drop on the toppers. Rose then threw a single and the Fulton Fox slapped on his fifth straight double to go ahead 31–29.

After this streak, Ray missed both shoes and Rose quickly rammed in 6 points to again lead 35–31. Rose doubled, but Gorsline topped, then came back with a double and scored 6 as Rose missed. Gorsline led 37–35. Rose got 3 on a double and Ray made it 38–38 on a single and a point. Gorsline singled and Rose slapped on a double for 3. Rose doubled again and scored 3 more to lead 44–38. Rose had another double but Gorsline topped. Ray could only single and Rose hit another double, his fifth straight, to go out 50–38. Score:

Player	Pts	R	DR	SP	Pct
Rose	50	46	18	66	.697
Gorsline	38	40	12	66	.606

Hirschman, Gothard and Latzko each coasted to wins over Shepard, Zessin and Otto.

Like the old of the mountain, Skinner climbed all over Raab to knock him out of the unbeaten class 50–29, hitting .61 as Raab fell to .532. Lundgren, Miller and Middleton all showed power in winning their games.

ROUND SIX

Rose started out to trounce Hirschman with 17 out of the first 24 and led 27–12. Then Louie suddenly cut loose with 19 out of 20 and was ahead 40–27! Hirschman won 50–30 with .722. Latzko nosed out Gothard 50–44 with .680; Gorsline and Otto won, Otto going .654. Lundgren hit .731 to murder Miller 40–14, as Raab and Middleton went at it hammer and tongs with Raab winning 50–36, pitching .712 to Ray's .650; Craft and Skinner won, the latter taking fourth place by his victory over Kelly 50–44.

ROUND SEVEN

Rose started fast against Otto and with 17 out of 22, took a 21–8 lead. Five doubles by Otto, however, put him ahead 23–21! Rose crawled ahead 28–27, but two sixes in a row put Otto ahead 39–28 and a point on a single made it 40–28.

Otto shot another double and things didn't look so good for the "Tiger"!! Rose covered, however and then, after a ringer each for no-count, Otto grabbed 3 more on a double to lead 43–28.

Rose took two 3's on two doubles, then missed with both shoes! Otto, with a good chance to sew it up, also missed with both shoes, but got a point to make it 44-34. Rose got a point off from Otto's single ringer and singled back. Otto hit a double to make it 47-35! Rose doubled to make it 47-38, then singled and Otto got in for a point. Otto singled again and got another point to make it 49–38.

Otto singled again, but Rose hit a double. Rose doubled again and scored 6 as Otto missed to creep within 49–47. Rose only singled, but Otto again missed both as Rose crawled out to victory 50–49. Rose hit .625 to Otto's .600.

Gothard barely eked out a win over Shepard 50–47, while Zessin defaulted to Latzko. Hirschman had plenty of trouble in disposing of Gorsline 50–42, pitching .672 to Ray's .643. Lundgren pounded out .750 to beat Davis 50–1. Middleton, needing a victory to tie for fourth place, hit .679 to whip Craft, as Raab defeated Kelly. Miller made the finals by beating Skinner and this left Skinner and Middleton tied for fourth place.

- - - - - - -

A long, gay party, lasting into the "wee hours" was at Otto's home.

- - - - - - -

August 16 – Finals

Middleton defeated Skinner two out of three to become the 8th finalist. Skinner led 46–26 in the first game, but fell off at the end as Middleton connected for 13 out of 18 to nick a win 50–49. Skinner overcame a 47–38 lead to trip Middleton 40–47 in the second game, but was never in it in the third game as Middleton won 50–32.

ROUND ONE

Gothard hopped on Lundgren and downed him 50–41 as Lundgren hit only .566. Hirschman hit the same to be beaten by Miller 40–40.

Rose started out even worse against Raab, throwing only 10 out of 26 and Raab had a game-winning lead of 30–1. Rose out-played Raab after that, but not enough to do any good. Rose brought it up to 42–30, but stopped there, Raab winning 50–30 with .600 to Lee's .515.

Latzko, however, was even worse! Starting with only 10 out of 30, Joe found himself trailing Middleton 31–8 and although he nearly succeeded in pulling the game out, Latzko lost 50–47, shooting only .464. it was evident that a new champion was coming out of this tournament! Who would it be!

ROUND TWO

Gothard continued to pitch the least worst horseshoes, going .650 to trounce Miller 50–32. Raab stayed tied for the lead by beating a Joe Latzko who hit only .470, Raab going only .529 to win 50–39. Lundgren hit 22 out of the first 30 to roll up a 34–3 lead on Hirschman and finally won 50–35 with .618.

Rose and Middleton engaged in a tight dog-fight all the way. Rose took an 8–4 lead and Ray then got ahead 9–8. It was tied at 12-all, then Rose ran up to 21, only to have Middleton tie at 21–21. Rose led 24–21, but Ray crawled ahead 26–24; Rose went ahead 28–26, but Ray again went to the front 30–28. Rose got to 31, then Middleton went into the lead 37–31. Ray later led 40–32, but three doubles by Rose put him ahead 44–40. It was tied at 44, then Rose went to 47 on a double, Middleton tied it at 47–47 with a double and Rose finally went out with a double!

ROUND THREE

Raab got off a .760 game to beat Hirschman 50–24 and eliminated him. Rose fell before his seemingly insurmountable jinx, Lundgren. Rose led 25–21, but faded away after that to lose 50–28.

Miller definitely eliminated Latzko 50–32 and Gothard stayed unbeaten by defeating Middleton 50–39.

STANDINGS

Raab	3	0	Rose	1	2
Gothard	3	3	Middleton	1	2
Lundgren	2	1	Latzko	0	3
Miller	2	1	Hirschman	0	3

ROUND FOUR

Lundgren slammed on .767 to smear Latzko 50–19 and Hirschman eliminated Middleton 50–22, hitting .680. Raab took the undisputed lead by beating Gothard who could only hit .440, 50–22. Rose, pitching only .485, was eliminated by Miller 50–34.

ROUND FIVE

Lundgren began to establish himself as a favorite by pitching .792 to butcher Miller 50–16. Raab, however, continued to lead by winning over Middleton 50–17 with .697. Gothard stayed in the running by beating Hirschman 50–36 with .672. Latzko, aided by eight consecutive doubles, ran up a 28–6 lead on Rose to win 50–34.

STANDINGS

Raab	5	0	Hirschman	1	4
Lundgren	4	1	Middleton	1	4
Gothard	4	1	Latzko	1	4
Miller	3	2	Rose	1	4

ROUND SIX

Lundgren's stock continued to soar as he trounced Middleton 50–24, going .731. Raab put Miller out 50–40, hitting .676. Latzko, leading Gothard 48–39, suddenly threw off and let Gothard win. Rose and Hirschman, out of the running, staged a beauty. Rose got 3 on a double, then Hirschman poured on six doubles in a row, but could only score 9 points as Rose, pouring 'em on too, hit 25 of the first 30 to lead 18–10. Hirschman never caught up after that and Rose won 50–31, throwing 49 out of 70 for .700.

ROUND SEVEN

Lundgren engaged Raab in the feature game and got off to a commanding 37–15 lead, but could hold that lead and Raab gradually whittled him down and nosed out a win 50–49. All eyes suddenly turned to Gothard, for could he succeed in beating Rose, he would go to the title series! Alas, for Gothard! He was in the midst of being handed a lacing by the latently aroused "Tiger" 50–39, leaving Lundgren and Gothard to battle for 2nd. Middleton helped Rose by nosing out Miller 50–47, to give Rose a tie for 4th. Latzko defaulted to Hirschman.

STANDINGS

Raab	7	0	Miller	3	4
Lundgren	5	2	Hirschman	2	5
Gothard	5	2	Middleman	2	5
Rose	3	4	Latzko	1	6

There were a few playoff games before the final title series. Hirschman defeated Middleton two out three for 6th place 50–44, 48–50 and 50–19, hitting .761 in the last game.

Rose walked over Miller in two straight games in a playoff for 4th place, 50–42 and 50–24, hitting .618 and .686.

Lundgren and Gothard fought it out to see who would meet Raab for the title. Lundgren went .780 to smack Gothard 50–12 and proceeded to roll to a 41–27 lead in the second game only to see Gothard suddenly hit a streak of 17 out of 18 to come up and nose out a 50–47 win. Lundgren led all the way in the final game to win 50–39 with 60 out of 82 for .732.

– – – – – – –

Before moving on to Rose's account of the championship series, this writer would like to comment on the playoff process used in Michigan in 1942. A single playoff game to decide the second-place tie between Lundgren and Gothard may make some sense. But a best of three game series to decide 6th place and 4th makes little sense—especially considering they were 50-point games following a seven-game round robin. These guys loved to pitch horseshoes!

– – – – – – –

Title Series

Lundgren opened with 18 out of 20, but could only lead 9–1. Carl later led 15–4, but here Elmer laid on a streak of 22 out of 24 to slide ahead 29–18. Three doubles put Lundgren ahead again 33–29, but Raab put on a finishing burst of 16 out of 20 to win 50–38 with 58 out of 78 for .744.

Lundgren piled into the second game and ran away from Raab all the way, hitting 56 out of 74 for .751, winning 50–23. Raab put up more of a struggle in the third game, with the lead see-sawing back and forth. Raab led 29–27 and there he seemed to weaken and Lundgren moved on to a 50–35 victory with 55 out of 76 for .724.

Carl completely moved Raab down in the fourth game, squelching "Roundy" 50–17, with 38 out of 48 for .792.

The fifth game opened with Lundgren moving into a lead and gradually increasing it. The championship was well within his grasp and as the score reached 41–26, not one person there would have given Raab any chance. But's here what happened! Lundgren fired a double, but Raab topped it and came back with another double. Lundgren threw his first shoe on and then threw his second on also and both shoes leaped up and off the stake! It was 41–32 and Raab, with a sudden gleam of hope in his eyes, drove another double on. Again Lundgren threw his first one on and his second shoe hit on and both shoes flew off AGAIN!!

It was now 41–38. Raab aroused and inspired, drove on another double and the score was tied as Charley could only get on one. Again the relentless Raab hit a double and scored 3 to go ahead and again he doubled and scored 3 more to lead 47–41. Here he finally missed one, but picked up a point as Lundgren missed one too. Again Elmer missed one and Lundgren finally dropped on a double to make it 48–44. Lundgren doubled again and scored 3 more to make it 48–47.

Lundgren again threw a perfect double, but his second shoe rose slowly up and fell over and off the stake and the Ann Arbor pitcher quickly smacked on a double and won out 50–47! Raab had 52 out of 78 for .667.

His almost miraculous rescue from the brink of oblivion had seemingly fired Raab into a ringer throwing demon. Lundgren shot 19 out of 22 to open the sixth game, but could only lead 13–6. Two consecutive double misses by Carl then allowed Raab to make it 13–12 on two singles, then Elmer hit five doubles in a row to go ahead 21–13.

Lundgren never got out from under after that. He brought it up to 35–33 at one point, but four doubles by Raab here put the game away, finally winning 50–36 with 65 out of 84 for .774. Lundgren hit 60 out of 84 for .714.

The last and deciding game found Lundgren about exhausted and unable to stand the pace. Carl led 7–1, but Raab slipped ahead 12–7. Lundgren made it 12–11, but from then on it ceased to be a contest. Lundgren could not keep pace with the inspired Raab and fell further behind as it went along. Raab finally won 50–24 with 42 out of 60 for .700 as Lundgren fell down to .550.

Thus was written the most remarkable reversal of fortunes ever seen in a title series.

- - - - - - -

Next Rose penned some incredible coverage of the AAU National Amateur Championships. In an era when there were few World Tournaments being held, this rather new arrangement with the AAU offered interesting events and a fairly unknown side of the sport. Rose enters the competition and his handwritten personal accounts are just incredible.

- - - - - - -

A.A.U. National Tourney

On September 11, Sunny and I took off in the "Escritoire" for Cincinnati, Ohio and we arrived there after an all-day and not very eventful trip. We landed at Schuster's in Deer Park and I warmed up at a court a block down the street. That night Sunny went to a show and I went to the Old Dutch Mill.

Afterward we went to the Club Melody. I certainly didn't feel very good in the morning but Sunny and I went downtown and crossed the free bridge to Newport, Ky., where I qualified for the finals of the National A.A.U. Tourney.

Results of the 1942 qualifying competition:

Score	Contestant	City
256	John Lindmeier	Chicago, Illinois
249	Arner Lindquist	Morgantown, West Virginia
234	Dorne Woodhouse	Chicago, Illinois
233	Frank Breen	Elgin, Illinois
221	Harry Henn	Cold Spring, Kentucky
219	Harold Lange	Elgin, Illinois
218	Harold McPherson	Newport, Kentucky
217	Charles Eha	Bellevue, Kentucky
214	Lee H. Rose	Detroit, Michigan
218	Stanley Manker	Chillicothe, Ohio
200	E. L. Martin	Norwood, Ohio
191	Walter Lindmeier	Chicago, Illinois

After a show, eats, drinks, etc., we went to bed and arose the next morning to go back to Newport for the finals. It was held at the Northern Kentucky Horseshoe Club.

Finals were held on a basis of 50-shoe games with a count-all system! Phooey!!

I met Walter Lindmeier of Chicago in the first game and led nearly all the way to best him, 95–84. Then I beat Harold Lange, 108–85. I lost my next start to Dorne Woodhouse, 105–104.

Disgusted with that one-point defeat and the whole crazy system of playing, I lost to Harry Henn, 107–84. Then I lost to Stan Manker, 96–88

Then my natural instincts got the better of me and I started to click. I defeated Martin, 112–95 and Eha, 100–90. Then I met the defending champion John Lindmeier and I battered him down 114–91 with 72%. My next game with Frank Breen was my best of the day; I beat him 129–119, shooting 42 ringers for 84%, winding it up with 8 straight doubles.

Then I met the very slow pitching Arner Lindquist, who was leading the event. I had only 1 ringer out of the first six shoes and he led 12–4. From then on I pulled up on him but due to the game only lasting 50 shoes, I didn't have time to catch him and lost out 110–106. I wound up the day by nosing out Johnson 112–111 and tied for 3rd place.

1942 National A.A.U. Men's Championship Finals

Name	W	L	%
1. Arner Lindquist	11	1	66.5
2. Dorne Woodhouse	9	3	65.0
3. John Lindmeier	8	4	68.0
4. Stanley Manker	8	4	67.0
5. Lee H. Rose	8	4	64.0
6. Frank Breen	8	4	63.0
7. James "Pops" Johnson	7	5	55.0
8. Harold McPherson	5	7	54.0
9. Everett L. Martin	5	7	52.0
10. Harold Lange	4	8	52.0
11. Harry Henn	3	9	53.0
12. Charles Eha	1	11	52.0
13. Walter Lindmeier	1	11	44.0

1942 National AAU Men's Doubles Championship Finals

	W	L
1. John Lindmeier & Dorne Woodhouse	3	0
2. Arner Lindquist & Stanley Manker	2	1
3. Frank Breen & Harold Lange	1	2
4. Tom Luck & J. R. Kirkpatrick	0	3

Sunny and I started for home that very evening and reached home about 6 a.m. the next day.

- - - - - - -

Rose had little to say about his decision to attend this event or about the AAU's involvement in the sport. No doubt he had intended to win the event and a national championship, but this was a rather competitive group of amateur pitchers. John Lindmeier and Frank Breen were two of the all-time greats in the AAU competition, and Stan Manker is a NHPA Hall of Fame inductee and a five-time senior men's world champion (1971, 1974, 1975, 1978, and 1975). Breen never participated in the NHPA, but Lindmeier and Lindquist were annual championship-class pitchers in the 1950s World Tournaments held in Murray, Utah. The question is: Will Rose try for an AAU title again?

- - - - - - -

On September 20, Detroit was supposed to go to Flint for a team match, but besides me, only Kelly went along. We had a pick-up match and a nice party at Middleton's.

In a practice game with Joe Latzko, I beat him in a 25-point game 25–9, shooting 64 ringers out of 70 shoes! Believe it or not! [That was 91.43%.]

Our Detroit District Tournament was scheduled for September 27, but it was too windy so on October 4 we gathered again. Again we called off the official tournament because of the wind, but we played a round-robin to see who would have won if we had played it that day. Walls, Lundgren, Getz, Fitch, Don Walls, Fagan and Kelly played along with me.

I served notice that I was going to be a title threat by easily winning seven straight games from these opponents.

Detroit District Tournament
October 11, 1942

There were only eight entries and we played under sanction of the A.A.U.

Game 1 – Paul Fitch of Pleasant Ridge was my first victim 50–15, with me hitting 33 out of 50 for .660.

Game 2 – My old nemesis, M. B. Getz, was my next victim 50–37.

Game 3 – I met Lundgren, the undefeated defending champion. I was supposed to be the underdog in this game, but it wasn't even close as I simply tore Lundgren down with a steady stream of doubles, winning 50–12, hitting 50 out of 62 [an 80.6% game].

Game 4 – I easily defeated Shell in my next start 50–17, with 42 out of 62.

Game 5 – I met Ed Walls — — — He, too was undefeated, but he was simply engulfed by my deluge of doubles. I walloped him 50–14, with 43 out of 54 [for 79.6%].

Game 6 – Leading nearly from the start, I beat Kelly 50–34.

Game 7 – I rolled complacently to a victory over Fagan 50–21 as I kept one eye on the Walls–Lundgren game. Walls defeated Lundgren and so was to meet me in a 3 out of 5 match for the championship.

— — Title Series — —

Now, here are the facts ——— Walls and I have been rivals for a long time and many times we have had terrific arguments about his habit of always stepping over the foul line when pitching. I did not like these arguments and hated to mention it now because he was stepping over all during this tournament. While I beat him that one game easily, I knew that trying to beat him in a series while giving him six inches less distance on each shoe was a different story. After turning things over in my mind, I finally determined to keep quiet and not mention his fouling at all. I did —— and here it is.

The Lee Rose Story

Walls got 3 on a double to open and I took a point on a single and 6 more on two doubles to lead 7–3. Walls got 3 on a double and I covered his next double. Walls got 3 more on a double to go ahead 9–7. I then hit three doubles to move ahead again 13–9. Walls and I each got a point, then I got 3 on a double and another point to lead 18–10.

Walls then hit three doubles, but it was still 18–13. I got 3 on a single and 3 more on a double, to be ahead 24–13. Walls got a point, then doubled twice to make it 24–17. I got 3 on each of two doubles and another point to lead 34–17.

Walls chugged in three doubles to make it 34–23. A little later it stood 46–29; then it came. Walls, desperate, started to step nearly a foot over the foul line and looped on seven straight doubles and won the game 50–46. Score:

	Pts	R	DR	SP	Pct
Walls	50	70	26	94	.744
Rose	47	68	23	94	.723

Walls opened with 19 out of 24 and was leading the game 18–4, but I rallied back with 22 out of 24 and went ahead of him 26–21. Then Ed got a 6 and I got a 6 back and a couple more points put me ahead 34–27. Then Walls topped a double, got three on another double and had his third double topped. Another double gave me 3 points to lead 37–30. Then I singled and Walls doubled for 3 more points. He doubled again, but I topped him. Walls got a point on a single; then I doubled over his single for 3 more to lead 43–34.

Walls got 3 on a double, I got a point and then doubled, Ed topped it. Then he got 3 on a double, 3 on a single and 3 more on a double and he led me 46–41. Another Walls double was topped by me; then I hit two more doubles and scored 3 on each to lead 47–46. Two more doubles by Walls put him out. Score:

	Pts	R	DR	SP	Pct
Walls	50	70	26	94	.744
Rose	47	68	233	94	.723

I just didn't have the heart to keep on fighting against such a handicap and I just banged away expecting only defeat and that is just what I got. I led 10–9, but he went ahead then and I never headed him off. Score:

	Pts	R	DR	SP	Pct
Walls	50	53	22	68	.779
Rose	36	47	15	68	.691

- - - - - - -

Rose ended his third journal with a listing of all his game played in 1942, which isn't reprinted here because we have read about each and every game. His record for the year was 39 wins against 16 games lost.

He also recorded his won-lost record against lifetime opponents—a sampling of which is reprinted here.

- - - - - - -

Opponent	Years	Won	Lost
Ed Walls	13	18	33
Joe Latzko	11	6	24
Jim Skinner	15	16	11
Ray Gorsline	11	11	1
M. B. Getz	10	16	7
Carl Lundgren	8	23	27
Bobby Hitt	7	3	25
Elmer Raab	3	2	4

Fellow Michigan Pitcher
Wins a National Title

- -

The year of 1943 found the game of horseshoe pitching sinking down into a deep hole which threatened to almost wipe the game off the list of active sports.

I did not pitch very much myself, but the few times I did go out with the shoes I found myself pitching better than I had ever pitched before.

Carl Lundgren making a pitch.

Torrential downpours rendered pitching impossible during May, but in June I got in a few practice games with Lundgren, whom I defeated 20 out of 28.

On July 4, I played Ed Walls at his place and beat him four out of six and on July 6 at Northwestern Field, I walloped him three straight averaging .762 to his .682. I hit .738, .775 and .826.

By July 14, I had beaten Walls seven out of nine, Gothhard 12 out of 15 and Lundgren 21 out of 29.

Now —— it was just a bunch of games by two pick-up teams. A high wind blew —— as it always does in Ann Arbor —— but many good games were played.

- - - - - - -

The 1942 Michigan State Tournament was set for two Sundays, August 15 & 22. One round robin of all entries on August 15 and the six high to get a clean slate for August 22 for one round robin, with the two high to play the best 4 out of 7 game series for the title. Entry fee to be $3.00. Six prizes.

My Twentieth
State Tournament
Wines Field — Ann Arbor
August 15 — Round Robin

ROUND ONE

Joe Latzko opened his quest for a fifth state title by beating his fellow towns-men, Bill Miller, 50–18, clicking off .742. Carl Lundgren rolled over old Jim Skinner 50–5 with .711. Lee Rose met Ray Gorsline. With three out of four, Gorsline took a 4–0 lead, but with nine out of the next twelve, Rose forged ahead 17–4. Gorsline was never in the game after that and Rose won 50–13, hitting 29 out of 42 for .690. Elmer Raab opened the defense of his title by coming from behind in the stretch to beat Carl Gothard 50–47. Raab had .639 to Carl's .605; M. B. Getz trimmed Jonas Otto 50–36 with .597; Joe Kelly nosed out N. E. Shepard 50–47; Jim Davis eked out a 50–49 win over Ray Middleton and Ed Jones shaded Joe Fagan 50–48. Ed Walls drew the bye as there were seventeen entries.

ROUND TWO

Latzko draped Lundgren over the ropes, winning 50–17 with .767; Gothard trampled over Gorsline 50–9 with .739; Rose easily squelched Skinner 50–14 with 25 out of 34 for .736; Walls went .680 to slaughter Shepard 50–9; Kelly turned in a fine performance in beating Otto with .656 and Davis upset Getz 50–49 with .616; Raab disposed of Middleton 50–35 and Miller beat Jonas 50–42. Fagan—bye.

ROUND THREE

Raab hung up his third straight in beating Getz 50–11 with .688; Lundgren butchered Jonas 50–9 with .687; Walls trounced Otto 50–18 with .675; Middleton won his first game by beating Gorsline 50–10 and Kelly hung up his third game in giving Davis his first defeat 50–24.

Latzko met Rose. With five out of six, Rose leaded ahead 10–0, but Latzko came on with eight out of ten to gain a one-point lead at 12–11. Rose with 15 out of the next twenty, led Latzko 25–14 and seemed headed for a win. But here, however, he fell off and Latzko, though not pitching well, drew up quickly and went ahead to win 50–38, hitting .636 to Rose's .591. Gothard beat Skinner 50–16 and Miller beat Fagan 50–39.

ROUND FOUR

Ed Walls hung up the high game by running over Davis 50–4 with 34 out of 44 for .772. Latzko strode forward another notch by bouncing Gothard 50–19 with .759. Rose hit an even .750 with 30 out of 40 to wipe up Ed Jones 50–7. Lundgren hit .722 to beat Fagan 50–12. Raab knocked Kelly out of the undefeated class 50–39 after a very stubborn battle by Kelly, who was proving to be a regular "dark horse." Middleton beat Skinner, Getz won from Gorsline and Otto beat Shepard. Leaders:

Latzko	4–0	Rose	3–1	Getz	2–2
Raab	4–0	Kelly	3–1	Middleton	2–2
Walls	3–0	Miller	2–1	Davis	2–2
Lundgren	3–1	Gothard	2–2		

ROUND FIVE

Walls stepped along with 62 out of 80 for .775 to administer the first defeat to Raab 50–26. Latzko went .727 to beat Middleton 50–29. Lundgren hit .725 to wallop Miller 50–31 and Rose coasted over Fagan 50–3 with 20 out of 30 for .667. Gothard, Shepard, Kelly and Getz all won.

ROUND SIX

Walls continued to hog the lime-light by pounding out 33 out 40 for .825 to smother poor old Gorsline 50–1. Latzko hit .750 to take Getz in camp 50–12. Raab went .729 to beat Shepard 50–28 and Rose rolled to an easy win over Miller 50–20 with 37 out of 56 for .661. Gothard, Otto and Kelly each won. Jonas dropped out at this point.

ROUND SEVEN

Walls kept up his pace by slaughtering Skinner 50–7 with 31 out of 38 for .815. Rose met Lundgren. Rose grabbed 9 on two doubles to open the game, but Lundgren poured on four doubles to tie it. Two more doubles put Rose ahead 15–9, then three doubles by Lundgren tied it again.

Each got a point and then Rose forged ahead and this time Lundgren could not catch up. Rose won 50–35 with 43 out of 60 for .717. Latzko trailed Kelly until it stood 31–30, then hit eleven out of twelve to run out as Kelly weakened. Latzko hit .714. Miller upset Gothard 40–42 and Raab beat Otto. Middleton and Shepard each won. Leaders:

Latzko	7–0	Kelly	5–2	Getz	3–3
Walls	6–0	Lundgren	4–2	Middleton	3–3
Rose	6–1	Gothard	4–3		
Raab	6–1	Miller	3–3		

ROUND EIGHT

Joe Latzko became the only undefeated man by walloping Ed Walls 50–32 with .731. Lundgren beat Gothard 50–33 with .709; Miller beat Middleton and Jim Davis upset champion Raab 50–43. Otto, Getz and Shepherd won. Skinner and Gorsline were both eliminated by losing their eighth straight game. Rose had a bye.

ROUND NINE

Latzko butchered Shepard 50–11 with .783; Rose marched over Gothard easily 50–16 with .739; Lundgren trounced Middleton 50–13; Getz upset Miller 50–36 and Kelly eliminated Fagan. Otto and Gorsline won.

ROUND TEN

Latzko went .778 to beat Otto 50–10. Miller defeated Kelly 50–28 with .711. Rose had a rather tough game with Middleton. With seven out of eight, Ray went ahead 6–0, then Rose hit 16 out of 18 and rolled ahead 25–6. Middleton then started a determined come-back and came on to tie it up at 31-all. Rose finished with 15 out of 22, to win 50–34 with 57 out of 82 for .695.

Getz jumped on Lundgren to lead him 21–4 with 22 out of the first 28 and later he led by 44–20. But Lundgren suddenly hit 19 out of 22 and came up to nose Getz out 50–48 with .663. Raab rolled over Gorsline until it stood 47–11, when Gorsline suddenly clicked with 17 out of 20 and rushed up to 44 before Raab went out on a double. Walls and Davis won. Leaders:

Latzko	10–0	Lundgren	7–2	Miller	5–4
Rose	8–1	Raab	7–2	Getz	5–4
Walls	8–1	Kelly	6–3		

ROUND ELEVEN

Lundgren beat Kelly 50–24 with .682 and Latzko smeared Davis 50–16 with .682. Rose met his perennial jinx, Getz!! Two opening doubles put Rose ahead 9–0. Then Getz got 3 on a single and after a four-dead, got 3 more on another single. Getz then laid on five doubles in a row to lead Rose 15–9. Another point on a single made it 16–9.

Ten out of the next twelve made it 19–16 in favor of Rose, then Rose hit on off-streak and Getz rushed out in front 42–24. After three straight four-deads, Rose doubled again to pick up 3 and doubled again to pick up 6 more as Getz missed. It was 42–36 with Getz still leading. Rose hung on his sixth straight double to score 3 and a seventh double tied the score at 42-all.

Rose then only singled, but got 3 as Getz missed. Rose got a point on a single, then doubled, only to see Getz top it. Getz then missed and Rose could only get a single to lead 49–42. Then Rose missed! Getz slugged in a double to make it 49–48. Getz laid on another double but Rose miraculously topped it! Rose came back with only a single but Getz up and missed both shoes and Rose won out 50–48.

Miller took an early lead on Walls and led 21–9 and later 31–19. Walls ran ahead 39–31 and Miller came back to lead 46–39, only to lose 50–46. Gothard defeated Middleton 50–37. Raab and Shepard each won.

ROUND TWELVE

Latzko opened the big valve on Raab and 45 out of 52 for .865, defeated him 50–15. Walls pounded on 49 out of 68 for .721 to defeat Lundgren 50–34. Rose easily smothered Kelly 50–20 with .712. Gothard defeated Getz 50–42. Fagan upset Otto 50–48. Miller and Gorsline both won.

ROUND THIRTEEN

Latzko shot 38 out of 46 for .826 to win out Gorsline 50–8. Walls hit .767 to easily defeat Rose 50–20 as Rose went only .571. Getz eliminated Ray Middleton 50–20 and Miller nosed out Otto 50–49. Lundgren, Gothard and Davis each won.

ROUND FOURTEEN

Latzko murdered Skinner 50–3 with 31 out of 36 for .861. Raab hit 23 out of 28 for .821 to beat Fagan 50–9. Kelly defeated Middleton 50–25 with .709; Walls trimmed Gothard 50–27; Miller beat Davis 50–25; Rose eliminated Shepard 50–23 and Lundgren eliminated Otto 50–43.

ROUND FIFTEEN

Raab polished off Miller 50–20 with .808; Walls walloped Middleton 50–23 with .712; Lundgren beat Davis; Gothard beat Shepard; Fagan beat Gorsline; Rose won from Otto 50–31 with .642; Kelly assured himself of a place in the finals by trimming Getz 50–39.

ROUND SIXTEEN

Miller hit Gorsline with .808 to win 50–14; Rose eliminated Davis 50–24 with .712; Walls eliminated Getz 50–21; Old Jim Skinner finally won a game, beating

Fagan 50–15 with .640; Otto upset Gothard 50–43; Middleton beat Shepard and Raab won from Lundgren 50–36 as Charley fell down to .486.

ROUND SEVENTEEN

Latzko hit .772 to beat Fagan 50–5 and finished up an undefeated day. Walls trounced Kelly 50–34 to wind up 2nd with only one defeat. Raab gained a tie for 3rd with Rose by winning from Lee Rose 50–44, going .662 to Rose's .648. Lundgren took 5th position by beating Gorsline and Miller took 6th by winning from Skinner. Gothard tied for 7th with Kelly by subduing Davis 50–18.

- - - - - - -

Rose didn't give any hint about the time span for this round robin. In today's World Tournament, a pitcher's shift is usually limited to five 40-point games. Fifty-point games are longer and a round robin of seventeen games is brutally long overall.

Yet again the Rose journals contain unbelievably complete data and statistics. For the 1943 Michigan state tournament, Rose records every game played by each and every player and then compiles a summary of totals. Here are the games played by Rose and his recap of the standings after the preliminary round robin, before he moves on to relate the finals.

- - - - - - -

Rose's Games

	Pts	R	DR	SP	Pct	Opp	Pts	R	DR	Pct
1.	50	29	9	38	.690	Gorsline	13	15	2	.357
2.	50	25	9	34	.736	Skinner	15	16	2	.470
3.	38	39	10	66	.591	Latzko	50	42	13	.636
4.	50	3	11	40	.750	Jones	7	16	2	.400
5.	50	20	7	30	.667	Fagan	3	5	1	.167
6.	50	37	13	56	.661	Miller	20	31	6	.553
7.	50	43	15	60	.717	Lundgren	35	38	13	.634
8.	Bye									
9.	50	34	13	46	.739	Gothard	16	23	8	.500
10.	50	57	19	82	.695	Middleton	34	50	14	.609
11.	50	58	20	88	.659	Getz	48	56	19	.637
12.	50	37	14	52	.712	Kelly	20	27	7	.519
13.	20	32	8	56	.571	Walls	50	43	15	.767

(Continued on next page)

	Pts	R	DR	SP	Pct	Opp	Pts	R	DR	Pct
14.	50	37	11	58	.638	Shepard	33	33	11	.569
15.	50	27	10	42	.642	Otto	31	21	7	.500
16.	50	37	14	52	.712	Davis	24	26	7	.500
17.	44	48	15	74	.648	Raab	50	49	16	.662

Player	City	W	L	R	DR	SP	Pct
1. Joe Latzko	Flint	16	0	633	240	842	.752
2. Ed Walls	Detroit	15	1	612	210	864	.708
3. Lee Rose	Detroit	13	3	590	198	878	.672
4. Elmer Raab	Ann Arbor	13	3	599	193	920	.651
5. Carl Lundgren	Detroit	12	4	617	199	948	.651
6. Wm. Miller	Flint	10	6	656	196	1072	.612
7. Carl Gothard	Detroit	9	7	657	202	1080	.608
8. Joe Kelly	High Park	9	7	571	163	982	.581
9. M. B. Getz	Ferndale	8	8	565	164	980	.576
10. Jonas Otto	Ann Arbor	7	9	542	150	974	.556
11. James Davis	Battle Ck.	6	10	488	131	934	.522
12. Ray Middleton	Flint	5	11	521	137	950	.548
13. N. E. Shepard	Flint	5	11	436	114	882	.494
14. Ray Gorsline	Fulton	3	13	352	53	812	.433
15. James Skinner	Athens	2	14	359	75	806	.445
16. Joe Fagan	Detroit	2	14	355	73	832	.427
17. Ed Jones	Flint	1	15	146	32	302	.483
Totals				8699	2530	15058	.577

Final – August 22nd

GAME ONE

Joe Latzko got off to a flying start by taking an easy game from Carl Gothard, who hit only .368. Latzko went .763 to win 50–5. Lundgren showed class in defeating Walls 50–39, going .682 to Ed's .646. Raab went .616 to beat Kelly 50–26 and Rose had it easy with Miller, having to go only .550 to win 50–30.

GAME TWO

Latzko and Rose clashed in the best game of the tournament and the greatest game of horseshoe ever pitched in a Michigan meet. Rose opened with a double which was topped. Then Joe missed both shoes and Rose piled in for 6. Rose kept on doubling; hitting four more, but they were all dead ones. Then Rose missed both shoes and Joe tied it up at 6–6.

Joe's sixth double was then topped by Lee and then picked up 3 more on another double to tie at 9–9. Rose got a point on a single to lead 10–9. Then — — the ringer machine from Flint opened up! Sixteen times in a row, Latzko banged on a double!!! The first scored 3 and the next four were stopped by Rose and the sixth scored 3 to put Joe ahead 15–10. Joe scored more on the 7th and 3 more on the 9th. The next five doubles were voided by Rose, but Joe scored 3 each on his 15th and 16th doubles to lead 24–10. There was no question about who was going to win after that, but Rose would not give in and Latzko was forced to keep going in high gear. The final result:

Pts	R	DR	SP	Pct	4-On	
Latzko	50	87	39	102	.862	23
Rose	24	79	30	102	.774	23

Lundgren hit .773 to down Miller 50–22. Gothard beat Kelly and Walls downed Raab 50–40 in a poor game. Leaders:

Latzko	2–0	Rose	1–1	Raab	1–1
Lundgren	2–0	Walls	1–1	Gothard	1–1

GAME THREE

Rose, undismayed by his defeat, walked into Kelly in the same groove he had held against Latzko and it was good enough to swamp Kelly 50–15. Rose had 30 out of the first 34 to lead 44–4. Rose hit 34 out of 44 for .772. Walls climbed over Miller 50–22 with .734.

Latzko apparently had extended himself beyond his limit against Rose and didn't start out so well against Lundgren and Carl soon had an early lead of 25–10 with 21 out of 26. Then Joe started a come-back and pulled up on Lundgren to finally tie it up at 36 all. Latzko kept on and led 47–43 and then came an anti-climax as Lundgren dropped on seven straight doubles to beat Latzko 50–47! Lundgren went only .718 to Joe's .697. Gothard rallied at the finish to take a see-saw battle from Raab 50–48. Leaders:

Lundgren	3–0	Rose	2–1
Latzko	2–1	Gothard	2–1

GAME FOUR

Latzko practically assured the state of a new champion by plastering Raab 50–27 with .750.

Rose met his next great hurdle — — Walls. Walls got off to a good start with seven out of eight to lead Rose 10–0 and things didn't look so good for the "Tiger." Ten out of twelve, enabled Rose to make it 11–10 in Ed's favor and here a double miss by Rose made it 17–10. Rose hit four doubles to make it 17–16 and a double by Walls made it 20–16. Rose got 3 on a double to make it 20–19 and Walls got two 3's on two doubles to lead 26–19. Rose took 3 on a double to make it 26–22 and again Walls got two 3's on two doubles to lead 32–22. Rose topped a double and Walls picked up another point on a single to lead 33–22.

Walls doubled again and got 3 more to lead 36–22. Walls missed one but Rose could only get a single point. 36–23. Walls got a point on a single, then Rose shot four doubles, but only got 3 points. Here he missed both shoes, but Walls only got a single to 40–26. Walls then missed both shoes, but Rose could only get a single. Walls took another point on a single to lead 41–30. Rose lashed out once more with four doubles and this time Wall's resistance was weakening and Rose went ahead 42–41!! Walls got a point to tie it at 42-all, then missed both shoes!! Rose could only get on a single and Walls tied it again at 45-all with a double. Then Walls could only get two singles in the clutch and the toy bulldog went out with two doubles to win 50–45! Rose had 65 out of 90 for .722 to Ed's 62 ringers for .688.

Lundgren stayed unbeaten by defeating Gothard 50–32 and Miller beat Kelly 50–29.

GAME FIVE

Lundgren really "stepped out" on Raab, squelching him 50–6 with 32 out of 36 for .889. Latzko stayed right on his heels by beating Miller 50–25 with 51 out of 68 for .750.

Rose remained in the running by taking an easy game from Gothard 50–18 with .700. Walker beat Kelly 50–38.

GAME SIX

Latzko completely slaughtered Walls with 36 out of 40 for .900 to beat him 50–6 as Lundgren easily beat Kelly 50–29. Gothard beat Miller. Then it came — — Rose met Raab!!

The game went along in see-saw fashion. Raab lead 6–0; Rose led 10–6; Raab led 12–10; Rose led 14–12; Raab led 18–14 and 22–14; Rose led 26–22 and 35–28 and 36–29. Raab led 37–36 and Rose tied at 36-all. Rose here doubled and Raab topped it. Raab doubled and scored 3 and then doubled again. Rose's second shoe hit right on and took both of his shoes off and Raab's scored 6 to lead 46–37. Rose could not rally after that heart-breaker and lost 50–38 and was thus eliminated.

GAME SEVEN

Rose met Lundgren who hadn't had a loss yet. After three consecutive four-deads, Lundgren got a point on a single and 6 on a double. Then came four more four-deads before Rose scored 3 on a double. Lundgren scored 3 on a double, then came two more four-deads. Rose then got 6 on a double and after another four-dead, got 3 on a double and 4 on a single to go ahead 16–10.

Rose had hit 29 out of 34 up to here and Lundgren had hit 24 out of his first 26. It later stood 29–29 as both players fell off a little and then Rose rushed ahead 39–29. Lundgren staggered ahead 49–48 and then Rose won out with 2 points on two singles.

Latzko routed Kelly 50–13 with .774 and Walls defeated Gothard in a whiz-bang game, 50–39, with Walls having 67 out of 8 for .779 to Gothard's 62 ringers for .720.

Raab defeated Miller 50–32. Final Standings:

Player	W	L	Pts	R	DR	SP	Pct
Latzko	6	1	347	369	145	474	.778
Lundgren	6	1	349	356	129	490	.726
Rose	5	2	312	350	121	508	.689
Walls	4	3	290	342	122	520	.657
Raab	3	4	271	311	96	502	.619
Gothard	3	4	244	283	84	466	.607
Miller	1	6	199	267	72	456	.585
Kelly	0	7	176	229	59	428	.535
Totals			2188	2507	828	3844	.652

Championship Series

Lundgren was just "never in it" in this series and was butchered four straight. Latzko won 50–38 with .737; 50–32 with .811; 50–20 with .892 and 50–9 with .780.

Latzko averaged .806 for the four games as Lundgren averaged .683. Averages for Latzko and Lundgren (Round Robin & Championship Series):

	Pts	R	DR	SP	Pct
Latzko	547	606	243	768	.789
Lundgren	448	557	200	784	.710

- - - - - - -

Rose had more success soon, as he describes in his account of the 1941 tournament for a district title.

- - - - - - -

Rose Regains Detroit District

Horseshoe Title

Lee Rose returned to the pinnacle of Detroit horseshoe pitchers on August 29. By taking the Detroit District title at northwestern Field. Only eight starters faced the barrier, one of them being Lee Rose II.

The "Tiger" had no trouble in running over Getz, Kelly, Joe Wolfe, Louis Kinsman, Lee Jr. and Lundgren. Then, after a short rest, Rose and Lundgren squared off for the best three of five championship series.

FIRST GAME

Lundgren opened the first game with five doubles and scored 3 on the fifth one. With 16 out of 18, Lundgren led 8–0. Then Carl fell off a little and Rose, with 15 out of 18, shot ahead 19–10. After a double miss, Rose again started to roll and hit 21 out of his next 24 to show a lead of 34–14. After Lundgren made it 35–23, Rose shot 12 out of 14 to end it 50–26. Rose had 62 out of 80 for .775, while Lundgren had 53 ringers for .663.

SECOND GAME

Lundgren stepped out with a beautiful game and it was touch and go all the way. Rose led 13–12 and six straight doubles put Carl ahead 24–13. Rose never quite tied the score after that, although he came within one point of doing so several times at 25–24, 34–33, 40–39, 44–43 and 47–46 and here Lundgren won out with three final doubles. He hit 73 out of 96 for .760 and Rose had 72 ringers for .750. A very good game!

THIRD GAME

The third game saw Rose "blow-up" at the start and he changed shoes with Lundgren walking all over him. With 29 out of 36, Carl was leading 27–3. Rose pitched only to get the new shoes working for the next game and lost 50–15 with Lundgren hitting 59 out of 78 for .756.

FOURTH GAME

Faced with the task of beating the high-flying Lundgren two straight, Rose was in a bad spot. Lundgren didn't let up at all and at 34 shoes, had a lead of 24–16. Here he suddenly slumped for eight shoes, making only two ringers, as Rose zipped ahead 31–24. Lundgren then staged a come-back and crept up to tie it up at 41-all. A double put him ahead 44–41 and Rose tied it with a double at 44–44.

Rose doubled again and Lundgren topped it. Carl hit another double and scored 3 and then scored a point on a single to lead 48–44. Then — — out of a clear sky — — he missed!!! Rose then won with a double.

FIFTH AND FINAL GAME

The fifth game was a desperate struggle all the way. Rose took a lead of 25–17, but Lundgren rushed ahead 33–26 as Rose fell off a little.

Then Rose seemed to suddenly find his confidence and he came on like a hurricane up the final stretch. Two doubles made it 33–29. After two singles let Carl lead 36–29, Rose pounded on five doubles, a single and another double to go out in front 43–36.

After Lundgren scored 3 on a double Rose finished it up with 13 out of 16 to win 50–43. Rose had 66 out of 90 for .733 and Lundgren had 63 for .700. For the series, Rose averaged .722 and Lundgren averaged .710. This is the best City Series ever pitched in Detroit.

- - - - - - -

Then Rose entered another National AAU championship tournament. The event was held in Chicago again and Carl Lundgren joined Rose on the adventure.

- - - - - - -

The National A.A.U. Tournament was held at the Lincoln Park courts in Chicago on Sat., Sun. and Mon., September 4-5-6. Lundgren and I attended.

We left on Friday night, being lucky to get on a crowded bus and got to Chicago at 4:30 a.m. on Saturday. We got a room at the Bancroft Hotel and after 3 hours of sleep, arose and went to Lincoln Park on the streetcar. We both qualified for the finals in singles and doubles both.

On Sunday, Lundgren and I played in the doubles tournament "just for the fun of it." We played 7 games and we won our first 5 games to be the only undefeated team at that point. Then we lost to Arner Lindquist and his partner and then lost to Lindmeier and Woodhouse to tie for 2nd. We won the 3-way tie for second place by slaughtering Lindmeier and Woodhouse and then Danhauer and Loerzel.

We played two rounds of the singles that day also and Lundgren and I each won our two games easily.

On Monday, we resumed our play. We each won our first game in the morning, then we played each other. Lundgren won a nip and tuck struggle from me, 50–46. I lost another to Breen and later, one to Lindquist and one to Henn. Lundgren went through everybody until the second to last game, when he was upset by Burkhalter.

Lundgren tied for first and defeated Lindquist for the title in a single game playoff.

- - - - - - -

Rose wasn't overjoyed with Lundgren's unexpected success. If Rose had done better, surely the tone of his tournament description would have been different. He didn't include a record of the final standings, and the tournament had limited newspaper coverage. I was able to find only a partial record of the tournament results when I was conducting research for *AAU National Horseshoe-Pitching Championships 1937–1977*:

1943 National AAU Men's Championship

	Player	City	W	L	%
1.	Carl E. Lundgren	Detroit, MI	15	1	63.8
2.	Arner Lindquist	Morgantown, WV	14	2	67.4
3.	Frank Breen	Elgin, IL			65.5
	Lee Rose	Detroit, MI			
	Dorne Woodhouse	Chicago, IL			
	Burhalter				
	Harry Henn	Cold Spring, KY			

1943 National AAU Doubles Championship

	Player	City	W	L
1.	Arner Lindquist–	Morgantown, WV		
	Charles Grosselin	Morgantown, WV	6	1
2.	Lee Rose–	Detroit, MI		
	Carl E. Lundgren	Detroit, MI	7	2
3.	John Lindmeier–	Oak Park, IL		
	Dorne Woodhouse	Chicago, IL	5	3
4.	Wm. Danhauer–	Chicago, IL		
	Leonard Loerzel	Chicago, IL	5	3

- - - - - - -

After his brief recounting of the National AAU experience, Rose's journal turns to more local events.

- - - - - - -

Several other meets were held in September and October. I won the Ford Local 600 C.I.O. [Congress of Industrial Organizations] tournaments at the Local 600 picnic at Belle Isle, beating four opponents easily, one of them being Joe Wolfe and one Fagan.

At the same picnic, the city-wide C.I.O. meet was held and was won by Carl Lundgren by beating me 50–46. I won three other games, one from Wolfe and one from Fagan.

Lundgren and I each won one leg on beautiful trophy cups.

There was a meet held at Northwestern Field, billed as the Wayne County Open. Lundgren won it, beating me 50–44. I was 2nd beating Kelly, Valleau, Shepard and Fagan.

There was a state championship team match at Flint. I beat Miller, Jones, Middleton and Wood and lost to Latzko and Raab. Flint won the match.

The season closed on a cold windy at the beautiful courts at Port Huron with a meet labeled "Eastern Michigan Open."

Latzko won it. I was second, losing to Joe and beating Miller, Middleton, Lundgren, Jones and Winter. Winter is champion of the county.

The 1943 Record = 59 Wins and 15 Lost

Won and Lost Against
Leading Life-Time Opponents

Opponent	Years	Rose Wins	Opp Wins
Jim Skinner	16	17	11
R. H. Rizor	15	50	9
Ed Walls	14	19	34
Jim Burt	12	48	29
Ray Gorsline	12	12	1
Joe Latzko	12	6	28
M. B. Getz	11	18	7
Carl Lundgren	9	30	31
Ray Middleton	8	11	4
Joe Kelly	7	11	1
William Miller	6	16	6
Orville Valleau	5	8	0
Carl Gothard	5	17	3
Elmer Raab	4	2	7
Jonas Otto	4	4	2

Jacobs Earns a National Championship

I t is a new year and a new horseshoe-pitching season—and 1944 was a great season with some important career highlights for Lee Rose, the Flower of Detroit.

- - - - - - -

An experiment was supposed to be tried this spring, by holding both a city and state tournament in April.

I set the date for the city meet as April 16 and the state as April 23.

The city tournament was not held, owing to cold weather, as only Lundgren, Rose and Rose II showed up.

On April 17, I pitched one hundred shoes on my own courts as follows:

00	00	00	00	0	00	0	00	00	00	0	0	00	00
6	12	18	24	28	34	37	43	49	55	58	62	68	74

00	00	0	0	0	00	00	00	00	00	00	00	00
80	86	90	93	97	103	109	115	121	127	133	139	145

00	00	00	00	00	00	00	00	00	00	00	00
145	151	157	163	169	175	181	187	193	199	205	211

00	–	0	00	00	00	00	00	0	0	00	0
217	218	222	228	234	240	246	252	256	260	266	270

87 Ringers — 38 Doubles
Twenty Consecutive Doubles
A Life Record For Me!

Rain and cold also canceled the state tournament for April 23, so the beautiful experiment did not have a chance to work.

Rose Wins Meet

Lee Rose had no trouble in winning an invitational tournament at Northwestern Field on May 28.

Only four starters faced the barrier: Rose, Kelly Prediger and Koppitsch. It was a double round robin and Rose easily hung up six straight wins, beating Kelly 50–9 and 50–1; Prediger 50–17 and 50–9 and Koppitsch 50–21 and 50–9.

No score sheets were kept, but Rose had a percentage of between 75 and 80 percent. Standings:

1. Rose	6–0	3. Prediger	3–3
2. Koppitsch	3–3	4. Kelly	0–6

Wayne County Open

June 12 — Northwestern Field

Twelve entries started, but the heat or something got the best of 'em and nearly all had dropped out at the finish. Latzko won the meet, beating all who would play him. He won from Rose 50–46, when a late rally by the "Tiger" almost pulled the game out of the fire. Latzko led 49–27 at one time. Joe had 61 out of 84 for .726 and Rose had 59 ringers for .702.

Rose had no trouble in taking 2nd place, easily snowing under Miller, Middleton, Koppitsch, Otto, Shepard, Gothard, Getz and Kelly.

In an exhibition match after the meet, Rose and Latzko split two games, Rose taking the first 50–42 and Latzko the second game 50–36. These two pitchers stamped themselves as THE TWO to beat for the state title.

On Sunday, July 23, Joe Latzko visited at Northwestern

Field and Rose played him an exhibition match and rolled over Joe in three straight games; 50–22, 50–40 and 50–46.

On July 25, at Roseland, in a practice game, Rose defeated Lundgren as follows:

	Pts	R	DR	SP	Pct
Rose	50	130	55	150	.863
Lundgren	29	124	50	150	.823

A very remarkable game!

- - - - - - -

The next item in the journal is a clipping about a state AAU-sponsored event, followed by Rose's recap of the tournament.

- - - - - - -

Horseshoe Champ at Ford CIO Picnic

Feature entertainer for Ford UAW-CIO Local 600's field day at Belle Isle tomorrow will be Carl Lundgren, national horseshoe-pitching champ, state and city champions will also compete in the A.A.U. sanctioned contests.

Other attractions will include a beauty contest, field and track meets, outboard motor boat racing and tennis tournaments.

Michigan A.A.U. Tournament

July 30 — Belle Isle

Played on six wretched courts which prohibited anything resembling horseshoes, this meet was won by Joe Latzko. There were nine starters and Joe lost only to Raab. Rose, Raab and Otto tied for second. Rose defeated Fagan, Bray, Kelly, Miller and Raab and lost to Latzko, Lundgren and Otto. Raab lost to Otto,

Rose and Fagan and Otto lost to Latzko, Kelly and Lundgren. In the play-off, Rose beat Otto, Otto beat Raab and Raab beat Rose. The tie was then settled by a 50-shoe pitch and Raab took second and Rose got third.

- - - - - - -

Rose is announcing this next entry as his twenty-first state tournament, which is significant because few pitchers ever play in that many state tournaments. Also remember that Rose was only 38 years old at the time.

- - - - - - -

My Twenty-First State Tournament
August 12–13, 1944
Mueller Courts, Port Huron, Michigan

The Mueller Courts were very beautiful, partitioned off, painted, etc., but someone forgot to fix the clay, there being too little of it and too hard packed. Pitching was rendered more difficult by a very strong wind and a burning sun.

Lee Rose opened the festivities by singing the National Anthem over the P.A. system and the battle was on. There were 13 entries.

ROUND ONE

Defending champion Joe Latzko opened the defense of his title with the high game of the round, beating Miller 50–35 with only .609. Lundgren slaughtered Otto 50–12 with .562. Rose trailed Craft 12–3, but a streak of 15 out of 18 made it 36–12 and Rose coasted out 50–18 with an even .500. Koppitsch took a lead of 28–14 over Shepard, then saw Shep whittle the lead down and go ahead 49–38. Then Shepard missed twice and the Dearborn giant lashed on two doubles to win 50–49. Hirschman beat Davis 50–41 and Jule Winter defeated Zessin 50–26. Kelly drew the bye.

ROUND TWO

Latzko stepped up the pace a little by downing Koppitsch 50–26 with .697. Lundgren kept along with him by defeating Kelly 50–13 with .591. Rose had no trouble in disposing of Zessin 50–17, with .542. Otto defeated Craft 50–38, Miller beat Winter 50–24 and Shepard won from Davis 50–33.

ROUND THREE

Latzko got up more steam as he quickly set Davis down 50–6 with 25 out of 32 for .781. Koppitsch easily beat Winter 50–17 with .578. Craft beat Kelly 50–29. On an especially bad court, Rose met Miller. Rose led 11–7 and then threw only one out of the next ten and Miller was ahead 23–11. Rose banged away after him and brought the score up to 36–29, but fell apart again here and Miller won out 50–34 with .537 as Rose went .426!! Shepard defeated Hirschman 50–34 and Otto beat Zessin 50–34.

ROUND FOUR

Latzko continued to get stronger and laid Hirschman low 50–1 with 28 out of 32 for .875. Miller ironed out Otto 50–17 with .717 and it began to look like the Flint pre-tournament prediction of Latzko–Miller running one–two might have some basis of fact. Rose, who had not lost to Koppitsch all year, now proceeded to "blow" and was never in it as Hank beat him 50–24 with .594 as Lee went .468!!

Lundgren remained undefeated by besting Craft 50–21; Zessin upset Kelly 50–32 and Davis beat Winter 50–33.

ROUND FIVE

A queer round this was! Latzko mysteriously fell down to .391 in losing to Shepard 50–37. The fact that Shepard could use the game to get into the finals couldn't have anything to do with it, of course. So Lundgren became the only unbeaten pitcher in the meet by beating Zessin 50–13 with .613.

Rose bounced against Davis, clicking off 31–44 for .704 to win 50–4. Miller continued to do well, hitting .620 to beat Kelly 50–12. Hirschman beat Winter 50–47 and Otto nicked Koppitsch 50–38. Leaders:

Lundgren	4–0	Rose	3–2
Latzko	4–1	Otto	3–2
Shepard	3–1	Koppitsch	3–2
Miller	4–1	Hirschman	2–2

Here, a halt was called for lunch.

ROUND SIX

Rose again hit the high game in easily rolling over Hirschman 50–13. Rose had 20 out of the first 26, and ended up with 27 out of 42 for .642. The wind and sun were very bad and the courts were getting worse. Miller more firmly established himself as a favorite by dragging Lundgren off his unbeaten perch 50–35 with .584. Shepard kept coming along, beating Winter 50–46 and Otto helped himself by beating Davis 50–42. Koppitsch settled his dinner with a 50–41 win over Kelly. Zessin beat Craft. Leaders:

Miller	5–1	Koppitsch	4–2
Lundgren	4–1	Otto	4–2
Latzko	4–1	Rose	4–2
Shepard	4–1	Hirschman	2–3

ROUND SEVEN

Miller continued to lead the parade by slaughtering Craft 50–5 with .609. Latzko had the high game of .676 to beat Winter 50–30. Lundgren dragged out a win over Koppitsch 50–45. Rose had no difficulty in taking Shepard down a peg 50–20 with .583. Otto hit .613 to wallop Hirschman 50–11 and Kelly won his first victory in beating Davis 50–38. Leaders:

Miller	6–1	Rose	5–2
Latzko	5–1	Shepard	4–2
Lundgren	5–1	Koppitsch	4–3
Otto	5–2		

ROUND EIGHT

Miller fell down to only .406, but eked out a win over Zessin 50–41. Latzko met Rose. With a rush of 17 out of 20, Latzko went ahead 12–4 and never lost the lead. With 27 out of 34, Latzko held a lead of 30–9. Rose whittled away at him and brought it up to 39–33, but faded off as Latzko won 50–41. Joe had .634 to .579 for Rose.

Lundgren remained with the leaders as he went .480 to beat Davis 50–26. Otto grabbed 4th place all alone by winning over Shepard 50–27. Koppitsch beat Craft 50–32 and Kelly upset Hirschman 50–45. The leaders:

Miller	7–1	Rose	5–3
Latzko	6–1	Koppitsch	5–3
Lundgren	6–1	Shepard	4–3
Otto	6–2		

ROUND NINE

With Miller drawing a bye, chief interest centered on the Latzko–Otto game, as Otto was threatening to become a contender. With 15 out of 22, Otto tore ahead of Latzko 31–6 and it seemed to be all off for Joe, but here he went to work and 20 out of the next 26 put Latzko ahead 38–34. Otto once more got ahead 40–39, but 15 out of the last 18 enabled Latzko to win 50–40. Joe had .694 to Otto's .613.

Lundgren entered a three-way tie for 1st place by beating Hirschman 50–25. Rose met Winter. With seven out of eight, Rose loped ahead 12–0, but three straight doubles by Jule tied it up. Rose then strung on five doubles, the first three scoring 15 points to lead 27–12. The last two were voided by the first of 2 of 5 doubles by Winter which tied it at 27-all. Another single and double put Winter ahead 33–27, then three doubles and a single put Rose ahead 40–33. Winter plugged away to tie it again at 46-all, but two final doubles put Rose out. Rose had 40 out of 62 for .666 to Winter's .613.

Koppitsch fought an uphill battle to overcome a 28–8 lead and nose out Zessin 50–46 to stay in a tie for fourth place. Shepard beat Kelly 50–46 and Craft beat Davis 50–37 to get a tie for eighth place. Leaders:

Miller	7–1	Rose	6–3
Latzko	7–1	Koppitsch	6–3
Lundgren	7–1	Shepard	5–3
Otto	6–3		

A halt was called for eats and stuff and the last four games were played under floodlights.

ROUND TEN

Miller seemed to take to the floods and hit 39 out of 50 [78%] to smear Koppitsch 50–18. Latzko mopped up Kelly 50–20 and Lundgren easily beat Shepard 50–35. Otto, undaunted by losing to Latzko, walloped Winter 50–19. Craft got a firmer hold on eighth place by beating Hirschman 50–45 and Zessin stayed with him by defeating Davis 50–26. Leaders:

Miller 8–1, Latzko 8–1 and Lundgren 8–1.

ROUND ELEVEN

Lundgren fired a big shot by upsetting Latzko 50–24 with .609 as Latzko went only .516!! Miller kept going by pitching .625 to beat Davis 50–14. Rose hit the high game by stepping along at a .741 clip to clip Otto 50–21. Rose had 43 out of 58.

Craft slipped by Shepard 50–21; Zessin beat Hirschman 50–34 and Kelly beat Winter 50–35. Leaders:

Lundgren	9–1	Otto	7–4
Miller	9–1	Koppitsch	6–4
Latzko	8–2	Shepard	5–5
Rose	7–3		

ROUND TWELVE

Hirschman came from far behind in the dying moments to upset Mr. Miller 50–49 as Lundgren ran over Winter 50–20 to take the lead all alone. Latzko walloped Craft 50–25 and Koppitsch walked over Davis 50–16. Rose, coasting along in his typical fashion, beat Kelly 50–25. Zessin lost his chance to gain a position for the finals, by losing to Shepard 50–27.

ROUND THIRTEEN

Rose leaped on Lundgren like a tiger and rammed on a 24 out of the first 30 to run up a lead of 29–4, to win finally 50–16, hitting 39 out of 56 for .696. Otto trounced Kelly 50–38; Latzko eliminated Zessin 50–33; Hirschman upset Koppitsch 50–11; Shepard "upset" Miller 50–36 and Craft made the finals by beating Winter 50–25.

Preliminary Round Robin Summary
Top Eight Qualify for the Finals

Player	W	L	Pts	R	DR	SP	Pct
1. Joe Latzko	10	2	561	459	147	739	.622
2. Carl Lundgren	10	2	551	376	100	686	.548
3. Lee Rose	9	3	547	393	119	672	.584
4. William Miller	9	3	560	395	111	716	.551
5. Jonas Otto	8	4	490	322	81	674	.477
6. Frank. Koppitsch	7	5	488	374	84	766	.488
7. N. E. Shepard	7	5	515	341	84	780	.437
8. Louis Craft	5	7	402	309	70	724	.426
9. Louis Hirschman	4	8	408	310	69	740	.419
10. Henry Zessin	4	8	437	387	51	732	.392
11. Joe Kelly	3	9	406	299	63	726	.411
12. Jule Winter	1	11	390	303	51	784	.386
13. Jim Davis	1	11	333	249	37	698	.357
				4417		9436	.469

Finals

Sunday dawned clear and very hot, with a strong wind that seemed to blow out of a giant furnace.

ROUND ONE

Miller opened right up on Shepard and rounded him up 50–8 with .761. Otto upset the dope by beating Lundgren 50–26 with .629 as Charlie pitched only .500. Rose pitched carefully against Craft to win 50–15 with .609. Latzko won from Koppitsch 50–21, but only threw .500, as his finger was bothering him.

ROUND TWO

In the terrific heat and strong wind, Rose met Lundgren. Rose got a point, then Lundgren got 3, Rose got 3, Lundgren got 3. There came a four-dead and Lundgren then got another point. Rose got a point, then hung on four doubles to go ahead 12-5. Lundgren hit three doubles to make it 12-8 and Rose hit two doubles to make it 15-8. Lundgren hit 8 out of the next 12 to move ahead 18-15, but here a double miss allowed the "Tiger" to leap in for 6 to go ahead 21-18. Later it stood 24-24 and then Rose suddenly pulled on three doubles and two singles to lead 40-24! Rose won out 50-28, hitting 41 out of 68 for .602.

Latzko dropped to only .488 and Miller staggered to a win over him 50–42. Otto kept unbeaten by rolling over Craft 50–19. Koppitsch beat Shepard.

This was the worst round, as wind blew tremendously. Otto overcame a 42–36 deficit to beat Miller 50–42 and stamp himself as a contender.

Rose stayed unbeaten by beating Koppitsch 50–43 in an uphill fight which saw Koppitsch leading 23–11, 29–19 and 43–35. Rose went only .525.

Latzko beat Craft 50–18 and Lundgren slaughtered Shepard 50–17. Leaders: Otto 3–0, Rose 3–0, Latzko 2–1 and Miller 2–1. Others out of the running for now!

Rose met Latzko!! It was expected to be a hard fight, but those on the inside "know," knew that Latzko has about reached the end of his rope. He is known as a "one day pitcher" who tears his hand so badly from his unorthodox grip that one day is all he can stand. Five out of six put Rose ahead 9–0. Five out of six for Joe made it 9–6 and three out of four for Lee made it 12–6. Joe got 3 on a single and Rose got 3 on a single. Joe got 4, then Rose got 4 and it was 19–13 in favor of Rose.

It was a new Rose facing Latzko now — — — one who was confident and not shaking. The champion was tottering — — — and the knock-out was near — — —. It came !!!

Rose poured on three doubles and scored 3, 6 and 3 to pound out a lead of 31–13! Rose got another point to make it 32–13 and then, aghast at such easy going, missed and saw Latzko pile it on for 6 to make it 32–19. Rose then put his nose down and ground out 11 out of the next 14 and then looked up to find himself leading 42–19. The game finished up 50–23, with Rose getting 37 out of 58 for .638.

Otto piled over Shepard 50–20 to stay undefeated. Lundgren kept alive a faint hope by beating the fading Miller 50–41. Craft Beat Koppitsch 50–30.

ROUND FIVE

First place was at stake as Rose met Otto. However, there wasn't much exciting about the game! Rose was heading downhill now and had a championship light in his eyes that burned with all the pent-up fire of 11 years of fruitless title-chasing. Wind and sun and hopping shoes could not faze the stem and machine-like swing and pitch of the "Flower of Detroit." Steadily Rose ground Otto under foot, hitting 35 out of the first 50 without a double miss and led 38–20. Rose had two doubles misses after that, but won 50–27, shooting 45 out of 66 for .682.

Lundgren, Latzko and Miller all won, to each retain a slim chance for second place.

ROUND SIX

Latzko fired on 39 out of 50 to eliminate Lundgren 50–14, as Miller made his last stand against Rose. Miller opened with five straight doubles to rush ahead 12–0, but Rose never faltered in that steady, driving stride. Three doubles put Rose ahead 15–12 and Miller tied it at 15-all.

Rose drove on steadily and went ahead 25–15 and from there on it ceased to be a contest. Rose won 50–17 as Miller collapsed, hitting 36 out of 54 for .666. Otto stayed in 2nd place by beating Koppitsch 50–19.

ROUND SEVEN

Rose wound up undefeated by striding along steadily to grind Shepard down 50–10 with 33 out of 46 for .717.

Latzko faced elimination as he met Otto and made a determined and desperate bid to stay in the running. Latzko walked all over Otto from the start, running up a lead of 12–1 and steadily increased it until it stood 35–15 at 50 shoes.

Latzko seemed certain to tie for 2nd place, but the indefatigable Otto never gave up and began pouring ringers on. Two doubles made it 35–21 in favor of Otto, then Latzko fired four more doubles, but only got 3 points on the first one. It was 38–21. Then Latzko broke down! Otto piled up 4, a 3 on three and 3 on a single, to make it 38–31. Otto got another point on a single and Latzko then topped a double, but missed both shoes next frame and Otto piled in for 6 to tie it at 38–38! Otto got a point on a single and then doubled, but Latzko topped it.

Joe got a point on a single and 3 on a single to lead 42–39. Joe singled and Otto doubled to tie it at 42–42. Otto singled and Latzko hit a double to go ahead 45–42. Latzko took another point on a single to lead 46–42.

Latzko doubled again and all seemed over for Otto, but the big man from Ann Arbor calmly banged on a double on top. Otto picked up a point on a single, then doubled and Latzko up and missed both shoes!! It stood 49–46 for Otto. Otto doubled again but the champion once more came in with a double on top. Then Latzko missed both shoes! Otto went out with a double!! Otto had 64 out of 98 for .653.

Lundgren and Miller both won to tie for 3rd place.

Finals Round Robin Standings
Top Two Move to Championship Playoff

Player	W	L	Pts	R	DR	SP	Pct
1. Rose	7	0	350	262	82	418	.626
2. Otto	6	1	327	258	75	446	.578
3. Latzko	4	3	311	260	74	454	.572
4. Lundgren	4	3	268	228	60	412	.553
5. Miller	4	3	300	236	59	450	.524
6. Craft	2	5	209	132	30	380	.347
7. Koppitsch	1	6	204	182	29	430	.423
8. Shepard	0	7	139	128	25	354	.361
Total	28	28	2108	1686	434	3344	.504

Championship Match

Rose and Otto did not wait long before squaring off for the championship series.

As a series, it perhaps lacked the glamor and drama of series played in the past and the doubts of an ultimate winner were lacking almost completely. Otto had played remarkably well, and had also been rather lucky to reach the series at all and no one gave him a ghost of a chance against the steady stone-wall of the veteran Rose.

And indeed — — — it was so!

Rose opened the first game in a business-like manner and soon showed a lead of 18–4. Otto rallied gamely to come out in front 22–21 and then fell back before Rose's steady game and Rose won 50–24 with 42 out of 66 for .636.

Otto opened the second game with a rush that bade fair to square it up and opened up a lead of 20–4 as Rose put on only six out of sixteen. Then Rose started crowding 80% and shot 31 out of the last 40 to quickly crumple Otto up 50–30. Rose had 37 out of 56 for .661.

Otto pitched everything he had in the next game and Rose wisely did not try to head him off. Otto won 50–25 with 44 out of 68 for .648.

Rose had marked time for this game and let Otto have it with both barrels. After it stood 4–4, Rose showered on 27 out of the next 34 and easily won after that, 50–13. Rose had 34 out of 46 for .739.

Otto took a 9–4 lead in the 5th game, but Rose soon rolled ahead 13–9, 19–12, 29–15 and 34–22. Otto threw himself out striving to close the gap and did succeed in coming up to jump ahead 44–42! Then two doubles put Rose out as Otto failed to make a ringer, and

Rose Became the Michigan State Champion!!!

Championship Series Summary

| | Rose | | | | | Otto | | | |
	Pts	R	DR	Pct	SP	Pts	R	DR	Pct
1.	50	42	13	.636	66	24	35	9	.530
2.	50	37	12	.661	56	30	31	10	.553
3.	25	36	9	.529	68	50	44	13	.648
4.	50	34	12	.739	46	13	22	5	.478
5.	50	43	12	.582	74	44	39	10	.527
	.619					.551			

- - - - - - -

This was Lee Rose's second state championship. His first was ten years earlier, in 1934. This win had a bit of good luck in that Bobby Hitt hadn't entered, while Latzko and Lundgren, both usually better pitchers, struggled and had miserable finals. Also, the title could have been determined after the first round robin, as is the practice for most other state championships. If that had happened, Latzko and Lundgren would have had a playoff for the title and Rose would have been in third place.

That isn't to say Rose was undeserving of the win. He had become a very accomplished pitcher. We shouldn't question his win, but it was another 11 years before Rose won his third state championship.

This next interesting entry is a clipping that covers a tournament held August 27th. Then we have Rose's account of a win over Lundgren, followed by a description of another district championship.

- - - - - - -

Yale Host to Champion
Shoe Tossers

Tournament in City Park
Last Sunday Gave the Crowd
Many a Thrill

Yale residents who journeyed to the city park last Sunday afternoon to witness the Horseshoe Tournament got a thrill out of the many miraculous feats enacted by the players, comprising the best horseshoe tossers in the state of Michigan.

The day was so perfect, the park so beautiful, the crowd so well pleased, that Lee Rose, Detroit, secretary-treasurer of the Wolverine State Horseshoe Association and 1944 State Champion, speaking for the Association, voiced the sentiment of the visitors, when he said that they would like to have the Eastern Michigan Tournament an annual event in Yale. This, the Yale members believe, would be a great boast for the town and undoubtedly they will arrange to invite the Association to hold the Eastern Michigan Tournament here next year as suggested.

Former State Champion, Joe Latzko, of Flint, put on the big show of the day. Not only did Joe cop tournament honors with 11 straight victories and hang up a high ringer average of 82.4 per cent for one game, but he was responsible for the most scalp-tingling stunt ever seen locally in an athletic way.

While his traveling mate, Ed Woodward, lay his chin on top of a stake, Joe tossed seven out of eight shoes around said stake without marring Ed's physiognomy one whit. And he did it over the regulation distance—40 feet.

Then, if that wasn't enough, Joe tossed eight straight ringers—over a blanket which completely hid the opposite stake 40 feet away. Latzko threw effortless and accurately, as if the three-foot barrier wasn't there.

Out-of-town players, in order of games won, pitched as follows:

1944 Eastern Michigan Invitational

August 27th — Sand Courts

Player	W	L	Pts	R	DR	SP	Pct
Latzko	11	0	550	396	125	586	67.5
Rose	9	2	492	383	110	644	59.4
Lundgren	8	3	539	371	103	614	60.3
Otto	8	3	504	342	97	632	54.1
Winter	7	4	441	316	73	638	49.3
Miller	6	5	515	374	112	716	52.2
Getz	5	6	409	325	75	690	47.1
Kelly	4	7	366	479	58	626	44.5
Koppitsch	3	8	387	302	71	668	45.2
Shepard	3	8	328	263	44	650	40.4
Lewandowski	2	9	301	239	41	622	38.5
Jones	0	11	280	233	42	624	37.3

Rose Defeats Lundgren

On September 4th at Northwestern Field, Rose defeated Lundgren in a 6 out of 11 game match that went the whole 11 games. A very strong wind blew all day.

Rose opened the first game with 23 out of 28 to take a lead of 29–4 and then slumped off and Carl came on to eventually win 50–44. Rose overcame a 27–19 deficit to beat Lundgren the second game 50–36 with .700.

It was nip and tuck in the third game with Lundgren winning, 50–45. Here a rest for beer was called. Rose led all the way to take the fourth game 50–42. Lundgren walked away with the fifth game 50–33 and threatened to do so again the sixth, but Rose came from behind in the late stages to even it up 50–41.

Lundgren held the upper hand in the seventh game until it stood 37–23 and here Rose ripped on 23 out of 24 to win 50–37 and take the series lead at four games to three. Rose hit the high game of the day in the eighth game to slaughter Lundgren 50–19. Rose had 57 out of 76 for .750.

Here, Lundgren insisted on resting and getting some more beer. Lundgren took the next game 50–33 and the tenth game 50–16 to even it up at five games each.

Rose hit six straight doubles to lead in game eleven 21–3, but Lundgren came back to lead 35–33. Rose then hit 15 out of the last 20 to win 50–39. Totals:

	Pts	R	DR	SP	Pct
Rose	471	487	154	760	.643
Lundgren	464	482	157		.634

Rose Retains District Title

September 10th — Northwestern Field

Lee Rose retained the Detroit District Championship at Northwest Field on September 10, by overpowering eleven consecutive opponents in the round robin and then pulling Lundgren down 3 out of 4 in the championship series.

No score sheets were kept in the round robin games, but Rose had no trouble in rolling up eleven straight wins. Although just out of bed with a severe cold, Rose easily ran over Koppitsch, Howdyshell, Mohn, Peary, Getz, Dalby, Lundgren, Kelly, Yorkison, Ashcraft and Fagan and was never threatened at any time.

Lundgren won 10 and lost 1 and thus qualified for the 3 out of 5 series with Rose. Final standings:

Player	W	L	Player	W	L
Lee Rose	11	0	Joe Kelly	6	5
Carl Lundgren	10	1	Howdyshell	5	6
M. B. Getz	7	4	Jerome Ashcraft	4	7
Andy Yorkison	7	4	Ted Mohr	2	9
F. Koppitsch	6	5	L. Peary	1	10
Joe Fagan	6	5	Otis Dalby	1	10

Championship Playoff

Both started slowly and not too well. Rose took a lead of 12–6, then Lundgren laid on ten out twelve to run ahead 23–12. Rose trailed along until it stood 43–25, then a sudden spurt of 12 out of 14 put Rose in front 44–43. Both staggered at the end, with Lundgren going out with five out of eight to win 50–47. Score:

	Pts	R	DR	SP	Pct
Rose	47	47	17	72	.653
Lundgren	50	47	15	72	.653

GAME TWO

The pace became faster and there wasn't much to choose from between them. Eight out of the first ten put Lundgren ahead 3–1. There was a single each for no-count and then Rose picked up 3 on a single. Rose then hit 16 out of the next 18 and had a lead of 14–9. A single and two doubles by Charlie tied it at 15-all. Both fell off a little and Lundgren got ahead 27–24. A miss allowed Rose to go ahead 28–27, then Lundgren plastered on twenty out of twenty-two to lead 43–31. Rose then started a rally and banged on seventeen out of twenty to go out. Score:

	Pts	R	DR	SP	Pct
Rose	50	70	26	98	.714
Lundgren	44	70	26	98	.714

GAME THREE

Rose laid it into Lundgren all the way, pouring doubles on in a steady stream. Five doubles put Lee ahead 9–0, but 18 out of twenty enabled Lundgren to lead 19–12. Five more doubles by Rose made it 19–18 and five doubles back by Lundgren made it 25–18. Rose now clicked on seven more doubles to lead 33–25 and after a single, Rose hit five more doubles to lead 42–26, making 25 out of 26. Score:

	Pts	R	DR	SP	Pct
Rose	50	68	28	84	.809
Lundgren	33	62	23	84	.738

GAME FOUR

Lundgren looped on 38 out of the first 50 and had a lead of 39–21 over Rose and it looked as though the series would be even up. But here the "Tiger" opened up and began to bang doubles on. Four doubles made it 39–27 and a single took a point — 39–28. Six more times Rose dropped on doubles and went ahead 40–39. Here, he missed and Lundgren hit a double to lead 45–40. Lundgren hit another double, but Rose reared back once more, covered that double and fired four more to win 50–45 and retain his Detroit title. Score:

	Pts	R	DR	SP	Pct
Rose	50	61	25	84	.726
Lundgren	45	61	22	84	.726

CHAMPIONSHIP SERIES

	Rose					Lundgren			
	P	R	DR	Pct	SP	P	R	DR	Pct
	47	47	17	.653	72	50	47	15	.653
	50	70	26	.714	98	44	70	26	.714
	50	68	28	.809	84	33	62	23	.738
	50	61	25	.726	84	45	61	22	.726
Totals	197	246	96	.728	338	172	240	86	.710

- - - - - - -

Lee Rose seems not to have been well liked by his fellow players. His extremely competitive nature meant he was probably easier to get along with on days when he was winning rather than days when he was losing. He had a tremendous stem of self-confidence, so to speak, as he called himself the "Flower of Detroit," a play on his assumed surname. But he also displayed strong promotional skills and effort and for five decades contributed to the advancement and organization of horseshoe pitching.

One of the reasons Michigan was a powerhouse in the sport at the time was Lee Jacob's effort to promote horseshoe pitching at all levels of the sport. Even as early as the 1920s he made distinctive efforts to establish teams and league competition. He worked to grow his local league efforts into local and state competitions. He served for 25 years as the Michigan association's secretary-treasurer, from 1935 to 1960.

That's all context for the highlight of Lee Rose's horseshoe pitching career: winning a national amateur championship.

His journal contains a couple of short newspaper articles announcing the tournament, but most of this chapter is his recording of the win. When Rose entered AAU events, notice that he used his real name (Lee Jacobs), something we are not accustomed to reading. Two newspaper clippings appear first and then Lee's handwritten account of the action.

– – – – – – –

National A.A.U. Tournament
Held at Northwestern Field
September 16–17, 1944

Horseshoe Pitching
Champs Are Coming

Defending champions in both the singles and doubles and one record holder will be in the field competing in the National A.A.U. Horseshoe Pitching Championships at Northwestern Field Saturday and Sunday, beginning at 1 p.m. each day.

Carl E. Lundgren, of Detroit, will defend his title that he won last year at Chicago. Arner Lindquist and Charles Grosselin, both of Morgantown, West Virginia, 1943 national doubles champions, also will be present. Lindquist won the 1942 singles title. Lundgren and Lee H. Jacobs, of Detroit, were doubles runners up last year.

Sergeant Frank Breen, of Elgin, Illinois, who holds two national records, has been granted a furlough by the U.S. Army to come here. Breen set his marks in 1941 when he got 750 ringers in 1,074 shoes pitched for the tournament and 80 ringers in a qualifying round of 100 shoes.

Each contestant will pitch 100 shoes in the qualifying round and 50 shoes against each opponent in the final round robin series. Ringers will count three points and shoes within six inches or less will be one point.

Everyone Pitches in This Game

Detroit's leading pitchers—of horseshoes, not baseball—are getting ready for the world series.

The National A.A.U. Senior horseshoe pitching championships are carded for Northwestern Field Saturday and Sunday and against the day, the city's most potent pitchers are limbering their arms and polishing up their accuracy.

Chief Detroit title threats are Carl E. Lundgren and Lee H. Jacobs of the Park and Recreation department. Lundgren is the defending national singles champion, while Jacobs finished in third place a year ago. They teamed to take second in the doubles at Chicago in 1943.

Qualifying play will start Saturday at 1 p.m., with each contestant pitching 100 shoes. The high scorers will fill out the championship bracket of 16 or 32 players, depending upon the number of total entries.

The championship bracket will stage a round robin series to determine the championship.

Other entries already received are Arner Lindquist and Charles Grosselin of Morgantown W. Va., defending doubles champions; Stanley Manker and James Johnston, Ohio champions for the past two seasons; Harry Henn, of Cold Springs, Ky.; Jonas Otto, of Ann Arbor and N. E. Shepard, of Flint.

On September 15, the evening before the big meet, I went over to Northwestern Field for some practice and there was Sgt. Breen warming up. I played him 2 practice games and really poured it on him. I hit around 90% to drop him 50–18 and overcame him in another game 50–33, which must have gone 140 shoes, with me still crowding 90%.

September 16 was the qualifying and the doubles. I warmed up a while and then qualified with a 256, 80 ringers to tie Breen's National record. Latzko hit 79 ringers and 255 points.

Koppitsch and I teamed up in the doubles, and only bad luck stopped us from taking the title! We just couldn't get started against Yorkison & Fagan and lost out. (Games were 50 shoes, count-all system.) After beating Breen and Manker, we lost a hard-luck game to Middletown & Shepard. Then we went to town and knocked off 4 good teams — Lundgren & Otto, Lindquist & Grosselin, Latzko & Woodward and Kelly & Getz. We wound up tied for 1st with Latzko & Woodward. The playoff game was played under the lights and Koppitsch and I were beaten.

Several of the pitchers were entertained by me at my house that evening, and most of the night.

Everything was set for the big finals on Sept. 17. Sixteen pitchers faced the barrier in 50-shoe count-all games. The day was hot and almost no wind at all — — — — just perfect for the "Tiger." A large crowd was on hand, even before play opened and heated speculation ran rampant as to who would win the meet. Chief choices were Latzko, Rose (or Jacobs, as he is known in A.A.U. circles) and Lundgren, Breen and Lindquist.

Rose opened with Shepard and had no trouble in coming out ahead. The second game with Manker of Ohio was just as easy. In the third game against Yorkison, Rose hit the high game of the entire day, scoring 133 points with 43 ringers out of 50 shoes. Grosselin was easy and then Rose struck his first snag in Middleton. Rose trailed most of the way. The game was played on the first court with people running through and interfering, making it very hard to rally. Rose tied the score on the last throw by hanging a double ringer over Middleton's leaner. The game went four extra innings. Rose galloped away with 4 straight doubles and finally won.

An hour of rest for lunch was called here and only Rose and Latzko were undefeated.

[When we] came back from a light lunch, Rose had to face Arner Lindquist! Lindquist jumped right off in front and his slow way of pitching made it difficult to rally against him. Rose, however, never wavered and even when things looked almost beyond recall, he kept bearing down. Then, near the end, Lindquist weakened and the Detroit ringer machine was quick to slip ahead and squeeze out a win, 103 to 101.

The 7th game, against Hirschman, was easy after 20 shoes and then came Breen. Rose tore into Breen early and ran up a lead and then sat back and defended it stoutly against the soldier's desperate rallies. Breen fell just a little short. Lindquist upset Latzko in this round and Rose stood alone at the top.

Kelly was the next victim of Rose, being powered under early by a flood of doubles. Rose was really going to town as he scented a national title in the offing. He met Getz in the 10th game and Getz jumped off to a lead at the start. Photographers were trying to snap pictures of Rose as he tried to catch up and that made things almost bad enough to cause Rose to blow up. But he didn't blow — — — instead, he came on with a consecutive drive of doubles that soon caught Getz and snowed him under.

Lundgren fired a broadside at Latzko in this round and bounced him down. This left Rose 2 games in front and 5 to go.

An immense crowd surrounded the courts. Persons who hadn't been around for years were to be seen. Harold Arnold, Joe Galesky, Ed Levagood and Sherer showed up. Stanley David and Johnny Schultz were there. Fitzgerald and Konz of Toledo were there. Greenfield, Goodell, Ingraham and others from Clark Park were there. Even E. L. Holmes, a schoolteacher back in Western High in 1921–25 came around to say hello.

Pekkala was easy in the 11th game and then came the Rose-Latzko clash. Latzko pitched a very good game, the game of a man who is very desperate and, getting an early lead over Rose, he clung to it all the way and won out.

This enlivened the situation to a great extent as Rose now had Miller, Lundgren and Otto to play and had to win them all to keep out in front. The story of these last three games Rose played cannot adequately be put into words! With an immense following crowded around his court and following his every pitch, the "Flower of Detroit" put on a show that has few equals in history.

Rose showered on 40 out of 50 to run a hard fighting Miller to the ground, then hit 39 out of 50 to swamp Lundgren. Then back to the hazardous 1st court, he tossed a thunderous barrage of 41 out of 50 to smash down Otto and become the NATIONAL CHAMPION!!!

In all these last games, Rose was the perfect horseshoe machine and indeed all through the tournament, never once gave vent to any temperamental outburst that had distinguished him in the past.

His manner was outwardly a cool, collected, icy-cold, machine-like attitude, fortified by a never-say-die quality that kept him coming over the rough spots. Mechanically, his pitching was beautiful, a high wobbly shoe that just seemed to adore the stake.

A just reward for a great pitcher!

- - - - - - -

The Lee Rose Story

Wow! It doesn't get any more personal than that. One could safely say that Lee Rose was a very competitive soul who was unabashedly proud of his accomplishments. We could question how competitive the tournament was and thus if this national title was all that meaningful. Any doubts on that front are answered by simply looking at their pitching averages. This was a competitive group of pitchers. They came from several states, and most were states champions back home.

Next is a short press clipping pasted into the journal.

- - - - - - -

'Shoe' Title Stays Here

Lee Jacobs, who began pitching horseshoe 25 years ago when he was 13 years old, finally crashed the elusive national championship circle yesterday, winning the A.A.U. singles title at Northwestern Field.

A lathe operator at the Ford Motor Co., Jacobs triumphed in 14 of his 15 matches, edging out Joseph P. Latzko, of Flint, by a margin of one match. The latter, who handed the new champion his lone setback, won 13 and lost two.

Third place went to Arner Lindquist, while Carl Lundgren, last year's title-holder, took fourth place from Sgt. Frank Breen, after the two had finished in a tie.

Sixteen contestants out of a field of 23 qualified for the finals. The competition was staged under the direction of George D. Chumard, Cincinnati, A.A.U. horseshoe chairman.

Championship medals were presented to the first three place winners.

- - - - - - -

A question follows these AAU events around: Are all the participants amateurs? This short clipping appears next in the journals. While there may have been a whispered question or two along the way, no player we know of had been formally challenged before about whether or not he was actually an amateur.

Horseshoers Called Pros

Professionalism charges were brought against Lee Jacobs of Detroit and Joe Latzko after they placed one–two in the National AAU horseshoe pitching tournament at Northwestern Field Sunday.

It was charged that Jacobs, who won 14 and lost 1 yesterday, had played in a tournament in Port Huron a month ago. Latzko is second with 13 and 2 was in the same meet, it is said.

Arner Lindquist of Morgantown, W.Va., and Frank Breen, of Elgin, Ill., were tied for third with 11 and 4 and will play off for the title if Jacobs and Latzko are disqualified. Jonas and Carl Lundgren, both of Detroit were next with 11 and 4.

Joe Kelly of Saginaw and Otto Woodward of Flint also are charged with playing in the pro meet.

Similar charges may have been made in previous AAU contests and in future years, but this is the first and only documented case of a formal challenge to amateur status turned up by research. It's intriguing that Rose thought enough of the article to clip it out and tack it in his journal.

Also, it's interesting to ponder who brought the charge forward. It's doubtful that it was a player who had participated in the event. If another event player was the source, he almost surely would have brought the charge forward when Rose entered the contest. It's also unlikely that it was any of the leading players, because they were from out of the area and wouldn't have been aware of what tournaments Rose or any other Michigan players had participated in.

Nevertheless, nothing must have come of it since Rose is still listed as the winner, and he was allowed to participate in later AAU tournaments, as was Latzko. In fact, Latzko won the 1946 national championship in 1946.

The article is not accurate in terms of the final tournament standings, but that was clarified in the official final standing report.

Here is how the tournament results appear in Lee Rose's journal.

(Note: Middleton withdrew after 13th round of play.)

(Jacob's 256 qualifying score equals the National A.A.U. record. 133 high individual score for one game, set by Jacobs, 3rd round.)

Non qualifiers as follows:

Ed Wall, Detroit	250	76
(3rd high qualifier – failed to show up in time for finals)		
Harry Henn, Cold Spring, Ky.	198	57
Frank Koppitsch	187	53
Harley Rizor, Toledo, Ohio	185	49
Henry Zessin, Saginaw	182	46
Joe W. Fagan, Detroit	162	42
Lin Roberts, Detroit	102	15

1944 Senior A.A.U. Horseshoe Pitching Championship Tournament – Singles and Doubles, under the auspices of the City of Detroit, Department Parks and Recreation, at Northwestern Playfield, Grand River & Wreford, Detroit, Mich., Saturday and Sunday, September 16–17, 1944.

1944 A.A.U. National Singles Final Standings

Place	Player	Qual	Pts	SP	R	%	W	L
1.	Lee Jacobs, Detroit	256	1728	750	520	69	14	1
2.	Joe Latzko, Flint	255	1666	750	511	68	13	2
3.	Arner Lindquist, W.Va	245	1634	750	462	62	11	4
4.	Carl Lundgren, Detroit	DC	1490	750	435	57	10	5
5.	Frank Breen, Elgin, Ill.	237	1433	750	421	56	10	5
6.	Jonas Otto, Ann Arbor	220	1497	750	434	58	10	5
7.	Andrew Yorkison, Detroit	210	1464	750	403	54	9	6
8.	Ed Woodward, Flint	204	1522	750	439	59	9	6
9.	Joe Kelly, Detroit	219	1432	750	399	53	8	7
10.	Stanley Manker, Ohio	238	1518	750	443	59	7	8
11.	Charles Grosselin, W.Va.	222	1345	750	356	48	6	9
12.	Norris Shepard, Flint	219	1262	750	348	46	6	9
13.	Alfred Pekkalo, Detroit	208	1300	750	344	44	3	12
14.	B. Hirschman, Saginaw	203	1288	750	336	45	3	12
15.	B. Getz, Ferndale	202	1291	750	341	45	2	13
16.	Roy Middleton, Flint	206	931	600	247	41	1	14

11,850 6,439 54.34%

Doubles Competition – Final Standings

Place	Players	Pts	SP	R	%	W	L
1.	Ed Woodward – Joe Latzko	863	350	239	68	6	2
2.	Lee Jacobs – Frank Koppitsch	788	350	230	66	6	2
3.	Frank Breen – Stan Manker	783	350	215	61	5	3
4.	Jonas Otto – Carl Lundgren	794	350	228	65	5	3
5.	Arner Lindquist – C. Grosselin	715	350	175	50	3	5
6.	Joe Fagan – Andrew Yorkison	641	350	168	48	3	5
7.	Ray Middleton – N. E. Shepard	648	350	191	55	2	6
8.	Joe Kelly – B. Getz	699	350	196	56	2	6

(Note: Final standings in doubles listed as result of playoffs to break ties.)

- - - - - - -

Rose closed out 1944 with a record of 86 games won and 19 games lost. He met many players for only one or two games, but here's his record with some of the pitchers he met several times that year.

- - - - - - -

	W	L
Lundgren	13	8
Joe Latzko	5	6
Jonas Otto	10	2
Frank Koppitsch	6	1

Let Me Reintroduce Myself—Lee Jacobs

The year of 1945 was a poor one for horseshoe pitching and for horseshoe pitchers. Few pitchers had new shoes and not many more had good shoes. No team matches were held and only a few tournaments. A few informal meets and friendly get-togethers were played.

The Detroit District Tournament was held at Northwestern Field on August 12. Twelve entries started, included Jonas Otto of Ann Arbor, a guest entry.

Ed Walls and Lee Jacobs finished in a tie for first place in the round robin, each winning 10 and losing 1. Walls lost to Jacobs and Lundgren beat Jacobs [in the round robin]. Walls hung up .716 for a new record ringer average in the round robin.

- - - - - - -

1945 Detroit District Tournament
Held August 12 — Northwestern Field
Round Robin Standings

Player	W	L	R	DR	SP	Pct
1. Ed Walls	10	1	467	165	652	.716
2. Lee Jacobs*	10	1	419	147	674	.622
3. Carl Lundgren	9	2	480	143	752	.637
4. Jonas Otto+	8	3	467	148	766	.606
5. Carl Gothard	7	4	442	140	686	.648
6. Andrew Yorkison	7	4	405	122	648	.625
7. Frank Koppitsch	5	6	336	88	634	.530
8. Joe Kelly	4	7	363	104	672	.540

(Continued on next page)

(Continued from previous page)

Player	W	L	R	DR	SP	Pct
9. M. B. Getz	2	9	377	97	750	.502
10. Joe Fagan	2	9	372	96	740	.502
11. Ernie Phipps	1	10	270	66	588	.459
12. Dell Morton	1	3	93	23	202	.460
Stan Pustelink	0	5	97	19	260	.373
Mark Goodell	0	2	27	3	86	.314
Totals			4615		8110	.569

Notes: *Formerly LEE ROSE, now using right name.
+ Guest entry from Ann Arbor.
Three players combine to fill in to make it an even round robin.

The final series between Walls and Jacobs was a hectic battle. Jacobs nosed Walls out 50–45, then Walls took the next two 50–31 and 50–42. Jacobs came back with 72 out of 98 for .734 and 50–36 with 59 out of 78 for .756.

Jacobs thus took the title for the third time in a row and the fifth time in his life.

1945 Detroit Championship Series

Game		Pts	R	DR	SP	Pct
1	Jacobs	50	56	18	80	.700
	Walls	45	56	17	80	.700
2	Jacobs	31	44	14	68	.648
	Walls	50	51	21	68	.750
3	Jacobs	42	61	21	90	.678
	Walls	50	65	24	90	.722
4	Jacobs	50	72	26	98	.734
	Walls	32	65	22	98	.663
5	Jacobs	50	59	22	78	.756
	Walls	36	55	21	78	.705
Totals	Jacobs	223	292	101	414	.705
	Walls	213	293	105	414	.707

My Twenty-Second State Tournament

August 18–19 Northwestern Field — Detroit

With twenty entries, the nineteen-game round robin couldn't be finished in one day, so 16 rounds were played.

ROUND ONE

Louis Hirschman of Saginaw hit the best game of the first round by beating Edward Woodward of Flint 50–24 with .678; Lee Jacobs of Detroit hit .672 to defeat Jonas Otto of Ann Arbor 50–30; Joe Kelly of Highland Park went .635 to slaughter Ed Titus of Parchment 50–18; Carl Gothard of Detroit hung up .604 to defeat the aged Jim Skinner of Leonidas 50–23; Norris Shepard of Flint scored an upset victory over Carl Lundgren of Detroit 50–27; Andrew Yorkison, giant southpaw from Detroit rolled over Jule Winter of Port Huron 50–23; Joe Fagan of Detroit upset Frank Koppitsch of Dearborn 50–40; Louis Craft of Kalamazoo nosed out Ray Gorsline of Fulton 50–45; Henry Zessin of Saginaw upset M. B. Getz of Ferndale 50–44; Latzko of Flint won by default from the late-arriving Frank Lewandowski of Port Huron.

ROUND TWO

Latzko ran up .761 in walloping Shepard 50–10; Hirschman stayed right along with .709 in trouncing Winter 50–15; Jacobs easily bested Kelly 50–30 with .634; Gothard stayed along by nosing out Koppitsch 50–46 with .632; Yorkison stayed unbeaten by whipping Woodward 50–30; Fagan remained unbeaten also by defeating Skinner 50–32; Lundgren beat Lewandowski; Otto beat Titus; Getz defeated Craft and Gorsline beat Zessin. Undefeated leaders: Latzko, Hirschman and Jacobs.

ROUND THREE

Lundgren really laid it on to Jacobs with 44 out of 52 for .846 for a 50–13 win; Latzko, Hirschman and Gothard remained unbeaten by winning from Titus, Fagan and Yorkison; Otto defeated Woodward; Getz beat Lewandowski; Kelly beat Winter; Koppitsch won from Craft; Shepard downed Gorsline and the venerable Skinner beat Zessin. Leaders: Latzko 3–0, Hirschman 3–0; Gothard 3–0, Jacobs 2–1, Lundgren 2–1, Otto 2–1, Yorkison 2–1, Shepard 2–1, Kelly 2–1, Fagan 2–1 and Getz 2–1.

ROUND FOUR

Latzko was running in high gear as he ground Getz under 50–1 with 23 out of 26 for .884; Hirschman slipped to .605, but stayed unbeaten by winning from Koppitsch 50–31; Gothard kept along by defeating Titus; Jacobs went .625 in winning over Craft 50–11; Lundgren beat Winter; Otto won from Gorsline; Yorkison hit 28 out of 36 for .777 to slam Shepard down 50–1; Kelly beat Skinner; Fagan showed unexpected power in beating Woodward 50–18 with .640; Lewandowski beat Zessin. Leaders: Latzko 4–0, Hirschman 4–0, Gothard 4–0, Jacobs 3–1, Lundgren 3–1, Otto 3–1, Yorkison 3–1, Kelly 3–1 and Fagan 3–1.

ROUND FIVE

Latzko continued to pitch in high power style in hitting .861 to mow down Winter 50–7; Gothard beat Kelly 50–40; Hirschman downed Craft 50–18 to keep pace with the Flint machine; Jacobs landed on Gorsline with 27 out of 32 for .884 to win 50–2; Lundgren stowed Woodward away 50–42; Otto beat Fagan; Yorkison won from Zessin; Getz and Koppitsch won. Leaders: Latzko 5–0, Hirschman 5–0, Jacobs 4–1, Lundgren 4–1, Otto 4–1, Yorkison 4–1.

ROUND SIX

Jacobs met defeat at the hands of Latzko 50–30. Latzko had .716 and Jake had .635. Gothard beat Gorsline; Hirschman beat Titus to stay undefeated; Lundgren was leading Zessin 28–17 when Zessin decide to concede the game and buy Lundgren a beer; Otto trounced Lewandowski; Yorkison was upset by the surprising Fagan 50–44 in a 92-shoe game; Woodward won from his first game, beating Kelly; Koppitsch, Getz and Skinner won. Leaders: Latzko 6–0, Hirschman 6–0, Gothard 6–0, Lundgren 5–1, Otto 5–1.

ROUND SEVEN

Latzko became the only undefeated player by overwhelming Gothard 50–16 with .727. Hirschman fell to .486 and was upset by Shepard. Jacobs beat his buddy Koppitsch 50–22 with .700 and Frank was a bit sore about it too. Lundgren had some trouble with Fagan, but won 50–34; Otto beat Craft; Yorkison whipped Lewandowski; Getz won from Winter; Kelly, Woodward and Titus also won. Leaders: Latzko 7–0, Lundgren 6–1, Gothard 6–1, Hirschman 6–1, Otto 6–1, Jacobs 5–2, Yorkison 5–2, Getz 5–2.

ROUND EIGHT

Latzko ironed out poor old Skinner 50–3 with .750; Lundgren was forced to the limit to nose out Koppitsch 50–46, Lundgren going .690 to Frank's .678. Otto easily beat Zessin; Gothard downed Lewandowski; Hirschman bested Gorsline; Jacobs hit .709 to defeat Getz; Yorkison beat Kelly 50–40; Shepard and Titus all won. Leaders: Latzko 8–0, Lundgren 7–1, Gothard 7–1, Otto 7–1, Hirschman 7–1, Jacobs 6–2, Yorkison 6–2.

ROUND NINE

Latzko rolled along .781 in stowing away Zessin 50–3; Lundgren defeated Craft; Gothard stayed along by nosing out Getz 50–49; Otto slaughtered Shepard; Hirschman was turned back by Jacobs 50–35 with Jacobs shooting 62 out of 84 for .738; Yorkison beat Titus; and Kelly, Woodward, Winter and Fagan each won. Leaders: Latzko 9–0, Lundgren 8–1, Gothard 8–1, Otto 8–1, Hirschman 7–2, Jacobs 7–2, Yorkison 7–2.

ROUND TEN

Lundgren hit the high game of the round in knocking off Otto 50–19, Lundgren had 57 out 70 for .814 and Otto had 47 ringers for .672. Latzko had 59 out of 76 for .776 in beating Woodward 50–32 as Woodward had 52 ringers for .684. Yorkison went .736 to dispose of Craft 50–9; Jacobs coasted over Shepard 50–38 with .632; Gothard beat Zessin 50–36. Kelly, Winter, Getz, Hirschman and Koppitsch also won. Leaders: Latzko 10–0, Lundgren 9–1, Gothard 9–1, Otto 8–2, Hirschman 8–2, Jacobs 8–2, Yorkison 8–2.

ROUND ELEVEN

Latzko still stepped along, beating Gorsline 50–4 with .766. Lundgren took 2nd place all alone as he defeated Getz 50–14; as Woodward upset Gothard

50–48, Jacobs crashed out .712 to overpower a stubborn Zessin 50–32; Yorkison downed Hirschman 50–42; Otto ran over Skinner 50–7; Shepard, Kelly, Titus and Fagan won. Leaders: Latzko 11–0, Lundgren 10–1, Gothard 9–2, Otto 9–2, Yorkison 9–2, Jacobs 9–2.

ROUND TWELVE

Latzko curbed Yorkison's aspirations by taking him into camp 50–24. Joe hit 61 out of 80 for .762 as Andy hit 53 ringers for .663. Gothard showed power as he jumped on Otto with .739 to hand him a 50–14 lacing. Jacobs traveled at an even .700 to down Skinner 50–13; Lundgren beat Titus; Hirschman beat Zessin; Kelly, Koppitsch, Woodward, Craft and Lewandowski each won. Leaders: Latzko 12–0, Lundgren 11–1, Gothard 10–2, Jacobs 10–2.

ROUND THIRTEEN

Latzko ironed out Koppitsch 50–5 with .804; Lundgren defeated Skinner easily; Gothard shaded Fagan 50–40; Jacobs rolled over Lewandowski 50–17 with .685; Otto trounced Yorkison 50–25; Kelly upset Hirschman 50–46; Woodward, Shepard, Getz and Winter also won. Leaders: Latzko 13–0, Lundgren 12–1, Gothard 11–2, Jacobs 11–2, Otto 10–3.

ROUND FOURTEEN

Lundgren blasted out the high game in taking Gothard 50–10 with .769; Latzko slipped down to .647 in beating Fagan 50–11; Jacobs took 3rd place in disposing of Woodward 50–41 with .678; Otto took Hirschman 50–20; Shepard, Kelly, Lewandowski, Getz, Titus, Winter were all winners. Leaders: Latzko 14–0, Lundgren 13–1, Jacobs 12–2, Otto 11–3, Gothard 11–3.

ROUND FIFTEEN

Jacobs racked up 39 out of 44 for .887 in downing Titus 50–9; Latzko went .806 to wallop Hirschman 50–11; Lundgren hit .761 to slaughter Yorkison 50–16; Gothard beat Craft. Leaders: Latzko 15–0, Lundgren 14–1, Jacobs 13–2, Otto 12–3, Gothard 12–3.

ROUND SIXTEEN

This round was played under floodlights. Yorkison, fresh from the beer parlor, defeated Jacobs 50–34 with .735. Latzko nosed out Kelly 50–40, as Lundgren beat Gorsline; Otto downed Winter; Hirschman beat Gothard 50–32. Leaders at the end of play on August 18: Latzko 16–0, Lundgren 15–1, Jacobs 13–3, Otto 13–3, Gothard 12–4, Yorkison 10–6, Hirschman 10–6.

This round ended and most of the pitchers came to the Jacobs residence, where an all-night party took up the proceedings. Dancing, cards and drinking were the main features.

The meet was continued on August 19, with most of the contestants feeling pretty foggy.

- - - - - - -

Before moving on to the final three rounds, note Lee's new practice of using his actual last name, "Jacobs," even outside of AAU events. He includes a brief note at the end of the Detroit Tournament (the first event of 1945) but no explanation of why he made the change. Getting accustomed to the shift from Rose to Jacobs in his descriptions is a challenge for readers of his journal.

- - - - - - -

ROUND SEVENTEEN

Lundgren was the least worst player in topping Kelly 50–33 with .695. Latzko remained undefeated in beating Otto 50–30 with .651. Gothard ran over Shepard 50–19; Jacobs trounced Winter 50–8; Yorkison, Zessin, Hirschman, Woodward, Fagan and Skinner all won. Leaders: Latzko 17–0, Lundgren 16–1, Jacobs 14–3, Otto 13–4, Gothard 13–4, Yorkison 11–6, Hirschman 11–6, Kelly 10–7, Woodward 10–7.

ROUND EIGHTEEN

Latzko walloped Craft 50–25 to stay unbeaten; Lundgren kept up in 2nd by knocking down Hirschman 50–29; Jacobs stayed in third with the high game of the round in beating Fagan 50–29 with .667; Otto and Gothard kept in a tie for fourth by winning; Yorkison took sole position of 6th place by winning; Kelly eliminated Getz 50–37 and stayed in a tie for 7th with Woodward, who also won.

NINETEENTH AND FINAL ROUND

Lundgren whacked Latzko down for his first defeat 50–27, with .721, to tie for 1st place. Jacobs looped on 42 out of 52 to smother Gothard 50–19 with .808. Otto took 4th by beating Getz; Yorkison remained 6th by winning; Woodward, Kelly and Hirschman all won to stay tied for 7th.

In the play-off for 7th and 8th places, Woodward defeated Kelly 50–33 and Hirschman also defeated Kelly 50–35. The finals started soon after the robin completion.

1945 Michigan State Tournament
Preliminary Round Robin Final Standings

Player	W	L	Pts	R	DR	SP	Pct
1. Joe Latzko	18	1	877	683	244	950	.719
2. Carl Lundgren	18	1	905	691	231	1056	.654
3. Lee Jacobs	16	3	877	746	253	1172	.687
4. Jonas Otto	15	4	843	716	213	1172	.611
5. Carl Gothard	14	5	825	677	203	1184	.571
6. Andrew Yorkison	13	6	837	683	204	1136	.601
7. Edward Woodward	12	7	808	671	203	1120	.599
8. Louis Hirschman	12	7	825	68	119	1190	.578
9. Joe Kelly	12	7	840	720	215	1210	.595
10. M. B. Getz	10	9	774	595	163	1126	.528
11. Joe Fagan	8	11	776	640	163	1242	.515
12. N. E. Shepard	8	11	663	529	126	1094	.483
13. Frank Koppitsch	6	13	712	572	157	1132	.505
14. F. Lewandowski	6	13	487	400	76	996	.401
15. Jule Winter	5	14	589	498	116	1070	.465
16. Ed Titus	5	14	537	456	104	1078	.413
17. Henry Zessin	4	15	579	410	86	1066	.387
18. Ray Gorsline	3	16	533	394	72	1080	.364
19. Jim Skinner	3	16	498	375	60	1054	.355
20. Louis Craft	2	17	570	501	110	1106	.452

Play-Off for 7th and 8th Places

Player	Pts	R	DR	Pct	SP		Player	Pts	R	DR	Pct
Woodward	50	42	16	.656	64	vs.	Kelly	33	35	10	.547
Hirschman	50	51	12	.579	88	vs.	Kelly	35	48	10	.545

Finals – Game One

The feature of the first round was the sudden collapse of the defending champion—Lee Jacobs!! Jacobs opened against Woodward and was pouring ringers on steadily and seemed to be headed for an easy win. He led 28–16 and 31–19. Here, he suddenly seemed to go to pieces and Woodward quickly tied the score at 31–all. Jacobs got ahead again 35–31 and that was he end. With 13 out of 16, Woodward ran right out to win.

Latzko hit .704 to defeat Gothard 50–27, Otto beat Hirschman 50–33 and Yorkison upset Lundgren 50–44.

GAME TWO

Latzko poured on .796 to slaughter Otto 50–10. Yorkison stayed unbeaten by trouncing Woodward 50–20. Lundgren led all the way to send Jacobs down to his second defeat 50–35 and Gothard won from Hirschman 50–39.

GAME THREE

Latzko went .741 to dispose of Woodward 50–26 and Yorkison trimmed Otto 50–28. Jacobs went .688 to beat Gothard 50–36 and retain a chance. Lundgren eliminated Hirschman 50–29.

GAME FOUR

Jacobs, with nine out of twelve, sprang to a 17–0 lead over Latzko, then collapsed again and only threw one ringer out of the next ten shoes as Latzko rushed ahead 25–17. Jacobs then seemed to catch hold of himself for a while and battled along until he got ahead 38–36. Then he threw only four out of ten as Joe went out. This eliminated Jacobs. Yorkison still went unbeaten by winning from Hirschman 50–35. Lundgren eliminated Otto 50–43 and Woodward eliminated Gothard 50–41.

GAME FIVE

Latzko trounced Yorkison 50–28. Lundgren vaulted into a tie for 2nd by winning over Woodward 50–31 and eliminated him. Hirschman took a lead of 24–0 over a disheartened Jacobs and finally won 50–30. Otto beat Gothard 50–48.

GAME SIX

Latzko trimmed Lundgren 50–20 and Yorkison took a strangle hold on 2nd by banging out a win over Gothard 50–26. Jacobs beat Otto and Hirschman best Woodward.

GAME SEVEN

Latzko remained undefeated by beating Hirschman 50–10. Jacobs jumped on Yorkison at the start for a lead of 33–1 and coasted to a 50–36 win, thus enabling Lundgren to tie for 2nd by beating Gothard 50–42. Otto beat Woodward 50–24.

In a single play-off game, Yorkison defeated Lundgren 50–41 to qualify for the championship series.

Championship Series

Latzko carried too much experience for Yorkison and defeated him four straight games. Yorkison had a lead of 21–9 in the first game, but lost 50–41. Latzko led 38–37 in the second game and won out 50–37 with 68 out of 90 for .755 as Andy had 64 ringers for .711. Latzko led all the way to take the third game 50–35. Yorkison never gave up and tore into a lead of 42–28 in the fourth game, only to fall off as Latzko drove to the title with a 50–42 win.

Finals Round Robin Standings

Player	W	L	Pts	R	DR	SP	Pct
1. Joe Latzko	7	0	350	281	110	402	.696
2. Yorkison	5	2	314	286	86	474	.603
3. Lundgren	5	2	314	285	91	464	.613
4. Jonas Otto	3	4	268	320	100	528	.606
5. Lee Jacobs	3	4	288	296	89	498	.594
6. Hirschman	2	5	246	249	62	464	.536
7. Gothard	1	6	280	286	84	486	.581
8. Woodward	2	5	229	238	69	428	.556
Totals	27	27	2289	2241	691	3744	.588

Play-Off Game for Second Place

	Pts	R	DR	Pct	SP			Pts	R	DR	Pct
Yorkison	50	43	14	.615	70		Lundgren	41	40	12	.572

Championship Series

Best of Seven

	Latzko					Yorkison			
	Pts	R	DR	Pct	SP	Pts	R	DR	Pct
Game 1	50	56	19	.718	78	41	53	20	.679
Game 2	50	68	19	.755	90	37	64	23	.711
Game 3	50	61	24	.709	86	35	54	14	.628
Game 4	50	61	22	.709	86	42	53	21	.619
Totals		246		.723	340		224		.659

- - - - - - -

Lee Rose attended and pitched in the 1945 National AAU Tournament. He wrote very little about it, though, maybe because he wasn't successful in retaining his title. What he recorded about the tournament doesn't matter much—except that he indicates where the event was held. My research wasn't turning up much information about the tournament that year. In fact, the dates and site of the 1945 event were unknown until I discovered this section of Lee's journals.

The tournament was held in Norwood, Ohio, and the Cincinnati newspapers gave good coverage. The first media announcement was on September 2nd, and the second was printed September 19th.

- - - - - - -

Tourney at Norwood

Entry blanks have been mailed for the Senior National A.A.U. horseshoe pitching championships at Norwood Municipal Horseshoe Courts, Allison and Sherman Aves., September 22–23. The tourney will be conducted in connection with Ohio A.A.U. championship meet. Defending singles champion is Lee Rose, Detroit. Jim Johnson, Ludlow, Ky., is the defending Ohio A.A.U. champion.

Horseshoe Meet Opens Saturday

Norwood Municipal Horseshoe Courts will be the scene of the National Senior A.A.U. horseshoe pitching champion tournament Saturday and Sunday.

A crew of men, under Norwood City Engineer Al Ellis, Recreation Director H. C. Dillion and Leo McGrath, president of the Norwood Horseshoe Club, have been putting the courts in shape for the feature horseshoe attraction and they compare favorably with any court in the country, according to those who have seen the best. Ten courts comprise the Norwood layout.

The entry of Sgt. Frank Breen of the U.S. Military Police, Chicago, was received for the national tournament Tuesday, G. D. Chumard, chairman of the national committee stated. Breen's civilian address is Elgin, Ill., where he is a member of the Watch City Horseshoe Club, one of the leading clubs of the Mid-West. Breen is co-holder with two others for the high qualifying score in the national tournament. The mark is 256 points out of a possible 300.

Missing from the list of entries will be that of 79-year-old George Everhard of Linwood, who qualified last year for the final round-robin competition of the state tournament. Everhard will be on hand as a spectator and may pitch a few games but the tough tournament grind is a little too much for his age, he contends.

The entries include the 1943 and 1944 singles champions, Carl Lundgren and Lee Jacobs. Arner Lindquist, the 1942 champion has also entered.

The doubles tournament schedule calls for qualifying competition for both singles and doubles events to get underway Saturday at 1 p.m. Saturday, doubles finals to be at 4 p.m. Saturday, final round robin in the state tournament 9 a.m. Sunday and final round robin in the national at 1 p.m. Sunday.

Lee Rose pitching on the Ford Motor Company Court.

- - - - - - -

Lee describes just how close he came to winning again.

- - - - - - -

I lost the National A.A.U. title in Norwood, Ohio, to James Johnson. I was the only one to defeat him, but I lost to Manker and Mulroy, each by one point. The games were 50-shoe count-all.

1945 A.A.U. National Singles Final Standings

Place	Player	City	W	L	%
1.	James "Pop" Johnson	Ludlow, Ky.	14	1	58.5%
2.	Lee Jacobs	Detroit, Mich.	13	2	
3.	Stanley Manker	Chillicothe, Ohio			
4.	Joe Latzko	Flint, Michigan			
5.	Ralph Lackey	Middletown, Ohio			
6.	Arner Lindquist	Morgantown, W. Va.			
7.	Frank Breen	Elgin, Illinois			
	Mulroy				

1945 A.A.U. National Doubles Final Standing

1. Arner Lindquist & Charles Grosselin, Morgantown, W.Va.

2. Carl Lundgren, Detroit, & Jonas Otto, Ann Arbor, Mich.

3. James Johnson Ludlow & Harold MacPhearson, Covington, Ky

4. Joe Latzko & Ed Woodward, Flint, Michigan

– – – – – – –

In 1945 there didn't seem to be any issue with players declaring to be amateur pitchers. For the most part, players were participating in the AAU early their careers and joining the NHPA events when they were more experienced.

Pops Johnson, the 1945 champion, went on to play in NHPA events. He qualified 10 times for the men's Championship Class finals from 1948 through 1966. In his first year, 1948, he averaged 78.2 percent ringers and won 19 games, placing eleventh in the world standings. In 1974, Pops was the intermediate men's world champion, going undefeated (7–0) in the finals with a 67.7 percent ringer average.

Pops Johnson was elected NHPA's vice president in 1961 and served on the Hall of Fame committee for ten years. Johnson was inducted to NHPA Hall of Fame in 1985, is a charter member of the Kentucky Horseshoe Pitchers Hall of Fame, and is also a member of the Ohio Horseshoe Pitchers Hall of Fame.

This was the final AAU event for Arner Lindquist. In all, Lindquist won three gold medals, two silver medals, and two bronze medals. In 1942, at the age of 46, Lindquist became the oldest national champion to that point. He went on to win five West Virginia state championships: 1949, 1950, 1953, 1956, and 1957. His career continued with his participation in NHPA World Tournaments. From 1946 to 1965, Lindquist qualified 11 times for the men's championship finals, winning 154 games, which still ranks 52nd on the list of all-time wins. His highest finish was in 1946 when he placed seventh on a 16–7 record. He had another top-ten finish in 1950, when he placed ninth. His best overall season record was in 1957, when he averaged 74.28 percent ringers, had a record of 17–13, and placed twelfth.

Lindquist worked hard to promote horseshoe pitching. In 1955, the NHPA initiated its program of having regional directors lead the promotion of the sport, and Lindquist was one of the original seven regional directors. His wife Anna was the women's world champion in 1948 and 1949 and she was elected NHPA's vice president in 1953. Arner Lindquist has not been elected to the NHPA Hall of Fame, but he is on the ballot and hopefully in time he will get the nod and the public recognition he deserves.

It's somewhat surprising to read a mention of Leo McGrath as one of the event's organizers. McGrath was born in 1903, so he would have been 42 years old in 1945. I mention his age as a point of reference for the present-day members who knew Leo. He always seemed to be an old man. To realize that he was active and associated with sport that far back is surprising. McGrath was part of the NHPA scene in the 1960s and 1970s as a very active worker and he was a strong promoter of the sport for over 50 years. He served as president of the Buckeye Horseshoe Pitchers Association of Ohio for 27 years, from 1955 until 1982. That alone is an extraordinary service accomplishment. McGrath was elected NHPA's vice president in 1969. He is a charter member of the Ohio HPA Hall of Fame and was inducted to the NHPA Hall of Fame in 1974. McGrath passed away in 2000 at age 98.

After mentioning some of the career achievements of other players, it's only fair to restate that the Lee Rose so far had won four National AAU medals, one gold and three silver.

Third AAU National Title for Michigan Pitchers

R ose began the 1945 section of his journal by mentioning that the sport was going through difficulties, mostly resulting from World War II. For instance, the war effort's need for metal meant that pitching shoes were not being manufactured due to the shortage of steel for domestic use. At the start of 1946, that should no longer be an issue.

Also, no World Tournaments were held from 1942 through 1945. That certainly took a toll on the sport's popularity among players and the public. Since 1946, though, a World Tournament has been held every year—at least for the men's division. The women's division was not reinstated until 1947.

Rose begins the year in his journal with a newspaper article about him winning another Detroit championship. The article is followed by a few notes about the event in his own hand—and very words at that, considering that this was one of his most outstanding performances.

Rule by Ringers Reaches Sixth Term

It is generally recognized among followers of the sport that 40-year-old Lee Jacobs is tops among Detroit's horseshoe pitchers and it was not surprising that he won the Metropolitan title for the sixth time and the fourth in succession at Northwestern Field Sunday.

The champion defeated Ed Walls in four games 50–31, 12–50, 50–24, 50–35. The victory did not give Jacobs as much satisfaction as ordinarily. He had hoped that his wfe and 16-year-old son, Lee, Jr., would join him in the championship ranks, but they failed in the finals.

"I don't think he will speak to me for a week," laughed Mrs. Jacobs after taking the first two games and then losing the next three to Mrs. Viola Sands, 11–25, 18–25, 25–4, 25–21 25–12, in the women's event.

Young Lee, who will try out for the Western High football team next month, was beaten by Gerald Mitchell, 15, in the junior finals, 25–10, 25–17, 26–6.

Alex Clark, defeated Edmund Baranski, 7–25, 2–25, 25–15, 24–15, 25–9, for the men's novice title.

The tournament was conducted by the Department of Parks and Recreation.

Lee Rose, his wife Bertie Rose, son Lee Jr., all pitching in the 1946 Detroit city championship.

This tournament was not a round robin but by elimination matches. There were nine entries, so Lee Jacobs played Louis Kinsman for the eighth spot. Jacobs won two straight games 50–6 and 50–3.

First Round (Best of Three Games)

Jacobs beat Kelly
Walls beat Wrobbe

Lundgren beat Fagan
Yorkison beat Pierson

Semi-Final Round (Best of Three)

Jacobs beat Lundgren 50–32, 14–50, 50–49, 50–49
Walls beat Yorkison 3 straight games

Championship Series

I averaged .809 against Wall's .788. It was by far the best city series ever played. In the second game, Walls had 60 out 66 for .909. In the third game I had 81 out of 90 for an even .900.

	Jacobs					Walls			
	Pts	R	DR	Pct	SP	Pts	R	DR	Pct
Game 1	50	60	23	.811	74	31	54	18	.729
Game 2	12	48	17	.727	66	50	60	28	.909
Game 3	50	81	36	.900	90	24	72	29	.800
Game 4	50	75	28	.781	96	35	71	24	.739
Totals	162	264	104	.809	326	150	257	99	.788

- - - - - - -

Next some historic articles from Des Moines newspapers during the 1946 World Tournament are tacked in the journals.

- - - - - - -

Anxious to Give Truman
Horseshoe Pitcher's Card

President Harry S. Truman will be given a life membership card in the National Horseshoe Pitchers Association if Harry Woodfield, its president, can find an occasion for the presentation.

In Des Moines for the World Horseshoe Pitching Championships, which started Sunday morning, Woodfield pulled the specially engraved card from his hotel dresser drawer.

Knuckleball Grip

"The president isn't too hot a pitcher, in fact he uses a kind of a knuckleball grip, but we are giving him a life membership for the great contribution he has made to the dignity of the game," Woodfield said.

Woodfield and Arch Stokes, 80-year-old pitcher from Salt Lake City, Utah, talked over pitching techniques and agreed that the "finger on the calk" grip used by President Truman has never won any tournaments.

Woodfield demonstrated the one and three-quarters turn technique he hopes to teach the president when he presents the life membership card.

The 70-year-old expert and promoter said he had planned to give the card to Mr. Truman a couple of months ago at the time the horseshoe court was erected on the White House lawn. Woodfield helped construct the court.

Better to Wait

"The president was having strike and railroad and coal troubles about that time and I thought it would be better to wait until things cooled off a little bit," Woodfield said.

He said he had inspected the White House court on several occasions and had provided horseshoe and rules for playing but had not yet contacted the president.

"There have been a lot of people making remarks about a 'horseshoe pitching cabinet' and the 'horseshoe vote' and I think those are the reasons the president hasn't been playing much lately," the promoter said.

"I know he likes the game a lot but I'm afraid some of his secretaries don't think the horseshoe publicity does him any good. They got a little nasty a couple of times when I called and I could tell they didn't like it, but I know the president does."

98% Exercise

Woodfield said that the court, right outside of the president's office, affords 98 percent exercise for the time he takes off. "It's the ideal sport for a busy man. Great for the waist line and for a good-neighbor policy," Woodfield said.

Woodfield said he wishes President Truman would correct his grip on the shoe and quit using a pair of chrome plated shoes that were sent as a present.

He's straining his arm the way he throws and the chrome shoes slip. They'd be alright on the wall but for pitching they're no good." Woodfield said.

- - - - - - -

This next little clipping stands very large in the career of Lee Jacobs. This article announces his purchase of a horseshoe-manufacturing business. He had already accomplished so much. He was a championship-class pitcher, a national champion, a state champion, a national association officer, and a lifetime promoter of the sport. Now he owns his own horseshoe-manufacturing company. The original old-style Lattore shoes still show up now and then for horseshoe collectors. They were novel shoes, and then in the 1960s Jacobs made very distinctive changes to the shoe's design. Shoes of that vintage are probably even more difficult for collectors to find.

Lee's short note about attending the 1946 World Tournament in Des Moines follows the business announcement. Then, in the absence of his colorful reporting, we will rely on newspaper coverage of the 1946 event that he added to the journal.

Jacobs and Koppitsch
Buy Out Lattore & Levagood

Lee Jacobs and Frank Koppitsch have bought out Lattore and Levagood's horseshoe manufacturing business and will operate under the name "The Ringers."

The new partners will manufacture and sell the pitching horseshoes that have made Lattore & Levagood famous in this sport.

I attended as representative of the "Lattore" Shoe, "THE RINGERS." I did not compete, as I wanted to remain amateur for the meet at Norwood again.

Allen Sets Mark
Colorado Horseshoe Vet Scores 540
to Top World Meet Qualifiers

Ted Allen of Boulder, Colorado, cracked a world record as he turned in a score of 540 to lead qualifiers in first-day action at the World's Horseshoe Tournament Sunday at Birdland Courts.

Allen, who wore the crown from 1933 through 1940 and who finished second to Fernando Isais of Mexico City, Mexico, in the 1941 meet, the last held before the war, broke Isais' record of 532, set in 1940. Isais is not defending his title.

The top qualifiers enter match completion today while a new champion will be crowned July 4.

Second place in the qualifying round went to Charles (Casey) Jones, Waukesha, Wis., who turned in a score of 515. Sidney Harris of Minden, Neb., who has held the championship in that state for the past 15 years, was third with 504.

Clifford Hanson of Gilbert, Iowa's state champion, qualified nineteenth with a score of 448. Dale Dixon of Des Moines finished ninth with 476.

In turning in the best qualifying score ever recorded, Allen tallied 174 ringers out of 200 throws for an average of 87%. He threw 16 double ringers in a row in his qualifying round.

The tournament, held in connection with Iowa's Centennial celebration, will get underway on the Birdland Courts at 8 a.m. today.

Qualifiers

Player	City, State	Points
Ted Allen	Boulder, Colorado	540
Casey Jones	Waukesha, Wisconsin	516
Sidney Harris	Minden, Nebraska	504
Johnny Sebek	Canton, Ohio	502
John Lindmeier	Maywood Illinois	485
Arner Lindquist	Morgantown, W. Virginia	478
Roland Kraft	Lecompton, Kansas	478
Arlo Harris	Indianapolis, Indiana	477
Dale Dixon	Des Moines, Iowa	476
Vito Fileccia	Brooklyn, New York	475
W. O. Maxwell	Hicksville, Ohio	474
Evan Tishock	Columbus, Ohio	469
Howard Robinson	Nebraska City, Neb	468
Andy Stolarik	Canton, Ohio	455
Thomas Brownell	Gloversville, New York	455
Marion Lange	Bondurant, Iowa	451
Bill Kolb	Newark, New Jersey	451
Alvin Dahlene	Lawrence, Kansas	448
Clifford Hanson	Gilbert, Iowa	448
Henry Harper	Los Angeles, California	445
Bob Cash	Cleveland, Ohio	445
Earl Green	Indianapolis, Indiana	442
Wm. Danhaurer	Chicago, Illinois	442
Orville Harris	Indianapolis, Indiana	441

Failed to Qualified

Joe Hill, Iowa	439		Theo. Harlan, Iowa	436
Arnold Thompson, Ill.	432		M. Tamboer, Kansas	429
Archie Gregson, Oklahoma	426		Ron Cherrier, Minnesota	412
Carl West, Minnesota	406		Harold Darnold Iowa	408
Vyrl Jackson, California	402		Russ Butterfield, Iowa	392
Guerdon Jones, Wisconsin	392		Orval Lundrey, Kansas	381
Leon Shanahan, New York	373		Chester Dunlap, Arizona	370
Ralph Kampschroeder, Kan.	353			

Shoe Tossing Easier
Than Farming: Allen

As a youngster, Ted Allen started his farm chores around daybreak. He turned in usually around sunset.

"There must be an easier way to make a living," Ted kept telling himself.

One day Ted's dad handed him a pair of much-abused horseshoes. From that day on the former world's champion shoe pitcher earned his bread and butter by flipping ringers around an iron peg some 40 feet away.

He did it so well that he dominated the field from 1933 to 1940.

Serves as Male Nurse

Ted lost his national title in Des Moines in 1941, the final pre-war tournament. It went to Fernando Isais, a Mexican from Los Angeles.

During the war Ted served with the 179th Station Hospital in the Aleutians. He was a technician serving as a male nurse.

Allen was released from the Army last winter. He immediately went to work with the Gene Autry Rodeo, giving a horseshoe pitching demonstration.

Leaves Rodeo

Ted left the rodeo to come to Des Moines to compete in the first postwar national tournament.

Sunday afternoon the erstwhile Boulder, Colorado, farmer, not only paced the field at the Birdland Courts, but established a new world's record qualifying score of 540. On Sunday, Ted recalled some his outstanding achievements:

1. Ninety-eight ringers out of 100 shoes pitched.
2. Sixty-six straight ringers.
3. National Champion eight straight years.
4. An 88.4 percent ringer average in his match with Guy Zimmerman in Des Moines in 1940.

The 1940 Zimmerman–Allen match is rated the greatest duel ever played. Zimmerman started off by pitching 36 ringers without a miss. Fifty times four ringers were on the peg, including nine in a row. Ted put on 65 double ringers, Zimmerman 64.

Players Relax

"Horseshoe pitching has made great strides in recent years," said Allen. "It's a sport to relax you. Many of our top officials during the war played horseshoes so they could relax."

"President Truman had a horseshoe court erected on the lawn recently. Although he isn't an expert, he finds the game refreshing and relaxing."

"And there's more to horseshoe pitching than most people believe," added Allen. "Your reflexes and vision must coordinate. "I exercise my eyes as well as my muscles. I must be a good judge of distance. Like a photographer, I must be able to focus my vision accurately 40 feet away. Timing naturally is important too."

- - - - - - -

The journals don't contain an article covering the final standings, although Jacobs did jot down a very concise note: "Allen won the meet."

The final standings for the 1946 event and a short description is reprinted from Gary Kline's *Official N.H.P.A. History of the World Tournament 1909 to 1980*:

- - - - - - -

1946 World Tournament
Des Moines, Iowa, June 30–July 3

	Qual	W	L	R	SP	Pct
1. Ted Allen	540	22	1	1173	1398	83.9
2. Casey Jones	516	21	2	1304	1612	80.9
3. Sidney Harris	504	19	4	1197	1666	71.8
4. John Sebek	502	18	5	1313	1762	74.5
5. Vito Filecca	475	17	6	1079	1552	69.5
6. Dale Dixon	476	16	7	1163	1670	69.6
7. Arner Lindquist	478	16	7	1096	1628	67.3
8. W. O. Maxwell	474	15	8	1222	1774	68.9
9. Arlo Harris	477	15	8	1090	1670	65.3
10. John Lindmeier	485	13	10	1229	1736	70.8
11. Tommy Brownell	455	13	10	1073	1612	66.6
12. Andy Stolarik	455	13	10	1002	1544	64.9

(Continued on next page)

(Continued from previous page)

	Qual	W	L	R	SP	Pct
13. Roland Kraft	478	12	11	1132	1654	68.4
14. Orville Harris	441	12	11	1012	1568	64.5
15. Henry Harper	446	11	12	1066	1602	66.5
16. Bob Cash	445	8	15	990	1592	62.2
17. Alvin Dahlene	448	7	16	1050	1606	65.4
18. Earl Green	442	7	16	968	1554	62.2
19. William Kolb	451	7	16	888	1474	60.2
20. Wm. Danhauer	442	5	18	851	1478	57.6
21. C. Hanson	448	4	19	809	1545	55.6
22. Marion Lange	451	3	20	766	1388	55.2
23. Howard Robinson	468	2	21	1016	1660	61.2
24. Evan Tishock	469	0	23	562	1114	50.4

- - - - - - -

After being eliminated, Johnny Sebek the "Ohio" Express," thoroughly walloped Allen by a score of 50–24. This put Ted Allen and Casey Jones in a tie with two rounds remaining. In round 22, Allen creamed Sidney Harris 50–14, eliminating him while Jones overpowered Sebek 50–21, despite Johnny pitching 77 percent. His set up one of the greatest matches ever for the World Championship—superstar Ted Allen, trying to regain his title, pitted against superstar Casey Jones, trying to win his first. In this 158-shoe game, Ted tossed 139 ringers including 60 doubles for 87.9 percent. Hard Luck Casey threw 137 ringers including 59 doubles for 86.7 only to lose the World Championship 50–44! Allen had waited five years to successfully regain his title.

So the name Sebek appears again. He made some noise at the 1946 World Tournament and his fourth-place finish is a significant performance. Of course we first read his name in the coverage of Lee Rose's national team league in 1940. Andy Stolarik was one of Sebek's teammates in that team competition, and two other pitchers—Orville and Arlo Harris from the Indianapolis team—were also participants in the league.

There are a number of tournament players who were active in the National AAU championships who made an World Tournament appearance in 1946. First is Arner Lindquist, the 1942 National AAU champion, who is makes a strong statement with his seventh-place finish. John Lindmeier, a three-time national champion (in 1937, 1940, and 1941) half of the National doubles championship team (in 1941 and 1942), also had a top-ten finish at the 1946 event. But Lindmeier didn't peak in his skill level until the 1950s at the tournaments held in Murray, Utah. The Harris brothers entered some of the earliest AAU competitions in the 1930s. Little-known William Danhauer, from Chicago, was also an AAU veteran. In fact, Danhauer was on the winning 1940 National AAU doubles team. Even Bill Kolb, who was just 32 years old in 1946, has an AAU background, but not until 1968 when he won a National AAU men's title. He also won a bronze medal being part of the third-place team in the 1978 National AAU championships.

Along with Lindquist and Lindmeier, Tommy Brownell made his rookie appearance in the 1946 World Tournament. As Gary Kline notes, Lindquist and Lindmeier eventually earn their way to World Tournament All-Time Wins List, with 154 and 168 wins, respectively. Brownell also went on to earn a spot on the NHPA's list of the top 100 players with 141 games won. He was inducted to the NHPA Hall of Fame in 2007. Lindquist and Lindmeier have not been inducted, though both are deserving.

Now back to the journals and Lee Jacobs's account of his 23rd state tournament.

- - - - - - -

My Twenty-Third State Tournament
At Port Huron
August 24–25, 1946

In the round robin I breezed along to a tie for 1st place with Lundgren, each winning 17 and losing 2. I lost to Hirschman, 50–49 and to Lundgren 50–29. Lundgren lost to Latzko and Yorkison.

In the finals, I met Ed Woodward in a two-out-of-five series and defeated him three games to one. I then defeated Carra three games to one.

In the championship series I met Joe Latzko for a best-of-seven series. Latzko hit 51 out of 78 to my 49 out of 78 to win the game 50–47. Latzko had .654 to my .628.

In the second game I evened it up in an odd game where I had 53 out of 82 for .646 while Joe had 55 ringers for .671. I won 50–43.

The third game was a bitter battle all the way with Joe taking it 50–46 with 71 out of 96 for .739. I had 70 ringers for .729.

I evened the series again by winning the fourth game 50–40 with 73 out of 98 for .744 to Joe's .704.

Joe went .728 to my .717 to win 50–45 and then hit .744 to my .709 to win 50–41 and retain the state title.

It was a very good series!

- - - - - - -

My goodness, that was a very gracious comment for Lee to make—and a bit unusual since it followed a defeat. Maybe he was mellowing out a bit as he was getting older, although he is still young, at 37 years old. He certainly pitched well enough to win another state title, but Latzko was a great pitcher—and on that day, he was a great pitcher even by today's standards. As was Lee Jacobs.

Some of Lee's records for this tournament were lost before being entered in his journal. The players' individual records in the preliminary round robin were all recorded, but the finals match play and the championship series between Jacobs and Latzko were not. So only Lee's individual games are summarized.

- - - - - - -

Lee Jacobs' Record in Preliminary Round Robin

Lee Jacobs

Pts	R	DR	Pct	SP	Opp	Pts	R	DR	Pct
50	29	11	.806	36	Shepard	1	14	1	.388
50	75	28	.735	102	Latzko	37	71	22	.696
50	35	13	.700	50	Yorkison	22	24	6	.480
50	38	12	.679	56	Carra	19	27	3	.482
50	38	10	.655	58	Lewandowski	20	28	9	.482
50	31	10	.645	48	Craft	14	20	4	.416
50	36	12	.643	45	Kelly	37	31	9	.553
50	46	16	.622	74	Woodward	38	40	8	.625
49	59	17	.615	96	Hirschman	50	60	17	.625
50	41	14	.602	68	Otto	36	34	6	.625
50	30	9	.600	50	Winter	11	17	4	.340
50	38	12	.572	66	Field	36	32	7	.484
50	40	11	.572	70	Koppitsch	34	38	11	.542
50	19	6	.559	70	Heuer	8	6	1	.176
29	37	10	.544	68	Lundgren	50	43	15	.632
50	27	7	.519	52	Getz	32	20	6	.384
50	33	7	.466	74	Zessin	44	32	7	.432

Games won 17; Games lost 2.
Won games from Fagan and Pinkstaff by default.

Lee Rose Pitching at Port Huron, 1946.

- - - - - - -

Jacobs made a return trip to Norwood, Ohio, for the 1946 National AAU tournament. He didn't win, but he was involved in deciding who was champion. He was directly involved in helping his longtime Michigan adversary, and perhaps a horseshoe buddy, become a national champion.

The notes of this event in the Lee Rose journal are brief.

- - - - - - -

The 1946 National A.A.U. Tournament was held at Norwood, Ohio. Intermittent rain and cold weather made things bad.

I didn't do so good in this meet, but had the pleasure of knocking off the defending champion Jimmy Johnson after he had won 13 straight games. This put him in a tie for first place with Joe Latzko and when Joe nosed out Johnson, he became the new champ.

So much for 1946.

- - - - - - -

What an extraordinary development. Latzko's victory meant that 1946 marked the third time a Michigan pitcher had won the National AAU title in the past four years—each time a different Michigan pitcher. That certainly speaks to the competitive skill level of pitchers in Jacobs's home state.

Though Lee didn't dedicate much journal space to this championship tournament, it was was significant in the sport of horseshoe pitching. The newspaper article and standings below are borrowed from *AAU National Amateur Horseshoe-Pitching Championships 1937–1977*.

- - - - - - -

Shoe Champs Are Crowned

Joseph P. Latzko of Flint, Michigan, won the 1946 Senior National AAU Horseshoe Pitching Championship Sunday at Norwood Municipal Horseshoe Courts from a field of over 30 entrants. The Michigan boy won 17 of his 19 final round robin game.

In qualifying Saturday for the finals, Latzko set a new national A.A.U. mark of 262, exceeding the old mark of 256 held by jointly by three pitchers. He also set a new mark of 36 ringers, in a 50-shoe game.

Jim Johnson, 1945 winner, was second, winning 16 of 19 games. Stanley Manker was third and Ralph Lackey fourth. Tied for fifth place were 12-year-old Jacob Hoff and his father Charles Hoff. However, on ringer percentage basis fifth place went to the elder Hoff and sixth place to the youngster.

Ralph Lackey and June Marcum, of Hamilton won the National AAU doubles title, finishing in a tie for first place with Latzko and Ed Woodhouse, winning in a play-off. Johnson retained his Ohio AAU title, with the Ohio A.A.U. doubles title going to Lackey and Marcum.

1946 A.A.U. National Singles Championship Finals

Place	Player	City	W	L
1.	Joe Latzko	Flint, Michigan	17	2
2.	James Johnson	Ludlow, Kentucky	16	3
3.	Stanley Manker	Chillicothe, Ohio		
4.	Ralph Lackey	Middletown, Ohio		
5.	Charles Hoff	West Manchester, Ohio		
6.	Jacob Hoff	West Manchester, Ohio		
	Lee Rose	Detroit, Michigan		

1946 A.A.U. National Senior Doubles Championship Finals

Place	Player	City
1.	Ralph Lackey & June Marcum,Hamilton, Ohio	
2.	Joe Latzko & Ed Woodward, Flint, Michigan	
3.	Harry Henn Cold Spring, Ky. & Guy Morgan, Hamilton, Ohio	

A Trip to the Big Show

Early in the year we moved from Detroit to Belleville and I played very little horseshoes. I did practice up a little and took a bus trip to Des Moines for a tournament, but failed in my 100-shoe test.

This did not deter me however from going to Salt Lake City, Utah.

Now this record is being written in the year 1957, I have neglected to keep up my books the way I should have and many records have been lost in these years. I will try to bring things up to date with whatever records and memories I can call upon.

I went to Salt Lake City via train [to the 1947 World Tournament]. I qualified for the finals with 484 points in 200 shoes.

As can be seen, I didn't do very well, but at least I got to play in the big show. I rode back with Alvin Gandy in his car to Topeka, Kansas and thence by train home.

Jacobs attended one of the foremost World Tournaments ever. The state of Utah was celebrating their centennial and Archie Stokes proposed they bid on hosting the 1947 World Horseshoe Pitching Championships. They bid, Utah received approval, and the tournament went well. That is a bit of an understatement. The World Tournament probably was never held in a more picturesque setting. The newly constructed, lighted courts were exceptional. The county was heavily involved, and there was tremendous community support for the event.

Although the 1948 tournament was held in Milwaukee, Wisconsin, the 1949 tournament returned to Murray and the next eleven World Tournaments were held there as well. An unprecedented 12 tournaments were held in 13 years at the Murray courts. Those tournamants coincided with an era known as the "golden years" of the sport. And our hero, Lee Jacobs, was there. He qualified successfully and was part of another historic event.

His journal contains a few clippings on the tournament and those describing the final results are included.

- - - - - - - -

Isais Wins 34 of 35 to Take Horseshoe Title

Fernando Isais held the national horseshoe pitching title today after completing six days of competition with a single loss and 34 victories over the best tossers in the nation.

Final matches were completed late last night and the total scores were not tabulated until tonight by Archie Gregson, manager of the tournament in which 200 competed.

Isais, who owns a Los Angeles tennis shop and pitches for fun, lost his single match to defending champion Ted Allen of Boulder, Colorado, who finished in a tie for third with 32 victories and 3 losses. Wayne Nelson of Muncie, Ind., shared the tie.

Casey Jones of Waukesha, Wis., took second with 33 victories and two losses. Allen took honors for the highest percentage of ringers, 84.7, closely followed by Isais with 83.2.

Isais Beats Champ to Win U.S. Horseshoe Crown

Fernando Isais, the dark and handsome horseshoe star of years past, wrapped up the national horseshoe pitching championship Sunday and prepared to take it back with him to his home in Los Angeles, from where it has been missing since 1941.

He waded through 35 challengers to prove his supremacy at the Salt Lake City county fairgrounds courts and never a more intriguing group of tossers was assembled.

In winning the title, Isais dethroned Ted Allen, Boulder, Colorado, which in itself was a feat some thought impossible. Casey Jones, was in the runner-up spot. The Waukesha, Wis., star finished just a "shade" out of the top position.

The new champion last held the title in 1941, when he captured it in Des Moines, Iowa, but never defended the honors. He was not content with just first place this time, but also broke the world record for points in the qualifying round on opening day when he shot 544 points to blast Allen's year-old mark of 540.

Friday, Isais added to this by tossing 22 consecutive double ringers to dash another Allen record on the books. In the preceding game, Ted had thrown 20 straight doubles to break a seven-year-old mark established by Guy Zimmerman in 1940.

The 1948 meet will be held at Milwaukee, Wisconsin, in conjunction with their centennial celebration, Harry (Pop) Woodfield, president of the association, announced.

This year's tournament conducted on newly constructed courts in Murray, acclaimed as being the "best in the world," was a state centennial-sponsored event.

- - - - - - -

Fernando Isais won his second World Tournament title in 1947. That win was the first in a run of six consecutive championships. That was an unbelievable record that stood until 2008, when Alan Francis tied the record. Francis proceeded to break the record in 2009 and again in 2010, when he established the standing record of eight consecutive World Tournament wins.

- - - - - - -

1947 World Tournament Final Standings

	Qual	W	L	R	SP	Pct
1. Fernando Isais	544	34	1	1973	2372	82.3
2. Casey Jones	543	33	2	2086	2512	83.0
3. Ted Allen	D.C.	32	3	2126	2508	84.8
4. Wayne Nelson	521	32	3	2080	2576	80.7
5. James O'Shea	520	29	6	1993	2542	78.4
6. Guy Zimmerman	535	28	7	2125	2658	79.9
7. Louis Dean	497	27	8	1699	2354	72.2
8. Eddie Packham	529	26	9	2034	2630	77.3
9. Tommy Brownell	507	25	10	1834	2472	74.2
10. Ray Gatewood	540	24	11	2030	2674	75.9
11. Sid Harris	509	24	11	1983	2626	75.5
12. Ervin Hosier	447	24	11	1873	2598	72.1
13. Vito Feleccia	467	21	14	1759	2510	70.1
14. Stan Deleary	523	19	16	1938	2666	72.7
15. Henry Harper	481	19	66	1712	2526	66.8
16. Dean Brown	473	18	17	1833	2582	71.0
17. Don Titcomb	502	18	17	1856	2644	70.2
18. Arner Lindquist	492	18	17	1669	2114	69.1
19. Alvin Gandy	509	18	17	1703	2516	67.7
20. Roland Kraft	519	17	18	1798	2592	69.4
21. Dale Dixon	494	16	19	1560	2384	65.4
22. Marines Tamboer	482	13	22	1789	2614	68.4
23. W. O. Maxwell	489	13	22	1470	2334	63.0
24. Ray Ohms	441	13	22	1417	2254	62.9
25. Paul Mori	489	12	23	1432	2350	60.9
26. Ellis Hanna	492	11	24	1540	2448	62.9
27. William Kolb	472	11	24	1335	2200	60.7
28. Ray Arnold	457	11	24	1291	2164	59.7
29. Bruce Walters	438	9	26	1204	2124	56.7
30. Merle Palmer	484	8	27	1428	2350	60.8
31. Lee Jacobs	484	5	30	1246	2144	58.1
32. Hansford Jackson	433	5	30	1217	2138	56.9
33. Ron Cherrier	439	5	30	1221	2148	56.8
34. Harry Dolan	431	5	30	1225	2200	55.7
35. A. J. Byrns	469	4	31	1181	2158	54.7
36. Sam Pipe	443	4	31	1075	2026	53.1

My 24th State Tournament

This was at Northwestern Field. A week before the tournament I happened to try out a pair of experimental shoes with four notches in the toe and found I could pitch them real good with a 1-1/4 turn and I used these in the tournament.

In the round robin, Latzko took first with 16 win and one loss, Lundgren was 15–2, Carra and Irwin Carlberg, a new comer, were 14–3. I and Hirschman were 12–5 and Woodward and Winter were 10–7.

In the finals, Latzko breezed with 7–0, while Carlberg and I tied for 2nd with 5–2 each. In a single game play-off, I lost to Carlberg and then with darkness setting in, there was no time to complete a series between Carlberg and Latzko, so prizes were awarded on basis of the standings at hand and Latzko retained the title.

I also won the city tournament for the 7th time and for the fifth year in succession.

Take note of the name Irwin Carlberg. He became a star pitcher in Michigan and even earned a state championship in 1956. Carlberg entered the 1949 World Tournament, qualified for the Championship Class and placed 19th on a 17–18 record and averaged 67.9 percent ringers. He was an avid promoter of the sport and he was elected NHPA vice president in 1948. Carlberg was awarded the Stokes Memorial Award in 1965.

25th State Tournament

I made a lone trip to Des Moines in my 1936 Ford, a feat in itself, and again failed to qualify for the tournament.

The World Tournament was to be at Milwaukee and I practiced very hard to be ready to go to it. Then, a week before it was to open, I had an accident on the stairs and broke two ribs and injured a shoulder and my horseshoe pitching was about over for the year.

My 25th State Tournament
September 4–5, 1948
Port Huron

I was barely able to use my right arm to pitch and my left arm still in a sling, as I attended the meet at Port Huron.

To my surprise, I won enough games to get into the final eight, on a 8–5 won-loss record.

In the finals, I didn't get anywhere, of course. Won 2 lost 5 for 7th place.

Latzko and Carlberg played the series and Joe defeated Irwin in four straight games, all one-sided.

- - - - - - -

The journals do not contain a copy of the 1948 World Tournament final standings.

Fernando Isais was crowned the 1948 champion on a 29–2 record, while averaging 84.2 ringers. His losses were a 50–40 game to Tommy Brownell, who pitched 88.0 percent for the game, and a one-point loss (49–50) to Guy Zimmerman.

Two other highlights of this World Tournament require mention. Casey Jones, who never won a world championship, set a world record by averaging 87.5 percent ringers for the tournament and came in as runner-up again due to his three losses. Also, Guy Zimmerman pitched the first-ever perfect game in a World Tournament. He hit 44 straight ringers against Henry Pergal.

Brownell, mentioned earlier as an NHPA Hall of Fame inductee, pitched 87.9 percent to beat Ted Allen 50–40 in their match. It's quite a feat to beat both Allen and Isais in the same tournament, but Brownell also beat Casey Jones 50–36 with an 84.4 percent game.

26th State Tournament

I played in the Detroit District Tournament at Clark Park and I easily walked away with it, losing only one game to Bill Ball.

My 26th State Tournament
September 10–11, Ann Arbor

Not any records of this meet are at hand and memory alone will have to serve. It was held at Wines Field in Ann Arbor. Twenty-four entries.

An unexpected defeat from Joe Kelly early in the play kept me from tying for 2nd place with Jule Winter and a chance at the title. I wound up in third place with 19 wins and 4 losses.

Latzko beat Winter four straight games for the championship.

I took a lone trip in my old 1937 Pontiac to Rock Island for a tournament.

Takes Playoff for
Horseshoe Tourney Title

Earl Bomke of New Berlin, Illinois, won the Class A title of the 23rd annual Midwest Horseshoe Tournament at Long View Park yesterday. Bomke's win climaxed one of the most thrilling finishes in the history of the tournament.

Tied with Norm Dixon of Streator, Illinois, with a loss each at the end of the regular schedule, Bomke defeated Dixon two out of three games in the play-off, averaging 87.5 per cent ringers in his best game. Bomke, former Illinois champion and Midwest winner, had three games of 78 per cent in the tournament.

John Lindmeier, Maywood Illinois, present state champion and last year's Midwest winner, finished fifth.

Other winners were Class B, Aden Swinehammer, Aurora; Class C, Lee Jacobs, Belleville, Michigan; Class D, Frank Palka, Chicago.

Ellis Griggs, Plainview, Ill., threw 88 ringers out of 100 shoes to lead the 32 qualifiers with 274 points. There were 55 entries.

The tournament drew the largest crowd in its history and interest was keen through the playoff which concluded under lights at 8 p.m. Scores:

Class A
1. Earl Bomke   (264) 6–1
2. Norman Dixon   (266) 6–1
3. Ellis Griggs   (274) 5–2
4. Ellis Cobb   (241) 4–3
5. John Lindmeier (D.C.)   3–4
6. Helmer Magnuson   (248) 1–6
7. Milton Tate   (248) 1–6
8. Alfred Terry   (244) 0–7

Class B
1. Aden Swinehammer   (234) 7–0
2. Truman Standard   (229) 6–1
3. Nelson Vogel   (226) 5–2
4. Joe Bennett   (240) 3–4
5. Dale Terry   (227) 3–4
6. Lawrence Ferro   (227) 3–4
7. Glenn Anderson   (227) 1–6
8. Harold Darnold   (238) 0–7

Class C
1. Lee Jacobs (223)   7–0
2. Ralph Dykes   (215) 5–2
3. Leslie Long   (226) 4–3
4. Howard Collier   (224) 4–3
5. Ray McBride   (213) 3–4
6. Russell Sheetz   (215) 2–5
7. Paul Danker   (215) 2–5
8. Ralph Peters   (225) 1–6

Class D
1. Frank Palka   (205) 6–1
2. John Strode   (213) 6–1
3. Chester Hefner   (213) 5–2
4. Clark Kaiser   (205) 4–3
5. Charles Schneider   (205) 4–3
6. Roy Efflandt   (208) 2–5
7. Warren Wickstrom   (218) 1–6
8. Joe Sorem   (209) 0–7

- - - - - - -

A couple of noteworthy names appear in this group, including Ellis Cobb. He participated in his first World Tournament in 1948 and was a competitive pitcher, but his fame came in 1956 as he became editor of NHPA's *News Digest*, a role he filled for an extraordinary 32 years. Cobb was inducted into the NHPA Hall of Fame in 1970.

Another pitcher who isn't a recognized name to readers today is Glenn Anderson, who qualified for Class B. He would have been 28 years old at this event, and he was becoming a rising star. Later he was a serious challenger at World Tournaments at Murray, Utah, during the 1950s. Then one evening in 1958 as he was driving home from a local horseshoe tournament, he was killed in a one-car accident. Before his untimely death, Glenn won the Mid-West Tournament in 1954, among a field that included Truman Standard, Milton Tate, John Paxton, Harry Page, Nelson Vogel, and Ron Cherrier. He beat them all as he went 7–0 on the day.

Glenn qualified nine times (in consecutive years) for the World Tournament men's Championship Class. He had seven years with a winning record, and earned a top-ten finish four times. He had enviable talent and one can't help but wonder what he might have achieved in future years. His record is as follows:

Year	Place	Wins	Loss	Ringers	Shoes	Average
1950	33	7	18	1476	2396	61.60
1951	17	20	15	2038	2828	72.06
1952	11	22	13	1821	2536	71.80
1953	11	20	15	1860	2592	71.76
1954	8	8	4	790	1030	76.69
1955	6	26	9	2113	2780	76.00
1956	6	27	8	1927	2608	73.88
1957	13	13	15	1888	2528	74.68
1958	8	18	12	1706	2350	72.59
9 Events		161	111	15,619	21,648	72.14

This little meet that Lee Jacobs traveled to had four National Hall of Famers entered. And a few on the roster who someday may also be inducted. Of course, Lee Jacobs is a National Hall of Fame inductee as well as Ralph Dykes, Ellis Cobb, and Harold Darnold. John Lindmeier, Truman Standard, Glenn Anderson, Arner Lindquist, and Milton Tate are all worthy, have been nominated, are on the ballot, and who knows, someday may also be inducted.

Jacobs did not attend the 1949 World Tournament as Fernando Isais won his fourth title. The final standings had been clipped out of *Horseshoe Pitcher* magazine, the NHPA's successor to *Horseshoe World*. They are tacked into the journals and reprinted below. But first, the 1949 ladies Championship Class final results are shown.

- - - - - - -

1949 Ladies World Tournament

1. Anna Lindquist
2. Marie Kamschroeder
3. Pat DeLeary
4. Doris Dolan
5. Delsa McCleary
6. Helen Ohms
7. Hope Isais
8. Mary Jones

- - - - - - -

A women's World Tournament was held in 1948 as well, in Milwaukee, with little fanfare or media mention. Lee's journals make no mention of the event, but it marked the first women's world champion declared since 1935, a period of 14 years. Anna Lindquist was the 1948 women's champion and she repeated in 1949. If that name is familiar, that's because she was the wife of Arner Lindquist, of AAU fame. There probably are only three legitimate pitchers in this group of women, the top three. The rest of the players are spouses of men who were there to qualify for the men's division, i.e, Jones, Isais, Dolan, DeLeary, and Ohms. You can match up the names. They were conscripted to fill in the ranks so a full women's tournament could be played.

1949 World Tournament Results
Murray, Utah, August 15–29

	Qual	W	L	Pct.
1. Fernando Isais, California	D.C.	34	1	83.9
2. Ted Allen, Colorado	513	33	2	81.9
3. Casey Jones, Wisconsin	507	31	4	80.4
4. Dean Brown, California	497	30	5	79.5
5. Stanley DeLeary, Arizona	529	30	5	78.7
6. Don Titcomb, California	473	28	7	77.9
7. Tommy Brownell, New York	523	27	8	77.0
8. Ray Gatewood, California	523	27	8	77.0
9. Louis Dean, California	518	26	9	75.3
10. Roland Kraft, Kansas	501	25	10	77.1
11. Lowell Gray, California	512	21	14	72.8
12. Alvin Gandy, Kansas	492	21	14	70.0
13. Pat Brady, New York	494	19	16	70.4
14. John Sebek, Ohio	507	19	16	69.7
15. Dale Dixon, Iowa	512	18	17	69.1
16. Ray Ohms, Utah	465	18	17	68.9
17. Ervin Hosier, California	454	18	17	67.5
18. Merle Palmer, Wyoming	502	17	18	68.2
19. Irwin Carlberg, Michigan	454	17	18	67.9
20. Elmo Tilikainen, Colorado	465	17	18	66.6
21. John Elkins, Missouri	492	16	19	67.0
22. Arner Lindquist, W. Va.	501	15	20	66.9
23. Nels Peterson, Minnesota	463	15	20	66.5
24. E. J. McFarland, Texas	486	14	21	67.4
25. Paul Meri, California	477	14	21	65.2
26. Henry Harper, California	472	12	23	64.4
27. Ron Cherrier, Minnesota	483	11	24	64.1
28. Cherry Bennett, Utah	455	11	24	52.6
29. Jay Burns, California	464	10	25	65.0
30. W. O. Maxwell, Ohio	451	8	27	60.8
31. Harry, Dolan, California	472	8	27	56.8
32. Harry Henn, Kentucky	436	7	28	55.5
33. Ray Arnold, California	460	6	29	57.5
34. Louis Larson, Minnesota	433	4	31	54.2
35. George Callas, California	431	4	31	53.8
36. Larry Geer, California	430	1	34	50.6

- - - - - - -

It has been mentioned before that Roland Kraft was a one-armed pitcher. So was Louis Larson of Mankato, Minnesota, which likely makes this the only World Tournament with two one-armed pitchers in the Championship Class.

27th State Tournament

The year's journal coverage begins with this tournament article, which was probably clipped out of the NHPA *Horseshoe Pitcher*. Surely it's not from a newspaper, but it is entertaining just the same.

- - - - - - -

Michigan
The Blue Water Festival Open
Horseshoe Tournament
July 15, 16, 1950
By Frank Lewandowski

	W	L
1. Joe Latzko, Flint	13	2
2. Irwin Carlberg, Grand Rapids	12	3
3. Lee Jacobs, Belleville	12	3
4. Andy Yorkison, Detroit	12	3
5. Paul Focht, Dayton, Ohio	10	5
6. Carl Lundgren, Detroit	9	6
7. Bill Ball, Detroit	9	6
8. Jonas Otto, Ann Arbor	8	7
9. Joe Kelly, Highland Park	8	7
10. Les Peary, Detroit	7	8
11. Bill Crabbs, Todelo, Ohio	7	8
12. Henry Zessin, Saginaw	5	10
13. Jule Winter, Port Huron	3	12
14. Clarence Jazwiak, Detroit	3	12
15. Harry Seibert, Union, Ohio	2	13
16. George Stifel, Toledo, Ohio	0	15

There were five players who did not qualify for Class A. Of these only three were eligible for Class B, as the winner and runner-up of last year's Class B and the 16 finalists in Class A could not participate in the B class this year. I had my hands full trying to run the tournament, so did not get into the B set-up.

Guy Brown, last year's winner and Uno Stone, runner-up, were automatically out. This left Ray Donnen of Yale and Jim Greene of Port Huron as the finalists for Class B. Ray did not show up on Sunday although Jim waited for him until the Class A final round robin was almost over, when it was decided that he became the winner of Class B by default.

In line with the N.H.P.A.'s policy of trying to interest the teen-agers in the game of horseshoes, we also had a Class C set-up for these boys. We expected about eight entries in this set-up, but only two actually showed up. They were Ron Greene and Dick Brown, sons of Jim Greene and Guy Brown. In the play-off, Dick Brown won the match 4 games to 1. This left Dick as the winner and Ron as the runner-up. We hope to have a world's champion out of this class someday.

Some of the human highlights or human interest stories of this tournament were as follows:

- Andy Yorkison beating Joe Latzko in the first round of the final round robin on Saturday night.
- Harry Seibert pulling a leg muscle and having to drop out.
- George Stifel developing a blister on his foot and forced to drop out.
- Jule Winter dropping out because of business matters.
- Joe Kelly's superb mastery of the public address system.
- Mr. Henry Zessin's wonderful job as self-appointed secretary of this tournament. It was really appreciated by yours truly.
- The welts on Carl Lundgren's back from the springs in his hotel bed, because some of the boys put his mattress underneath the old frame.
- The wonderful cooperation that was had from everyone concerned, whether connected with the tournament or not.
- The good work the ground keepers did to keep the courts in shape and the good opinion the players had for that good old Port Huron clay, or gumbo, which originally was dug out of the bottom of St. Clair River, when the St. Clair Tunnel was built in 1890.

- Mr. Tomshack of our Port Huron City Recreation Department, deserves a lot of credit for the help he gave us in this and previous tournaments. If he did not help, I don't know where we would get the ground keepers or trophies for our events.
- I almost missed one of the main upsets of the whole event, namely that of Bill Crabbs of Toledo defeating Lee Jacobs with his 3/4-flip shoe.

I again took a long train ride to Salt Lake City to the [1950] World Tournament. As you can see by the following scores, I missed by one stinking point of making the finals. I sat out the meet as a scorekeeper.

- - - - - - -

The tournament summary appeared in an issue of *Horseshoe Pitcher* magazine.

- - - - - - -

The first upset was in the third round when Louis Dean, of California, took over Stan DeLeary by a score of 50–35. The second upset came in round eight when Ted Allen lost to Ed McFarland, of Texas, by the score of 50–39. This Texan had the pleasure of beating all the Allens as Ted's brother Ira and his nephew Richard Allen were also in the tournament

On Wednesday evening, eight more games were played. At the end of this day's play, three men remained unbeaten. They were Isais, Jones and Gray. Thursday evening opened up with the 17th game for eight more and in the nineteenth game both Casey Jones and Lowell Gray lost their first game. Casey lost to Gatewood and Gray lost to DeLeary.

On Friday evening, only five games were played because all hands were invited to a wonderful banquet which was held at the Elk's Hall in Salt Lake City after the games. Ellis Cobb, of Illinois, took Casey Jones for a ride in the 26th game by a score of 50–43 for Jones' second defeat and in the last stanza of the evening Allen was taken over by Casey, by the same score 50 to 43. This was Ted's 2nd defeat up to this point. By now, Isais had won his 29th straight game.

The final six games were played on Saturday evening before the largest bunch of spectators I have ever seen at a horseshoe tournament. James

Johnson, of Kentucky, started his final games by winning his first and second game of the evening from Stan DeLeary and Ted Allen. Stan had 31 points and Ted had 49 points. That made the third loss for DeLeary and the same for Allen. Don Titcomb, of California, accounted for the third loss of Casey Jones in the 31st game by 50 to 37. In the 32nd round, Jones beat DeLeary for his fourth loss by 50–22. Then it happened! In the 33rd game DeLeary took over the champion for his only loss. The count was 50 to 43. Then came the 35th and final game. Isais won over Casey Jones by 50–46. Fernando Isais won his fourth consecutive championship. This accounted for Jones' fourth loss which tied him with Ted Allen for second place. To break the tie, it was decided that they would play one game, the winner to garner second place. After a game lasting for 140 shoes pitched, Casey Jones came out ahead by beating Allen with a score of 50–48.

At the conclusion of this playoff, all hands made a bee line for the Auditorium where Mr. W. H. Adams presented Isais with a beautiful trophy. Here too, all the prizes were awarded to each finalist. At this final get-together, a wonderful lunch for all those present was donated by the Do Drop Inn. To give you an idea of what good horseshoe pitching looks like, just go over these final results.

1950 World Tournament Final Results

	Qual	W	L	Pct
1. Fernando Isais, California	D.C.	34	1	83.5
2. Casey Jones , Wisconsin	540	31	4	80.9
3. Ted Allen, Colorado	535	31	4	82.0
4. Stan Deleary, Arizona	535	30	5	76.7
5. Lowell Gray, California	495	28	7	75.9
6. Dean Brown, California	500	27	8	76.2
7. Ray Gatewood, California	496	25	10	74.3
8. Don Titcomb, California	504	24	11	75.1
9. Louis Dean, California	481	23	12	71.8
10. Jimmy Johnson, Kentucky	505	23	12	70.1
11. John Monasmith, Wash.	478	22	13	69.0
12. Roland Kraft, Kansas	491	20	15	72.7
13. Marines Tamboer, Kansas	496	20	15	71.1
14. Ron Cherrier, Minnesota	485	20	15	68.0
15. Alvin Gandy, Kansas	473	19	16	68.1
16. Ellis Cobb, Illinois	491	19	16	67.7
17. John Lindmeier, Illinois	536	17	18	73.7
18. Harold Shaw, Iowa	491	16	19	76.8
19. Ira Allen, California	474	16	19	69.0
20. Henry Harper, California	490	15	20	64.8

(Continued on next page)

(Continued from previous page)

	Qual	W	L	Pct
21. Dale Dixon, Iowa	490	14	21	70.2
22. Ray Ohms, Utah	486	14	21	66.4
23. Aden Swinehammer, Illinois	472	14	21	65.7
24. Nels Peterson, Minnesota	462	13	22	66.5
25. Tommy Bartlen, Wisconsin	507	13	22	66.3
26. Gerald L'Abbe, Colorado	477	13	22	66.2
27. Ed McFarland, Texas	468	13	22	66.0
28. George Hilst, Illinois	483	13	22	63.9
29. Norm Dixon, Illinois	471	12	23	67.4
30. John Paxton, Iowa	463	11	24	62.0
31. Ralph Allen, Colorado	490	10	25	67.0
32. Arner Lindquist, W.Va.	485	9	26	66.4
33. Glenn Anderson, Illinois	474	7	28	61.1
34. C. Hefner, Illinois	463	6	29	62.0
35. J. Byrnes, California	461	3	32	53.0
36. Nelson Vogel, Illinois	464	2	33	55.5

Without the ladies, there probably would not be a tournament without color. So, on Friday and Saturday morning ten of the women had a Ladies World Championship Tournament. There were ten finalists who played a round robin of nine games. Mrs. Pat DeLeary, wife of the fourth-place winner in the Men's Division, came out on top with all nine games won. Anna Lindquist lost the women's title to Pat by losing just one game. Katie Gregson was third, Marie Kampschroeder 4th, Viola Hilton 5th, Betty Walter 6th, Helen Ohms 7th, Hope Isais 8th, Delsa McCleary 9th, and Mary Lindmeier 10th. Top prize in this event was $50.00.

Ted Allen had a high game of 96.7%. Isais put on 27 doubles in a row to beat Jimmy "Pops" Johnson in their game. Sidney Harris, after qualifying with 505 (5th best), was taken ill and had to return home.

- - - - - - -

The report shows that Lee Jacobs scored 460 points in his qualifying round. As he said, he was just one point away from qualifying for the Championship Class. This was the last year where just one class was held. In 1951, a Class B was added. Jacobs was not the only Hall of Fame member snubbed in the 1950 tournament's qualifying process. There are a number of other notables and eventual Hall of Fame members who also failed to qualify, including:

Cletus Chapelle (with 455)—Chappelle was elected NHPA president 1957. He earned four Oregon state championships and qualified for the World Tournament in the next five consecutive years. He was inducted to the NHPA Hall of Fame in 1981.

Henry Knauft (with 455)—Knauft was an 11-time Washington state champion, who qualified 11 times for the World Tournament Championship Class between 1951 and 1977. Inducted to NHPA Hall of Fame in 1985.

Harold Darnold (with 440)—Darnold qualified for the Championship Class nine times from 1941 through 1984. He was inducted to the NHPA Hall of Fame in 1994.

Archie Gregson (with 403)—He made the Championship Class cutoff in 1941, but overall he was known more for his promotion efforts. Gregson served as NHPA president in 1958 and as national secretary from 1941 to 1947. He was inducted to the Hall of Fame in 1966 as a charter inductee.

Dr. Sol Berman (with 388)—Berman never did qualify for the men's Championship Class and did not return to a World Tournament until 1965. In all, he pitched in 20 World Tournaments. Berman also pitched in several National AAU events, winning the national doubles championship in 1976. He was elected to the NHPA Hall of Fame in 1986.

- - - - - - -

I took another trip in my 1937 Pontiac to Rock Island, Illinois. Again I landed in Class C, but this time I only came in 4th [at the Midwest Open.]

My 27th State Tournament
July 29, 30, 1950
Wines Field in Ann Arbor

Only eight starters entered and in the round robin, Latzko and I finished tied for 1st. The next day the six other players pitched a round robin and Jonas Otto and Irwin Carlberg entered the four-man finals along with Joe and me.

Others were: Lester Peary 1–6, Henry Zessin 1–6, Frank Lewandowski 1–6 and Joe Kelly 3–4.

In the semi-finals, Jacobs beat Carlberg in four straight games. Results:

Jacobs					Carlberg			
Pts	R	DR	Pct	SP	Pts	R	DR	Pct
50	68	21	.680	100	47	67	22	.670
50	51	16	.637	80	43	49	14	.612
50	47	15	.653	72	48	46	15	.639
50	58	23	.784	74	25	49	15	.662
	224	75	.687	326		211	66	.647

And Latzko beat Otto in six games. Results:

Latzko					Otto			
Pts	R	DR	.Pct	SP	Pts	R	DR	Pct
36	45	13	.605	74	50	48	13	.648
50	50	15	.657	76	37	43	9	.566
35	38	8	.528	72	50	43	12	.597
50	52	17	.650	80	41	48	13	.600
50	37	13	.617	60	30	28	7	.467
50	34	14	.739	46	23	24	7	.521
	256	80	.627	408		234	61	.573

And again Jacobs meet Joe Latzko in the finals, losing four straight games:

Latzko					Jacobs			
Pts	R	DR	.Pct	SP	Pts	R	DR	Pct
50	53	20	.716	74	38	47	16	.635
50	63	25	.787	80	29	57	21	.712
50	66	25	.733	90	34	60	19	.666
50	47	20	.839	56	11	33	8	.589
	229	90	.763	300		197	64	.653

– – – – – – –

If it had not been for Joe Latzko, one wonders just how many state championship Lee Jacobs might have won.

– – – – – – –

On September 16, Lundgren, Kelly, Peary, Otto, and Jacobs drove to Toronto, Ontario, in Kelly's car. Stayed overnight and the next day we played a double-header team match.

Our first match was an easy victory over Buffalo, New York, with Lundgren and Jacobs winning all five games.

We lost to Toronto in the second match, with Jacobs winning 3 games as the best Michigan player. Drove home again.

I sold $127.00 worth of shoes there, after Canadian money exchange.

28th State Tournament

J acobs made no note of attending the World Tournament, but his journal includes the results as printed in the NHPA *Horseshoe Pitcher*. There were some significant moments at the 1951 event so the results are also included here.

The first item of note is the historic reestablishing of a junior division, some 27 years after Minnesota's Frank Stinson the first junior title in 1924. Dave Loucks of California won the 1951 junior event and went on to win the next two junior championships. At the time it was impossible to foresee that Loucks would go on to become NHPA president, a position he held for 19 years (1986–2004). He was probably the most influential and productive leader the national association ever had.

- - - - - - -

1951 World Tournament
Junior Division

Name	W	L	R	SP	Pct
1. Dave Loucks, San Francisco, Ca.	15	0	162	338	47.9
2. Stan Hilton, Murray, Utah	14	1	157	396	39.6
3. Gordon Larson, Murray, Utah	11	4	118	502	23.5
4. Jim Healey, Murray, Utah	11	4	120	460	26.0
5. John Benvegnu, Murray, Utah	11	4	109	534	26.0
6. Jerry McCleary, Midvale, Utah	10	5	136	524	25.9
7. Larry Edmondson, Union, Utah	9	6	97	498	19.4
8. Howard Larson, Murray, Utah	9	6	80	490	16.3
9. Harold Paxton, Ottumwa, Iowa	8	7	103	510	20.1
10. Gene Merrill, Murray, Utah	6	9	81	520	15.4

11. Larry Birch, Murray, Utah	5	10	59	446	13.2
12. Carl Benvegnu, Murray, Utah	5	10	60	554	10.8
13. Jack Merrill, Murray, Utah	3	12	25	428	5.8
14. Gary Brown, South Gate, Ca.			Withdrew		
15. Garr Lundquist, Murray, Utah			Withdrew		
16. D. Gile, Murray, Utah			Withdrew		

1951 World Tournament
Women's Division

Name	W	L	R	SP	Pct
1. Sarah Byers, Portland, Oregon	7	0	166	374	44.3
2. Pat DeLeary, Phoenix, Arizona	5	2	157	380	41.3
3. Anna Lindquist, Morgantown W.V.	5	2	193	404	47.7
4. Katie Gregson, Crestline, Ca.	4	3	165	400	41.2
5. Rosa Froyen, San Francisco, Ca.	4	3	165	480	34.3
6. Viola Hilton, Murray, Utah	2	5	89	436	20.4
7. Daisy Chapelle, Portland, Ore.	1	6	74	412	17.9
8. Mary Lindmeier, Broadview, Ill.	0	7	63	342	18.4

1951 World Tournament
Men's Division
Isais Snares Fifth Straight
National Horseshoe Title

Fernando Isais again successfully defended his title at Murray, Utah, by winning all thirty-five games, he met his toughest competitor in the fourth round when he defeated Ted Allen by the close score of 50 to 49. There were 122 shoes pitched in this game. Right from the beginning of the tournament it looked like the final results would show a change in the final results, as compared with previous years because in the first round Monasmith took over DeLeary, Packham beat Casey Jones and Chubb took over Gatewood. These three games in themselves were upsets.

Another upset came in the eighth round when in a 106-shoe game Allen lost his second game to Eddie Packham by 50 to 42. The following summaries of all games will give up a better picture of the happenings than words so look it over.

Results of the 1951
World Horseshoe Pitching Tournament
Men's Championship Class

		W	L	Pct
1. Fernando Isais, Los Angeles	D.C.	35	0	85.7
2. Ted Allen, Boulder, Colorado	519	33	2	83.2
3. Marines Tamboer, Wichita, Kan.	509	29	6	76.0
4. Eddie Packham, Los Angeles	515	25	10	74.8
5. John Lindmeier, Broadview, Ill.	493	25	10	74.8
6. Casey Jones, Waukesha, Wis.	524	23	12	77.0
7. Ray Gatewoon, Lennox, Calif.	486	23	12	77.0
8. Dean Brown, South Gate, Calif.	508	23	12	76.1
9. Louis Dean, Pomona, Calif.	499	23	12	72.4
10. Dale Dixon, Des Moines, Iowa	490	22	13	73.3
11. Ellis Cobb, Aurora, Illinois	486	22	13	72.8
12. Stan DeLeary, Phoenix, Arizona	497	22	13	72.5
13. John Monasmith, Yakima, Wash.	497	21	14	72.7
14. Merle Palmer, Cheyenne, Wy.	389	21	14	72.1
15. Roland Kraft, Lawrence, Kansas	481	20	15	76.1
16. Dean McLaughlin, Ontario, Can.	458	20	15	73.4
17. Glenn Anderson, Moline, Ill.	496	20	15	72.0
18. Tommy Bartlen, Milwaukee, Wis.	524	20	15	70.9
19. Alvin Gandy, Topeka, Kansas	495	18	17	72.2
20. Cletus Chapelle, Portland, Ore.	488	18	17	69.9
21. Harold Shaw, What Cheer, Iowa	497	18	18	70.5
22. Ervin Hosier, South Gate, Cal.	486	17	18	70.1
23. Lowell Gray, San Gabriel, Cal.	472	16	19	72.1
24. Frank Stinson, Minneapolis, Minn.	487	14	21	72.1
25. Richard Allen, Boulder, Colo.	464	13	22	68.3
26. Henry Knauft, Spokane, Wash	476	13	22	68.2
27. Rob Cherrier, Northfield, Minn.	463	12	23	68.1
28. John Paxton, Ottumwa, Iowa	458	11	24	67.4
29. Ray Ohms, Salt Lake City, Utah	472	10	25	68.9
30. Gerald L'Abbey, Englewood, Co.	485	10	25	67.4
31. Lewis Getchell, Tacoma, Wash.	473	10	25	67.4
32. Paul Mori, San Francisco, Cal.	468	10	25	66.2
33. Cherry Bennett, Kaysville, Ut.	462	9	26	64.6
34. Eugene Patrick, Poppenish, Wash.	467	2	33	60.2
35. Lindza Greenlee, Springfield, Mo.	473	2	33	59.5
36. William Hill, San Francisco, Ca.	479	1	34	52.7

1951 World Tournament
Men's Class B

Name	Qual	W	L	Pct
1. Roy Getchell, Tigard, Oregon	455	21	2	67.8
2. John Elkins, Stella, Missouri	458	19	4	66.0
3. Alvin Dahlene, Lawrence, Kan.	446	18	5	69.2
4. Harold Darnold, Burlington, Ia.	436	18	5	67.9
5. Arner Lindquist, Morgantown, WV	425	17	6	61.4
6. George Callas, San Francisco, Cal.	446	16	7	61.2
7. Alden Van Iten, Green Bay, Wis.	401	15	8	61.5
8. George Hook, Ontario, Calif.	439	14	9	58.5
9. Hugh Rogers, Cedar Falls, Iowa	416	14	9	56.4
10. Ralph Dykes, Chicago, Illinois	431	13	10	61.8
11. Harry Page, Waterloo, Iowa	397	13	10	58.9
12. Earl Winston, LaMonte, Mo.	442	12	11	57.7
13. Marion Lange, Bondurant, Iowa	427	12	11	55.8
14. Marvel Bean, Patterson, Iowa	420	11	12	58.5
15. Nelson Vogel, Manito, Illinois	445	10	13	63.2
16. Louis Larson, N. Mankato, Mn.	439	10	13	53.4
17. Leonard Millspaugh, Portland, Ore.	418	10	13	50.9
18. C. V. Palm, Cheyenne, Wyoming	396	6	17	49.0
19. Ralph Phillips, Portland, Ore.	406	6	17	48.2
20. A. M. Eames, Pomona Park, Fla.	398	6	17	47.1
21. Hubert Galpin, Salt Lake City, Utah	404	5	18	48.6
22. Archie Gregson, Crestline, Cal.	422	3	20	48.4
23. W. D. Hubbard, Baker, Montana	359	3	20	42.6
24. Jesse D. Edwards, Portland, Ore.	354	3	20	41.4

- - - - - - -

Finally in 1951 the NHPA woke up and expanded participation in the World Tournament. So many pitchers, for so many years, would drive hundreds of miles to try and qualify. Then, when they failed to make the top 36, they'd simply turn around and drive back home. That wasn't good for the sport. Now with an additional class, another 24 pitchers could take part in the annual "big show."

It wasn't the first time a Class B was included, since back in 1935 a similar setup (the called the Dispatch Tournament) was used, but that practice wasn't continued in the following 16 years.

The Class B participants of 1951 included some Hall of Famers and other significant name players. This is the first year we see the name Earl Winston of LaMonte, Missouri, who went on to have a most distinguished career. The name Ralph Dykes showed up earlier in an AAU event, but by 1951 he was a member of NHPA and he certainly went on to serve the organization well. Both Winston and Dykes are hall of fame members, as are Harold Darnold, Marion Lange, and Archie Gregson.

Before concluding the coverage of the 1951 World Tournament, take note of these tournament highlights listed in the *Horseshoe Pitcher*.

- - - - - - -

The longest string of doubles for the tournament went to Marines Tamboer of Kansas. He had 18.

The longest game of the tournament was between Ted Allen, Boulder, Colorado, and Frank Stinson, Minneapolis, Minnesota—138 shoes.

Dean McLaughlin of Canada pitched the most shoes in the tournament—2866.

The entire [group of] 36 men averaged 71% for the tournament.

In convention: Ladies pitching distance was made optional, 30 feet or 40 feet.

Manufacturers must have their new or changed shoes in the officers' hands by the first of March.

- - - - - - -

A newspaper article included in the 1944 section of Jacobs's journal reports that he was employed as a lathe operator at Ford Motor Company. He must have remained a Ford at least through 1951, given the next couple of clippings he saved.

- - - - - - -

Ford Shoe Tossers
Invited to Tournament

If you're a horseshoe pitcher and would like to toss a few ringers in the annual horseshoe tournament sponsored by the Industrial Recreation Association of Detroit, you are urged to contact Charlie Pink, lines 7548 or 7572, immediately.

The industrial tourney is scheduled for Saturday, August 27 at Clark Park. All Ford employees, whether a member of the Ford Horseshoe Club or not, are eligible to participate.

Entry blanks and further details may be obtained from Charlie Pink, Recreation Unit. Entry fee is only $1.00.

Lee Jacobs Wins
Rouge Horseshoe Tournament

Lee Jacobs, one-time city horseshoe champion put on a dazzling exhibition last weekend to win the Rouge Horseshoe Tournament in the open class.

In a field of 12 pitchers, Jacobs stood out. Drawing a bye in the first round, Jacobs got into the tourney with a resounding win over John Maskelis, 50–21, in the second.

In the semi-finals Jacobs met Steve Silyes and took straight games by scores of 50–10 and 50–13.

Clashing with Alex Clark in the finals, Jacobs had more trouble. He won the first of the three-game series 50–42, dropped the second 39–50 and then came through with a vigorous 50–15 win in the third.

In the novice class, James Holdbird won out over fourteen entrants. He met Ken Oliverson in the finals and won 21–9, 19–12 and 21–16.

Winners in the National Telegraphic Horseshoe Tourney are not yet known. Joe Nagy and Lee Jacobs, both Rouge, came up with 98 points, which may or may not stand up under national competition.

Horseshoe Tournament at Clark Park
Produced Some Brilliant Playing

The Annual Local 600, UAW-CIO Horseshoe Pitching Tournament sponsored by the recreation Department was held at Clark Park on Saturday, August 6th.

Sixteen entries took part in the open contest and eight in the contest confined to Local 600 members.

Lee Jacobs, former state champion shoe tosser breezed through the local contest with seven straight wins. Alex Clark took the runner-up position with six wins and one loss. Joe Fagan, Frank Couture and Joe Nagy finished in a three-way tie for third place with four wins and three losses each.

Joe Kelley, a Highland Park resident took first place in the open contest with a brilliant display of horseshoe pitching. Kelley won fourteen in the fifteen game round-robin affair, besting Lee Jacobs in a hard-fought game. Kelley lost one game to Alex Clark when the latter broke loose with an eighty-three per cent ringer game to win 50–11. In a sudden death play-off game between Kelly and Jacobs for first place, Kelley won easily with a 50 to 31 score.

First, second and third place trophies for each tournament were presented by the Local 600 Recreation Department. Final standings:

Open Class	W	L	Local 600 Class	W	L
Joe Kelley	14	1	Lee Jacobs	7	0
Lee Jacobs	14	1	Alex Clark	6	1
Clarence Flynn	12	3	Joe Fagan	4	3
Alex Clark	11	4	Joe Nagy	4	3
Del Morton	10	5	Frank Couture	4	3
Les Peary	9	6	Steve Silye	2	5
Carl Lundgren	9	6	James Holbird	1	6
Jonas Otto	9	6	Joe Streeter	0	7
Joe Fagan	6	9			
Frank Couture	6	9			
Ray Wrobble	6	9			
Joe Nagy	5	10			
James Holbird	4	11			
Steve Silye	4	11			
Joe Steeter	1	14			
Norm Elliot	0	15			

Rouge Tops Telegraphic Horseshoe Tournament

Two Rouge shoe tossers dominated the nationwide Telegraphic Horseshoe Tournament just completed.

That is the story now that returns from both the Rouge and many branch plants have been tabulated.

Winner of the tournament was Alex Clark, Dearborn Assembly Plant, who racked up a total of 110, highest in the country. Lee Jacobs, Plastics Plant, was runner-up with 109.

Behind these two, came Henry Hurt, last year's top man, who scored 108 out of Kansas City, Charles Fitch and Al Winter, both Kansas tossers, were fourth and fifth respectively.

Others who placed above 90 were: Nelson Kesler, Rouge, with 96; John Distler, Buffalo, with 90; and Nolan Wood, Kansas with 90.

Kansas City branch dominated the telegraphic event last year, but Clark and Jacobs put it on ice in this year's tourney.

Rouge Tourney

In the special Rouge Horseshoe Tourney for Rouge-area employees exclusively, one winner has been named. He is Zegment Kotwica, Dearborn Engineering, who defeated another Engineering employee, Michael Laitur, in the finals to take the novice crown.

Open competition in the Rouge tourney has not been completed, but it also will involve the two telegraphic winners, Clark and Jacobs. They will get together in the finals of the Rouge tournament as soon as possible.

- - - - - - -

The terminology used in these articles is a bit cryptic for non-local readers. It seems that Rouge was a suburb of Detroit. But it's not clear exactly what a telegraphic tourney is. Now, moving on to Lee's account of the 1951 Michigan state tournament.

My 28th State Tournament
Port Huron
August 25–26

I sailed through the round-robin in good style (10 wins, 3 losses) and then in the finals I brought out my new trial pair of shoes, the "Rockets," and went through with only one defeat to meet Joe Latzko in the finals series.

Finals Round Robin

ROUND ONE

Latzko had the high game at .661 to beat Kelly 50–39. Jacobs eked out a winner with .471 over Raab 50–39. Lundgren beat Woodward 50–25 and Carlberg beat Woodward 50–25.

ROUND TWO

Jacobs won over Kelly 50–35; Carlberg pitched .700 to upset Latzko 50–43; Lundgren beat Woodward 50–41; Peary beat Raab 50–43.

ROUND THREE

Jacobs averaged .720 to beat Carlberg 50–15; Lundgren won over Raab 50–40; Latzko had the round high game at .773 in winning over Woodward 50–11; Kelly got his first win in beating Peary 50–25.

ROUND FOUR

Lundgren beat Kelly 50–27; Latzko had another high game at .711 in winning over Lee Jacobs 50–12, Jacobs had only .480; Carlberg beat Peary 50–31; Woodward beat Raab 50–34.

ROUND FIVE

Lundgren remained unbeaten in a 50–47 victory over Carlberg; Latzko pitched .695 to win over Peary 50–36; Jacobs beat Woodward 50–37; Raab beat Kelly 50–42. Standings:

Lundgren	5–0	Kelly	1–4
Latzko	4–1	Peary	1–4
Jacobs	4–1	Woodward	1–4
Carlberg	3–2	Raab	1–4

ROUND SIX

Latzko hit .721 to give Lundgren his first loss 50–33; Jacobs won again 50–27 over Peary; Carlberg stayed in the hunt by beating Raab 50–25; Woodward beat Kelly 50–27.

Latzko pitched .750 to beat Raab 50–25; Jacobs pitched .760 to win over Lundgren 50–23 and knock Carl out of the finals; But Carlberg had the high game of the round, pitching .777 to beat Kelly 50–16; Peary beat Woodward 50–16. Jacobs will meet Latzko in the finals series of best of seven games. Summary:

1951 Michigan State Tournament Finals

Player	W	L	Pts	R	DR	SP	Pct
Latzko	6	1	343	329	115	486	.703
Jacobs	6	1	312	246	71	420	.586
Carlberg	5	2	312	281	88	454	.619
Lundgren	5	2	306	276	76	476	.584
Peary	2	5	257	250	66	472	.529
Woodward	2	5	230	206	52	436	.472
Kelly	1	6	236	202	55	408	.495
Raab	1	6	256	220	44	474	.464

Latzko controlled the series, averaging .712 and losing only one game, game two and of course winning four games. Summary:

Latzko					Rose			
Pts	R	DR	Pct	SP	Pts	R	DR	Pct
50	39	11	.650	60	25	29	4	.480
46	53	18	.660	80	50	55	21	.690
50	40	14	.710	56	39	37	15	.660
50	56	23	.800	70	28	48	16	.690
50	40	16	.741	54	18	26	6	.481
		.712					.609	

Drove my car to Rock Island, for the Midwest Open, but the meet was rained out.

Lundgren, Jozwick and I went in Lundgren's Chevrolet to Clearfield, Pa., to the Eastern National. Got into Class B and didn't do so well.

Went with Lundgren to a meet at Grand Rapids on September 2 & 3. Didn't do so well.

Class A	W	L
1. J. Latzko, Flint	6	1
2. H. Sibert, Dayton, O	5	2
3. I. Carlberg, G.Rapids	5	2
4. P. Focht, Dayton, O	4	3
5. L. Jacobs, Belleville	4	3
6. C. Lundgren, Detroit	3	4
7. J. Kelly, Detroit	1	6
8. L. Peary, Detroit	0	7

Class B	W	L
1. J. Otto, Ann Arbor	6	1
2. J. Davis, Battle C.	6	1
3. J. Miller, Detroit	5	2
4. A. Kerr, Lowell	3	4
5. H. Hunter, G.Rapids	3	4
6. F. Levandowski, Huron	3	4
7. K. Miller, G.Rapids	2	5
8. A. Nickson G.Rapids	0	7

29th State Tournament

I took a long, lonely trip to Clearfield, Pa., in my 1941 Plymouth to the Eastern National. Again I made Class B and didn't do very well.

- - - - - - -

Pennsylvania

Carl Steinfeldt of Rochester, New York carried home the 1952 Eastern National Horseshoe Pitching Championship, Saturday, August 2, after two days of strenuous pitching at the Clearfield County Fair.

The new champion, who succeeds Dale Carson of Baltimore, Maryland, spread-eagled the field in the Class A division to win his title. Included in his 77.09 percentage for the seventeen games was one game of 91.8%.

Runner-up in Class A was Dean McLaughlin of Oshowa, Ontario, Canada, with a 13–4 record. Ralph Lackey of West Middleton, Ohio, last year's runner-up, was third, also with a 13–4 record in games won and lost but with a ringer percentage of 68.4 as compared to McLaughlin's 74.9. McLaughlin led the field in qualifying with 86 ringers and a score of 272 out of 100 shoes.

Lowell Edmondston of Danville, Indiana, won first place in Class B with a 15–2 record and a 65.7 ringer percentage.

Harold Blackman of Toronto, Canada handled the public address system for an exhibition game between Bill Kolb of New Jersey and Dale Terry of Illinois and did a fine job before an audience of over five thousand people. The game was very close with Kolb emerging the winner by a score of 51–47 in a game that saw both men pitching over seventy-five percent ringers. Final standings:

1952 Eastern National

Class A

	W	L	Pct		W	L	Pct
1. C. Steinfeldt	17	0	77.9	10. W. Woodward	8	9	67.5
2. D. McLaughlin	13	4	74.9	11. Ralph Maddox	8	9	62.5
3. R. Lackey	13	4	68.4	12. S. Fennicchia	8	9	62.5
4. V. Fileccia	10	7	70.5	13. Harold Reno	7	10	64.0
5. H. Sibert	10	7	69.3	14. G. Anderson	6	11	66.9
6. R. Frye	10	7	66.3	15. J. Fulton	6	11	62.8
7. D. Carson	9	8	71.7	16. G.F. Anderson	5	12	64.2
8. G. McFatridge	9	8	71.4	17. E. Tishock	4	13	53.0
9. P. Focht	9	8	67.9	18. C. Gerrish	2	15	59.5

Class B

	W	L	Pct		W	L	Pct
1. L. Edmondson	15	2	65.7	10. L. Crooks	6	11	58.1
2. B. Kolb	14	3	67.8	11. D. Mitchell	6	11	57.0
3. L. Long	14	3	66.6	12. J. Mitchell	6	11	55.5
4. J. Durham	13	4	59.0	13. Clippinger	6	11	52.3
5. A. Natale	12	5	64.9	14. L. Peary	5	12	54.6
6. H. McPherson	11	6	62.8	15. G. Mawson	5	12	52.9
7. A. Dahlene	10	7	59.3	16. Lee Jacobs	5	12	52.9
8. W. Murphy	8	9	57.9	17. R. Carson	5	12	50.2
9. D. Mayes	8	9	57.9	18. W. Nellis	4	13	50.0

- - - - - - -

The article and tournament summary above are from a clipping from the *Horseshoe Pitcher* that Jacobs placed into his journal.

Lee Jacobs may not have pitched as well as he would have liked, but he certainly was sharing a field with greatness. In Class A for this tournament, were six hall of fame pitchers: Carl Steinfeldt, world champion in 1976; Dean McLaughlin, who we read about in the match play with Canadian teams; Dale Carson, who was a two-time National AAU champion (1949, 1950); Paul Focht, world champion in 1962; Ralph Maddox (West Virginia) has the distinction of being the youngest state champion ever, at age 12—followed by Fred Hay (Minnesota, age 13) and Ira Allen (Colorado, age 13); and Harold Reno, two-time world champion, 1961 and 1964.

In Class B, Jene Durham (Maryland) was the National AAU champion in 1951 and Bill Kolb (New Jersey) was mentioned before as a National AAU doubles champion in 1968.

- - - - - - -

There was a meet on July 4 at Ruby, which is near Port Huron. Makeshift courts and lights and heat and beer were the main features. Jule Winter won, with Clark 2nd and Joe Latzko and I 3rd.

- - - - - - -

Jacobs made no comments about attending the 1952 World Tournament, although he clipped the results out of the *Horseshoe Pitcher* and tacked them into the journal.

The biggest news of the 1952 national event was that Fernando Isais won his sixth consecutive championship. It was an unbelievable accomplishment and was a record that stood for many decades. The fact that Ted Allen was competing in each of those tournaments makes a major statement in favor that Isais may have been the better pitcher of the two all-time greats. Then throw in Frank Jackson, C. C. Davis, Harold Reno, Curt Day, Elmer Hohl, Walter Ray Williams Jr., and Alan Francis, and you can try to decide who is the greatest all-time horseshoe pitcher.

Isais pitched 83.5 percent ringers in winning this title. Ted Allen and Casey Jones also bettered the 80 percent mark. Twelve more players shot over 70 percent ringers, a statistic that would not be matched in today's World Tournaments.

One more Isais tribute—he won 69 straight games over the last three World Tournaments. His streak came to an end in the 33rd round at the hands of James "Pop" Johnson, the 1945 National AAU champion from Ohio.

Sarah Byers won her second straight world championship while pitching a respectable 53.5 percent ringers. This was her last championship. Shortly after the 1952 tournament she was in a car accident that caused injuries that didn't permit her to continue pitching horseshoes.

Dave Loucks won his second junior championship.

Now, we move on to Jacobs's account of the 1952 Michigan tournament. He was 46 years old, and it was his 29th state tournament.

My 29th State Tournament

This meet was all my own idea. I saw in the paper that the Michigan State Fair had decided to hold a "state championship" meet. I straightaway called them and told them that they couldn't do that without out state association sanction, so they asked me to come there and talk it over, which I did. The result was that a tournament [with] a good prize list was set for September 6–7.

I took my vacation the week before the meet and spent each day at the fair working to get the courts in some kind of shape. I even purchased horseshoe stakes to use. The courts were the worst we have ever pitched on.

So all that week I had no practice and it showed in the round robin of 25 points games. I failed to reach the finals.

In the finals, comprised of Winter, Latzko, Otto, Kelly, Lundgren, Clark, Carlberg and Peary, Winter and Latzko came to the final series.

This match was scheduled for 4 out of 7 games, but darkness cut it short and Winter was declared the new State Champion.

	Winter					Latzko			
Game	Pts	R	DR	Pct	SP	Pts	R	DR	Pct
1	50	48	15	.615	78	47	46	15	.590
2	50	47	15	.671	70	45	44	14	.629
3	32	44	12	.629	70	50	50	18	.714
4	50	49	14	.681	72	32	44	16	.611

30th State Tournament

About the only thing I remember about this year is:

My 30th State Tournament
Isabella County Fair
Island Park in Mt. Pleasant

Entries:

Mike Barnes, Mt. Pleasant

W. Hautmaki, Mt. Pleasant

Louis Hirschman, Saginaw

Harry Hunter, Grand Rapids

Lee Jacobs, Belleville

Joe Kelly, Highland Park

Albert Kerr, Lowell

Dan Latzko, Mt. Pleasant

Joe Latzko, Flint

Carl Lundgren, Detroit

John Miller, Detroit

James Ostrander, Lansing

Jonas Otto, Ann Arbor

Lester Peary, Detroit

Ted Stone, Mt. Pleasant

Richard Van Raalte, Grand Rapids
Jule Winter, Port Huron
Edward Woodward, Flint
Harry Zessin, Saginaw

Qualified the 16 best by four 50-shoe games. A round robin of the 16 best found Joe Latzko finishing first and Jule Winter coming in second.

In the championship series, cut to 3 out of 5, Winter retained the state title by beating Joe 3 games to 1.

- - - - - - -

The journal doesn't provide much information for 1953. Jacobs admitted that his record-keeping efforts had slipped, but there weren't any clippings either. Given his ongoing dedication to the sport, we have to imagine that the 1953 World Tournament must have been of some interest to him even though he didn't include a clipping of the results in his journal.

The tournament can be quickly summarized: the string of consecutive world championship for Fernando Isais came to a halt as Ted Allen won his sixth men's title; with little fanfare or mention in the NHPA publications, young Dave Loucks won his third junior title; and Hazel Harris of Colorado won the women's championship.

Still Pitching, but No Glory

T he 1954 World Tournament results were included in Lee's journal. This was the seventh year that the "big show" was held in Murray, Utah, and the NHPA was starting to show some stability. The World Tournaments in Utah were having a strong and positive impact on the sport across the country.

The 1953 champion Ted Allen did not earn consecutive titles. Guy Zimmerman won his first and only world championship in 1954, while averaging 84.2 percent ringers for the tournament. Zimmerman was a tremendous exhibition and competitive pitcher and sadly his competitive days came to an end after an accident in which his car rolled over his legs.

The 1954 tournament had a very different format from the usual round-robin method. Pitchers played qualifying matches to identify the top 36 pitchers and that group was then seeded into six groups of six players each. After a round robin in each group, the field was reduced to three groups of eight pitchers (24 players). Another round robin was played and the top two in each group advanceed. Those six played another round robin to determine the top two, who then played a match series for the championship. In that finals playoff, an incredible series, Zimmerman beat Isais in three straight games, averaging 87.8 percent to Isais's 84.9 percent.

In his book *Official N.H.P.A. History of the World Tournament 1909 to 1980*, Gary Kline writes that after that playoff match, Isais and Zimmerman each gave their shoes to the top two finalists in the junior division. They were Byron Bowman, of Murray, who won the title on a 12–0 record and Roger Vogel, had just one loss.

To give more contemporary context to that anecdote, note that Roger Vogel (son of Nelson Vogel, a championship-class pitcher) went on to be a star on the Murray courts. As Ottie Reno has said, "Roger was not the greatest pitcher, but he was a great pitcher." Vogel pitched for many years, winning state championships in five different states (more than any other pitcher). He hung up his shoes back in the 1980s. Then in 2013, at age 75, after nearly thirty years, he decided to come back to the sport to pitch as an elder. It took him a while to regain his ringer average, but his natural skill for the sport remained and by the time the 2013 World Tournament came around, he was averaging over 70 percent. He qualified for the elder's Championship Class. Vogel's son, Bret, has also qualified for the men's Championship Class, making the Vogels the only family known to have three generations of horseshoe pitchers to accomplish that feat.

Next, the journal contains a clipping (not included here) that reports on a tournament in Lakeside, Ohio, in which Jacobs was part of Class B and placed eighth, pitching 41.5 percent ringers. That is far below the performances we are accustomed to read about. Jacobs was 48 years old in 1954, so age should not have been a factor.

The journal also had a copy of the 1954 Eastern National Horseshoe Tournament final standings. For years this event had a tremendous following, and the 1954 tournament was an extraordinary one. Of the 16 players in Class A, eight are hall of fame members and four others have been nominated and are on the ballot for induction.

1954 Eastern National Horseshoe Tournament

	W	L	%
1. Carl Steinfeldt, Rochester, N.Y.	12	3	72.7
2. Casey Jones, Random Lake, Wisconsin	12	3	74.9
3. Curt Day, Frankfort, Ohio	10	5	76.8
4. Thomas Brownell, Amsterdam, N.Y.	9	6	75.6
5. Ellis Griggs, Plainville, Illinois	9	6	75.1
6. Harold Reno, Sabina, Ohio	9	6	71.4
7. Stanley Manker, Martinsville, Ohio	9	6	69.8
8. Truman Standard, Canton, Illinois	8	7	74.6
9. John Fulton, Carlisle, Pennsylvania	8	7	71.0
10. Glenn Anderson, Moline, Illinois	8	7	70.6
11. James Johnson, Covington, Kentucky	7	8	70.6
12. Arner Lindquist, Morgantown, W.Va.	6	9	66.3
13. Dale Dixon, Des Moines, Iowa	4	11	67.2
14. W. O. Maxwell, Hicksville, Ohio	4	11	65.3
15. Harold Wolfe, Cedarville, Ohio	3	12	66.0
16. Milton Tate, Peoria, Illinois	2	13	62.6

Steinfeldt won the playoff game 73.0% over Jones 69.0%.

A Third State Championship

The year's coverage began with the results of the Lakeside, Ohio Open, held on July 4th. Ohio pitchers did well in the event, which isn't surprising since four of the Ohio players went on to be world champions. Lee Jacobs participated, but had no comment on his performance.

- - - - - - -

Lakeside, Ohio Open
Horseshoe Tournament
July 4, 1955

Class A	Qual	W	L	Pts	R	SP	Pct
1. John Fulton, Penn.	256	6	1	348	370	510	72.5
2. Harold Reno, Ohio	254	6	1	344	337	436	77.2
3. Harry Sibert, Ohio	236	5	2	323	324	490	66.1
4. Carl Lundgren, Mich.	234	3	4	245	283	464	60.5
5. Leonard Glass, Ohio	236	3	4	255	286	474	60.5
6. Paul Focht, Ohio	D.C.	2	5	287	365	530	67.1
7. Jim Schamp, Ohio	222	2	5	240	290	392	61.9
8. Lester Peary, Mich.	235	1	6	186	205	392	52.3

	Pts	R	SP	Oct		Pts	R	SP	Pct
1. Fulton	52	33	46	70.7	Reno	21	23	46	50.0
2. Fulton	50	66	96	67.3	Reno	42	64	98	65.3

Class B	Qual	W	L	Pts	R	SP	Pct
1. Harold Wolfe, Ohio	208	6	1	336	279	430	64.8
2. Stan Manker, Ohio	217	6	1	338	265	392	67.6
3. Curt Day, Indiana	220	6	1	324	274	418	65.5
4. Joe Kelly, Mich.	216	3	4	266	236	410	57.5
5. Lee Jacobs, Mich.	192	3	4	257	213	406	52.4
6. Eddie Fouse, Ohio	216	2	5	278	282	488	57.7
7. Denver Ford, Ohio	196	2	5	237	210	432	48.6
8. John Miller, Mich.	180	0	7	117	146	354	41.2

Three-way tie played off:

	Pts	R	SP	Pct		Pts	R	SP	Pct
1. Wolfe	52	66	92	71.7	Day	33	60	92	65.2
2. Wolfe	50	66	88	75.0	Manker	34	60	88	68.2

– – – – – – –

Now we come to one of the highlights of the Lee Rose journals. Jacobs was a three-time Michigan state champion. His wins were somewhat unusual, in the sense that each was earned in a different decade and in a very competitive state. In his own words, Jacobs recounts his third state championship win.

– – – – – – –

1955 Michigan State Horseshoe Tournament
Mt. Pleasant
August 26–27

My 32nd State Tournament [at age 49]. There were 22 entries and we were divided into 2 squads of 11 men each.

The records of this meet are not at hand and are presumed to be lost, but if they turn up later, will put them in. The Red Squad consisted of: Beckey, Bell, Carlberg, Eckhoff, Flynn, Jozwiak, Kerr, Lundgren, Otto, Peary and Van Roalte. The Blue Squad consisted of: Clark, Craft, Davis, Hunter, Jacobs, Kelly, Joe Latzko, John Latzko, McBride, Ostrander and Schultz.

The six high from each squad out of a qualifying round robin were to qualify for the final 12-player round robin and the top two to play a 3 out of 5 game series for the state title.

The preliminary round robin was played on August 26 and the following qualified:

Red	Blue
Carl Lundgren	Joe Latzko
Irwin Carlberg	Alex Clark
Clarence Flynn	Joe Kelly
Lester Peary	Lee Jacobs
Albert Kerr	James Ostrander
Nick Beckey	Harry Hunter

On the morning of August 27, when the final 12 appeared to start the finals, Lundgren came up with a bad back and after dropping two games had to retire and was replaced by Jozwiak.

Finals

In the first round, Jacobs met Ostrander and got off to a sad start by being soundly trounced.

In the second round, Jacobs met Carlberg and very meekly took another bad beating.

In the third round, Jacobs met Flynn and although he pitched a little better, he was beaten again.

In the fourth round, Jacobs met Beckey and in no time at all, was trailing 37–3!!

AND THEN IT HAPPENED

Like a jig-saw puzzle that cannot make a complete picture until the last piece falls into place, Jacobs suddenly became a complete picture; and from a floundering, almost hapless contender, changed into a ringer-throwing machine. With his new Super Rocket shoes, Jacobs began doubling against Beckey and doubled and doubled and doubled!!

From a deficit of 37–3, Jacobs rolled like a wave over Beckey to leave him glassy-eyed on 43 as he went out. From that point on there was only one question: Could Jacobs make 2nd place?

ROUND FIVE

The machine that was now Jacobs rolled over Albert Kerr until it was 47–0! Then Jacobs let Kerr score before going out.

ROUND SIX

Jacobs threw two shoes away with the score 48–0 against Harry Hunter to let him score.

ROUND SEVEN

Jacobs threw two shoes away with the score 49–0 against Jozwiak to let him score.

ROUND EIGHT

Jacobs met Peary, who was here the surprise pitcher of the tournament, being tied for the lead with Latzko, each having won seven straight.

The WCEN radio station sound car had come upon the scene and the game was featured on the P.A. system. Peary was going real well and looked on several doubles early in the game and took an opening lead.

Then Jacobs picked up his Super Rockets and went to work. Double after double leaped on the stake and Peary was ground under in short order.

ROUND NINE

Jacobs met the undefeated Joe Latzko. As the game started, the P.A. system announced that they would move the "mike" down to pick up the game between "the champion and the hottest pitcher on the courts." In the few minutes it took to move the "mike," Jacobs was already leading 40–6! It was over soon, 50–12.

Peary lost again and Jacobs now tied for 3rd place with Kelly.

Jacobs met Kelly. The Super Rockets exploded on Kelly and rolled him under 50–18!

Peary lost again and Jacobs was now tied for 2nd place and in the running for the title! And among the spectators it was being rumored that Jacobs could not be stopped now!

ROUND ELEVEN

In this last round, a stubborn Clark faced Jacobs, but was blasted by a withering storm of doubles that left him on 24. Peary was knocked off by Flynn and the final standing was:

1. Latzko	10–1	Clark	6–5
2. Jacobs	8–3	Ostrander	6–5
3. Kelly	7–4	9. Beckey	5–6
Peary	7–4	10. Hunter	4–7
5. Carlberg	6–5	11. Kerr	1–10
Flynn	6–5	12. Jozwiak	0–11

This left Latzko and Jacobs to play a best of five series for the championship.

Championship Series

In looking back through the years, it will be seen that Jacobs (or Rose) had lost again and again to Joe Latzko in the final drive, but in this series, it was almost a certainty that Latzko was a doomed man! Jacobs was pitching like a fiend incarnate and Joe was hitting his bottle to bolster his nerves.

Around the court, Joe's mother, brothers, relatives and friends silently hoped for the best but expected the worst. And that's what they saw!

The relentless Jacobs simply snowed Latzko under each game. There never was any doubt about it. The first game ended 50–22. The second game was 50–18. The third and final game was 50–14.

And after an 11-year lapse, the (now) "Belleville Tiger" became the champion pitcher of Michigan.

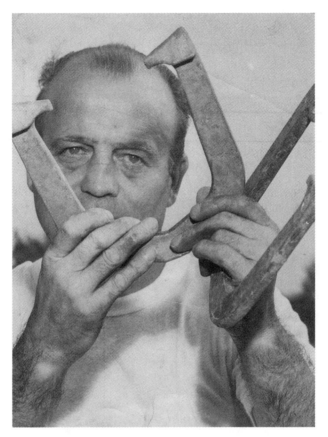

Lee Jacobs Takes Aim at Mt. Pleasant, Winning His 3rd State Championship

- - - - - - -

A clipping of an interesting human-interest story appears next in the journal. You should be reminded that this article was written 59 years ago.

- - - - - - -

City Boys Streamline
Horseshoe Pitching

Horseshoe pitching has come a long way from the barnyard.

The city boys have taken to the game and streamlined it just as they did the horseless carriage.

Uncle John and Pete the hired hand, hardly would recognize the game today. Chances are too, if they challenged one of the better pitchers from the city, they would get whomped.

For one thing, they're not making shoes like they used to. In some future civilization, people will dig up horseshoes and conclude that the extinct animal known as the horse must have had square feet.

The boys who pitch for ringers have put together a shoe that would have hobbled old Dobbin. They've opened up the prongs and put hooks on the tips, so that the shoe will spin on the stake and stay there.

Used to be, when a shoe started spinning, it was a good time to move your shins out of range.

Instead of hooking one end of the shoe and spinning it like crazy, today's pitchers control the spin-three-quarters of a turn or a turn and a quarter or one and three-quarters- and plop it around the stake more times than they miss.

This year's champion in Michigan is 49-year-old Lee Jacobs of Belleville, who has been studying the fine science of ringing a stake since he was 13.

Jacobs, a factory worker at Willow Run General Motors plant, beat out another city boy, Joseph Latzko of Flint, a Buick employee.

In their tight match for the championship at Mt. Pleasant, Michigan, Jacobs and Latzko pitched more than 65 per cent ringers.

There have been more spectacular records. Ted Allen, of Boulder, Colorado, once threw 29 consecutive double ringers. It also was claimed that Allen could kill a rabbit on the run by dropping a horseshoe over its neck.

Almost any of today's top-notch pitchers can light a match tied to the stake with one shoe and put it out with the next pitched shoe. They also do things like ringing a cigarette out of a stooge's mouth or tossing ringers under a fool's chin resting on the stake.

As a city sport, horseshoes has proven an effective way to dig up a carefully tended lawn and has caused to least one lawsuit in Detroit when it was said that the clang of shoes on stake kept people awake.

But devotees say it also has prevented countless attacks of rheumatism and appendicitis and trimmed many a waistline. It's the stooping and stretching, they insist, that does the trick.

Factory workers in some Detroit plants have adapted the game to concrete floors, using rubber horseshoes and skidding them onto removable stakes.

This next article, which gives a nice view of the Lee Jacob's family, was probably clipped out of an employer magazine or company newsletter. That's followed by the final entry for the year, a succint report of another loss.

— — — — — — —

State Professional Horseshoe Champion

Lee Jacobs (Dept. 210), who lives at 1110 Quirk Road, Belleville, Michigan, is the Michigan State Professional Horseshoe Champion of 1955.

Lee won the championship at Mt. Pleasant, pitching 25 games to eliminate 23 entries. He won the 1933 State Professional Horseshoe Championship and returning to amateur status, the National Amateur Championship in 1944.

Lee pitches a "one and three-quarters" turn shoe and averages 65–70 ringers out of 100 pitches. He is looking forward to entering the 1956 World's Professional tournament at Salt Lake City, Utah.

Lee has two sons, Lee Jr., who is studying to be an artist, Robert, who is aiming at a professional singing career and a daughter, Diane. The Jacobs boys are active in rodeo entertainment.

Julius Jacobs, the well-known horse dealer on Quirk Road, Belleville, is Lee Senior's father. The increasing interest in the sport of horseshoes is evidenced by the fact that there were 600 entries in the 1955 Michigan State Fair Tournament.

Bertie and I took a trip to Peoria, Illinois, to the Eastern National and after driving all night, I failed to qualify for the finals.

Not Even Close in His
33rd State Tournament

This chapter starts with coverage of the Mid-West "Ringer Round-Up" Open tournament. This event was held in Frankfort, Indiana. Previous Mid-West Opens have been mentioned as events Jacobs participated in—those earlier events were held in Illinois. I can't absolutely confirm this, but I believe these tournaments called "Mid-West Opens" are a spin-off or even a continuation of the major Mid-West Opens held in Des Moines, Iowa, back in the 1930s when no World Tournaments were being held. The Iowa events were major events of championship quality and apparently were handed off to others to carry on a respected tournament.

This 1956 Open was filled with stars of the game. In Class A, eight of the twelve were World Tournament championship-class pitchers, and Curt Day and Paul Focht were men's world champions. Lee Jacobs must not have attended, because we will not find his name in the summary. He clipped this article out of NHPA's *Horseshoe Pitcher*.

Mid-West "Ringer Round-Up" Open
Frankfort, Indiana
Dorner Park
July 7, 8, 1956

Curt Day, Indiana State Champion from Frankfort, Indiana, copped first place in the Mid-West Open from a field of 65 contestants from six different states.

Day's three-quarter reverse turn won high honors and swept all eleven games in the Class A round robin. Milton Tate of Peoria, Illinois, finished second.

Seventy-five-year-old, W. O. Maxwell of Hicksville, Ohio, won Class B. The Fouse brothers, Leo and Eddie, from Wilmington, Ohio, captured Classes C and E, while Paul Van Sickle of Indianapolis, Indiana, annexed the Class D title.

Ernie Danielson Jr. of West Burlington, Iowa, took the Junior crown from a field in which the oldest was only 14 years and all pitched the full distance of 40 feet.

A heavy wind that blew in gusts plagued the tournament and cut ringer percentages considerably. A new method of prize distribution was used in which each game won decided the amount of prize money to the winner. The prize list consisted of three trophies and totaled $425.00.

Class A

Player	Qual	W	L	R	SP	%
1. Curt Day, Frankfort, Ind.	402	11	0	625	840	74.4
2. Milt Tate, Peoria, Illinois	372	9	2	579	792	73.1
3. Ed Sharp, Mulberry, Indiana	371	6	5	642	880	73.0
4. Virgil Taylor, Ohio	383	6	5	628	872	72.0
5. Jim Johnson, Kentucky	375	6	5	602	860	70.0
6. Truman Standard, Illinois	382	6	5	588	848	69.3
7. Harris Maitlen, Indiana	378	5	6	593	834	71.1
8. Gene Brumfield, Indiana	381	5	6	592	868	68.2
9. Graydon McFatridge, Indiana	371	5	6	553	814	68.0
10. Glen Anderson, Illinois	370	4	7	564	860	65.6
11. Paul Focht, Ohio	390	3	8	597	882	67.7
12. Nelson Vogel, Illinois	375	0	11	399	688	58.0

*Qualifying round consisted of 150 shoes.

Class B

Player	Qual	W	L	R	SP	%
1. W. O. Maxwell, Ohio	359	9	2	486	736	66.0
2. Floyd Fowler, Indiana	345	8	3	485	776	66.5
3. Lowell Edmondson, Indiana	362	8	3	465	752	61.7
4. Oris Harshman, Indiana	351	8	3	469	786	59.7
5. Stan Manker, Ohio	356	6	5	441	762	57.9
6. Roger Vogel, Illinois	350	5	6	436	786	52.6
7. Carl Lundgren, Michigan	346	5	6	383	714	53.6
8. Frank Polka, Illinois	360	4	7	411	692	59.7
9. Richard Konieczny, Ind.	356	4	7	408	744	54.8
10. Ellis Cob, Illinois	340	3	8	396	732	54.1
11. Nelson Brown, Indiana	350	3	8	375	712	52.7
12. Ernie Danielson, Iowa	342	3	8	331	674	49.1

Class C

Player	Qual	W	L	R	SP	%
1. Leo Fouse, Wilmington, O.	331	4	1	226	366	61.7
2. Leslie Long, Sterling	333	3	2	232	384	60.4
3. Lester Peary, Detroit	329	3	2	201	362	55.5
4. Ben Farmer, Union City	332	3	2	210	344	61.0
5. Gene Lawver, Canton, Ill.	329	2	3	214	360	59.4
6. Joe Kelley, High Park	331	1	4	206	352	57.9
7. Harold Renner, Muncie,	331	Withdrew				
8. H. McPherson, Covington	330	Withdrew				

- - - - - - -

The 1956 World Tournament was held July 18 through 25. There was no commentary from Lee Jacobs, so again we can assume that he did not participate. The final standings printed in the *Horseshoe Pitcher* were added to the journal and are reprinted below.

For the second year the World Tournament held a special playoff was held at the conclusion of the regular play. That format was determined in advance. In fact, the arrangement was presented by Ted Allen as a gesture of good will. He felt he held an unfair skill advantage and he wanted to make sure all the players had a fair shot at the title. Based solely on the regular round-robin results, Don Titcomb would have been the World Champion, after losing only one game against such a competitive field. The same format had been held the previous year as Ted Allen won the round robin undefeated in 35 games and then went undefeated in the four-player playoff that followed.

Ted Allen is Still
World Ringer Champion

Ted Allen, of Boulder, Colorado, is still the World's Champion after almost five hours of pitching in the finals of the World Horseshoe Pitching Tournament held at Murray, Utah on July 25th.

Ted Allen and Don Titcomb, of Sunnyvale, California, ended the final night's four-man round robin for the right to move into the championship playoff, with two matches won and one lost. Allen then won the two-out-of-three championship playoff against Titcomb two games to one. Game scores: 50–45, 40–52 and 50–49.

In the four-man round robin, Titcomb was victorious over Curt Day, of Frankfort, Indiana, 52–16 and former champion, Fernando Isais of Los Angeles, 52–27. He lost to Allen 52–25.

Besides defeating Titcomb, Allen also won from Curt Day, 51–19, but succumbed to his old rival, Isais 50–26.

Following is a complete summary of the results of the World's Tournament at Murray, Utah, including the four-player play-off:

Finals Playoff Round Robin

Name	W	L	R	SP	%
1. Ted Allen	2	1	252	290	86.9
2. Don Titcomb	2	1	194	230	84.3
3. Fernando Isais	1	2	249	300	83.0
4. Curt Day	1	2	198	256	77.3

1956 World Tournament Finals

Qual. Name	Pts	W	L	R	SP	%
1. Don Titcomb, California	1781	34	1	2089	2486	84.0
2. Fernando Isais, Calif.	1771	33	2	2114	2536	83.4
3. Ted Allen, Colorado	1780	32	3	2121	2544	83.4
4. Curt Day, Indiana	1702	28	7	1986	2578	77.0
5. Truman Standard, Illinois	1721	28	7	2078	2610	79.6
6. Glenn Anderson, Illinois	1643	27	8	1870	2538	73.7
7. Louis Dean, California	1613	26	9	1937	2610	74.2
8. Dean McLaughlin, Canada	1598	26	9	1959	2630	74.5
9. John Lindmeier, Illinois	1629	25	10	2006	2694	74.5
10. Clive Wahlin, Utah	1642	24	11	2125	2816	75.5
11. Virgil Taylor, Indiana	1527	24	11	1954	2660	73.5
12. Ed Shape, Indiana	1547	23	12	1846	2608	70.9
13. John Elkins, Missouri	1506	20	15	1809	2586	70.0
14. Alvin Gandy, Kansas	1495	19	16	1769	2560	69.1
15. Floyd Fowler, Indiana	1463	19	16	1701	2560	68.6
16. Dean Brown, California	1495	18	17	1982	2734	72.5
17. Jerry Schneider, Calif.	1468	18	17	1868	2650	70.5
18. Jim Weeks, California	1495	17	18	1912	2664	71.8
19. E. J. Wiley, Idaho	1359	16	19	1694	2536	66.8
20. Milton Tate, Illinois	1407	15	20	1754	2526	69.4
21. Oris Harshman, Indiana	1373	15	20	1714	2550	67.2
22. Ray Ohms, Utah	1343	14	21	1580	2446	64.6
23. Ron Cherrier, Minnesota	1300	13	22	1806	2628	68.7
24. George Hook, California	1333	11	24	1485	2378	62.4
25. W. O. Maxwell, Ohio	1209	11	24	1485	2378	62.4
26. Howard Robinson, Nebraska	1142	10	25	1571	2470	63.6
27. Harold Wolfe, Ohio	1163	10	25	1516	2378	63.8
28. Harry Page, Iowa	1331	20	25	1678	2622	64.0
29. Harry Russell, Colorado	1116	10	25	1471	2312	63.5
30. Stan Dahl, Canada	1195	9	26	1486	2370	63.8
31. Hubert Galpin, Utah	1114	9	26	1327	2212	60.0
32. Dave Baker, Missouri	1168	9	26	1563	2422	64.5
33. Ervin Hosier, California	1181	8	27	1532	2348	65.3
34. Roger Parson, Utah	1139	7	28	1465	2410	60.8
35. Clarence Giles, Utah	1029	5	30	1280	2188	58.5
36. Frank Bonaly, California	927	5	30	1280	2188	58.5

My 33rd State Tournament – 1956
August 24, 25 at Mt. Pleasant

I got off to a shaky start against Fagan but managed to come from behind in the stretch to win. After a bye, I flopped badly and lost to Jozwiak and Ostrander. Enraged, I slammed into Latzko and walloped him, which was his only defeat in the round robin.

From here on I was untouchable. My "Super Rockets" were working fine and I simply ran over everybody I played. I roundly trounced Kelly, Beckey, Flynn and shut out Van Raalte. I beat Krimmel, Hautmaki and shut out Kerr. I smothered Hunter, Schultz and in the last round of the day, beat Carlberg 50–11.

Late that night, I slipped and fell down a long flight of stairs, fracturing two ribs and my chances were gone.

The next day, I played anyway, but you can imagine how tough it was.

I lost Peary, then nosed out Chamberlain and Craft. Lost to Davis, Clark and Lundgren and beat Bell.

In the title series, Carlberg took the championship by beating Latzko in a best 3 out of 5 game series.

1956 State Tournament Round Robin

	W	L		W	L
1. Joe Latzko	20	1	12. Nick Becky	10	11
2. Irwin Carlberg	19	2	13. Albert Kerr	10	11
3. Alex Clark	18	3	14. Harry Hunter	8	13
4. Carl Lundgren	18	3	15. William Hautmaki	7	14
5. James Ostrander	17	4	16. Joe Fagan	6	15
6. Lester Peary	16	5	17. William Bell	5	16
7. Lee Jacobs	15	6	18. Walt Chamberlain	4	17
8. Joe Kelly	15	6	19. Louis Craft	3	18
9. C. Jozwiak	12	9	20. R. Van Raalte	2	19
10. James Davis	12	9	21. Ralph Krimmel	2	19
11. Clarence Flynn	11	10	22. Jack Schultz	0	21

- - - - - - -

A newspaper clipping, likely from Mt. Pleasant, enclosed in the journal describe the championship series between Carlberg and Latzko and a bit more about the tournament.

- - - - - - -

Latzko Beat by Detroiter
New State Horseshoe Champion

In a blazing three out of five game dual for the state horseshoe pitching title Irwin Carlberg of Grand Rapids beat Joe Latzko of Flint, and former Mt. Pleasant resident, for the state title at the fair. Latzko's mother works at the Phillips Café.

Lee Jacobs, last year's champ, who beat Latzko in the state finals at the Isabella County Fair in 1955, was not in the running this year.

Bill Hautmaki of State Home won the Mt. Pleasant Regional Tournament Friday. In the state tournament, Hautmaki finished eleventh, Bill Bell of Mt. Pleasant twelfth, and Walt Chamberlain of the Indian Reservation, thirteenth.

22 ENTRIES

Twenty-two men entered and took part in the state tournament. They were from every section of Michigan and winners of their own regional tournaments.

To decide the winners, the 22 men played 21 games of horseshoe against every man in the tournament. The first two men who won the most games out of the 21 games were Carlberg and Latzko. They played off for the state title starting at about 6:30 p.m., Saturday.

TIGHT CONTEST

Carlberg won the first two games from Latzko, who had previously won the state title about 15 times. Latzko came back to win the next two games. Carlberg won the third game for the title by pitching 42 ringers out of 52 shoes pitched.

Both men were sharp at tossing ringers. In horseshoe, if both men get two ringers, there is no score. Twenty-eight times in the fourth game, the two men got double ringers and did not score. Mort Neff, TV outdoor sportscaster, arrived about 5:30 p.m., but had to leave before Carlberg had won the title.

34th State Tournament, and Still Counting

T his next chapter's coverage begins with an Ohio tournament Jacobs participated in. The tournament results he clipped from the NHPA *News Digest* was written by Emma Focht, a National Hall of Fame member and wife of another Hall of Famer Paul Focht. The article describes the playoff process of a 100-shoe pitch to eliminate one of the players in a the three-way tie for first place in Class A. This certainly was an unusual circumstance. In those years ties were broken through head-to-head match competition, at least for first place. Even today, ties are broken by ringer percentage, except for first place in the Championship Class; those ties are played off by all players tied. At least the play-off resumed with a best two out of three series.

All three pitchers in that three-way tie were NHPA Hall of Fame members. Dale Carson also should be remembered for being a two-time National AAU champion (1949 and 1950).

- - - - - - -

Dale Carson, Maryland Ringer Artist
Takes Top Honors in Lakeside, Ohio Open

By Emma Focht

The annual Lakeside, Ohio Open Tournament was held on Friday and Saturday, June 28–29, in Lakeside, Ohio. As had been predicted the meet attracted many of the top-flight players of the Mid-West. The tourney was conducted by the Ohio Buckeye State Association and was sanctioned by the National Association.

The courts at Lakeside, near Port Clinton, were much to Dale Carson's liking as he proceeded to defend and before the meet was over, had successfully retained his title for another year. He hails from Baltimore, Maryland. He did not have it too easy inasmuch as he tied with Paul Focht of Dayton, Ohio, and Harold Reno of Sabina, Ohio, at the end of the round-robin play. Each of the three pitched 100 shoes to see which two played for the championship. The final two were Carson and Focht. In the two-out-of-three game match, Carson averaged 80 percent ringers to win while Focht put 78 percent of his shoes on the peg in a valiant to subdue the titleholder. Final standings are as follows:

1957 Lakeside (Ohio) Open

CLASS A

Player City	W	L	R	SP	%
Dale Carson, Baltimore, Md.	7	2	447	588	76.0
Paul Focht, Dayton, Ohio	7	2	460	632	72.7
Harold Reno, Sabina, Ohio	7	2	434	612	70.9
Harrion Maitlen, Berne, Ind.	6	3	498	686	72.6
Ed Sharp, Mulberry, Ind.	6	3	487	672	72.0
Curt Day, Frankfort, Ind.	4	5	397	602	65.9
Harry Sibert, Union, Ohio	3	6	351	558	62.9
John Fulton, Carlisle, Pa.	2	7	447	670	66.7
Graydon McFatridge, Rushville	2	7	348	574	60.6
Leonard Glass, Xenia, Ohio	1	8	232	466	49.7

CLASS B

Player City	W	L	R	SP	%
Alex Clark, Garden City, M.	4	1	164	328	50.0
Joe Kelly, Highland Park, M.	3	2	192	352	54.5
Clarence Flynn, Detroit, M.	2	3	162	3000	54.0
Stan Manker, Martinsville, O.	2	3	178	334	53.2
Harold Wolfe, Cedarville, O.	2	3	146	288	50.6
Carl Lundgren, Detroit, Mich.	2	3	154	322	47.8

CLASS C

Player City	W	L	R	SP	%
Loren Crooks, Fultonham, Ohio	5	0	193	334	57.7
Lee Jacobs, Belleville, Mich.	4	1	153	264	57.9
Lester Peary, Detroit, Mich.	3	2	165	302	54.6
Oris Harshman, Frankfort, Ind.	2	3	143	300	47.6
Carl Cline, Dayton, Ohio	1	4	103	258	39.9
Leo Fouse, Wilmington, Ohio	0	5	117	290	40.3

Player City	W	L	R	SP	%
Sam Blake, Detroit, Mich.	4	1	127	300	42.3
Howard Bryant, Washington, O.	3	2	150	334	44.9
Ray Middleton, Bradentown, Fl.	3	2	123	302	40.7
Denver Ford, Fayette, Ohio	3	2	136	352	38.6
Wm. Phillips, Youngstown, O.	1	4	126	342	36.8
John Miller, Detroit, Mich.	1	4	124	350	35.4

– – – – – – –

Next is a summary of another Mid-West Ringer Round-Up clipped and added to the Jacobs journal. The 1957 event was a highly competitive affair—nine of the twelve players in Class A averaged over 75 percent.

Bill Neilson, the fourth-place finisher in the tournament, averaging 77.5 percent ringers, was the 1938 National AAU junior champion and also teamed up for the National AAU doubles championship that year. In third place was Glenn Anderson, averaging 77.9 percent. Anderson was the nationally rising star who died far too young in an unfortunate car accident in 1958.

– – – – – – –

1957 Midwest Ringer Round-Up

Ed Sharp of Indiana emerged as a champion of champions in the Mid-west "Ringer Round-Up," held at Dorner Park in Frankfort, Indiana, July 6 and 7 over a stellar field of 82 players hailing from eight different states.

The victory was a popular one as it marked the first time the lanky Hoosier ringer artist had stood in the winner's circle after a major tourney, for Ed had five times been runner-up in the Indiana state meet as well as second place in many other events during the past six or seven years. Even so he was forced into a playoff by "Red" Brumfield who defeated Sharp in a similar spot in last year's state tournament.

High winds of gale proportions marred the qualifying hours and created a jam at deadline time, but perfect conditions prevailed during the round-robin play, resulting in a sensational brand of horseshoes in all six classes.

Four players entered the last game of Class A tied for the first place. Curt Day of Indiana, the defending champion who placed fifth, eliminated Glenn Anderson of Illinois in this round with an 84.1% game, while the new champion took care of Bill Neilson of Indiana with an 85.7% effort. Sharp and Neilson had a run of ten consecutive "four deads" in this game and Neilson had 34 straight ringers.

Jim "Pops" Johnson of Kentucky defeated youthful Virgil Taylor in a playoff for Class B after the two had ended in a deadlock. Taylor's uncle, Earl Green of Indianapolis took third in the class and 77 year old W. O. Maxwell of Ohio was fourth.

An unprecedented five-way tie for first place resulted in Class C. Lateness of the hour forced awards to be made on ringer percentage, with Floyd Fowler of Indiana having the edge over Les Young of Illinois, Walt Horner, Marvin Craig and Paul Van Sickle of Indianapolis.

Leroy Clewell in Class D, Milt Tate in Class E and Nelson Vogel in Class F, all of Illinois, were champions, Tate, runner-up in Class A last year, averaged 80.0 percent ringers.

Glen Anderson of Moline, Illinois, led the qualifiers with 391 points and 122 ringers in his 150 shoes.

Tournament prizes amounted to six trophies and $536.00 in cash. Oris Harshman, Nelson Pickering and Tom Moon of the host club, who did such a good job on this year's meet, will be in charge of next year's affair.

CLASS A

Player	W	L	R	SP	%
Ed Sharp, Mulberry, Indiana	9	2	796	1002	79.4
"Red" Brumfield, Markleville, Ind.	9	2	772	984	78.5
Glenn Anderson, Moline, Illinois	8	3	756	970	77.9
Bill Neilson, Dugger, Indiana	8	3	838	1082	77.5
Curtis Day, Frankfort, Indiana	7	4	729	944	77.2
Harrison Maitlen, Berne, Indiana	6	5	779	1026	75.9
Art Dugle, Chicago, Illinois	6	5	634	906	70.0
Paul Focht, Dayton, Ohio	5	6	674	892	75.4
Lowell Edmondson, Danville, Ind.	3	8	600	860	69.8
Arner Lindquist, Morgantown, W.Va.	3	8	562	844	66.6
Truman Standard, Canton, Illinois	1	10	707	960	75.4
Graydon McFatridge, Rushville, Ind.	1	10	677	930	72.8

Sharp defeated Brumfield in first place playoff 50–28, with 76.4 percent ringers.

Jim Johnson, Covington, Kentucky	10	1	498	676	73.7
Virgil Taylor, Greencastle, Ind.	10	1	481	646	74.3
Earl Green, Indianapolis, Indiana	9	2	498	734	67.8
W. O. Maxwell, Hicksville, Ohio	7	4	476	708	67.2
Harold McPhearson, Covington, Ky.	7	4	433	658	65.8
Curt Atwell, Flora, Indiana	6	5	406	631	64.3
Frank Palka, Chicago, Illinois	5	6	441	688	64.1
Carl Lundgren, Detroit, Michigan	4	7	437	752	58.1

- - - - - - -

Milton Tate won the 1957 Class E title. While that is good, it certainly was not as good as being the runner-up in the Championship Class the previous year. Tate was indeed a championship-class pitcher. He was a three-time Illinois state champion: in 1930 (at age 24), 1931, 1933, and 1937. After a twenty-year absence from World Tournament play—he had qualified in 1927 and 1933—he entered the 1953 event. He missed the cut for the Championship Class, but won Class B. Tate went on to qualify six more times and achieve two top-ten finishes during the "golden years" of horseshoe pitching. His best year was 1959, when he placed fifth on a 30–5 record, pitching 78.68 percent ringers. Tate achieved 121 games won during World Tournament play, which puts him in 79th place on the World Tournament All-Time Wins List.

- - - - - - -

My 34th State Tournament
September 7–8, 1957
Riverside Park, Plymouth, Michigan

This was a real successful meet, which drew 33 entries, many of them for the first time. The men were divided into 2 squads and played round robins of 25-point games, with the five highest in each squad to go to the finals. The next five of each squad moved on to Class B.

Squad Standings

SQUAD ONE

Player	City	W	L
1. Alex Clark	Garden City	13	2
2. Clarence Flynn	Detroit	12	3
3. Sam Blake	Detroit	12	3
4. Andy Yorkison	Detroit	11	4
5. Delmar Hallock	Watervliet	10	5
Jim Davis	Battle Creek	9	6
Roy Smith	Muskegon	9	6
Eddie Combs	Fraser	9	6
Irwin Carlberg	Grand Rapids	8	7
Nick Beckey	Detroit	8	7
John Miller	Detroit	8	7
Harry Hunter	Grand Rapids	3	12
Joe Fagan	Detroit	3	12
Harvey Pankow	Plymouth	3	12
Ray Schmidtman	Benton Harbor	2	12
Al Buck	Muskegon	–	–

Note: Carlberg, defending champion did not make the finals!

SQUAD TWO

Player	City	W	L
1. Joe Latzko	Flint	14	2
2. James Ostrander	Lansing	14	2
3. Carl Lundgren	Detroit	13	3
4. Lester Peary	Detroit	12	4
5. Lee Jacobs	Belleville	12	4
Ken Jensen	St. Joseph	11	5
Joe Kelly	Highland Park	11	5
Clarence Jozwiak	Detroit	9	7
Cliff Moylan	Detroit	7	9
Jonas Otto	Ann Arbor	7	9
Henry Zessin	Saginaw	5	11
Jack Schultz	Grand Rapids	5	11
Ralph Krimmel	Battle Creek	4	12
Louis Craft	Kalamazoo	4	12
Alvin Malvitz	Carelton	3	13
R. Van Raalte	Muskegon	2	14
Art Berg	Muskegon	2	14

Note: Moylan failed to appear for the Class "B" finals, so Miller took his place.

Finals

ROUND ONE

Ostrander hit the best game of this round in disposing of Jacobs 51–12, going .711. Delmer Hallock trounced Lundgren 50–21, Yorkison beat Blake, Flynn upset Latzko 50–26 and Clark, the pre-tourney favorite, bested Peary 50–38.

ROUND TWO

Ostrander continued to hit well, going .684 to slaughter Yorkison 50–10. Peary hit .660 to walk over Jacobs 50–11. Jacobs looked bad on these courts with no hard surfaces to stand on. Clark nosed out Hallock 50–49 and Flynn stayed along with him by beating Lundgren 50–30. Latzko beat Blake 50–38 with only .500.

ROUND THREE

Ostrander flopped to .486 and lost to Latzko 50–25 as Joe went .625. Yorkison whipped Jacobs 50–12. Clark grabbed 1st place all alone by downing Flynn 50–34, hillock walloped Peary 50–40 and Lundgren dropped Blake 50–37.

ROUND FOUR

Ostrander hit Lundgren with .743 to win 50–35 and Hallock mowed Jacobs down 50–3 with .690. Flynn defeated Peary 50–43 and Latzko nosed out Yorkison 50–46. Clark beat Blake 50–25. Leaders: Clark 4–0, Ostrander 3–1, Hallock 3–1, Latzko 3–1, Flynn 3–1.

ROUND FIVE

Clark stowed away Ostrander 50–36, as Hallock nosed out Flynn 50–44. Latzko stayed in the running, beating a hard-trying Jacobs 50–47. Yorkison beat Lundgren 50–22 and Peary beat Blake. Leaders: Clark 5–0, Latzko 4–1, Hallock 4–1.

ROUND SIX

Clark quickly went past Yorkison 50–26, with .704. Latzko got by a battling Lundgren 50–25, hitting 63 out of 86 for .732 to Charlie's .639. Hallock stowed Blake away 50–23 and as Ostrander lost a hot fight to Peary 50–47, it became apparent that the title lay among Clark, Hallock and Latzko. Flynn racked up Jacobs 50–10.

ROUND SEVEN

Clark downed Latzko 50–42 with a late rally, but Ostrander upset Hallock 50–39. Jacobs took another shellacking from Lundgren 50–15. Blake beat Flynn 50–40 and Yorkison edged out Peary 50–44.

ROUND EIGHT

Jacobs was high man in this round, winning his only game of the day. Jacobs hit 28 out of 42 to beat Blake 50–13 with .667. Clark snowed Lundgren 50–19 and Hallock downed Yorkison 50–35. Latzko kept his hopes alive by beating Peary 50–46 after Peary led 46–37. Flynn overwhelmed Ostrander 50–9.

ROUND NINE

With Clark already "in" and remaining "in" by walloping Jacobs 50–32, the main interest was in the Latzko–Hallock game. The game was tied at 22–22 and then Latzko broke down and Hallock galloped away to win 50–28. Lundgren hit .700 to beat Peary 50–26, Flynn beat Yorkison 50–38 and Ostrander beat Blake 50–35. The finals standings:

Player	W	L	Pts	R	DR	SP	Pct
Clark	9	0	450	357	110	582	.613
Hallock	7	2	438	349	107	564	.618
Latzko	6	3	396	393	107	670	.585
Flynn	6	3	418	336	96	576	.583
Ostrander	5	4	367	335	93	548	.605
Yorkison	4	5	355	312	89	546	.571
Peary	3	6	387	366	102	634	.577
Lundgren	3	6	302	298	88	546	.545
Blake	1	8	281	252	59	538	.468
Jacobs	1	8	192	189	44	436	.433

Championship Series

The poorest series ever played found Clark blowing up entirely as he lost the first game to Hallock 50–32. Hallock pitched only .516 to Clark's .406!

The second game was 34–31 for Hallock and he hit 13 out of the last 14 to win 50–34, with 49 out of 72 for .680 to Clark's .597.

Title Series

Hallock	2	0	100	82	24	136	.602
Clark	0	2	66	69	16	136	.507

Class B Finals

(No score sheets were kept)

Player	W	L	Player	W	L
Smith	8	1	Jozwiak	4	5
Davis	7	2	Beckey	4	5
Carlberg	6	3	Otto	3	6
Jensen	6	3	Miller	1	8
Kelly	5	4	Combs	1	8

Class B Title Series

Davis defeated Smith two straight games.

35th State Tournament

A couple of informal meets were held at Plymouth in one of which I ran a bad second and the other a good third.

- - - - - - -

At Lakeside, Ohio, on June 28, I qualified and made Class C and ran a hopeless last, lost all five games, averaging only .451.

At Frankfort, Indiana, didn't get to play at all.

On July 26–27, at Plymouth, was held the Eastern Michigan Open. This meet was my idea to try out a new system for running the qualifying round of a meet by using a device of chess tournaments called the "Swiss System." In this, all players start even and players are drawn in the first round and then winners are drawn against winners, etc. until all players have played seven games. Then the highest games-won number goes to the finals with ties decided by the so-called chess "median system." In this tournament at Plymouth, 17 players started.

Alex Clark and Ken Jensen finished with 6–1 each, Clark losing to Latzko and Jensen losing to Clark. Lundgren, Latzko and Smith came in 5–2; Flynn, Kelly and Kerr were 4–3. This left Carlberg, Beckey, Schmidtman, Jozwiak, Coutre and Jacobs tied for the last two places and by the "median system," Carlberg and Jozwiak went to the Class A finals.

Results of the Finals

Class A	W	L		Class B	W	L
1. Alex Clark	9	0		1. Lee H. Jacobs	7	0
2. Ken Jensen	7	2		2. Nick Beckey	6	1
3. Carl Lundgren	6	3		3. Lee J. Jacobs	4	3
4. Irwin Carlberg	6	3		4. R. Schmidtman	4	3
5. Clarence Flynn	6	3		5. Jonas Otto	3	4
6. Roy Smith	4	5		6. R. Van Raalte	3	4
7. Joe Latzko	3	6		7. D. Larrick	1	6
8. Joe Kelly	2	7		8. E. Larrick	0	7
9. Albert Kerr	1	8				
10. Clarence Jozwiak	1	8				

The Detroit Open is set for Plymouth on August 16–17 and the State Tournament will be held at Kiwanis Park in St. Joseph, August 30–31 and September 1.

1958 Detroit District Open

August 16th – Round Robin Standings

Player	W	L		Player	W	L
1. Alex Clark	13	0		8. Lester Peary	6	7
2. Carl Lundgren	11	1		9. Samuel Blake	5	7
3. Joe Kelly	9	4		10. Lee H. Jacobs	4	7
4. Joe Latzko	8	4		11. Nick Beckey	4	9
Andrew Yorkison	8	4		12. Clarence Joziak	4	9
6. Clarence Flynn	7	5		13. Joe Fagan	1	12
7. James Davis	6	6		14. Bernard Sheridan	0	12

FINAL ROUND ROBIN

Player	W	L		Player	W	L
1. Clark	9	1		Beckey	5	5
2. Lundgren	8	2		8. Peary	4	6
Flynn	8	2		9. Jacobs	2	8
4. Kelly	7	3		Blake	2	8
5. Davis	5	5		11. Sheridan	0	10
Yorkison	5	5				

And so on to St. Joe's!

My 35th State Tournament
St. Joseph, Michigan
August 30, 31 – September 1, 1958

All contestants except defending champion Delmar Hallock qualified by 5 games, 50-shoe count-all. Twenty-nine entries. The scores:

Name	City	Points
1. Delmar Hallock	Benton Harbor	D.C.
2. Ken Jensen	St. Joseph	565
3. Carl Lundgren	Detroit	548
4. Alex Clark	Garden City	544
5. Irwin Carlberg	Grand Rapids	500
6. Joe Kelly	Highland Park	496
7. Roy Smith	Muskegon	496
8. Clarence Flynn	Detroit	477
9. Jim Davis	Battle Creek	476
10. Lester Peary	Detroit	467
11. Nick Beckey	St. Clair Shores	457
12. Andrew Yorkison	Detroit	444
13. Roy Bisnett	Decatur	434
14. Edward Combs	Fraser	430
15. Lee H. Jacobs	Belleville	425
16. Norb Nelson	Hartford	393

The top 16 scores qualified for the finals. They were split into two squads for the finals round robin. The remainder of the qualifiers all going to Class B:

Name	City	Points
17. Jonas Otto	Ann Arbor	378
18. Claude West	Sturgis	362
19. Albert Kerr	Lowell	355
20. Vern Fuller	Battle Creek	340
21. Howard Jones	St Joseph	337
22. Richard VanRaalte	Muskegon	329
23. Ray Schmidtman	Benton Harbor	305
24. Henry Zessin	Saginaw	300
25. Harry Parmer	Muskegon	294
26. Louis Craft	Kalamazoo	293
27. Mal Broadhurst	St. Joseph	279
28. Delmar Terhune	Colon	249
29. Herbert Klemm	Stevensville	145

On August 31st each Class A squad played a round robin and the top four from each squad moved into the final eight for a round robin on September 1st.

FINALS ROUND ONE

Winner	P	R	Pct	Sp	Opp	P	R	Pct
Hallock	50	29	.764	38	Yorkison	4	13	.342
Clark	50	35	.673	52	Smith	16	23	.420
Flynn	50	28	.583	48	Kelly	28	22	.459
Jensen	50	30	.577	52	Lundgren	15	19	.365

ROUND TWO

Winner	P	R	Pct	Sp	Opp	P	R	Pct
Jensen	50	47	.783	60	Smith	13	37	.617
Flynn	50	34	.709	48	Yorkison	21	26	.542
Clark	50	64	.667	96	Kelly	44	60	.625
Lundgren	50	49	.645	76	Hallock	39	47	.618

ROUND THREE

Winner	P	R	Pct	Sp	Opp	P	R	Pct
Jensen	50	36	.783	46	Kelly	6	23	.500
Hallock	50	43	.694	62	Smith	25	36	.581
Flynn	50	49	.612	80	Lundgren	47	49	.612
Clark	50	40	.612	66	Yorkison	32	33	.500

ROUND FOUR

Winner	P	R	Pct	Sp	Opp	P	R	Pct
Jensen	50	27	.844	32	Yorkison	7	12	.375
Clark	50	54	.729	74	Lundgren	23	46	.622
Hallock	50	48	.727	66	Kelly	19	39	.591
Flynn	50	43	.717	60	Smith	22	34	.566

ROUND FIVE

Winner	P	R	Pct	Sp	Opp	P	R	Pct
Flynn	50	48	.686	70	Hallock	33	42	.600
Jensen	50	34	.654	52	Clark	45	32	.615
Kelly	50	48	.648	74	Yorkison	47	48	.648
Lundgren	50	28	.482	58	Smith	46	28	.482

ROUND SIX

Winner	P	R	Pct	Sp	Opp	P	R	Pct
Clark	50	59	.702	84	Flynn	28	52	.619
Smith	50	38	.679	56	Kelly	27	29	.482
Jensen	50	46	.639	72	Hallock	35	41	.569
Lundgren	50	31	.430	72	Yorkison	49	32	.445

Winner	P	R	Pct	Sp	Opp	P	R	Pct
Clark	50	51	.750	68	Hallock	28	43	.632
Jensen	50	55	.671	82	Flynn	39	52	.634
Kelly	50	46	.657	70	Lundgren	41	42	.600
Yorkison	50	31	.516	60	Smith	35	24	.400

Final Standings

Player	W	L	Pts	R	DR	SP	Pct
1. Jensen	7	0	350	275	98	396	.694
2. Clark	6	1	345	335	112	492	.679
3. Flynn	5	2	317	306	104	472	.626
4. Hallock	3	4	335	293	94	452	.648
5. Lundgren	3	4	276	264	77	482	.547
6. Kelly	2	5	224	267	88	456	.585
7. Smith	1	6	207	220	63	408	.533
8. Yorkison	1	6	210	195	55	390	.500

1958 Championship Playoff
Best of Five Series

Winner	P	R	Pct	Sp	Opp	P	R	Pct
Jensen	50	27	.562	48	Clark	33	21	.437
Jensen	50	41	.706	58	Clark	17	28	.500
Jensen	50	57	.770	74	Clark	25	50	.676
3 games won			.710					.568

In Class B, Jones placed first in the 12-game round robin on a 11–1 record, but second-place Kerr won the playoff in two straight games, 50–30 and 50–28, averaging .537.

The banquet was held at the Benton Harbor Moose Club and the meeting followed. Officers elected were: President, Joe Kelly; 1st Vice President, Norb Nelson; 2nd Vice President, Roy Smith; 3rd Vice President, Henry Zessin and Secretary-Treasurer, Lee H. Jacobs.

– – – – – – –

This newspaper clipping tacked in the journal, offers a bit more infromation about 1958 Michigan state tournament.

- - - - - - -

Jensen Wins State Horseshoe Title

Ken Jensen, St. Joseph postman, yesterday won the Wolverine State Horseshoe Class A tournament staged at Kiwanis Park by defeating Alex Clark of Garden City.

Jensen scored over Clark 50–33, 51–17, and 50–25. In the first game, Jensen made 83 per cent ringers.

On Saturday, Jensen was high point man in a count-all, five-match preliminary round for position in the Class A or Class B bracket.

In a round robin on Saturday, with seven other players, Jensen's only defeat came at the hands of Joe Kelley of Highland Park, the association president. He was undefeated in Monday's play.

Jensen's victory kept the state championship in St. Joseph. The title last year was won by Delmar Hallock.

The final Class A standings:

	W	L		W	L
Jensen	10	0	Lundgren	3	4
Clark	6	4	Kelley	2	5
Flynn	5	2	Roy Smith	1	6
Hallock	3	4	Jorgenson	1	6

In Class B, Albert Kerr of Detroit and Howard Jones of Benton Harbor tied for the title in regular play. Kerr then defeated Jones two out three games for the championship.

The tournament was sponsored by Lou Kerlikowske of St. Joseph, the St. Joseph Recreation Department, and the St. Joseph Horseshoe League.

36th State Tournament

- -

1959 State Tournament
Kiwanis Park – St. Joseph, Michigan
Saturday, Sunday and Labor Day

Round Robin Standings

Red Division	W	L	Blue Division	W	L
Carlberg	15	0	Hallock	14	1
Jensen	14	1	Latzko	14	1
Flynn	13	2	Lundgren	12	3
Ostrander	10	5	Yorkison	12	3
Kelly	10	5	Clark	11	4
Smith	10	5	Peary	10	5
Davis	10	5	Beckey	8	7
Jones	7	8	Kerr	8	7
Craft	7	8	Nelson	7	8
Parmer	6	9	Broker	5	10
Jacobs	5	10	Yerby	5	10
Haverly	5	10	Van Raalte	4	11
Otto	4	11	West	3	12
Stough	3	12	Klemm	3	12
Krimmel	2	13	Fuller	2	13
Terhume	0	15	Mason	1	14

The top five in each squad qualified for the finals. To break the 3-way tie for 5th place in the Red Division; Davis dropped out, so Kelly beat both Ostrander and Smith, and Ostrander beat Smith to get in finals.

After the banquet, at the meeting, Jacobs came to the end of a 25-year reign as Secretary-Treasurer when Carlberg was elected.

In the Class B, I beat Krimmel and then lost to Beckey.

Class B was won by Peary who beat Smith in the final match.

- - - - - - -

The following tournament summary was drafted by new secretary for the Michigan association, Irwin Carlberg, and distributed to the membership. A copy was inserted in Jacobs's journal.

- - - - - - -

Results of the 1959
Michigan Horseshoe Championships
Labor Day Weekend – St. Joseph

Championship Class (Finals – 10-man Round Robin)

Name	City	W	L	%	Point System
Ken Jensen	St. Joseph	8	1	69.3	13.10
Irwin Carlberg	Grand Rapids	8	1	68.4	11.33
Joe Latzko	Flint	7	2	67.8	11.02
Delmar Hallock	St. Joseph	5	4	62.7	10.03
Clarence Flynn	Detroit	5	4	62.6	8.28
Alex Clark	Detroit	4	5	57.1	7.07
Joe Kelly	Detroit	3	6	58.1	7.40
Carl Lundgren	Detroit	3	6	55.0	7.06
James Ostrander	Lansing	1	8	58.9	7.23
Andy Yorkison	Detroit	1	8	54.2	6.07

Ken Jensen retained his State Championship by winning 3 out of 4 games from Irwin Carlberg. Jensen averaged 72.1% ringers in the playoff series.

Point system above awards 1 point won [per] win and difference between your opponent and 50 points. (For example—Flynn defeated Ostrander 50–42. Flynn scores 1.08 points while Ostrander score .42 points.)

Class B consisted of the 22 players not qualifying for Class A. Les Peary, Detroit, won Class B beating Roy Smith in a best 2-out-of-3 game series.

TOURNAMENT FACTS:

Shortest Game – Latzko vs. Lundgren, 30 shoes pitched
Longest Game – Flynn vs. Ostrander, 100 shoes pitched
Highest Ringer % (One Game) – Joe Latzko, 83.3%
Most Consecutive Ringers – 16 by Joe Latzko

NEWLY ELECTED OFFICERS FOR THE NEXT THREE YEARS:

President – Delmar Hallock, St. Joseph
1st Vice President – Alex Clark, Detroit
2nd Vice President – Roy Smith, Muskegon
3rd Vice President – Al Kerr, Lowell
Secretary – Irwin Carlberg, Grand Rapids

- - - - - - -

Jacobs offers no comment on what purpose the point system he describes is supposed to serve. I can't decipher what that was all about, but it's interesting and evidently temporary.

An Era Concluded

L ee Jacobs didn't play this year and ended his string of State Tournaments. Lee Jacobs Jr. played in the state meet and didn't do anything much.

- - - - - - -

That single sentence is all Lee Jacobs wrote to introduce 1960. Jacobs archived a copy of Irwin Carlberg's report on the 1960 state tournament was inserted in the journal...

- - - - - - -

Michigan State 1960 Horseshoe Championship

Championship Class

		W	L
Alex Clark	Detroit	8	0
Irwin Carlberg	Grand Rapids	8	1
Ralph Bacon	Grand Rapids	7	3
Clarence Flynn	Detroit	6	3
Ken Jensen	St. Joseph	5	2
Roy Smith	Muskegon	5	2
Joe Latzko	Flint	4	3
Carl Lundgren	Detroit	4	3

Class A Consolation Playoff

Group 1	W	L	%	Group 2	W	L	%
Clarence Flynn	4	0	67.8	Ralph Bacon	4	0	62.9
James Davis	3	1	57.6	Joe Kelly	3	1	55.6
Roy Smith	2	2	53.4	Carl Lundgren	2	2	62.7
Andy Yorkison	1	3	53.0	Les Peary	1	3	46.7

Clarence Flynn defeated Ralph Bacon 50–36 to win Class A with 66.6% to 57.6% for Bacon.

Class C-1	W	L	%	Class C-2	W	L	%
Alvin Malvitz	3	0	47.9	Bob Hanna	4	1	35.8
Ralph Krimmel	2	1	37.0	Jack Adams	3	2	40.8
Clar. Haverly	1	2	36.3	Otis Saeter	3	2	30.7
Henry Zessin	0	3	32.6	Nick Beckey	3	2	31.0
Jonas Otto	2	3	34.9				
Lee Jacobs Jr.	0	5	32.9				

In Class C, Alvin Malvitz defeated Bob Hanna 50–16 with 52.2% ringers.

Junior Boys Divisions – Jim Ostrander of Lansing, defeated Tommie Smith of Muskegon, 50–49 and 50–28.

Class B	W	L	%	Class D	W	L	%
G. Van Gelder	4	0	47.3	Henry Freeman	5	0	45.9
Floyd Bartley	3	1	49.9	Louis Craft	4	1	43.4
Al Kerr	2	2	38.5	Vern Fuller	3	2	40.2
C. Jazwick	1	3	33.6	Milton Greenman	2	3	29.6
Harry Parmer	0	4	35.9	John Barber	1	4	31.4
Jim Ostrander	0	5	29.4				

- - - - - - -

The Championship Class win/loss numbers are confusing. The number of wins should equal the number of losses, but they don't in this report. No explanation is provided of how the round robin or the finals were conducted.

The Consolation Class seems to be something very different and rather innovative, but again there is explanation of the seeding. It's likely that after the finals round robin and the two top players were determined for the championship playoff series, the remaining players split into the two groups for additional play. Latzko and Ken Jensen did not participate, but that could simply have been their choice to decline to play any further.

This tournament summary represents the final entry in the Lee Rose journals. Jacobs did pitch some after 1960, but not much and without the skill level and success of his younger years. Also, the relative sparseness of his entries in recent years suggests that his interest in maintaining the journals had faded.

There is some evidence that Lee Jacobs was still pitching competitively in the 1970s. The the Michigan Horseshoer Pitchers Association Hall of Fame has given Jacobs credit for participating in 59 Michigan state tournaments. This confirms that the pitching career for Lee Jacobs exceeded 60 years.

CONCLUSION

----

*I*ncredible is the first word that comes to mind when trying to describe the experience of actually seeing and reading through the Lee Rose journals. No other horseshoe pitcher or promoter kept a comparable volume of tournament records with such intense detail for each event. His record keeping began in 1920, one year before the NHPA was formed and he maintained his journals for four decades—in perfect handwriting. These original journals are now housed in a display maintained by the Michigan State Horseshoe Pitchers Association Hall of Fame.

The journals capture the highlights of Lee Rose's career in detail. We almost feel as if we were actually there to witness his National AAU championship win in 1944, or the Michigan state championship in 1955; or his great performance in the 1940 World Tournament. Not every event he wrote about was a personal highlight for Lee, but his complete set of journals offer a rare glimpse into pivotal decades of our sport's history.

Few NHPA members had the total involvement that Lee Jacobs had during his career. And few excelled in as many aspects of the sport. Lee Rose was a great pitcher—a championship-class pitcher. His three state championships each took place in a different decade and he participated in at least 36 Michigan state tournaments, according to the documentation in this journals. In the brief bio posted by his name on the Michigan Horseshoe Pitchers Association Hall of Fame website, Jacobs is given credit for participating in 59 Michigan state tournaments.

Lee excelled in promotion of the sport and in a very broad sense. His efforts were largely responsible for Michigan's vast history of state tournaments back in the 1920s, 1930s, 1940s, and 1950s. He promoted league and team play on a large scale during an era in which travel wasn't as easy as today—and when league play wasn't a popular notion among most NHPA leaders. Lee Rose served as a state officer for twenty-five consecutive years and was even elected a national officer. During the time he served as NHPA's secretary-treasurer, he wrote *The Horseshoe Compendium*. Written in 1940, the book is now classified as a precious document of the NHPA and still serves as the sport's historic resource. Jacobs also owned a horseshoe-manufacturing business that he bought in 1946 from fellow competitor and buddy Leo Lattore. He operated that business well into the 1970s. As if that isn't enough, he also sang the National Anthem a cappella for some World Tournaments and other events. He was an amazing character of the sport.

For all of his accomplishments and efforts, Lee (Rose) Jacobs was inducted to the NHPA Hall of Fame in 1984. He was also appreciated by pitchers in his home state of Michigan and was a charter inductee to the state association's Hall of Fame in 1967. Fittingly, his fellow charter inductees were Joe Latzko, Bobby Hitt, Carl Lundgren, and Jonas Otto—his long-time colleagues and competitors.

So how do we thank Lee Rose for the journey his journals provide? How do we express our gratitude for the generous gift he gave us by recording and sharing his career? Simple: We do what he did. Love and be involved in the sport of horseshoe pitching, give time and service to promote the sport's longevity, and stay involved. Be part of the effort to hand off the sport to future generations, in better shape than when we received it.

PREFACE

Horseshoe Compendium
as Written in 1940 by
NHPA Secretary Lee Rose

HORSESHOE
COMPENDIUM

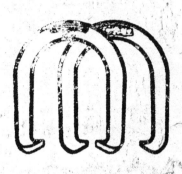

PUBLISHED BY

THE NATIONAL HORSESHOE PITCHERS'
ASSOCIATION

PRICE 50 CENTS

PREFACE

When the National Horseshoe Pitchers' Association of America was first incorporated, one of the ideas in mind for the betterment and advancement of the game of horseshoe pitching was the yearly publication of a book devoted exclusively to the sport. While the Association was formed in 1921, there was no book published until 1928, when the National Secretary, Mr. D. D. Cottrell, compiled and published a book for the National Association called "Horseshoe Pitching—How To Play the Game." This book was re-edited and re-published in 1929. Since that time, however, no book containing the official stamp of the National Association has appeared on the market.

Believing the time has come for the issuing of another book containing information needed by both pitcher and promoter alike, your present National Secretary has taken it upon himself to gather and compile such material as deemed necessary for the productions of a small but complete volume which, it is hoped, will satisfy those seeking horseshoe knowledge, and contain the answers to numerous queries which come in to the Secretary's office. We believe each article is self-explanatory.

The pitchers of some states seemingly overlooked by this book may feel slightly discriminated against, but it must be stated here that every state having a charter or a legal representative, and even many other states were asked to contribute articles or facts about horseshoe pitching in their states, and if your state is not represented it is due to the fact that no official news was received, and rather than take the risk of publishing statements for which no proof was at hand, we decided to print only those sent in.

We wish to thank Claude E. Hart, of New Jersey; Gaylord Peterson, of Illinois; L. D. Lane, of Connecticut; Alvin Dahlene, of Kansas; Harry Woodfield, of Washington, D. C.; A. L. McNeil, of Wyoming; W. A. Banta, of

Indiana; Raymond E. Adams, of Maine; S. S. Randell, of Massachusetts; L. O. Rigney, of South Dakota; Fred Butler, of Vermont, and Leland Mortenson, of Iowa, for contributing valuable articles for use in this book.

It is the earnest hope of this Association that a book devoted to the game shall be published in the spring of each year, and that each edition will contain complete information concerning the happenings of the year before. In other words, just as the "Horseshoe World" is the monthly magazine of horseshoe pitchers, so this will become the year-book of the sport. Your Secretary would like comment on this book; whether it pleased you, or whether it did not, and if not, why.

In closing, let me urge each and every one to join the National Association, subscribe to the "Horseshoe World," use only sanctioned horseshoes, and spread the gospel of this grandest of all sports wheresoe'er you may go.

Signed

LEE ROSE, National Sec.-Treas.

5228 Shaw Ave., Detroit, Mich.

❧ ❧ ❧

PUBLISHED BY

NATIONAL HORSESHOE PITCHERS ASSOCIATION

5228 Shaw Ave.

DETROIT, MICHIGAN

1-9-4-0

PRICE 50 CENTS

Kansas City, Kansas, and Kansas City, Missouri, had become quite a center of the sport and nearly every hamlet or village within a hundred or more miles had its local champion.

Horseshoe pitching contests for teams representing different cities were held on clay courts in Convention Hall, Kansas City, Mo., in 1900, and again at Independence, Mo., in the summer of 1902. Other similar contests were held at different times and places.

In 1905 an Ottawa, Kansas, team of four men challenged any other four-man team to play for a cash prize of $100. A team, consisting of W. Fox, W. M. Baldwin, Robert Pierce and A. B. Argenbright, of Kansas City, Mo., accepted the challenge. The Ottawa team was Mr. Hollingsworth, Judge Robert Harrison, Seth Cope and another man whose name the writer could not learn. Kansas City team had shoes made out of rasps.

The contest was held on pegs two inches high above the level ground and 38½ feet apart. Players were required to stand back of the peg with toe against it.

Ringer counted 3 points, leaner 2 points and any shoe within 6 inches of peg one point.

The men of the Ottawa team pitched first. One was was placed at each peg and each pitched 80 shoes. Then the other two men in the Ottawa team pitched the same way. The four men made a total of 444 points. Then the four men of the Kansas City, Mo., team each pitched 80 shoes in the same way and scored a total of 447 points. The high man of the Kansas City team was Argenbright, who made 144 points, beating Hollingsworth, the high man of the Ottawa team by three points. These three points were accounted for by the last shoe when Argenbright pitched a ringer, scoring three points and winning the meet for Kansas City when the score stood at 444 points for each team until the last shoe was thrown.

About 1907, Manhattan (Kansas) College offered a prize for the best two men teams and also for the best individual pitcher. Argenbright and Pierce won first prize for team pitching and Frank Jackson who has been World's Champion so many years and, who then lived at Blue Mound, Kansas, won the prize for best individual pitcher. Each team played every other team one 21-point game, and each individual pitcher played every other one 21-point game.

According to the writer's best information the first horseshoe pitching tournament in which competition was open to the world was held the summer of 1909 in Bronson, Kansas, and Frank Jackson, the winner, was awarded a World's Championship belt with horseshoes attached to it. Mr. Jackson had never heard of being able to hold a shoe so it would open toward the peg at this time but had been practicing to find some way by holding his shoe with his finger around the heel calk so he could pitch ringers. The games were played on dirt courts on stakes 2 inches high above the level ground and 38½ feet apart. Jackson had acquired the skill of pitching a ringer over the stake and laying his second shoe on top of the stake time after time so his opponent couldn't keep his ringer on. Each man drew a number in this tournament and No. 1 played No. 2, No. 3 played No. 4 and so continued until every man had played. Then numbers were drawn again by the winners, and play continued in the same way until the last winner was declared the World's Champion.

Two or three years later the height of the stake was raised to 6 inches; ringers counted 5 points; leaner or hubber counted 3 points and closest shoe regardless of distance counted one point. Top ringer received the count of all ringers that were on the peg under it, which means two ringers 10 points, three ringers 15 points, all counted for the man whose ringer was on top. Games were still 21 points. There was no regulation as to weight or size of shoe. One pitcher had a shoe in which the curve on one side was four inches more than on the other side. At a Topeka tournament, Jackson used a pair of shoes he had made by a blacksmith, who bent the calks so the shoe would slide better in the sand and help him to slide ringers on the peg. Tournaments were held in Kansas City, Missouri, or Kansas nearly every year and Jackson successfully

[4]

defended his title of World's Champion each time. The writer has not been able to find any records of these tournaments held before the one in Heathwood Park, Kansas City, Kansas, Oct. 23 and 24, 1915, the record of which is published elsewhere in this book.

Because there was no uniformity in the rules of the game as played in different localities, the best and oldest horseshoe pitchers from different parts of Missouri and Kansas got together in 1913 and agreed to adopt a uniform set of rules. After many games were played and each particular difference in each rule had been tested and tried out a committee formally adopted what they believed to be the best. Then the question was asked by what authority these rules were adopted and were to govern the game.

The first ruling body of the horseshoe pitching game of which we find any record was organized in the court room of the First District Court, Kansas City, Kansas, May 16, 1914. A constitution, by-laws and rules were adopted and officers elected. The name chosen was The Grand League of the American Horseshoe Pitchers' Association. The Association granted charters to local leagues in many states and their rules were accepted as standard in governing all regular horseshoe pitching tournaments. They established the rule that like values always cancel like. They raised the peg to 8 inches which met with approval of most pitchers. They established the weight of shoes so that in the 1915 Annual Tournament no shoe was used that weighed less than 2 pounds or more than 2 pounds 3 ounces. They kept the rule that leaners counted 3 points, ringers 5 points and no shoe more than 6 inches from the peg would count. Pitchers' box was 3 feet each side of the peg and 6 feet back. Pitcher could stand anywhere in the box. Stakes were 38½ feet apare. They published a book called the "Horseshoe Guide" containing playing rules, report of annual convention and officers and annual tournament and other contests.

In 1907 the winter visitors to St. Petersburg, Florida began to amuse themselves by pitching horseshoes in the sand on a lot next to the Poinsettia Hotel on Central avenue. There were two courts for horseshoe pitching and two courts for quoits. The pegs used on the horseshoe courts were 35 feet apart and 3 inches high above the level ground. Game was 21 points, ringers counting 3 point. First part of the winter season of 1909 and 1910 the courts were moved to the corner of Third street and Second avenue North where the Park Cafeteria now stands and the latter part of the season to the vacant lot next to the Allison Hotel. No pitcher had up to that time heard of so controlling the delivery of a shoe so it would fall open toward the peg.

In the winter of 1909 on the lot side of the Allison Hotel, Dr. F. M. Robinson, Poughkeepsie, N. Y., and O. T. Battles, Chardon, Ohio, as partners were playing a game with Frank Elliott, Rochester, N. Y., and another man as partners pitching on courts where sometimes all four shoes would bury themselves so deep in the sand that they would all be covered out of sight. While the game was in progress Battles, who stood side of Elliott, while digging out of the sand the shoes Dr. Robinson had pitched spoke up with the ardor of a man that has just made a new discovery and said: "Doc, your shoes all come fork to." This had not been previously noticed even by the doctor himself. The other pitchers then began to question the doctor to find out how he did it, but he didn't know, only that it came natural to him to release his shoe so that it fell open toward the peg with a one and three-quarter turn. The doctor held his shoe with his first finger around the heel calk as all other players did at that time.

From that time the other players began to practice holding their shoes on the side with the opening toward them and from them and by most every conceivable way in order to try to control the shoe so it would fall open toward the peg for they said if the doctor's shoe naturally fell open toward the peg they could acquire the skill necessary to control the delivery of a shoe so it would fall open.

As far as the writer has been able to learn this is the beginning of trying to control the open shoe in pitching which art is now known in a more or less degree by every good pitcher.

In the fall of 1910 the horseshoe courts were moved to Williams Park. The Sunshine Pleasure club had been organized in 1909, having among its members the devotees of horseshoe pitching, roque, checkers, and dominoes. All the members, representing the other games, except horseshoe pitching have now withdrawn and formed other clubs representative of each sport. The Sunshine Pleasure club is believed to be the the largest and oldest horseshoe pitching club in existence. It has 13 clay courts with concrete for the pitchers' box, except in the clay area and the space between the pegs paved. It also has about 25 sandy loam courts. All but two of the National Tournaments held in the south have been played on their courts. The first officers were Samuel Clement, of Pennsylvania, president, who is now 88 years old and may be found pitching quoits practically every day. E. J. Betts, of Ohio, vice president; C. M. Hite, of Ohio, treasurer, and O. T. Battles, of Ohio, secretary.

Through the efforts of the members of the Sunshine Pleasure club on Feb. 26, 1919, the National League of Horseshoe and Quoit Pitchers was organized at the National Tournament in St. Petersburg with representatives from 29 different states. Harry G. Haynes, Akron, Ohio, and Dr. E. C. Beach, St. Petersburg, Fla., were especially active in perfecting its organization which was given a charter under the laws of the State of Ohio, June 27, 1921.

On May 10, 1921, The National Horseshoe Pitchers Association of the United States was also incorporated under the laws of the State of Ohio with headquarters at Akron, Ohio. A year or two later these two national organizations were consolidated under the name of the latter.

At the National Convention at Lake Worth, Florida, February 26, 1925, the name was changed to The National Horseshoe Pitchers association of America, which is now the only governing body of the sport in this country.

The present rules of the game and all the records that are available of the National Tournaments that have been held are printed elsewhere in this book. The interest in the sport is rapidly growing and clubs are being formed in many localities which are either affiliating directly with the National Association or forming State Associations which are affiliating with the National. It is estimated that there are some two million horseshoe pitchers in this country. The official organ of the National Association is the Horseshoe World, published monthly by R. B. Howard, London, Ohio, at $1.00 per year and contains a mass of matter interesting to every lover of the sport and should be taken by every horseshoe fan.

CONSTITUTION AND BY-LAWS
of the
NATIONAL HORSESHOE PITCHERS ASSOCIATION
OF AMERICA
(Incorporated under the Laws of Ohio,)
As Revised September, 1939
Incorporated under the laws of Ohio as revised September, 1939

PREAMBLE

"Knowing the art of horseshoe pitching affords a healthy recreation and a competitive sport suitable to all persons, young and aged, male and female, at a cost comparable to other games, and with a desire to standardize its laws authorize and conduct tournaments of National scope and encourage the promotion of leagues and associations throughout the nation, we do establish this Constitution and By-Laws for the following association hereinafter called THE NATIONAL HORSESHOE PITCHERS ASSOCIATION OF AMERICA.

ARTICLE I.

Section 1. The name of this association shall be THE NATIONAL HORSE-SHOE PITCHERS ASSOCIATION OF AMERICA.

Article II. Legislative

Section 1. All legislative powers herein granted shall be vested in an assembly of delegates to be appointed, elected or selected by the members of this association that are duly chartered under this body and such other delegates as are provided for in Article II, Section 2.

Sec. 2. When there is a State Association in good standing, it shall be entitled to five (5) delegates. When a State is not affiliated with the National Association, next preference in furnishing delegates will be conceded to affiliated State clubs. Class A clubs shall be entitled to two (2) delegates. Class B clubs shall be entitled to one (1) delegate. A completion of the State's allowance may be made from individual memberships. If the State's delegation cannot agree on its membership, the President of the Association shall have power to act. Five (5) votes is all that any State can have on a voting subject. Voting may be by ballot, rising vote or ayes and nays. Proxies not allowed, nor shall substitution be made for any delegate representing a State as an individual. State associations or clubs may substitute a member in good standing if a vacancy in the delegates arises. A delegate must be in person to have voting power.

Sec. 3. The officers of this Association shall consist of a President, First Vice President, Second Vice President, Third Vice President, and a Secretary-Treasurer, who shall constitute the Board of Directors and have voting power as National officials and not as State delegates. The President may add as many honorary vice presidents as he may deem advisable.

Sec. 4. The officials, consisting of the President, First, Second and Third Vice Presidents, and Secretary-Treasurer, shall be the Executive Committee, and be in charge of the affairs of this association, and shall be empowered to transact such business in the interest of the game and the Association as deemed advisable, and not contrary to the Constitution and By-Laws and Rules.

Sec. 5. The officials shall be elected at the first convention after the first day of January, 1925, for a term of two (2) years and every two (2) years thereafter. They shall take office immediately at the close of the meeting when elected. The officers may call a meeting in convention at any time it is deemed advisable.

By unanimous vote of the Convention at Duluth, Minn., August 15, 1927, the first sentence of Section 5, Article II, was changed to read as follows:
The officials shall be elected at the first convention after the first day of January, 1929, to hold office until the next convention and then for a term of one and one-half years.

Sec. 6. Fifteen (15) delegates shall constitute a quorum and have authority to transact the business of the Association when seated in convention.

Sec. 7. Any member of this Association shall be eligible to hold office. Delegates to National Conventions, representing State Associations or State Clubs, must present certificate of election or appointment signed by the President of the organization he or she is delegated to represent.

Sec. 8. In the event of the death or resignation of an officer or committeeman between conventions, the President is empowered to make appointment to fill the unexpired term; said appointment to be approved by a two-thirds vote of the Executive Committee within thirty (30) days, or another appointment made by the majority of the said committee.

Sec. 9. All committees and appointments made by the President shall serve during his term of office unless dismissed for neglect of duty or conduct unbecoming a member.

Sec. 10. The Constitution, By-Laws, Rules and Regulations covering equipment may be amended or repealed at any session of the assembly of delegates by a two-thirds vote of those present.

Sec. 11. The following committees shall be appointed by the President from the members in Convention:

Constitution and By-Laws and Rules; Membership; Auditing and Finance; Grievance; Credentials; Publicity; Resolutions; or any other committee he deems advisable for the good of the Association. It is not necessary that members of special committees be actually in convention.

Article III.

Section 1. The President shall be Chief Executive of this Association, and preside at all its meetings when able. He shall sign warrants on the Treasurer for payment of all accounts and sign all State or Club Charters as prepared and signed by the Secretary.

Sec. 2. The First Vice President shall perform the duties of the President in the event of death or absence or disability of said officer.

Sec. 4. The Secretary shall be the custodian of and keep all the records, property, correspondence, books, accounts, printing materials and other documents belonging to this Association. He shall keep the complete minutes of the meetings and perform all other duties pertaining to said office. He shall preserve all past records, correspondence and other property belonging to this Association and be able to turn over to the Executive Committee any data in his possession on demand. He shall receive and pay to the Treasurer all moneys belonging to the Association and prepare and transmit the President's warrants upon the Treasurer for payment of bills and shall also endeavor to promote harmony and good will in the membership of this Association.

Sec. 5. The Treasurer shall be the custodian of the funds of this Association and shall disburse the same on signed warrants prepared by the Secretary and signed by the President. He shall furnish a complete statement of moneys received and paid out at each convention or at any time on demand of the Executive Committee.

Sec. 6. All bills of account or expense against this Association amounting to over twenty dollars shall be submitted to the Board of Directors and paid when approved by four of the five directors. If not approved in this manner, amounts contested shall be brought before delegates in convention assembled and submitted to a vote.

Sec 7. All committees named in this constitution and By-Laws shall be under the direction of the President and their duties shall be defined by him.

Sec. 8. The Secretary-Treasurer shall be bonded, provided the Executive Committee approves, and in such amounts as funds carried from time to time warrant.

Sec 9. All Officers shall have their books and records and any other property belonging to this Association in convention or, if unable to be there, must forward same to headquarters before the first day of the convention. They shall also turn over to successors in office all records and property of the Association that may be in their possession.

Article IV.

Section 1. Any person or group of persons may become a member or members in the National Horseshoe Pitchers Association of America on the payment of a 25c fee for a fiscal year from June 1 to June 1, 15c of this to be paid to the National Association and 10c to be retained by the State Association or the representative of each state elected by the State Association or temporarily appointed by the National Secretary, to whom will be issued the state charter and through whom will be issued all membership cards. No membership shall be issued in any state except through such a state representative by the National Secretary at no charge to the State Association, upon proper proof that such state association or representative will meet the requirements of the National Association and make an earnest effort to secure memberships.

All sanctions for tournaments to be held in any state shall be issued by the state association or state representative, who shall require that National Rules be followed and that each participant is a member of the National Horseshoe Pitchers Association. A copy of the sanction shall be forwarded to the National Secretary for recording.

All interstate sanctions shall be issued through the National Secretary, who shall notify the state associations or state representatives in each state included in such territory assigned to an inter-state tournament.

Championship certificates shall be issued through the National Secretary upon certification that National rules were followed, legal shoes used and that participants in the tourney were members of the National Association.

Sec. 2. The Constitution, By-Laws and Rules, as adopted shall be published by this Association in booklet form. This booklet also to contain statistics covering tournaments and other information of interest and necessary to those conducting tournaments.

Sec. 3. No National Tournament games shall be played in rain or on the Sabbath Day.

Sec. 5. No person shall be eligible to take part in a National Tournament until the entry and guarantee fees have been paid or deposited. The entry fee shall be not less than five ($5) dollars covering male entries, and two ($2) dollars for female entries. The forfeit guarantee shall not be less than five ($5) dollars for each entry. The amount deposited as a forfeit guarantee shall be returned the depositor as his or her schedule is completed. Failure to complete will be cause for forfeiture of the amount.

Article V.

Section 1. State Associations shall be organized under the National Body and known as (Name of State) Division of the National Horseshoe Pitchers Association of America.

Sec. 2. Chartered State Associations are granted authority to organize and develop the advancement of the horseshoe game in their territory to permit and foster the affiliating with their organization all clubs, leagues or associations within their State, thus becoming by their affiliation with the State Organization a part of the National Body and entitled to representation in accordance with provisions of Article II, Section 2.

Sec. 3. State Associations and their affiliated members must comply with this Constitution, its By-Laws and Rules.

Sec. 4. The officials of organizations affiliated with the National Body shall be governed the same as National Officers and perform their duties in accordance with this Constitution and By-Laws.

Article VI.

Section 1. Not less than two National Tournaments and conventions shall be held each year: one in the southern section where warmth permits in the winter season, and one in the northern section in its summer season. The winter season tournaments are to be held between January 1st and March 15th of each year. The exact dates of authorized National Tournaments shall be furnished the Secretary by those awarded the privilege of holding the tournament at least sixty (60) days prior to the date of starting.

[9]

Sec. 2. The winner of an authorized National Tournament shall be declared the Champion Horseshoe Pitcher of the World and shall hold said title until the next authorized tournament, at which time he shall have the privilege of again contesting for the title on the same basis as the others, except he shall not be compelled to pitch a qualifying round to enter the championship finals.

Sec. 3. A ladies' tournament may be held in connection with the men's tournament and the winner shall be declared The Champion Lady Horseshoe Pitcher of the World and shall hold said title until the next authorized National Tournament as aforesaid.

Sec. 4. The assembly of delegates in convention shall award the privilege of conducting a subsequent tournament by a two-thirds vote. In case no bid is received at the convention, the Executive Committee has authority to make award. A city or organization, desiring to hold a National Tournament, shall have its bid in the hands of the Secretary at the first session of delegates assembled in convention.

Sec. 5. No sealed bid will be considered by the assembly of delegates unless the following articles are clearly defined:
   (a) State facilities available for conducting a tournament.
   (b) Amount of cash prizes.
   (c) Amount of trophy prizes.
   (d) Miscellaneous advantages.

Sec. 6. This Association may conduct the National Tournament under its own auspices in strict accord with rules herein stipulated and at a place agreeable to its membership.

Sec. 7. The favored bidder or bidders for a National Tournament must pay to the National Association an amount equal to twelve and one-half per cent of the total cash and trophy prizes to be awarded sixty (60) days prior to the date of starting the tournament, unless the Executive Committee authorizes a later payment.

Sec. 8. The favored bidder or bidders for a National Tournament must place the total amount of the prize money on deposit in a National bank at least 30 days prior to the opening date of the tournament and so certify to the National Secretary.

BY-LAWS

Article I.

Section 1. The Executive Committee shall be the judicial body and shall define and interpret the Constitution and By-Laws. Technical points may be submitted to it for decision and the ruling declared official unless delegates in convention assembled, by a two-thirds vote, rule otherwise.

Sec. 2. It shall be the duty of all committees to serve willingly and in the best interests of the Association.

Article II.

Section 1. A member may be suspended for:
(a) Non-payment of dues or fees as per Article 4, Section 1; (b) wilfully violating the Constitution, By-Laws, or Rules; (c) by participating in a tournament under an assumed name or being found guilty of fraud, fixing games or other conduct unbecoming a member; (d) for directly or indirectly betting on a contestant or self when an entry in the competition; (e) for participating in a tournament not sanctioned by the National Association or one of its state subdivisions or using unsanctioned shoes in a tournament, a member shall be suspended for a period of one year and the secretary of the National Association shall notify all State Associations and state representatives of said suspension.

Sec. 2. No member shall be suspended until after a trial before the Executive Committee.

Sec. 3. Members suspended under clause (a) shall be reinstated upon payment of back dues. Under clause (b) after a period of six months, and under clauses (c) and (d) after a period of one year unless delegates in convention by a two-thirds majority vote contrary.

Article III.

Section 1. To accommodate the largest number of contestants possible, and on the least number of courts, and to make satisfactory to officials, players and spectators, the deciding of the World's Championship, one of the following methods shall be pursued in determining same:

[10]

(a) The rotation or round robin plan. When forty (40) or less entries are to compete, each entry shall play the other one game, the winner of the most games being declared the champion.

(b) Double Rotation Plan. When the playing is stretched over a period of two weeks, this method shall be given preference. During the first week of play, the players shall compete as in paragraph (a); the ten, twelve, fourteen or sixteen players finishing highest in games won, qualifying for the second week's play. During the second week of play those chosen as qualifying shall play each other at least three (3) and not more than five (5) games, preferably, each player playing the other once each day. The player winning the most games shall be declared the Champion of the World. All other players, qualifying for the second week of play, shall receive prizes graduated according to their order of finishing.

(c) When there are over forty to compete, the group method of elimination shall be employed; that is: the players may be divided into groups of preferably six, eight or ten, each player in the group playing one game with every other in the same group. By selecting the two, three, four or five highest in each group, eliminations can be made to 12 to 16 players; these to play according to paragraph (a) in deciding a championship.

(d) A diversion from these systems may be granted by the Executive Committee.

Sec. 2. The title of Champion Horseshoe Pitchers of the World can be contested for only in National Tournaments authorized by the National Horseshoe Pitchers Association of America, or in a series of games, (not less than six wins in a scheduled 11-game match), same to be authorized by a majority vote of the Board of Directors, it being understood that the Board of Directors will give preference to those finishing among the first six in the last previous previous tournament. The Board, however, may, at its discretion, select some other opponent for the champions. Not more than three such contests may be held annually. A representative selected by the board shall be in attendance to conduct the match. No bid under five hundred ($500.00) will be accepted, and 25 percent of this amount shall go to the National Horseshoe Pitchers Association of America.

Sec. 3. In a National Tournament games won and lost shall determine the winner..

Sec. 4. If three-cornered ties, or more, cannot be decided by the game method in first play-off, they shall be determined by the point method. The contestant having the highest number of points shall be declared the winner. If the championship is involved, however, play must continue among those tied until a champion is declared by games won.

Sec. 5. Special Feature Games may be arranged each day, they having no bearing upon the schedule or championship, and while they are being conducted, the Tournament Committee shall have the privilege of clearing the courts of other contestants, but players may continue with any game already started.

Sec. 6. Profane or abusive language will not be permitted upon the tournament grounds by players or members.

Sec. 7. Roberts Rules of Order, Revised, and reading as follows, shall govern the order of conducting meetings:

1. Reading of the minutes of the previous meeting (and approval of same).
2. Reports of officers and boards and standing committees.
3. Reports of special (select) committees.
4. Special orders.
5. Unfinished business and general orders.
6. New business.

ARTICLE IV.

Section. 1. "Any horseshoe manufacturer, in introducing a new pitching horseshoe or change made in any pitching horseshoe must submit blueprints of same to the National Secretary for an official approval. Following acceptance of the blueprints by a unanimous decision of the committee, the manufacturer must submit the finished product to the committee for a final acceptance before he may affix the official five cent manufacturers' tax stamp to each pair of shoes disposed of by the manufacturer and/or his agent or agents. The aforementioned tax is to be used for conducting a National Tournament only.

"In submitting blueprints to the National Secretary, five (5) blueprints will be submitted so that the National Secretary shall in turn submit these blueprints to each of the five members of the National By-Laws and Rules committee that they may in turn give their official recognition of the blueprints submitted.

"The manufacturer may waive the rule requiring him to submit blueprints, and submit the finished product directly."

Sec. 2. "Each manufacturer shall post with the National Secretary a bond of one hundred ($100.00) dollars as a guarantee of his willingness to comply with the National Rules in manufacturing and disposing of his product, said bond to be forfeit to the fund for conducting National Tournament if manufacturer does not comply with all rules and regulations laid down by the National Horseshoe Pitchers' Association of America."

ARTICLE V.

Section 1. Beginning with the year of 1940, and each year thereafter, the National Association shall conduct a National Team League under the following rules:

Rule 1. Eligibility. Any member in good standing in the National Association is eligible to compete as a player or hold position as manager, coach, director, owner, or some such office on or in connection with any team in this league.

Rule 2. Source of Team. Any source, such as a horseshoe club, county, district or state association, city, town, village, fraternal organization, private or commercial sponsor, or any reliable functionary may enter a team in this league.

Rule 3. Registration. Each source desiring to enter a team shall file notice of prospective entry with the National Secretary before April 1st. Each prospective entry shall be sent a team contract which shall be filled in and returned no later than May 1. This contract will simply affirm that team's willingness to participate in the league play and accept the schedule and rules as given, and will be signed by no more than ten (10) players and such other officials connected with that team.

Rule 4. General Plan of Schedule. On or before May 15, each team will receive its official schedule for the year. The entries for this league will be divided into divisions according to geographical locations, and each team will play a home-and-home series of at least two matches with each other team in its division. After division champions have been decided, a plan for play-offs between them to decide the National Championship team will be drawn up and played.

Rule. 5. Method of Deciding Winners. The team matches shall be decided on the basis of seven-men-a-side. There will be seven rounds of play, and seven games per round. The team winning 25 or more games is the winner of the match. Matches won and lost shall decide the team's standing in the league.

Rule 6. Each team will be allowed to sign ten players. There will be no limitations placed upon their ability or distance of residence from the home courts of the team they represent.

Rule 7. Each team will be required to be uniformed, and it is recommended that each player's name be engraved on his uniform.

Rule 8. Method of Conducting Team Match. The home team management shall be responsible for having the courts in perfect shape, and shall also make arrangements for groundkeepers, scorers, ushers, etc. They shall also furnish scoresheets. Just before the match is to begin, each manager shall write out his line-up, numbering his players from one to seven, the number indicating the court on which that player will start. Neither manager shall see the opponent's line-up until both have been turned in to the official referee or announcer. After each round of play, the members of the visiting team shall move one court to the right, and the members of the home team shall move one court to their left. Each manager may make substitutions before each of the last six rounds, provided that such substitution does not place a man upon a court where he has already played one game, or bring together two men who have already played each other. If both managers substitute simultaneously, bringing up such a case, the home team must withdraw or change its substitution.

Rule 9. The home team shall send either the score sheets or a compiled result of each match to the National Secretary. If a compiled result is sent, it should include each player's games, won and lost, his points and opponents' points, his ringers, double ringers, shoe pitched and ringer percentage. The National Secretary shall have all the results and standings published in the Horseshoe World.

Rule 10. Financial Arrangements. A team entry fee of ten ($10.00) dollars shall accompany each team's entry into the league. Each team shall defray

[12]

its own expenses for uniform, traveling, etc. (It is to be left up to each team to obtain its own commercial sponsor for these things). Each team shall be at liberty to charge admission to the general public for its home games, or take up a collection, or hold raffles or drawings, and is not under any obligations to share receipts with the visiting team unless special pact between the two has been previously agreed upon.

Rule 11. Any point not fully covered by these foregoing rules may be decided upon by the National Secretary or if demanded, by the Executive Committee.

Rule 12. It is desired by the National Association that each state association form within its own state, a league similar to the National league, using the same general rules, and that results of these leagues be also sent to the National Secretary. It is requested, however, that no member of a National League team shall play on a state league team.

It is further desired by the National Association that each district or locality with enough players to form a league shall form local leagues on the same patterns as the National League, with the understanding that no player from either a National League or State League team be allowed to play in this local league.

HORSESHOE PITCHING RULES

Authorized by the National Horseshoe Pitchers' Association of America in Convention Assembled, August, 1939.

HORSESHOE COURTS

Rule 1. Sec. a—Lay-out of Courts—A court shall consist of two pitchers' boxes with stake in the center of each and shall cover a level area over all of ten (10) feet in width and fifty (50) feet in length.

Sec. b—When a number of courts are constructed as required in tournament play, the stakes shall be at least ten (10) feet apart between courts, and front pitching box foul lines preserve a straight line across the entire lay-out. Construction shall be made to permit of north-south pitching.

Rule 2. Pitching Distance—The pitching distance shall be forty (40) feet between stakes. Ladies' pitching distance thirty (30) feet.

Rule 3. Indoor Pitching—When indoor courts are constructed, the height of pitching boxes should not be over six (6) inches above floor level. Ceiling height at least twelve (12) feet.

Rule 4. Sec. a—Pitchers' Box—Pitchers' box shall be six (6) feet square, with stake in the exact center.

Sec. b. The pitchers' box shall be filled to a depth of six (6) inches with potter's clay or substitute of like nature and kept in moist and putty-like condition in the stake area. (When boxes are hard surface, as related in Section C, the opening about the stake shall be filled with clay).

Sec. c.—When the pitchers' box is hard surface, an opening not less than thirty-one (31) inches in width, and forty-six (46) inches in length must be left about the stake and filled with clay.

Sec. d. Foul line surrounding the pitchers' box shall be well defined and the frame at the front must extend approximately one (1) inch above the surface.

Sec. e. Foul lines shall be determined by inside measurement to the near side of the box frame from the stake.

HORSESHOE EQUIPMENT

Rule 5. Stakes—The stakes shall be of iron or steel, one inch in diameter, and shall extend twelve (12) inches above the clay surface with a three (3) inch incline toward the opposite stake.

Rule 6. The Official Shoe—No horseshoe shall exceed the following dimensions: seven and one-half (7½) inches in length; seven (7) inches in width; two and one-half (2½) pounds in weight. No heel or toe caulks shall project more than one and one-sixteenth (1 1-16) inches in height over all; that is including the body of the shoe. The opening between the heel caulks shall not exceed three and one-half (3½) inches, inside measurement. Said opening shall not be more than nine-sixteenths (9-16) inches from the extreme end of the shoe determined by measurement from a straight edge placed across the extreme ends of the heel. No hook shall project more than thirteen-sixteenths (13-16) inches from inside the body of the shoe. No projection shall be allowed extending beyond an imaginary line following the general inner contour of the shoe, with the exception of the hooks which shall be no farther than one (1) inch from a line drawn between the extreme ends of the shoe heels.

PLAYING RULES

Rule 7. Sec. a. Conduct of Players and Members—No contestant, while opponent is in pitching position, shall make any remark or utter any sounds within the hearing of opponent, nor make any movement that does or might interfere with the opponent's playing. Penalty—Both shoes of the offender shall be declared foul in the inning complained of.

Sec. b. Any member of the National Horseshoe Pitchers' Association of America who indulges in heckling or unfair rooting against any pitcher in a tournament whether with malicious intent or otherwise, shall be expelled from the grounds and from the National Association.

Sec. c. No contestant shall touch own or opponent's shoe or shoes until winner of point or points has been agreed upon by contestants or decision rendered by the referee. Referee shall declare foul, shoes thrown by a contentant failing to comply with this rule, and award points to the opponent according to the position of his or her shoes.

Sec. d. No contestant shall walk to the opposite stake or be informed of the position of shoes prior to the completion of an inning.

Sec. e. A player, when not pitching, must remain on the opposite side of the stake to the player in action, and to the rear of a line even with the stake.

Sec. f. Any player repeatedly violating rules or guilty of unsportsmanlike conduct may be barred from further participation in the contest.

Rule 8. Sec. a. Foul Lines—Any shoe delivered while the pitcher's foot extends on or over the raised foul line (See Rule 4, Sec. d) shall be declared foul, and removed from counting distance.

Sec. b.—In delivering the shoe the pitcher shall stand within the pitchers' box, but outside an eighteen (18) inch radius of the stake.

Rule 9. In delivering a shoe, the pitcher must remain behind the foul line until the shoe pitched reaches the court at which it is delivered.

Rule 10. Choice of Pitch—Choice of first pitch or follow shall be determined by the toss of a coin. In successive games between the same players, the loser shall have choice.

Rule 11. Broken Shoes—When the shoe lands in fair territory and is broken into separate parts it shall be removed and the contestant allowed to pitch another shoe in its stead.

Rule 12. Sec. a. Foul Shoes—A shoe pitched while contestant stands beyond the box foul line limits. A shoe striking outside the opposite pitching box or on the hard surface when courts are so constructed.

Sec. b. Foul shoes shall be removed from the opposite pitchers' box at the request of the opponent.

Sec. c. A foul shoe shall not be scored or credited except in the score sheet column headed "shoes pitched."

Rule 13. Measurements—Measurements to determine points won shall be made with calipers and straight edge.

SCORING RULES

Rule 14. Sec. a. A regulation game shall consist of fifty (50) points in all contests where a National or Sectional title is involved. Any other contests may be decided in any manner acceptable to the state association in that state, provided that the National Rules, Constitution and By-Laws are not violated.

Sec. b. Game points in other tournaments, leagues or contests may be determined by local authorities to fit their conditions.

Sec. c. A game is divided into innings and each inning constitutes the pitching of two shoes by each contestant.

Rule 15. Sec. a. A shoe must be within six (6) inches of the stake to score.

Sec. b. Closest shoe to stake scores 1 point.

Sec. c. Two shoes closer than opponents, 2 points.

Sec. d. One (1) ringer scores 3 points.

Sec. e. Two (2) ringers scores 6 points.

Sec. f. One (1) ringer and closest shoe of same player scores 4 points.

Sec. g. Party having two ringers against one for opponent scores 3 points.

Sec. h. All equals count as ties and no points are scored.

Sec. i. In case each contestant has a ringer, the next closest shoe, if within six (6) inches of the stake shall score 1 point.

Sec. j. In case of a tie, such as four (4) ringers, or contestants' shoes are equal distance from the stake, causing no score for either, party pitching last in the inning will start the next inning.

[16]

Sec. k. A leaning shoe has no value over one touching the stake.

Rule 16. Sec. a. The points shall be scored according to the position of the shoes at the inning's end, that is, after the contestants have each thrown two shoes.

Sec. b. Ringer credits shall be given on the same basis.

Sec. c. The winner of points shall call the result. In case of a tie, the party pitching last shall call.

Rule 17. Definition of a Ringer.—A ringer is declared when a shoe encircles the stake far enough to allow the touching of both heel calks simultaneously with a straight edge, and permit a clearance of the stake.

Rule 18. Recording the Results—The recording of results shall be as follows: W, Games Won; L, Games Lost; P, Points; R, Ringers; DR, Double Ringers; SP, Shoes Pitched; OP, Opponents' Points; PCT, Percentage of Ringers.

JURISDICTION

Rule 19. Sec. a. A tournament committee, satisfactory to the Board of Directors, shall supervise National contests.

Sec. b. A referee appointed by the committee shall decide points when contestants are in doubt. He shall also see that rules are complied with.

Sec. c. Appeal may be made to the committee if a ruling of the referee is not considered proper. Decision of the committee shall be final.

Sec. d. All protests shall be made immediately the occasion arises. Protests covering shoes or conditions of play can only be made before the start of the game.

Sec. e. If rain or other elements interfere, players must stop play and not resume until officials authorize. On resuming play, score at time of interference will be in effect also the same courts will be used by contestants unless they agree otherwise.

Sec. f. The interpretation of the tournament committee covering technical points and their ruling on matters uncovered by these rules shall be final.

Sec. g. An official scorer shall cover each game. When open scorers are also maintained, the official scorer shall watch closely the open score and correct immediately any error.

Rule 20. Three-handed Games—In three-handed games, when two of the players each have a ringer and the third player no ringer, the party without a ringer is out of the scoring and others score according to conditions pertaining if only two were in the game. Otherwise the regulation rules apply.

Rule 21. An official contest between two players shall consist of best six (6) out of eleven (11) games.

[17]

HISTORY OF PAST WORLD TOURNAMENTS

While many complete records of past world tournaments are in the files of the National Association, it is believed that page after page of figures would not be as interesting as a running story, and this idea is the excuse for not publishing more complete figures. If the general public wishes more figures, however, they will be published in later books.

On October 23, 1915, a world championship meet was held at Kansas City, and was played under the rules of the Grand League of the American Horseshoe Pitchers' Association. Stakes were 38½ feet apart and three-quarters of an inch in diameter. Ringers counted five and leaners counted three. Games were for 21 points. This tournament was won by Frank Jackson who won 24 games and lost only one.

The next tournament of which we have any record was held in St. Petersburg, Fla., Feb. 22-26, 1919. Stakes were 40 feet apart, eight inches high, and had a one- inch lean. Games were for 21 points. Eighteen players entered, and played a triple round-robin. Fred M. Brust, of Columbus, Ohio, easily outclassed the field, winning 53 games and losing only one. Dr. F. M. Robinson, of Poughkeepsie, N. Y., was second with 47 wins and seven losses. At the close of this tournament, with representatives from 25 states, there was formed the National League of Horseshoe and Quoit Pitchers.

Tournaments now began to come regularly, and at St. Petersburg, Fla., Feb. 23-28, 1920, another meet was held. The winner of this tournament was George May, of Akron, Ohio, who sailed through 24 opponents without suffering a defeat. Games were for 50 points. Joe Wilkinson, of Akron, was runner-up.

The first modern world tourney held in the North came in the same year when at Akron, Ohio, on Aug. 8-14, was held the next meet. George May, the defending champion, slipped down to eighth place as Frank Jackson, then of Kellerton, Ia., came through to win. No record of the games won and lost appear in the files. Charles Bobbitt, of Lancaster, Ohio, was second. The first woman's tournament was held in connection, and with only two entries, the champion became Miss Marjorie Voorhies, of Asbury Park, N. J.

In the Mid-Winter Tournament held Feb. 21-27, 1921, in St. Petersburg, Fla., Charles Bobbitt became world title holder. The meet was held in Williams Park, and there is no record of the games won and lost, or the shoes pitched. Bobbitt scored 1,040 points in 21 games, so he must have won 20 and lost one. He threw 439 ringers, an average of 21 per game, so it is deduced

[19]

of that state, Mrs. Francisco living in Muskegon, Mrs. R. A. Bishop, of Battle Creek, Mrs. E. Tuttle, of Walled Lake, and Mrs. Doris Cole, of Grand Rapids. Mrs. Francisco had a ringer average of .452. The women divided $145 in cash prizes, $75 and a gold medal going to the winner.

The scene of world championship play shifted to Cleveland, Ohio, where September 19-23, 1923, was held the next meet. Fifty-three men entered the tournament, fifty of them starting. The contestants were divided into five groups of 10 each, and after playing a round robin in each group, the eight highest advanced to the next round. The 40 survivors were then divided into eight groups of five men each and 12 more were eliminated. The 28 men left were again divided into four groups of seven men each, and the four highest in each group made up the 16 in the finals.

C. C. Davis was high in the preliminaries, with a ringer average of .591, but close on his heels came George May with .572, and Loren May with .561. Frank Jackson was next with .549. In the finals, records were broken right and left as George May won the title with an average of .600, winning 14 and losing one. C .C. Davis came in second with an average of .610, winning 13 and losing two. Loren May was third and Frank Jackson was fourth. William Yocum, a player who was to play in many more meets, was sixth; Blair Nunamaker, of Cleveland, was 11th, and Carroll Jackson was 12th. Yocum set a world record by shooting .777 against C. Jackson, but Frank Jackson fired an .800 against Nunamaker soon after. Davis threw the most ringers ever thrown in one game, hurling 63 against F. Jackson's 59.

There were eight entries in the women's tournament. Mrs. Francisco, now of Columbus, Ohio, won seven straight games, beating Mrs. Lanham 50-48 for the title. Mrs. Francisco averaged only .378, while Mrs. Lanham, in second, averaged .465. Mrs. Lanham pitched .708 against Mrs. Heenan to establish a record for women.

Lake Worth, Fla., was the site of the winter tourney of 1924, the exact dates being February 18-23, and it was in this ·meet that C. C. Davis again crashed through to the title. Charley defeated 22 consecutive opponents, and averaged .579, while Frank Jackson came in second, winning 20 and losing two and having an average of only .514. Tied for third place were Loren May and a young newcomer from Eldora, Iowa, named Putt Mossman.

The contestants divided $1,830, of which $500 went to first

[21]

place. The only record set in this meet was made by Loren May who threw six consecutive doubles against Buckman.

In the women's tournament, Mrs. Lanham dethroned Mrs. Francisco as champion by winning six consecutive games, defeating the title holder, 50-15. Mrs. Lanham set a record by averaging .527. Total prizes for women was $180, first place taking $75 and gold medal.

One interesting fact connected with this tournament was that the Lake Worth Herald put out a special horseshoe edition every evening after results were in.

The summer tournament of 1924 was held in Minneapolis, Sept. 17-21. It was agreed that the 24 contestants were to play one round-robin, and the two highest would play a three-out-of-this tourney, winning 23 consecutive games in the round-robin, this tourney, winning 23 consecutive games in the round-robn, and whipping Frank Jackson three straight in the series, which was played in the rain. Mossman averaged .625 for the tournament, setting a new record. Hansford Jackson placed third, Floyd Billings, of Waukesha, Wis., was fourth, while down in ninth place was Carroll Jackson.

Mrs. Lanham easily retained her title in the women's meet, winning 11 straight games in the round-robin with an average of .560, and then beating Mrs. Brouillette in two straight games in the series.

A feature of this tournament was the greatest game of horseshoes pitched up to that time. It was between Mossman and F. Jackson, and Mossman won with 73 ringers in 102 shoes to Jackson's 72 ringers.

The winter tournament of 1925 was held February 16-28, at Lake Worth, Florida. The plan of this tournament was that the 32 entries would play one round-robin the first week, and the 12 highest would then play a round-robin each day for five days to decide a champion. Frank Jackson sailed through the preliminaries with 31 consecutive victories, with Putt Moss an second with 29 wins. It was in the finals, however, that Mossman proved his superiority over the horseshoe players of that day by going through 55 games with only two defeats to finish far ahead of C. C. Davis who was beaten 10 times. Putt hung up a new record of .676 average for the finals, and averaged .659 for the entire 86 games of the tournament.

On February 25, Mossman beat Bert Duryee in a great game which broke several records. It was the longest game ever pitched, 108 shoes, and at one stretch there were four ringers on the stake eight consecutive times. Mossman ended the game with an unfinished run of nine straight doubles. Mossman threw

[22]

80 ringers while the silent man from Kansas tossed on 75. Putt had 30 doubles to Bert's 26. It must be remembered that hooked shoes had not yet been invented, and this game must stand forever as a remarkable performance.

Frank Jackson wound up in third place with 42 wins and 13 defeats; Loren May took fourth, winning 34 and losing 21; Wm. Yocum was fifth with 29 wins and 26 losses; and Duryee was sixth with 26 wins and 29 defeats. Blair Nunamaker was seventh.

The contestants divided the greatest purse ever given in a horseshoe tournament, $3,500.00, of which $625.00 went to contestants finishing lower than 12th.

Mrs. Lanham continued her mastery over the fair sex by again successfully defending her title. She won eight straight games in the preliminaries with .589, and dropped only one game in the finals of nine games, averaging .572. Mrs. Lanham hit .579 for the whole 17 games, all new records. Mrs. Francisco came in second, Mrs. Brouillette took third, and Mrs. Besancon, of Detroit, Mich., won fourth. The women divided $495.00 in prize money, $110.00 going to those below fourth place. The total prize money for this meet at Lake Worth amounted to $3,995.00.

There was no tournament held again until February 8-18, 1926, at St. Petersburg, Fla. In this meet it was agreed that the 33 starters would play once around, and the 12 highest would then play three times around in the finals.

Putt Mossman gave no indication of weakening in the prelims, sailing through 32 games with only one defeat, and setting a new record for this event with .674. In second place with two defeats came Bert Duryee and Blair Nunamaker, while Frank Jackson brought up in fourth with three defeats. Mossman broke the record for consecutive doubles by throwing 10 in a row against Harry Robinson.

The finals developed into a fine battle right down to the wire, with Mossman hitting the best percentages, but unable to shake off Jackson, Duryee, Nunamaker and Art Cumming. Due to one man's dropping out, only 11 competed in the finals. When the final results were tabulated it disclosed Mossman and Jackson tied for first with 24 wins and six defeats each, while Duryee was only one game behind. Putt had averaged .679 for the finals, which was a new record, and .676 for the entire tournament, also a new record. Jackson had only made .614 in the finals, while Duryee had made .626.

The two tied for first agreed to play a two-out-of-three series for the title, and Mossman won the first game only to

[23]

see Jackson win the second. In the third and final game the excitement was intense as an immense crowd surrounded the courts, and the score seesawed until the score stood, Jackson 49, Mossman 48. Mossman, pitching first, missed with both shoes, and the veteran Jackson, pitching second, also missed both of his, and when the final count was made, Jackson had won the world championship on a shoe a good four inches away from the stake, and Putt Mossman had come to the end of his championship trail.

The men divided $3,060.00 in prize money, $445.00 going to men below 12th.

Mrs. Lanham did not defend her title, and Mrs. Brouillette swept through to her first championship without losing a game in 14 starts. Mrs. Francisco was second, Mrs. Besancon, of Detroit, Mich., was third, and fourth went to Mrs. Cole of Grand Rapids, Michigan.

The women divided $405.00 in prizes, $150.00 going to first, and $100.00 to second.

The total prize for this tournament was $3,465.00.

Again there was no summer tournament in the North in 1926, and the two champions rested easy until February 14-23, 1927, at St. Petersburg.

Twenty-six starters faced the barrier as play got under way in the preliminaries. Only a few games had been played when it became apparent that a new power had arisen in the top-notch ranks. A young schoolboy from Montpelier, Indiana, named Jimmy Risk was bowling over the best of them, and he continued to mow 'em down all through the first week of play, winning 25 consecutive games with an average of .652. The lanky Blair Nunamaker thundered along in second with 23 wins and two defeats. Tied for third were the two main actors of the year before, Mossman and Frank Jackson, each with 22 wins and three defeats. C. C. Davis, back to the horseshoe wars after a two-year absence, trailed along in fifth with 21 wins and four defeats.

C. C. Davis stepped out high, wide and handsome in the finals to win the title with 29 victories and four losses, with Risk coming in second, only one game behind. Davis set a new record by averaging .692 in the finals, while Risk had but .622. Blair Nunamaker took third with 27 wins and six defeats, averaging .625; Frank Jackson came in fourth with 25 wins and eight losses, averaging .646. Mossman took fifth and Duryee was sixth. The players divided $1,670.00 in prize money.

In the women's division there were only five entries. Mrs. Francisco won four straight games in the preliminaries, but Mrs.

[24]

Brouillette came through with a successful defense of her title, winning eight out of nine games, with Mrs. Francisco second with seven wins and two defeats. The women divided $190.00 in prize money.

In 1927 a summer tournament was held in Duluth, August 7-14. A field of 38 players started this tournament, but the high wind and cold weather forced three of them to withdraw the first day. Frank Jackson was high man in the preliminaries, winning 33 games and losing only one game, and that to his son, Vyrl. Davis, Risk, Duryee, H. E. Jackson, Hilst, C. E. Jackson, Cumming, Freel, Mossman, Collier, and Reese finished in that order to qualify for the finals.

Davis put on the pressure in the finals to retain his title with 30 wins and three losses, but the wind and cold kept his average down to .648. Frank Jackson took second place with 26 victories and seven defeats, averaging .611. Duryee was third, Cecil Freel, of Murray, Iowa, was fourth; Carroll Jackson took fifth, Risk was sixth, and Mossman slipped down to seventh with only .501. The players divided $1,815.00 in prize money.

Eight entries started in the women's tournament, and Mrs. Lanham, the left-handed star, was back after a two and a half year absence to demonstrate her superiority over the field. She swept through seven games in the preliminaries without defeat, and lost only one game in the finals in nine starts. Mrs. Lanham averaged .583 in the preliminaries, and .560 in the finals. Her average in the preliminaries was a new record, while her average of .569 for the whole tournament was also a new record. In a game against Mrs. Young, she also set a record for one game, hitting .833. The women divided a prize list of $216.00.

The winter tournament of 1928 was again held in St. Petersburg, Florida, February 20 to March 1st. Thirty contestants opened play, and in the very first game, Bert Duryee upset Champion C. C. Davis 50-41. Davis, however, swept through the next 28 games without defeat, finishing first in the preliminaries. Blair Nunamaker came in second, losing only to Davis and Leslie Robison. Bert Duryee and Harvey Elmerson, of Kenosha, Wis., tied for third with 24 wins and five losses.

Frank Jackson, Jimmy Risk and Carroll Jackson were next with 23 wins and six defeats, while the others to qualify for the finals were C. R. Thompson, Vyrl Jackson, Harold Falor, Jim Hough and Hansford Jackson. Putt Mossman, for the first time, failed to qualify for the finals, coming in 13th.

On the first day of the finals, rain held the games down to nine instead of 11, and Davis went through undefeated, averaging .731. Duryee, Risk and Nunamaker were tied for second with two defeats each. Against V. Jackson, Davis set a new world record by hitting .889. Each man played 13 games the second day of the finals. Duryee won from Davis, but dropped a game to Elmerson, and at the end of the day Davis had won 21 and lost one, while Duryee was second with 19 wins and three defeats. On the third and last day of the finals, each of these two won their first six games, Davis having a close call with Thompson, 50-47; then in the seventh round Nunamaker hit Davis with a string of 65 ringers in 78 shoes for .833 and sent him down to defeat. With Duryee only one game behind, the excitement increased. Elmerson came within an ace of toppling Davis, losing 47-50, but both men came down to their final game with each other just one game apart. If Duryee could win from Davis it would mean a tie for the title. But Bert got off to a bad start and the wily Davis had run up a long lead before Duryee hit his stride, and then it was too late, and Davis had clinched his title again, and established himself as the king of the horseshoe world. Davis won 31 games and lost two, averaging .702 for a new record. Duryee won 29 and lost four, averaging .694. Far behind the two leaders came Nunamaker with 23 wins and 10 defeats, with an average of .662, and Elmerson took fourth with 20 wins and 13 losses, averaging .640. Frank Jackson, C. R. Thompson, Jimmy Risk, Carroll Jackson, Hansford Jackson, Harold Falor, Jim Hough and Vyrl Jackson finished in that order.

The players divided $1,750.00 in prize money.

There were only five entries in the women's tournament. Mrs. Lanham was not present, and a new champion was assured. Mrs. Brouillette took four straight games in the preliminaries, with Mrs. Francisco, Mrs. Young, Mrs. Cumming and Mrs. Rose following in that order. In the finals, however, Mrs. Francisco crashed out nine straight wins to again become champion, with Mrs. Brouillette coming in second. The women divided $255.00 in prize money.

A women's tournament was held during the summer at the Exposition at Rochester, N. Y., September 3-6, 1928. The great Mrs. Lanham again appeared on the scene and walked away with the title, winning seven consecutive games in the preliminaries, and eight out of nine in the finals. In this tourney, Mrs. Lanham turned back the challenge of Miss Doris Perkins, of Springfield, Mass., in a record-breaking game, 50-48. Each contestant hurled 54 ringers, a new record, and Miss Perkins shot 19 doubles, a new record. The game went to 92 shoes, the longest game ever pitched between women. The women divided $500.00 in prize money, $150.00 going to first place, and $110.00 to second.

There was no tournament for the men until February 4-9, 1929, when the next official meet was held at St. Petersburg, Florida. This tournament was not staged on the sumptuous courts of the Sunshine Pleasure Club, but rather across the tracks in Waterfront Park. It was conducted on the single round-robin plan, and the prize list offered was considerably lower than in other years, there being $1,210.00 for the men, and $175.00 for the women, a total of $1,385.00.

This tournament was won by Blair Nunamaker of Cleveland, Ohio, who hit an average of .695. Blair met only one defeat in 14 games, losing only to Bert Duryee.

Mrs. Francisco took the title in the women's division.

Following this tournament, horseshoe pitching encountered a slump in big meets. The leading players were heard from now and then as being on a tour or winning a state title, but it wasn't until July 27-31, 1933, that another world tournament was held. This time it was put on by "A Century of Progress" in Chicago. The prize list offered amounted to $1600.00, with $1,420.00 going to the men. Each contestant was to pitch 100 shoes for total points, and the 24 highest qualifiers were to pitch a single round robin for the title.

Since there had been no world tournament for four and one-half years, speculation ran high as to the probable winner. Besides the defending champion, Blair Nunamaker, there were several ex-champions in the field, Davis, Jackson, Mossman, and several strong contenders such as Risk, Duryee and the three Jackson boys. From Arizona came James Lecky, and from the coast came Fernando Isais and Ted Allen, and from Ohio came Grover Hawley, all new names to world tournaments, but highly-touted stars in their own section.

The hundred shoe pitch proved a nightmare for many good pitchers who belonged in the finals, while several poorer ones slipped in due to a good streak in their hundred shoes. A near-tragedy occurred when Nunamaker, the defending champion, barely qualified for the finals.

The finals were played off in three days, and the field was led by C .C. Davis, the high qualifier, for the greater part of the time. Blair Nunamaker put up a great fight to hold his title, but slipped down to a tie for third with Jimmy Risk and Fernando Isais.

By a great finish, Ted Allen tied for first with Davis, and in the play-off that followed, became the new world champion by winning two straight games from the former title holder.

	W	L	R	DR	SP	Pct.
Ted Allen, Alhambra, Cal...............	20	3	1127	408	1532	.735

C. C. Davis, Kansas City, Mo.......	20	3	937	341	1382	.719
Fern. Isais, Los Angeles, Cal......	18	5	1087	379	1502	.720
Jas. Risk, Montpelier, Ind..............	18	5	1016	372	1580	.709
B. Nunamaker, E. Cleveland, O.	18	5	1034	359	1504	.689
Russell Sigler, Pittsfield, Ill........	16	7	947	312	1488	.675
James Lecky, Phoenix, Ariz.	16	7	1004	333	1516	.654
Bert Duryee, Wichita, Kan............	15	8	1003	316	1538	.644
Grover Hawley, Bridgeport, O......	14	9	932	295	1472	.639
Edward Walls, Detroit, Mich.......	13	10	933	280	1574	.621
Harold Sheets, Waukesha, Wis....	12	11	946	299	1492	.641
Howard Collier, Fiatt, Ill............	12	11	869	267	1414	.488
H. Jackson, Blue Mound, Kan......	10	13	781	220	1410	.600
Lloyd Woodard, Columbus, Kan..	10	13	823	257	1388	.585
John Calao, Chicago, Ill..............	10	13	805	226	1384	.527
L. Steinmann, St. Louis, Mo..........	9	14	808	226	1424	.539
C. Jackson, La Grange, Ill............	9	14	786	244	1280	.525
Vyrl Jackson, Kellerton, Ia............	9	14	852	243	1456	.488
Verne Licht, Lodi, Wis....................	8	15	990	304	1654	.561
Orville Harris, Indinapolis, Ind.....	6	17	813	229	1466	.499
Clarence Pfeiffer, Dubuque, Ia.....	5	18	928	271	1540	.511
Alton Wood, Chicago, Ill............	4	19	738	190	1378	.468
J. Hoeksema, Grand Rapids, Mich	2	21	504	149	942	.538
Milton Tate, Knoxville, Ill............	0	23	446	116	850	.481
Totals..........................	276	276	21150	6636	34166	.594

The women's tournament was captured by Caroline Schultz, of Harvey, Ill., and her sister Charlotte came in second. Mrs. Esther James, of Hastings, Mich., was third.

In the first annual Mid-West Tournament held at the Iowa State Fair in 1933, C. C. Davis walked off with first place, and he repeated this performance in 1934.

A tournament held in California in 1934, and advertised as a world tournament was not an officially sanctioned one, and no results of this meet are on hand.

Ted Allen came out of the West again in 1935, and captured the Mid-West Meet while on his way to Moline, Ill., where the world tournament was to be held August 27-Sept. 3.

This tournament at Moline copied after the Chicago meet by forcing the pitchers to qualify by the hundred shoe method, although there was time for a better way, and the scores ran high. C. C. Davis was again high in this event, scoring 266 points with 84 ringers. Jimmy Risk threw 85 ringers, but scored less points, 264.

Twenty-four men reached the finals, and the last man in, Gaylord Peterson, had to shoot 242 points to make it. The second high 24 played in the Moline Dispatch Tournament which was pitched at night, and the last man to qualify for this was R. H. Rizor, of Detroit, with 222 points and 65 ringers. These figures show clearly how much improvement had taken place in the game in the past two years.

Mrs. Esther James, of Hastings, Mich., broke all women's records by hurling 266 points with 86 ringers, and practically frightened the Schultz sisters right out of the tournament, for they left after qualifying, and refused to play. Caroline forfeited her title without a struggle, and gave no good reason for doing so.

Play in the men's round-robin was to be on the basis of six games a day, and the first day found Ted Allen and Charles "Casey" Jones, of Waukesha, Wis., tied for the lead with six wins each. C. C. Davis and Joe Bennett, of Moline, were close behind with five out of six, while with four out of six, stood Guy Zimmerman, Frank Jackson, Harold Sheets, Jimmy Risk and Harvey Elmerson. Risk broke the record for consecutive doubles by firing 12 against Zimmerman, but Jimmy lost the game. On the second day, Allen hung up three more wins before being stopped by old Frank Jackson, and this left Jones unbeaten, but in the very next round, Davis took Jones down. At the end of the second day, Allen and Jones still were tied for the lead with 11 wins and one loss each, while tied for third were Davis and Jackson with 10 victories and two defeats.

The third day found Jones losing his first two games to Elmerson and Sheets, but rallying to win four in a row, the fourth victim being Allen. This left Ted with two defeats, and Jones, Elmerson, Zimmerman and Davis tied for second with three losses. On the final day, Allen and Elmerson came down to the final game without any further losses, and a huge crowd packed the courts to see their game. It was a tight battle, with Allen steaming on 13 consecutive doubles in mid-game to grab a small lead which he held to the end, winning 50-47. Ted Allen's average of .755 was a new high, and his streak against Elmerson was also a new record.

Mrs. James walked away with the women's ttile, winning five straight games with ease. The women' final standings:

		W	L	P	R	DR	SP	Pct.
1.	Mrs Esther James	5	0	250	178	61	268	.636
2.	Mrs. Chas. Johnson	4	1	242	176	55	308	.593
3.	Mrs. Betty Davis	3	2	220	159	40	290	.548
4.	Mrs. Guy Zimmerman	2	3	212	161	50	296	.555
5.	Mrs. Glenn Rust	1	4	139	110	21	268	.410
6.	Mrs. Lee Rose	0	5	51	52	6	206	.253

	W	L	P	R	SP	Pct.	Prz.
Ted Allen, Alhambra, Cal.	21	2	1144	1222	1618	.755	$290
H. Elmerson, Milwaukee, Wis	19	4	1043	1256	1740	.721	240
G. Zimmerman, Sac City, Ia.	18	5	1085	1213	1654	.733	200
C. C. Davis, Kansas City, Mo	18	5	1103	1198	1626	.736	150
F. Jackson, Blue Mound, Kan	17	6	1111	1285	1762	.729	100
Chas. Jones, Waukesha, Wis	17	6	1125	1244	1712	.726	75
Jas. Risk, Montpelier, Ind.....	15	8	1115	1225	1720	.712	50
Jos. Bennett, Moline, Ill..........	14	9	947	1114	1612	.691	45
W. O. Maxwell, Hicksville, O	14	9	973	1059	1524	.693	40
Ellis Griggs, Plaineville, Ill....	13	10	1038	1232	1728	.712	35
A. Dahlene, Lawrence, Kan	12	11	920	987	1482	.665	30
L. F. Gray, Long Beach, Cal	12	11	896	1205	1734	.694	20
Jas. O'Shea, Brocton, Mass....	12	11	1365	1003	1492	.672	15
Earl Bomke, New Berlin, Ill	10	13	929	932	1470	.634	10
Howard Collier, Cuba, Ill......	10	13	879	991	1490	.665	10
Leo Lattore, Dearborn, Mich	9	14	945	1068	1646	.648	10
O. Bozich, Kansas City, Mo.	8	15	892	1011	1580	.639	10
Leo Rollick, Chicago, Ill..........	8	15	668	794	1231	.645	10
H. Sheets, Waukesha, Wis....	7	16	747	793	1414	.560	10
A. Swinehamer, Aurora, Ill	7	16	675	910	1376	.659	10
R. Addington, Dunkirk, N. Y.	5	18	784	1014	1561	.649	10
Glenn Rust, Milwaukee, Wis	5	18	790	871	1510	.576	10
G. Peterson, Varna, Ill......	4	19	717	849	1492	.562	10
E. R. Baker, Macomb, Ill......	1	23	485	628	1116	.562	10

The Moline Dispatch Tournament was held at night, and the entries in this meet played very well. The averages were lower than the men could have ordinarily thrown because it was at night, and because the second half of the schedule was finished in one night in a downpour of very cold rain. The summary:

Robt. Bales, Kansas City, Kan	22	1	1023	894	1336	.633	$60
R. Frye, Orkney Springs, Va.....20		3	1036	905	1324	.683	50
D. Brown, Long Beach, Cal........20		3	760	693	1086	.640	40
Wm. Garvey, Boone, Ia...............17		6	1006	863	1402	.629	30
Myron Ferguson, Columbus, O....17		6	739	784	1208	.638	20
Carl Hoff, Lewisburg, O.............16		7	1022	902	1436	.621	10
John Calao, Chicago, Ill.............16		7	997	821	1442	.593	9
C. Henson, Arlington, Va.............16		7	1040	924	1458	.606	8
F. Harburn, Cromartz, Ontario	15	8	739	644	1066	.600	7
Lee Rose, Detroit, Mich.............14		9	915	820	1418	.578	5.50
L. Mahoney, Red Bank, N. J......14		9	864	815	1374	.571	5.50
T. Jarrell, Hyattsville, Md..........10		13	634	640	1040	.612	5
L. Steinmann, St. Louis, Mo......10		13	838	723	1380	.515	5
John Simon, London, Ont.............10		13	578	524	1090	.484	5
John Paxton, Fairfield, Ia.........	8	15	1425	763	1308	.593	5

R. Wilson, Washington, D. C.	8 15	528	475	1018	.500	5
R. H. Rizor, Detroit, Mich.	6 17	726	623	1308	.500	5
Jos. Clayton, Morris, Ill.	5 18	464	464	752	.617	5
Alfred Terry, Morris, Ill.	4 19	427	375	718	.534	5
Carey Davis, Moline, Ill.	3 20	418	421	756	.564	5
Dale Terry, Morris, Ill.	3 20	359	351	702	.500	5
Alton Wood, Chicago, Ill.	2 21	297	327	654	.500	5
Lloyd Woodard, Columbus, Kan	2 21	403	416	832	.500	5
John Garvey, Boone, Ia.	0 23	32	43	128	.343	5

Ted Allen successfully defended his Mid-West title in the tournament at Des Moines in 1936. In the 16-man round-robin, Allen and Casey "Jones" tied for first with 13 wins and two defeats each. Allen averaged .730, and Jones hit .740. In the play-off, Allen won two straight games, averaging .800. Sam Somerhalder of Guide Rock, Neb., was third, and Alvin Gandy, of Topeka, Kan., and Ellis Griggs, of Plainville, Ill., tied for fourth.

Fernando Isais walked away from the field in the Mid-West meet at Des Moines in 1937. The great Mexican did not lose a game, and hung up a 15-game average of .835, the highest ever hurled in a tournament of national scope. Ted Allen finished second with 13 wins and two losses, averaging .824. Guy Zimmermann was third with .790; "Casey" Jones took fourth with .746; John Sebeck, of Canton, Ohio, came in fifth with .741; Ellis Griggs took sixth with .740; Robert Bales was seventh with .706; Gaylord Peterson was eighth with .753; Sam Somerholder came in ninth with .743 and others to finish above the seventy mark were Alvin Gandy with .717 and John Paxton with .726. The sixteen men in the finals hung up a grand average of .726.

The 1938 Mid-West Tournament at Des Moines was the high spot of the year. The pace that horseshoe pitching had reached can be discerned by a few of the games played in the preliminaries. Casey Jones defeated Ellis Griggs with 107 ringers in 116 shoes; Eddie Packham won a game from Garland Goble which lasted two hours and fifteen minutes; James O'Shea shot 102 ringers in 116 shoes against Dean Brown; and Ted Allen beat Jones with 111 ringers in 130 shoes. Ted Allen won 32 consecutive games in the preliminaries, and then breezed through the finals with 15 more straight victories. In the finals he hung up an average of .846 to set a world record. Ellis Griggs came in second with 12 wins and three losses, averaging .757. The next six in order were: Alvin Gandy .770, Fernando Isais .781, Dean Brown .740, Casey Jones .823, Eddie Packham .770, and James O'Shea .775.

The year of 1939 brought another Mid-West Tournament to

Des Moines, and this time the Convention of National Horseshoe Pitchers' Association was held in conjunction.

The horseshoe world felt the need of a convention badly, for there were several points that needed fixing in the rules and laws that had been rendered obsolete by the march of progress.

The preliminaries, of which no official score was kept, was lightning fast for ringer averages, and it is estimated that most of the high 16 shot close to an 80 per cent average to reach the finals. Ted Allen, who suffered four beatings in the preliminaries, crashed through the finals with 15 stroight victories to retain his title. Dean Brown broke the world record against Lyle Brown by hanging up 20 consecutive double ringers, and after these two boys had tied for fifth place, a play-off game between them saw another record broken which had stood since the winter of 1925. The two Browns had four ringers on the stake for 10 successive innings. The players in the finals finished as follows:

1.	Ted Allen	15	0	.827
2.	Guy Zimmermann	13	2	.800
3.	Charles Jones	12	3	.809
4.	Alvin Gandy	10	5	.767
5.	Lyle Brown	9	6	.755
6.	Dean Brown	9	6	.801
7.	Grover Hawley	7	8	.772
8.	Aden Swinehamer	7	8	.737
9.	Ira Allen	7	8	.774
10.	Ellis Griggs	7	8	.746
11.	Raymond Frye	7	8	.708
12.	Roland Kraft	6	9	.708
13.	Dale Dixon	5	10	.726
14.	Sidney Harris	4	11	.693
15.	J. Robert Tompkin	2	13	.650
16.	Robert Bales	2	13	.737

The National Convention was a great success as far as passing the right laws and rules was concerned. It remains, of course, to see whether the new laws and rules can be enforced. If they can, the horseshoe game can look forward to 1940 with hope of reaching the road leading to greater heights than ever before attained. With the help of the pitchers themselves this can be done. Even as this book goes to press, at least three sources are trying to obtain the world tournament for 1940, and at least one source is certain. If the others come through also there may be the unusual sight of three world championship meets in one year. To say the least, this would be a vast change from the tournamentless years from 1935 through 1939.

[33]

HOW TO WIN AT HORSESHOES

The following hints will tell you how to win at horseshoe pitching, and enable you to become a popular and well-liked personality.

Always bang your shoes together just as your opponent is about to pitch. This distracts his attention and makes him miss If he glares at you about it, look very innocent and make a remark about how the mud sticks to your shoes or how your shoes continually burr.

After you have pitched your shoes, just stand up at the front of the box, and if your opponent desires to pitch from that same side, make him remind you of it each time, and then just step across to the other side of the stake and stand there at the front of the box. This always worries your opponent and takes his eye while he is trying to pitch. If he still pitches good shoes, try waving your hand to an imaginary friend on the sidelines and shouting hello at him.

If your opponent proves to be a poor sport or a fussy guy, and insists on you standing back while he pitches, always start walking for the other stake just as he swings his second shoe. Thumping the feet hard as you start out lends effectiveness to this idea.

If your opponent is having a hot spell and you want to cool him down, call for the score and then hold a long-winded argument with the scorekeeper over the way the score stands. Getting your opponent into the argument will help a great deal. Or if you get the chance, call for a careful measurement of shoes by the referee and keep him at it as long as possible. Even if your opponent is willing to concede you the point or the ringer, do not accept. Insist on everything being perfectly square. You might even seize this opportunity to make a speech about your fairness in all things, and how you wouldn't want anything you didn't earn.

Never give your opponent credit if he beats you. Make him distinctly understand that you gave him the game out of pure goodness of your heart, or that you were simply below your normal form and could have beaten him easily if you could have got going.

Always show the spectators what a swell sport you are by coaching your opponent, as he pitches, with some remark like "Atta boy!" "Put 'er on!" "Let's have four dead!" And always loudly express sympathy when he misses.

Always show your anxiety to see the courts kept in good condition by stamping and scraping the clay around the stake every inning. This must be done, of course, while your opponent is pitching his shoes.

In delivering your shoes always plant half your foot over the foul line. This saves considerable distance, and makes ringers of those shoes which would ordinarily be a couple of inches short. Then, too, this has a psychological effect on your opponent, as he will watch your feet and debate mentally whether or not he should call attention to your fouling, and this tends to reduce his concentration on pitching.

Before playing a game with a tough opponent who may beat you, tell everyone nearby how hard you had to work that day and how tired you are, or how you have been ill all day, or how sore your fingers are or something along that line so that if your opponent wins the game, it is what was to be expected considering your wretched condition, while if you win, then the spectators can see what a courageous fellow you really are.

By doing all these things, and other things along this same line, you will soon become a great personality, well liked and popular, and you will be doing something to add to the dignity of the game.

COURSE OF INSTRUCTION FOR BEGINNERS
By LEE ROSE

INTRODUCTION

Horseshoe pitching is one of the oldest sports in the world, but it has only in the last decade reached its present scientific status. The popularity of horseshoe pitching is increasing by leaps and bounds and every season finds new stars rising in all parts of the country. The increased interest in this sport naturally demands expert instruction, and, while many experts can and do give oral lessons and demonstrations, very few have attempted to set forth their instructions in written form. This dearth of written instruction is a handicap to correct development of players, and it must eventually come to pass that more written material will put in its appearance.

Foreseeing this ultimate demand we have compounded this work, believing it may be the forerunner to many greater ones. Our earnest desire to aid the game of horseshoe pitching to prosper through putting the beginner on the right track from the start is our only aim in this work.

In this treatise, we have attempted to set down the various problems which confront the beginner from the very start, and to point out to him the correct way to do everything which must be done before he can become a full-fledged player. We have taken these problems one by one in their logical sequence and have tried to explain each one in the most common-sense manner possible, and have progressed through the various items necessary in their chronological order.

With the hope that our suggestions will be received in the same spirit as given, we present the following treatise for the special edification of beginners in the great American game of horseshoe pitching.

THE HORSESHOE COURT

We shall assume in writing this that you, the student, have not yet acquired any knowledge of how to pitch—that you are a beginner who has had little or no experience in tossing the "Dobbin Slippers." Working under this assumption, we shall have to begin at the very beginning and attempt to show you the right way to do everything, and to try to explain to you the reason why.

The first necessary item to a horseshoe player is a proper pitching court. You may believe that since you are a rank beginner you can start your practise on any old pair of stakes driven into the ground, but this idea is as wrong as is an idea that a baseball team should practise in a forest.

[36]

Horseshoe pitching science has developed among other things, an official court, which, when properly built and maintained according to the rules, helps in no small way to increase the efficiency of the modern pitcher. If you attempt to pitch or learn to pitch on a poor court you will be working under a handicap right from the very beginning.

In the official rules you will find the proper measurements for an official horseshoe court in case you wish to construct one yourself, while in nearly every city and town in this country you will find horseshoe courts constructed either by the recreation department or by a private horseshoe club which you can easily join for a small cost.

Assuming that you need no further help in solving the problem of your horseshoe court we will pass on to the next item.

THE HORSESHOE

The second item necessary for a horseshoe pitcher is a pair of pitching shoes. The official rules tell you the weight and various measurements of a pitching shoe, but you will not be required to measure or weigh a pair of shoes before you buy them if you buy a nationally known make of shoe that has been officially sanctioned by the National Horseshoe Pitchers' Association.

The question concerning shoes is to decide which make of shoe one should pitch. There is an old saying which says that one man's meat is another man's poison. In other words, one shoe may be the best for one certain player, but another player may not be able to get as good results with that same shoe. Which make the beginner should use is, of course, an open question. One can get a better idea and quite a bit of amusement in hearing manufacturers or their salesmen discourse upon the advantages of their shoe. The only dependable way to decide is to try out all the shoes for yourself and pick out the ones you can pitch the best. The beginner, however, must pick out one before he can do any pitching, and to him our advice is—use a pair of shoes of a make which seems to be the most popular. Be sure that they have the largest possible hooks, and they should have a notch or two in the inner circle of the toe. We are not describing any certain shoe here, for several of the leading makes have one or both of these features. There is no doubt that these hooks and notches tend to hold your ringers on the stake, and a good pitcher should use the best that horseshoe science has developed in the way of shoes.

Use a new pair of shoes when you start out. You cannot expect results from a pair of second-hand shoes which have been warped and battered out of proper balance. When you purchase shoes which are made in different tempers of hardness,

[37]

it is best for beginners to obtain those of medium temper, as these stand up quite well and are still not hard enough to cause excessive bouncing.

THE OPEN SHOE

In pitching horseshoes the object is, of course, to cause the shoe to encircle the stake for a ringer. Consistent pitching of ringers can be attained only after you have mastered the art of throwing the "open shoe," meaning, of course, a shoe which arrives at the stake with open end foremost so as to more readily create ringers. It can be seen that the pitching of a horseshoe to make a ringer is quite an exact science which has become more and more exacting as the years have added knowledge to players.

A few years ago there were many ways to throw an open shoe which were deemed good enough for first class competition. Among some of the ways used was the three-quarter flop shoe, a shoe which turned clockwise three-quarters of a turn and flopped over end for end at the same time. This was a very popular throw some years ago, and is still used extensively among the older players. It is commonly called the "Lazy Dan." Another pitch closely allied to the "Lazy Dan" is the three-quarter turn without the flop. This turn is somewhat better than the flop shoe. Other clockwise turns include the "one turn," the "two turn," and "two and one-quarter," and "two and three-quarter." Of these four turns, the first two are very difficult to master for it is apparent that to throw a one or two-turn shoe you must grasp the shoe somewhere around the toe calk, and such a grip envolves the risk of cutting fingers on the sharp edges of the toe calk. The wearing of gloves eliminates the danger of cuts, but gloves subtract from a pitcher's efficiency, for too many shoes slip from the player's grasp if he wears gloves. The second two of these four turns, the two and one-quarter and the two and three-quarter turns necessitate too much spin on the shoe to allow for good control. There are a few players who have done well with these turns, but they are exceptions.

There is an occasional player who uses a counter-clockwise turn on his shoe. This is commonly known as a "reverse" turn, but it is little more than a freak, and should never be used as it is too hard on the wrist.

There are two other turns known as a "tumble" and a "double tumble." In these two turns the pitcher obtains an open shoe by causing the shoe to turn over end for end either once or twice. This idea is not very effective, as this way of pitching is difficult to master, and the least bit of wind will interfere too much.

[38]

The ever-increasing science of horseshoe pitching, and the constant demand for more and more ringers have eliminated all these afore-mentioned methods of throwing an open shoe from the consideration of first class players. At the present time there are but two turns which meet the requirements of modern horseshoe players. These two turns are the one and one-quarter and the one and three-quarter turns. Which of these two turns is the best is a moot question among the experts. You will find the leading players fairly well divided in their opinions regarding the possibilities of these two turns, but all will agree that these turns are far superior to any other turns.

Our choice of turns must therefore be limited to these two. Our advice to the student is this: If you are now a pitcher and have been using the one and one-quarter turn, stick to it! But if you are just starting in, or have been using some other turn, make up your mind to pitch the one and three-quarter turn.

It is not difficult to switch from one of these turns to the other, because your swing, step and delivery will be the same, while the grip you are going to learn here is applicable to either turn.

THE GRIP

There will be no need to go into detail concerning the various ways the leading experts take hold of their shoes to throw them. Each of these experts has developed a grip peculiar to himself that will be hard to imitate, and a beginner will do very well to avoid trying to imitate an expert, because the man he tries to copy has gone through an evolution of grips to arrive at his present one, and the beginner cannot successfully copy him without first experiencing the same evolution.

The beginner must make his start with a grip which he knows is fundamentally sound, and can afterward shift his hold slightly to conform with the ideas he acquires after considerable practice. Practically all of the leading experts take hold of the shoe in the same basic manner, but each of them has added a quirk here and there to differ slightly from others. It is a question whether this little change does him any better, or whether it is just the thought that he has invented a grip peculiar unto himself that enables him to do better. However that may be, the fact remains that the beginner must start out on the right track, and for the beginner we advocate this grip for him to use.

We have taken the privilege of naming this grip the "gun-handle grip." As the name implies, the hand and fingers are bent into much the same shape as they would be, were you to grasp

[39]

a pistol butt preparatory to firing it. Here is how the gun-handle grip is obtained.

Hold the shoe in your left hand, calks outward from the body and the open end of the shoe pointing straight up. Now double your right hand into the same position it would be if you were holding a pistol with your index finger on the trigger. Now straighten the thumb out and open your other three fingers enough to allow a horseshoe to be inserted into the hand. Insert the shoe which you hold in your left hand so that the underside of the shoe rests on the middle segment of your index or trigger finger. Straighten your little finger out until the tip of it rests against the end of the toe calk. Clamp your thumb down flat on the topside of the shoe, having it point directly at the opposite or right heel calk. Allow the other two fingers to rest against the shoe wherever they naturally go. This is your grip for a one and three-quarter turn. If you are going to pitch a one and one-quarter turn, take exactly the same grip on the opposite side of the shoe having the tip of your little finger against the right heel calk. With the one and one-quarter turn it is desirable to spread the hand out as far as possible.

Your fingers must not be allowed to slip from their place during the time it takes to swing the shoe. When the shoe is finally released, let go of it just as though it had suddenly become red hot; do not let it slide from your fingers. You may find that the trigger finger remains in contact with the shoe longer than does the other fingers and thumb, but this is as it should be, for the index finger imparts the final message to the shoe from your hand.

This should be your grip to start out with. It will seem terribly awkward to you at first, and you will no doubt find your hand and fingers tiring very quickly from this unaccustomed exercise, but it will come to you easier as your grip becomes more familiar. After you have learned to pitch quite well you may find that a slight shift of your fingers will suit your own style a little better, but until you learn to pitch quite well our advice to you is to adhere religiously to this grip until you master it. Remember, if there seems to be something wrong, it is you and not the fundamental principles behind your grip.

THE STANCE AND STEP

The next thing we must learn is the part our feet play in pitching the horseshoes. The first thing to determine is which side of the stake we shall hurl our shoes from. The orthodox side for a right hander is the left side of the stake. Pitching from the right hand side is called a cross-fire. While many pitchers use the cross-fire side, they would find themselves hurl-

[40]

ahead to a point close to the foul line. Keep your feet parallel at all times. After you have delivered your first shoe, replace your feet as they were before, and go through exactly the same step for the second shoe. You will find it advisable to keep your right foot on the ground at all times. You may raise your right heel in delivering the shoe, but you should keep the toe on the ground. This enables you to back up and replace your feet in starting position without looking down at them between pitches, and this aids in developing a rhythm to the delivery of your two shoes.

There is another new method of stepping which is a recent idea, but because of the risk of getting you confused regarding the step, we will delay telling you about this new method until later. Just keep in mind how your feet should work, and when you learn about the swing you will then be able to fit the two together.

THE SWING AND DELIVERY

Up until now we have told you about several points that are relatively small when compared to the next point we shall attempt to set forth. This next is the pulse of all horseshoe pitching—the "swing." The swing is the vehicle which whisks your shoe across intervening space to the opposite stake, and it is going to present to you, the beginner, the one most difficult part of pitching horseshoes. It is here that most horseshoe pitchers fail. Most pitchers, whether they be experts or dubs use much the same grip, step and shoe, but the thing which distinguishes them apart is their swing.

Your arm and shoulder contains many sets of muscles which have been built up through work you have done. In developing a horseshoe swing you must bring into play many muscles which you heretofore have never used, and the gradual strengthening of these muscles takes time and patience. Most players develop their arms up to a certain point and then fall into a rut from which they never recover, either because they lack the necessary desire to practice unrelentingly until they conquer the swing, or because they get into competition too quickly, and in the heat of battle allow their swing to degenerate into a pushing motion from which it is hard to recover. It is fatal to allow yourself to form bad pitching habits. It is much better to take longer in getting ready to pitch, when you will have formed good habits of pitching. But let us take up the swing itself.

There are two parts to the swing, the front swing and the back swing. The front swing is easy, because it is easy to raise one's arm up in front of one's self, but the back swing is the dif-

[42]

have gained enough knowledge of the game to be able to learn to pitch quite well. The following paragraphs contain information which is more for the use of an advanced pitcher rather than a beginner, and we suggest that the student should refrain from attempting to use any of this following information until he has learned to pitch fairly well.

If you have followed the lessons exactly as prescribed herein, you will be pitching fairly well, but your shoe will seem to lack something. There will be many times when you will get your shoe to go very well, and then there will be other times when you can't for the life of you seem to make it work right. We will try to explain to you just what it is that you lack, and how you can go about getting it.

The necessary thing which you lack is the "break." Here is the definition of the "break." As you pitch your shoe now it leaves your hand, rises into the air, spins around as it flies through the air, opening up just as it reaches the stake. It spins around fairly evenly as it travels through the air. The "break" is a motion you impart to the shoe which causes it to travel through the air in a series of jerks rather than in an even spin. The idea behind these series of jerks is to cause the shoe to make its last jerk as it reaches a point about three feet from the stake to which it is going, and sweep straight into the stake open end foremost without making any further turn or jerk from that point on.

The breaking shoe has a distinct advantage over the spinning shoe for this reason. When you develop a spinning shoe, you become used to seeing it open when the shoe travels at one certain height. If your shoe happens to travel a little higher or a little lower your shoe spins either not quite enough or too much, and your shoe is not open when it reaches the stake. With the breaking shoe, however, it can readily be seen that it will be open whether it is high or low.

It is a very simple thing to know how to obtain the break on your shoe, but it is not so easy to master. As your shoe reaches the top of its back swing you tilt your wrist upward as far as you can before starting your shoe on its down swing. As your shoe is on its down swing, and until it is about half way up on its front swing, keep your wrist tilted. Then straighten your wrist up just an instant before you give it the flip which gives your shoe its turn. You must be careful not to get the flip and the tilt confused; the flip which turns your shoe is a twist of the wrist, while the tilt is a bending of the wrist, two different motions. However, the two motions must be performed so quickly and so close together that they seem almost impercept-

[44]

These first two weeks is the toughest period in learning to pitch, and it is necessary that you make up your mind that you are going to try faithfully, for only by this drudgery can you forge yourself into a pitcher.

After these first two weeks you can go around where there are other players, and you can pick out a few of the poorer ones to play against at the start. As you improve you can play better ones, and soon you will find yourself a full-fledged "slipper slinger."

COHESION

As you play, you will find that it is difficult to get all the various parts of your horseshoe pitching system working smoothly and at the same time. Some days your shoe will open beautifully, but you will not be able to line it up with the stake, or perhaps you have your shoe lined up perfectly and you can't seem to get the right distance, or perhaps your shoe doesn't land flat. The thing which you lack is "cohesion," or the knack of correcting one flaw without causing something else to go wrong. The attainment of cohesion is something which every person must work out for himself, but we can give you an idea here as to how to go about it.

There are three things your shoe must do in order to make a ringer. First, it must be open; second, it must be lined up with the stake; and third, it must have the proper balance. Here are the three parts of your delivery which affect these three items the most directly. Your open shoe is obtained through your grip and the twist you give to your wrist and arm just before releasing the shoe. Your line is obtained by stepping in the proper direction and swinging your arm in a straight line close to your body. Your distance is obtained through the swing you give your shoe. With this chart to guide you, you can correct your faults as soon as you recognize them.

If your shoe is opening properly, you know your grip and wrist flip is working. If your shoe is in line, you know your step, and the direction of your swing is all right, and if you get the proper distance you know the length of your swing is all right. As we have said before, you should get these three things working before trying to obtain a "break" on your shoe. As for the heighth your shoe should reach in its flight, this item will work itself out automatically. However, we would say that your shoe should travel no higher than twelve feet and no lower than eight.

You have read these instructions on how to learn to pitch. Careful study of these instructions, and faithful practice will make you a good player. The matter is entirely in your hands.

[46]

HOW TO CONDUCT A HORSESHOE TOURNAMENT

Only one other book, to our knowledge, has ever contained specific information on how to conduct a tournament, and that was written over a decade ago. Much has transpired since then in the way of advancement of ideas both in play and in the conducting of same. Naturally, ideas and plans which were popular over ten years ago have become obsolete with the march of time.

In the early days of horseshoe pitching the entrants to practically all the world tournaments were either the professionals who made it their business to be there, or a number of well-to-do vacationers with a few local players to fill in. The tournaments were usually leisurely affairs taking the better part of two weeks for the completion. The first week was devoted to one round-robin wherein each player met each other player in one game. After that the twelve highest players in the round-robin played each other three to five games each for the next three to five days.

Later, with increased numbers of entries and a little shorter time, the squad plan of play was instituted. Under this plan the players were segregated into squads of from six to 12 players who played a round-robin schedule in each squad with the three, four or five highest in each squad moving into the finals. This system would have been fine had all players been equal in skill, but sometimes a player who might have been entitled to a place in the finals was eliminated in the squad play due to his being cast in a squad with several strong players, while weaker players reached the finals through being placed in a squad with weaker men.

After that, there came the so-called "100 shoe pitch" plan. All entrants were forced to pitch 100 shoes for total points with the highest ones picked for the finals. This plan was strictly in favor of the top-notch players who managed to get through the tournament with a minimum of effort, and it was a distinct disappointment to the ones who had come to the meet with only the intention of meeting the good players for the fun of the thing.

Horseshoe pitching had become a business for the professinals, and they cashed in on their abilities with as little effort as possible. However, somebody had to pay for these tournaments, and the ones who were putting up the prizes were the poorer players who knew they couldn't win the title, but who would liked to have played a few games against the champions just for the fun of the thing. Results and facts speak for themselves—only TWO world tournaments have been held in the past TEN YEARS!

ing a few rounds wherein the good ones polished off the poorer ones just to get a line on how their favorites are pitching, and here begins the working up of spectator interest.

A well-run tournament should pass through three phases of play designated roughly as the Preliminaries, the Round-Robin and the Finals. In the Preliminaries, all entrants shall be looked upon as equal and treated as such. In other words, whoever has charge of the tournament should act just as though he had never seen nor heard of a single player in the meet. No favors should be shown any player which are not accorded to the others. In a world tournament and also in some state meets the defending champion is not required to go through the qualifying stages of the tournament, and, of course, he is allowed this favor.

The first phase of the tournament is therefore devoted to the Preliminaries. In this stage of play each pitcher is required to pitch a certain number of games in actual competition, following a regular schedule. The number of games pitched by each man is dependent upon the number of courts, the number of entrants, and the time allowed. In the case of a world tournament it may take two days; in a state meet it may take one day.

The general plan is given here and the tournament manager can fit it into his conditions easily, always remembering that the more games played gives a better line on the qualifiers, and more satisfaction to those eliminated. In order that each player may have the same chance, each must pitch the same number of shoes, and the games must be limited to 50 shoes. In these games it is recommended that both players count all points made each inning, three for each ringer and one for each shoe within six inches of the stake. The first pitch should, of course, go to the player with the closest shoes as in a regular 50-point game.

The tournament manager will always be able to guess fairly close as to the number of men who will be entered, and knowing how much time he will have, he can regulate the number of 50-shoe games accordingly. To give a specific instance, let us say that this system is to be used in a big tournament, and 16 courts are available for a whole day's play. The expected entry list would, let us say, be the same as that of Moline in 1935, 78 players. Since 32 players could play at one time, there would be three qualifying shifts, and if nine hours were used for actual play, that would allow three hours of play for each shift. In three hours' time each player could play as many as nine games, but to be safe, the tournament manager could cut it to eight or even seven games. By the end of the day each pitcher would have played the same number of games and would have thrown the same number of shoes.

[53]

out of five games. The two finalists will meet in a four-out-of-seven series.

The two losers in the second round of the finals will meet in a three-out-of-five series for third place. The four losers in the first round of the finals shall meet in a two-out-of-three series with the fifth meeting the eighth, etc. The two winners in these series then play another two-out-of-three for fifth place, while the two losers play one game for seventh.

All ties for positions in the preliminaries and the round-robin shall be decided in the most efficient manner, proceedure to be determined by the tournament manager.

It can easily be seen that the spectator interest will be gradually raised as the tournament goes through its different phases. At first there will be a scramble among all the players simply to get into the first 30 places. The topnotchers will easily make it, and it will be no more than a warm-up to them. Then the battle narrows down to a race to get into the first eight places, and several good pitchers will be crowded out here. Subsequently, the race is reduced to four, and then to two, and finally the interest reaches its height as these two final pitchers square off for the final series.

This entire system has been used in the Michigan State Tournament for the past four years, and has been praised by all pitchers who have participated in it. Under this system, a top-notch player does not lose his chance for the title because some poorer player who has no right to do so gets a hot streak and upsets him in a game, and a poorer player who gets through the round-robin with several lucky wins must hold his place on merit in the finals. Furthermore, the fans who have come to see the meet like to see the good ones play each other, and like to see records made, and will have more chance to see all this when two top-notch pitchers play a three-out-of-five series than when they just meet in a single game.

A tournament manager should come to a tournament completely prepared to conduct it in the most efficient manner. He should, of course, be perfectly familiar with the plan under which the meet is to be run, and he should have his schedules ready. If he knows in advance just how many pitchers will be in the round-robin, he should prepare individual schedules for each player, listing his games and the courts on which he will play them, and all he has to do then is hand out the numbers and the corresponding schedule.

After a sufficient number of score keepers have been lined up, the manager will instruct them as to the proper way to keep the scores, and then he will call all of the players together and

THE NATIONAL LEAGUE

Many people have possibly heard of or read about the National Association forming a National Team League to begin operation in 1940 for the first time. Many have sent letters to the National Secretary concerning this league. Some have been critical, but more have been in praise of such a laudable effort. All letters, however, invariably ask for further information concerning the different rules. In this article we shall attempt to take each rule and explain the whys and wherefores of each.

I believe Rules 1 and 2 need no explanation, but Rule 3 might be explained to some extent. In filing a notice of prospective entry, the sender does not obligate himself in any way to enter a team. This is just to aid some source which would like to enter a team, and does not know for certain whether or not they will be able to do so. This also gives the National Secretary a line on how many teams will be lined up for the coming season, and he will be able to draw up team contracts in advance.

The team contract will be signed by each person connected with the team either in the role of a player or in the capacity of manager, coach, trainer, or some such office.

Rule 4 deals with the drawing up of the schedule for the season. The National Secretary will draw up a schedule for each team in each division. As nearly as it is possible to do so, he will have each team play one league match every two weeks, one game at home, and the next game on the road. This allows each team a month between road games, and is not too much traveling for them since teams who have been playing matches for years now have frequently made journeys more often than this.

There is no way to tell beforehand just how many divisions will be formed, for it will depend entirely upon the number of entries, and their geographical locations. All matches will be scheduled for Sundays, but if two teams wish to arrange between them to play the match upon some other date, this will be perfectly agreeable to the National Association.

Each team will be furnished with a copy of every team's complete roster so that the strength and personnel of each prospective opponent will be known, and no team can substitute a "ringer" upon the other team.

It is the general plan to bring the divisional winners together to decide a world team championship if at all possible. This plan will depend a great deal upon how far apart the winners are located, and circumstances attending each team's situation.

In determining the number of men per side, the number chosen was seven. An odd number of men will automatically eliminate any tie matches, and since five men on a side seemed too few, and nine men on a side seemed too many, the number seven seemed to be ideal.

Rule 8 was compiled from the National Secretary's long experience with team matches, and we believe it is self-explanatory.

Rule 10 has been the subject of many questions, most of them dealing with the $10.00 entry fee. Most inquiries deal with what will be done with the money. Well, to begin with the National Association has taken upon itself an extra task involving a great deal of labor, a few more books for records, and good deal more postage. All the expenses connected with the league will be taken out of the entry fees, and the balance can be used for whatever the majority of teams desire it to be used for. On each team's contract they will be asked to state what they want the money to be used for. A suggestion would be to use it for defraying part of the expenses of bringing the division winners together, or put it up in cash prizes to be played for by the winners. Any other suggestions will be welcome.

Rule 12 has been the favorite subject for letters received. Some states have written in saying that they would like to enter teams in this league, but could not see their way to barring the members of these teams from state league competition or local league play. Now we wish to make one thing clear—we simply say, "It is REQUESTED that no member of a National League team play on a state league team," etc. We do not POSITIVELY wish to bar any person from playing in as many leagues as he wishes to play in.

This rule can be left up to each state association to interpret, and since they are more familiar with their own conditions, they can decide if they will allow a pitcher to play in both leagues or only in one. Some of the states may find it to their advantage to allow men to participate in only one league. In Michigan, for example, the seven best pitchers from Detroit would be able to whip any other Michigan team with ease, but the second best seven in Detroit would be about on a par with the smaller towns. Also, in the local league in Detroit, with the cream of the pitchers barred from league play, the league would find itself better balanced. To repay these men for the loss of local league play, there would be an all-star individual league formed among the better players, and this should be more interesting to them, and more beneficial to their development since they will be meeting stronger players at all times.

Plans along this same line can be worked out in other large cities, and we feel certain that the result will be newer and greater interest aroused in horseshoes.

[59]

A word in closing. We do not expect this National League to be a wonderful success the first year, for a thing like this needs building up. We DO believe, however, that in this league, and the formation of smaller leagues of all classes on the same pattern, lies the future of the game of horseshoe pitching. The National Association, by forming these leagues, will be doing something for the "run-of-the-mine" pitcher, and he is the one upon whom the burden of success or failure rests.

NATIONAL H. S. P. ASSOCIATION OF AMERICA
FINANCIAL REPORT

Aug. 19, 1935. Balance on hand	$ 76.33
Receipts, 1935 Aug. 19 to Dec. 31	63.00
	$ 139.33
Expenses, 1935; Aug. 19 to Dec. 31	75.00
Jan. 1, 1936. Balance on hand	$ 64.00
Receipts from stamps, 1936	414.00
Receipts from memberships, 1936	539.50
	$1017.83
Expenses, 1936	703.13
Jan. 1, 1937. Balance on hand	$ 314.70
Receipts from stamps, 1937	337.00
Receipts from memberships, 1937	289.60
	$ 941.30
Expenses, 1937	724.91
Jan. 1, 1938. Balance on hand	$ 216.39
Receipts from stamps, 1938	384.00
Receipts from memberships, 1938	216.20
	$ 816.59
Expenses, 1938	358.69
Jan. 1, 1939. Balance on hand	$ 457.90

Receipts from stamps to Aug. 15... 150.00
Receipts from memberships to Aug. 15................................. 108.15

$ 716.05
Expenses, 1939, to Aug. 15.. 250.00

Aug. 15, 1939; Balance on hand..................................$ 465.69
Receipts from Aug. 15 to Sept. 1, 1939............................... 25.16

Sept. 1, 1939. Balance on hand...$ 491.12
        Signed   R. B. Howard, Sec.-Treas.
Sept. 1, 1939. Balance on hand ....$ 491.12
Receipts from stamps, Sept. 1 to Dec. 31, 1939..................... 275.00
Receipts from memberships Sept. 1 to Dec. 31, 1939........ 65.00

$ 831,12
Expenses, Sept. 1 to Dec. 31, 1939................................. 301.70

Jan. 1, 1940. Balance on hand......................................$ 529.42
        Signed   LEE ROSE, Sec.-Treas.

NEW JERSEY

New Jersey Horseshoe Pitchers Association was organized May 27th, 1934, and applied for and received a charter from the National Horseshoe Pitchers Association in July, 1934.

Current Officers

President, D. Eric Brown, 2900 Carmen St., Camden, N. J.

First Vice President, Paul Puglise, 88 Lyon St., Paterson, New Jersey.

Second Vice President, Reynold Santoro, 211 Broad St., Perth Amboy, New Jersey.

Secretary and Treasurer, Claude E. Hart, 17 Van Reypen St., Jersey City, New Jersey.

Executive Committee—Lee R. Davis, 2 Brookway Ave., Englewood, N. J.; Michael Mahoney, Lincroft, N. J.; John Landers, 11 Moore Terrace, West Orange, N. J.; Walter Angilly, 114 Romaine Place, Newark, N. J.; Frank Maisch, 601 Madison St., West New York, N. J.; Harry Oberhauser, 70 Laurel Ave., Arlington, N. J.

Prior to organization of the State Association, most of the activity consisted of match games between the top players. Frank Boyce, of Oldbridge, was recognized as the state champion from 1925 to 1933, closely followed by George MacNeil, of Absecon. During 1933, Joe Puglise, of Paterson, began to challenge the leaders and went on to win the official state championship in a tournament held at the State Fair in Trenton in September of that year. Other tournaments were held in Paterson, Egg Harbor, Camden and Perth Amboy, but the most popular ones were held at the Boyce Farm in Oldbridge.

With the organization of the association, horseshoes really began to flourish. A 14-year-old school boy, named Lawrence Mahoney, of Lincroft, began to astound the players and fans alike by winning from men twice his size and in tournaments would average around 50 per cent ringers. At the state chamionship tourney held at the State Fair in Trenton, in September, 1934, the folowers of the sport were even more amazed when he made a clean sweep of his nine championship games and copped the state title with an average of 59 per cent ringers.

Joe Puglise saw his title go overboard even though he averaged 62 per cent for the day. Since that time the lad from Lincroft has dominated horseshoe pitching in New Jersey and won the state championship for the sixth consecutive year in 1939. During those six years he has not lost a single game in any state championship tourney. Several players have tried to unseat him. Puglise has been a constant threat and Johnny Rosselet, of Elizabeth, Otto Peters of Jersey City, Eugene Hillman of

Paterson, Arthur Haagsma, of Jersey City, William Kolb of Newark, Joe McCrink of West Orange, and Clare Hume of Jersey City have tried in vain. Hume gave the crowd a thrill in the 1937 tourney by holding Mahoney even for the better half of the title game, but could not quite match his youthful opponent to the end.

In 1937 another school boy sensation loomed on the horizon in the person of Arthur Scolari, of Paterson, a protege of Joe and Paul Puglise. He won the Class "B" state title averaging 60 per cent ringers. Being forced out of competition in 1938 by illness, he was back in 1939 to nose Hume out for the runner-up spot to Mahoney in the title play averaging 66 per cent. The 1937, 1938 and 1939 tournaments were held on the Lincoln Park courts in Jersey City.

During the past six years the association has sponsored, in addition to the annual state championship, several "open" tournaments, including the New Jersey Open and the Central Jersey Open, both usually held at Emil's Log Cabin in Middletown; the South Jersey Open at Clemendon Park, Camden, and various local tourneys. The Annual Eastern Pennsylvania Open, sponsored by the Willow Grove Amusement Park at Willow Grove, Pa., is directed by D. E. Brown, President of the New Jersey Association.

The most popular open tournament is the Annual Hudson County Open, which is held in Jersey City and sponsored by the Hudson County Horseshoe Club, Inc., 671 Montgomery Street, Jersey City. The first one was held on July 15tn, 1934, and 38 men entered the competition. Vito Fileccia, of Brooklyn, was the winner after a play-off with Joe Puglise, and made it four-in-a-row by winning the 1935, 1936 and 1937 tourneys. The '34, '35 and '36 tournaments were held on the courts at Bergen and Montgomery Streets, while the last three, 1937, 1938 and 1939, were held on the new courts constructed by the Hudson County Park Commission, in Lincoln Park, Jersey City.

The 1938 tournament found Ted Allen, world's champion, entered in the competition, but it was not his day and the title went to William Hamann, of White Plains, New York. 1939 was destined to be truly a New Jersey year and the most coveted open title in the several states adjoining New Jersey went to New Jersey's own state champion, Larry Mahoney. The entries, numbering over 90, included Fileccia, former New York state champion; William Hamann, defending title holder, and then New York state champion; Kenneth Hurst of Providence, Rhode Island state champion; Raymond Frye, of Richmond; S. Lane, of Stamford, Conn. Harold Seaman, of Hyde Park, former New York state champion; John Fulton, of Carlisle, Eastern Pennsylvania champion.

Mahoney won with an average of 80.9 per cent and a high game of 89.7 per cent, both of which set new records for New Jersey competition. Fileccia finished second, averaging 75 per cent with a high game of 83.7 per cent. Hamann was third, with an average of 75.4 per cent, and a high game of 89.2 per cent. Hurst was fourth, averaging 73.2 per cent with a high game of 85.8 per cent. Frye was fifth with an average of 70 per cent, and a high game of 78 per cent. Fulton and Seaman failed to qualify for Class "A" and finished first and second in Class "B" in the order named. Fulton averaged 64.2 and Seaman 63.7 per cent.

This fine competition amply rewards the Hudson County men notably Benjamin Murphy, Thomas Ellis, Otto Peters, Clare Hume and Claude Hart, for their tireless efforts to make their tournament worthy of the best competitors. New Jersey would like to take this opportunity to thank their neighboring state leaders for their fine co-operation in this and other tournaments.

A prime factor in the development of the game was the organization throughout the state of numerous horseshoe clubs. Among the first to organize was the Pellington Horseshoe Club of East Orange, Paterson Associated Clubs of Paterson, Camden Horseshoe Club of Camden, Liberty Horseshoe Club of West Orange, and the Bergen, Audubon and Pershing Clubs of Jersey City. Others were the Englewood Horseshoe Club of Englewood, The Forest Hill Club of Newark, and the Watchung Horseshoe and Social Club of West Orange.

In October, 1936, the Bergen, Audubon and Pershing groups united to form the Hudson County Horseshoe Club and in February, 1938, this latter group was incorporated and at the end of the decade was one of the strongest units in the State Association, along with the Englewood Club and the Forest Hill Club. Of the earlier groups, Camden and Paterson had indoor courts for winter pitching, followed by the Hudson County Club in 1936 and Forest Hill in 1939.

Indoor pitching during the winter months has done a lot to keep the game going and through numerous friendly matches between the various clubs. During the winter of 1938-1939 several individual matches were staged by the Hudson County Club and the Englewood Clubs. The first was a match between Larry Mahoney and Ted Allen on the Hudson County Courts. Mahoney won three games out of five averaging 75 per cent against 76.6 per cent for Allen. Vito Fileccia then took a crack at the Jersey champ on the same courts but could not win a game even though

[64]

he averaged 70.4 per cent. Mahoney was hot and averaged 81 per cent. William Hamann, then New York state champion, was the next to feel the sting of the New Jersey champ. Mahoney shot 78% to win three out of five games. Hamann's average was 74 per cent. Hamann, however, avenged his defeat in a match sponsored by the Englewood Club by winning three straight games.

New Jersey, while it was not one of the first states to take up horseshoe pitching, certainly has come a long way in the short space of a few years. We might mention in passing that in 1933 Joe Puglise won the state championship with an average of only 36 per cent, while in 1938 Mahoney pitched 73.5 per cent to win the state title.

Before signing off we feel it is imperative to mention some of the men in the promotional field, without which horseshoes would still be a "back-yard" sport. These men may never have heard the plaudits of the crowds for their pitching ability, but for their efforts to promote the game so that others can enjoy their chosen sport under the best possible conditions we believe they deserve equal credit with the most talented pitchers. We mention D. Eric Brown, of Camden; W. E. Santoro, of Newark; Paul Puglise, of Paterson; George MacNeil, of Absecon; Reynold Santoro, of Perth Amboy; Lee Davis and Albert Anderson, of Englewood; Benjamin Murphy, Thomas Ellis, Otto Peters, Clare Hume and Claude Hart of Jersey City, and a host of others.

Signed,

CLAUDE E. HART, Secretary-Treasurer
New Jersey Horseshoe Pitchers Asso.

ILLINOIS

Organized horseshoe pitching in Illinois found its inception at a big open tournament held at Fairbury on Labor Day, 1925. This tournament was won by Frank Jackson, with Walter Torbert second, and Gaylord Peterson third. A meeting at this tournament resulted in the formation of The State Horseshoe Pitchers' Association of Illinois, Inc.

Every year since then, Illinois has held a yearly, sanctioned state tournament. Walter Torbert, of Clinton, was the first state champion, winning the title in 1926 from a field of 130. This meet was also held at Fairbury. In 1927 the meet was held at the State Fair in Springfield, and again Walter Torbert came through against a field of 150. In both of these tournaments Torbert did not lose a game.

The promising career of this young pitcher was ended in the

spring of 1928 by the Grim Reaper, and this great loss was mourned by horseshoe fans everywhere.

Gaylord Peterson came through to win the 1928 tournament which was again held at Fairbury. In 1929 the tournament was brought back to Springfield to become a permanent fixture of the fair, and a grand old player, C. R. Thompson, of Chicago, became the champion. Milton Tate, of Knoxville, began a reign as champion with the 1930 tournament, and he retained his title until the 1933 meet when he was dethroned by Joe Bennett, of Congerville.

Gaylord Peterson again took the title in 1934, and Ellis Griggs, of Plainville won out in 1935. Another grand old player ascended the throne in 1936 when Howard Collier, of Canton, won out. In this year was first instituted the junior tournament for boys under 18, and the first winner was Herbert Patrick, of Fairbuny. The yeas of 1937 saw Milton Tate come back to the top, and also saw Patrick retain his crown. William Moore, of Danville, won out in 1938, with Patrick again winning the junior meet. Aden Swinehamer, of 1203 Grand Blvd., Aurora, is the present state champion, having won in 1939.

The Illinois Association has had a fine tournament every year since its formation. Each year the meet is pitched under a huge tent to prevent rain from halting the proceedings, and also to protect players from sun glare.

The success attending the Illinois efforts are due in no small way to the magnificent work done by President L. E. Tanner, of Anchor. Mr. Tanner really needs no introduction to any horseshoe fan, for everyone knows of his unselfish and unstinting labors during the trying years of 1933-39 when he was National President. He has been the head of the Illinois Association ever since it was first organized, and the efforts of one great horseshoe patriot in the organization of a state can be clearly seen in Illinois.

The only sad mark upon the Illinois slate is found in Chicago. Here, most of the players have hooked up with the A.A.U. How these professional pitchers have succeeded in joining an amateur association is not known, but even if they have slipped by as amateurs, their very conscience should tell them that they are defeating the purpose for which amateur pitching was organized. It is hoped that these players will see their way to coming back with the organization to which they rightfully and morally belong.

MASSACHUSETTS

Massachusetts joined the National Association in 1936, the first year the new membership plan was put into effect. They

[66]

had been ably represented at the Moline Convention by Philip Gilpatrick, and in 1936 became the second highest state in the membership list. Their membership dropped to two-thirds in 1937, and was halved again in 1938. In 1939 they voted at their state convention to drop out of the National Association entirely. Communications between the National Secretary and the State Secretary indicate, however, that the Bay State would be willing to rejoin the National fold if they can be shown that it would be to their advantage to belong.

Here are the winners of the state title for the past seven years:

James Shea won the title in 1933, 1934 and 1935, with percentages of .580, .617 and .630; 1936, Stanley DeLeary, .607; 1937, James O'Shea, .816; 1938, James O'Shea, .811; 1939, Stanley DeLeary, .723.

Here are the winners of the New England championship for the past ten years: 1930, John Kilpeck, Massachusetts, .502; 1931, Bernard Herfurth, Massachusetts, .504; 1932, Charles Gerrish, New Hampshire, .514; 1933, Bernard Herfurth, Massachusetts, .530; 1934, Bernard Herfurth, Massachusetts, .662; 1935, James O'Shea, Massachusetts, .676; 1936, Stanley DeLeary, Massachusetts, .632; 1937, James O'Shea, Massachusetts, .745; 1938, James O'Shea, Massachusetts, .743; 1939, Kenneth Hurst, Rhode Island, .762.

The ever-increasing ringer percentage tells the story better than words of the way the game is developing in the Massachusetts sction of the land.

CONNECTICUT

Horseshoe pitching owes its modern beginning in Connecticut to Sam Bartram who, in 1925, moved from Kokomo, Ind., to Connecticut, and introduced the game there by giving exhibitions throughout the state and interesting people in taking up the sport. By 1939 he had created enough interest to be able to hold a state tournament at Bridgeport. The winner of this tournament was S. C. Lane, of Stamford, a recent resident of Ft. Lauderdale, Fla. Mr. Lane organized the Stamford Horseshoe Club, and from that time on the game grew steadily.

A state tournament was held yearly in Bridgeport, and Mr. Lane continued as champion until 1933, when G. Georgetti, of Manchester, won the crown. He successfully defended it the next year also.

In 1935 the Connecticut State Horseshoe Pitchers' Association was formed, and the site of the state tournament was moved to Greenwich. This meet was won by Irving Wood of New Canaan. William Crofut, of Shelton, captured the title in 1936, and S. C.

[67]

Lane came back as champion in 1937. The championship for the past two years has gone to Crofut, who set a record by averaging 62 per cent in the 1938 meet at Litchfield.

Connecticut has made great strides in organizing regular team leagues. Starting in 1935 by entering two teams in the Tri-County League, an organization which included part of New York, they continued to grow, and entered teams in the Hudson Valley League in 1938. The year of 1939 found Connecticut forming their present fine state league, and found them also staging the New England Tournament at Hartford.

Connecticut expects a banner year in 1940. They will continue their state league, and will also have entries in the National League, meanwhile increasing their membership to greater heights.

State Secretary is Mr. L. D. Lane, of 715 Hope St., Springdale.

SOUTH DAKOTA

The present state association of South Dakota was organized in 1937, having been affiliated with the National Association since that time. The President is Lee Washburn, of 402 Sawyer St., Lead, and the Secretary Treasurer is L. O. Rigney, of Deadwood, Box. 436.

George Paulson, of Rapid City, won the state tournament in 1937, and Leigh Dunker of Warner took the title in the last two years.

The South Dakota Association has been growing steadily since its formation and boasts that it will soon outstrip other more thickly-populated states in the matter of membership.

UTAH

Horseshoe piching started in Utah in 1925, and the game flourished until the zenith was reached in 1932. From then until a couple of years ago the game waned, but now amateur pitching has taken a hold, and it is estimated that besides the professionals, there are 3,000 amateur pitchers in the state. This is altogether a healthy state of affairs, for these players will eventually join the National Association, and we may find Utah our leading state in a few years.

The Utah Association is a member of the National Association, and is working hard to promote the game.

There is a movement on foot to organize the students, both men and women, at the University of Utah in 1940.

E. W. Wahlin, of Magna, is president, and C. M. Wilson, of Salt Lake City is secretary treasurer.

[68]

DISTRICT OF COLUMBIA

Horseshoe pitching has finally reached into the nation's capitol and found ready workers, promoters, and a fine public. Prior to 1929 the game was virtually unknown in the city, but the Washington Evening Star sponsored a huge tournament which drew more than 5,000 entries. One of the divisions of the meet was for legislators, and the final match between Senator McMillen and Senator Hiram Johnson was broadcast over a national hook-up.

The Evening Star has sponsored tournaments yearly since that time, and horseshoes has prospered accordingly. Sports writer Rod Thomas has continually boosted the game, while in Harry M. Woodfield, 734 19th St., N.E., the sport has a highly energetic leader.

In 1939 the city built 12 new courts within sight of the White House, and they were dedicated by a visit from the Canadian team from Toronto. The dedication was attended by many prominent political and social figures. The visiting team was royally entertained by Senator Ernest Lundeen of Minnesota.

The District of Columbia promises to have its best season in 1940.

Winners in past tournaments are as follows:

1929   Charles A. Fort
1930   Harry Saunders
1931   John Gourvenac
1932   Hubbard Quantrille
1933   Harry Saunders
1934   Harry Saunders
1935   William V. Moore
1936   William V. Moore
1937   Harry Saunders
1938   Irwin Carlberg
1939   Irwin Carlberg

METROPOLITAN CHAMPIONSHIP

1929   Millard Peake, Maryland
1930   Harry Saunders, Washington, D. C.
1931   Harry Saunders, Washington, D. C.
1932   Clayton C. Henson, Virginia
1933   Clayton C. Henson, Virginia
1934   Clayton C. Henson, Virginia
1935   Raymond L. Frye, Virginia
1936   William V. Moore, Washington, D. C.
1937   Raymond L. Frye, Virginia
1938   Harry Saunders, Washington, D. C.
1939   Clayton C. Henson, Virginia

KANSAS

On May 16, 1914, in Kansas City, Kansas, was organized the Grand League of American Horseshoe Pitchers, the first National organization the horseshoe game ever had. But beyond this fact, and the fact that Kansas furnishes the game with many leading pitchers, the state has not done a great deal in organization. Although many hard-fought state tournaments have been held, none of them were ever sanctioned by the National Association, but with the election of Alvin Dahlene, of Lawrence, to the post of National Second Vice President, it is hoped that this state will decide to enter the fold of sanctioned states by joining the National Association.

Lloyd Woodard, of Columbus, won the state title in 1929, and Bert Harriss, of Minneapolis, captured the honor in 1930. In 1931, Lester McCollam, of Kincaid, a former champion, came back to take the title which he successfully defended in 1932. Frank Phillips, of Topeka, took the laurels in 1933, after a play-off with Merle Stoner, and in 1934 the veteran Bert Duryee once more ascended the throne. Alvin Gandy, of Topeka, won out in 1935, and the following year saw Frank Phillips win in a play-off with Roland Kraft, the one-armed star from LeCompton. Gerald Brown, of Lawrence, came through in 1937. In 1938 there was no meet for the title, but in 1939, the scene shifted from Topeka, where all previous tourneys had been held, to Columbus. Alvin Gandy won the title after a play-off with Alvin Dahlene.

With such a wealth of horseshoe pitching talent, Kansas certainly could hold with any other state, and promises to have at least one great team in the National Team League.

The National Representative in Kansas is Alvin Dahlene, of Lawrence. ·

KENTUCKY

Kentucky first joined the National Association in 1928, but their membership has been allowed to lapse since that time. However, things have been pointing toward their rejoining at an early date.

The first state tournament in Kentucky was held in Louisville in 1923, and was won by J. W. Netheron. Since that time the title was won three times by Mr. Akers, of Nolin, three times by Mr. Young, of Shelbyville, twice by Mr. McCoy, twice by Sam B. Mattingly, twice by Mr. Beckman, and once each by Mr. Miller and Mr. Soete.

A strong and willing worker for horseshoes in Kentucky is E. B. Patterson who has been president for 12 years.

WYOMING

The first championship horseshoe tournament, under National jurisdiction, in Wyoming, was held in Cheyenne in 1933, and was sponsored by the Cheyenne Horseshoe Club. This contest was won by Lester Forsythe, of Laramie. In 1934 and 1935 the state meets were also held by the Cheyenne Horseshoe Club both of these meets being won by Clarence Carllson, of Cheyenne.

In the fall of 1935 the Wyoming Division of the National Horseshoe Pitchers' Association was organized. This organization became active in the spring of 1936. The officers elected at that meeting were as follows: President, D. R. Kinports, Cheyenne; First Vice President, O. E. Forsythe, Laramie; Second Vice President, H. L. Rowe, Sheridan; Third Vice President, R. H. Platt, Encampment; Fourth Vice President, Jack Jones, Douglass; Secretary, Ernest Harrison, Cheyenne; Treasurer, G. D. Percival, Lusk.

In 1936 the Cheyenne Club again sponsored the state tournament, but was managed by the State Association the championship being won by Lester Forsythe, of Laramie.

The state meet in 1937 was sponsored by the merchants of Glenrock, and held at that place. The state organization also had charge of and conducted the tournament. Jack Jones, of Douglass won the championship.

The State Fair Association contributed cash prizes for the 1938 state meet which was again run by the State Association. As a result of this meet Merle Palmer, of Cheyenne, was declared state champion.

At this time the state officers for the following two years were elected as follows: President, Geo. H. McConnaughey, 503 S. Park, Casper, Wyoming; First Vice President, O. E. Forsythe, 703 S. Seventh St., Laramie; Second Vice President, Harry Phillips, Mission Barber Shop, Sheridan; Third Vice President, R. H. Platt, Encampment; Fourth Vice President, Hilmer Hanson, 143 Conwell St., Casper; Secretary, by appointment, A. L. Mitchell, 421 E. 18th St., Cheyenne; Treasurer, G. D. Percival, Lusk.

The Wheatland Horseshoe Club, with the financial assistance of the business firms of that city conducted the 1939 state meet. This was the hardest fought contest ever held in Wyoming, Shell Patton, of Dwyer, winning with an average percent of 60.1, while Merle Palmer, the runner-up and former champion, averaged 62.2 per cent. In some individual games the percentage ran as high as 70 per cent.

A county association was formed in Laramie County in 1939 and a county tournament was held at the county fair in Pine

Bluffs. L. W. Farrell, of Cheyenne, won the county championship.

Beside the county association of Laramie County, there are two local clubs in the state; the Cheyenne Horseshoe Club which was organized in 1931 has been active every year since; the Wheatland Horseshoe Club which was organized in 1939, is a progressive and strong club.

MAINE

State officers of the Maine Association are:
President, Frederick Robie, State House, Augusta.
Vice President, H. VanDerwerker, 541 S. Main St., Brewer.
Secretary-Treasurer, Raymond E. Adams, 35 Pine St., Auburn.
The state champion in 1926 was Mr. Cummings of Norway, and in 1927 the title-holder became Milton Bush, of Auburn. Guy Sturtevant, of South Paris, won the honor in 1928 and successfully defended the title until 1932, when Ralph "Doc" Robinson, also of South Paris, won the championship at the Lewiston Fair Grounds. Robinson held the title until 1935 when the first officially sanctioned meet was staged at Portland. Harold Goodier, of South Portland, became the winner. The 1936 meet was played at Auburn, and was won by the late Leonard "Tony" Lombardi, with an average of .628.

South Brewer held the 1937 meet which had to be played in the rain, and Robinson became the champion, averaging .603. In 1938 the tournament went to Rumford, and the title went to Goodier. The 1939 meet was held at Portland, and Merrill Barnes of Bangor came through to win the championship, averaging .606.

The State of Maine has made remarkable strides forward in the horseshoe game, and bids fair to become one of the outstanding states in the National Association fold.

NEW MEXICO

New Mexico is the most recent joiner of the National Association, having entered the fold during 1939. Horseshoes is beginning to take hold there, and fine things are expected from New Mexico in the future.

The first state tournament was held at the State Fair in Albuquerque in 1939, and the title was won by the state president, Charles Curran. The officers for New Mexico are as follows:
President, Charles Curran, 321 Rencher, Clovis.
Vice President, A. F. Scott, 608 S. Edith St., Albuquerque.
Secretary, E. L. Drake, 2104 Etob St., Albuquerque.
Treasurer, Paul Mackey, 1816 N. 4th St., Albuquerque.

INDIANA

Officers of the Indiana Division, National Horseshoe Pitchers' Association are:

President, W. A. Banta, 618 Arch St., Indianapolis.
Sec. Treas., Paul S. Van Sickle, 32 Whittier Pl., Indianapolis.
Vice Pres., Ray Peckham, 2505 Chestnut St., Ft. Wayne.
Vice Pres., William Everett, 2228 E. Main St., Lafayette.
Vice Pres., James Stringer, N. Home Ave., Columbus.
Vice Pres., Charles Cowan, Veedersburg.
Vice Pres., Noah Malott, Mishawaka.

Jimmy Risk won the state title for the years 1926 through 1930 in the meets held at the Indiana State Fair, but the years from 1930 to 1937 were lean years for horseshoe pitching in the state.

In 1937 the state joined the National Association, and a state meet was held at the courts of the Fall Creek Club in Indianapolis, and the winner was Arlo Harris who averaged 74 per cent. In 1938 the title went to James Cox, of Perrysville. He did not lose a game in nine starts. Ernie Recht, of Ft. Wayne, set a new state record for ringer average when he hit .755, but could only finish fourth. Ray Peckham was runner-up.

Jimmy Risk regained the state title in 1939 in the meet at Ft. Wayne with Wayne Nelson, of Muncie, runner-up.

Anderson is the scene of the annual A.A.U. National Junior Horseshoe Tournament.

MARYLAND

Maryland has never been a member of the National Association, but yearly tournaments have been held with the following winners:

1929 Millard Peake, Bethesda
1930 Millard Peake, Bethesda
1931 Joseph Merryman, Bladensburg
1932 Joseph Merryman, Bladensburg
1933 Lee Fleshman, Rogers Heights
1934 Lee Fleshman, Rogers Heights
1935 Temple R. Jarrell, Hyattsville
1936 Temple R. Jarrell, Hyattsville
1937 Lee Fleshman, Rogers Heights
1938 Lee Fleshman, Rogers Heights
1939 Lee Fleshman, Rogers Heights

[73]

MICHIGAN

Officers of the Wolverine State Horseshoe Pitchers 'Association are:

President, Ray Middleton, 619 Fox St., Flint.

Eastern Vice President, Joe Lasko, 619 Fox St., Flint.

Western Vice President, Jack Hoeksema, 511 Eastern Ave., Grand Rapids.

Upper Peninsula Vice President, Kenneth Campbell, Stambaugh.

Secretary Treasurer, Lee Rose, 5228 Shaw Ave., Detroit.

From 1923 through 1927, yearly state tournaments were held as follows: 1923, Battle Creek, won by Lew Wilkes, of Battle Creek; 1924, Detroit, won by Ralph Baxter, of Hillsdale; 1925, Detroit, won by Ben Emmerson, of Battle Creek; 1926, Battle Creek, won by Frank Seals, of Cassopolis; 1927, Battle Creek, won by Ed Walls, of Detroit.

The first chartered association formed April 15, 1928, with H. E. Smith, of Battle Creek, President; R. H. Rizor, of Detroit, Vice President; Carl Stenzhorn, of Port Huron, Second Vice President; T. M. Howard, of Battle Creek, Secretary; and Fred O'Melay, of Hillsdale, Treasurer.

The 1928 tournament was held at the Michigan State Fair. Ed Walls won, with Lee Rose second. In 1929 the tournament was held at Battle Creek with Joe Lasko of Mt. Pleasant the winner. In 1930, due to many circumstances, the state charter was allowed to lapse, but tournaments went on as before. Ed Walls and Lee Rose ran one-two in 1930 at Detroit; Ed Walls and James Skinner, of Athens, ran one-two, in 1931 at Detroit; Ed Walls and James McDonald, of Pontiac, ran one-two, in 1932 at Pleasant Ridge; and Lee Rose became champion in 1933 at Detroit.

In 1932 a minority group obtained a charter and held a tournament at Battle Creek, which was won by Jack Hoeksema, of Grand Rapids, and in 1933 they held another meet at Grand Rapids which was won by Ralph Baxter.

With the state demoralized by fighting between rival groups, nothing was done in 1934, but in 1935, Lee Rose finally convinced R. B. Howard that the Detroit group was the proper one to hold the charter, and the present Wolverine State Association was formed. Under their administration, horseshoe pitching has progressed swiftly in Michigan. The 1935 tournament was held at Dearborn, and the 68-year-old Jim Skinner won the title. In 1936 the tournament went to Marquette in the Upper Peninsula where the new system of playing a tournament, an innovation of Lee

Rose, was first tried. Bobby Hitt, 14-year-old "boy wonder" of Plymouth, won the meet, with Lee Rose coming second.

Iron River held the 1937 meet which was again won by Bobby Hitt, with Carl Lundgren, of Detroit, second. In 1938, at Plymouth, was held the most successful of Michigan meets. Bobby Hitt again defended his title with Joe Lasko, now of Flint, taking second. Iron River again staged the meet in 1939, and Joe Lasko took the title away from Bobby Hitt, who was second.

The 1940 meet is scheduled for Flint. Several county fairs in the state stage tournaments spasmodically, and several cities, especially Flint, Grand Rapids and Detroit, will be strongly organized in 1940.

VERMONT

Horseshoe pitching has just begun to take a hold in Vermont, and, while they have not yet formed a regular state association, they have a live-wire club at Bennington which promises to blossom forth into a full-fledged state association.

The first official state tournament was held in 1930, and was won by Leon Kerry, of Randolf. Mr. Kerry was recognized as state champion until 1939, when the Bennington Club held a sanctioned state meet. This meet was won by Maynard Brown of 31 Belmont Ave., Brattleboro. Mr. Brown went undefeated in nine games, averaging .559, while Fred Butler of 307 North St., Bennington, was second, losing only one game, and averaging .552. Mr. Butler is the National Representative in Vermont.

RHODE ISLAND

The officers of the Rhode Island Division of the National Horseshoe Pitchers' Association are as follows:

President, Joseph A. LaClair, 20 Metcalf Ave., North Providence.

Secretary, Albert Bourgeois, 77 Hunnewell Ave., Providence.

Treasurer, Samuel Pendleton, 71 Oriole Ave., Pawtucket.

The present state champion is the 18-year-old star, Kenneth Hurst, who resides at 66 Fairmont Ave., Providence.

Rhode Island has shown a great deal of interest in the game this past season, and is looking forward to greater things for 1940.

[75]

VIRGINIA

While Virginia has never been a member of the National Association, they have had yearly championships with the following winners:

1929 Alex Kirchner, Barcroft
1930 Alex Kirchner, Barcroft
1931 Charles C. Darr, Ballston
1932 Clayton C. Henson, Arlington
1933 George C. Thompson, Falls Church
1934 Raymond L. Frye, Orkney Springs
1935 Raymond L. Frye, Orkney Springs
1936 Clayton C. Hanson, Arlington
1937 Raymond L. Frye, Orkney Springs
1938 Clayton C. Henson, Arlington
1939 Clayton C. Henson, Arlington

MRS. FRANCISCO

IOWA

By Leland Mortenson

It is a pleasure to write this history of Iowa in Horseshoes for the N. H. P. A. I have hopes that horseshoe pitching will some day develop into a much greater sport, and I believe there is a chance that some day, perhaps not for a hundred or more years, but some day at least, it will be where boxing now stands. If so, then the present and near past of horseshoes can be compared to boxing of about the time when pugilists spent most of their time hiding from the police. If my dream, and, of course, the association's dream, comes true, will it not surely be interesting for the people of the future to read about our successes and failures, of outstanding events, and of interesting personalities of the past?

This shall be a history of the game in Iowa and shall touch upon the national scene when Iowans have had connection with it.

Mr. Lee Rose, the National Secretary, has asked me to present human interest phases as often as possible. This I shall do up to and including 1935, but I am going to purposely eliminate much of such material from 1935 to 1940. My reason is that many of the humorous and interesting scenes I could picture taking place during those years are closely related to problems still facing the National Association, and may therefore be said to be unfinished.

So far as we are able to learn, the horseshoe game was with America before Iowa became a state. Perhaps it was adopted here after the arrival of blacksmith shops with their large numbers of cast-off horseshoes.

The game, once it began in Iowa, didn't change much until the twenties. The courts varied in length from 30 to 55 feet; the stakes were generally rusty, easily bent pipes, three inches high, or perhaps three feet; maybe bent and leaning in any direction. The earth around the stake was generally at least two feet deep and as hard as a brick. The players generally competed in two-men teams, tossing cast-off shoes of different sizes and weights. For the most part the men were old. Games were of 21 point duration; five points for a ringer, three for a leaner, ten for a ringer covering an opponent's ringer, and twenty for a double ringer upon an opponent's double ringer.

No official champions existed. About the only honor to be gained from being an expert was to be a most desired partner. The only prizes ever won were such items as a keg of beer or something of similar or less value, offered at an occasional picnic, and the man who won was generally he who was fortunate in having the largest and heaviest shoes, for these would slide the best and bounce the least.

In 1909 the promoter of a colt show somewhere in Kansas, conceived the idea of staging a world's championship horseshoe pitching tournament in connection with the show. An Iowa farmer, Frank E. Jackson, of Kellerton, won the title and a championship belt.

Jackson, in 1909, was 39 years old, and had been tossing cast-off horseshoes since a boy. His method was like all others, to spin the shoe with one finger and pray for an open shoe. At that time he was fortunate if he could hook 20 per cent ringers. Jackson claims to have kept his title until 1919, and that he gradually improved and finally regulated his shoe to turn 1¾ times..

In 1920 Jackson induced the Iowa State Fair Board to put up some cash prizes for a two-man team tournament. This competition was held in front of the race track and Jackson and his oldest son Carrol, won first prize. The contest was changed to singles competition in 1921 and Jackson won the "bacon."

The two state tournaments had been successful enough in drawing entries and in entertaining the State Fair visitors that the Fair Board made a successful bid in 1922 for both World and State Tournaments. Frank Jackson held both titles, and he was an overwhelming favorite to defeat all rivals. For these tournaments new courts were installed directly north of the brick horse barn. A small section of bleachers were set up, but there was no fence to keep spectators from getting too near the pitchers. Model T Ford axles were used as stakes.

Frank Jackson was considered to be so skillful that he was barred from the State Tournament, but a $50 prize was set aside for a two-out-of-three contest between the winner of the tournament and Jackson for the Iowa championship.

A newcomer to the State Fair contests was a rather thick-lipped 20-year-old shabbily dressed boy from New London, Iowa. His name was Frank Lundin. He never said much, just pitched, and with every pitch he bit his lips, so that while he was in a game it was a common sight to see his lips bleeding.

The state meet was held before the national, and Lundin easily won. He was said to be absolutely nerveless. After disposing of his rivals, Lundin cracked Frank Jackson in two straight games, 50-13, 50-17, averaging 61 per cent ringers and starting the first game with seven consecutive double ringers. Sixty-one per cent would be poor today, but Lundin was using horseshoes, although made especially for pitching, were greatly inferior to the best of today.

C. C. Davis, a very famous pitcher, then from Ohio, saw Lundin defeat Jackson for the state title, and said something to this effect, "We'll take him in the National." But Davis became a Lundin victim, 50-12.

By the way, I rank Lundin's state championship 1922 victory over Jackson as one of the three outstanding games in Iowa history for suspense and surprise. When the old-timers get together now it is the game they like most to talk about.

The people in New London were so proud of Lundin that they erected a huge sign beside the road leading into the town. It read, "This town is the home of Frank Lundin, World's Champion Horseshoe Pitcher."

FRANK LUNDIN

In the 1922 National Meet Lundin did lose one game to Lyle Brown, then 17 years old, and from Des Moines, 50-48. The Lundin boosters claim that Lundin threw the game in order to

[79]

put Brown into third place, but this can be discounted. Brown led 49-48 and threw a ringer and a close shoe. Lundin topped with a double which should have won the game, but his second ringer hopped away, giving Brown the point he needed.

Frank Jackson lost two games to Lundin and to his second oldest son, Hansford. If Hansford had lost to his father then there would have been a tie between Jackson and Lundin for the championship. This single instance is pretty good proof that the Jacksons didn't practice game-throwing to much extent, if any.

It may be stated that by this time National rules about the same as those of today were in use.

An Iowa Horseshoe Pitchers' Association was organized that year and Dr. J. H. Becker, of Des Moines, was elected secretary and treasurer. Becker held his association together until 1927, when he withdrew. However, Becker never called for any more conventions, but collected dues. The money was used for tournament prizes. This was not a case of dishonesty but simply a matter of keeping oneself at the head of an organization by not calling a meeting. The other officers were not interested enough to argue with Becker about the matter.

Lundin and Jackson went to Florida early in 1923, where a 15-year-old boy from Ohio, Harold Falor, copped Lundin's title. Lundin's friends say that this tournament was a joke, that sand was placed around the stake instead of clay; that Falor had practiced for a month to slide his shoe to the stake which he learned quite well, and that the other pitchers threw their ringers directly on, only to have them bounce off. I don't know whether this is true or not. However, most Iowans don't remember Lundin lost his title. They think he retired undefeated except for the game they think he threw to Brown.

In 1923 the State Fair held a state tournament with Lundin easily defending his title and again trouncing Frank Jackson. This was the last tournament play for Lundin.

Why did Lundin retire from horseshoes? The answer is that he lost the fine touch of one of his finger nerves. He is not a cripple today, but just simply can't regulate the turn of the shoe.

A popular fable about Lundin is that he never injured a nerve, but that some gamblers bought him off for a period of years, that he pitches about 100 per cent ringers in secret daily practice, and that he will be back at the fair when his time expires. Believe it or not, I have heard that tale over 200 times from different sources in the past ten years.

The only significance of this fable is that Lundin is No. 1 in the hearts and memories of the older Iowa fans.

It was shortly before Lundin retired that a Des Moines man whose name is now forgotten, promoted some matches at the fair grounds. In one of these Lundin beat Jackson six straight games, and in another, C. C. Davis vs. Jackson, an amusing incident occurred.

Davis and Jackson had put up a side bet and there was a small sum of gate receipts to be divided. Jackson's shoes continually fell short of the stake, but Davis shot a righ ringer percentage. Immediately after the game, Jackson measured the court and found the stakes to be 41 feet apart. Why 41 instead of 40? Tom Fogarty, of Des Moines, and long associated with horseshoe pitching, says that Jackson's friends claimed that Davis had purposely practiced on 41-foot courts and that the night before the match Davis or some of his friends went to the fair grounds and moved the stakes.

At any rate, Fogarty says, the promoter couldn't get anything settled; that Mr. Corey, of the Fair Board, was called to make the decision, which he promptly did by tossing the funds into the school fund.

The three Des Moines high schools adopted horseshoe pitching as an inter-school sport in 1924, and Lyle Brown was secured to serve as coach for all three schools. The athletic board evidently didn't have much interest in trying to make a success of it for they merely drove a couple of stakes in some cinders behind out-of-the-way corners of the schools. The poor courts made a poor appearance, as did the out-of-the-way location.

Why was the game dropped? It couldn't have been because of lack of interest for there were more entries for horseshoe pitching than for track, for which reason the track coaches grumbled about horseshoes "taking away material." Did the sport attract the rougher element of the school? Well, hardly, for of the ten men on the North High team, all graduated with excellent records, five graduated from college, and one, the City High School champion, is now a foreman in a Des Moines factory. The City School athletic director opposed horseshoes upon the grounds that it lacked enough action, but she favored golf, a sport with less action.

It was about 1924 or shortly before that the Des Moines horseshoe pitchers organized a club and held regular Sunday morning tournaments at what are now called the Birdland Courts. The results of these tournaments were published regularly in the press. This was not necessarily the first such club in Iowa, but it was the best known, as it still is. Since that time many other active clubs have sprung up such as those at Cedar Rapids, Cedar Falls, Adair and Ankeny, with its electric lights.

Two interesting officers of two of these clubs were D. J. Cowden, of Adair, and Dr. J. H. Becker, of Des Moines, already mentioned.

Cowden organized a mail league tournament on a nation-wide scale and called his league the "National Horseshoe Pitchers' Athletic Association of America." He studied horseshoe scores as they were mailed in, spent hours on each one, wrote letters of eight to ten pages to the sender with what he called scientific criticism of the pitchers' score. And he had revolutionary ideas on how to completely change the game. His plans were so complicated that nobody but Cowden bothered to try to study them.

Dr. Becker, although I said he used dictatoral methods in holding his office, was a practical horseshoe booster. Many times he personally canvassed the Des Moines merchants to get prizes for tournaments, and in a state meet here in 1927, he collected $275 in merchandise prizes. A fault he had, but which did no harm, was to get enthusiastic about some plan, announce it to the press, and then discover it was unworkable. For instance, he once announced that the following year he was going to take America's best 50 pitchers on an exhibition tour of Europe. Becker began getting numerous applications, and he made promises to some, then he found out he couldn't do it.

By August of 1924, Frank Jackson was again world's champion and came to the fair confident of regaining the title left vacant by Lundin's retirement. But he was disappointed, for Putt Mossman, a flashy 18-year-old boy from Eldora, swept through the tournament. Mossman had won fifth in the 1923 state tournament.

A world's championship tournament was held at Minneapolis in September, 1924, and Mossman won first, Frank Jackson second, and Frank Campbell, of Waukee, Iowa, fourth. Emmett Mossman, age 13, won the world's junior title, and the oldest brother, Warren, took the world's amateur title.

Putt Mossman was born in Hardin County, Iowa, July 8, 1906. Besides his brothers, Emmett and Warren, he had a younger sister, Dessie. The children all went in for sports with emphasis upon horseshoe pitching, almost total exclusion of education, and as much as possible also of work. In fact, Putt probably never did any work except a little on the farm, and none at all after he became world's champion.

A few years after winning the world's amateur championship, Warren took up professional wrestling and once claimed the middleweight championship of his county.

Emmett beat Frank Jackson at the Iowa State Fair at the

age of 13, but he never seemed to improve much and never beat Jackson again. Several years later he tried to copy Putt's horseshoe and motorcycle exhibitions, but he flopped. He tried amateur boxing and in his only fight he was knocked out in the first round. He tried Putt's motorcycle stunts on the highways and there he had similar accidents to those Putt had on race tracks.

After Putt won the world's horseshoe title he traveled from coast to coast staging horseshoe exhibitions, sometimes on a guaranteed contract, but mostly by taking up collections. In 1927 he pitched for a semi-pro baseball team in New York, and in 1928 he failed in a try-out with the Boston Braves. In 1927 he invented a hook horseshoe and also a horseshoe uniform. In 1929 he started to stage motorcycle exhibitions. By 1930 he was shooting revolvers by aiming through mirrors, doing high kicking stunts and numerous other things. In 1929 he nearly served time in the Ohio Penitentiary for killing a pedestrian while driving 40 miles an hour in a town, and with defective brakes, and then he drove the car the remainder of the year without having the brakes repaired. He starred in motion pictures in Hollywood in the early thirties, fought main events on Des Moines boxing cards in 1930, and went around the world putting on exhibitions in Japan, Australia and other countries.

Putt has been nearly killed on his motorcycle several times, and he is reported to have crippled his wife for life when he failed to clear her in a stunt motorcycle leap in California. He is said to have taken up an airplane in Australia without instruction, and to have crashed. He claimed the title of "World's Champion All-around Athlete" in 1930. (See Omaha World-Herald April 6, 1930). An Iowa college professor said Putt was a genius, and if he had studied chemistry or law he would have been as remarkable in that as he was in horseshoes. Another professor said he was insane. One newspaper reporter wrote an article about Putt's marvelous personality. Another reporter said Putt had a very poor personality.

This is just an outline about Putt, but this outline is worth further investigation as to whether Mossman must not certainly be rated Iowa's No. 1 athlete of all time.

In August of 1939 Mossman was reported to be a member of an exploring expedition in Africa, but this is not presented as fact as it has not as yet been confirmed.

For a short time after winning at Minneapolis, Mossman took Frank Jackson with him for exhibitions, and beat his rival most of the time but the two couldn't get along and soon parted company.

The 1925 National meet in Florida, and the state tourney at

[83]

the Iowa State Fair of the same year were repetitions of 1924, Mossman first, Jackson second.

In the fall of 1925, Omaha, Nebraska, held a tournament for the interstate championship of Iowa and Nebraska. Lyle Brown won, but neither Mossman nor Jackson were present.

In the spring of 1926 Jackson regained his world's title from Mossman in a Florida tournament, but he was not master without dispute, for Putt beat him in four straight games a few weeks later. Jackson was absent from the 1926 Iowa State Fair Tournament, so Mossman won with ease.

On December 18, 1926, Mayor Hale Thompson promoted a special match in Chicago for the world's championship between Mossman and Jackson, with Putt winning and claiming the championship. Jackson then claimed that a match for a championship was a violation of National rules. So, in fact, there were two world's champions until C. C. Davis beat both of them in Florida early in 1927.

FRANK JACKSON

[84]

In September, 1926, Jackson entered a Mid-West Tournament at Omaha. First and second prizes had been advertised as $100 and $40. When the pitchers assembled, they complained about the lopsided setup of prizes. But Jackson insisted that the prizes remain as advertised, which they were. Cecil Freel, a lanky, six foot, five inch, 118 pound, 18-year-old youth from Murray, Iowa, provided a surprise and won every game, connecting with 65 ringers to defeat Jackson. Freel was really not in Jackson's class. It was just his day, and if any man ever was blue it was Jackson with his $40.

After Davis won the world's championship from Mossman and Jackson, in 1927, no Iowa man ever won it again. A state championship tournament was held at the Des Moines Birdland courts in June, 1927. Jackson won and Mossman was absent, and at the State Fair the same year, Jackson kept his title although he lost two games to Mossman.

C. E. DAVIS

1927 saw the establishment of electric lights at the Birdland courts and many pitchers took advantage of them by tossing until past midnight many times. Before the end of the summer, hoodlums had destroyed the light and they were removed by the Parks Department. In 1938 lights were again installed and are still in use.

In 1928 a Central Iowa tournament, with an airplane ride for first prize, and a state junior tournament were held in Des Moines. John Garvey, a youth from Boone, won the first meet, and Floyd Saffell of Des Moines, took first and Emmett Mossman second in the latter tournament.

Frank Jackson won the 1928 State Fair Tournament, with Mossman fourth. This meet saw our first experience with a public address system, but we didn't have another one until 1936.

On July 14, 1929, a state tournament was held at the Birdland Courts. Jackson was first and Mossman sixth.

From the time Mossman became a first-class pitcher he had never been backward about belittling Frank Jackson. Time and time again he issued challenges to play for side bets. Sometimes these were published. During the summer of 1929 Mossman did more challenging than ever, and inferred through a newspaper story that Jackson feared him. The results of this was that Jackson was rather "burned up," and that there were a large number of red-hot fans ready by State Fair time. Jackson downed Putt in the preliminaries, but the finals were to be a sensation.

At this time, and this was the last one, we had no schedule, game by game, for the finals. The finals started and a crowd of over 1,000 was present.

There was always tremendous interest in the Mossman-Jackson games. There were several reasons. Both were former world's champions; both hated each other and the fans knew it; there was a contrast wherein Jackson was old and a common farmer type, while Putt was young, good looking, fast and active, and dressed in a flashy manner. Jackson was modest, Mossman a braggart; Jackson was fairly large, Mossman small.

I was superintendent of the tournament and had arranged for Mossman to put on a trick exhibition in the midst, the result of which was to draw about a thousand people about him on the courts. The State Fair farmer police gave up in their attempt to get the crowd back. In fact, they refused to help me.

The fans presence on the courts stopped several games, and slowed down the finals. Many of the pitchers became angry at Mossman and me for arranging the exhibition, but my purpose was to get the fans entertained so I let the exhibition continue. Jackson was furious.

FRED BRUST

Finally, after the exhibition, Mossman and Jackson argued as to when to pitch their game. Jackson wanted it at once. Mossman wanted it last. The crowd got into the argument and all knew what the trouble was. Finally, Mossman, Jackson and Guy Zimmerman, then a quiet 21-year-old boy from Sac City, Iowa, had only one another to pitch against. Mossman and Jackson got into a heated argument in the center of the courts as to which one should play Zimmerman first.

The crowd had followed the dispute closely, and thinking there was an impending fight, rushed out upon the courts, their mass stopping most games. Some of the crowd were Jackson supporters, evidently eager to fight for their favorite. Some were for Mossman. I went out to settle the argument and I was threatened by both sides. The Fair cops vanished from sight. It seemed that the slightest thing could have started a first-class mob fight. I called for a flip of a coin. Mossman lost.

As I walked away from the center of the court I absent-mindedly walked in front of a peg to which Harry Reese, of Iowa City, was ready to pitch. Reese's patience with the interfering fans was at its end, and as soon as he saw me, but yet not recognizing me, he let the shoe go with all his might. It struck me a terrific blow on my arm.

Putt downed Guy Zimmerman, 50-29; Jackson then beat Guy 50-1$\overline{4}$. Then Putt hurled 51 ringers out of 60 shoes to beat Jackson 50-16. This clash between Mossman and Jackson, I rate among the three greatest of Iowa games, as was said before, for suspense.

The settlement of the argument just in the nick of time, and diverting the attention of the mob, was, I believe, the only thing which prevented a riot, which, if it had happened, would probably have ended horseshoes at the Fair. This was my poorest job in ever handling a tournament, and with this blight on my record, it would be well for me to count a long time before I ever criticize other tournament superintendents.

Mossman and Jackson split games at the Fair in 1930, but Jackson won the title.

In 1931 Mossman filed his entry for the tournament at the Fair but was seriously injured in a motorcycle spill on the race track a few days before the start of the tournament. Hansford Jackson won the title from his dad who took second.

Dessie Mossman, Putt's comely sister, was permitted to pitch 30 feet against the men in 1930 and 1931. The first year she won seventh prize; the second she took third, and in a hot streak she connected for ten straight double ringers. The men pitchers objected so strongly to a woman having a handicap that such method has not been permitted since.

Frank Jackson regained his title at the Fair in 1932 by handily defeating Hansford. That year, as in 1931, a state college tournament was also held with Victor Jones, of Iowa State College, defeating a field which included the 1931 winner, Jimmy Rainbow, of State Teachers' College; and a State High School Tournament was likewise held. In addition, I presented the State College champion discus thrower, a leading shot-putter, and a boy who the next year won the Drake Relay hop, step and jump event, in exhibitions. The exhibitions were good, but the Fair visitors were not greatly interested.

[88]

In spite of my efforts to boost fan interest in the tournament, the spectators were dwindling. I concluded that new blood was needed among the contestants, so I was successful in getting the meet opened to adjoining states in 1933. This tournament was called the "Mid-West." C. C. Davis came here and went away with the title, but not until he had to beat Jackson two out of three games, winning the last 50-49 with 79 ringers apiece. That year a Davis-Zimmerman game was broadcast, play by play, over the radio.

In 1933, Mossman, Jackson and Lyle Brown all entered a Chicago National meet, and all failed to qualify among the best 24 pitchers.

Davis repeated his victory in 1934, but Jackson had now left the state, and to date he has not returned. In order to defeat Guy Zimmerman in a game which was to decide the 1934 championship, Davis used clever tactics. With Zimmerman leading 30-17, Davis started an argument with the announcer, and then with the crowd, with the simple purpose of rattling his opponent. It worked. Guy became nervous and Davis walked out 50-37. This tournament had among its entries little Charles "Casey" Jones, of Waukesha, Wis., then 15 years old, who took third place.

Frank Jackson and Zimmerman both entered a National meet in California in 1934. Jackson tied for third, Zimmerman was fifth.

The Mid-West Tournament had been an improvement over the State, but I was not satisfied, and induced the Fair Board to put up $500 in prizes for a Mid-West National Tournament in 1935, and since then it has been the same each year, and each year since the courts have been enclosed with a five-foot fence.

In 1935 Ted Allen, 27-year-old world's champion from California, dethroned Davis, and in 1936 he defeated "Casey" Jones in a play-off of a tie. In 1936 we secured a first-class public address system and have had one each year since. Leroy Page, a young man from Des Moines, who had helped me several times before in conducting the tournament, handled it exceptionally well, and has done so since.

In 1937 Fernando Isais, 22 years old, and from Mexico City, Mexico, dethroned Allen and won every game he played in the finals. In that tournament, Isais was the coolest pitching machine I have ever seen. He averaged 83.5 per cent ringers in 15 games on new iron stakes put in by John Gordon, a California enthusiast. Isais in his final game against Allen that year appeared to consider his time as a boring waste, and Allen as a beginner. He looked exceedingly bored as he proceeded to pitch ringers, walked slowly, and put Allen into a nervous state of mind. Isais won 50-28; every shoe he threw was a ringer, and the only time Allen scored was when the Mexican's ringers hopped off. Isais lost a large number of ringers as the clay was a little too dry. This game is one of the three greatest in Iowa history for the unusual aspect of it.

John Gordon was mentioned above. He is a wealthy retired California man who manufactures horseshoes, and in a dozen other ways is liked up with the game. He has taken an active part in the Iowa State Fair Tournaments since 1935. If I say that Mossman is the most unusual personality in the history of the pitchers, I must also say that John Gordon is the most interesting personality of the non-pitchers connected with the game. No doubt, he is head and shoulders over anyone else in that respect. A full story about John Gordon must wait for at least ten years, for it seems that a story now would be only the beginning of a much longer story which can later be assembled.

Ted Allen was an improved pitcher in 1938, while Isais had gone back. Ted averaged 84.1 per cent to win every game. In 1939 he again won every game to average 82.7 per cent.

The 1939 tournament was covered by Life Magazine, and a picture of a California star, Dean Brown, was broadcast by radio. In connection with this tournament, a convention of the National Horseshoe Pitchers Association was held at Hotel Fort Des moines. At this convention LeRoy Page, of Des Moines was elected president, while another Iowan, Robert Tompkin, a young lawyer from Dysart, was appointed to be a member of the important Rules Committee.

An amusing incident occurred on the Sunday morning of this tournament. The Fair Board had permitted a preacher to use a huge dance hall tent to hold his services, and with the time for the sermon about to commence, he came over and furiously demanded that I compel the pitchers to stop practicing as the congregation was watching the pitchers instead of going to church.

I agreed to stop them, so he announced to the crowd that there would be no more pitching that morning, and that church services would start immediately. Some of the people argued with him, but most of them went back into the church.

By 12 o'clock he was still preaching, and I thought that two hours of that was enough, so I signalled for games to start. The preacher heard the sound of the shoes hitting the pegs, and shouted, "There they go, worrying about their box scores; some day they will worry about their box score above." The congre-

[90]

gation snickered. The closing prayer came. The congregation hurried back to watch the game.

Since 1934 the Iowa championship has also been decided at the State Fair. Zimmerman won in 1934, 1936, 1937 and 1939; John Garvey, of Boone, in 1935, and Lyle Brown, in 1938.

In 1939, Dale Dixon, of Des Moines, personally interested eight Des Moines business firms to pay the expenses of an industrial league tournament in which there were six men on each team. It was a success and is to be continued in 1940.

The State Horseshoe Pitchers Association, after its collapse in 1927, was re-organized in 1936, but it did not become affiliated with the National Association. In 1938, Byron Stoney, of Cedar Rapids, replaced Lyle Brown, of Des Moines, as president, and it joined the National, and that year held a tournament at the Cedar Rapids Fair which was won by John Paxton, Fairfield. It was a state-wide tournament, but was not for the state championship.

Some of Iowa's best horseshoe pitchers not already mentioned have been Elzie Ray, of Shenandoah, who once beat Frank Jackson 50-0; John McCoy, of Des Moines, Bill Garvey, of Boone, and Russell Sheetz, of Cedar Rapids.

During the past 20 years, the only prominent pitchers of the nation who have not competed at the state fair have been Blair Nunamaker, of Cleveland, Ohio, and Harvey Elmerson, of Milwaukee, Wisconsin.

Since 1935 the Mid-West National has had as its visitors many non-pitching prominents such as Gordon, Lattore and Levagood of Michigan, and Tanner of Illinois.

In closing, it may be said that the Mid-West National is different in the type of pitchers competing than were the state meets of the twenties. Then the contestants were mostly farmers the Mid-West National has less farmers among the players, and has had such others as Professor Carl von der Lancken, of Columbia University, New York; Jimmy O'Shea, a Massachusetts penitentiary guard; Eddie Packham, a California aeronautical engineer; Sam Somerhalder, of Guide Rock, Neb., a high school football coach; and Dean Brown, who made his living by pulling Zeppelins to earth; just to mention a few. In addition there is a noticeable difference in the ages of the best pitchers. In the twenties, Mossman was one of a few youths in a field of forty to fifty much older men, while today, if a man past 40 years of age gets into the finals it is a surprise.

[91]

The crowds watching the games today are larger than in the twenties, so large now, that we estimate the total number of ever-changing spectators of six-day competition at 60,000, with 2,500 the most at any one time.

The remarkable skill of Isais, Allen, Zimmerman and others of today has discouraged the poorer players to become spectators, so that the 105 entries of the 1923 state tournament have dropped to 38 in the Mid-West Naional in 1939.

LADY PITCHERS AT MOLINE

TED ALLEN   MRS. JAMES

L. E. TANNER   MRS. GEO. BROUILLETTE

PUTT MOSSMAN

[95]